RAINCOAST CHRONICLES
FOURTH FIVE

RAINCOAST CHRONICLES
FOURTH FIVE

Stories and history of the BC Coast

from Raincoast Chronicles issues 16–20

EDITED BY HOWARD WHITE

HARBOUR PUBLISHING

Harbour Publishing
P.O. Box 219
Madeira Park, BC
V0N 2H0
www.harbourpublishing.com

Cover Design by Peter Read
Cover image "Potlatch Dancers" by Gordon Miller
Printed and bound in Canada

Raincoast Chronicles 16: Time and Tide: A History of Telegraph Cove
Page design by Lionel Trudel, Aspect Design
All photographs courtesy of Pat Wastell Norris, except for page 70 courtesy of Jimmy Burton, page 61 courtesy of Jimmy Burton and Liv Kennedy, page 50 courtesy of Harbour Publishing, and page 90 by Jim Borrowman courtesy of Liv Kennedy. Photo of SS *Cassiar* on page 18 by Walter E. Frost, City of Vancouver Archives. Map of Telegraph Cove area and illustration on page 26 by Lionel Trudel. Excerpt from *Whistle Up the Inlet* © 1984 by Gerald Rushton, reprinted by permission of Douglas & McIntyre.

Raincoast Chronicles 18
Page design by Martin Nichols, Lionheart Graphics

Raincoast Chronicles 19
Page design by Martin Nichols, Lionheart Graphics
Additional photography credits: Page 6, City of Vancouver Archives, St Pk P311N196; page 7 City of Vancouver Archives, Wat P128N109; page 10, City of Vancouver Archives, Dist P135N156.1.

Raincoast Chronicles 20: Lilies and Fireweed: Frontier Women of British Columbia
Page design by Roger Handling
Image page 339 BC Archives B-00182. *At Birth* by Mary August Tappage, from *The Days of Augusta,* edited by Jean E. Speare, reprinted by permission of Douglas & McIntyre.

Harbour Publishing acknowledges financial support from the Government of Canada, through the Book Publishing Industry Development Program and the Canada Council for the Arts, and from the Province of British Columbia through the British Columbia Arts Council and the Book Publisher's Tax Credit through the Ministry of Provincial Revenue.

Library and Archives Canada Cataloguing in Publication

Raincoast chronicles fourth five / edited by Howard White.

Reprint of issues 16–20 of Raincoast chronicles.
Includes bibliographical references and index.
ISBN 1-55017-372-3 / 978-1-55017-372-7

1. Pacific Coast (B.C.)—History. I. White, Howard, 1945–

FC3803.R35 2005   971.1'1   C2005-903628-1

CONTENTS

INTRODUCTION

Howard White

Raincoast Chronicles started life in 1972 as a 64-page softcover journal, boldly announcing that it would place BC coast character on the record. The late Lorne Parton, reviewing the first issue in the Vancouver *Province*, gave the sepia-toned upstart top marks for character but wasn't so sure about longevity. "Get a copy while supplies last," he advised, "publications like this blossom and wither like mayflies." It was an easy prophecy, but life would be very boring if all easy prophecies came true. Thirty-three years on, we are still chronicling BC character, while the worthy Parton has long since graduated to the great newsroom beyond the clouds.

Recording character is a sufficiently vague objective, but to the surprise of many including myself, it turned out I had something special in mind. I had grown up in coastal camps and roadless villages supplied by steamer and I was bedevilled by the fact that our part of the world never showed up in the world of books, or when it did, it was so changed by alien perspectives you could barely recognize it. I wanted to see if it couldn't be portrayed a bit more like it seemed to those of us who lived in it.

When the time came to actually begin describing this elusive character, I fell back upon *things*. "No ideas but in things," said one of my literary heroes. I knew it was not just the things that made us, rather the stories in them, but it had to start by naming the things, the talismans, the landmarks. *Chokerknob. Rockcod. Floatcamp. Stumpranch. Steampot. Campboat. Netfloat*, I recited in an early editorial. We produced articles and art about Easthopes and eulachon, towboats and giant trees.

It struck a chord. The first issue sold 3,000 copies, the second, 5,000 and the third, 10,000. By the fifth issue, all the previous issues were sold out and people were still clamouring for them, but we didn't have enough money to reprint them. It would have been cheaper to print all five in one bound volume, but wiser heads warned us it would be hard to sell a pricey hardcover comprised of material that had already been broadly exposed in journals. We went ahead anyway, and *Raincoast Chronicles First Five* sold 70,000 copies, making it one of the all-time bestsellers in BC history. This is how collecting individual *Chronicles* in enigmatically-titled bound volumes every five issues became a tradition, with *First Five* followed by *Six/Ten* and *Eleven Up*.

Raincoast Chronicles Fourth Five, containing journals 16 through 20, is the largest collection yet. It also differs from previous collections in that two of the component journals—Pat Norris's history of Telegraph Cove (Number 16) and Stephen Hume's history of pioneer BC women (Number 20)—are long essays on single topics by single authors. The rest follow the more familiar *Raincoast* formula of shorter pieces by diverse hands. There are *things*. Sawmills. Canneries. Lighthouses. Crows. Cougar. Deer. Donkey boiler coffee. There are stories. The murder of early BC's greatest architect. The backyard sub that upstaged the US Navy. Gold rush dancehall queens. The shelling of Estevan lighthouse. No single item captures west coast character by itself, but taken altogether these 420 pages, especially added to the previous three collections, make as full a picture as you'll find.

RAINCOAST CHRONICLES

Sixteen

TIME & TIDE:
A HISTORY OF TELEGRAPH COVE

PAT WASTELL NORRIS

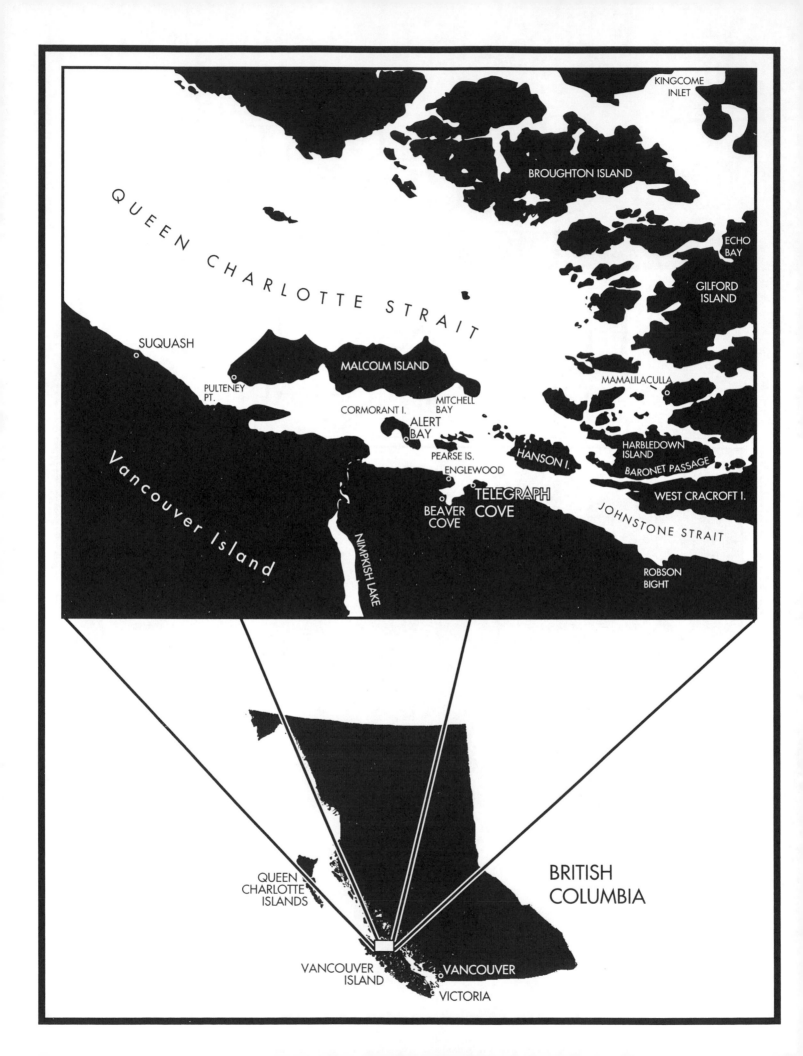

Telegraph Cove ranks as one of the notable man-made landmarks of the BC Coast, a tiny notch in the desolate Vancouver Island coastline between Kelsey Bay and Port McNeill almost totally encircled by an elaborate system of boardwalks and wooden buildings built on shorefront pilings. It is a *tour de force* of barnacled architecture, a kind of accidental gumboot theme park. A first-comer to Telegraph Cove feels just a tiny bit like a first-time visitor to Venice: the natural landscape has been taken over by a structure of great elaborateness, but there is scarcely a clue left as to who made it and to what purpose. The mystery is made more enticing by the feeling something remarkable must have gone on here, to have left such remarkable remains.

In the following pages Pat Wastell Norris answers the questions about "who?" and "why?" with gratifying completeness, and also confirms all suspicions about remarkable goings-on. It turns out that the rough-sawn mini-metropolis was built by her father, Fred Wastell, who needed something to do after the Great Depression inter- rupted his rather genteel existence as the son of a well-bred factory manager in nearby Alert Bay. Pat grew up there in a world of kelp dolls and killer whales with her younger sister and a very odd assortment of millworkers, coastal drifters and well-bred relatives, who good-humouredly rolled up their sleeves and learned some very un-genteel survival skills. Remarkable events, ranging from her aging grandmother's mastery of gasboat handling to her mother's emergency medical heroics, performed aboard storm-tossed towboats on battered loggers and expectant mothers, were a daily occurrence.

Pat Norris' memoir of growing up wet does more than fill the intriguing blank left in BC Coast history under the name of Telegraph Cove; it provides us with one of the more charming and insightful portraits we have yet had of upcoast life between the wars, a busy and colourful period justifiably described as the golden age of the BC coast.

Howard White

TELEGRAPH COVE

The brochure contained several beautiful photos of the BC coast and a description of the charter trips that were offered. One of them was a sail up the coast to the Indian village of Mamalilaculla. This village, it stated accurately, had been deserted for many years but it had now been reclaimed by descendants of its original inhabitants and was prepared to welcome visitors. The trip offered, the brochure went on, "an incomparable opportunity to interface with the Indians."

"Oh my god," I thought, "what would father have made of this!"

My father interfaced with the Indians every day of his life and with a lot of other coastal inhabitants too, and you can bet that his experiences were very different from the sanitized version of real life being offered to these earnest Tilley-hatted tourists. There was the time, for example, that he made every effort to interface with at least one Indian at Kingcome and all that turned up was a couple of starving dogs—but I'm getting ahead of myself.

It was my grandfather who named it Telegraph Cove. When he arrived in Alert Bay in 1909, Vancouver Island's north coast lay silent and virtually empty—its scattering of inhabitants were Indian tribes in their villages and a handful of white people. In 1912 the staccato click of a telegraph key and the faint crackle of a bad telephone line penetrated that silence to some slight degree when the federal government completed a telephone-telegraph line from Campbell River to northern Vancouver Island. When J.T. Phalen, the Superintendent of Telegraphs, was looking for a suitable location for a lineman's station close to Alert Bay, my grandfather suggested a little

cove where the lineman's boat could be safely moored. Since it now needed to be properly identified, my grandfather promptly added place-naming to his services and called it Telegraph Cove.

And so, in 1912, telegraph lineman Bobby Cullerne became the Cove's first inhabitant. He lived in a one-room shed-roofed structure that, in a different guise, is still there. He not only lived alone, he worked alone; the telegraph line was simply strung from tree to tree along the shoreline and he patrolled the shore in his boat. His job required some rudimentary domestic skills, some familiarity with the internal combustion engine, a certain degree of seamanship and the ability to climb trees rather than telephone poles.

Apart from his government salary, Bobby's circumstances were no different from anyone else's in the vicinity. His life, like theirs, demanded strength of character, capability, versatility—and a sense of humour. The coast was not for the frivolous or the irresponsible. Lost in its immensity, unable to communicate with their fellows, cut off from the conveniences of the city, its people were do-it-yourselfers to a man/woman/child. They had common sense which served them better than intellectual brilliance—and they worked nonstop. In one sense, they lived a life of privilege, for they had the luxury of a pristine environment. Unfortunately it was a luxury they failed to recognize, for aesthetic appreciation pre-supposes leisure—and leisure was in short supply. Despite their best efforts, a lot of them died because their occupations were dangerous and nature, itself, is merciless.

A frontier offers opportunity to the entrepreneur and independence to the self-sufficient. And so it was possible for my father, dispossessed by the Great Depression, to start a business and, of necessity, a community at Telegraph Cove. He brought his bride there and that's where my sister and I, their two daughters, grew up. As a result we had an unconventional—and vastly entertaining—upbringing.

Not in his wildest dreams, however, could my father have envisioned what was to come. When my grandparents' picnics at deserted Indian villages were rained out, my grandmother and her friends played bridge on a wooden box in one of the longhouses. My father wouldn't have believed that, just a few decades later, boatloads of people would devote considerable time and money to glimpse a reconstructed Indian culture. And for my

father, a boat was a means of earning a livelihood. He had the best one he could afford and kept it well maintained—for one day our lives might depend on it. Kayakers, paddling around in their cockleshells with no purpose other than the enjoyment of nature, he considered damn fools. As for whale-watchers, when Bill Mackay proposed a business based on this activity, my father felt compelled to disabuse him of his naiveté. "Bill," he said, "nobody's going to come up here to look at Blackfish."

He was wrong, but understandably so, for the early days were different—very different—from those that followed.

THE WILD WEST (COAST)

Alert Bay – This settlement, on the southern side of Cormorant Island, is on the northeastern side of Broughton Strait opposite the mouth of the Nimpkish River. In addition to being a commercial fishing port, it is a distributing centre for the many logging communities in the outlying districts.

British Columbia Pilot

His name was Alfred Marmaduke Wastell, which says it all. He was a typical English gentleman with all the strengths and weaknesses that the term implies—and he was my grandfather. He was immaculate in his dress and tolerant and whimsical in his outlook, and how he ever came to be the manager of anything as down-to-earth as a box factory is difficult to imagine, since no one else in his large family ever seems to have engaged in any practical activity. But that's exactly what he was—the manager of a fish processor's box factory in Alert Bay, a little community on the British Columbia coast some two hundred miles north of Vancouver. When he arrived there in 1909, it had exactly nineteen white inhabitants and about two hundred native Indian ones; it was, essentially, a Kwakiutl village.

My grandfather's parents and their growing family had originally lived on the south coast of England. Family documents describe my great-grandfather's occupation as "Gentleman." Spelled with a capital G, that simply meant that he didn't have to work for a living and could spend his days doing whatever suited his fancy. Somewhere along the line he fancied living in Canada, so he packed up the household and travelled to Ontario. He didn't emigrate, you understand; he didn't have to. The British Empire included all the pink bits on the globe and, as one of the largest pink bits, Canada was not an independent country but simply another part of the Empire.

The family settled in Haliburton, Ontario where my grandfather Duke, the last in a family of ten, was born. To me the words "ten children" and "nervous breakdown" occur simultaneously, but that wasn't the case with the Wastells. They had a big house, plenty of "help," and a laid-back attitude. My grandfather remembered a happy and rambunctious childhood of sliding down the staircase on a metal tea tray and being held by the heels down the well by an Irish maid as punishment for some mischief. His father, however, was middle-aged when my grandfather was born and, as he got older, he grew nostalgic for his native land and decided to move his family back to England.

As the youngest in the family, my grandfather had never known England. Canada was *his* native land; he was no longer a child and he had had all the education he was going to get. He resolved to stay where he was, and went out and got himself a job "licking stamps," as he put it, at a local lumber mill. He was an agreeable and conscientious employee, and before long he began to learn the box-making business. He began, as well, to squire around the local young ladies, one of whom was Mary Elizabeth Sharpe.

Mame, as she was called, was the daughter of a Great Lakes captain who was away on his ship most of the time. Her mother, worn out by the birth of seven children, was in ill health. With an absentee father and an ailing mother, much of the household management fell to Mame, who was the eldest, and this experience shaped her personality. She became immensely capable and hard-working—and she became used to running the show. She was left, as well, with a marked distaste for large families in general and babies in particular.

By 1897, Mame and Duke had known each

other for five years, during which time she had flirted with many others, but he had remained constant in his affection. The choice of a mate is so often dictated by unspoken—if not unconscious—motives. That was the case here. My grandfather knew, by then, that Mame possessed the practicality and common-sense that he needed. She, in turn, was sure by this time that Duke would be a more considerate and devoted husband than her father had been to her mother. Once they had decided to marry, my grandfather wrote a touching letter to his future father-in-law which said, in part:

Should you think it proper to accept me as a son-in-law, I will forever do my utmost to make Mame happy and make you feel that you have not misplaced your trust and that you have placed the future of your daughter with one who will love and cherish her and that you may rest without the least thought of her being unhappy or neglected.

He was accepted, of course. The only difficulty was the distance that now separated them. My grandfather, by then established in his career in the box-making industry, was working for Barnet Sawmills on the west coast. So my grandmother said good-bye to her family and the big house on the shore of Lake Ontario and made the long train journey to New Westminster where they were married.

Almost immediately, my grandfather's devotion was put to the test. It had been a bleak little wedding with no friends or family present, and after only a few months in New Westminster my grandmother was overcome by homesickness. She missed canoeing on Lake Ontario, she missed the muskmelons that grew there, and most of all she missed her family. And so her husband, as good as his promise to make her happy, left his job. The two packed their household possessions in big wooden boxes and made the journey back to Ontario.

My grandfather found another job there and then his devotion was *really* put to the test. Mame, having tasted the wild west, decided that the east was stuffy and tiresome and that she much preferred British Columbia. Once again, my grandfather quit his job; once again, they packed the wooden boxes and left for New Westminster. Here, my grandmother's indecision ended. The west was now her life and she never saw Ontario again. She did, however, see her family; eventually all of them came west to live.

My father Fred was born in New Westminster a year or two after his mother had finally decided where she wanted to live. They weren't settled yet, however, for when he was nine, the BC Fishing and Packing Company, a fish processing company, offered my grandfather the job of managing the box factory it had recently acquired at Alert Bay. The enterprise had been badly managed, but its new owners felt that, given a year, my grandfather could get it running properly. This is what they proposed to him.

The whole family responded to the idea with

The BC Fishing and Packing Company's box factory crew at Alert Bay. My grandfather, Duke Wastell, at left.

The BC Fishing and Packing Company's box factory at Alert Bay.

enthusiasm. For Duke, it was a professional challenge; for Mame, who had finally cut her emotional ties to Ontario, it promised two activities that she especially enjoyed: boating and bathing, as it was then called. For my nine-year-old father Fred, it promised an adventure straight out of the *Boy's Own Annual*—an Indian village!

So late one Vancouver evening, the three Wastells embarked on a Union steamship. While they slept, the ship pushed northward up Georgia Strait, paused for slack water and then proceeded through Seymour Narrows and on into Johnstone Strait. By noon the next day, they had reached Alert Bay, a wide crescent-shaped bay that stretched along the southern shore of Cormorant Island. All along the bay, a broad pebble beach ran down to the water, and behind it lay the dense coastal forest. Following the shoreline, between the beach and the trees, stood a string of buildings: assorted frame houses, a small church with elaborate white gingerbread trim, the blank faces of huge Indian long-houses staring out from behind towering totem poles, and finally, the buildings and wharves that marked the box factory and the fish cannery. The ship docked at the cannery wharf, the gangway was lowered into place, and the Wastells disembarked to join a world that, unbeknownst to them, was to be their home not for a

year, but for the rest of their lives.

My grandfather busied himself with the problems of the box factory, while around him the community of Alert Bay changed and grew. The original white inhabitants—a handful of missionaries and fishing company employees—were joined by the operators of a new government wireless station, by a doctor and nurses who worked in the mission hospital, by oil company employees who provided marine fuel services, by teachers for the expanding school, and by government forest and fisheries wardens. Even with all the new arrivals, it remained a small community. All its white inhabitants had originally been city people whose jobs had required them to come to Alert Bay. Once there, they tried to approximate life in the city as closely as possible. They were what was then termed "respectable" people, an appellation that differentiated them from the non-respectable loggers who surrounded and out-numbered them, and who weren't considered respectable mainly because they were drunk all the time. They were drunk all the time because they did physically exhausting, deadly dangerous work and lived in isolation in camps that were lost in the vast coastal wilderness. Consequently, it was hardly surprising that whenever a logger received payment for a boom of logs that had been sent to "town"—Vancouver or

New Westminster—his friends gathered round in the nearest beer parlour for a little celebration.

As the liquor flowed, these parties got strenuous. At one of them, someone with a new pair of caulk boots initiated a contest. Caulk boots are high-laced leather footgear, as stiff and heavy as ski boots, and like ski boots, they give their wearers a clumping gait. It's the soles of the boots, however, that make them indispensable in the woods. Protruding from the thick leather are dozens of razor-sharp nails that allow the wearer to cling like a fly to the rounded and unstable surface of a log. In this competition, each man in turn put on the new boots and tried to see how far he could run up the wall. Those who failed to let go quickly enough when they had reached the limit of their ascent fell off, landing on their heads rather than on their feet, thereby losing the game and having to buy drinks all around.

Fortunately, the walls were lined with boards but as this activity didn't do much to improve their appearance and as he feared further damage to his property the proprietor, Charlie Cavanaugh, resorted to the lame excuse that he was obliged to shut down the bar because his liquor supply had run out. He fooled no one. The loggers decided that if he couldn't keep a more abundant supply of liquor on hand, the hotel wasn't worthy of the name and had better be dumped into the sea. Since the building lay on the edge of a big, flat table of rock almost overhanging the water, this procedure posed no particular problem for a gang of loggers. Each man went to his boat and brought back his pump jack, a piece of equipment usually used to extricate logs from tangled slopes and send them down into the water below. They set the jacks under the shore side of the building and commenced to raise it off its foundations. It wasn't long before the hotel started to creak and groan, and Charlie, by now aware that all was not as it should be, went out to investigate. What he saw convinced him that he'd better go inside and "find" some more liquid refreshment.

The crew of the Union steamship *Cassiar* was more successful at closing the bar and making it stick. Gerald Rushton, in his book *Whistle Up The Inlet* says:

Stories about the roistering aboard the SS Cassiar *were not exaggerated in the days when hand-logging was at its peak. The vessel's bar did a roaring trade, particularly when loggers headed for the city with a season's earnings after camp was paid off. Frequently, the master would have to order the bar closed, and it sometimes took two husky mates to restore order.*

SS *Cassiar*

My grandmother (standing in Panama hat), my grandfather (wearing spats), and three young guests on the newly launched *Klinekwa*—so newly launched that her mast has not been stepped (c.1912).

My grandfather's lifetime consumption of alcohol didn't exceed a couple of glasses of sherry, but he was tolerant and practical when it came to the drinking habits of others. This was just as well since, by 1912, he was not only the mill manager, but the local Justice of the Peace.

One weekend, the Provincial Police at Alert Bay consulted with him in his latter capacity. They had received a message from Minstrel Island concerning an attempted murder, and they wanted my grandfather to accompany them to the scene in order to lay charges, or do whatever a Justice of the Peace was required to do under the circumstances.

So, on a particularly beautiful Sunday morning, some eight hours after the reported incident, they set off in the police boat for Minstrel Island. The first thing they noticed upon their arrival was a dozen or so loggers sleeping on the sun-warmed rocks beside the hotel. Questioning revealed that the hotel's owner had gone to Vancouver and left his wife and, in my grandfather's words, "a little sawed-off cook" to look after the premises. Once they were roused from their sleep, the loggers readily acknowledged that on the previous night they had had a little party. Their powers of recall ranged from hazy to nil but they did agree that, once again, an unscheduled bar closure had caused all the trouble.

"That little runt who was tending the bar decided that we'd had too much," said one of the group, "and he told the boss's wife that they had better close up till we sobered up a bit."

The management did just that, which was a mistake because one of the boys went down to his boat and got a boom auger, an instrument used to bore four-inch holes in boomsticks—the long, straight logs that frame a log boom. He proceeded to bore a hole in the barroom door so that he could pull back the bolt that was locking it. When the two people inside voiced their displeasure over this turn of events, the loggers proposed draping a boomchain over the cook's shoulders and throwing him into the chuck. At this point the owner's wife fled to get a message to the police.

Having heard the evidence, the Justice of the Peace assembled all those involved, thrashed the matter out, and fined the boom auger expert ten dollars—with an order to replace the barroom door.

About the only other entertainment the loggers had were the dances at this same Minstrel Island. They were dances in name only for, probably because of the acute shortage of females, they invariably deteriorated into fist-fights and ended up as fully fledged brawls. The best you could say for them was that they were a change from logging.

It was understandable, then, that the "respectable" people felt it necessary to maintain their standards. But that didn't mean that they were stuffy or intolerant. Quite the reverse. Life on the coast fostered a sense of permanent irreverence. Knowing intimately so many diverse characters made us very aware of the sterling qualities of those with no pretensions, and forever impatient with snobbishness and self-importance.

Ten years after his arrival in Alert Bay, my father was off to the University of British Columbia, the temporary terms of my grandfather's employment were long forgotten, and the decade of the 1920s was about to begin.

The Roaring Twenties bowled through North America, bringing the message that prosperity and pleasure were out there for everyone. Overnight, the wind-up Victrolas changed their tune. The refined squealing of Galli-Curci was replaced by a tinny voice warbling, "You scream, I scream, we all scream for ice cream."

The young, the affluent, the sophisticated, the urban, all got the message first but it wasn't long before sober citizens began to get that fun feeling as well. Small business owners, people whose lives had been an unremitting struggle to collect their modest receivables, now exulted because their years of thrift had provided them with nest eggs and their success in the stock market had turned those nest eggs into portfolios that would ensure them not only comfortable retirement, but luxury. And since the bonhomie that comes with prosperity can't be contained, it rolled on without a pause into the furthest reaches of BC.

My father and his parents were perfectly positioned to enjoy the new decade. The company supplied them with a large comfortable house surrounded by a pretty garden and a tennis court. It also supplied the services of a Chinese cook. Their circumstances were made even more pleasant by the fact that they now owned a little yacht, the *Klinekwa*. Each summer she was meticulously scraped and varnished and otherwise prepared for a season of picnics and overnight jaunts. And when my father returned from university, he brought his car, a 490 Chevrolet, back with him on the coastal steamer. Since the community had no real roads, he and his friends piled in, cranked the engine into life and racketed

Chong with a kitchen knife and Alex MacDonald with an unidentified object, (c.1919) Alert Bay.

Pretty girls and handsome young men, c. 1915. The girl on the right is Mary Easthope of the Easthope engine family. She later married Alex Macdonald.

around the mill yard.

Winter and summer, my grandparents' house overflowed with guests. They had the wherewithal and the inclination for a lively social life, and my father—handsome and full of fun—was the belle of this ball. Yet, when Fred Wastell finally became engaged, it was not to one of the carefree flirts that surrounded him, but to Emma McCoskrie, an earnest young nurse who had come to work in the local hospital.

Emma's upbringing could not have been more different from Fred's. Whereas he had been an indulged and adored only child, encouraged to have as much fun as possible, she had lost her mother at the age of three and, bewildered and lonely, had been sent to live in the joyless household of a childless aunt and uncle.

Now, however, she was the fiancée of the local "catch." She had, in Mame, a domineering and slightly jealous future mother-in-law and, in Duke, a gentle and welcoming future father-in-law, and for the first time in her life she found herself part of a jovial household dedicated to good times. Friends and relatives, missionaries and businessmen, middle-aged bridge players, and young teachers and nurses all enjoyed the hospitality and high spirits of my grandparents' home. Old photos show civilized life in the foreground and untamed wilderness in the background. Here they sit, stand or lounge, pretty girls with smart haircuts and chic country clothes; handsome young men with crinkly, sexy smiles wearing white flannels and clutching tennis rackets. In the garden in front of the honeysuckle stands Chong, the cook, resplendent in starched white. My grandmother poses serenely on the deck of the *Klinekwa* wearing a finely striped cotton dress with a big white collar, and a deep-crowned straw hat trimmed with a band of fabric that matches her dress.

Ten years of economic depression and another six of war were about to obliterate all traces of that pleasant life—and it all began in 1928.

My grandmother and my father, seated, Chong in his off-duty cap and three of the ever-present guests (c.1912).

II

TELEGRAPH COVE MILLS LTD

Telegraph Cove is on the eastern side of Beaver Cove about 3½ cables southwestward of Ella Point. It is a small cove extending about 1½ cables in a southeasterly direction, with a width of approximately 200 feet at its narrowest point.

The Broughton Lumber and Trading Company's wharf, the face of which is about 170 feet long, has depths from 17 to 22 feet. The local steamer calls regularly. There is a sawmill, store and post office, connected to the general telephone system. Diesel oil, gasoline and water are procurable for small vessels.

This cove provides excellent shelter for small craft in all weathers.

British Columbia Pilot

In 1928, BC Packers switched from wooden boxes to corrugated cardboard. Their need for lumber was gone; within weeks, the box factory was closed and within months its assets—including the manager's house—were disposed of. Chong, the cook, like the manager and the other forty company employees, was dismissed.

In 1928, there were no severance packages, no unemployment insurance cheques, no pension plans to roll into an RRSP. My grandfather was nearing sixty, not the most employable age. He was a man however, of limitless equanimity. He responded to this sudden change in fortune by withdrawing a sizeable sum from his bank account, buying a transcontinental train ticket, and booking passage to England on the brand new Canadian Pacific ship, the Empress of Great Britain. There he would spend several months relaxing and visiting family. He brought home a beautiful souvenir book containing blueprints and full page watercolour paintings of the interior of this fast new ship and, as a child, I spent hours lying on my grandparents' green carpet poring over these illustrations. Having spent my life, to that point, in a rugged and remote world, I was both puzzled and entranced by the grandeur depicted between its handsome blue and gold covers.

My grandmother had not been aware of these travel plans until her husband announced them one morning, at breakfast.

"Well then, Mame," Duke said, "how would you like to pack your valise and take a trip to England with me?"

My grandmother was astounded. "England?"

"Yes," said my grandfather. "Now that I'm no longer working we have time to take a little holiday."

"I think that since you're not working it would be a lot more sensible for us to stay at home and save our money," said Mame.

"Oh, it won't be an expensive trip. We can stay with the family. They have plenty of room."

"I'd go mad sitting around all day with those people," she said. "Useless lot. Perfectly able-bodied people spending their days doing absolutely nothing.,"

"They don't sit around all day," he protested mildly. "They go out in the garden. They play croquet. Father even has his Peterborough canoe," he added. "Takes it out on the pond every day. You could go canoeing."

My grandmother was not to be enticed. "You go if you want to."

And so he did, while she stayed in Alert Bay and began to adjust to life with a cook, a tennis court— or a salary.

It was now that Mame supplied her contribution to the marriage. Duke's parents, having been spared the necessity of earning a living, had consequently imbued their children with a lofty disregard for money. As a result, my grandfather had a tenuous grasp of the financial facts of life and a dangerous attraction to mining stocks. Mame's upbringing, on the other hand, had made her the *de facto* head of a large family, and had indelibly impressed upon her consciousness the value of a dollar. Early in her marriage, she had realized that she must wrest away as much of my grandfather's discretionary income as possible, lest his financial follies bankrupt them. She had invested this little hoard in mortgages and rental real estate, the returns from which kept them both for the rest of their lives.

My parents, meanwhile, were struggling with the problem of their own future. At the time of their wedding in June 1928 my father, (with fine disregard for charges of nepotism), was the bookkeeper for the same box factory that his father managed. He and Emma were married by a friend of the family in a lovely old church in Victoria. My mother wore a chic silk crêpe de chine dress that had been designed and made by a French dressmaker. They went to California for a leisurely honeymoon and, when they returned to Alert Bay, it was to a brand new house that had been built for them. But, within months, this well-ordered world fell down around their ears.

For a year after the box factory closed, my father was retained to close the books and finalize the business there, but in the fall of 1929 another disturbing event took place. Three thousand miles away the New York stock market crashed and the shock waves travelled all the way from the east to the west. Jobs disappeared overnight.

My father would say later that it wasn't a great start for a family that now included an infant daughter. But he failed to mention that BC Packers had offered him employment in their Vancouver offices; I don't think he ever even considered this an option. From the moment he stepped off the coastal steamer with his parents at the age of nine, the coast was where he belonged. It was not an unreasonable view, for it was a boy's paradise, offering space, freedom and adventure. By the time he was a man of thirty, this way of life was so much a part of him that to relinquish it was simply not an alternative.

Instead, he turned his attention to a piece of land that my grandfather owned just down the coast: four hundred acres of waterfront that he had acquired as payment of a bad debt. Duke always played down the bad debt aspect, maintaining that the Royal Bank had urged him to buy out their stake in the property. I'm sure they did. They had been stung, too, and their fellow creditor no doubt seemed the likeliest prospect to buy them out. Mame, a much shrewder judge of character than her husband, would never have lent $1200 to such an obviously poor risk, and when the debtor predictably defaulted and signed over this chunk of wilderness instead, she was furious. As it turned out, her distress was unjustified.

Over the years my grandfather had taken timber off the property and, in the mid-1920s, he and a group of Japanese had built a salmon saltery and a primitive little mill there. My father had a financial interest in the mill—he had suppled the money for the machinery—but for the preceding two years it had lain idle. Now he proposed to resurrect this mill and make a living cutting lumber. He contacted his childhood friend in New Westminster, Alex MacDonald, and together they embarked on this new endeavour.

That the undertaking involved up-grading a sawmill that was then hardly worthy of the name, providing housing for themselves and a crew, setting up a water system and a generating plant—in fact establishing

June 1928. My mother wore a chic crêpe de chine dress. My father's best man was his future business partner, Alex Macdonald.

The bleak beginnings of Telegraph Cove Mills.

a town as well as a business, all on a shoestring, didn't seem to strike them as an insurmountable problem. Or perhaps it was my father's sanguine temperament that made it all seem feasible.

At any rate, it began to come together. My grandmother's brothers could build or fix anything, and they proceeded to do just that. Three Chinese, including Chong the cook, all former employees of the box factory, arrived unbidden, fixed up an old shack (forever after known as the China House) and presented themselves as crew members. Chong, still wearing his immaculate whites, became camp cook. They were joined by others. The going rate of pay was twenty-five cents an hour, although by this time, with the Depression grown even worse and without the cushion of unemployment insurance there were men willing to work for nothing more than room and board. That approach couldn't have struck the new company as a very professional arrangement, however, for they continued to pay wages.

That the great shortage of jobs could have tragic consequences was borne out by the experience of David, a young family friend who had just graduated from UBC with a bachelor of arts degree. Back then BAs were not the dime-a-dozen credentials they are today. They entitled the holder to teach at any public school and should have opened many other doors to employment. Now every one of those doors was tightly shut and, unwilling to live off his parents, David asked about a job at the mill. As sympathetic as he

was, Alex couldn't afford another crew member, but David finally got work in the big Wood & English mill at nearby Englewood. Unused to manual labour, he lasted three days before being killed while working on the green chain.

Telegraph Cove Mills, meanwhile, had acquired letterhead and business cards and a former seine boat, the *Mary W*, which was used for towing logs and delivering lumber. But towing logs and carrying lumber was not what she was designed for. This became apparent when, early on, they put an overly ambitious deck load on her and she nearly rolled over in a sea. She had defects as a towboat, too, for she was underpowered for the job.

Towing logs is a slow and tricky business. For one thing, the coast tides are strong and capricious. The tide out of Baronet Pass, for example, sweeps out of Blackney Pass and out around the east side of Malcolm Island. As the *Mary* emerged from Baronet Pass and rounded Cracroft Point, she had to pull sharply to port, almost doubling back in the direction from which she came in order to free herself from the tide's grip and get out into Johnstone Strait. A little more power would have made this manoeuvre unnecessary, but the *Mary* didn't have it. Then there was the wind. Johnstone Strait isn't the calmest body of water and any sizeable seas will tear a boom to pieces. Getting a boom in safely was always a combination of good luck and good management.

For the uninitiated, a log boom is a rectangle of

floating logs arranged side by side and end to end. Around their perimeter, boomsticks—extra long, extra straight logs secured end to end with great chunks of chain—maintain the rectangular shape. At regular intervals, lying at right angles to the logs and on top of them, are "swifters." They, too, are long straight logs fastened in place with boom chains; they give the boom stability and at the same time divide it into prescribed units called "sections."

To manoeuvre a boom out of a confined space, the tug keeps its unwieldy charge right alongside or pushes it bow-on, or both, until it's in open water. A cable "bridle" is attached to the two corners of one end of the rectangle, then the towline is attached to the bridle. Slowly, line is paid out, until the boom is far enough astern to be free of the negative effect of the wash from the tug's propeller. Then the towline is secured, and tug and tow are under way. Since towing, especially with a boat like the *Mary*, was a painfully slow business, my father made himself as comfortable as possible. He tipped back the high stool in the wheel-house, steered with his feet, and read *The Hiballer*, a modest trade publication for loggers which contained, among other things, a lot of dirty jokes.

That was on good days. But with no marine radio in existence, and therefore no accurate weather reports, there was only the barometer to warn of coming weather. So there were, inevitably, some bad days. There is no shelter in Johnstone Strait, and on rare occasions they were caught there by the weather. If conditions deteriorated quickly and unexpectedly, the boat and tow found themselves in exposed water and a rising wind. When the seas got to a certain height the logs, in their rectangle, would start to rise and fall, until finally one would catch on a boomstick. Its weight would hold the boomstick below the surface of the water, and now the other logs, like a herd of willful cattle, would surge, one by one, over the gap and into the open sea. Other escape routes would occur as logs washed over the boomsticks and the crew of the tug, looking astern, would see the boom disintegrating. By hauling in the towline and closing in on the boom it was sometimes possible to pry the logs off the boomsticks with a pike pole and salvage something of the tow. But if the weather was bad enough, the tow was lost and the financial repercussions, for a small sawmill like ours, were heartbreaking.

Nor did it take a storm to lose a boom; even the light chop caused by the clashing of wind and tide could do it, as happened one bright afternoon in Blackney Pass when the whirling tide met a brisk little westerly wind. A log bounced onto a boomstick and suddenly the boom was breaking up. The boat turned, manoeuvred into position alongside the boom, and the deck-hand, pike pole in hand, jumped down onto the logs. My father put the engine in neutral and hustled to the stern deck to hand him a line.

It didn't get that far. Instead there was one of those quick frightening moments that occur when huge inanimate objects wrestle control from their keeper and take charge. The boat and the boom, both in the grip of the tide, parted company. The towline caught a corner and pulled a fifty-foot boomstick up out of the water.

"Lifting *Jesus!*" yelled the deck-hand, fighting for balance.

My father sprinted for the wheel-house, the boat churned astern, and the towline strained along the log and finally

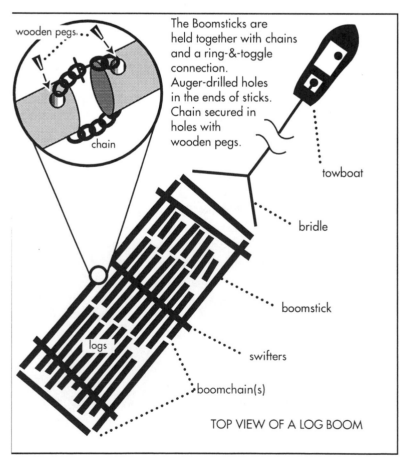

The Boomsticks are held together with chains and a ring-&-toggle connection. Auger-drilled holes in the ends of sticks. Chain secured in holes with wooden pegs.

wooden pegs

chain

towboat

bridle

boomstick

logs

swifters

boomchain(s)

TOP VIEW OF A LOG BOOM

The *Klinekwa* scouting for logs among the maze of islands between Johnstone Strait and the Mainland, c. 1931.

snapped back into position. Some distance astern, the deck-hand, looking exceedingly lonely, bounced around on his little island of logs. He was rescued; the boom was not. In all directions the logs spun away with the tide, like truants out of school.

If, by some stretch of the imagination, these undertakings could have been considered adventures for the men, they were certainly adventures that my mother could have done without. With a year-old child she moved from her new house to a three-room shack perched on a bluff above the harbour. It had a wood stove, outdoor plumbing, and after some time, sporadic bursts of electricity from the newly installed but secondhand generating plant—a ten-horsepower Petters engine. Even when it was operating, this plant supplied only enough power for a few dim light bulbs. As a child, I was startled to learn how much illumination a light bulb could really give; it was as if I had been blind and then regained my sight. We were, it seems, like the *Mary*, perpetually underpowered!

The water supply came from a little creek that had been dammed and piped down to us through the woods. The pipe itself was buried underground to keep it from freezing, although it frequently did anyway, but there were other problems to contend with besides cold temperatures. When all danger of freezing was past, the bears came out. They were curious about the water gurgling underground and, with a couple of swipes, they would rip the pipe out of the ground; the connections would break, and our water supply would dwindle and cease. In later years when plastic pipe replaced the original iron, it was even worse; they not only ripped it out, but chewed it before they were satisfied that it had no nutritional value.

Nor were these inconveniences repaid with a setting of great natural beauty. Instead the senses were assaulted from every side. The hills that sloped down to the small cove, today so lush and green and lovely, were then a sea of blackened stumps—the ravaged remains of logging and of a fire. Below the house, on the dock, the saltery still operated intermittently, filling the air with the stench of rotting fish guts, and forcing my mother to keep all the windows tightly closed.

There was no other English-speaking woman in the vicinity and the rain poured down unceasingly. To make matters worse, the first two winters that my parents spent there were unusually cold. Some perverse law of nature decrees that under such circumstances the weather will always try for a record. It did. The logs froze into a solid mass in the bay and so did the pipes under the flimsy house.

For Emma, then, the honeymoon ended abruptly in 1929. For Mame, the transition from her former life to this new one was easier because, for her, it carried some real psychological benefits. True, the lawn tennis parties were a thing of the past, she had pressing financial worries and she, herself, had replaced the Chinese cook in the kitchen and at the scrubbing board. But she and Duke were still living in the relative comfort of the more civilized community of Alert Bay, where they had moved into the house originally intended for my parents. They still had the *Klinekwa* and made frequent trips back and forth to keep in touch with the new enterprise at Telegraph Cove. And Mame was by nature frugal and resourceful. Most importantly, if doing meaningful tasks that confirm our worth in our society brings satisfaction, then she had that satisfaction in spades, for both she and the *Klinekwa* soon acquired a new career. Together, my

grandparents scouted the labyrinth of islands between the mainland and northern Vancouver Island on log-buying expeditions; in the days before radio telephone, the only way to find out which logging camps had booms to sell was to visit the camps themselves. It was an occupation that suited my grandmother perfectly. The daughter of a sea-captain, she loved being on the water and handled the boat with professional skill. She wore a neat, navy blue "afternoon dress" on these expeditions and did her grey hair up in a soft bun. In those pre-feminist days, the sight of this dignified figure running a boat with such assurance must have presented a puzzling picture. Docking smoothly at one logging camp, she rang "stop engines" and in the ensuing silence she was vastly amused to hear a logger on the log dump above her say to his companion, "Where in the world did that old lady come from?"

Not all their landings were so harmonious, however. Today's yachts tuck their powerful high-speed engines under the floorboards and run them with pilot-house controls. The *Klinekwa*'s big engine, with its huge iron clutch lever, required a spacious engine-room and an attendant with a strong arm. The engine-room was just aft of the pilot-house and its big windows gave a clear side view. Unfortunately this permitted my grandfather, who acted as engineer, to second-guess my grandmother, who acted as captain. As the boat approached a dock, Mame rang one bell as a signal to disengage the clutch. The engine did not respond. Leaning down through the engine-room door, my grandmother yelled, "Duke, I gave you one bell!"

There was no time for further conversation. The *Klinekwa* was, by this time, almost on top of the dock. My grandmother rang one bell and then two to put the engine full astern. The *Klinekwa* slid forward, still under way, and banged heavily against the piles.

While the lines were being secured there was silence but when the boat was safely tied up, Mame's frustration burst forth. "Duke, you old fool," she cried, "when I'm landing the boat, do what I say! I know what I'm doing. You can't see properly back there, so just answer the bells. If this keeps up, we're going to take someone's pilings out—and

My mother in her trousseau finery en route to California by ship.

28

damage the little *Klinekwa*." My grandmother considered the *Klinekwa* a member of the family and, as such, the boat had her deep affection—and her protection.

"Yes, yes, dear girl," said my grandfather. He never argued. There was no point in arguing because he knew what my grandmother did not: that men were always right, anyway.

The area of the north coast that they covered, the part within feasible towing distance of the mill, has neither the oppressive grandeur of the deep inlets to the east nor the exposed water of Johnstone Strait to the west. Instead, it is a maze of islands, large and small, scattered like the pieces of a jig-saw puzzle, their convoluted shapes forming endless waterways.

As a child of four I went along on many of their voyages. My mother, by now expecting my sister Bea, was no doubt delighted to have a brief respite from my company. And so we three wended our way down narrow channels, skirting kelp beds, checking the charts and consulting the tide book, as the *Klinekwa* slipped past mile after mile of impenetrable coastal forest. In those days—the days before bulldozers and heavy equipment—the pristine green wilderness seemed impregnable, for man had only nibbled at its edges.

The great trees crowded down to the high water mark, their branches dripping with Spanish moss. Around us bobbed the sea birds; eighty feet above us in the spiked tops of the cedars, bald eagles sat stern and alert. Occasionally, a mink streaked across the rocks where our wake, rolling out from the bows, bounced against the shoreline. Before us the water lay as pliant and lustrous as satin, and behind us our wake formed two ribbons of white lace.

It was only when we reached our destination that the spell was broken. Rounding one last point, we would come upon a cluster of floats tied to the shore, on them a few weather-beaten buildings, smoke rising from tin chimneys. There was the A-frame and the donkey engine, the latter protected from the unending rain by a patched corrugated iron roof. There was a hillside of logging slash, and in the water floated half-made-up booms of huge logs.

The people we met on these expeditions were an odd mixture. The coast has always mirrored the times.

From the very beginning I loved boats with a passion.

In the 1970s and 1980s it harboured, in its green recesses, not only loggers and fishermen but marine biologists studying whales, Viet Nam War veterans recovering from their horrors, and drug dealers posing as back-to-the-landers. In the 1930s besides the loggers and fishermen there were missionaries, remittance men and genuine back-to-the-landers.

The back-to-the-landers were, even amongst themselves, a disparate group. There were, for example, the Hallidays, who had a large farm in the remote reaches of Kingcome Inlet. They raised cattle, and in the "early" days they had *rowed* their produce the sixty

A summer outing on the *Klinekwa*, c. 1925. The man standing is my grandmother's brother Fred—one of my father's talented uncles.

miles to the nearest market in Alert Bay—a four day return trip. The very thought of rowing a heavily laden skiff thirty miles a day beggars the imagination. Against tides and winds, it must have been an unbelievably laborious undertaking. By the thirties they were making the journey by gasboat, but Salo, a Finn who had a homestead on Malcolm Island, still rowed to Alert Bay once a week to sell his butter and cream door-to-door. Granted, the return journey was more like five miles than sixty, for he rowed his big dory from Malcolm Island to the east side of Cormorant Island, secured it there and then hiked across the island to the settlement with his produce on his back. Nonetheless the trip must have required not only stamina but timing, for he needed a fair tide on both legs of his trip. No row boat is a match for the tides that race through those waters.

In an idyllic little bay on Pearse Island lived an English couple, the Youngs. They were a tiny little pair who grew daffodils as a cash crop. The fact that in the 1930s there was virtually no ready market for daffodils in that part of BC didn't seem to have occurred to them. Although their vegetable garden and the fish at their doorstep kept them from starving, theirs was a meagre existence. Yet they stayed there, I suppose because of financial constraints, until the end of their lives; long after they were gone, the daffodils bloomed each spring; a sudden sweep of gold in an otherwise unremittingly green landscape.

In contrast to the Youngs, who were unfailingly pleasant and polite, there lived, up in the then-inaccessible reaches of the Nimpkish River, a scowling German always referred to as "old Schalling." He appeared only rarely, rowing his dory on some private errand. It was reported that he had a wife, and even children, but no one seemed to have actually seen them. It was said, too, that someone, perhaps a timber cruiser, had inadvertently stumbled on his homestead one day and was greeted by Schalling brandishing a rifle and ordering him off. Certainly my mother, when she was still nursing in the local hospital, had a memorable encounter with him. He had appeared at the hospital one day, taciturn as ever, with a blood-soaked rag around one hand. When it was removed, it was discovered that he had lost two fingers in some kind of an accident. Somehow he had managed to row himself to the hospital from his remote homestead without bleeding to death en route. Even then, my mother swore, he did not seem in any particular distress. She had remained awed by such stoicism.

Each spring, when wild lilies bloomed in profusion in the meadows at the mouth of the Nimpkish River, we took the boat there for a picnic. We returned home with armfuls of the delicate mauve flowers; but all afternoon, as we picked them, I kept one eye out for Schalling—expecting him to appear from the depths of the forest like the gnomes in my books of fairy tales.

Although at four I was too young to appreciate it, I realize now that the greatest possible contrast in the human condition occurred in the relatively short distance between Soderman's Camp—wherever it happened to be at the moment—and the Indian village of Mamalilaculla on Village Island. We bought a lot of logs from Oscar Soderman, a tall bony Norwegian in his mid-fifties who had a peculiar claim to fame. He had married, whether while under the influence or in full possession of his faculties we could never be quite sure, a former Madam who now ran the camp—and Oscar—with an iron hand. Sidney Soderman was reported to be a holy terror of a boss, and loggers are not easily intimidated. The only indication we ever got of this came one day when my father and Sidney were conferring about logs. There was a knock at the door and Sidney yelled, "Who is it?"

"It's Bob," came the reply.

"Well bob the hell out of there", shouted Sidney, and there was the sound of rapidly retreating steps.

On my grandparent's visits, however, Sidney was always hospitality itself. If we arrived anywhere near a meal hour, we were always invited to join Oscar and her in the cookhouse; and while Oscar and my grandfather discussed how much timber was in the water, what species it was and when the log scaler would be around, my grandmother and Sidney Soderman had their own conversation. Although Mame was the soul of rectitude, she and Sidney seemed to get along fine; perhaps each recognized in the other a strong character and a good business sense.

Two very different women lived a few miles away at Mamalilaculla. The Misses O'Brien and Dibben shared a little frame house above a white clamshell beach, the only white people in the village. These two spinster ladies had left England, their families and everything familiar, and had travelled across the Atlantic, across the continent and up the BC coast to this isolated Indian village. They were Anglican missionaries, sent on this bizarre journey as others of their kind were shipped off to darkest Africa.

Miss O'Brien had a small private income which she used to build a church, a school and a small sanatorium for tuberculosis patients. In theory this was a perfect example of practical Christianity; in practice it didn't fly, though certainly not for lack of devotion on the part of the ladies. Since the Indians already had their own rich spiritual heritage and few of the young were terribly anxious to be educated—and since the men, in particular, were disinclined to pay any attention to women—the project was not a howling success. Nonetheless, the two missionaries continued their endeavours for the remainder of their lives, and the Indians came to realize that their presence had its advantages. They could always earn a small but

In the early days, the saltery was still operating and in season the warehouses were stacked floor to ceiling with huge boxes of salted salmon.

dependable cash income from chopping the ladies' wood and delivering their mail and provisions from the nearest settlement at Echo Bay.

Since the Misses O'Brien and Dibben had no logs to sell, our visits to them were purely social in nature and were, in fact, opportunities to check on their welfare. It was usually afternoon by the time we reached Village Island and the ladies always invited us into their untidy little sitting-room for tea. I was given an atlas or something of the kind to look at while the adults chatted. What they talked about is hard to imagine, for the two women had no radio, no current reading matter, and no regular contact with other white people. Yet the social niceties seem not to have been impaired.

One day, for some long-forgotten reason, my grandmother and my father and I made the long trip to Halliday's farm at the head of Kingcome Inlet. It proved a memorable experience for me; it introduced me to an enormous beast called a cow. I had seen any number of wild creatures but I had never seen any farm animals, nor had I ever seen a farm. In fact, I had never seen a field, and I found the huge, flat expanse of grass most unusual.

We went into the barn where my father and Mr. Halliday got into an interminable conversation. Fascinated by the huge animals that surrounded us, I could finally stand it no longer. I approached a tan-coloured cow very cautiously and stretched out one finger. I didn't know I was being observed until we were on our way back to the boat.

"Well, what did the cow feel like?" asked my father.

I considered. "It was soft and warm," I said.

My grandmother, meanwhile, had made her own discovery. It must be explained here that Mame was not a passive participant in the game of life. She was ever alert to opportunities and took full advantage of those that presented themselves. Typically, she had found an opportunity at Halliday's farm.

"Fred," she said, indicated a large cardboard carton, "will you put that box on the boat. It's going to the Bay with us."

"What's in it?" asked my father.

"Frogs," said my grandmother.

"*Frogs?*"

"For the garden," she explained. "Frogs are wonderful for eating bugs, and this place is just alive with them. The Halliday boys have caught me a box full."

Under her direction, he put the box on the back deck where the frogs would get plenty of fresh air, and we headed homeward down Kingcome Inlet. Before long, it began to blow hard. The boat started to lunge and roll, and when my grandmother went to check her charges on the back deck she was distressed to find that the box had fallen over. She hurried to the wheel-house.

"Fred," she said, "those frogs are getting out of their box."

"That's very unfortunate," said my father, "for the frogs."

"Don't joke," said Mame, "I want you to go out and get them back in the box."

When it came to his mother, whom he called Elizabeth, my father was endlessly forbearing. He handed her the wheel and headed for the stern. I followed him as far as the galley where a window gave a view of the deck.

By now, frogs were flying in all directions. A frog is probably constitutionally constructed to land on a level surface. On the back deck, there were no level surfaces. There weren't even any stationary ones. Consequently, the frogs had become disoriented. They were leaping into the sea, rolling around in the scuppers, and clinging precariously to coils of rope and the winch. My father and the frogs proceeded to leap around the back deck with mad abandon, my father somewhat disadvantaged by the fact that he was laughing uncontrollably. Glued to the window, I watched the proceedings which, for amusement value, certainly exceeded anything the Muppets could have produced. Eventually, my father did get some of the frogs back into their box and they were duly released into my grandparents' garden. Today some of their descendants must still live in the marshy spots on Cormorant Island.

The boat that took us on all these journeys was thirty-five feet long. She had graceful lines, comfortable accommodation and a heavy-duty Atlas Imperial gas engine. Nothing like that engine exists today. It pushed her along at the remarkable speed of ten knots, hence her name *Klinekwa* which means "lightning" in the Kwakiutl language. The Atlas had two big cast-iron cylinders painted bright engine-enamel green, and it threw a thirty-inch flywheel. Once the engine was started by hand-cranking, the igniters were adjusted manually until the engine was running smoothly. It ran with a resounding "tha-thunk," "tha-thunk," "tha-thunk," that could be heard for miles across the water. There was a gas tank with a glass gauge on the wall of the engine-room, and gas was pumped by hand from the large tank in the hull into this smaller, gravity-fed one.

On one log-buying trip, my grandfather went into the engine-room to check the gas level and found, to his considerable agitation, a thin stream of gas spraying out of a pinhole in the tank. As it sprayed out and mixed with air, it turned the engine-room into one huge carburetor. The mix cannot have been just right, however, for as yet it hadn't demonstrated the principles of the internal combustion engine. Instinctively, Duke put his finger over the hole. His finger continued right on through the wall of the tank. He shoved his handkerchief in the now gaping hole and stopped the engine. Mame, who was in the wheelhouse steering, was startled by the sudden loss of power.

"Duke, what in the world are you doing?" she said, peering down the steps that let from the pilot-house to the engine-room.

"We have a little problem with the gas tank," he said, gesturing at his handkerchief, now sodden with gas.

"Mercy on us," she said.

"I'm going to have to stop this up with something," said Duke. "You keep an eye on the boat while I see what I can find for a patch."

Mame headed back to the pilot-house.

"If she gets near the rocks, call me," he said, "and we'll push her off with the pike pole."

So while they drifted, my grandfather made a more substantial patch from some gasket material, a piece of tin, and a great deal of electrician's tape. At my grandmother's suggestion they "aired out" the engine-room. And then my grandfather warily started the engine once again, and they "tha-thunked" home with only a small drip of gas forming

My father Fred Wastell, at about the time of his marriage.

now and again at the bottom of the tank.

Next day the tank was removed and placed on our dock, and a water hose was run into it. For twenty-four hours, water ran into one opening and out of the other, in preparation for a more permanent patch job. Meanwhile, a good piece of iron and some solder were assembled. At the first touch of the blowtorch, the tank exploded with an ear-shattering bang, showering hundreds of pieces of metal in all directions and scaring the hell out of the holder of the blowtorch. "That gas," said my father thoughtfully at dinner, "is amazing stuff."

days. The lineman's shack is on the left; below it the saltery and the warehouse for fish storage.

III

EDUCATION COMES IN MANY FORMS

The tidal streams in Blackney Passage are strong and attain a rate of 5 knots at times, with heavy races off Cracroft Point on both the flood and the ebb. Two portions of the flood, or east-going stream, flowing northward and southward, respectively, off Hanson Island, meet near the southern end of Blackney Passage causing a strong tidal race in mid channel.

British Columbia Pilot

Up to this point, all my adventures had been experienced not just as an only child but as *the* only child, for I had no playmates. However, I had parents and grandparents and knew everyone else that I encountered in my little world, and they all knew me. It was an entirely satisfactory existence as far as I was concerned. But parents can never leave well enough alone. Each summer my mother took me, and later my baby sister Bea, to Victoria, where she spent a month visiting relatives and getting some respite from her isolated life. All well and good, but on these holidays she always took great pains to introduce me to the sub-species called "children," an experience that I found to be an unremitting strain.

Frankly, children frightened me. I understood adults; they were logical and dependable. Children were unpredictable and, well, childish. As well, they travelled in huge groups of perhaps five or six. Then there was the culture gap; they were city and I was country. They took something called chalk and made marks on something called sidewalks and did something called hop-scotch. Sidewalks, in themselves, were a great source of wonderment to me. That ribbon of cement with the neat, regular divisions stretching in all directions as far as the eye could see was a puzzling phenomenon for someone who had only walked on a dock or along a trail through the woods.

By the time I was six, though, there were married members of the sawmill crew and, even in the country, there were other children of school age. Somehow we had to be educated. So in the summer of my sixth birthday, while in the city for her holiday, my mother arranged an appointment with the Superintendent of Education about our getting a local school.

The Superintendent of Education was formidably neat. He wore a navy serge suit that had been pressed, in some places, to a shine. On his big oak desk, small piles of paper lay in perfect alignment. In an anteroom a secretary typed busily, and in the street below cars passed. The Superintendent of Education gestured toward a chair and my mother sat down.

"You are...," he consulted his appointment book, "Mrs. Waistle."

"Wast*ell*," said my mother.

"And what can I do for you?" he asked.

"My husband has a little sawmill on the northern end of Vancouver Island," she said. "We have a small community there. I've come to see if we can get a school established for our children."

"And just where is it that you live?"

"Telegraph Cove," said my mother.

The Superintendent of Education consulted his maps and papers. It had taken him a lifetime of effort to reach his position and he was not a man to be trifled with. Looking at his maps, he decided that Mother was trying to do just that.

"There is already a local school in your area," he said. "There is, in fact, a one-room school approximately three miles away at Beaver Cove. The government would certainly not consider setting up another one. I happen to be of the opinion that it has never hurt a child to do a little walking. That's what feet are for." He smiled ever so slightly at his own wit.

Now it was my mother's turn to face the culture gap. How to replace this bureaucrat's vision of sturdy children trudging along a dusty country road, with something closer to reality. How to explain to a man with traffic streaming along outside his window that

in the woods behind our house the ground was steep and covered with rotting deadfalls. Under the fir and the hemlock and the cedar trees, salmonberry, devil's club and salal grew eight feet tall in dank darkness. The alternative to this jungle was the sea—often rough, always gurgling ominously with tide.

"The children can't walk to Beaver Cove," said my mother. "Nobody can walk to Beaver Cove. There's no road between the two communities."

"No road?" said the Superintendent of Education, puzzled.

"It's very rough country," said my mother. "Very

Jimmy painting the *Hili-Kum*'s mast. Our schoolhouse is the building directly beneath him with the three large windows.

steep. Straight down into the sea. The underbrush is terribly thick. Even if we managed to hack a trail through the woods, it wouldn't be safe for children."

The Superintendent of Education digested all this a bit at a time.

"I see," he said, more to himself than my mother. "I see."

"Well," he said finally, "I suppose in that case we could give you some assistance. We couldn't build a school in your community, of course, but if your company is prepared to supply a building and equip it, the government would supply a grant to pay a teacher's salary. You must understand," he added firmly, "that you will have to have a minimum of seven students to qualify for this grant."

"I'm sure we can meet those requirements," my mother said.

"Well that's settled, then," said the Superintendent of Education, rising and extending his hand. "Good-bye, Mrs. Waistle."

"Good-bye," said my mother.

The teacher's grant was duly processed. A side effect of the seven-children edict was the preference always given to job applicants with large families. My father had no intention of letting birth control endanger our government grant. And now everything else was up to us: the building, the furnishings, the school supplies and the maintenance.

There was a small house under construction at the mill at this time, and when my mother returned with her teacher's grant in hand, this building was modified slightly and became a school. The large front room became a classroom, and the three big windows that faced the stunning view were raised lest we students be distracted from the tasks at hand. There was a little covered porch for our coats and rubber boots, and behind the classroom there was a bedroom and a kitchen with one cold water tap. This was to be the teacher's accommodation. Outside there was a new privy with a brand new can of chloride of lime on the seat.

It's ironic that the next step, getting the furnishings and the equipment, was the easiest of all. We were far too isolated and too short of money to pursue these things in the conventional manner. But the Depression came to our aid. By then, it had ground on for six years, and the north coast was littered with evidence of its presence. In a nearby bay, there were the looming remains of a pulp mill that had never operated. The boilers for our mill had come from an abandoned coal mine. Everywhere, there were empty habitations left to the encroaching forest by disheartened owners. At Mitchell Bay on Malcolm Island, the population had shrunk to the point where the school had closed. We went over in the boat and found the abandoned schoolhouse. Inside, it was bright and hot and dusty. Someone had been into the building before us and had scattered books and papers on the floor, but everything we needed was there. The blackboards were removed from the walls, the desks unscrewed from the floor, the scattered books were carefully packed in cartons, and even the blackboard brushes were found in the grass outside and salvaged. We had our school.

But as yet we had no teacher. It was mid-September by now and once again things worked in our favour. Teaching jobs, like all jobs, were in short supply. There had been a scramble for positions advertised earlier in the year; now that the school year was actually underway, those who had failed to get places had given up hope and were desperate for employment—desperate enough to consider our isolated way of life and the salary offered. For as my mother pointed out, eighty dollars a month wasn't really a lot of money. So she advertised, chose a perfectly satisfactory candidate (who much later became a professor at Columbia University in New York!) and by October we children had all been introduced to formal education. Since none of us aspired to be neurosurgeons, and since there was no drug problem and no gang warfare, parents and students alike found education to be a very straightforward and stress-free experience. Year after year, our teachers were young, lively and resourceful. They taught seven or eight children, in five or six grades, the basics and whatever extra their talents could provide. If our grasp of history was a bit tenuous, our knowledge of frog spawn was complete. We missed a lot. We weren't exposed to great music or introduced to the wonders of a library, but we found these things later for ourselves; in the meantime, we learned to work on our own, to think for ourselves and to help the younger members of the class. Except for the time a teacher slipped on a patch of ice, fell on me and broke my collarbone, my education proceeded without incident.

In school or out of it, physical activities didn't include organized sports. Sports, as such, were as foreign to us as a night at the opera, for several reasons. We were all of elementary school age; there were often no teenagers in the community to introduce us to

such things as baseball. Those teenagers who occasionally lived among us did hard physical work all week, and in their few hours of leisure they were more inclined to lie down and read pulp magazines or do their laundry. Then, even if there were an enthusiast or two among the adults, there was no suitable space. Our playing field was not only not level, it was vertical. And finally, and perhaps most importantly, we children had so many more interesting things to do that organized games palled by comparison. No book of children's adventure stories offered experiences that we couldn't duplicate for ourselves. We built log cabins, explored the trackless jungle, dammed streams and played Robinson Crusoe on deserted beaches.

The ocean was too cold for swimming; instead it offered another recreational opportunity. Under the dock, down in the clear green depths, a dazzling array of marine life presented itself—sea urchins, crabs, sea anenomes, starfish, barnacles (which made excellent bait) and rock cod. The fishermen among us bought fishing line from the store, keeping it, when not in use, wound around a bit of scrap lumber. Thus equipped, they spent hours fishing through the cracks in the dock and were invariably rewarded for their patience.

Even the youngest of us pursued their interests with enthusiasm. One little boy of about three, whom my father had nicknamed "Hardtack" for his tough and independent spirit, roamed the bushes and the boardwalk with very little supervision. His abiding interest was natural history, and at regular intervals, tottering the considerable distance between his house and ours, he would proceed to a stump in our front garden. Between the roots, at the base of the stump, was a small opening. "Hardtack" would lie on the ground, head turned and pressed against the stump, and would insert his small arm into this crack and probe about earnestly. Sometimes he would withdraw his arm and try to peer into the blackness within, only to resume his efforts, his arm stretched to its limit.

My mother, seeing his tow head at the back door, knew just what to expect—and she would cringe. Hardtack would hammer on the door with his free hand, and when my mother appeared he would extend the other with its writhing prize.

"Nake,.....nake," he would say, proudly.

"Yes, Hardtack," my mother would say, backing into the laundry tubs, "a very lovely snake. Now put it back where you found it."

Hardtack always did as he was told, but in a week

Under the dock a dazzling array of marine life presented itself. The fishermen among us were invariably rewarded for their patience.

or so the whole process was repeated. The snake's refusal to abandon its chosen home in the face of these disruptions can be interpreted as heroism, or obstinacy—or as proof that reptiles have limited reasoning power.

While most city children have only a hazy idea of what their fathers do all day—and in the 1990s often their mothers as well— we children were anything but vague about our parents' occupations. On one side of the harbour stood the mill, on the other side the mill office and the dock. Everyone's father left the house when the 7:50 mill whistle blew and tramped along the boardwalk to one or other of these destinations. If there was any doubt about what employed them for the rest of the day we could check it out and, in fact, we regularly did.

Everybody's work, with the exception of the bookkeeper's and the storekeeper's, involved noise and machinery; it was heavy and dangerous; it was fun to watch. In the mill, the most interesting person to watch was the sawyer. He stood behind a screen in a welter of noise and a stinging fan of flying sawdust. Just ahead of him whirled two five-foot circular headsaws. The fact that every sawyer was missing fingers proved the unforgiving nature of those saws. Beside the sawyer, and at his bidding, the carriage strained forward carrying a log through the saws, and then raced backwards. Standing on the carriage, balanced and braced against its movement, the dogger made

instant adjustments in response to the sawyer's hand signals. It was a spell-binding ballet.

At the other side of the harbour, the tug wrestled log booms in through the narrow entrance and scows out of it. Like a sheepdog, she circled the perimeter of her charges, pushing here and shoving there. Periodically, she put on an even more entertaining show when our wooden scows had to be turned over for their annual tarring. They were first filled with sea-water, then out in the entrance of the bay the tug put a short tow-line on the half-sunken craft and revved up her engine. The whole scow lifted slowly out of the water like a great black whale and rolled over. Once the bottom was re-tarred, there was a repeat performance to get the scow upright again.

When the tug wasn't towing she was being loaded with lumber. At high tide she lay almost level with the dock, but at low tide she lay a good fifteen feet below it and the slingloads of stacked lumber swung out high in the air before they were lowered to their resting place on the stern deck. If the slings were placed dead centre on the stack of lumber and the load was thus perfectly balanced, it was easy enough to handle; but an unbalanced load, once lifted off the ground, acted like an unbroken horse, willfully catching on every protuberance, dragging its hapless attendant hither and yon. Once over the edge of the dock, it took up a vertical position rather than a horizontal one, and threatened to slide downward onto the heads of those below. Again men and machines performed their intricate dance; the tug's engine puffed away in neutral, the winch growled, the boom swung back and forth, hands signalled, feet kept carefully out of the bight of the line.

All day long there was the reassuring hum of machinery with the clack of conveyors and the whining of saws providing grace notes. As a child, I was always disturbed by communities where earning a living wasn't accompanied by noise. I found their atmosphere purposeless and their silence depressing.

People never believe me when I say I can't ride a bicycle.

"What do you mean?" they say irritably. "Everyone can ride a bicycle. I've been riding a bicycle since I was six."

Well, I haven't. I can't ride a bicycle because where I grew up there were no roads. None. That's the message my mother finally got across to the Superintendent of Education. There was an icy ocean sloshing at the rocks and a dense wall of cedar, fir, hemlock and salal right down to the high-water mark. There were floats and gangways and docks and a boardwalk that was supported by pilings, but there was no road. No possible way to leave the confines of that small horseshoe-shaped cove, except by water.

Bea and I didn't have bicycles; instead we had a flat-bottomed twelve-foot skiff. It was old and heavy and so badly designed that it was like rowing an island, but it gave us freedom and a clumsy mobility. Not that there weren't ground rules. We were taught never to stand up in a rowboat, never to run on a larger boat, never to play on log booms (logs having a tendency to roll you off into the water and then close over your head), and never, *ever* to scream. We kept our shrill children's voices down. We knew that if we ever needed help that would be the time to scream. Our home was always filled with my parents' friends, and when these were city people

their children, hummed up by the novelty of it all, ran up and down the deck of the tug screeching endlessly. We regarded them gravely, and with a certain amount of contempt.

Day after day, weather permitting, my sister and I sallied forth in our skiff. There was no real destination possible, for the coastline was deserted on both sides of our harbour. Instead of going somewhere, we examined starfish and at low tide knocked abalone off the bottom with one swift jab of an oar. We made kelp babies from the huge globes of kelp with their briny steaming hair, we watched whales before it was fashionable to do so, and we kept an eye on the tide.

The tide ruled our lives. Those unfamiliar with BC coastal waters were always astounded by their tidal currents. Not for nothing were our docks built to accommodate a twenty-two foot rise and fall. From a distance, the ocean appeared static and for a few minutes twice a day it was; but the innocents who found themselves out in a rowboat when the tide turned and started to run had the unsettling experience of rowing as hard as they could in one direction while being swept inexorably in the opposite one, and were the source of much amusement until they learned better. Small whirlpools, forming and reforming around the boat, were nature's reminder that this was one big river that wouldn't alter its direction for another six hours.

Of course, an engine would have changed all this, but in the 1930s outboards were rare and notoriously

My sister, myself, our rowboat and the makings of a kelp doll.

unreliable. More important, they were expensive; during the Depression there was no money for recreation—or even for conveniences. Hard labour was the substitute. And so my sister and I considered ourselves very fortunate in having the luxury of our own boat. We rowed for miles and, of necessity, we watched the tides. We knew when they were slack, when they would be working to our advantage and how, if all else failed, we could get in very close to shore and pick up a back eddy. None of this was taught, but was simply learned from watching a parent who did not row, but who ran a tug and made part of his living towing booms of logs and scows.

On one of our expeditions we took our dog, Puppy, with us. He was anything but a puppy. Our previous dogs, Yissie and Cultus, had been killed by cougars. Puppy was, as my grandmother termed it, a Jap dog. He had belonged to a departed Japanese fam-

Alex MacDonald and I in the millyard with
Yissie and Cultus, Both dogs were later killed by cougars.

ily—hence his generic name, I suppose—who had left him behind. He was a very solid dog—the word stout comes to mind—and an ocean voyage was a pleasant novelty for him. He sat in the bow seat of our stubby little boat and regarded the watery world with interest. Suddenly, directly in front of him, not three feet away, a large salmon jumped into the air and hit the water with a splash. Puppy let out a series of wild barks and leaped over the bow in the general direction of the salmon. When he surfaced, he was paddling hard—and grunting, the frigid water and his new form of locomotion causing him acute anxiety. He had completely forgotten the salmon and wanted just one thing, to get back into the skiff. Realizing that we would capsize if we tried to pull him over the side, we spun the boat around and approached him stern first. Country dogs don't wear collars, so there was nothing to grasp. The one who was not at the oars leaned over, grabbed him by the leg and pulled. Feeling in imminent danger of having his leg yanked out of its socket, Puppy wisely resisted. Maybe a rope, we thought; all we had was our painter. The oarsman reversed the skiff and now approached Puppy bow on. The rope approach was as futile as the leg approach. There was no way we could reach far enough to secure the painter around Puppy's ample middle. All three of us were becoming exceedingly anxious. Once more we spun the boat around and approached Puppy stern to. Now we both crouched in the stern seat, balancing our weight as evenly as possible. Without a word, we both reached out our skinny arms, grabbed Puppy by the rolls of fat around his non-existent neck and hauled with a strength born of desperation. Puppy came scrabbling into the boat, clawing us painfully in the process and streaming cold water. For the rest of the voyage, we took turns rowing and sitting in the stern seat with our arms held firmly around Puppy's wet neck. Although he seemed disinclined to repeat the performance, we were taking no chances.

All of our efforts, that day and on other similar jaunts, were hampered by the fact that Bea and I were wearing bulky homemade life-jackets. There were no child-sized life-jackets in the 1930s. For economic reasons, recreational boating wasn't a feature of those years, and children who lived as my sister and I did represented an infinitesimal share of the life-jacket market. So my mother, ever resourceful, bought some heavy white canvas and sewed it into child-sized vests. She ripped open one or two of the older, grubbier vests that we carried on the *Klinekwa* and inserted slabs of cork, sewing them firmly into place. We wore them for two reasons. Firstly we knew the dangers the sea presented. The local doctor calculated that anyone thrown into it had twenty minutes of life before dying of hypothermia. The comments of city-dwelling relatives of local drowning victims, that they "couldn't understand how this could happen. He was a very strong swimmer," made no sense to us. We could understand all too well how such things could happen, and we understood, too, that our life-jackets were no guarantee of survival. They simply gave us an edge of safety.

The second reason we wore our life-jackets was that our mother wouldn't have let us out on the water without them. That she let us go alone, at all, is a source of wonderment to me now, for she was a conscientious and protective parent, inordinately concerned with germs and other lurking dangers. However, given the circumstances of our life, I suppose she saw nothing unusual about two skinny little girls in a twelve-foot rowboat exploring miles of coastline, out of the sight or hearing of all other human beings.

As we got older, our expeditions took on a much more business-like air, for our father now offered us real money for any beachcomb logs we brought in. By this time our heavy little skiff had been replaced by a big old open boat with a little two-hp Briggs & Stratton engine. Emboldened by the knowledge that we now had power and were not at the mercy of the tides, and dazzled by the prospect of being paid the going price for logs and of earning the astounding sum of ninety dollars for a big one, we pursued this new avocation with enthusiasm. There were only two provisos: from mother, the usual admonition about wearing our life-jackets; from father, a stern warning that we were not to use our oars—which we always carried for back-up should the Briggs & Stratton fail—to pry logs off the beach.

Each afternoon after school we would race home, change our clothes and putt-putt out of the cove, around the point and into the open strait in search of "a good log." Our voyages were not without incident.

One sunny afternoon we spotted a gigantic fir log drifting lazily down the strait. We cut the engine and maneuvered alongside it. Even rough calculations promised hundreds of board feet of prime fir. We got our tow rope around it, fastened it securely with a timber hitch and then moved to start the engine. The starting cord had to be wrapped around the flywheel and then yanked briskly. Sometimes one yank would do it, but if the plugs were dirty it might take several to get it to spring into action. This time the first yank failed and, as the flywheel reversed itself, it whipped the starting cord through the air and wedged its small wooden handle beneath the floorboards of the boat. One would assume that if the handle had gotten in under the floorboards it could be gotten out. Not easily, we discovered. The flywheel's force had driven it far into a crack and it was severely stuck. This, in itself, posed no particular problem; the urgency lay in the fact that, as we wrestled with the engine, the tide turned. Slowly, but with increasing velocity, it moved our little boat and its huge tow around and around down the strait. As we struggled with the jammed cord, small whirlpools appeared around us and the distant shoreline moved past in the wrong direction. By the time the handle was finally extricated and the engine started, we were a couple of miles from our starting point. Gradually we took up the slack on our tow rope and gave the engine its maximum two horsepower. Slowly, at full throttle, we slipped backwards down the strait. Our little engine could buck the tide unencumbered, but towing a giant log rendered it impotent. We had drifted so far from home that we were now concerned about our gas supply. There was only one thing to do. With keen regret we cut the engine once again, untied the log, re-started the engine, being careful to cover the floorboards with a jacket to prevent further mishap, and headed for home. We were bucking a strong tide now and our progress was slow. Behind us, our three hundred dollar log, the source of unimaginable wealth, the basis of our future fortune, whirled lazily round and round in the current until we could no longer see it at all.

We had other beachcombing problems. One afternoon, attempting to roll a log off the rocky shoreline and into the water, the temptation to use the oar as a pry grew too strong; I did what I'd been told not to do with predictable results. The oar broke and the log stayed right where it was. I was disturbed but determined. I searched the shoreline for a piece of driftwood that would serve as a pry and renewed my efforts to free the log. Then one of my feet slipped on the kelp that covered the rocks and, looking down, I saw that my leg had taken on a peculiar configuration. I suspected I had dislocated my knee. It was extremely painful but I dared not cry or even appear unduly upset. Bea, five years younger that I, was the only source of help, and I was afraid that if I alarmed her she might not act with the dispatch and efficiency required. I got myself firmly seated on a log and, trying hard for nonchalance, I said, "Bea, I think I've hurt my knee. Will you pick up my foot and pull it out, towards you, just as hard as you can? Pull it really hard," I said, anxiously. She did just that and with the resilience of all things youthful it snapped back into position. Now she put the pieces of the broken oar into the boat and I eased myself down the rocks and over the gunwale. We started the engine and headed home in a very subdued mood. I knew my father would be extremely annoyed about the oar, my knee was throbbing painfully, and our log remained where we had found it, securely wedged in the rocks.

As we approached our teen years, Bea and I learned to swim in a public pool in Victoria. This was considered not so much a recreational experience, but rather, a means of ensuring our survival. As our proficiency in the water improved my mother relaxed her insistence on life-jackets. First, as the oldest, I was permitted to go without mine, which made it all the more onerous for my sister to have to wear hers. One day when we were on some family trip on the tug, my sister prevailed upon mother to let her out of this constriction.

"Well, yes," said mother, "I guess you're old enough to be on the boat without your life-jacket..." Jubilant, my sister ripped off the offending garment and flung it overboard. We watched with shock and fascination as it sank like a stone beneath the wake of the tug.

IV

THE SIMPLE LIFE

Weynton Passage—This passage leads northwestward from the junction of Johnstone Strait and Broughton Strait into Blackfish Sound and the eastern end of Cormorant Channel. The fairway, which is deep, has a minimum width of 7 cables. In Weynton Passage, the tidal streams attain a velocity of 5 knots at times, and set over and across the shoals extending from Stephenson Islet. There are heavy tide rips at times near both shores, and in the vicinity of Stubbs Island.

British Columbia Pilot

Searching records of the past brings the bewildering feeling that Telegraph Cove never existed, that these men and women and children never lived. In libraries there are one or two newspaper articles written long after the fact. In the provincial Archives, there are my grandfather's notes to his friend Major J.S. Matthews. There is a sentence or two in the *British Columbia Pilot*. And that is all. It's as if the whole thing were a figment of the imagination; and yet, day and night, with a billow of smoke or a shower of sparks, the sawmill burner advertised our presence. By day, we were a cluster of small brown buildings and a dock huddled at the base of a mountain. By night, we were a few dim lights in the miles and miles of blackness.

Every day of the week but one, men hefted timbers in the rain and wrestled with second-hand machinery. Their wives tried to get one Monday's wash dry before the next Monday rolled around, and had their babies as cheaply as possible—one inadvertently giving birth in the sawdust of the mill floor. After school, we children helped at home and engaged in our own strenuous projects. One January, for example, we formed a bucket brigade and emptied the frog pond onto the ground in a misguided attempt to create a skating rink.

Our hard work was our security. We produced something tangible and were paid for it. We each had a house to call our own and a kitchen stove to fill the rooms with warmth and drive away the dampness. These basics were our bulwark against the times, for in the cities people were lining up at soup kitchens, and on the prairies some of them were starving.

Although our little community had intruded to some small degree, the landscape belonged to the natural world and its inhabitants. Raccoons boldly picked our raspberries in full view of their rightful owners, deer demolished our roses, otters played on our log booms and cougars prowled our woods and occasionally ate our pets. If they were hungry enough, they tried to eat people as well, as Hillier Lansdowne discovered. "Hilly" was a descendant of the illustrious and aristocratic British Lansdownes, although the connection was not immediately apparent when you met him. He had a small logging camp on one of the islands across the strait, where one morning a cougar leapt out of the woods and attacked Mrs. Coon, the wife of one of the Indian loggers. Although he had no gun or any other weapon at hand, Hilly rushed to her rescue. By this time the cougar's jaws had a firm grip on the woman's shoulder. Hilly got his hands around both sides of the animal's neck and, after some considerable effort, strangled it. He brushed off any suggestion of exceptional bravery. "Since I outweighed the son-of-a-bitch by about a hundred pounds, I expected to win that fight," was his comment.

Visitors found all of this madly picturesque. People tend to romanticize what they don't understand, and they certainly didn't understand our life. They walked into our shabby kitchen, smelled bread baking and were enchanted. "Back to the simple life," they enthused. But it wasn't a simple life; it was actually very complicated, and it stretched our capabilities to the limit. Or our guests gazed out at the view from our living-room windows and said, "It's just breathtakingly beautiful, of course, but what do you do to fill your time?" Somehow it escaped their notice that at that very moment my mother was filling her time by doing what she did so often—cooking dinner for a crowd. And perhaps cooking it on a sawdust-burning stove that wasn't burning because the sawdust was wet hemlock. Her culinary tasks were always made especially difficult when the sawmill was cutting hemlock.

My mother's chief source of dissatisfaction however, was not the sawdust burner, but the house itself. It was far too small and very ugly, for it was still essentially a lineman's shack. My mother's grandfather had been an architect and she had inherited his eye. She spent all her spare moments drawing floor plans, clipping pictures and planning her dream home. At first she thought that a log house would be the most suited to our environment, but my father said that log construction was poor advertising for a sawmill, so then she dreamed of a Dutch Colonial. She got neither. It was ironic that someone who cared so much about houses should live all her married life in one of the ugliest buildings imaginable.

It must have been about 1932 that my father and Alex MacDonald went to look at the boilers at Suquash, and there my mother and I found a real-life dream home. I can date it because I can remember it so I must have been about three.

The men had heard that the abandoned coal

mine there was selling two brand new boilers at a bargain price, so a "picnic" was organized one weekend and we took the boat to Suquash, anchored and rowed in to shore. While the men went off to inspect the boilers, my mother and I investigated the big house that sat empty on a rise above the sea. Much later, when I explored the interior of BC, where there are so many more mines, I was always puzzled by the difference in the quality of the housing provided for the managers of mines compared to what was laid on for those who managed logging operations—and I'm still puzzled. Whereas the superintendent of even a large logging camp lived in a tacky little frame house, the manager of any mine lived in a house that verged on the luxurious. The house we found at Suquash was a perfect example. We pushed open the door and went inside and, even as a small child, I knew that this was what was left of a lovely home. The walls were panelled, there were square bay windows with window seats, and a huge river rock fireplace capable of supplying endless cheer in the unendingly rainy climate. Indians had been in the house before us and had ripped off some of the panelling for firewood. They had cooked clams in the great fireplace, and the shells were piled high on the hearth. I loved the house

and couldn't understand why it had been abandoned by its occupants. For Emma, living in her ugly shack, it must have been an even more painful experience to wander through those empty rooms. However, she said nothing; she simply took a photo of the great stone fireplace and we turned and left the house to its fate.

Finally, in 1937, my father came up with what he considered a brilliant solution to the housing problem. He would have Mame's brother, who was also named Fred, raise our house and put another storey under it. As a consequence what started out as a lineman's shack ended up as a large two-

The added storey at least made the lineman's shack into more of a family home.

storey lineman's shack.

The whole undertaking was an ambitious one and certainly wouldn't have been possible without the skill of my father's uncle. This remarkable man, with nothing more than a couple of pump jacks and a big pile of mill ends, cut the house loose from its moorings and raised it eight feet into the air. The fact that it stood on an irregularly shaped rock bluff (as rock bluffs usually are) didn't make the job any easier.

While all this was going on, my father lived in the upper part of the building. Having the rest of us do the same thing must have seemed, even to him, to be stretching the point a bit, so my mother, my sister and I spent the summer in Victoria. My father kept us posted. He wrote to my mother:

Was glad to get your letter today and if we had four or five carpenters here might be able to keep up with your suggestions but we are following as closely as we can and doing our very best. Some of the minor ideas we can leave for awhile but just for now Fred is getting in the plumbing which I miss terribly. The house looks funny now from the outside—like a box but when Fred gets those false eaves on I think it will be fine. Our old bedroom is as good as new, just has to be nailed on to the house again. (It had been removed from the now-second storey in order to maintain a rectangle and was now going to be re-attached to the ground floor!)

To me he wrote:

You would have a great time if you were here now. Every time you wanted to go in the house you would have to climb up the woodshed roof and in our bedroom window. The King and Queen are looking out over the roof and you have to crawl into that room from the basement. Some morning I expect to wake up and find I can't get out at all. The black cat doesn't know what to make of it all.

We returned to a house with five bedrooms, two bathrooms, some very nice French doors leading from the front hall to the living-room and a fireplace. It wasn't, however, by any stretch of the imagination, a Dutch Colonial.

By now our little ten-hp Petters light engine had been replaced with a new larger one. The "new" light engine was, of course, not new but was the Atlas Imperial that had formerly powered the *Sundown;* nor did it give us much more access to the wonders of electricity. The community was allowed electricity for one morning a week for

The mine manager's house at Suquash. The stair railings and panelling had been used for firewood and the hearth was littered with clamshells.

domestic purposes and, as a consequence, half a dozen frantic housewives plugged in their washing machines at the same time, which often proved more than the generator could bear and left us with a tub full of washing and no power.

For this reason, electricity played a very small part in our housekeeping. We kept our perishables in a screened safe, ironed our clothes with sad irons, cooked on a sawdust burner and took our rugs outdoors to beat them free of dust. When the incessant rain made clothes drying outdoors impossible, we hung the laundry on a ceiling rack in the kitchen and dodged wet sheets as we cooked. In place of a vacuum cleaner, we filled a bucket with damp shreds of torn newspapers, scattered these over the fir floors and then swept them up along with the dust that clung to them. At an early age I was practised in all these domestic arts,

45

and I could run a winch and load a boat with lumber as well, but when I went to high school in Victoria, I found these to be non-transferable skills.

Given this casual country life and the absence of labour-saving appliances, the housewife of today would adopt a casual country style and use pottery and table mats. No one had this imagination or good sense in the 1930s; instead, we used white damask tablecloths and napkins, silver flatware and, for Sunday dinner, white and gold Limoges china. It made for a lot of unnecessary work. Nor did we use any better sense when it came to food.

If we on the north Island were poor in monetary terms, we were immensely rich when it came to natural resources. Year after year, seiners dotted the waters of Johnstone Strait and hauled in nets full of salmon; in Belize Inlet, prawn fishermen caught eighteen hundred pounds of prawns in four days; the local paper bragged that our timber resources could "build a boardwalk to the moon." Our tiny population took all this largesse for granted and saw no end to its abundance. Yet, as a family, we certainly didn't take advantage of it. Far from living off the land, we ate cases of canned vegetables and a lot of gristly roast beef, and if we had had to depend on my father to catch us a fish or shoot us a deer we would have long since starved. The only people who really understood how to live off these resources were our Japanese employees.

At eleven o'clock each evening, our electric lights faded once as a warning and then went out. What had been a cheerily lit living-room moments before was plunged into the deep darkness of a country night until, with much stumbling and fumbling, the coal oil lamps were lit. Guests from the city found this delightfully idiosyncratic—so amusing and romantic to carry a lamp upstairs to bed. This return to the lamplight of yesteryear wasn't, as one might guess, an effort to save on the fuel that powered the light engine; rather it was insurance against our being burned in our beds. Our house, and all the other buildings in the community, had been wired by amateurs. Even someone of my father's optimistic nature felt that the sleeping occupants were safer without power surging through this creative electrical work.

We were lucky at Telegraph Cove in that, before roads and radio-telephones and helicopters, we had two life-lines that many coastal communities did not. We had a sixty-foot boat that was well maintained and operated by someone with skill and judgement—and we had a telephone. The telephone line was simply strung along the coastline, and was frequently taken out by falling trees. Each party was assigned a particular series of rings—we answered our phone when it rang one short and one long ring—and to call others we cranked out the appropriate rings. Everyone on the line could listen to everyone else if they were so inclined—but they weren't, probably because the phone was never used for casual conversation. It was for business or for emergencies, and it surprised no one when it was dead and couldn't be used at all until the lineman, patrolling by boat, found the break and fixed it.

Then, in the early 1940s, Spilsbury and Hepburn began to install a magical new device called a radio-telephone in all the isolated habitations that dotted the coast. Up until that time, people in the remote settlements were cut off from the rest of the world by distance and silence. Suddenly that silence was broken, communication was possible, distance shrank. Life would never again be quite so sternly lonely. The radio-phones facilitated business, of course, but for people engaged in work as dangerous as logging, people whose only previous connection with civilization was a gasboat, they could also mean the difference between life and death.

Since we were connected to the telephone line we continued to use that form of communication, but we had a radio-telephone installed in the boat, as did almost everyone else. Now, when we were off on our various trips, we could listen to the marine weather reports and notify customers of our estimated time of arrival. And we could relieve the tedium of towing by listening to fishing boats, separated by a distance of two miles, enquiring, with unconcealed delight at this new toy, "How's the weather over there?" Although this was a straightforward (though superfluous) question, there was a lot of duplicity wafting over the radio waves, too. Passing a seiner brailing in enough salmon to sink it, we could hear her skipper being evasive about his position and success, in order to keep his fellows as far away as possible.

Listening in, of course, was quite acceptable,

because to make a call one had to wait until any existing conversation was completed. And only half of the conversation was actually heard. The other half was merely a series of beeps and had to be imagined. That this was not a real limitation was exemplified by a conversation we overheard one day between a man on a fish packer and his wife in Vancouver. We could hear only the wife's side of the conversation.

She said she missed him.

A couple of perfunctory beeps.

She found herself greatly inconvenienced in his long absences by her inability to drive a car.

Three beeps.

She would like to learn to drive.

Three beeps.

The man next door had offered to teach her. How did this idea strike him?

A torrent of beeps poured from the marine band ....

Our other connections with the larger world were the daily newspaper and the radio. Neither one was as straightforward as that sentence implies. The newspapers arrived once a week on a Union steamship, in a big bundle containing the previous seven days' news. This was not an unsatisfactory arrangement. There is something infinitely relaxing about reading news that's a week old. As if we weren't distanced enough from the alarums of the world, this distanced us even more. There was rarely a problem that hadn't been resolved by the time we read about it. My grandfather, in particular, sitting in front of the fire, puffing his pipe and reading the week-old newspapers, found the time lapse just right for his stage of life.

The radio, a floor model Stromberg Carlson, had two limitations. Firstly, it was powered by a storage battery which gave us a week or two of strong reception and then, as the battery weakened, just a few tantalizing moments of sound before it faded away to nothing; and secondly, since we lived right at the base of a mountain, radio reception was uniformly poor and no amount of amateur aerial adjusting could overcome the challenge of topography.

Our contact with he outside world via the media, then, was sporadic, limited, out-of-date and filled with static. Our contact with the rest of the human race, however, was continuous and immediate. Each visitor who appeared at our door had come a long way to get there; the wonder of it was that there were so many of them. Without warning, pile-driver operators, yachtsmen, school teachers, wire rope salesmen and clergymen, to name a few, turned up on our doorstep. As a consequence, growing up in our house was a lot like working in a hotel. If our visitors were stranded, they were offered a bed; if they were cruising in a small boat they were offered a bath; all of them were offered a meal. We had a visitor, or visitors, for at least one meal a day—sometimes for all three. Because we owned the store, we had access to groceries twenty-four hours a day. That was a good thing, because in the kitchen a meal planned for five became one for eight; the breakfast porridge for four was stretched, with piles of toast, to feed six; extra pies, cakes and cookies rolled out of the oven, and the dirty dishes formed an endless stream. All of this was accomplished with a sawdust-burning cookstove, a far from inexhaustible supply of hot water provided by that same stove, and no electrical appliances

Having this throng of dissimilar people passing through the house meant that we learned, like Barbara Walters, to make conversation with anyone about anything. And it meant that, to this day, I have a compulsion to ask anyone who appears at the door to come in for a meal.

Mother had been raised a Methodist, but she switched to the Anglican church when she married. I was glad she did, because Methodists were very strict and forbade card playing and dancing, which seemed to me to put quite a damper on a life that wasn't already over-filled with entertainment. Besides, the Church of England appeared to be the official religion of the north coast. This was because their missionaries had got there first. In Alert Bay, they had built an Indian residential school, a much-needed hospital and a small but beautiful church. And then, in the early years at least, they sent the clergy for this church directly out from England.

Unlike their brethren who joined the army and set out for India, these men hadn't joined the church for adventure, so the difference between life in a quiet English village and life on the BC coast left them in a permanent state of culture shock. It made them an easy target for ridicule, too, which didn't help the religion they were promoting. Like our table linen, they were nice but unsuited to the surroundings.

They were also hard to talk to. They were the only visitors who defeated our Barbara Walters-ish attempts at conversation. Sitting in our living-room, sipping tea and eating cucumber sandwiches (which my mother thought would make them feel at home) we had absolutely nothing to say to each other. After a couple of hours of this, we felt we had done our bit for the Anglican church.

We had better luck with the mission boat *Columbia* which brought us the Rev. Heber Greene, who was equally sincere but much more suited to the environment. Still, it isn't any of his religious teachings that I remember. Rather, I remember watching in awe as Rev. Greene, sitting at our breakfast table, put cream and brown sugar on his bowl of oatmeal and then poured his glass of orange juice over it. "It will all end up in the same place," he said cheerfully.

A scow load of lumber and a scow load of slabs, mid-'30s. The latter were sold to the Indian Residential School at Alert Bay to fuel their heating plant.

V

MARINE TRAFFIC

Johnstone Strait—The southern shore is a continuous series of high, steep mountain ranges rising abruptly from the water's edge, some of the highest peaks being covered with snow all year round. These ranges are separated by valleys through which flow streams of considerable size.

British Columbia Pilot

All along the northeast coast of Vancouver Island, the mountains drop straight into the sea. At the foot of one of them, our small horseshoe-shaped harbour looked out, due north, onto Johnstone Strait. It was a stunning view. Beyond the strait lay the delicate outline of an intricate web of islands; beyond that lay the mainland and the coast mountains. Mount Waddington, the highest peak in the range rose, like Mount Fuji, in the distance.

Johnstone Strait was our thoroughfare, our link with the rest of humanity. In theory, it could have started us on a journey to the ends of the earth, and in practice it sometimes brought us ships from just such places. We travelled Johnstone Strait to shop, to do business, to visit friends, to see a doctor, or just to while away a Sunday afternoon. On sunny summer mornings when the sea was glassy and rolled away from a boat's bow in oily curves, on bright fall afternoons when the westerlies got up as regularly as clockwork and blew the sea into a blazing blue, or on bleak November days when the southeasters shook the house and turned the sea into an army of great grey rollers smoking with spume; at all these times, in a variety of craft, we emerged into the strait on our errands, be they casual or critical.

A constant stream of marine traffic worked its way up and down the strait: freighters, passenger steamers, tugs and tows, seiners, trollers and yachts. Some of these vessels called in at our little harbour at regular intervals, some simply passed by, and some of them appeared unexpectedly from nowhere, moored for an hour, a week or a summer, and then vanished as completely as if they had never existed.

The most regular of our callers were the Union steamships. Each week, without fail, either the *Cardena* or the *Catala* arrived. Their black hulls, white superstructures and red funnels were familiar to every coastal inhabitant, for they were the north coast's supply line to the city. Each week on "boat day," the ship's radio operator broadcast the estimated time of arrival and then, there they were, rounding the point and blocking the entrance to the harbour with their bulk. Suddenly the air was full of acrid smoke from their funnels, the store was full of fresh food, and the Post Office was full of the mail they delivered.

As children, we made many trips with our mother to and from Vancouver on these ships, and they were always thrilling adventures. Encumbered as we often were by an aged aunt—and sometimes even a canary—we required two staterooms. My sister and I shared one of them, revelling in our independence. However, when it came time to go to bed, we needed help from an adult. Employing some secret procedure that died with them, the stewards on these ships made up the berths so tightly that it took a strong and determined adult to pry the sheets apart. No child was equal to the task. Even when one finally wriggled in under the blankets, it was only those with the general body contours of a postage stamp who could be comfortable.

We were shy country children, and when we descended the broad brass-trimmed stairway to the dining saloon we were always overwhelmed by its magnificence. There were big, round tables with snowy napery, clusters of silver cutlery, glasses tinkling with ice cubes, and stewards in black uniforms and immaculate white shirts. The menu always included the item "celery and olives" and we astonished our adult table-mates by quietly devouring every olive in sight. Travelling thus we had acquired a taste for them and we never, ever, had them at home.

In retrospect, the service that the Union Steamship Company provided was remarkable. They pressed doggedly on through violent winter storms and, perhaps even more remarkably, they kept to their appointed schedules in blankets of fog. Long before radar, these sizeable ships negotiated the convoluted channels and narrow passages that formed our difficult coast, and made their regular appearances in the tiniest, most remote settlement. Year after year, with no fanfare and little recognition, their tired-looking captains performed remarkable feats of seamanship.

The company didn't operate entirely without incident, of course. Although we ourselves had never been involved in any of their marine mishaps, an acquaintance of ours had.

Mr. Pesnic was a huge, raw-boned man in his seventies who had been a logger and a homesteader. He had a booming voice, a thick middle-European accent, and a unique pattern of stress and intonation that made his conversation particularly compelling and invariably reduced my father to helpless laughter,

no matter how mundane the subject. Sitting chatting on his back steps one day he happened to mention that he had been on the Union steamship *Cheslakee* when she sank at the dock at Van Anda. My father sensed that a man of Pesnic's phlegmatic temperament might possibly provide an uncommon perspective on the event and he was absolutely right.

Mr. Pesnic, it appeared, had left Vancouver on the 8:45 p.m. sailing. He went to bed in his cabin, planning to get off at Manson's Landing on Cortes Island early the next morning. Once into Georgia Strait, the *Cheslakee* encountered grimly heavy weather. Hit by one particularly bad squall, her cargo shifted and she couldn't be righted. Asleep in his bunk, Mr. Pesnic was unaware of these grave events, but when he finally awoke it was to a feeling of unease. The ship was docked, but not at Manson's Landing. A great deal of shouting and commotion was going on outside the porthole, and the floor of his cabin was not in the same position as it had been the night before. With some difficulty, Pesnic got out of his berth, put on some clothes, struggled out into the corridor, up the companionway and onto the deck. A scene of considerable chaos met his eyes. The ship was heeling over, and as the deck slanted ever more

The Union steamship S.S. *Cheslakee* when she sank at the dock at Van Anda, January 1913.

markedly, passengers were clambering up it in a desperate attempt to reach the ladder on the dock.

Obviously, the women passengers were having the most difficult time. Pesnic had probably never heard the expression "women and children first," but he subscribed to the idea. He and another man helped the women to get themselves and their families up the deck and onto the ladder. Nor did they confine their efforts to women. A man in city clothes, who seemed to be reacting quite emotionally to the whole experience, was also helped to the ladder. He climbed to the top, walked across the dock in a state of shock and fell into the water on the other side. There he clung to a piling screaming for help.

"Shut up!" bellowed Pesnic. "We saved you once. You're just going to have to wait."

By now the deck had assumed an almost perpendicular position, and Pesnic decided that the time had come to save himself. He got a firm grip on a hatch cover that was now above his head rather than in its customary position underfoot, and tried to haul himself up. Some distance above him was a logger with the same intent. When that logger had thrown on his clothes that morning they included the only footwear that he had—a pair of heavy caulk boots with razor sharp nails protruding from the soles. They give the wearer a firm grip on a log but they don't give much purchase on a steel deck. Besides, the logger was inclining just a bit towards panic. He scrabbled up the deck, slipped and came crashing down on Pesnic's fingers.

"*Well* now," Pesnic explained to my father, "he was a big man and I got sort of mad."

Once again the man scrambled for safety, and once again he fell back onto Pesnic's fingers.

"You bastard," shouted Pesnic, finally provoked, "you wait till I get up there! I will give you a punch you won't forget."

"What happened?" asked my father, who was at this point convulsed with laughter.

"When I finally got up on that dock," said Pesnic, "the bugger was gone."

My father composed himself, we had a cup of Mr. Pesnic's good strong coffee and walked back to our boat.

Unlike the Union steamships, most of the boats that called came unexpectedly. Waking to a strong southeaster, we might find three seiners tied to the dock below the house, their big brailers swaying at their masts, their fishing company flags snapping in the wind. Having sought shelter for the night, they would start up their engines and head out again with daylight. As they let go their lines the incomprehensible shouts of their crews identified them as Italian or Yugoslavian.

When boats arrived at night, they often advertised their presence by flicking on their searchlights and probing the darkness for the narrow entrance to our harbour. Since two of our upstairs bedrooms faced directly out to sea, we would be wakened suddenly from a sound sleep to find the whole room brilliantly illuminated. This blinding light would move back and forth, like a great eye, checking the rocky shore and the docks, and then, having established its boat's position, it would snap off, leaving us to our sleep.

One day a "back to basics" family sailed into the Cove; quite literally, for their vessel had no power, only its sails. Sailboats were a curiosity, since they weren't suitable as workboats and the wealthy, who had money for recreational craft, favoured power boats. The crew of the sailboat consisted of a man, his wife and their son who was about two. They embraced the hippie philosophy of living off the land and they had been subsisting on clams, fish, seaweed and berries—a highly nutritious diet but one that palls after a time. At any rate, they didn't seem averse to joining the market economy, if only temporarily. The husband became one of the sawmill crew and the wife moved—with some relief, it appeared—into one of the employee houses. Here, at least, they had plumbing and more spacious quarters than their boat afforded. It was the child, however, who gained the most from this change of scene. At sea he had played at the nose of the boat, a tiny area fenced off with rope to keep him from falling overboard. He was so used to spending his days sitting down that when he came ashore he continued the practice. It was some time before he recognized the possibilities inherent in standing up and walking around. When they resumed their voyage, which they did before long, it must have been hard for this two-year-old to relinquish his new-found freedom and adjust once more to the boat.

On another day, we woke to find a little boat tied, not to the dock or to the floats, but to a boom-stick on the other side of the bay. For a couple of days there was no sign of life aboard. Finally, worried about its occupant, Jimmy, our boat's engineer, rowed over to investigate. The owner, as small as his little boat, was asleep in his bunk.

"How's your grub?" asked Jimmy, after looking

around the confined space not seeing anything at all that was edible. "Got anything to eat?"

"I've got a bit of flour," said the occupant.

"That doesn't sound like a lot to me," said Jimmy. "You'd better come across and tie your boat to the float and get some food."

And so Tinkerbell, as he was nicknamed, stayed around all summer and did odd jobs. Then, one fall morning, we awoke to find that Tinkerbell, in his little boat with its tiny engine, had sailed away.

Not all our visitors were as impecunious—or as reticent—as Tinkerbell. In summer large, glossy yachts came gliding around the point. Crew members readied snazzy rope bumpers all along their sides, lest anything mar their perfect paintwork; people in bright clothes lounged on their afterdecks. If our boat was out, they sometimes made themselves at home at her mooring. The owner of one of these over-powered toys, having blithely moored in the *Hili-Kum*'s spot, came into the store for ice.

"I'm sorry, we don't have ice," said Thelma, the storekeeper.

"No *ice*?" the man asked, incredulously. He looked around the store as if to assure himself that she wasn't hiding some behind a counter somewhere.

"No ice," said Thelma.

"So, I'll have some gas," the man said. He regarded the store's little display of wilted vegetables with disdain. "You *do* have gas?"

"Yes," said Thelma, "but you'll have to move to the front of the dock."

She got the keys to the gas shed, he moved his boat, and they met at the end of the dock.

"You can fill up the water, too," the man said.

When his gas tank was full, Thelma switched hoses and filled up his water tank. Then they went back to the store where she made out his bill.

"What about the water?" the man said, checking the bill.

"We don't charge for water," said Thelma. "It's just there for our own convenience. We're not really in the tourist business." She was getting her own back.

The word "tourist" did it. The man seemed suddenly compelled to present himself as a master mariner.

"Just came through the Yuculta Rapids," he said, notching up his voice. He pronounced it as it's spelled, which was unfortunate. "We're going to Alaska. Going across the Sound," he added, just in case we yokels thought he was going overland. "Of course, that boat I've got can take anything. I've been out in a lot of dirty weather in that boat."

My father had been working in the office. Now he came around and peered through the Post Office wicket to see where all the noise was coming from.

"Spread it thin," he murmured. "You've got a large farm."

This kind of thing left us members of the "life is real, life is earnest" school with a permanent distaste for high life. Secretly, I took great pride in the fact that ours was a workboat and that, as a consequence, our trips had a purpose. By definition, then, others might be amateurs but we were pros. I never revealed this reverse snobbery to anyone else in the family, and only once do I remember any of them making a comment in this regard. We were tied alongside a big yacht in the some harbour after a very long day on the water and, as my grandmother prepared dinner, she noticed a white uniformed chef doing the same thing in the galley opposite.

"Oh, sometimes I do miss having a Chinaman," she sighed.

Fortunately, there was a different kind of yachtsman we looked forward to seeing and with whom we became fast friends. They were regular visitors—their boats appeared every summer without fail. Most of them were Americans who made the trip up the Inside Passage to Alaska each year. They were competent seamen and interested and interesting people—magazine editors, teachers, professional people of all kinds, who filled our living-room with their adventures, their enthusiasm and their laughter.

Our own boat lay moored at the dock below our house. When the winter southeasters howled up the strait our boat—and our log booms—remained safe and secure, perfectly sheltered in their bolthole. Only the great gusts of wind that soughed through the tops of the trees, that sent sheets of ripples across the surface of the bay, that caused the tug to glide away from the dock, straining at her mooring lines, were a reminder of the fury being vented on the sea half a mile away.

By the late 1930s the *Mary W* had been replaced by the *Hili-Kum*, a handsome new tug built in the style of a seine boat. My father had by now discovered that this type of vessel, with its big hold and its sizeable stern deck, was more practical for his purposes than a conventionally designed tug. The *Hili-Kum* was designed and built by my grandmother's shipbuilder brother James, and her materials were the best the sawmill could supply. Her entirely self-taught designer turned out a boat that towed well, and could carry nine thousand feet of lumber on her stern deck and still remain stable in almost any sea. She was fifty-seven feet long and had a 75-hp Atlas Imperial diesel engine; her name meant "trustworthy" in the Kwakiutl language and she was.

The *Hili-Kum* was a workboat. She was there for emergencies, of course, and she took us on picnics and outings, and occasionally on trips to Vancouver, but she was first and foremost a work boat, and as such she earned a good part of our living.

Her accommodations were spartan. Up in her bows, in the foc's'le, were four narrow bunks with only enough headroom to get in and out of them. On each side, a porthole with glass so thick and scratched that it was opaque, admitted a little feeble light. Aft of the foc's'le was the engine-room containing the big Atlas, a bank of storage batteries, an air compressor and a long workbench with an array of tools above it and under it.

The Atlas was an engine with presence; it stood five feet tall and threw an eleven-hundred-pound fly-wheel. The camshaft opened the valves with a reassuring "ta-pocketa, ta-pocketa" sound that was a lot easier on the nerves than the frenzied whine of the high speed engines that were to come.

Off the engine-room was the one convenience: a head with its complicated system of valves and hand pump, an apparatus that mystified and embarrassed most of our passengers. Aft of the engine-room and separated from it by a bulkhead, was a big hold with the shaft rumbling under its floorboards.

Above deck, the pilot-house had one high berth and a stool for the helmsman. There was the usual paraphernalia: big brass wheels for the engine-room controls, gauges, a searchlight mounted on the roof, the compass and the radio-telephone.

Much later, on my father's new boat, the *Gikumi*, radar was added to the pilot-house equipment. Until the novelty wore off, we gazed with fascination at the sweeping red line and at the tiny dots that appeared here and there on its screen. One day, soon after it was installed, my father was peering into its depths, trying to get a feel for its navigational usefulness, and got so caught up in the wonder of it all that when he finally raised his eyes he found the *Gikumi* almost on top of a hapless troller. He had forgotten that a wooden boat wouldn't show up on the radar screen. He spun the wheel, the *Gikumi* veered sharply to starboard and surged past the smaller boat where the fisherman, white with fright and anger, yelled obscenities.

Aft of the pilot-house there was a cabin with a double bunk. The charts were in a drawer beneath it, and the chart table dropped from the wall above it. Aft of that, in the galley, there was a square Seacook stove with a rail around its top and a small stainless

The *Hili-Kum* under construction on Jim Sharpe's ways at Alert Bay

steel sink with a hand pump that delivered cold water. There were lockers for dishes and food, a long table and a bench. One of my friends, inspecting the boat years later, said that the accommodations reminded her of a refugee camp. Yet, even as a small child, I loved "the boat" with a passion. Pete Fletcher, writing for *The Westcoast Mariner*, said, "The highest moments of seat-of-the-pants adventure, pure fright and outright humour, occur on the sea in small boats." From an early age I knew that to be true.

"Time and tide wait for no man," my father would groan, getting out of a warm bed at four in the morning to catch a tide. Then he—and I as often as I could—would let ourselves out of the house and descend the long flight of stairs to the dock, where Jimmy was waiting in the damp morning air. We would climb down the ladder to the boat, the rungs clammy with moisture. The mooring lines dripped cold sea-water; even the boat's cabin was dank and cold. But within minutes, the big engine was thundering away, filling the air with the hot, rich smell of diesel and, just a few more minutes later, the galley stove was muttering and the coffee perking. The galley, so recently cold, soon became so uncomfortably hot that the door had to be fastened open. Outside, the boat thrust forward purposefully; the deck vibrated with the power of her engine; the wake hissed by; the air blew fresh and briny.

In the pilot-house, my father, who had complained so extravagantly such a short time before, steered with one hand and drank coffee with the other, happier than any man had a right to be. And so for endless days, lapis lazuli summer ones and leaden winter ones, we sat on those high seats in the pilot-house and saw the natural world unfold. We watched the sun split the horizon, bringing with it a brisk little breeze that rippled the water and sent glittering light all over its surface. At the other end of the day, we watched the sun drop back into the sea, staining the sky with improbable colour and then, confidently, we sailed straight on through the inky darkness.

We watched pods of killer whales rolling along on mysterious errands, their glistening black backs curving smoothly out of the sea, and sometimes we were

The *Hili-Kum* entering Telegraph Cove.

Al Gauthier, Colin Armitage and my father's partner, Alex MacDonald in the millyard.

accompanied by porpoises, shooting back and forth under our bows. Seabirds bobbed along on the waves beside us or sat in solemn rows on bits of driftwood. We threaded our way past tiny tufts of green islands and sometimes, close in to shore to take advantage of a back eddy, we could almost reach out and touch the Spanish moss that trailed from the big cedars.

My father took guests along on these voyages whenever possible, often a group of off-duty nurses from the local hospital. Sometimes they had idyllic trips; sometimes quite the opposite, for my father couldn't control the weather and most of the guests failed to recognize the important part it could play in such outings. As a consequence, the passengers sometimes climbed aboard as a merry band and returned as virtual stretcher cases. One horrendous day in Queen Charlotte Strait, inching our way down from Fort Rupert with an empty scow, I was sent to check on one of our passengers who was lying on a bunk in the stateroom. Actually, "lying" was a euphemism. As the boat slammed down into the trough of the sea, her whole body was raised as if by levitation and then dropped back onto the mattress with a *thud*. I bent over her, clinging to whatever would prevent me from falling on top of her. She opened her eyes. "How are the other girls?" she asked. They were all, I told her,

desperately sick.

"Hell's bells, the poor sinners," said the occupant of the bunk, and turned her face to the wall.

However it's an ill wind, if you'll pardon the expression, that blows nobody any good. Whenever I stepped aboard the boat, Jimmy abdicated his role as cook and passed that responsibility on to me. As engineer, he hated getting meals, especially for guests; as a teenager, I wasn't a lot more enthusiastic about the job, or a lot more experienced than he was. In consequence, I was always discreetly delighted when our passengers began showing signs of acute *mal de mer*. It meant that I could proceed with meal preparation for three rather than for two or three times that number. In the heaving galley, Jimmy would affix an extra bar to the top of the stove to hold the pots in place, and I would wet down a couple of dish towels, spread them on the table and lay out the cutlery, secure in the knowledge that my culinary efforts wouldn't be scrutinized by strangers.

One of the mill's big customers was the Indian Affairs Department. They bought thousands of feet of lumber and countless building supplies, and the beauty of it was that, since it was a government agency, we got paid without having to resort to searching the local beer parlours to collect our receivables. The only problem lay in the delivery. Since it took at least three to unload the boat and our tug carried a crew of two, we relied on the customers themselves to give us a hand at the receiving end. The problem was that, at the Indian villages, there was seldom anyone there to help; in fishing season, there was *never* anyone there to help. Before one trip to Kingcome Inlet, my father made searching inquiries of the Indian agent regarding the docking facilities and the help that would be available. Despite the agent's assurances, we arrived to find a very small float moored to the shore and not another living thing in sight except two starving dogs who greeted our arrival with pathetic enthusiasm.

There was nothing to be done but to somehow struggle that deckload—all nine thousand feet of it—onto the float. As the pile of lumber rose, the float sank, until it was completely submerged. Then, with some difficulty, the tug cast off her lines (now some feet under water) and very gently, so that her wake wouldn't cause the whole lot to tip over into the sea, moved out into the inlet. That much of that lumber ever survived to become part of a house is doubtful. Certainly the shrinkage in any such building, as the sodden lumber dried out, would have been phenomenal.

For a while we operated a shingle mill as well as a sawmill, but when the Hadleys started their little shingle mill down Baronet Passage I guess it was easier to buy shingles from them for resale. Besides, just having a conversation with Merle Hadley was worth the trip. Like Pesnic, Hadley had a distinctive delivery. He spoke in such a slow drawl, and had such laconic comments to make, that anything he had to say turned out to be vastly entertaining.

When the *Hili-Kum* arrived at their place to load shingles, we always found their two little boys playing around in a dinghy, their float house immaculate and Hadley and his wife working together in the shingle mill. Merle cut the shingles; his wife packed them into bundles. Their movements were swift and sure.

Mrs. Hadley was a pretty woman with a beautiful complexion and smooth, dark brown hair. Her well-worn overalls revealed a small curvy body. As Jimmy and Hadley and my father trekked across the float with bundles of shingles they chatted.

"You're darn lucky, Merle," said my father, "to have such a hard working wife."

"Yeeaas," said Hadley, "aand she's the most eee-ven tempered woman in the wooorld—maaa-d *all* the time."

The *Hili-Kum* landing a scow on the beach. She would retrieve the empty on the next tide.

Several times a year, the *Hili-Kum* made the twenty-two-hour trip to Vancouver. To make these trips pay for themselves, she carried freight both ways. Going south, she carried a load of door stock to be delivered to E.A Sauder; on the return journey, her hold and her deck were piled with plywood, mouldings, doors and windows, for we now sold building materials as well as lumber.

Like the tortoise, slowly but surely, the *Hili-Kum* chugged down Johnstone Strait, through Greene Point Rapids and the Yucultas, past Cortes Island and Savary Island, and into the Gulf of Georgia. She pushed on past Sechelt, Howe Sound and Point Atkinson, past the houses that now appeared dotting the hillsides of West Vancouver, and under the arc of Lions Gate Bridge. Now, unfamiliar city smells wafted from the shore—the smell of industry, of coffee roasting, of automobile exhaust. Turning to starboard, she passed the floating oil stations and found a berth at one of the crowded floats in Coal Harbour. Once she was safely moored, her passengers and crew prepared to face the culture shock that they knew awaited them. Five minutes from the *Hili-Kum's* deck the chaos that was Georgia Street roared by. Legs still sagging from the motion of the sea, we found the stream of traffic always took some getting used to. Cars shot at us from all directions, but navigating cautiously, we reached the safety of the Stanley Park streetcar and were borne toward the dazzle of downtown Vancouver. For us, the dazzle didn't include hotels or restaurants. "Waste not, want not," was my grandmother's motto and we all subscribed to it. Accommodation ashore would most certainly have been an extravagance, so those on the boat stayed on the boat and ate their meals there. This could be confining and dismal in winter, but in summer it was pleasant to leave the noise and confusion of the city behind and have a cool, quiet dinner on the stern deck. Across the harbour lay the lush greenery of Stanley Park; the screams of its peacocks and snatches of music from Malkin Bowl drifted across to us on the breeze. On the water, the sculls from the Vancouver Rowing Club skimmed by on practice runs.

When we were children in school, my sister and I didn't go on many of these trips to the city, but in the spring of 1939 our parents made a startling announcement. They told us that the King and Queen were to visit Vancouver in May and not only had they planned the next trip "to town" to coincide with this visit, but they intended to take us out of school so that we could make the trip and take part in the momentous occasion.

"This is a very historic event," my mother said, "and I want you children to have a lasting memory of it."

As it turned out, the trip did supply us with a lasting memory, but it was a memory peculiar to *our* way of life, not the Royal Family's; and it was my grandmother, rather than the King or Queen, who was the central figure.

There was just enough accommodation on the *Hili-Kum* for the family, grandparents included, and for Jimmy. We set off in high spirits with all our best clothes hung carefully on their hangers. Thanks to the Atlas these clothes, when we put them on two days later, would reek of Diesel oil. This rather marred our attempts to put our best foot forward, but it wasn't enough to dampen our enthusiasm.

As the boat neared Vancouver and entered the expanse of unprotected water that is Georgia Strait, we found a high sea running. The *Hili-Kum* reared and plunged and my mother, who hated rough water, predictably got seasick. After a while, she realized that her misery was being made even more acute by the penetrating smell of brass polish. Jimmy, anxious that everything be shipshape for the King and Queen, was polishing the boat's brass to a gleaming perfection. Mother crawled to the pilot-house and made him stop.

The rough weather was unfortunate for another reason. Our marine radio told us that the royal couple would be arriving on a warship at 3:00 p.m., that the harbour would be closed just prior to their arrival, and it wouldn't be re-opened to marine traffic until they had safely docked. This presented us with an unexpected complication. The seas had slowed our progress so much that we knew we wouldn't get under Lions Gate Bridge in time; in fact, off our starboard bow, we could already see four warships on the horizon, surging towards us from the west.

We decided to tie up in Caulfeild Cove and take a bus into the city. As the *Hili-Kum* struggled on past the entrance to Howe Sound and around Point Atkinson, all aboard, except the helmsman and my mother, were busy getting dressed in their best. Even inside Caulfeild Cove, there was a big swell running but the mooring looked safe enough for the boat. There was not another boat, or another soul around; presumably, they were all off preparing to greet the King and Queen. My mother's queasy stomach had delayed her a bit, but my grandparents and my sister and I were ready. We gathered on the back deck, which was rising and falling with the heavy swell, and my father and Jimmy stood on the float, which was also rising and falling quite markedly, and got ready to hand us down.

My grandmother went first. She reached out her hands to them, stepped forward—and the boat surged away from the float. What happened next was like a perfectly choreographed ballet. My grandmother missed her footing and dropped straight into the sea in the three-foot space that now appeared between the float and the boat. Still holding the men's hands—hers now high above her head—she disappeared below the surface. In the perhaps four seconds at their disposal, they yanked her all the way out and onto the float. Having reached the limit imposed by the mooring lines, the *Hili-Kum* hesitated, then surged once again towards the float. She heaved against it with the full weight of her heavily planked, sixty-foot hull, and the bumpers squealed.

Despite our way of life, I had never seen anyone fall in before. I raced to my mother in the galley.

"Nana has fallen in," I reported tremulously. "Right over her hat."

Before my mother could reply, Nana herself appeared in the doorway streaming water, her Madame Rungé suit a sodden mess. For some reason it wasn't the condition of her suit—or her hat—that disturbed her.

"Well, I've just ruined my best corset," she announced sourly.

It occurs to me now that a person who has just escaped being drowned and/or crushed to death might be justifiably excused for suffering a shock reaction. It didn't occur to my grandmother—but she *was* upset about her corsets and about the fact that we waited for an hour, sitting on a low stone wall by the roadside, and no bus came along to take us to the city. And so we returned to the boat and continued our journey into Vancouver, tying up at our usual place in Coal Harbour, where we cooked our dinner.

The radio told us that on the following day the royal couple were to be in New Westminster, so next day we took the bus and sat in the bleachers at Queen's Park in New Westminster and waved little Union Jacks. The Queen wore a powder blue dress with a hat to match, and the King was in his naval uniform. As they drove slowly past, smiling and waving graciously, I reflected that neither the King nor the Queen had any idea how much trouble we had gone to, to be there for them.

Off our starboard bow we could already see four warships surging towards us.

VI

"AND HOW WAS YOUR DAY?"

The Blow Hole, a passage between the northwestern extremity of East Cracroft Island and Minstrel Island, leads into Clio Channel. The passage is narrow and shallow, and in it, near its southwestern end, is a rock which dries 17 feet. Kelp grows right across the passage. This passage may be used only by small craft with local knowledge.

British Columbia Pilot

That perfunctory question, "And how was your day?" took on a richer meaning at Telegraph Cove. How were our days? They were, in a word, eventful. We were fifty men, women and children cut off from the rest of humanity by forest and ocean. That, in itself, made our days demanding and unconventional. Add the perils of the sea and a whole array of balky machinery, and the opportunities for humour and drama were boundless.

At twelve, I wrote in my childhood diary, "Left at 12:30 p.m. for Bryant's camp. Enroute rescued Mackay's A-frame. Quite exciting and funny."

So there it was. Life was always either exciting or funny; often it was both.

On one date in my diary, there's the straightforward statement, "Morris Goodrow drowned at Bones Bay today." Morris Goodrow's brother Ed owned a pile-driver. Like his brother, Morris was wiry and dark. Their coveralls and mechanics' caps stiff with grease, their faces streaked with soot and grease and creosote, they seemed even swarthier than they were. Periodically, when our dock needed repairs, my father towed Goodrow and his towering machine into our harbour. There, against the dock, he and his crew heaved creosote pilings into place with a steam donkey, and then pounded them relentlessly into the sea bottom. It was heavy, dangerous work and, when they were working on the cannery dock at Bones Bay, it killed Morris.

We veered from tragedy to domestic misadventure. On the 22nd of one month I noted, "The *Alaska Prince* was in loading all morning. Mary fell off her back porch but mother says she didn't break anything. Fortunately it was high tide. [Mary's porch rested on pilings over the water]. Our cat had kittens."

Just two days later, the entry is: "Pouring rain. Just finished dinner when Englewood called. Rush trip to the hospital with a man who blew himself up."

Small wonder that, as children, we had difficulty relating to our contemporaries in the city, for whom a strawberry soda appeared to be the highlight of the day.

For all of us then, adults and children alike, each new day presented fresh new challenges. Take, for example, one of my grandfather's contributions to the good of the cause. Being a yacht, and a wooden one at that, the *Klinekwa* was a high-maintenance proposition. Gone were the days when someone was hired to scrape her hull and apply red lead, or to paint and varnish her superstructure. So when my grandfather announced at lunch one day that he intended to spend the afternoon varnishing the interior of the *Klinekwa's* cabin, his help was welcomed with enthusiasm.

With money in such short supply, a job like this never involved the purchase of a new can of varnish, as long as there were left-over dribs and drabs around. In fact, my grandmother's thrift was perhaps most noticeably manifest when it came to interior decoration. Embarking on a painting project, Mame didn't buy paint, but instead mixed together all the odds and ends that could be found. As a consequence, her bookcases were a dismal mauve-grey; and her wallpapering projects tested my father's paper-hanging skills to the limit. If a room's dimensions required six double rolls, he was never permitted that extravagance, but was supplied with five. He solved this problem with his usual ingenuity. Behind every door in every room the wallpaper was of another pattern. As long as the doors remained open, it was an effective solution.

So, after lunch, my grandfather, mindful of these economic constraints, dutifully searched the boat's lockers for leftover varnish. He unearthed a collection of containers, old pickle jars and jam tins, containing a variety of paint products. Finally, he found a tin with perhaps enough varnish in it to do his job. Lighting his pipe, he set to work. All afternoon he puffed and varnished, while the sawmill hummed companionably in the background.

When my grandmother had had her nap and her usual orange, she went down to the boat to inspect the project. The first thing she noticed was an inordinate number of flies stuck to the surface of the walls. Wet varnish is notorious for collecting dust and debris on its surface, but in this instance the problem seemed excessive. She went over to inspect my grandfather's operation more closely.

"Duke," she said in a fury, "you're a jackass."

My grandfather, ever one to humour the more volatile temperament of the ladies, stopped in mid-brushstroke and looked puzzled but benign.

"How *could* you paint this whole cabin with Roger's Golden Syrup?" said my grandmother, almost in tears. "If you didn't smoke that filthy pipe all the time, you would have realized this didn't smell like varnish."

It took a great deal of scrubbing to get it off and my sister and I refused to be conned into helping, even with the bribe of unlimited Orange Crush. As my sister said, "I'm not going to; I just *hate* all those bugs."

My grandfather was more successful in another of the roles thrust upon him by our isolated existence. He "did" kittens. This was necessary because my grandmother was a one-woman SPCA. She was continually rescuing starved, abused, or abandoned animals and then my grandfather was required to "put down" the unfortunates that were beyond redemption—and to do it in the most humane manner possible. This was easier than it sounds for, at that time, chloroform could be purchased over the counter. My grandfather must have been a bulk purchaser, since he spent a good part of his retirement years chloroforming cats, and became something of an authority on anaesthesia.

Of course, painting and doing kittens were Alfred Marmaduke Wastell's unofficial duties. Officially, he was a Stipendary Magistrate. When he was appointed

to this position some government agency sent him a whole set of law books beautifully bound in tan leather. He kept them in a glass-fronted bookcase in the front hall, where they looked very impressive. I don't think he ever opened any of them, though. The crime in our area was pretty straightforward and he found that common sense and that ingrained sense of authority—or is it superiority—that came with being English was all he really needed.

My father's days were more varied, for he had many duties. He towed logs and delivered lumber, caught rats, cut our hair, supervised the bookkeeping, wallpapered our house and his parents', serviced the tug's big engine and provided impromptu ambulance and marine rescue services—all the while charming the endless procession of friends, acquaintances and strangers who appeared from nowhere and flooded through our house as inexorably as the tide. His only concession to his former profession was his firm commitment to a business shirt and tie, which he always wore, no matter how manual the labour. Even on the night the trim-saw building burned down, he was only prevented from completing his usual toilette by my mother who shouted, "For heaven's sake, Fred, forget your tie! The mill's on fire!"

There was an immediacy about our way of life—a very clear relationship between cause and effect—so that, when we were awakened at 2:00 a.m. by shouts and the crackling of fire, it was obvious to all that if the mill burned there would be no jobs in the days that followed. And jobs, in the 1930s, were highly valued. All and sundry, therefore, bent to the task of saving the mill. It was not easy. Our fire-fighting equipment consisted of a pump mounted on a large wheelbarrow-like contrivance and some lengths of half-rotten, second-hand canvas hose.

The first snag occurred when someone raced the pump from the dock at one side of the harbour to the mill at the other, only to find that the storage battery that powered it had been used for other purposes and was missing.

Someone else found a charged battery on the boat, hefted it up the ladder to the dock, and ran with it half a mile to the pump—not an inconsiderable feat when you reflect on the weight of a storage battery. The hose was lowered into the sea and the pump started. A more powerful pump would have burst the hose to shreds but, with the serendipity that ruled my father's affairs, the pump was just powerful enough to deliver water to the fire but not powerful enough to burst the hose.

Three things saved the sawmill: a) the tide was high so the hose, which was short as well as rotten, could reach the water supply; b) every inch of the surrounding area was in its customary state—sodden with rainwater (when it rains virtually 360 days a year, even a sawmill's combustibility is minimized); and, c) the building that housed the trim saw was some little distance from the main mill buildings.

This bracing interlude over, everyone went home to bed for an hour or two. At ten minutes to eight, the mill whistle blew as usual. The crew assembled, the machinery started to hum and the conveyor belts to clack, then at eight o'clock the starting whistle blew and the saws began to whine.

The millwright turned his attention to repairing what was left of the trim saw.

Not all disasters ended so happily. One dark winter afternoon when my mother had only been part of this new life for a few months, my father phoned her from Alert Bay. He had gone there in the boat earlier in the day and now, in the late afternoon, it was blowing so hard that he thought it better to stay put for the night. When it was too rough for him, it was too rough. His call spared my mother from worrying about his safety, yet it meant a long evening alone with her baby.

As she sat listening to a wind that was now literally shaking the house, she happened to glance out the window at the blackness that was Johnstone Strait—and thought she saw a light. She extinguished the lights in the room, stood by the window and strained to see. Out in the distant darkness there was, indeed, a light that flashed intermittently. She thought it unlikely that a boat would be out there in such a storm, and she was sure there was no beacon or buoy in that general direction. Puzzled, she watched for some time, trying to discern some pattern or direction in the blinking of the light. Finally, it disappeared.

Next day, the mystery was solved. A small open boat was found upturned, a larger boat was discovered aground on one of the Pearse Islands, and then the bodies of a man and woman were recovered. Instead of staying with their larger vessel when its engine failed, they had launched their dinghy and attempted to reach our lights across the Strait. The woman had put on her fur coat and a life-jacket and when her body was found she still clutched the flashlight she had used to blink her desperate SOS.

The night before, our boat had not been in her usual berth at the dock below our house, and it's unlikely that my father could have reached the couple in time had he come from as far as Alert Bay, although

The morning after the trim saw building burned down.

61

he most certainly would have tried. Yet my mother was haunted by that stormy night for a very long time. Years later, something would trigger the memory of it and she would berate herself once again.

"How could I have been so stupid?" she would say miserably. "Those poor people were out there calling for help. I thought of an SOS and I know the signal, but it wasn't an SOS—just a few blinks. I didn't realize that they were dropping down into the trough of those seas and then their light was cut off from my vision, and their message was garbled."

And then there was the night the light engine ran away. That is not to say that the engine actually left home. Rather the pin in the governor broke and the engine, accustomed to running at 350 rpm, began whirling around at three times that speed. The most immediate result was that all our lights flared suddenly from a normal level of illumination to a blinding white glare. Sensing that all was not well in the light plant department, Jimmy (who looked after this engine as well as the engine on the boat), set off at a dead run for the warehouse where the light engine was housed. In the few minutes it took him to get there, the screaming engine, vibrating uncontrollably, had shaken off its extremities. The exhaust pipe had snapped off and the day fuel tank had been ripped from its moorings on the wall and lay on the engine itself, where it was blazing furiously. The huge flywheel, almost a ton of spinning iron, was approaching its maximum potential and was ready for orbit.

"Oh my god," said Jimmy, surveying the scene, "what's going to happen here?"

It was a rhetorical question. He stepped into the maelstrom and pulled the wedges by hand and very gradually—for it had built up tremendous momentum—the flywheel slowed and then stopped.

If the engine had exploded, as it was very close to doing, it would have sent large chunks of iron and large chunks of Jimmy in all directions, and it would certainly have set the warehouse on fire, and possibly the whole town, for our fire-fighting equipment had done nothing but depreciate since the trim-saw burnt down.

However, the engine didn't do any of these things, and this brush with catastrophe didn't alter my father's habit of thrift one bit. The engine, obtained second-hand from the Marshall Wells boat, the *Sundown,* had been a good engine and he felt that the results of this little mishap—a flattened crankshaft and burnt out bearings—could be rectified. He phoned Tommy Penway, possibly Coal Harbour's best heavy-duty mechanic, and Tommy arrived on the Union boat and spent three days filing the flat spot on the shaft with a hand file and checking it with calipers. Then he replaced the bearings, told my father he had done all he could, and went back to the city. When the engine was started, it ran for only a few hours before burning out the bearings again. Undeterred, my father and Jimmy pulled the piston and forever afterwards this three-cylinder engine ran on two cylinders. The lights were never the same, though.

The passage of time did nothing to alter the drama of our days. In the space of a little over a year, the three Hanuse brothers were drowned off the mouth of the Nimpkish River, the Sticklands' boat exploded and caught fire, Hilly Lansdowne received a medal from the Humane Society for strangling the cougar, and John Nicholson's gillnetter was found drifting near Malcolm Island. John Nicholson was seventy-two. When his boat was found, the light on his net was still burning, as was his mast light. The engine and the stove were shut off. Having left things in good order, John had lain down in his bunk and died.

VII

THE AMBULANCE SERVICE

Baronet Passage—This narrow channel is entered from Blackney Passage northward of Cracroft Point, from whence it leads eastward into Clio Channel and Beware Passage, both of which are connected to Knight Inlet.

On account of the dangers within it, the passage should be used only by those in possession of local knowledge.

British Columbia Pilot

On stormy winter nights, the man who drives home on rain-slicked streets, puts his car in the garage and settles down with the evening paper, secure in the knowledge that if a crisis occurs in his immediate vicinity it will be handled by the appropriate authorities, that man is different from the man who settles himself with a week-old paper knowing full well that there are no appropriate authorities and that, if a crisis occurs in his immediate vicinity, he will have to take himself, and probably his boat, out into the gale. And the wife and children of the first man are different from those of the second.

As children, we learned very early on that in crises large and small we must cut the chatter and do exactly as we were told. Thus, if the boat was hurling herself into a bad sea and the helmsman suddenly handed over the wheel with the admonition, "Keep her heading just the way she is," and disappeared to attend to pressing matters elsewhere, we did just that. With a wheel as big as yourself and a wildly gyrating horizon, it might not be easy to follow instructions, but it certainly fostered concentration. If, on the other hand, some illness or emergency required us to cook dinner, we fired up the kitchen stove and got some kind of a meal on the table without scalding ourselves or the cat.

The real requirement was that we do whatever was asked of us—and sometimes a lot was asked—without protest or panic. In my father's books, "getting excited" in an emergency was the ultimate sin and, like all children, we wanted to live up to our parents' expectations.

Of course, it was easy enough for my father. He *never* got excited. He came from a long line of people who never got excited. His uncle James was a good example. Early one morning, before our parents were up, he appeared at our front door. My sister and I ushered him into the warmth of the kitchen where we were cooking breakfast, got him a comfortable chair and offered him coffee.

"No thank you," said Uncle James mildly. "I won't have any coffee this morning. I just want to see your father and tell him that the boat seems to be sinking."

If my father was calm, my mother was a contradiction. She had the nervous temperament of a race horse, yet when faced with a woman hemorrhaging her life away after childbirth, she was cool and in complete control. She was a registered nurse, the only source of medical help that was near at hand and, as such, her life was full of crises.

Sawmills are dangerous places to work; add the additional dangers peculiar to the sea, and you have the rich mix of disasters that presented themselves at our door. There were deep gashes and crushed ribs, fingers severed by the saws, and concussions from the force of flying objects. When the mill whistle blew a series of staccato blasts and the machinery was suddenly silent, mother braced herself. Sometimes, happily, the interruption was only a broken conveyor belt; but often, looking across the harbour, she would see a worried little knot of men surrounding some unfortunate. Within minutes they would be in our kitchen, or—if it was a stretcher case—at the bottom of our long flight of front stairs.

One man arrived with a finger that was hanging by just a few thin shreds of flesh. My mother returned it to its normal position and splinted it in place, and the tug took him to the hospital where the doctor sewed it back onto his hand. The operation was a success. The finger, he commented later, was always a bit cold and numb; but a finger is a finger, and even an unfeeling finger is better than none at all.

On another day, Norm, a tall, fair member of the crew, cut *his* hand badly; it was bleeding heavily so someone supplied an empty carton to catch the flow. He arrived at our door, holding his carton, just as Jimmy, the tug's engineer, was about to leave. Mother, seeing Norm's face, sat him down and whisked off to get some brandy. She returned to find Norm sitting there with his carton—and Jimmy out cold on the floor.

There were lots of "after-hours" medical emergencies, too. The 'flu that became pneumonia, terrible burns from red hot stoves, or the employee with the DTs who literally tore the bunkhouse to pieces one evening. And then there were the expectant mothers. Pregnant women were my mother's *bête noire*; that is, pregnant women who were nearing their due dates. In my mother's perfect world, they would all have gone to stay at the hotel near the local hospital a little beforehand and, when their time came, they would have gone to that hospital where there was the staff and equipment to deal with possible obstetrical complications—and there they would have been safely delivered. But they didn't. Instead they stayed at home until the last possible moment, then relied upon my father's skill as a seaman and/or my mother's as a midwife, to see them through their ordeal. This wasn't simply perversity. These mothers-to-be didn't have the money for extras like hotel rooms, they often had other small children at home to care for, and sometimes they didn't even speak English, and consequently felt safer in familiar surroundings. The interesting part is that the hospital was only five miles away which, by city standards, would be considered right next door. Like a conjuring trick, though, the perception of distance is not what it seems and can't be measured in immutable units like miles. Distance stretches and shrinks. In the city those five miles would be covered in a few minutes, rain, storm or shine, on a paved road in an automobile or ambulance. In our case, those five miles were five miles of temperamental salt water and the mode of transport was a ponderously slow tugboat. In the best of weather, the trip to the hospital took an hour; in a howling gale it would take a least twice that. And so, mother kept an inordinately sharp eye on the midsections of the employees' wives

and did everything possible—short of inquiring directly into their sex lives—to determine who was pregnant and at what stage. This was a cat-and-mouse game. In the 1930s, pregnancy was not advertised as widely as it is today. Quite the contrary. It was kept discreetly under cover until its presence could no longer be kept hidden.

It's ironic, then, that one of these tests of seamanship and midwifery took place at a time when my mother felt secure in the knowledge that there were no imminent births. She and my father were sleeping peacefully when someone came pounding up our long flight of stairs and started hammering on the front door. My father struggled into his dressing-gown and went downstairs. There followed a short animated conversation. Certainly it was animated on our visitor's part. He was practically shouting at my father. Hearing both our parents stirring now, my sister and I emerged from our respective bedrooms and met in the upstairs hall. Through the bedroom door we could see mother throwing on her clothes.

"A lady is having a baby," she said sweetly, ever anxious to put the best face possible on the brutal facts of life, "so you children will have to look after yourselves. Be sure to have a good breakfast, and be sure to close the draft on the sawdust-burner when you leave for school ... and get my box, will you dears, it's in the linen closet."

Her "box" was a wooden one, enamelled white. It contained packages of dressings and rolls of gauze bandage and adhesive tape, a sling and some splints, a bottle of iodine and one of aspirin tablets, a pair of surgical scissors and a thermometer, some string and bottle of brandy. These items, and her knowledge, were the first aid, and the last aid, she had to offer.

Both parents let themselves out the front door and started down the front steps to the dock. My sister and I stationed ourselves at the upstairs window. During the night, fog had filled our little bay and now, at four in the morning, we could barely see the end of the dock. Wisps of it drifted past the window and formed and reformed around the house. We could hear our father's brisk footsteps breaking the woolly silence as he went to rout out our boats' engineer and then, within moments, we heard the heavy thump of the diesel engine reverberating around the bay. We heard the "plank" as the lines were let go and dropped from the dock to the deck. The engine was put in reverse, and we heard the churning of water under her stern as she turned in the narrow confines of the harbour. There was a small boat moored to the front float. The *Hili-Kum* edged carefully alongside and the two boats were tied together. We watched as they moved away from the float—looking for all the world like a mother hen with a chick under her wing—and then disappeared into the fog.

As we learned later, the expectant mother was from a neighbouring logging camp. Logging camps seldom had boats of any decent size because all their towing was done on contract by large towing firms in the city. They had, at best, camp tenders used for pushing logs around in the booming grounds. This husband and wife had made arrangements to use this type of small boat to take them to the hospital. Since this was the first baby, they thought that if they left promptly at first contraction they would have ample time to get to the hospital. But they reckoned without the fog. Unaccustomed to travelling blind and with no courses to refer to, the boat's operator was lost within minutes. Sightless, they plowed around for a couple of hours, all three becoming increasingly agitated, and finally more by good luck than good management, they found our dock looming at them out of the fog.

My father, of course, had courses laid out for just such emergencies. He was, in fact, a fine seaman, but one would never have guessed it from his nonchalant approach. On a bright summer day, the boat loaded with lumber and with a full complement of the ever present guests, he would decide to run a course for that particular trip. He would check the compass and his watch and, while trading funny stories and eating a nutbar, he would jot down some figures on a chart or in the

back of the log book. Now one of these sets of figures took him unerringly to his destination.

Meanwhile, my mother was employing skills of another sort. As soon as she climbed onto the little camp tender and met her patient, she realized that it was too late to transfer her to the relative comfort of the *Hili-Kum*. So she sent the men for blankets from our boat and constructed a makeshift bed in the foc's'le of the smaller boat. Then, as the *Hili-Kum* felt her way through the fog, she straddled the camp tender's engine and delivered the baby.

Fred and Emma Wastell on the dock at Englewood—July 1939.

In the late morning, sitting at our school desks, we children could hear the *Hili-Kum* returning. We could hear regularly spaced blasts from her air horn out in the foggy void—first faintly and then loudly as her bows suddenly materialized out of the mist and she moved carefully into the bay.

Sound travels at 1000 feet per second, which is of little interest to the general population but can have great significance for the mariner. Before radar, when fog erased all reference points, a boat had only its whistle—and it's echo—to guide it along our intricate coastline. Courses could take you to your destination, but in fog so thick that only the bow of the boat was visible, the fine tuning had to be done with the whistle. Head out of the pilot-house window, ears straining over the sound of the slow-turning engine, the skipper blew his whistle, listened for its echo and felt his way forward. In theory, then, a one-second interval between whistle blast and echo meant the boat was five hundred feet from shore; but the interval was never timed—simply sensed from experience.

The entrance to our sheltered harbour presented a very narrow gap in the contours of the coastline. Approaching it in thick fog, engine idling, whistle blasting, we would hear the echo returning once, twice, three times. Then, as the boat edged slowly ahead and to port, there would be a fourth blast of the whistle—and silence. We had pinpointed the entrance. Around the lunch table we discussed the morning's events.

"Are they going to call the new baby *Hili-Kum*?" asked Bea.

"I doubt it," said my father.

My mother looked tired. "I've left the blankets down in the office," she told my father. "Will you have someone bundle them up and send them to the dry cleaners?" "You know," she added, "we don't expect to be paid for jaunts like this but I do think they might have offered to pay for the cost of the dry cleaning."

My father was confident on the water but never overconfident. When the straits were smoking with flying spume, he stayed home. Unfortunately those were often just the times he got called out.

A few miles from our little community there were two large logging camps. They had first-aid men, of course, and their camp tenders were equal to the trip to the hospital in good weather. But in a howling southeaster, they weren't—which is where my father came in. Our old crank telephone would ring and my father would go off in search of the tug's engineer. We would watch soberly as the boat left her sheltered moorage and headed out into the gale—even more

Two freighters loading lumber, one of them from a scow.

anxiously when her immaculate white cabin disappeared into darkness as well as wind.

The weather was not the only problem connected with these trips. Our boat was, after all, built as a tug not an ambulance and, as such, her cabin doors were too narrow to admit a stretcher. Stretcher cases then, which usually meant the most seriously injured, were denied the relative comfort and warmth of the cabin, and instead had to make the trip to the hospital lashed to the hatch on the back deck. To have been badly injured, to have endured the difficult trip out of the woods to the boat and then to lie on a hatch in the middle of a howling gale must have been a unique experience. The stretcher was covered with a tarpaulin and was securely tied down, but each time the boat plunged into the seas water would pour down the adjoining deck and out of the scuppers, and the propeller, racing as it lifted out of the water, must have shaken the poor victim unmercifully.

The other thing that made these trips difficult was the time they took. There were no public roads into the woods, no helicopters, no available float planes. Just getting an injured man from the site of the accident to our waiting boat could take many hours. One evening, our telephone rang with the message that the neighbouring camp had an injured man en route. The caller estimated that the crummy carrying him down the tortuous logging road would arrive within the hour. My father agreed to be there waiting with the boat for the last lap of the journey to the hospital. It was approaching 7:00 p.m. My mother was good at reading my father's mind.

"Who's going with you?" she asked.

"Oh, I'll just take the boat myself," said my father. "It's a nice night, no problem with the weather, and I don't want to drag Jimmy out after a day's work. Besides, it's not a stretcher case; the fellow on the phone said he thinks it's just a broken arm or something."

"Don't go alone," said my mother firmly. "Find someone else to go along if you don't want to bother Jimmy, but don't go alone."

As it turned out, my father and Jimmy were joined at the last minute by Stan, one of the mill crew, who decided to go along for the ride. And so there were three on board when they arrived to pick up their passenger—which was just as well. They found a logger who had been injured hours before and was in great pain; he had been given the first aid man's supply of morphine, but its effects had long since worn off. All the way to the hospital, it took the combined efforts of Jimmy and Stan to keep the patient from ending his misery by jumping overboard. As Jimmy explained, although no explanation seemed necessary, the man was Italian and "Italians are very hyper people." It was a tiring trip.

And then, of course, there was old Gordon Eiger, an ancient prospector who blew himself up with a charge of dynamite. On our weekly trips to Alert Bay, Gordon was a regular passenger. Bent and feeble, he would struggle aboard the boat and, once in Alert Bay, he would shuffle up the road to the beer parlour, buy half a dozen cases of beer and transport them back to his claim in the bush. One day we got an emergency call and arrived to find that he was the injured man, not that he was recognizable because for starters, he had burned all the skin off his face and arms. When he was bundled into a stretcher and onto the back deck, we were sure this was Gordon's last trip to Alert Bay. Several weeks later, we were stunned to see him tottering down the dock at Englewood for his regular run to the beer parlour.

On the raw frontier of the north Island, it wasn't surprising that injury and accidental death were such common occurrences. Our little local paper, *The Pioneer Journal*, was published in Alert Bay; almost weekly, it reported a litany of calamities.

"Witnesses say that the cable was rusted and it broke."

"It was thought that the log was stable but it was not."

"The boat was found drifting but no bodies have been recovered."

"The child was scalded to death when a drum of boiling water overturned."

Our own little community had few real tragedies, but we weren't entirely spared. In the very early days of the mill, a Japanese crew member slipped while loading lumber, fell off the dock, hit his head on the fender log, and was instantly killed. Much later, two boys escaped the adults' notice and were playing on the log booms that floated in the bay. Like all strictly forbidden activities, this one had an irresistible attraction. Nothing is more fun than racing across a log boom, hopping off one rolling log and onto the next before you can be pitched off into the water. One of them lost the game, was trapped under the logs and drowned. This saddened us all, not least us children, for we were a small group and the loss of one of us left a gaping hole in our ranks. We were sobered, too, by the realization that the retribution for disobedience could be so swift and final.

Then there was Jerry, a merry little boy with round, rosy cheeks and brown eyes that twinkled with mischief. He didn't live in our community but arrived each morning on his dad's gasboat to attend school. I remember that he stymied our teacher one day by telling her, in reply to her question, that his favorite colour was white. One day his father failed to deliver him to school and our teacher told us the truth.

"Jerry has died," she said.

We were shocked—but not too shocked to ask for further information. What had happened, we wanted to know.

"He ate too many salmonberries," said our teacher.

On the way home for lunch, we regarded the salmonberry bushes and their ripe fruit with deep distrust.

When I discussed it with my mother over the lunch table, her explanation was a little more technical, as a nurse's explanation would be.

"He had a burst appendix," she said, "and he didn't get to the hospital in time."

THE CREW

Dent Rapids is a stretch of turbulent water between the Dent Islands and the southern shore of Cordero Channel. It is 2 cables wide in its narrowest part and depths are over 50 fathoms. The tidal streams attain a rate of 8 to 9 knots with dangerous overfalls and eddies.

Duration of slack water in all the rapids is very brief and does not usually exceed 5 minutes.

British Columbia Pilot

If the Eskimos, surrounded by the stuff, have dozens of words for snow, then we certainly should have had more than one for rain. We were rained on for ten months of the year (and in August the fog rolled in). There was the generic rain that rattled out of the sky for days on end, and dripped ceaselessly from the trees and the eaves. There was the slashing rain that came with the southeasters; it gusted off the sea, tortured the trees, and crashed against our windows in furious bursts. And there was the drenching rain that fell, not in drops, but in continuous streams that had no beginning and no end. Beaten flat, the sea lay prostrate under its onslaught. The air was thick with its moisture.

The crew, depending on their natures, complained, ignored, cursed or joked. If they worked in the shelter of the leaky corrugated iron that roofed the mill, they were fortunate. If they worked outside, they bowed to the inevitable and struggled into their hot, heavy rubber pants and jackets.

In those dark Depression days, steady jobs were prized possessions. The mill offered twelve of them—but that was all it offered. The term "fringe benefits" hadn't been invented. Of necessity the initiative required of employees was astounding. Jimmy Burton's introduction to Telegraph Cove was not atypical.

Jimmy was the only child of a tiny, feisty Irish woman who had earned a living for them both cooking in logging camps and for railroad gangs. At nineteen, he had already worked on fish packers for several seasons but it was sporadic employment, and he jumped at the chance of a steady job on our boat. Late one evening, he boarded the Union steamship *Cardena* in Vancouver with his bedroll, a six-dollar second-class ticket to Telegraph Cove, and the bag of sandwiches his mother had provided. His ticket entitled him to a bunk in the hold with the freight, but he decided instead to spend the night sitting up in the saloon. At some point in the evening he was engaged in conversation by one of his fellow passengers, a logger who was more than a little pissed.

"Want a drink, kid?" offered his new friend unsteadily but generously.

Up to this point in his life, Jimmy hadn't tried alcohol, but he felt that perhaps now was a good time to start. He accepted, the two repaired to the logger's cabin—for he was travelling first class—and his host poured them each a stiff rum.

Jimmy's next conscious thoughts were prompted by the cheery sound of breakfast chimes being played in the corridor outside the cabin. He discovered that he had spent a restful night lying on the lower berth of the logger's cabin. The logger, meanwhile, had spent *his* night folded up on the rock-hard, four-foot settee. The breakfast chimes had wakened him, too, and he wasn't in a particularly good mood.

"Who the hell are you?" he asked, belligerently.

"Don't you remember?" said Jimmy. "You invited me in for a drink."

Jimmy was by now ravenously hungry and would have liked to have hit up his erstwhile friend for breakfast, but it didn't seem feasible, so, refreshed by his restful sleep, he returned to the saloon where he sat down and ate his sandwiches. Before long, he discovered that he wasn't the only new employee on board. Doug MacLean was bound for Telegraph Cove as well. He was a year younger than Jimmy and had

had a gentler upbringing. This was his first experience away from home. At their destination, they disembarked together and searched out their employer.

Embroiled in the numerous tasks that "boat day" involved, my father was too preoccupied to give the two much of his attention. He did tell them that the bunkhouse was full, that they would occupy another building next door to it and then he sent them off in that general direction.

They found the building without too much trouble. It had no windows, no doors, no stove, no running water. It was March. "Jeez, it was cold in there," Jimmy remembers. There were several iron bedsteads with straw mattresses in the otherwise empty rooms. They selected the better looking of these and put down their bedrolls. Doug appeared disconsolate.

Jimmy & Thelma Burton, 1943

Walking through the freight shed on the way to this spartan accommodation, Jimmy had noticed some large flattened bread cartons. They returned to my father and asked if they could have some of these.

"What do you want them for?" asked my father, ever suspicious of any form of conspicuous consumption.

"Thought we'd tack them over the windows," said Jimmy. "Cut the wind a bit. Got a hammer we could borrow?"

Even this improvement—even the good hot dinner they had later in the cookhouse—failed to raise Doug's spirits. That evening he sat on his bed and cried. "Oh god, I want to go home," he sobbed.

Jimmy's experience in the college of hard knocks had made him a pragmatist.

"Well, Doug, how much money have you got? It costs twelve dollars to get back on the Union boat and it isn't even coming back for another week. I got no money. Nothin'. So the two of us aren't going anywhere. Tell you what, Doug," he said, "Let's give her a try."

My father eventually found them a little stove. Doug stayed till war was declared. Jimmy stayed for forty-eight years.

The bunkhouse that was too full to admit the two newcomers was not a great improvement over the place they presently occupied. It was an ugly board-and-batten building with a shed roof. True, it had windows, doors, a cold water tap and a big wood stove made out of an old oil drum, but it was a building inspector's nightmare. The sanitary facilities consisted of a privy that hung over the edge of the dock. The icy draft that blew in from the ocean below not only discouraged lingering, but had the disconcerting habit of blowing the discarded toilet paper back through the hole in the seat and whirling it around the occupant's head.

Wind whistled through the uninsulated walls of the bunkhouse, too, which meant that the crew kept their makeshift stove going full blast most of the time. Periodically, one of the occupants would be wakened in the middle of the night by the smell of smoke and would discover that a spark from the stove had ignited part of the floor. The first time this happened someone yelled, "The floor's on fire!" and there was much confusion and outcry. But as the crisis repeated itself, the crew took a more phlegmatic approach. The one who smelled the smoke got up, threw a bucket of water on the floor and went back to bed. By the time the building was finally torn down, the entire floor around the stove was charred, and the stove remained upright more from force of habit than anything else.

Most of the occupants of the bunkhouse were in their teens and twenties. Pat was the exception. He was older—and dirtier—than the rest. Unlike the others, who used blankets, Pat was the proud possessor of a sleeping bag lined with rabbit fur, which he referred to as his "rabbit robe." The other members of the crew didn't share Pat's fondness for this item; they knew it contained other living creatures besides Pat, and they tried, without success, to get Pat to air it out or make some other attempt to clean it up before its livestock appeared in their own rooms. Finally they decided to dramatize the problem. Jimmy went outside and lay full length on the boardwalk; the others draped the sleeping bag over him. Then they called Pat.

"Pat," they said as the sleeping bag inched slowly down the boardwalk, "take a look at this. That sleeping bag of yours is crawling away."

In marked contrast, Mike Bloomfield's living habits were downright fastidious. He had taken the trouble to line his room with scraps of cedar V-joint; he kept everything within

it neat and tidy, and he commanded that unheard-of luxury, a battery radio. But he made a fatal mistake. He informed the other occupants of the bunkhouse that they were not to enter his room and, most especially, they were not to touch his radio. This was a lot like waving a red flag in front of a bull; Mike seldom entered his room without finding half the crew lounging around on his bed, listening to his radio.

For Chong, the camp cook, life was certainly no easier. If anything it was harder, for Chong

On a rare sunny Sunday in 1938, some of the mill crew pose on the boardwalk. Standing (LtR): Doug MacLean, Arnie Wasden, Colin Armitage, Michael Bloomfield. Front row: Jimmy Burton and Malcolm "Scotty" Carmichael.

worked not six days but seven. Every day, he prepared and cleared away three big meals, hauled wood in a handcart from the mill, and chopped it to fuel his huge iron cookstove, and in his "spare" time he cultivated a vegetable garden behind the cookhouse. Once a week, he brought his grocery orders into the office to be forwarded to the appropriate wholesalers in Vancouver. These orders had first to be translated, because they were ingenious examples of creative writing. One such list read as follows:

fifty pon cow meat backside end [hindquarter]

1 sak plato

1 sak callot

1 sak bled flor—come wet no good [bread flour in double sacks to keep it dry]

1 sak oat—all same for hose but not fo [one sack of rolled oats].

Next came a separate order for "flute."

1 box tomat

1 box peche

1 box plum

1 box apel

Footnote on this order: *No got, no send*

One of Chong's rare complaints concerned the deer who continually broke through the fish net that was supposed to protect his garden and ate his vegeta-bles. Finally, he announced to my father that the deer must be shot. Since my father would no sooner have shot a deer than he would have shot his wife, he hid behind the excuse that it wasn't hunting season.

"You can't kill a deer out of hunting season," he told Chong.

"Wastell," said Chong, "you just shoot him little bit. He go far away and never come back."

The idea of wounding a deer appealed to my father even less than killing one; besides, he thought, probably correctly, that even if the deer was thus dissuaded, his relatives would take his place in the garden and perpetuate the problem. Chong was out of luck.

If Chong was bedevilled by deer and the English language, across the harbour our new steam engineer and his family, the Kerrs, were grappling with *their* problems, and trying, against all odds, to establish a home for themselves. The Kerrs had arrived sometime previously on the Union steamship *Catala*. Mr. Kerr brought his family of four: a boy of about ten and three daughters. There was no wife or mother in evidence. Nor did their household goods arrive with them. His wife apparently, had left him forever; the possessions had left him only temporarily. They had gotten lost in transit and the shipping company promised to search them out and return them to him.

As soon as my mother heard of the family's plight she made a big casserole and got together a pile of

The four Kerr kids with my sister and me.

blankets from the *Hili-Kum.* Then she and my sister and I set off around the harbour to the engineer's house carrying our offerings. The engineer's house was, for convenience's sake, built right beside the mill, but we didn't find them there; rather, we found them in the blacksmith's shop. The father, a big raw-boned Scot, was frying eggs and bacon in a large, flat sawdust shovel over the fire in the forge. He had scouted around and found some empty glass jars in the basement of the house, and they were using these as cups for the tea that he had made. It was obvious that they were a family not easily beaten.

When their possessions finally did arrive, we noticed that everything including their clothing had been shipped in barrels. Possibly a man's solution to the problem of packing up a household. At any rate, they were now able to set up housekeeping in their own slap-dash but cheerful way. It was plain that the children could have used a mother but, like their father, they were tough and resourceful and they proceeded to look after the household duties, go to school and somehow bring themselves up.

Several of the houses for married employees were occupied by Japanese families. They planted vegetable gardens which flourished despite the almost continuous rain, furnished their homes with furniture they made themselves, and built themselves skiffs so that they could row out into the strait and bring back a steady supply of seafood. Their food, fresh from the garden and the sea, was far more nutritious and much less costly than ours, but it never occurred to us Occidentals to learn from their example.

As the Depression ground on, men quite literally drifted in from nowhere. One cold winter morning, walking through the lumber shed on the way to school, my sister and I found a man sleeping on a pile of lumber. He turned out to be named Blackie. He had come around the point in a gasboat so old and decrepit that it promptly sank to the bottom in front of the cookhouse. Seeking drier accommodation, Blackie had removed himself to the lumber shed. When my father found him there later that same morning, he told him that he had better move into the marginally better shelter that the bunkhouse afforded.

Blackie was as swarthy as his name implied; he looked the type to be carefully avoided on a dark night. When questioned, he told my father that he was a flagpole painter, but that he had got into a little trouble and was advised to leave Vancouver. What

kind of trouble was never made clear. Despite his murky background, he stayed and worked, and thoughtfully supplied my mother with some homemade ratfish oil for her arthritis. Except for one incident, he caused no trouble at all.

One evening, Blackie sat alone in his room, consumed a bottle of rye, and discovered in the process that life was an intolerable burden. He appeared at the door of Arnie's room carrying his .30-.30 rifle.

"Arnie, I've come to say good-bye," he said. "I'm going to kill myself."

Presented with this stunning news, Arnie's hands began to shake so violently that he could hardly pull on his pants. His mind, however, was working quickly and efficiently.

"Blackie, you'll have to say good-bye to all the crew," he said. "Not just me. You can't shoot yourself without saying good-bye to everybody."

So Blackie, carrying his gun, proceeded from room to room, bidding farewell to each startled occupant. He was down to the last couple of crew members and things were looking pretty desperate, when someone had another bright idea.

"You'll have to say good-bye to Alex," said someone with an inventive mind. "You just can't shoot yourself without saying goodbye to the boss."

Blackie was propelled out the door and sent off in the direction of Alex MacDonald's little bachelor house. Alex was a gentle and kindly man with a propensity for reading late into the night. He was more than surprised to open his door to an employee who was threatening suicide. But Alex was not a man to shirk responsibility. He invited Blackie into the living-room and, using all his powers of persuasion, tried to talk him out of ending his life. But Blackie was adamant.

"It's no good, Alex," said Blackie. "My mind's made up. It's not worth it. Life's just not worth it."

Alex, having lost the first round, now tried another tack. The night, he argued, was not the time to commit suicide. Nights were somehow not conducive to successful suicide.

"Wait till the morning, Blackie," he said. "Shoot yourself in the morning. You can see so much better in the daylight."

This made some sense to Blackie. They both had a cigarette while he considered the situation.

"Take my word for it, Blackie," said Alex, "the morning is the time to shoot yourself."

Since Alex was the authority when it came to cutting lumber, perhaps Blackie felt he was also an authority on suicide. At any rate, he was finally persuaded to wait for the morning and Alex accompanied him back to the bunkhouse.

Their entrance was regarded warily by the crew, and it was not until Alex had actually got Blackie into his room and into bed that they sighed a collective sigh of relief and went to bed themselves.

At 2:00 a.m. the blast from a .30-.30 shook the insubstantial walls of the building and, as a body, the crew fell out of their beds and formed a little huddle in the hall.

"Oh Jeez, he's done it," somebody said.

No one had the guts to open Blackie's door and face whatever lay behind it. They stood and shivered and smoked and whispered until someone got brave and inched open the door. Blackie lay on his back, his rifle on the bed beside him; there was a gaping bullet hole in the ceiling above the bed. As the others craned their necks to see into the room, their movements woke Blackie from a sound sleep.

"For Christ's sake, Blackie," said Norm, furiously, "what the hell do you think you're doing?"

"I tried to kill myself," explained Blackie, "but I missed."

And then in September 1939, war was declared and our little community was flung from one set of problems into another. For ten years, we had struggled with the spiritual and material impoverishment of the Depression. Then, almost overnight, we struggled with overwork and shortages. The most serious shortage was labour. Gradually, our younger crew members disappeared into the services, and the older ones left for higher paying jobs in shipyards and factories. And then, in 1941, the Japanese bombed Pearl Harbour and within months all our Japanese employees were gone.

Whether or not these people, given the opportunity, would have murdered us "round eyes" in our sleep remains a debatable question, for they weren't given the chance. Within days, they were required to pack up their possessions and be on their way to the Interior. For months afterward, many of their hastily packed cartons still stood piled in the warehouse. A month or two after one family's departure, a letter arrived. It had been, the letter said in laborious English, a difficult time. As soon as the family had reached their strange new destination, Kenny had gotten sick and had had to have his throat cut. Since Kenny was their seven-year-old son, we interpreted this to be a description of a tonsillectomy. They asked my father to dispose of some of their possessions and to forward others to them and, in appreciation, they wanted us to have for ourselves "the flowerish cushion."

This final exodus left the mill desperate for crew members; my father and Alex turned to a friend in the city for help. Living in Vancouver certainly gave this man access to whatever labour supply there was; nonetheless, his efforts couldn't really have been termed a success. For one thing, he was a realtor and, as such, his knowledge of a sawmill's requirements was sketchy, to say the least. As a consequence, the results of his search for labourers were bizarre. He sent us men who could barely walk, let alone heft timbers. In his Mother Theresa phase he sent us a young man called Bing, a former inmate of a mental institution. He assured us that Bing would be able to function if a suitable job were found for him. Alex felt, quite rightly, that a suitable job was not one where Bing was surrounded by whirling saws. So he was made bull cook, and was supposed to help out in our garden when not otherwise occupied.

Bing turned out to be strong and cheerful, but he had a serious body odour problem and a genius for avoiding work. He also had a fetish concerning people's age. Since he had soon exhaustively interviewed all the crew in this regard, he was always delighted to see a new face—a face which usually belonged to one of our guests. He would approach them with a cheery smile, look them over carefully and announce, "I would say you're about forty-two." Since the person in question might often be a woman of thirty, this estimation of her age was not met with enthusiasm. Indeed, some found it deeply depressing.

My mother tried valiantly to avoid Bing when guests were present or, at the very least, to keep the conversation off the subject of age, but her efforts were to no avail. "Please disregard him," she would say. "Bing has a little problem," and she would wave her hand vaguely in the direction of her head. Despite this explanation, many of the guests were crushed by their encounter with Bing, and it took some time to cheer them up afterwards.

It was perhaps just as well that about this time the Royal Canadian Air Force arrived.

THE MADNESS OF WAR

Pearse Islands, a group of ten islands of various sizes and heights lying close together, are thickly wooded, and are located westward and northwestward of Stephenson Islet.

No attempt should be made to pass between the Pearse Islands, or between them and Stephenson Islet, unless in possession of local knowledge.

British Columbia Pilot

You've heard the phrase "the madness of war," referring to the practice of one group of human beings setting out to kill another. During the war years, we were mercifully spared the killing. We certainly weren't spared the madness, however, for we were suddenly introduced to the Military Mind. Our small, highly individualistic society had always been openly contemptuous of bureaucracy, and had existed largely out of reach of its clutches. Now it bore down upon us with full force.

Not that it started out badly. The Air Force decided to build an airport on an heretofore uninhabited stretch of land some fifty miles north of us, and the sawmill was to supply the lumber. Considering that my father had spent the previous ten years beating every conceivable bush for lumber orders, no matter how small—the bush or the order—this was an unbelievable bonanza.

There was one tiny hitch, however. In the years previous to 1939, to secure a lumber order and be promptly paid for it was the challenge. Securing the crew to cut the lumber required no effort at all. Now the situation was reversed. The airport construction would take everything we could cut—our total production—but putting together a crew to cut it was the challenge. Our able-bodied crew had filed off to war and the mill was struggling along, manned by the halt and the blind.

Nonetheless, this was an opportunity too good to be missed, and all the hands fell to with a will. Week after week, the crew loaded scow after scow, and the *Hili-Kum* edged them out of the harbour at high tide and started the long, slow tow northward, up Johnstone Strait and into Queen Charlotte Strait. In summer, this was a more or less routine trip; in winter, southeasterly gales turned these straits into an unending procession of angry grey combers hissing with windswept foam. Going north with the loaded scows was the easier tow, for it involved a following sea; but returning with the empties was another story. Tug and scow now headed into the full force of the gale. Even with the engine slowed to half speed, the tug bucked and reared, water smashing against the pilot-house windows and running down the decks. Behind the boat, the scow was invisible behind explosions of white water, the towline tightening and slackening, the strain threatening to part it or—even worse—to tear the winch to which it was moored out of the deck.

Inadvertently finding herself present on one such voyage, my mother alternated between the pilot-house and the stateroom just aft of it. Most of the time, she lay prostrate with sea-sickness but, whenever some particularly spectacular gyration threatened to drown us all, she came reeling into the pilot-house to shout over the pounding of the engine and the roar of the storm, "Cut the tow, Fred, cut the tow!" My father paid very little attention to this momentary distraction.

Nor was the towing, itself, the only problem. The landing arrangements at Fort Rupert consisted of a hastily built grid on the beach, which meant that in the few minutes of high tide the empty scow had to be pulled off the shore, and the loaded one pushed onto it. This had to be done with precision; if the scows had drifted just slightly out of position, they would have got hung up and holed by the huge boulders that littered the beach.

Week after week the crew loaded scow after scow and the *Hili-Kum* edged them out of the harbour.

Other scows that had carried machinery and equipment up from Vancouver were often moored in the vicinity, and the Air Force sometimes wanted these juggled around. Usually the *Hili-Kum* and her crew were happy to oblige, but as winter approached and the weather worsened, the picture changed. One late January day, with the weather deteriorating rapidly, an RCAF officer appeared and began to bawl instructions from the dock.

"Take Number 43 out to the buoy, stand by Number 94 and then bring Number 63 into the lee of the dock."

His grasp of nautical terms was impressive.

My father was always patient and polite. "Sorry," he said, "there's a real wind getting up and I've got to get out of here."

He thought this explanation was sufficient. He was wrong. Under difficult conditions and in appalling weather, the airport project had been kept supplied with construction materials. The officer in charge was actually very fortunate in this respect, but he failed to see it that way. The problem, of course, was a deep and fundamental difference in philosophy. My father, who wouldn't have recognized an order it if jumped up and hit him in the face, simply ignored the unreasonable. For the officer, baffled and enraged by this seeming insubordination, an order was a sacred thing and left no room for a difference of opinion.

Given the season of the year, it was only a matter of time before the situation repeated itself. This time, short of manpower as usual, my father had enlisted Benny Brotchie as crew. Benny was a tall, impressive-looking native Indian who had the innate seamanship and laid-back demeanour so characteristic of his people. As my father leaned out the pilot-house window and manoeuvred the scow into place, Benny handled the lines on deck. Suddenly my father looked up.

"Oh Lord," he groaned. "Here comes our friend."

The officer, oblivious of the wind that was starting to come at them in great gusts, began bellowing instructions.

"Move Number 64 alongside Number 74, and then take Number 25 out to the buoy and bring Number 43 in."

"Got any more bad news?" yelled Benny as the *Hili-Kum* went full astern and hightailed it for home.

There were times, of course, when the weather was so bad that the return trip was out of the question. Then the tug, scow tied alongside, anchored behind the Cattle Islands until the wind subsided enough for them to venture forth. A phone message, relayed by some stranger, would advise my mother that the *Hili-Kum* was in the shelter of the Cattle Islands and would return when she could.

While the contractor was clearing the future airport of trees, and the laborious towing trips were creating an accumulation of building material, the Air Force administration was not idle. They decided, for some inexplicable reason, to run a telegraph system up

76

our rugged and uninhabited stretch of coastline. Unlike the earlier telegraph line that had simply been strung on trees along the shoreline, this new one ran further inland. There they built a series of line shacks, and manned them with airmen whose duty it was to patrol the line and prevent sabotage. These men were provisioned by boat, and the supplies they were issued were bizarre. They were given great bags of flour and slabs of bread, eight loaves to a slab. Presumably they were supposed to augment this carbohydrate diet by living off the land. Instead, they did what the Indians before them had done; they bartered with the white man. They hacked their way through the bush and presented themselves and their bags of flour at our store, where they traded for bacon or whatever other food appealed to them. Our Chinese employees always kept chickens. The airmen concluded their trading sessions by exchanging the eight-loaf slabs of bread for eggs and the occasional chicken. Years later, when the Chinese employees left, we found they had insulated their bunkhouse with the bread. All the exterior walls were stacked tightly, floor to ceiling, with dried bread.

The war brought other changes. Fifty miles to the south, York Island was fortified with gun emplacements. A military vessel patrolled the waters on either side of the island, accosting passing fishboats and tugs with a loud hailer and requiring them to identify themselves. Our first encounter with this new phenomenon was our most memorable. Since my father and his tug were known the length and breadth of the coast, he felt the burden of responsibility lay with the military. If they didn't know who we were, they could come alongside with their faster vessel and find out. Quite obviously, there was a difference of opinion. The military must have thought that *we* should be the one to make the effort, for one minute we were happily plugging along, my father in his usual tipped-back position, steering with his feet, and the next minute we heard a resounding boom and a shot was fired across our bows and landed with a splash in the water just off our port side.

"Son of a *biscuit* box!" exclaimed my father, knocking over the stool and slamming the boat into neutral.

He had managed everything this difficult coast threw at him—gales and reefs and tide races and fog—and his boat had never been so much as scratched. To be shot at was a hazard he had never anticipated, but such are the fortunes of war.

Since my father was often out half the night tow-ing, my parents were not early risers. It was my sister's and my responsibility to get our own breakfast and to get ourselves off to school. And we were required to prepare a good substantial breakfast—nothing of the Pop Tart persuasion. So early one pitch black winter morning, with a howling gale shaking the house, we were busy making porridge and toast on the kitchen range and listening to the news on our old battery radio, when someone pounded on our front door. Our front door was entirely of glass, and it sometimes seemed that half the world presented itself, in full-length living colour, on the other side of that glass. Friends, customers, strangers, the injured, guests and employees materialized there with their various demands, requests, greetings and emergencies. On that dark morning, we looked through the glass and saw two young men standing outside. They were wearing sou'westers and oilskins, and water was streaming off them onto the porch floor.

We brought them into the warmth of the kitchen, offered coffee and listened while they told us how they'd got there. An Air Force boat, possibly one of the many tugs and fishboats that had been requisitioned, *had run out of fuel* somewhere out in Johnstone Strait in this raging southeaster, and these two had been sent off in an open boat to get help for the drifting vessel.

My sister and I listened, appalled. Even as children we knew three things: one, that to start on a trip without measuring the fuel was something only an idiot would do; two, that sending anyone out in an open boat in those seas was something only an idiot would do; and, three, that surviving a trip across the strait under those conditions was something only an excellent seaman would do. We were right on all counts; our two visitors turned out to be young Maritimers, which is probably the only thing that saved them.

We went upstairs to break this interesting news to our parents.

"Well, wonders never cease," said my father, getting out of bed, "Give them some breakfast."

While all of us ate a nourishing meal, my father and the Maritimers tried to establish just where their boat was when its engine stopped and how far, given the wind and tide, it might gave drifted. Then they picked up our boat's engineer and we heard the big Atlas kick into life and the lines drop to the deck.

For a few minutes, sheltered in the lee of the point, the *Hili-Kum* headed out almost jauntily, water churning out beneath her stern, exhaust whipping away from her stack. But then, as she emerged into the strait, the full force of the southeaster hit her broadside. Her mast swayed in a huge arc and her hull rolled until the red lead on her bottom was clearly visible. Finally, my father turned her with the seas and they began their search.

They careered along in a following sea for half an hour, seeing nothing but breaking waves. Apparently they had miscalculated; the Air Force boat must be behind them rather than in front. When my father was concentrating, he tended to hum to himself; now he hummed softly and searched for his window of opportunity, that small area in the seething sea where the waves were slightly less violent. Then he spun the wheel. The *Hili-Kum* didn't manoeuvre quickly; for a long few minutes, broadside again, everyone hung on for dear life. The chart table leapt from its fastenings and slammed down on the berth below and, in the galley, crockery, canned goods and pots crashed from one side of their lockers to the other. Then, heading into the seas, my father stopped humming and just steered into the oncoming waves. The difficulty now was to get a good look around. As the bows dove into the trough of the seas, water flung itself against the windows and poured down the glass, obscuring everything. But each time the boat shook off the water and rose on the crest of the wave four pairs of eyes—or to be more accurate, three and a half pairs, for Jimmy had an artificial eye—scanned the horizon for a boat painted camouflage grey in seas of the same colour.

Finally, the object of their search was spotted rolling wildly off to port. Jimmy went to attach a heaving line to the towline while my father, humming softly, manoeuvred the *Hili-Kum* into position. This wasn't the easiest thing to do. Nor was it easy to get the heaving line to its destination. The line snaked across the seas, hit the wet and rolling deck of the other boat for a second and then slithered off into the waves. Hand over hand, Jimmy yanked it out of the water as fast as he could lest it foul the *Hili-Kum's* propeller. The Maritimers stood ready to grab for Jimmy, should he lose his footing on the heaving deck. In the pilot-house, my father did a little ballet trying to keep the bows into the seas with the wheel, kick the stern into position with the clutch and keep track of the action on the back deck, all at the same time. After a couple of tries, the boats had drifted too far apart. The *Hili-Kum* made a wide circle and came in again, as close as was possible. Jimmy threw the line

once more. There were several men along the side of the Air Force boat now, holding on to the ratlines and the piperails. On the third try, someone caught the heaving line and pulled it in. Someone else helped to wrestle in the heavy water-soaked towline and get it fastened to a cleat on the bow. Jimmy and the Maritimers paid out some line, got it through the hook that hung from the boom, and secured it to the *Hili-Kum's* winch. The tow began.

As the two boats struggled toward the shelter of the Cove, my father reflected on our chance of winning the war.

"If our side can't even remember to fill their fuel tanks," he said, "I think we're at a distinct disadvantage."

As time went on, the airport contractor really got under way, and our rag-tag crew wasn't equal to the task of keeping Fort Rupert supplied with lumber. To solve the problem, the Air Force took over the mill—and the boat.

The *Hili-Kum* disappeared for a short time and reappeared with her glossy white paintwork painted a dark wartime grey, her mast bristling with aerials and her cabin roof piled with life-rafts. All this life-saving equipment wasn't as excessive as it seemed, we soon found, for the boat, which had always operated with a crew of two, now had seven on board. Apparently, the Military Mind deemed whatever number a boat would sleep to be the appropriate number for her crew. To my father's and Jimmy's astonishment, the *Hili-Kum* now had, besides her captain, a slew of mates, deckhands, first and second engineers, a radio operator, and a cook to keep this mob fed.

The same largesse was applied to the mill. Where our regular able-bodied crew had numbered twelve, there were now sixty-five. It certainly gave the place an air of purpose. Every house, as well as the bunkhouse, was packed with sawmill crew or "support staff." Carpenters arrived to build another bunkhouse and a huge mess hall, since ours was not nearly large enough to feed this army.

The individuals most markedly affected by this turn of events were our three Chinese employees. Our Japanese workers had long since been deported to the BC Interior, and the rest of the regular crew were in the services; but the Chinese, who had been with us ever since the box factory closed, were still with us. Now, once again, with very little warning, they were out of a job. They were old and their grasp of English had never been good, so other employment was out of the question. Welfare didn't exist. Nor did the three expect any regularized assistance. Instead, they adapted to this change with flexibility and imagination. They continued to live in the China House, which cost them nothing, they had all the free firewood they needed for fuel, they had always kept chickens and had a garden—and now they became bootleggers! Cut off from the nearest liquor store by miles of water, surrounded by the military, they followed the classic recipe for success: find a need and fill it. Their new occupation wasn't immediately apparent, for the dealings were always handled with the utmost discretion, but finally my parents realized where all those footfalls in the night were heading, and why. In theory this activity was not a good idea, because it took place on private property, the owner of which was my grandfather, the local magistrate. In practice, however, it all worked out, because all concerned maintained their ignorance, if not their innocence.

My parents' adjustment to the new regime was perhaps more difficult. Neither of them had ever had the slightest contact with the military, and for them it a was a dizzying transformation. Overnight, common sense, independence and thrift were replaced by foolishness, bureaucracy and waste—and, as my mother said, a distinct lack of neighbourliness.

"I find it very hard to understand why they don't offer to take us along when they're making a trip to Alert Bay," she said. "We always have so many errands to do there, and after all, it *is* our boat."

"It's not our boat," said my father. "The Air Force is leasing it."

"Fred," said my mother irritably, "you know perfectly well we have always taken along anyone who wanted to go to the Bay. It's just common courtesy. Besides," she sniffed, "In wartime you'd think they would want us to save fuel rather than have us use the *Klinekwa* when it wasn't necessary."

"Just be glad we have the *Klinekwa*," said my father.

The only good thing that came out of this, from my mother's point of view, was the fact that when the Air Force took our boat out, all of her crew were required to wear their life-jackets. Though theirs were the more glamorous "Mae Wests," this requirement made it easier for my mother to enforce her rule that my sister must wear hers, lethal though it later turned out to be.

At first, uncertainty over the course of the war and tensions over various scares and alarms made these new inhabitants seem a prickly lot. We were required to black out our windows, and one night we answered the front door to find two *armed* airmen on the porch. They told us we were showing some cracks of light.

"How silly," said my mother, going around jerking at the curtains, "considering the mill burner is blazing away all day and all night." Of course, she was right. The burner, the only such beacon in miles of dark coastline, pin-pointed our location exactly, and provided a perfect reference point for the whole area.

Gradually, however, we began to shake down and form a new community. The airmen ceased to be fighting men and became just sawmill workers and seamen; for some of them, this had been their prewar occupations anyway, and they reverted to them easily. And the shake-down took place more rapidly than it might have, because they all got the 'flu. Suddenly, half of the crew were seriously ill. No provision seemed to have been made for such an occurrence; there was only a first aid man who was as sick as the rest. So my mother quite naturally assumed her previous role of medical practitioner to the community. Granted, she had never had so *many* patients before—as she said, it was like doing hospital rounds. But she rose to the occasion with her usual unassuming efficiency, making daily visits to each bed with her thermometer, ordering fluids from the messhouse, dispensing aspirin and checking for pneumonia and other complications. Several of the men got serious nose-bleeds that were almost impossible to stop, but stop them she did. After that, both sides relaxed, and we began to go on picnics together.

What made these picnics such an event were the crashboats. Somewhere along the line, the Military Mind had conjured up crashboats. Perhaps it was an effort to keep up with the American Joneses who had PT boats, for that's what these boats resembled. They were seventy feet long, had twin 1400-hp Packard engines which raced them along at a dazzling speed, and they must have cost an enormous amount of money to build. They were the *Takuli*, the *Huron*, and the *Montagnais*, and one or other of them was always stationed in our little weatherproof harbour.

As the name implies, they were designed to come to the aid of planes that had crashed. Since no planes ever crashed, it made a very pleasant life for the crew—and certainly a very exciting one for us, for by now neighbourliness had set in and we were often slipped aboard for rides. Only someone who has spent her life on a towboat can imagine the thrill as the Packards thundered into life, and the vessel backed out of the harbour and hurled herself up the Strait, a great rooster tail of wake arching out astern.

To celebrate Dominion Day holiday, the whole community—for there were Air Force wives now, and children—formed a flotilla of RCAF boats and ours, and headed for the lighthouse at Pulteney Point. There had been a good deal of consultation over the locale for this picnic, because some of the airmen wanted to play baseball. This wasn't an unreasonable ambition, but it posed a problem. Open flat land, even a small plot of open flat land, is a rarity on the north coast. Pulteney Point is one of the few places that has a stretch of hummocky grassland between the beach and the trees. So that was our choice. The boats anchored offshore, and dinghies ferried passengers and picnic supplies to the beach. The last contingent had barely landed before the first to arrive made a discovery: the crisp, salty grass was alive with snakes! Disturbed in their peaceful isolation, they writhed away in all directions, causing havoc among the picnickers. The ball players weren't inconvenienced and some of the smaller boys were delighted, but the rest of the group confined themselves to a narrow strip of beach close to the water and complained bitterly for the rest of the day, because they weren't able to roam around without being attacked by garter snakes.

On an evening in August, we took our picnic supper to Pearse Island. Afterwards, in the starry summer night, the boats, engines throttled back, picked their way through the narrow channels by searchlight. The chart shows a cluster of small islands; between them are convoluted passages, some navigable and some choked with rocks. My father led the flotilla because he knew the way. Like Cyclops, the bright eye of his searchlight probed first one rocky shore and then swung across his bows to check the other as we proceeded through the maze. The cushions of moss and the gnarled trees that clung to the bluffs that hemmed us in on either side showed brilliant green in the white glare of the searchlight; then we emerged from the islands, crossed the black strait, and found our small harbour. We gathered our hampers and blankets, called our good-nights and climbed the long, wet ladder to the dock and the long flight of stairs to the house, and went to bed.

What these junkets cost the taxpayer in fuel, one shudders to think—but as a morale-booster they were a wild success.

Other occasions took on a distinctive twist, too.

The *Huron*—one of the Air Force's crashboats.

Our July 1st picnic at Pulteney Point.

One Hallowe'en night, after the younger children in the community had done their rounds of trick or treat, we were startled to hear a loud explosion. Looking out, we saw every building illuminated, every tree in stark relief, in the flickering blaze of a flare. The crashboat crew were providing a spectacular finale to Hallowe'en with their Very pistol. Adults and children alike watched with delight as flare after flare shot up into the night sky and drifted slowly down into the bay. It was a measure of our isolation that no one from the world at large responded to these international distress signals—and just as well, too. A breathless rescuer, arriving on our doorstep to discover that we were celebrating Hallowe'en, would have been considerably put out.

By August 1945, we were waiting, along with the rest of the world, to hear that World War II had ended. Although we expected the news, we weren't sure how quickly it would reach us or who would hear it first, for people with battery radios limit their listening. As it turned out it was Grace, an airman's wife who worked in the mill office, who broke the news. At four o'clock in the afternoon of August 14th, she heard an alert on the telephone. She picked it up and listened in. It was the word we had been waiting for. Within minutes, the mill whistle began blasting out its message to the mountains and the sea, to a wilderness that neither knew nor cared about the end of a war. One of the airmen fired off his rifle; the radios, now all on, blared band music; and, when the *Hili-Kum* came in later in the after-

noon, all her signal flags were flying.

The next day was a holiday. The community cooked, and the airmen prepared the mess hall. That afternoon, an air force swain found me out on an errand when he called around. For some reason, perhaps simply exuberance, he left me a note to keep me abreast of the preparations that had taken place. I have that note. It reads:

This morning we started in and swept the floor in the dining room part. I had been down earlier and took the ping-pong table apart and moved that awful old cot out of there. George set out to cut evergreens and we tacked them up on all the windows and at both ends. We've strung the boat's flags from corner to corner and tied the balloons up in the middle. We started out with about seven balloons and now there are only four. They popped for no reason I could see. We have put streamers up between the windows. The streamers are American Beauty colour. It looks just plain red in that light, though. The guys fixed up shades of the same paper for the lights and they look just like pantaloons. They bulge in the middle and have a frill around the bottom. Of course Harold had to criticize them but we like them so they stayed that way. We got sheets off the boat to cover the tables and I twisted streamers to put around the edges. See you later.

It was a great party, an innocent celebration. We didn't know, then, that we were marking not only the end of a war but the end of our isolation.

TIME AND TIDE WAIT FOR NO MAN

Crane Islands, three in number, lie about 3½ cables northward of the eastern extremity of Bell Island, with a rock, covered less than 6 feet, situated about one cable northward. These islands should not be approached within a distance of 3 cables.

British Columbia Pilot

Someone once said that prospect of being hanged concentrates the mind wonderfully. In a less desperate way, and for a much longer period of time, a depressed economy focuses the mind as well. In the ten years from 1929 to 1939, everyone's attention was fixed on earning a living. We had a lot of home-made fun; every year my parents and most of the mill crew had saved enough for some kind of a holiday; my sister and I got dolls and books for Christmas; there was always plenty of food for ourselves and our many guests. Yet the overriding concern, the unspoken concentration, was still on having a job, getting paid, "making it" financially from one year to the next.

The war wiped away the Depression mentality. When it was over, everything had changed. Suddenly everyone had a good job and there was money to squander on things like outboard motors and record players. And, just as suddenly, everyone was tired of isolation, and began to push for a road that would connect us with the rest of the world. Getting a road became a collective obsession. Our local paper, *The Pioneer Journal*, exhorted the powers-that-were to do something and the powers-that-were gave speeches and made promises.

In the 1990s, things change with dizzying speed. In a year, an old log dump is transformed into a golf course, and a chic woman with a briefcase and a lot of jewelry is selling condos around its perimeter. Go away for a month, and you return to find that a whole chunk of forest has disappeared and a shopping centre is rising in its place. Forty years ago, change took place more slowly—so slowly that its presence was almost undetectable. Bit by bit, mile by mile, year by year, we got the road, but in the meantime life went on.

The mill, worn out from overwork, was repaired, the big Air Force mess hall became our community hall, the crew shrank back to its normal size once again and, a little later, my father replaced the *Hili-Kum* with a new boat called the *Gikumi* ("Chief" in the Kwakiutl language). We were so busy picking up the threads of our lives and getting things back to normal that no one noticed that "normal," itself, had changed.

Before the war, the *Hili-Kum* had ranged far and wide in her search for logs and customers. Her log read: Cutter Creek, Minstrel Island, Fort Rupert, Port Harvey, Knight's Inlet, Bones Bay, Scott Cove, Simoom Sound, Call Creek, Parson's Bay, Bute Inlet, O'Brien Bay and Loughborough Inlet, to name a few. We called at Bryant's camp and Mackay's, Soderman's, Campbell's, Sawchuk's, Wilson's, Bendickson's, Swanburg's, Carson's and Lafarr's. Now many of these small independent camps were closing, and the ones left were being annexed to huge timber companies with unfamiliar names like Crown Zellerbach and Alaska Pine. And so we bought our logs from these companies, situated right next door in Beaver Cove. There were no more arduous tows from far in the hinterlands. And the companies that sold us logs also bought our lumber—quantities of it, for they were building camps and logging roads all over the interior of the north Island. We supplied thousands of feet of bridge timbers—the most profitable kind of cutting a mill can do. But, of course, there was a dark side to all this good fortune. Because the mill was dependent on these companies for its log supply, its existence became dependent on their need for our lumber.

At the same time that these changes were taking

place in the forest industry, a whole new resource sector was springing up, bringing with it a whole new source of income for the *Gikumi*. There were iron and copper mines now in the Nimpkish Valley, at Benson Lake and on Neuritsos Arm. Huge Japanese ore carriers came to load at Beaver Cove and Port McNeill. When they sailed, they needed a tug to push them out and away from their moorings. Once under way, a Canadian pilot guided them through the Inside Passage until they came to Crane Islands and the open ocean. Here the pilot had to be taken off and returned to Port Hardy to catch a plane for Vancouver. And so the *Gikumi* took on, as well as her sawmill duties, the role of a sort of combined harbour tug/pilot boat. The job lasted for twelve years, and sometimes proved to be a demanding test of seamanship.

The first problem involved power. The ore carriers were enormous. The biggest of them, the *Yawatasan Maru*, was six hundred feet long and carried twenty-seven thousand tons of ore. Getting that dead weight moving was like trying to shift the position of an island. The *Gikumi* manoeuvred into position, placed her well-bumpered nose against the wall of steel that towered over her, and gave it everything she had. Water churned from her stern, but for a few minutes that was the only discernible movement. So

my father replaced the *Gikumi*'s Atlas Imperial with a new 290-hp Nissan.

"That thing will *never* last," Jimmy told my father. "It's just going crazy down there in the basement. Just a'screamin'. We'll see it come up through the decks any minute." Actually, it proved to be a very satisfactory engine but, after the Atlas, it took some getting used to.

Once under way, the ore carrier throttled back to allow the *Gikumi* with her maximum nine knots to keep up, and headed north. The *Gikumi* was on call 365 days of the year, which meant that on any one of those days—or nights—in fair weather or foul, the two vessels might follow each other out to the bleak tip of Vancouver Island. And before the smaller of the two got radar, it was a toss-up as to which weather was the most trying, fog or wind.

In fog, they lost sight of each other immediately. So the *Gikumi* would run her courses to the appointed spot in the ocean; then, with engine idling, Jimmy standing at the bows, and my father leaning far out the pilot-house window, they strained to hear the measured blasts from the Japanese ship's whistle. Having reached a consensus, they put in the clutch, revved up the engine once again and headed off blindly in the direction of the sound, Jimmy still standing

The *Gikumi* leaving Telegraph Cove and heading down Johnstone Strait.

The *Gikumi* alongside one of the ore carriers, waiting to perform her harbour tug duties.

outside in the mist. All of this groping about would have been easier if the vessels could have communicated by radio-telephone, but each was on a different frequency. Any conversations they had had to be relayed through a third party at the government stations at Bull Harbour or Alert Bay.

This difficulty was overcome by radar. At first, my father was highly distrustful of this new device. Nearing the appointed rendezvous, my father would say, "Jimmy, I think you'd better get out there and listen."

Jimmy, in his usual position at the bows, would concentrate for a few minutes and then point, "Yep, there's something blowing over there."

Taking a look at the radar screen, my father would say with astonishment, "Yeah, I can *see* it."

In short order, like a microwave oven, it became so indispensable that they couldn't imagine how they had functioned without it.

"Oh my god," moaned Jimmy, in mock dismay, "if this thing ever goes on the fritz, how are we going to make out?"

Travelling at six or seven knots, neither vessel ever stopped throughout the whole procedure of picking up the pilot. In howling winter storms, this exercise proved more than usually tricky. The *Gikumi* was

given the lee side, of course, but in those exposed waters it gave scant protection. My father put the wheel over hard and shoved the *Gikumi*'s front quarter straight into the side of the ship. The rubber bumpers screamed. Far above them the pilot, clinging to his rope ladder, timed his arrival. The *Gikumi* rose and fell like an elevator. He waited until she was on her way down and then came down the ladder hell-bent-for-leather in order to reach her deck before she started to come back up. If his timing was faulty, the *Gikumi* chased him right back up the ladder.

The most difficult feat was yet to come. In the wind, it was a formidable task to extricate the *Gikumi* from her limpet-like position against the wall of steel. She couldn't just slip astern, or she would be sucked into the propellers. She couldn't go right straight ahead, because she would get caught in the anchors or simply run over. Instead, her bow had to be gotten out into a position that would allow her to break away.

Given these circumstances, it wasn't surprising that the Japanese crew, sorry for the tiny vessel struggling so far below, were moved to acts of kindness. They sent lunches down to the *Gikumi* at the end of a heaving line. The first time one of these small boxes was lowered down to them Jimmy placed it carefully

The *Hosei Maru* raising anchor.

on the deck until the *Gikumi* had freed herself from the Japanese ship, then he took it to the pilot-house. My father opened it and peered at the contents.

"Well, Jim," he said, "what do you think?"

"I think them are the damndest sandwiches I ever seen in my life," said Jimmy.

"What do you suppose this is?" said my father, removing a capped bottle from the box and holding it up to the light.

"Tea?" guessed Jimmy dubiously.

My father unscrewed the cap and sniffed cautiously. "Cold tea," he said. "Tell you what," he added, "when that ship is right out of sight just toss this to the seagulls. You've got the lunch that Emma made for us back there, haven't you?"

"Why sure," said Jimmy. "Want a cup of coffee to go with it?"

"That'd be nice, Jim."

It's the thought that counts, of course, and the thought was very much appreciated. Nonetheless, as soon as the ore carrier was well out of sight, Jimmy threw "them crazy Suzuki sandwiches" to the seagulls, then laid out the peanut butter ones my mother had provided. Over the years those gulls stuffed themselves on sushi. It was enough to make a yuppie weep.

In 1948, BC Airlines based a Seabee in Alert Bay, and two years later QCA began *its* air service to the area. The mail now travelled by air, and great lumbering Stranraers carried passengers to the city and back. For the first time, a journey which had taken twenty-odd hours now took two. These planes changed the nature of medical emergencies, too. QCA was frequently pressed into service as an ambulance, and the

Seabee, while too small to carry a stretcher, was able to bring the doctor to his patients, thus supplying medical attention much sooner than would otherwise have been possible.

From the hospital in Alert Bay, Dr. Pickup was flown to accidents in many remote locations, but one of his most demanding emergencies took place at Beaver Cove, just ten air-minutes from the hospital itself. In March 1954, a crummy, returning to camp at the end of the day with its load of loggers, lost its brakes on a steep hill. The driver did the only thing he could: he turned the vehicle into the bank. It bounced against the hillside, rolled and then rolled again, strewing its passengers in its wake.

As soon as the news of this accident reached Alert Bay, Dr. Pickup and the BC Airlines pilot, Ed Bray, took off in the Seabee. There was a strong southeaster blowing, and if the take-off had been a bit dodgy, the landing was downright hair-raising. The pilot made eight attempts before he finally set the plane down on the stormy waters of East Bay.

Dr. Pickup found one man already dead and sixteen injured, eleven of them stretcher cases. Our phone at Telegraph Cove was ringing by this time; it took our boat, the camp tender and Robert Mountain's seiner, the *Tartoo*, to get them all to Alert Bay. At the hospital dock, a caravan of pick-up trucks and vans waited to transport the stretcher cases to the hospital where a little knot of men and women, recruited by the RCMP, were ready to donate blood. Those agencies and services which so effectively shield the city dweller from the harsh facts of life formed no part of our existence.

By now the little northern Vancouver Island communities, like eager ducklings, were making every effort to crack the shell of their isolation. Oddly enough, there was no shortage of roads. By the 1950s there were miles of good gravel roads snaking through the north Island. They were private logging roads built by the huge timber companies that had appeared after the war. The problem was that they didn't connect any of the communities, but simply reached into the wilderness to the timber resources. Their presence became the thin edge of the wedge, however, as we discovered at Telegraph Cove. In 1956 my father prevailed upon "Zip" Leino, the superintendent of the camp at Beaver Cove, and one day he sent a bulldozer operator over to punch his way through the woods to Telegraph Cove. There was no engineering involved, so the road wasn't all that well laid out; at our end water often poured down its slope into the mill yard. Nonetheless it was a road—a real road—and we were ecstatic. Now, on weekends, we could all escape the confines of that small cove. It was possible to *drive* through the wilderness that had been hidden from us for so long. We fished in the lakes, marvelled at the rushing glassy-green rivers, visited the mine sites, and met and made friends with people in the neighbouring camps. Now it was possible to go for a walk—not

a struggle through a trail hacked out of the underbrush, but a *walk* along a gravel road. Children could ride bicycles. Twenty years after the Superintendent of Education had envisioned it, children now went over that road to school. *Trucks* arrived from the two big camps at Beaver Cove to pick up lumber orders. On dark winter mornings a *bus* jounced down the hill and waited in the millyard, lights blinking, for school children to board it.

It was hard for us to believe. My father promptly bought a huge second-hand Chrysler. It had power everything, very little road clearance and was an entirely unsuitable car. He loved it. Several other of the Cove's inhabitants bought cars, including Jimmy.

Jimmy's choice of vehicle was entirely dictated by weight. He bought an Austin which was light enough for the *Gikumi*'s tackle to lift and drove it to Kelsey Bay, where it was loaded onto the back deck of the boat and unloaded onto our dock.

The Austin was a good car, but in time Jimmy was tempted by something bigger, and it turned out that his neighbour, Frank, was hot to buy the Austin. In fact, perhaps feeling that Jimmy might change his mind, or that someone else might beat him to it, Frank was seized by a sense of urgency. He arrived one evening while Jimmy and Thelma, his wife, were eating dinner and plunked a pile of cash on the table. He could barely wait for them to finish their coffee, so anxious was he to take delivery. He and Jimmy walked down to the lumber shed on the wharf where the Austin was parked, and Jimmy took all his fishing gear out of the trunk. The two of them got into the car, and Jimmy explained the esoteric English gear shift. Then, with Jimmy sitting beside him, Frank backed the car out of the shed, turned it around, hit the gas instead of the brake and flew over the twelve-by-twelve that edged our dock. It was a fairly low tide. The Austin did a flip, dropped ten feet and landed on its roof on the stern deck of the *Gikumi* moored below. Back in their

Despite the language barrier, the Japanese crew member at the bow relayed his captain's signals and the *Gikumi* pushed.

kitchen. Thelma heard a resounding crash, saw the *Gikumi's* mast arc wildly, and raced for the wharf. She arrived in time to see the two occupants crawl from the wreckage. Jimmy had hurt his ankle, but otherwise they were both intact. The car was not so fortunate; it lay smashed to pieces, its four little tires in the air.

Frank's enthusiasm for the Austin had waned; had, in fact, vanished.

"To hell with it," he said, or words to that effect. "Push it over the side."

Jimmy remonstrated.

"Push it over the side," repeated Frank, "I don't want it no more."

"Okay, Frank, I'll tell you what I'll do," said Jimmy. "I'll buy it back off you right where it is now."

Jimmy gave him seventy-five dollars of his money back.

Jimmy's ankle bothered him for some time but all in all, he reflected afterward, his first and last foray into second-hand car sales was, although more action-packed than he anticipated, not unsuccessful. He sold the Austin's engine to an old fellow in East Bay for a light plant and put the car's leather bucket seats in his boat.

The whole area continued to press for road access, and in 1962 a headline in the local paper read "North Island Dream Coming True." It went on to quote Dan Campbell, our MLA, who said that the government had approved a two-million-dollar highway construction project between Campbell River and Kelsey Bay. Further, the government had submitted plans for a bridge over the Nimpkish River. By using the existing logging roads, this bridge would connect Telegraph Cove and Beaver Cove to Port Hardy. True, there was still a twenty-five mile gap between Beaver Cove and Kelsey Bay but now, at least, and for the first time, Kokish Camp at Beaver Cover could play baseball with the camp at Woss Lake.

"The north Island," said Campbell, "has been asleep for fifty years. This is only the beginning."

He was right, but we weren't out of the woods yet. The road progressed in a manner typical of the north coast. For one thing, it kept right on raining. Whereas, in earlier days when the interior forest remained intact, this rain had had little effect, it now washed debris down denuded hillsides and flooded rivers and road beds. When the Nimpkish River Bridge was being built, Vancouver Piledriving had their dredge secured by "spuds": long steel pilings driven into the bed of the river. Heavy rains brought masses of debris down the swollen river and tore the dredge from its moorings. It was carried downstream, and finally came to rest on Flagstaff Island. The *Gikumi* was called out, and in the downpour and the dark they got a line on the dredge before the tide started to fall, and pulled it off the shore. By the early morning hours, they had it moored safely behind the breakwater at Alert Bay.

My sister Bea and Jimmy on the *Gikumi.*

Then another rainstorm washed out the Benson Lake road and left a gully ten feet deep across its width. Unfortunately, it happened after dark and a pick-up, driving along in the rainstorm later that night, fell into it. The passenger in the pick-up was knocked unconscious, the driver walked miles for help, and it took thirty loads of gravel to make the road passable again.

Periodically, school children had to get out of their bus and walk across bridges weakened by the rain, to transportation waiting on the other side.

Meanwhile, the twenty-five mile stretch of wild country that separated Beaver Cove from Kelsey Bay still presented an insurmountable barrier to the south. Once again, logging roads became the basis for access. There was only a little over a mile separating the north Island from Campbell River via the road to Gold River. When this mile of forest was penetrated we were connected—by a tortuous one-hundred-and-fifty mile gravel road that first zigged across Vancouver Island almost to its west coast, and then zagged in the opposite direction to the east coast. It was known as the Ho Chi Minh trail.

All these momentous changes—the roads, the air transportation—provided not only freedom from our isolation but competition for our faithful life-line, the Union steamships. Finally, on January 1st 1958, a large ad appeared in the local paper. Mr. J.A. MacDonald of the Union Steamship Company announced the end of its coastal service. He apologized "for the inconvenience this will create for our friends in the isolated communities of the coast."

You will note the word "friends." This wasn't a flattering term chosen by some marketing expert. It was a sincere description of the way the Union Steamship Company viewed its customers—and the feeling was reciprocated. The coast had lost a lot of its flavour.

Twenty years later, the mill at Telegraph Cove succumbed to these same changes. In 1940, the mill's advertising had read:

Telegraph Cove Mills Ltd.
Telegraph Cove, BC.
Rough & finished lumber for all building purposes
Mouldings, doors, windows, firewood
A private enterprise, buying logs locally and
Employing local labour
Write for estimates

It was a point of pride that the mill provided jobs and supported the local economy. By the late 1970s,

neither of these things was important. Good jobs were available everywhere, logs were the exclusive province of the large timber companies, and the mill's huge circular saws were too old-fashioned and wasteful for an environmentally conscious era.

It was a gut-wrenching experience to close the mill, disperse the decrepit office furniture, and dispose of the files and the fresh white letterheads that lay in piles, waiting for correspondence that would never be written. It was years before I realized that this hadn't been a business. True, bookkeepers wrote paycheques, and invoices were sent out, and the letterheads said Telegraph Cove Mills. But it was not a business and never had been. It was simply a way of financing my father's great love, which was plowing around the coast on a boat. It was a means of supporting a way of life that had now ended.

Fred Wastell had followed his bliss without hesitation—without considering the effect that our isolated life had on his wife and children. As a result, Emma Wastell's life was one of relentless domesticity. There were no labour-saving appliances, no meals "out," no pizzas ordered in. Three times a day, seven days a week, there were meals—big meals—for if my mother was often lonely she was never alone; the house was always filled with people.

Given these circumstances, my sister and I were no strangers to housework either. We scrubbed floors, baked pies and did endless tubs of washing. That this was a type of forced labour was illustrated by an exchange between my mother and my sister when Bea was still quite young.

"Would you like to earn twenty-five cents, Beasie?" inquired my mother.

"No," said my sister.

"Well you're going to."

However, we had countless hours of pleasure and adventure too. Mine centered around the boat. Each time I stepped onto the deck's thick planks and felt the boat move gently under my feet, I knew I had found my place in the universe.

My father and I never discussed our bond. As a parent and child, our communication was limited. But generations of captains, on both sides of the family, had given to him his effortless seamanship, and to me my appreciation of it.

Our isolated life couldn't prepare us for the sophistication of the wider world, so when we finally did make our way into that world we were not, at first, confident. But for all that we lacked, much more was gained, because our upbringing had bestowed great gifts.

For one thing, I grew up to be "handy." Capability was not only highly regarded in our family, it was assumed. It was assumed that anyone, with a little effort, could do anything. And it was also assumed that those who didn't were either lazy or lacking in character—or both. So when the camp cook fell ill, I coped, at sixteen, with a massive wood-burning stove, a half-witted bull cook and a messhouse full of hungry men. Nor were the demands only domestic. In Victoria, I was sent on errands to the Capital Iron and Metal to find various esoteric machinery parts (at a good price of course), and in the summer, when Jimmy and his family went on holiday, I took his place on the boat.

The second thing our life provided was a grounding in reality. We came smack up against birth and death, against bravery and bullshit. As a consequence, I've never been able to get too interested in the superficial aspects of life—and I cannot be conned.

Thirdly, and finally, I received the greatest gift of all—the gift of nature. If, from infancy, wild country and a wilder sea are a palpable presence, they become part of the soul. I am grateful that they are part of mine.

Her tugboating days over, the *Gikumi* now takes visitors whale-watching in Robson Bight.

RAINCOAST
CHRONICLES

Seventeen

Stories & History of the British Columbia Coast

Edited by

Howard White

Introduction

BY HOWARD WHITE

When *Raincoast Chronicles* started courtesy of a federal youth grant in 1972, we raised eyebrows by treating the 1950s as history, long before they had acquired a sufficiently sepia-toned air of antiquity in many people's minds. In this issue we rush another period into history—that capricious paisley-trimmed decade of our own beginnings. On page 98 Mark Bostwick recalls an unforgettable summer spent rediscovering Vancouver Island's West Coast Trail in 1972, courtesy of a federal government grant from the notorious Opportunities For Youth program. His humorous and nostalgic account looks with fresh wonder at a period when leaders could respond to the challenge of displaced youth, not by increasing jail space, but by paying the kids to go out and create their own jobs. Plenty of that seed money fell on fallow ground—but as booming recreational use of the West Coast Trail and a greying Raincoast Chronicles attest—some of it took hold.

As architect of the Parliament Buildings, the Vancouver Courthouse-cum-Art Gallery, the Empress Hotel and other turn-of-the-century BC landmarks, Francis Rattenbury has a claim to being BC's favourite architect. On page 93, Robin Ward—one of BC's favourite writers on architecture—critiques one of Rattenbury's less-known works, his own family home in Oak Bay, and in so doing provides a delightfully irreverent commentary on Rattenbury's brilliant and scandalous career.

In trying to record pioneer experiences, something which has bedeviled us from the first is the invisibility of women. We know they were there standing shoulder-to-shoulder with their men, but when it came time to record the scene for posterity, often as not they were left out of the picture. One glorious exception is Hannah Maynard, who solved the problem of being left out of the picture by taking her own. The tag "Maynard photograph" is stamped all over BC's historical face, but what of the woman behind the lens? On page 108 curator Petra Watson gives a rare glimpse of this self-taught pioneer photographer, whose busy Victoria studio recorded every facet of BC life for four crucial decades from 1862 to 1912.

Among the primary factors which shaped BC are the smallpox epidemics which reduced aboriginal populations to insignificance—normally viewed as an unavoidable natural occurrence. Were the plagues really a pioneering form of biological warfare manipulated by colonial administrators to guarantee BC would come out of the colonial period white? On page 117 epidemiologist Douglas Hamilton takes a closer look at this growing controversy.

No First Nation was more severely affected by smallpox than the Sechelt Nation, whose aboriginal metropolis at Kalpalin (Pender Harbour) made them one of the great powers of the northwest coast. On page 145 Howard White, a long-time resident of Pender Harbour, ponders the ruins of Kalpalin and fills in some gaps in the history of this little-studied group.

Some issues of *Raincoast Chronicles* have been planned around themes—logging, fishing, early Vancouver, forgotten villages—while for others unplanned themes have emerged after the fact in the form of nicknames—the soft logging issue (No.6), the E.J. Hughes issue (No. 10), etc. Maybe this one will become known as the bad medicine issue. Two of the articles deal with aboriginal health issues, while a third, "The Doctor Book" by Margaret McKirdy (page 162), revisits the day when "felons"—painful infections under the fingernail—had to be treated at home with the advice of *The People's Home Medical Book*: "Call the patient's attention to something at the other side of the room and while he is looking away press down hard with the knife . . . he will jerk and thus make the cut long enough . . ." McKirdy goes on to explore not just the vastly changed world of family health care since pioneer times, but also the changed role of family values in this beautifully-written piece.

Raincoast Chronicles 17 is rounded out with Lynn Ove Mortensen's biography of August Schnarr, the legendary Knight Inlet trapper (page 129), Paul Lawson's poem "The Rock Bandits," a "recipe" for donkey boiler coffee by the late Arthur Mayse, and two short amusing stories by Jack Springs and Dick Hammond. ❖

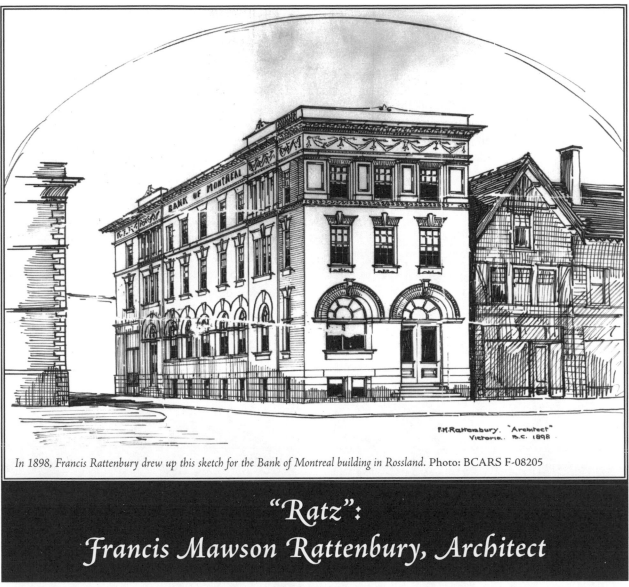

In 1898, Francis Rattenbury drew up this sketch for the Bank of Montreal building in Rossland. Photo: BCARS F-08205

"Ratz":
Francis Mawson Rattenbury, Architect

BY ROBIN WARD

Many of the Europeans who settled in Victoria in the mid- to late 1800s were opportunistic Scots, but it was an ambitious English architect, Francis Mawson Rattenbury, who gave the city its turn-of-the-century imperial character. If ever a city owed its appearance to one man, it is this one. Rattenbury's extravagant relics—especially the Parliament Buildings and the Empress Hotel, his two most photographed buildings—are prominent in an architectural heritage that includes some of the finest fin-de-siécle structures in Canada.

Rattenbury was born into a Methodist family in Leeds in 1867 and studied architecture with his two uncles, William and Richard Mawson. Lockwood & Mawson, as the uncles' firm was known before Rattenbury's apprenticeship, had made its reputation in mid-Victorian England with designs for a town hall and a model mill town built for "work, health, education, and moral instruction." But Rattenbury knew there were more exciting opportunities in Canada, where booming colonial cities brimmed with work for British-trained architects. In 1892, he sailed for Montreal.

Rattenbury gave himself a crash course in current North American styles by looking around Montreal before catching the train to Vancouver.

Within a year he had achieved astonishing early success by winning the competition for the new Provincial Parliament Buildings in Victoria. He was twenty-five years old.

When Rattenbury first sailed into Victoria's Inner Harbour in 1892 to scout out the site for the Parliament Buildings, he was inspired to create an "imperial garden of Eden." In those days visitors to Victoria arrived by sea, and Rattenbury envisioned the landlocked harbour not as a frontier town with an Indian village, but as a sort of European piazza dotted with picturesque statuary and monumental buildings—all of his own design.

To some extent he got his wish. Rattenbury was the toast of local society after his success with the Parliament Buildings and the CP Railway's Empress Hotel, one of the legendary imperial hotels. "Ratz," as he was ambiguously nicknamed, wasn't easy to work with—he played the temperamental artist when he was not given complete control of his projects and habitually fired off outrageously pompous letters to his clients if they interfered with his designs. He was given to profligate spending, noisy public tantrums and cavalier dealings with contractors and suppliers. But the Parliament Buildings and the Empress are still the centrepieces of Victoria's special architectural presence. With his design for the Crystal Garden and the CP Steamship Terminal, Rattenbury's Inner Harbour tableau was nearly complete.

In 1898, a few months after the Parliament Buildings had opened, Rattenbury married Florence Eleanor Nunn, daughter of a former British Indian Army captain. If Rattenbury thought he had gained a partner who would join in the whirl of his social life as the most prominent architect in the province, he was mistaken. Florence had enough grit to accompany him over the Chilkoot Pass during one of his wild schemes to run riverboats to the Klondike, but later she preferred to potter around in the garden of "Iechineel," the

English-born architect Francis Mawson Rattenbury gave Victoria its turn-of-the-century imperial character. Portrait circa 1924. Photo: BCARS F-02163.

This portrait of Mrs. Rattenbury (Florence Eleanor Nunn), was taken by Hannah Maynard. Photo: BCARS B-07984.

BC's first parliament buildings, known as the Bird Cages (in background), were moved to make room for Rattenbury's new parliament complex. Rattenbury appears in the centre of this 1893 photo. Photo: BCARS A-02574.

Rattenbury-designed BC Parliament Buildings under construction in the 1890s. Photo: BCARS D-05994.

Francis Mawson Rattenbury's work is well known and highly regarded in British Columbia today, but outside the province and Canadian architectural circles, the architect is a forgotten figure. In his prime, Rattenbury was an esteemed and envied member of Victoria's elite; in the 1920s his career and his domestic and social life took irreversible tumbles.

Rattenbury began building "Iechineel," his home in Oak Bay, in 1899. He was a flamboyant designer, almost always erring on the side of excess rather than understated good taste, but his home is cozy and charming, built in modest English Arts and Crafts style—the picture of domestic harmony. Florence, Rattenbury's first wife, loved Iechineel so much that when the marriage broke down she had a new home built within sight of it, and she brooded over it until she died in 1929. Glenlyon School took over the building in 1935. Photo by Robin Ward.

Oak Bay home Rattenbury began to build the following year.

What stories buildings tell. Rattenbury's Oak Bay home is picture perfect in its cozy image of rustic England, a scene of peace and contentment. And for a time, the Rattenburys were at ease here with their two children and their garden parties—"Iechineel" is an Indian word for "the place of good things." To this day, if you walk round to the back of the house, away from the carefree children's voices at Glenlyon School, which took over the house in 1935, you can sit on the shore and gaze on the islet Rattenbury bought and planted with gorse to colour the view.

But Rattenbury was never satisfied. He kept adding mock Tudor gables to the back of the house, spoiling its modest personality, much in the way that his growing self-importance began to erase whatever charm he once had. Still, with its rustic stone, leaded glass, patterned shingles and picturesque gables, Iechineel is the most attractive of all the smaller homes Rattenbury designed. While he often lacked the patience to attend to details, and was more comfortable wielding a flamboyant brush than a precise pen, he sometimes showed an instinctive ability to mellow his buildings' baronial bearing with coziness and charm.

Looking at Rattenbury's buildings and unrealized projects, one is left with the rather melancholy impression of a talent unfulfilled. His release from a plodding apprenticeship in England proved to be a creative dead end. Opportunity was there for the taking in the colonies—Rattenbury would have been lucky to land the Parliament Buildings prize in the old country, and even if he had, his uncles' firm would have taken the credit. But ultimately, he played safe with his styles. He never challenged his clients' old-world tastes any more than they encouraged him to broaden his own. Rattenbury was simply one of the legion of able British architects who prospered by building colonial works from Sydney to Singapore, and Melbourne to Montreal. In Victoria, he is remembered affectionately as a colourful fellow who designed some of the best-loved and most enduring buildings in town.

Ironically, one of those buildings was the setting for the beginning of Rattenbury's spectacular downfall. In late 1923, a dinner took place at the Empress Hotel to celebrate the commission for the Crystal Garden. Rattenbury, who was fifty-six, attended as guest of honour and was bewitched by Alma Pakenham, a wartime heroine and *arriviste*, twice married and thirty years his junior. He surreptitiously began visiting her house in James Bay where she lived as an apparently respectable piano teacher with her young son. Rattenbury made no secret of their trysts once the gossip got out. He might have retained his reputation had he been discreet, but locals drew the line when the couple began to appear together at the theatre after Florence had refused Rattenbury a divorce and, subsequently, when he tried every tactic short of murder to dispose of her. They were finally divorced in 1925. Rattenbury and Alma married but were ostracized by local society, and his career was in ruins. Percy Leonard James, the associate designer of the CP Steamship Terminal and the Crystal Gardens, sought credit for both buildings and Rattenbury had few friends left to contradict the claim.

Like many ageing empire builders, he retired to England in 1929, accompanied by Alma. But he was unknown and unfeted in his native land. In a poetic turn of events he was murdered by his chauffeur, who was also his wife's paramour, in an Agatha Christie setting in Bournemouth where he and Alma had settled. The "Villa Madeira" case caused a sensation in 1935, making the front pages of not only the Bournemouth *Echo*—"All Night Queue for the Villa Murder Trial... Sensational Allegations by the Prosecutor... Retired Architect's Death... Chauffeur accused of Murder"—but the *Times* of London. The case packed out the public viewing galleries in the Old Bailey and was the inspiration for a play, *Cause Célèbre*, by Terence Rattigan. Were it not for his well-publicized demise, Rattenbury would have ended his days in obscurity. But his work, even if only as an imperial footnote, deserves to be better known beyond the city where he made his reputation. ❖

Excerpted from Echoes of Empire: Victoria and Its Buildings, *by Robin Ward, Harbour Publishing, 1996.*

At Tsusiat Falls driftwood shelters with homey touches like hand-crafted benches, tables and a sauna suggested that other hikers were equally enthralled with the beautiful beach and freshwater pool at the base of the falls.

Opportunities for Youth, 1972, and the West Coast Trail

STORY AND PHOTOS BY MARK BOSTWICK

Across Canada during the soggy winter months of 1971 and 1972, thousands of young people living "collectively" (in shared accommodation) pushed aside the sand candles, Zig Zag papers and Grateful Dead albums, and sat cross-legged around homemade coffee tables filling in application forms for Opportunities for Youth grants. OFY had approached the chronic problem of summer unemployment with an unorthodox idea: let the unemployed themselves create jobs with government financial assistance. The concept suited the needs of a generation. Young people were in no hurry to choose careers because things were getting better, a

little better, all the time. Why lock into life too soon? Better to explore, especially if the government would pay you $100 a week to do so. OFY encouraged the prevailing "do-it-yourself" ethic since any proposal would be entertained, no matter how quixotic, droll or impractical.

I immigrated to Vancouver in the summer of 1971, arriving with a rucksack, duffel bag, fifty pounds of paperback books and a small grubstake of $1,800. For a couple of weeks I scoured the bulletin boards at UBC and along West 4th Avenue looking for a place to rent or a house to share. I rejected a dank basement suite with no light and a rock band upstairs, backed out of a house full of acid freaks, and placed my hopes in getting accepted by a group of women forming a house around interests in "the NDP and Women's Studies." The seriousness of the notice implied cleaner bathrooms, more regular hours.

The core group included a student nurse, a UBC student, a fish plant worker, and an unemployed office worker. The actual occupants changed with traumatic regularity and ultimately encompassed a longshoreman/actor, a bird caller, a revolutionary on the lam, a bank teller and a blacklisted ex-teacher and mountain equipment sales representative from Colorado. The house on West 12th in Point Grey had a big kitchen, one bath (no shower), a few sticks of cast-off furniture and a relentlessly inquisitive landlady. My 90-dollar share of the rent entitled me to a small room on the main floor beside the living room. My little pad was spartan, but sufficient: a mattress on the floor, a small desk with a rented electric typewriter, bricks and boards for bookshelves, and a couple of Fillmore posters on the wall.

The lifestyle of the house was a mixture of collective fun and interpersonal tension. On Tuesday evenings the whole house hitchhiked from West 10th and Sasamat to the UBC Women's Studies lectures: Women and the Industrial Revolution, the Myth of Penis Envy, Fear of Success, Women and Canadian Literature, Alternative Lifestyles. We drank beer at the Cecil Hotel, or if it was too crowded, at the Yale or Austin. We shopped for India print bedspreads along 4th Avenue, beads on West 10th, and watched old Marx Brothers movies at the Commie Kids Flicks on Carrall Street. We took long walks in the University Endowment Lands to collect autumn leaves and initiate romances. Collectively we pasted together paper lampshades, sang folksongs, and protested the nuclear tests on Amchitka Island. We also argued over the dullness of the food (brown rice and broccoli was the house staple) and dishwashing praxis (rinsers vs dunkers). There were disputes over who cleaned the bathroom (one of the women tore out a couple of pages of *Sisterhood is Powerful* and pasted it

over the ring around the tub); whether lounging around nude was social, anti-social, or showing off; and whether forming an intimate relationship undermined the household collectivity (I had formed one with Shelly Tees, the office worker).

Homes like ours did not exist in isolation. Everyone in our house knew people living in other collectives scattered across Point Grey, Dunbar and Kitsilano, and we maintained connections through parties, romances, borrowing, bartering and sharing information. Word about Opportunities for Youth spread across this network like wildfire. My old college friend Shelagh knew Larry, who knew Mary Jane and Sudsy, who knew Ellen Rosenberg. And Ellen, a biology grad student at SFU, was reputed to be a master at preparing successful OFY applications.

Over Christmas we began devising a proposal. We had no political illusions about OFY: it was a ploy by Pierre Trudeau to buy off the revolution; it was intended to disperse angry youth into tiny projects with low pay; it was a way to appease a group of young Liberal bureaucrats with "project officer" jobs that would permit them to keep their hair long and wear blue jeans. On the other hand, my bankroll was dwindling, Shelly was tired of her office job, and OFY seemed like an attractive way to spend the summer in the country.

Our initial ideas ranged from the sublime to the ridiculous. Why not rent a boat, load it with library books and cruise the inland waters stopping in at coastal villages to promote reading? This was such a good idea we even travelled to Nanaimo to talk the Regional Library people into supporting us, but it foundered on "practicalities." None of us knew anything about boats, sailing, or libraries. The crew looked a little shaky, too. One woman was trying to decide whether to join us or take an all-nude role as a character named "Cocaine" in a local film production.

A "Trans-Canada Hiking Guide" seemed more practical: a guide to short hikes accessible from the Trans-Canada Highway. It had some tourist promotion features and would allow us to spend the summer exploring the province. Dougald MacDonald, author of *Hiking Near Vancouver*, graciously wrote a recommendation and we sent in an application.

Ellen prepared our backup application, "The West Coast Trail Project." She had spent some time at the Bamfield Marine Biology station located near the northern end of the old West Coast Life Saving Trail on Vancouver Island. The Trail, which followed the coastline south for 44 miles to Port Renfrew, was slated to be the key feature of the recently announced Pacific Rim National Park. In our application we promised to establish "information centres" at either end of the Trail, and to register hikers and provide them with information. In addition, we would mediate between the visitors and residents of Bamfield and Port Renfrew. And finally, we promised to prepare a brochure on the Trail. The woman at the local OFY office thought this one was pretty good and told us "I'll probably be calling you from Ottawa."

We waited. The hiking guide proposal got turned down. We waited some more. The house broke up, Shelly and I moved down to Larry's place at 6th and Yew where we shared two small rooms and Larry's hand coffee grinder. We talked about what we'd do if the project did not come through. Finally, in late April we received word that the West Coast Trail Project had been approved.

Ellen Rosenberg and her fiancé Michael would run the Bamfield centre. Shelly and I, along with Evelyn Williams, a stringy blonde woman from small-town BC who had attended SFU and gestalt therapy workshops on Cooper Island, would staff the Port Renfrew centre. We purchased maps of the Trail, started buying equipment at the Mountain Equipment Co-op (which was then a room above a store on 4th Avenue), and began developing a strategy for moving to the Island.

While gearing up for our departure it dawned on us that we had signed up for something more than a lark. We knew no one in Port Renfrew, had no place to stay, had never hiked the Trail, and weren't sure when OFY would send us the first installment of our grant. It was our responsibility to become instant experts on the Trail and to run the information centre seven days a week for an unknown number of hours. No one had even the sketchiest idea of how many parties hiked the Trail each week.

Nevertheless, in late May Shelly and I took the MV *Queen of Victoria* to Victoria and put our thumbs out, hoping to cover the seventy miles to Port Renfrew by nightfall. A tattooed skin diver who choked sunken deadheads for $50 a day gave us a ride to Jordan River where we sat around in the Breakers Cafe until three hippies in a pickup truck took us as far as the squatter's encampment at China Creek. A working guy in another pickup truck took us the last twenty-four miles on a dirt road to Port Renfrew.

When we got there, we were not filled with hope. The pub in the hotel above the government wharf was locked because of a power outage and the hotel had no rooms anyway since the owner was raising chinchillas upstairs. We camped on the floor of an old fishermen's dormitory next door to the pub. It had no lights; scraps of drywall hung off the walls; the floor was littered with cigarette butts, beer bottles and several stained copies of *Jesus and His Friends*.

The next morning we set out on foot to visit the BC Forest Products logging camp, hoping to get help finding accommodation. For a small community of a few hundred souls, Port Renfrew was remarkably decentralized. A few houses clustered around the elementary school, hotel, and government wharf. A little farther on we passed the BCFP residential enclave, which looked like a tiny perfect California suburb with clipped lawns and sprinklers dropped onto the wild West Coast. Down the road we passed a patch of forest with the barnlike general store almost all by itself. The road beyond the store eventually crossed the San Juan River and parallelled a beautiful long beach strewn with chalk-white driftwood. The Pacheenaht Reserve embraced the Gordon River estuary below the BCFP forest operations. After the reserve the road passed a small cluster of old houses known as "Elliott's Cabins," circumvented the dump, and continued on into the BCFP site. We did not have to walk the entire way: the local school bus driver picked us up about halfway and gave us a ride to "Elliott's Cabins." Frank Elliott, one of the town's old-timers, wasn't around but we had a long chat with Fred King, who lived next door.

King was standing in his garden smoking his pipe and listening to the radio. He was a small Scotsman with grey hair, blue eyes and a taste for philosophizing. Within minutes he was showing us his beautiful dogwood and chestnut trees, and relating long stories about his adventures as a seaman, fisherman, policeman, Hollywood ladies' man and night watchman. His living room was full of electrical gadgets including three television sets and a half dozen tea kettles. Over coffee and Peak Freans he delivered with complete certainty the prediction that within thirty years the strain on the natural environment would reach a breaking point and there would be a major crisis. He offered to loan us a copy of Velikovsky's *Worlds in Collision*.

But our needs were more immediate. We hoofed on up to the BCFP logging site: a collection of two-storey frame buildings, including several dormitories, a cafeteria, rec room and administration building. We asked to see the boss. He was not immediately available so we had a cup of coffee and a slice of homemade pie in the cafeteria while we waited.

When we were ushered into Ken Halberg's office it was obvious to us that he already knew about our mission; news travels fast in a small community and it was Halberg's responsibility to know what was going on anywhere near his domain. He had invited his forester, Stan Nichols, to sit in. We

The old Life Saving Trail had been virtually abandoned in 1954… The federal government had sent in a few teams to reconnoitre and chop away some salal, but rot and deadfall had taken their toll: cable bridges and boardwalks were often barely passable, and always dangerous.

were ingratiatingly frank and friendly, avowing that we (and the federal government) wanted to save the community from problems with hikers and hippies. We also asked if he could help us find a place to stay. To our relief, both Halberg and Nichols were receptive to the idea of an information centre. They seemed thankful we were not agents of the Sierra Club. Halberg apparently believed our motives were benign, or at least perceived us as harmless. He offered to introduce us to Art Jones, the acting Pacheenaht Band chief, who ferried hikers across the river and who might help us find a place to live.

Despite its small size, or perhaps because of it, Port Renfrew had a subtle power structure. Halberg and Art Jones represented the two strategic communities. The company was the only real local industry, they could provide plum jobs like running the boom boats or doing office work, and they had the most technical expertise and equipment. The Band, on the other hand, controlled the estuary through which many of the logs were floated into the bay to form rafts; they had lines of communication with the federal government through the Department of Indian Affairs; and they had moral status as the area's oldest inhabitants. Relations between the two leaders were marked by careful courtesy and polite respect. Halberg almost self-consciously removed his hat when we entered Art's house.

Art Jones, a large middle-aged man, was fixing a car with the assistance of a bevy of toddlers when we pulled into his yard. Over the summer we would observe that Art spent most of his time fixing something, often for us. And he usually had several youngsters in tow. After Halberg summarized our plan and our needs, he offered (once the Band elders approved) to rent us a couple of small cabins on the reserve that had been recently vacated by Band families moving into new homes. The rent was $35 a month. It was easy to say yes. In private we agreed that Art was the friendliest person we had met so far in Port Renfrew.

Shelly and I had a little clapboard cabin facing the Gordon River estuary, with two rooms and a bedroom with linoleum floors, a shower and a propane stove. Art's housewarming gift was an old radio that could pick up signals from Victoria and sometimes Vancouver. Television had not yet reached this West Coast outpost. Evelyn would live in the second cabin and share our kitchen facilities. Shelly found a satiny driftwood plank on the beach on which I inscribed "West Coast Trail

Information Centre" with a felt-tip pen. We nailed the sign over the doorway and declared ourselves "ready for business."

Two days later we had our first customers: six hippies starting out on the Trail. We had little information, but did arrange for them to get across the river in Art's aluminum boat. After a ride to Sooke on Paul Miklevic' school bus and a quick trip back to Vancouver to borrow a friend's old Econoline van, fill it with bits and pieces of furniture, and collect our two cats, we returned to Port Renfrew and established a rustic but pleasant household.

We soon learned that ritual is a large part of village life. One of our rituals was morning coffee by the river across from our cabin. Watching the world go by is a corollary ritual: observing the gulls sprint across the sky and the crabs scuttle through the old seat springs and cam shafts on the sandy bottom of the river. In the distance a man and a boy rowed upstream against the outgoing tide, seeming

Camping on the beach.

to chase a lazy loon across the smooth water. The breeze rustled the broomflowers behind the cabin and we could hear the roar of waves crashing along the beach down the road. Occasionally a Beaver floatplane would land on the water right in front of the cabin, bringing some important person or message to the logging camp.

We wanted for very little. Art was forever turning up with a fresh salmon, a big crab or advice on where the berries were ripening. In many ways Port Renfrew was an economy of scarcity. Not poverty: it was just that things were hard to get. The nearest towns, Sooke and Lake Cowichan, were a long distance away. If something broke, people scavenged to find something to fix it. Help was not so much a conscious act of goodwill as a kind of unconscious habit. When the battery on our borrowed van died I simply hitched a ride into Cowichan on the morning BCFP crummy and somebody in Cowichan arranged to get me back to Port Renfrew where Art's brother helped me install it.

Time in a isolated place had many measures. One kind of time was marked by the trucks heading from town to the logging camp before dawn, followed an hour later by the school bus to Sooke, then a bit later by Leonard Jones's local school bus. After a rainstorm there was just enough time to hike to the grocery store and back before the dust returned. The changing tides followed a lunar schedule: the waterline varied ten or twelve feet in a single day and tide tables were an important survival tool for hikers on the Trail. Every few days we would stand on the porch of our shack and watch the boom boats manoeuvre a raft of logs down the river and out into San Juan Bay. In many respects a calendar seemed a more appropriate timepiece than a clock.

Our next task was to hike the Trail and gather information. The old Life Saving Trail had been hacked out of the forest before the turn of the century to permit the rescue of seamen from the many ships blown against the rugged coastline by Pacific storms. The Trail was forty-four miles long, following sandstone shelves and long driftwood-littered beaches, skirting headlands and rocky spots by angling into the forest. Dozens of streams and sev-

eral watercourses large enough to be called rivers cut across the pathway. These gorges were traversed by a system of ladders, steps and the occasional rickety bridge. With the exception of the Nitinat Lake area, the only access points were Bamfield in the north and Port Renfrew on the south. Once on the Trail a party was pretty much committed to struggling through.

The old Life Saving Trail had been virtually abandoned in 1954, rendered technologically obsolete by modern communications and helicopters. The federal government had sent in a few teams to reconnoitre and chop away some salal, but rot and deadfall had taken their toll: cable bridges and boardwalks were often barely passable, and always dangerous. Some ladders were missing three or four rungs in a row. From the moment we passed the fish boundary marker on the north side of the river, we found ourselves in physical combat with nature. It took us nine hours to cover five miles of mud, deadfall, tangled roots, slippery notched log ladders and thick ferns. We fell into bed at a bivouac camp tucked into a corner of a wet, misty forest.

The second day we got our first real glimpse of the ocean as we slogged along a vast sandstone shelf, skipping across surge channels, clambering around rocks, avoiding the impassable sections by re-entering the forest. The hardest section proved to be a large blowdown with logs stretched through the forest end to end in a zigzag fashion, sometimes a couple of yards above the forest floor. One misstep and I was convinced I would disappear into the underbrush never to be seen again.

We were living off backpacker's grub, a mixture of nuts and dried fruit, salty dried soups, crackers and Kraft dinner. No matter how much we ate, our packs did not seem to get any lighter. Our shoulders were sore, our feet were constantly wet and sprouting blisters. The local insect population treated us like Sunday supper. After a little flirtation the sun got shy, retreating in the face of a thick fog and steady drizzle.

On the fourth day I heard myself chanting a phrase from Milton's *Paradise Lost* about "rocks, fens, bogs, dens" and adding "beaches, briars, boulders and slippery boardwalks." Nevertheless, we began to get our hiking legs, to make better time on the open beaches, and wisely to stop early, cook early and go to bed early.

By carefully pacing ourselves and conserving energy we were better equipped to deal with some of the obstacles. The ladders down into Logan Creek were a fright, the slippery wet slanting corduroy boardwalk between Clo-oose and Whyac was perilous. I fell off—and through—the rotting wood several times. We hired a Native boatman to get us across the foamy whirlpools at Nitinat Narrows; he was nonchalant but my knees were shaking.

Respite came at two points: Carmanah lighthouse, a small freshly painted island of civilization overlooking the grandiose verge of rugged coastline and supremely powerful ocean, and Tsusiat Falls where the cascade created a freshwater pool on a beautiful beach. Tsusiat was like one of those oases that appear out of the burning desert in a film about the Foreign Legion. The number of driftwood shelters with homey touches like hand-crafted benches, tables and a sauna suggested that other hikers were equally enthralled.

On the sixth day, having pulled ourselves across Darling Creek on a decrepit little raft, we hightailed out to the West Coast Trail Information Centre (northern branch) just outside the Bible Camp. It was empty. We had expected to meet Ellen, Michael and Evelyn coming the other way, and it

The author and his partner Shelly at the information centre they established in 1972 at Port Renfrew with an Opportunitites for Youth grant. "Visitors appeared at all hours of the day and night… More than a few prospective hikers came without shirts, shoes or food. 'I thought I could just eat berries on the way,' said one. Some welcomed our advice, some didn't."

was not until we had hitchhiked back to Port Renfrew that we learned Michael had twisted his ankle at Logan Creek and been airlifted out by a Canadian Forces helicopter.

I concluded that the Trail was no birdwalk: it required skill, resourcefulness and stamina. Clearly the pioneers who had built and manned the Life Saving Trail were a hardy bunch. Every section of the path presented new challenges, new risks, new terrain. Having spent most of my outdoor life in the high mountains, I was entranced by the deep woods, tide pools, rocky cliffs and intricate ecosystems. At the same time I was discouraged at the intrusion of "civilization" in the form of lost lumber, plastic containers, old bottles, milk cartons and shards of cloth that littered the beaches. But mainly I felt good about myself. I had experienced a genuine adventure, one which I was willing to repeat.

Back at our Centre we settled into the rhythm of life in a small, isolated community. Conscious of our delicate position in the community, we tried to remain unobtrusive while keeping all lines of communication open. Stan Nichols, the BCFP forester, invited us over to the compound for dinner several times and told us about life in the logging camps. Working one's way up the corporate ladder meant accepting a series of postings in places like Port Renfrew. He loved the outdoors, and was persuaded by our boasting to hike the Trail himself, while we came to understand from him that living through a rainy winter ("seventeen inches in three days") in Port Renfrew took a different kind of stamina. Wives, especially, suffered from the isolation.

By mid-summer the number of hikers had swelled from a trickle to a steady stream. Art was kept busy taking hikers back and forth across the Gordon River, and appreciated the fact that we steered them to him, helped them find campsites, and gave them advice about finding a phone, buying supplies and staying out of the hair of the Pacheenaht and the loggers.

For city dwellers accustomed to the staccato rhythms of urban life, the measured life of Port Renfrew was an adagio of small events. The mail came three times a week and everyone, especially Evelyn, looked forward to the long walk to the post office, partly because we were not getting along that well: a matter of personal chemistry and world view. Movie night at the school was a chance for the community to get together. The arrival of books through the Vancouver Island Library system was a regular milestone; it was much easier to get a best-seller in Port Renfrew than in Vancouver. Shelly's huckleberry pie, made from berries we picked behind the cabin, improved an entire day. The first tiny perfect strawberries from the Reserve's patch were a huge treat. Sporadic power outages provided comic relief and consternation. Having planned a grand dinner, the resourceful Mrs. Nichols was sometimes forced to turn quickly to cold cuts and homemade wine.

Our neighbours killed a black bear wounded by poachers behind our cabin. The propane stove exploded and started a fire in the insulation, nearly burning the cabin down, while a covey of hikers continued to gaze at the maps on our wall as if a house fire were a normal occurrence here in the sticks. Our two city cats became adept hunters, bringing in prizes on a regular basis. A sudden increase in gulls announced the arrival of a fish packer boat and the fishing fleet. The pub was crowded for a couple of days, then the fleet moved on. The OFY sent a woman out to check our books; she arrived in a granny dress and granny glasses, spent an hour and left satisfied. Indian

Affairs cruised into the Reserve like a visiting eighteenth-century French *intendent* and left in a cloud of dust. First the fallers, then all the loggers went on strike. The woods stopped roaring with the sound of heavy machinery, and the black bears prowled hungrily around the dump.

The big political event of the summer mounted slowly. After years of petitioning by the community, the Bailey Bridge was fixed, and a few weeks later a section of the road was paved. Suddenly Victoria seemed to be taking an interest in little old Port Renfrew. The reason became clear in mid-summer when Social Credit Premier W.A.C. Bennett called an election. Phyllis Smith, the librarian at the elementary school, arranged for Tommy Douglas, who was then the New Democratic Party MP for Esquimalt, to pay a visit. He brought Jim Gorst, the local NDP candidate, with him. When asked if the NDP's plan for socialized auto insurance wouldn't put a lot of private insurance salesmen out of work, Gorst replied, "Oh, they can go to work in government offices." Tommy Douglas intervened hastily and smoothed things over by describing his achievements in Saskatchewan and discussing local issues like school funding and Unemployment Insurance. I was convinced that Social Credit would win again, but this was not the first or last time my political predictions would be wrong. Even Jim Gorst got elected.

Meanwhile we continued to serve the hiking public from the Centre. Visitors appeared at all hours of the day and night in numbers ranging from one to twenty. We looked first at their footwear, advising those who came in running shoes, cross-country ski boots or sandals that they would find the Trail a little tough. We warned people that dogs who couldn't climb ladders were in for a surprise, that babies would be miles and days from the nearest doctor. More than a few prospective hikers came without shirts, shoes or food. "I thought I could just eat berries on the way," said one. Some welcomed our advice, some didn't. A huge troop of Boy Scouts from Arizona with a troop leader who looked like Hermann Goering dismissed our advice. They went on to appall the other hikers by hoisting the Stars and Stripes at

The fresh paint and neatly clipped lawns of the Carmanah Lighthouse was an island of civilization overlooking the grandiose verge of rugged coastline and supremely powerful ocean.

each camp, and they got seriously hung up on the surge channels at high tide.

Returning hikers often stopped in at the Centre to recount tales of daring, like the young woman who swam all the surge channels, or the fellow who dog-trotted the Trail in a couple of days. More often we listened to harrowing stories of monstrous blisters, bruised shins, hordes of mosquitoes. The little logbook held comments like: "On the boardwalk by Whyac the boards which go crossways are less slippery than those which go lengthways, but I fell twice anyways." There was universal agreement that the trip was well worth it.

Shelly and I hiked the Trail a second time, starting from Bamfield. This time we were better prepared and graced with good fortune. The weather was warm and the forest muffled the sound of our footsteps on the plank bridges. At Klanawa River, floods had broken the line to the old raft, but an athletic young woman hiking with her mother arrived in the nick of time and swam across to reconnect the cord, while her mother floated across

on an air mattress. At Darling Creek, clusters of young people were bathing and laughing in the sun. Tsusiat Falls had more conveniences. The weather just got better and better.

There was more time for discoveries. We explored the rusting remnants of the USS *Michigan* and warmed ourselves with a driftwood fire banked against a plate from the *Uzbekistan*. Outside Clooose we poked around an old cabin nearly covered in vines and found scattered volumes of the *Encyclopaedia Britannica*, works by H.G. Wells and books on socialism. Near an old lineman's shack at Dare Point we happened upon a petroglyph figure carved in the soft rock below the tide line.

We hiked through a landscape drawing on the full palette of nature. Forest greens in a dozen hues, bone-white driftwood, frothy white breakers, sea green surge channels, powder blue skies, pink sunsets, jet black night skies with an infinity of twinkling stars. On the sandstone shelf we marvelled at potholes full of sea urchins, starfish, anemones, limpets and shiny black mussels. Near the mouth of the Cheewhat River Shelly stripped and dived in, catching a crab for dinner with her bare hands. We explored the sea caves at Owen Point and listened to the Pacific Ocean ricochet off the cliffs.

Although the last quarter mile through the forest seemed endless and we were covered in mosquito bites, we agreed the second trip had been incredibly satisfying. One more trip like that, we told ourselves, and we would probably stay in Port Renfrew forever.

The days were growing shorter, but the hikers continued to come. We estimated that 2,000 people had hiked the Trail that summer. The federal government was sending in a variety of scientists to check things out for the new park. There were several accidents, including a broken leg and a small forest fire which mobilized the BCFP crews. At last we realized the OFY cheques would soon cease; it was time to head back to the mainland. Shelly felt we were deserting the community, which had come to rely upon us to funnel the visitors onto the Trail with accurate information. We talked of coming back the next summer, but it was just talk. We said goodbye to our neighbours, packed up the Econoline van, and drove to Victoria.

What did we accomplish? We provided information to over a thousand parties, prepared a little guidebook for general distribution (it was followed shortly by a Sierra Club book), kept some people out of trouble both on the trail and in town,

and set a precedent for an information centre at either end of the trail.

The West Coast Trail Information Centre project began as a kind of paid vacation, but it became the beginning of a longer journey. For me the experience led, like the logs across the forest floor, to a series of community-based jobs that sum up my various careers.

We acquired a fair bit of knowledge about the Trail, its history, its beauty and challenge. But we learned some other things as well. In the 1960s many young people were high on the idea of communities; some believed, like the anonymous builders at Tsusiat Falls, that communities could be created out of a little driftwood and sweat. Our stay in Port Renfrew taught us that even tiny communities are intricate and mysterious, not easily made or maintained. I think we were a little more humble for the experience.

Looking back from the vantage point of the 1990s and my own middle age, I can perhaps be excused for viewing the summer of '72 through a lens tinted ever so faintly with nostalgia. It is not only for my own lost youth, but for a brief season when all humanity seemed to experience a flowering of its more constructive impulses, a time when leaders could respond to the challenge of displaced youth – not by building relief camps or bolstering police forces, but by paying them to go out and search for new roles befitting a new age. ❖

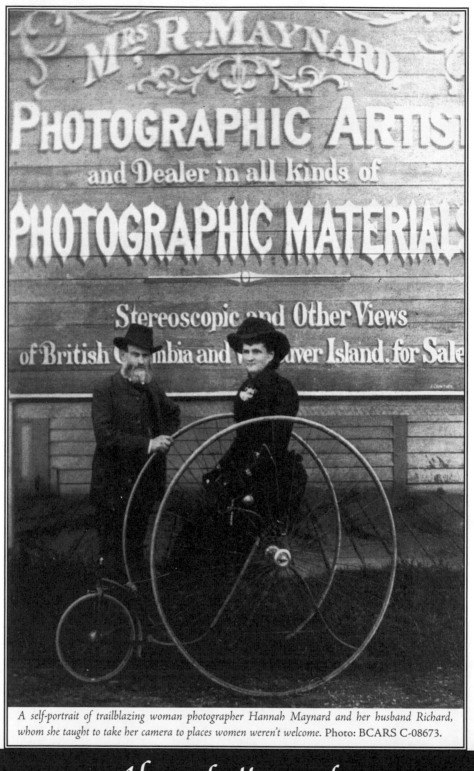

A self-portrait of trailblazing woman photographer Hannah Maynard and her husband Richard, whom she taught to take her camera to places women weren't welcome. Photo: BCARS C-08673.

Hannah Maynard:
Pioneer British Columbia Photographer

BY PETRA WATSON

By the 1860s, Victoria had changed from a hastily constructed fort serving the fur trade of the Hudson's Bay Company, to a busy port city and the centre of administration for the new colony of British Columbia. Lumbering and farming replaced fur exporting as the sustaining commercial activity in the area, and numerous businesses were established to serve local settlers, miners and fortune-seekers en route to the gold fields.

During the latter part of the nineteenth century, it was considered fashionable by the diverse and rapidly growing population of Victoria to visit the portrait studios of the city's professional photographers. One of them was Hannah Maynard. An anomaly as a professional woman photographer, Maynard ran "Mrs. R. Maynard's Photographic Gallery," a very successful studio practice in Victoria, from 1862 to 1912.

Hannah Maynard was born Hannah Hatherly in 1834 in Cornwall, England, and emigrated to Canada with her husband Richard James Maynard in 1852. They first settled in Bowmanville, Ontario where four of their five children were born: George, Zela, Albert and Emma. Their youngest daughter, Lillie, was born in Victoria. In 1859, Richard Maynard, a bootmaker by trade, travelled west to seek gold in the shallows of the Fraser River in southern British Columbia. After a brief but apparently successful sojourn, Richard returned to his family in Ontario. During his absence, Hannah had learned the techniques of photography.

The family moved to Victoria in 1862, and soon after, Hannah set up her first portrait studio on Johnson Street at Douglas. Richard Maynard spent that first summer placer mining for gold on the Stikine River – again, it is thought, with some success. On his return, he opened a boot and shoe store on Douglas Street near Johnson, and in 1874 Hannah moved her studio to the same building. Not long after, Richard learned photography, probably from Hannah. He was soon recognized as an excellent landscape photographer and was hired to document government-sponsored survey expeditions to northern British Columbia. The Maynards opened their third photography studio in 1892, on the upper floor of a two-storey brick building which they built on Pandora Avenue. (This building is still standing.)

Most of Maynard's clients were members of the burgeoning middle class in Victoria, and many of them made several visits to her studio. They wanted to be portrayed solemnly in photographs that would demonstrate social standing and economic prosperity.

Hannah Maynard's studio, in keeping with the traditions of nineteenth-century photographic portraiture, was a decorative parlour designed to make the most respectable people feel at home. Painted scenic backdrops, or decorative interiors almost rococo in design, created the portrait environment. Carved pedestals, diminutive fancy tables and ornate chairs were popular studio accessories. These props recalled the aestheticized tableau of the traditional easel painting, and in addition served as support structures that helped the client hold the pose without moving during the long exposure time. The painted backdrop of a landscape or a generously appointed salon was an environment suitable for showing off the elaborate fashions of the Victorian era.

The subjects of Maynard's photographic portraits – many of them middle- and upper-class men, women and children who often made consecutive visits to her studio – have remarkable physical and psychological presence. The affected poses and the self-conscious expressions so typical of nineteenth-century photography are in many portraits replaced by a feeling of ease, assurance and familiarity.

Maynard did not photograph only middle-class Victorians. She did portraits of sailors and other working-class people, and she invited Natives to the studio to be photographed in traditional dress – some of them wrapped in blankets and holding bundles of goods which they had brought to the city to sell.

Maynard also served as the official photographer for the Victoria Police Department between 1887 and 1892. Young boys, unusually stylish women and sullen men, most charged with theft or burglary, were walked from the police station, then along Cormorant Street to the Pandora Street studio for "mug shots." At first Maynard composed frontal full-face head and shoulder portraits, but later she experimented with a specially converted mirror that rested over the subject's shoulder and displayed both front and profile views in one image

"I think that I can say with every confidence," she is quoted as saying, "that we photographed everyone in the town at one time or another."

But Maynard did not limit her practice to the commercial portrait. She also undertook various forms of photographic experimentation – or as it was often called during the nineteenth century "photographic amusement." For example, she enjoyed producing composite photographs, or "Gems of British Columbia," made from the images of the many children Maynard photographed every year. It is thought that she composed the "Gems" from 1881 until at least 1894, and used them as studio promotion in the form of advertisements and seasonal greetings. To make them, she cut out and

pasted portrait photographs to a painted or photographed background, and then re-photographed the composition. "Gems" from previous years were incorporated in each new year's montage, creating a dense, visual display of tiny images of children. The "Gems," children as the jewels of nature, are steeped in both pathos and pleasure. They express youthful delight and comfort within the uncertainties and tragedies of childhood during the Victorian era, when diseases such as typhoid, diphtheria and tuberculosis were commonplace and usually fatal to young children.

During the late 1880s, Maynard also produced photographic images known as "statuette portraits." Described by her as "Living Statuary" and "Statuary from Life," these allegorical figures of pleasure, loss and despair appeared after a period of great sadness for Hannah: Lillie, her youngest daughter, contracted typhoid fever and died in 1883, at the age of sixteen. Maynard created a stat-

In addition to assiduously documenting daily Victorian life, Maynard was a tireless experimenter whose multiple exposure portraits display a wild sense of humour. Photo: BCARS F-05096.

uette portrait by placing the subject on a pedestal in front of a black background. To give a sculptural effect, the hair, face and/or other parts of the body were covered with white powder or rice flour. In the photograph, the figure of the body was dramatically visible against the dark background, and Maynard scraped or touched up the negative to heighten the cast-in-stone effect.

During the last few years, Maynard has become best known for the small number of double and multiple exposure self-portraits which she took during the 1880s. This form of experimentation, referred to as "freak" or "trick" photography, enjoyed a brief wave of popularity among professional photographers at the time. The photographer seeking information on multiple exposures could find numerous instructional articles in European and American scientific magazines and photographic journals such as *Scientific American* and the French journal *Nature*. The double exposure was

the usual application, but Maynard undertook the more complex multiple exposures. Her technique was to protect part of the film with a lens cap or a box with sliding doors. (One simple attachment was made from a cigar box, cut down to size and blackened inside.) By arranging her subject and studio props strategically, and later touching up the negative to smooth out the joining of the different exposures, she created some unique images.

In her self-portraits Maynard manipulated the patterns of her domestic environment, turning a habitual action such as pouring tea, writing a letter or winding a skein of wool into playful, humorous scenes that are both fragmented and narrative.

The multiple exposure form is especially poignant here. Maynard was a successful professional woman with a large family, a situation fraught with powerful contradictions at the time, and her portraits evoke those contradictions – the warmth and comfort of domestic life, the social

Maynard photo of the Great War Canoe Race, a headline event at Victoria's annual regatta in the Gorge. Photo: BCARS A-02896.

"Gems of British Columbia," one of the strangely haunting photo-collages Maynard composed from her annual crop of children's portraits. Photo: BCARS F-05054.

norms of the Victorian middle class, the creative energy of her work, and the demand and responsibilities of being a wife, a mother and a photographer.

A selection of these double and multiple exposure photographs, said to be of the "freak order," were published in the journal *St. Louis and Canadian Photographer* in 1894.

These multiple exposure photographs have been regarded as Maynard's major body of work and have largely contributed to her reputation as a feminine "eccentric" of the Victorian era – a capricious and untimely woman. This attitude has mistakenly conferred amateur status on Maynard's photographic practice, and has exacerbated the lack of recognition of her professionalism, her success as a portrait photographer, and her contributions as a pioneer settler and a respected citizen of colonial Victoria. For Maynard, like other professional studio photographers of the late nineteenth century, artistic and technical experiments were only brief explorations, not the focus of her work.

Hannah Maynard travelled extensively throughout British Columbia, alone or with Richard. A correspondent from Seattle's *Weekly Pacific Tribune*, visiting Victoria in 1878, stopped at Maynard's studio and learned that "she was on the upper Fraser and Cariboo road taking views." In August 1879, Richard and Hannah travelled together on a steamer around Vancouver Island. Richard often travelled alone on important commissions, such as accompanying the Indian Commissioner, Israel Powell, as far North as the Bering Sea in 1892 to undertake photographic work on the Seal Islands. But Hannah accompanied him on many trips and travelled on her own as well. Both the Maynards photographed landscapes, native villages and early northern white settlements, so the authorship of some images remains unclear. But collaborative photography was quite usual, so the photographs could be published during the late nineteenth century under either of their names. Also, as a woman photographer Hannah might have used Richard's name until her studio practice was established in Victoria.

Hannah Maynard's favourite outlet for publishing her own work, and sometimes that of Richard's, was the *St. Louis and Canadian Photographer*. In the September 1879 issue, the *St.*

Hannah Maynard travelled extensively throughout British Columbia, alone or with her husband Richard. Shown here, Richard Maynard poses in front of totems at Masset in the Queen Charlotte Islands. Photo: BCARS D-09210.

Louis Practical Photographer referred to Hannah Maynard as "one of the most industrious and preserving ladies we have in our business. She stops at no impediment, in our Art, but is a regular go-ahead, even beating our Yankee girls two to one in photography." On her retirement at seventy-eight, after fifty years of photographic practice, she was interviewed by the *Victoria Daily Colonist*, which reported: "Until the current year she never experienced a day's illness in her life. She [was] not tired of work or study… but she fancies that having worked for so long it is about time she made way for the younger generation." Hannah Maynard died in 1918 at eighty-four. ❖

Hannah Maynard travelled extensively throughout British Columbia, alone or with her husband Richard. Here she poses in front of totems at Skidegate on the Queen Charlotte Islands. Photo: BCARS G00822.

Illustration by Alistair Anderson

Donkey Boiler Coffee

BY ARTHUR "BILL" MAYSE

It was good coffee. A man with big feet could walk on it. It was the best coffee I ever tasted in my life, even if you did have to fish bits of burnt twig and charcoal out of it every now and then. But it had a taste, I think maybe from the quick, really savage boil in the white hot steam, that no other coffee anywhere else ever got, so we loved it.

Around about eleven o'clock in the morning when you were all tired out, ready for your break, you began to think about your lunch and, even more than your lunch, you thought about your coffee. Loggers' coffee in those days wasn't made on a stove at all and wasn't put in a thermos. They made it in the firebox of the donkey engine. The firebox is where they would have a roaring fire to keep steam in the boiler, because everything ran by steam in those years.

The loggers would be waiting and waiting and

waiting, and then 11:30 finally came and the engineer would blow his whistle; he would go *woooo woo*—one long and one short—and that meant lunch time. So everybody would drop their gloves and head to the donkey engine.

As soon as that whistle blew the fireman, whose job it was to stoke the fires, would start making the coffee. On the donkey engine deck he would have an old soup box or a big milk container. In it he'd store a big bag of coffee and a lot of half-pound tobacco tins for the loggers to drink their coffee from, we didn't have cups.

He would take a great big lard pail, one of the great big storage pails that holds two or three gallons of water, off a hook and he'd reach for what he called his injector hose. This is one of the hoses that had hot, hot steam from the donkey boiler. He'd put some spring water in his bucket first and he'd take the injector hose and woosh, he'd send a big jet of hot steam into it and it would bring it right from cold to boiling in nothing flat.

Then the important thing, he'd take about two pounds of coffee, which is quite a lot of coffee, and he'd dump it into this furiously boiling water. Then he'd take what they called the slice bar, one of the steel pokers that they used for poking up the fire in the firebox, and he'd hang his pail with his coffee makings on one end of the slice bar and he'd ram it right into the white hot donkey boiler.

In a second it would be blowing steam all over the place, it boiled so quickly. He'd hold it there for a while and let it have a good bubble, good boil. The heat was terrible, his face would be all screwed up from the heat. Then he'd set the pail on the donkey deck and he'd grab another of these bags of cold water, drinking water, and he'd pour about two quarts into the coffee; that was to settle it down. And then the coffee was ready for drinking.

The fellows would all swarm on the donkey engine and grab the empty tobacco cans and they'd take a dip into the big steaming bucket of coffee and get a half-pound can of coffee, which is quite a lot. And there'd be canned milk, "canned cow" we called it, and sugar in bags and we'd fix our coffee the way we wanted it. I liked mine quite sweet without very much milk in it.

Then we'd all sit with our lunches—we brought our lunches from camp if we were working out on a job. We called them "nose bags" because they were a brown paper bag with, oh, about four sandwiches in it, four big heavy sandwiches made of some meat or other, whatever was going in camp. And there'd be a great big piece of pie, about a quarter of an apple pie. That would be your dessert and a couple of jam sandwiches and some cookies. That made a pretty hefty lunch but we were hungry.

We'd been working hard all morning so we were ready to eat. We'd open our lunch bags and start in on our sandwiches and then we'd reach for our coffee and nothing tasted as good as that first drink of what we called donkey boiler coffee after a hard morning's work.

While we were eating, the big ravens that come around every logging operation in the woods, would come looking for food and we'd throw them scraps of our sandwiches. Everyone was quite relaxed and happy. And we'd have maybe a refill of coffee and some fellows would even have two refills of coffee. I'd give a lot for a can of it right now. ❖

Few Native villages escaped the smallpox plague, least of all those like Alert Bay (above), situated along the major trade routes. Photo: BCARS D-04293.

The Great Pox

BY DOUGLAS HAMILTON

On March 22, 1862 an inconspicuous notice appeared in the Victoria *British Colonist*. A resident of New Westminster, recently returned from San Francisco by steamer, had come down with variola, or smallpox. Fortunately, the paper reported, "the case is not considered serious." These words were to herald in the worst recorded disaster ever to strike British Columbia. By the time it was over, the smallpox epidemic of 1862 had claimed the lives of one-third of BC's Native people – at least 20,000 of an estimated population of 60,000 – and a few dozen white people as well.

Before the arrival of the white man, the population density of Natives on the West Coast was greater than anywhere on the continent. Most of them lived in what is today BC, where a benign climate and abundant local food supported large populations. We do not know exactly how many people lived on the BC coast before the first censuses were organized in the 1880s. Newspapers of the 1860s often quoted a pre-conquest figure of 35,000, but over the years we have learned the population was at least 100,000. White settlers underestimated the size of the Native population, possibly because it was easier, morally and legally, to take land from a few disparate people than from a large, recognized tribal group. In any case, official Canadian census figures show that by 1885, only 28,000 Natives were living in BC. A deadly combination of alcohol, firearms and previously unknown diseases devastated aboriginal people during the first century after contact, and the numbers did not begin to rebound until the 1920s.

Of all of the white man's terrible diseases, smallpox was the most destructive. No written records were kept by traders, miners or Natives, so the full extent of the catastrophe will never be known. But we do know that the smallpox epidemic was a watershed in British Columbia history. The sudden ravages of the disease effectively subdued

The sudden ravages of the disease effectively subdued the people of the First Nations like these near Cape Caution. Photo: BCARS D-08825.

the people of the First Nations and opened the door wide for conquest and settlement. The province of British Columbia would likely look very different today, but for one of earth's smallest and simplest life forms.

The little town of Fort Victoria was experiencing some growing pains in the early 1860s. It had been founded as a Hudson's Bay Company (HBC) trading post in 1843, and in 1851 Vancouver Island had become a Crown colony with HBC Factor James Douglas serving as governor. The town was populated by pioneer European immigrants and the local Natives who greatly outnumbered them. Trade between the two groups had prospered since the Europeans had first arrived, and in the spring of 1850 they had signed nine treaties, the Natives trading land for goods with the understanding that "our Village Sites and Enclosed Fields are to be kept for our own use, for the use of our children, and for those who may follow after us ..." One of these vil-

lage sites became the Songhees Reserve in the heart of Fort Victoria. Aboriginal people from many other groups travelled long distances to trade in Fort Victoria, and the gold rush of the late 1850s brought tens of thousands more white immigrants into town.

In a very short time Victoria grew to a bustling 5,000 with a hastily erected commercial hub of houses, tents, stores and warehouses. By spring 1859 more than 2,000 Natives were encamped within 200 yards of the fort and several hundred more were visiting at the Songhees reserve, including the warlike "Northern Indians" – Haida from the Queen Charlottes, Tsimshian from the northern mainland, and Kwakiutl from northern Vancouver Island. It was inevitable that whites and Natives would begin to clash over conflicting social values and over competition for parcels of land. And, with a growing concentration of people and hundreds of ships putting in to the port each year,

Mass infection was followed by panic and flight, which generated fresh outbreaks hundreds of miles from the source. Villages like Bella Coola became charnel houses. Photo: BCARS A-03980.

Smallpox survivors aboard the gunboat HMS Boxer. Photo: BCARS F-05167.

it was also inevitable that smallpox, the great world traveller, would eventually make an appearance at Fort Victoria.

Toward the end of March 1862, rumors of the dread epidemic among the Natives began to surface. Amor De Cosmos, the eccentric, flamboyant editor of the *British Colonist,* was one of the first to realize that the crowded town could be a perfect springboard for the "loathsome disease" among the neighbouring Native population. He noted the unusual "susceptibility to contagion of Indians" and called for the establishment of a smallpox hospital. Already the disease was rumoured to have taken hold in the Songhees reserve, and Dr. J.S. Helmcken, the HBC physician, had been ordered to vaccinate thirty Indians.

It had long been known that among popula-

tions never exposed to smallpox, the mortality rate was high – sometimes over 90 percent. When variola arrived in the New World with the early explorers in the early 1500s, the devastation it caused shocked and horrified even the hardened conquistadors. Early outbreaks in Mexico, Peru, Spanish Hispaniola, Cuba and Puerto Rico destroyed 50 to 90 percent of the Indians. Hernando Cortez's victorious march to the Aztec capital Tenochtitlán in 1520 was preceded and made possible by a crushing epidemic which eventually killed as many as half of Mexico's 30 million people. In his book *Of Plymouth Plantation 1620–1647,* William Bradford described the suffering of the Pequots in Connecticut: "For usually they that have this disease have them in abundance, and for want of bedding and linen and other helps they fall into a lamentable condition as they lie on their hard mats, the pox breaking and mattering and running one into the other, their skin cleaving by reason thereof to the mats they lie on. When they turn them, a whole side will flay off at once as it were, and they will be all of a gore blood, most fearful to behold. And then being very sore, what with cold and other distempers, they die like rotten sheep."

Bradford did not exaggerate. Smallpox was one of the most feared diseases in the world, with good reason. At the onset, the victim developed a fever, splitting headache and knifing pain in the back. A cough and runny nose developed. At this time the disease was difficult to diagnose because the symptoms were like those of many minor diseases, but those first days were the period of greatest contagion. Anything touched by the patient or his bodily fluids received a deadly dusting of viral particles. A single infected human lung cell could produce 10,000 to 100,000 seeds of death. On the second day the fever rose to 104°F. A terrible restlessness and sense of foreboding engulfed the victim, who was very sick indeed. If he was lucky, he slipped into a coma. Children often went into convulsions. On the third day a reprieve seemed to have been granted. The fever dropped and the patient felt a lot better – if he didn't know what he had. A mild rash began to show on his face. At this time the virus attacked the epithelial layers of the skin as well as the spleen, liver and other internal organs. On the fourth day the fever returned, and the victim's throat became terribly sore and his voice hoarse. The light pimply rash suddenly turned into hideous pus-filled pox wounds covering large areas of his face and neck. Thick scabs formed as if the victim had been badly burned, and in fatal cases there was extensive bleeding under the scabs which turned him black. The sores spread until they covered his legs, forearms and especially his back. As his face became swollen and distorted beyond recognition, the victim emitted a powerful stench. Severe sores in his mouth and throat made eating and talking impossible. Many victims in the last stages of the disease instinctively immersed themselves in water to quench the invisible fire. After the seventh day, the person began to die. If he survived for two weeks, permanent immunity was assured. After a month or so, the scabs fell away and the sores began to heal, but the resulting scars would disfigure the entire body, especially the face and neck. The survivor was seriously weakened by the virus and vulnerable to a host of other opportune ailments such as skin infections, pneumonia, influenza and measles. Smallpox often attacked the eyes and was once the leading cause of blindness in the world. It also predisposed the survivor to arthritis, sterility and heart problems.

It is no wonder that panic began to spread among Native groups up and down the coast. At about the same time, reports surfaced that "vaccine scabs" were being sold among them. Scabs were carefully collected from smallpox victims, dried for several days or weeks and hawked for "two bits apiece." A scab was then bound into scarified skin on the arm of a healthy person. If the disease took, the arm became red and swollen and a low fever developed. With luck, the patient recovered in a few days and was immune to smallpox for life. No one knew why this kind of vaccination, or "variolation" as it was called, was effective (viruses were not even understood until 1907), but it had been used for centuries in Africa, India and China. In fact, the "advanced" countries of Europe were among the last to accept variolation.

The procedure was certainly not foolproof. Some 3 to 6 percent of those variolated, contracted the full-blown disease and died. There was the chance of accidentally spreading some other dangerous infection such as tuberculosis or syphilis. Also the smallpox virus remained extremely contagious, and new epidemics could easily be sparked off by those who had recently been variolated. They felt only a little under the weather, and went on travelling, trading and living pretty much as usual – scattering the deadly seeds of the virus everywhere they went. This was well understood at the time. At the height of the epidemic, the *Victoria Press* reported that one patient at the Indian hospital, a variolated woman, "will not keep to her room, but walks about and was even engaged in making bread for some 'tillicums' who if they do not come to grief after eating it, may certainly esteem themselves lucky." Informed observers knew that variolation had to be combined with some form of quarantine to keep the pox from spreading. Yet there is no evidence that anyone proposed large-scale variolation combined with quarantine as a remedy.

By the end of April, Dr. Helmcken had variolated 500 Natives in Victoria. But with a transient population of over 2,500 and no effective quarantine, the effect was minimal and the pestilence continued unabated. It quickly reached Fort Simpson, Fort Rupert and Nanaimo by ship and canoe. Reverend A.C. Garrett wrote to the *Colonist* of "fearful ravages at the Chimsean village" near Victoria. "Twenty have died within the past few days; four died yesterday, and one body lies unburied on the beach having no friends and the others are afraid to touch it. Those buried are only covered with two or three inches of dirt and it is feared that the disease will spread. Great alarm exists at the village, and it is thought that nearly the whole tribe will be swept away."

Two days later, on April 28, De Cosmos published a long and scathing editorial on the developing crisis. He predicted that the "savage occupants" of the local reserve "will rot and die with the most revolting disease that ever affected the human race." Chances were, he warned, "the pestilence will spread among our white population, a fit judgment for their intolerable wickedness in allowing such a nest of filth and crime to accumulate within sight of their houses, and within the hearing of our church bells." De Cosmos declared that the Indians should be evicted immediately, their village burned to ashes and their shallow graves thoroughly covered.

The Native exodus from Victoria began in late April 1862. For many it was voluntary. The Songhees, sensing the danger, packed up suddenly and left their reserve. The Tsimshians were given twenty-four hours to leave their encampment and a British gunboat took up a position across from the camp to "expedite their departure." The Commissioner of Police, Mr. Pemberton, began to evict Natives from Victoria. Roadblocks were erected, and the Tsimshian camp was "fired in the afternoon and every vestige destroyed."

On May 8, De Cosmos again demanded total and immediate expulsion of Native people, pointing out that the disease had spread to all the different tribal groups near town – Haidas, Tsimshians, Kwakiutl, Songhees, Stikeens. He sneered at the $100 which Governor Douglas had personally donated for relief of the Indians. "But what trifling it is with the lives of our own citizens to think private benevolence can afford the security for the public health that is demanded! or that it can prevent the Indians from rolling with the disease at our very doors."

But it was impossible to enforce evictions in unincorporated Victoria, where there no health or sanitation authorities and few police constables. And complete expulsion presented economic problems. Fort Victoria would be paralyzed without the Natives, who provided an indispensable labour force for the wheels of commerce. It was this labour force that probably received most of the variolations administered by Dr. Helmcken. But it was difficult to distinguish between the variolated and the unvariolated. And what about the Indian woman who had shared hearth and home with a white man for years and had borne his children? It was impossible to separate a mother from her children, and difficult to separate a man from his woman. Besides, if women and children were banished to the Indian camp, they could fall into a "state of moral corruption and turpitude ... under the skillful education of the red-skinned friends of their maternal relatives."

Only holy matrimony would make things right, argued the *Colonist*. Marriage would be "make the best of a bad bargain and honest women of their paramours at the same time." And their children could live "free from the taint of illegitimacy." But the notion that marriage and "legitimacy" would protect against smallpox was only a cover for a deeply held prejudice against the mixing of races. Many of the settlers believed the "purity and goodness" of the white race would be diluted in the children of mixed marriages. "The breed remains," Dr. Helmcken said of the Natives, "and will require a great deal of crossing to make a superior race." When the wholesale evictions at Fort Victoria soon proved unenforceable, and the colonial government issued special permits for Native mistresses, many whites were horrified at what they saw as a moral cave-in. The best they could hope for was that the Natives would eventually die out, or become assimilated into the white population. The vicious ravages of smallpox and other diseases could only bolster such hopes.

Indeed, the death rate among Natives rose rapidly. Dozens of new cases appeared daily, and by May 10, over 200 had died, 100 on the reserve and 100 on islands in the Canal de Haro (Haro Strait). The northern Indians living on the reserve were given three days to leave, and when they ignored the order, "fire was resorted to for the purpose of compelling them to evacuate, which they prepared to do yesterday afternoon after their houses had been leveled to the ground." Whites were forbidden entry into the deserted reserve. Even at this advanced date there were no white people with the virus in town, and only one in the hospital.

After the last encampment had been deserted, some voices at last began to be heard criticizing the colonial government for inaction during the crisis. Two smallpox hospitals had been established, one for Natives and the other for whites, but the former provided no real remedy to the Indians. The *Colonist* reported: "Indeed, the hospital, so called, is only a place where the victims may die in a heap without being obnoxious to anyone,

Native cleaning woman employed by pioneer photographer Hannah Maynard. Victorians' reliance on Indian labour was one reason officials were reluctant to enforce quarantine when it might have done some good. Photo: BCARS D-04293.

and not where they may obtain relief and attention as its name implies." The total number of variolations outside the white community remained pitifully small – probably less then 6,000 in all of BC – and not all of these would have taken.

Another delicate question arose: what had the Indian missionary societies done to stem the disaster? From the beginning of the British missionary movement in the late eighteenth century, trade, commerce, and money had been emphasized as much as religion. The missionary societies were a valuable tool for Britain in capturing and taming the far-flung outposts of empire. But the clergy was completely unprepared for the scourge of smallpox in BC. The chaos and turmoil of the epidemic, combined with mass evictions, undermined the entire missionary effort. With classrooms empty, almost all the money remained unspent. The local newspapers began to question the missions' inaction. "What were our philanthropists about," De Cosmos wrote, "that they were not up the coast ahead of the disease two months ago, engaged in vaccinating the poor wretches who have since fallen victims."

Meanwhile, the mass expulsions had the effect of spreading the virus everywhere along the coast. Smallpox was among the most stable of viruses, able to lie in a state of suspended animation for weeks, months, possibly even years without damage, and with an incubation period of eight to fourteen days it was perfectly adapted to wreak maximum havoc among a displaced refugee population. Almost all who opened their doors to the fugitives welcomed a killer. Mass infection was followed by panic and flight, which generated fresh outbreaks as far as hundreds of miles from the source. The villages, forts and islands between Victoria and Alaska became charnel houses.

Reports from ships' captains were published in the newspapers: "The ravages of small pox at Rupert has been frightful. The tribe native to that section was nearly exterminated. Forty out of sixty Hydahs who left Victoria for the North about one month ago, had died. The sick and dead with their canoes, blankets, guns, etc. were left along the coast. In one encampment, about twelve miles above Nanaimo, Capt. Osgood counted twelve dead Indians – the bodies festering in the noonday sun" (*Colonist*, June 21). "Capt. Whitford, while on his passage from Stickeen to this city, counted over 100 bodies of Indians who had died from the small pox between Kefeaux and Nanaimo. In some instances, attempts had been made by the survivors to burn the dead, by heaping brush over their remains and setting it on fire. It had partially failed in most instances, and fuel had burned out leaving the blackened, roasted bodies to rot, and pollute the air with overpowering exudations" (*Colonist*, July 7). "Lo! the poor Indian – Capt. Shaff, of the schooner *Nonpareil*, informed us that the Indians recently sent North from here are dying very fast. 80 or so pustules appear upon an occupant of one of the canoes, he is put ashore; a small piece of muslin, to serve as a tent is raised over him, a small allowance of bread, fish, and water doled out and he is left alone to die" (*Colonist*, June 14).

In Nanaimo, Anglican minister J.B. Good and the Vancouver Island Coal Mining and Land Company (VCML) worked together to variolate the Indians in the town's reserve – many of whom were employed by the company. Plans were also made to remove the Natives to a camp outside town limits on the Nanaimo River – ostensibly to lower the risk of disease for all, but as it happened, the VCML coveted the reserve land for a deep-water

wharf. At New Westminster, the Catholic priest embarked on an intensive one-man variolation campaign. When he claimed to have variolated over 1,000 Natives in one day, an indignant citizen wrote to the *British Columbian*: "The vaccination [variolation] of a thousand Indians in one day, and by one man, needs no analysis to expose its absurdity. I abhor alike that sectional jealousy which sees good only in its own, and that fervor which elevates men at the expense of truth."

The virus moved quickly up the Fraser, Nass and Skeena river systems. It spread from Bella Coola to devastate the Chilcotins, then it attacked the Southern Carriers along the West Road (Blackwater) and Chilako rivers in the fall of 1862. From the panic-stricken Carriers, it passed to the residents of Uncho, Tatuk, Cheslatta and Eutsk Lakes. "At first corpses were hurriedly buried in the fireplaces, where the ground was free of snow and frost. Then survivors contented themselves with throwing down trees on them; but soon the dead had to be left where they fell, and the natives still relate in their picturesque language that grouse used to do their wooing on the frozen breasts of human corpses."

Among the fishing camps of the Shuswap along the Fraser River, smallpox spread like wildfire during the August salmon run and then hitched a ride home with the participants. Prospectors from the North Thompson reported, "There are no Indians on the North River, as they nearly all died of smallpox this year." Whole communities were virtually annihilated by the disease, and some bands lost so many of their members, they joined other groups to survive.

Much farther to the north, William Duncan, that towering figure in British Columbia's missionary history, moved his flock of 400 Tsimshians away from Fort Simpson to nearby Metlakatla in July 1862, to protect them from disease and keep them away from the evil influences of the trading post. The timing was perfect. Duncan variolated his charges and the isolation served as quarantine – with spectacular results. Only five of his followers died, while a hundred times that number perished at Fort Simpson. Events at Metlakatla serve as an example of what could have happened, had the colonial authorities combined forces and acted promptly and responsibly.

The short- and long-term effects of the smallpox epidemic on BC's Native population cannot be overestimated. At least 20,000 people were killed outright, and most of the rest were seriously weakened, some left blind and sterile. Whole villages were wiped out or abandoned. Elderly people were most vulnerable to the disease, so keepers of tradition, oral history, and complex skills like carving and canoe-making died in disproportionate numbers. The elaborate ranking system of crests and clans was severely disrupted. The deaths of so many title holders meant that younger, less experienced men suddenly became heirs to the names, crests, songs and dances of their lineages. When several bands united for survival, whole new cultural systems had to be worked out. Shamans and medicine men were completely discredited, paving the way for the goals of the missionaries. The social order in many groups was seriously eroded, just at a time when it was most needed.

Unable to cure smallpox, Native medicine men lost face before their own people. This Hannah Maynard photo of a shaman was taken at the Indian village at Hazelton. Photo: BCARS A-06031.

And there was a dramatic shift in the balance of power. Suddenly Natives found themselves strangers in their own land, marginalized by newcomers who could better resist European diseases. Growing opportunities in mining, logging and fishing drew even more white immigrants into the province. By 1885, the Native and white populations were about equal in size. "How have the mighty fallen!" De Cosmos wrote in the *Colonist*. "Four short years ago, numbering their braves by the thousands, they were the scourge and terror of the coast. Today, broken-spirited and effeminate, with scarce a corporal's guard of warriors remaining alive."

The smallpox epidemic also helped discourage the signing of any treaties between the Natives and the new settlers for many years. After the fourteen treaties Douglas arranged in the early 1850s, there were no more between the Crown and BC's Natives except for a minor one in the Peace River district in 1898. The ravages of the disease only strengthened whites' assumption that the Indians were a doomed race – accounts of the time refer to the extinction of the Natives almost as if it had already occurred – and if the Indians were all going to die out anyway, why bother signing treaties with them? The land was simply taken over by the Crown and passed on to white settlers. In the minds of many Europeans, the demographic disaster not only showed "God's anger" toward the heathen, it also provided vast lands for settlement, concrete evidence of God's good will toward the new Christian order.

There were complex reasons why white settlers in British Columbia were so unresponsive to the crisis, why whites were systematically variolated and quarantined while Natives were driven off, sometimes at gunpoint, to die by the tens of thousands. In the 1990s it may be easy to pass judgment, but a hundred years ago the authorities faced serious obstacles when dealing with the smallpox catastrophe.

Both of their two best weapons, variolation and quarantine, were regarded with fear and loathing by the Indians. Variolation killed a few of those who received it and often set off new outbreaks of smallpox. And because sores and skin rashes tend to look very similar, patients were accidentally variolated with syphilis, staphylococcus or tuberculosis. Variolation bore no resemblance to any Native healing practice of the day. Pressing a filthy scab into one's clean open wound must have seemed a barbarous and blasphemous act to those unacquainted with the treatment. Understandably, many Natives hid from the authorities, believing that variolation was a plot designed to spread the disease, not prevent it. Even when variolation was accepted, it was not effective without quarantine, which must have seemed a particular purgatory, to be avoided at all costs. For the whites who understood its purpose and value, quarantine worked very well. To the Natives, a place like the Indian smallpox hospital was a cruel prison filled with dead and dying people.

Another obstacle was the sheer speed and violence with which variola invaded a community. It struck without warning, and within two weeks virtually everyone in the village was either sick or dead. No prompt communication was available at that time, so it was impossible to co-ordinate an adequate defence. The chain of infection would burn itself out and move on, long before help could even be summoned.

But the strongest impediment to anyone wishing to stop the epidemic was the British colonial attitude toward public health. Today's view that promoting public health works for the common good was not a widespread belief in nineteenth-century England. Epidemics and plagues were seen as cleansing acts of God, both at home and abroad. For the powerful clergy, variolation and any inoculation were seen as direct interference with the plans of the Almighty. And "survival of the fittest"

was not just a figure of speech. England was a class-driven society much preoccupied with the "problem" of her own rapidly growing poorer classes. Thomas Malthus's *Essays on the Principles of Population*, which starkly laid out the frightening effects of overpopulation, was published in 1826. In it, Malthus offered a coolly logical solution to the problem: "Instead of recommending cleanliness to the poor we should encourage contrary habits. In our towns we should make the street narrower, crowd more people into the houses, and court the return of the plague. In the country, we should build our villages near stagnant pools, and particularly encourage settlements in all marshy and unwholesome situations. But above all, we should reprobate specific remedies for ravaging diseases, and those benevolent, but much mistaken men, who have thought they were doing a service to mankind by projecting schemes for the total extirpation of particular disorders." Malthus's views were in tune with the widely held beliefs of the time. If the poor in one's own country were seen as a disposable burden, the aborigines of conquered lands would be even more expendable. No wonder Britain was one of the very last "modern" countries to wholeheartedly accept either variolation or the cowpox vaccination.

Dr. Edward Jenner had published his groundbreaking *An Inquery into the Causes and Effects of the Variolae Vaccine* in London in 1798, presenting the first effective smallpox remedy that would almost never kill, and never spark off a new epidemic. Lymph from an infected bovine's running cowpox sore was rubbed into a person's cut skin and the mild disease, closely related to smallpox, gave immunity for about ten years. Cowpox could also be cultured using human subjects. Collecting and storing the infectious fluid was problematic in the mid-nineteenth century. It was easy to make the mistake of collecting fluids from sores that had nothing to do with the pox, but that were still deadly. Mysterious outbreaks of other infections were quickly traced to the practice, and questions of safety were raised. Moreover, to be effective the viral serum had to be collected at just the right time during its ten-day cycle of infection. And vaccination had to be repeated carefully every decade.

Still, many English people rushed to try the new vaccination during a smallpox outbreak in London in 1821. And other countries were quick to realize the benefits of it. US President Thomas Jefferson vaccinated his own large household in 1801 and distributed the first cowpox vaccine to local Natives a year later. The vaccination of Indians was provided for by an Act of Congress in 1832. King Carlos of Spain sent cowpox to his possessions in the New World in 1804, and Dr. Francisco Xavier de Balmis, the Johnny Appleseed of cowpox, stopped off at Puerto Rico, Cuba, Venezuela, Mexico, Peru and the Philippines, saving tens of thousands of lives. To keep the delicate virus alive, groups of indigent children were collected from local poorhouses in ports of call, and a few were inoculated every ten days during the long sea trip.

In Britain the story was quite different. Parliament passed laws making cowpox vaccination compulsory in 1841, 1853 and 1867, but no money was provided to enforce the acts until 1871, when dramatic events finally proved the value of inoculation beyond all doubt. During the grinding Franco-Prussian War in 1870–71, the inoculated German army lost only a handful of men to smallpox, while 21,000 non-inoculated French soldiers died of the disease. A new smallpox pandemic sparked by the French outbreak spread throughout Europe during 1870–75, killing half a million people.

All of these factors, combined with the HBC's emphasis on profit and indifference to social welfare, would have discouraged any public health crusader in Fort Victoria in 1862. But the administrators of the colonies of Vancouver Island and British Columbia could and should have done much more to contain the smallpox outbreak.

For one thing, large-scale inoculation would have been possible. The safe and effective cowpox vaccine was available from San Francisco within three days by express steamer. It was widely known that the vaccine had been used successfully elsewhere – several letters were published in the local papers to that effect – yet apparently no public official or enterprising entrepreneur considered offering the vaccine, even to Victoria's well-to-do white residents.

Teaching people simple hygiene for smallpox would also have been a cost-effective means of slowing the pestilence. If bodies of victims and their personal effects had been immediately disposed of, lives could have been saved. If the sick had been forbidden to travel instead of being forcibly evicted, many more lives might have been saved. And some rudimentary form of quarantine could have been enforced.

Fears of a runaway epidemic in white Victoria were completely groundless: natural immunity, variolation and quarantine insured that the virus would never gain a foothold. But instead of reassuring white residents and caring for aboriginal ones, the authorities allowed ignorance and yellow journalism to shift the public focus away from disease control and toward panicky self-preservation. Not only did the Indian victims of smallpox die in massive numbers, they also came to be blamed for causing the problem in the first place.

The terrible epidemic of 1862 was in fact the last of three smallpox epidemics that swept through the northwest coast between 1770 and 1862. The first arrived several years before the European explorers. Captain Vancouver noticed the telltale scars during his first circumnavigation of Vancouver Island in 1792. One of the earliest traders in sea otter skins, Captain Nathanial Portlock, stopped by Prince William's Sound in 1786 and observed: "The captain expected to have seen a numerous tribe, and was quite surprised to find only three men and three women, the same number of girls, and two boys about 12 years old and two infants. The oldest of the men was very much marked with the smallpox; as was a girl who appeared to be about fourteen years old. The old man endeavored to describe the excessive torments he endured whilst he was afflicted with the disorder which marked his face, and gave Captain Portlock to understand that it happened some years ago; he said the distemper carried off great numbers of the inhabitants, and that himself had lost ten children by it ... As none of the children under ten to twelve years of age were marked, there is great reason to suppose the disorder raged but little more than that number of years [ago]." In 1829, the American missionary Jonathan Green reported that about thirty years before, "the smallpox made great ravages" among the Haida. "This disease they call Tom Dyer, as some supposed from a sailor of the name who introduced it, through it is probable it came across the continent. Many of their old men recollect it, and they say, that it almost decimated the country."

The death toll of the first disaster is impossible to count, but calculating on the basis of other statistics in the New World, where Natives had no natural immunity, we can assume at least one-third of the people were killed. It is possible that the disease was brought by early undocumented visits from Europeans, but a more likely explanation lies to the south. In the 1770s a huge smallpox epidemic exploded throughout the western half of North America. The disease struck the Indians of the Missouri Basin and swept rapidly westward through the Dakotas, across the Rockies and up and down the Pacific coast. Annual migration patterns, and age-old trading routes for dentalium, abalone shell, slaves and other items, insured that the virus was spread far and wide.

The second great pox epidemic to lay waste to the northwest coast ran from 1835 to 1838. There are no documents on the event from BC, but farther north in Alaska, imperial Russia ruled the trade routes and careful records were kept. Smallpox was brought by the Tlingits to Sitka in November 1835. It spread like wildfire south to California, and north up the Principe Channel, to Norton Sound, the Aleutian Islands, Kodiak Island, the Alexander Archipelago, Fort Simpson and the Queen Charlotte Islands. The HBC in the south made almost no attempt to variolate, but Russia made vigorous attempts to arrest the epidemic in 1835.

The autocratic Tsars were among the first heads of state to endorse Jenner's revolutionary cowpox inoculation. Long before the vaccine became standard practice in England, Russian Indians were receiving it from St. Petersburg. Incredibly, the Russian Alaska Company's ship *Neva* brought the first cowpox inoculant to Sitka, Alaska in 1808. During the 1835 epidemic more

than 4,000 inhabitants were vaccinated, most of them Russians, Creoles and Aleut hunters. But the rest of the Native population was widely dispersed, and most regarded the practice of cowpox vaccination with horror. Problems with shipping and storing the vaccinia also reduced the effectiveness of the Russian program. In the end, of an estimated 30,000 Eskimos, Haidas, Tlingits and Tsimshians, about 10,000 died, mostly because of the Natives' fears, technical problems with the vaccine, and communication shortcomings. Interestingly, the mortality rate in Alaska was about the same as that of the 1862 epidemic in BC – one-third of the total Native population.

So, if each of these three smallpox epidemics immediately killed off a third of the Indian population between California and Alaska, and if further tolls were taken by the fact that many survivors were rendered blind and sterile, and if other imported diseases such as whooping cough, measles, diphtheria, tuberculosis and syphilis killed even more Native people, the accumulated death toll is staggering. The pre-conquest Native population of British Columbia may have been much greater than the 100,000 figure often quoted by learned authorities.

The last case of smallpox in the wild appeared in 1977 in Somalia. Only two repositories now hold the living virus for "scientific study" – one in Atlanta, Georgia, and the other in Moscow, Russia. Mankind has been patting itself on the back for almost two decades over this remarkable feat of deliberate extinction. But all over the Third World, and particularly in Africa, shamans and medicine men still treasure and preserve pox dust (powdered scabs of smallpox victims) collected decades ago. Attempts by medical authorities to collect and destroy this almost magical powder have been to little avail. It was, after all, one of the few treatments used by early practitioners which actually worked. Is the monster just waiting for the right circumstances to strike again? If any of the pox dust were still infective, a whole new and terrible cycle could be sparked off – this time in a world that is completely unvaccinated. ❖

August Schnarr with a good catch of trout from the Homathko or Southgate River. Photo: Campbell River & District Museum #11642.

The August Schnarr Family of Bute Inlet

BY LYNN OVE MORTENSEN

Some folks who lived up the coast in the early years of the century might say that August Schnarr was a hard case. But those who know would say he just did what he had to do and, most of the time, did it well.

Schnarr was born August 29, 1886, after his folks came west from Kansas to homestead near Centralia, Washington. Three more children followed in quick succession. With all those mouths to feed, Schnarr's father turned to logging. He also drank, and when he'd been hitting the bottle, he was abusive.

In about 1900, when Schnarr was fourteen, the family left the homestead and moved to a small house on twenty-six acres near Chehalis.

That same year, Schnarr got fed up with his father's abuses. He and his twelve-year-old brother Gus jumped their father on his way home from a drunk, and told him to clear out. August took over and ran the family with a tight hand from then on. The area around Chehalis was big fir timber country and pioneer machinery was primitive. In those days, Schnarr recalled, "you had to work; nobody'd hand you anything. We just had axes, bucking saws – not very good ones – augers." To take down a big fir, folks would bore a hole 18 inches deep into the base above the roots. Then they'd angle in another hole to meet it, to provide a draft. They'd light a little pile of tinder where the holes met. The fire would smoulder and burn for a while and "all of a sudden the tree would fall." First you cleared a little place for a garden, then enough ground for a cow.

August and his brothers cut cordwood and sold it for $3.50 a cord. They also hunted for meat, and their mother cooked and canned produce from their large garden. In 1905, Schnarr negotiated with a logging company to trade lumber for a rail right-of-way and the whole family worked together to build a large log house.

In 1907, when Schnarr was twenty-one, he got his first taste of British Columbia when he and Gus rowed up the coast, stopping at Gastown and Victoria. In June 1909, he and a friend hired on with a logging camp near Port Harvey on Cracroft Island. The mosquitoes, gnats and horseflies were so thick he remembered "you had to keep one hand going all the time."

He headed home to Chehalis when the camp closed for the winter but returned the following spring. With him aboard the old *Cassiar* this time were his younger brothers Gus and Johnny, and a 16-foot double ender. The brothers were soon hooked on the coast and were determined to find work over the winter. At the end of the season, they rowed across Johnstone Strait and set a trapline near the Adams River.

That same winter (1911–12) August, Johnny and a friend set out to explore Bute Inlet. They watched local natives hewing out canoes and built one of their own in similar fashion. Then they headed up the Southgate River, trapping marten and some mink along the way, and camped at the head of the inlet near the entrance of the Homathko River.

In 1912, August, Gus and Johnny, along with Paddy McCallum, tried their own hands at logging flood-downed trees in the Adams River. They took out two or three sections over the summer. When fall arrived, the brothers headed back up Bute to build a cabin twenty miles up the Southgate. They trapped in Bute the next two winters, and in the

The Schnarr float house at Shoal Bay circa 1924. Photo: Campbell River & District Museum #14388.

summer they explored the area as far as Knight Inlet by rowboat and sail.

In 1914, Gus and Johnny both left the region but August's patterns were established: handlogging in summer, trapping during the winter, mostly up Bute, and picking up the odd dollar for the bounty on cougars. He was a loner, and he learned to fall all kinds of trees with a springpole. First he'd make an undercut. Then he'd man one end of the saw with a limber young tree tied to the other, carefully arranged to get just the right tension to make a level cut. This he preferred to a human partner. He was always careful about accidents and "couldn't work with a reckless man."

Schnarr appreciated his freedom. He liked the absence of regulations, being able to cut any tree or kill any animal he wanted. He trapped cougar with dogs and liked a dog that was fast. He had no use for hounds who might follow an old scent. He travelled "clean through the canyon to the interior" up both the Klinaklini and the Homathko rivers. He built shacks all the way through, always near fresh water and plenty of wood. "That was lovely, beautiful country, that Waddington Trail." In lots of places there was just one trail and he'd set traps on either side. Though it was common to trap marten inland and mink and sometimes otter on the waterfront, Schnarr mainly caught marten up Bute. He was proud to announce that "the North West Fur Company said I brought in more marten than any ten men."

In 1917, after the US entered World War One, Schnarr was drafted. He left a 30-foot canoe, several guns and his handlogging outfit with a fellow on Stuart Island to sell on commission and dutifully trooped south to join up. But home from the war, he found his possessions gone and the man uncommunicative. Schnarr was enraged. In later years he stated that he didn't like lying and swore he'd never cheated anyone. One of his mottos was: "Be in the right and have the determination to carry through." He liked to hold up a clenched fist and declare, "Ya see that? It never failed me." But for the moment, Schnarr had to start over.

He got a job in a small machine shop at Shoal Bay. One day he heard about a pretty young woman who had settled with her parents at Cameleon Harbour on Sonora Island. He went on over and met Zaida Lansell. They were married in 1922 and moved into a float house at Shoal Bay. That same year, baby Pansy was born in Zaida's parents' home in Cameleon Harbour.

One day in the store at Shoal Bay, Schnarr spotted the guy who was supposed to have sold his belongings. This time, he didn't let the fellow get away. Many years later Schnarr recounted the scene in a high, crackling voice punctuated by an occasional giggle. "Here's where we settle up," Schnarr said. "I shoved him back and landed one on him. I popped him one and down he went. Three times I knocked him down. And then I said, 'tell ya what. Every time I see you I'm gonna hit you.' Schnarr saw the guy twice more, once on the Union boat and again in a hardware store in Campbell River, but both times the culprit managed to get away before Schnarr could carry out his vow.

Two more girls, Pearl and Marian, were born in the hospital at Rock Bay while the family lived in Shoal Bay. Shortly after, probably in early 1926, Schnarr towed the float house up Bute and skidded it onto a homesite halfway between the Orford River and the head of the inlet. The site, which came to be called "Schnarr's Landing," was to be August's home base and emotional cornerstone on and off over the next forty years.

Pansy was nearing school age. Since Zaida insisted on schooling for her girls, in 1928 the blond six-year-old was sent to board with a Mrs. Brians for 18 dollars a month so she could attend the school in Shoal Bay. Mrs. Brians took her along to dances, where she'd be put to sleep tucked in behind the piano. Also, probably unknown to any of them, Zaida was entering the initial stages of a terminal illness.

By the following September, Pearl was also ready for school and the girls went to live with Mrs. Asman, who later became Mrs. Muehle, wife of the sheep farmer at Big Bay, Stuart Island. Pearl's memories of Big Bay days contribute added sparkle to the always-exciting images of Stuart Island fishing. She recalls natives from the Old Church House Village on Sonora riding the eddies in big old

Zaida Schnarr and daughters (left to right) Pansy, Pearl and Marion at Stuart Island in the early 1920s. Photo: Campbell River & District Museum #14409.

dugouts, the women glowing in brightly coloured satin evening gowns ordered from Simpson's or Eaton's catalogues.

At Big Bay, board rose to 20 dollars a month per child. In a time when the family income hovered around $3,000 a year, that was a large chunk, more than twice the monthly rent. Rent on the homesite lease in April 1929 was $8.50. A new Gilchrist jack cost about 35 dollars (though Schnarr preferred stronger, geared models made by Ellingsons), and a pair of Raintest pants went for $4.50. Schnarr picked up extra money trapping cougar and wolf. Cougar skins brought 10 dollars while briefly, in 1929, the bounty on cougar rose to 40 dollars.

The indomitable Schnarr didn't sit still for long. He guided survey parties, including a 1927 – 28 hydro exploration for power sources in the Bute/Chilcotin region. When, years later, the W.A.C. Bennett Dam went through on the Peace River instead, Schnarr condemned it as a political plum. He felt there was more power potential in the Chilcotin and that a dam there would have caused less destruction of farmland and fish habitat.

Sometime during the twenties, he spent nights absorbing engineering theory and practice by the light of a coal oil lantern and earned an engineering diploma by correspondence. If he wanted something, he'd build it, including an unusual hand-hewn bathtub. He was practically penniless most of his life, yet he managed to build himself several rather exotic pieces of equipment, including an air-boat for travel up nearby rivers like the Homathko and Southgate, and an electromagnet for hauling boom chains.

In May 1932, in the depths of the Depression, Zaida died of cancer. She was only about thirty-one years old. Her body was carried to Cameleon

Harbour aboard the Columbia Coast Mission boat *Rendezvous* for a funeral service conducted by Reverend Alan Greene. The girls remember the last note Zaida wrote to them, using her left hand because she could no longer manage the right one.

To Pansy and Pearl, Zaida remains a dim presence since they spent so little of their childhood at home. They spent summers at the Bute homestead, but their memories are of playing in the water all day, coming in only to eat dinner and go to bed. Because of the dreaded "Bute wind," they remained on Stuart Island at Christmas when "Santa" Alan Greene would arrive, bearing oranges, candy and a small gift for each child.

Possibly because of Zaida's death, but also because Logan Schibler was trying to round up enough children for a school, Schnarr decided to move to Owen Bay. He skidded the house back onto a float and headed down the inlet, towing it with a little old Easthope. Generally, Schnarr liked to carry two small kicker engines aboard, so there would

At one time, August brought home four orphaned cougar kittens. Two died fairly quickly, but both a male and female survived to adulthood, bringing the girls a measure of notoriety when their unusual pets made international news. Photo: Campbell River & District Museum #15621.

In early 1926, Schnarr towed the float house up Bute and skidded it onto a homesite halfway between the Orford River and the head of the inlet. The site came to be called "Schnarr's Landing." Photo: Campbell River & District Museum #9005.

always be "one to come home on." But in this instance his precautions proved useless. Near Stuart Island a violent wind arose and Schnarr watched, helpless, as the float broke up and the house went to the bottom.

So he started over again. He and Logan Schibler tore apart buildings from an abandoned logging camp at Orford River, salvaging lumber, windows, bricks, even nails. Schnarr set the girls to straightening nails and, using all salvaged materials, whacked together a three-room shack over a cellar.

Various relatives came to watch the girls for a while but by the time Pansy reached age twelve, she took over running the household. It was "slim pickens," but they never went hungry. August shot deer and raised pigs; he made his own bacon and smoked fish. The family cultivated a huge garden and Pansy learned to can hundreds of quarts of meat, vegetables and fruit from the orchard each year. The only staples they bought were flour, oats, brown sugar, peanut butter and Pacific milk.

During the winter the girls attended the Owen Bay school, a small shack on floats. Daydreaming students could watch the water through cracks in the floor. But come summer, August dropped them at the old Bute homestead, sometimes for as long as six weeks. They lived in the only building left, an open boat shed, where they slept on straw, tended the garden and competed with local black bears for wild berries to can for winter. Schnarr treated them like boys, teaching them to hand log, bore boomsticks with an old crank auger, run the boats, even tend traplines.

Schnarr didn't believe in play, but one time, when Pansy was about thirteen, he brought home four orphaned cougar kittens. Two died fairly quickly, but both a male and female survived to adulthood, bringing the girls a measure of notoriety when their unusual pets made international news.

As the girls entered their teens, natural conflicts increased on the home front. August didn't approve

The Schnarr girls with their father. Photo: Campbell River & District Museum #15627.

of dances and feared his daughters' contact with young men in general. In 1936, he skidded the Owen Bay house back onto floats and towed it up Bute once more. Nevertheless, young men would sneak up the inlet to visit when August was away. At nineteen, Pansy "escaped" to a job in Sayward and married a childhood acquaintance shortly afterward. Her sisters followed suit, leaving August to fend for himself back at the Bute homestead, where he continued his familiar rounds of trapping and handlogging till the early sixties.

August Schnarr lived to be ninety-five. He spent his last years in a small home at Heriot Bay on Quadra Island. On a clear day he could see halfway up Bute from his living room window.

Pansy recalls her tough father with a touch of sympathy. "Everybody says how grumpy he was… but, you know… he lost his wife, he lost his house, left with three little girls, no money. It must have been very nerve-wracking for him… He had a pretty hard row to hoe.

"He liked the loneliness of Bute… The older he got, the more Bute belonged to him. So we took his ashes up there, we figured he would like that." ❖

August Schnarr with a cougar and neighbour, Mrs. Williams. Photo: Campbell River & District Museum #8493.

The Rock Bandits

BY PAUL LAWSON

Day after day,
hour after hour,
they grind away at their
unfinishable, unfathomable mission –
To make our world
a smaller place to live.

They are the rock bandits.
Those restless souls
who have come and gone
in search of their quarry.
Those dust eating deaf
who have lit the suffering fuse
and hidden from
the flyrock of life.

To places barren
they have gone
to reduce the magnificent
to mounds of rubble
All in the name of
some hangover thirst for
the nectar of the earth.

To places untravelled
they have travelled
so that others could
come that way
and marvel at their music
written boldly
on the faces
of those disappointed peaks

The powder that's gone
up in smoke
could fuel another war
or maybe it has already
fatalities by the hundreds,
death is a way of life –
All in the name
of flyrock and glory.

Some say the rock dust and nitro
makes them that way –
After conducting
a lifelong study
I'm here to say
that they're right

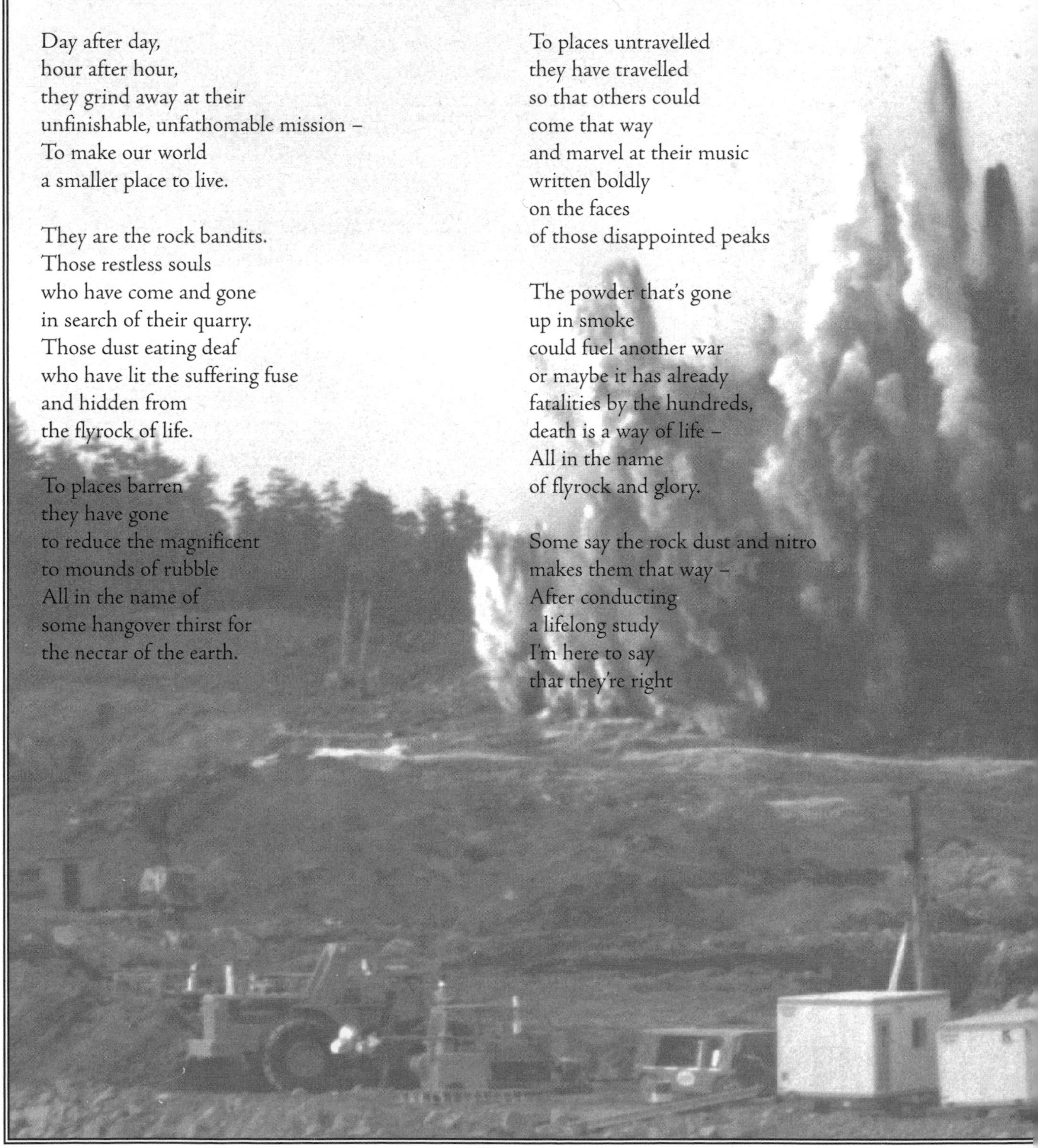

Those thirty-day headaches
just do something
to your attitude.

When will they stop
these raving rock bandits
from turning our
cordilleran home
into some piecemeal prairie
They've already made a good start –
flying time
has been notably reduced
by their air-tracked assault

It's a quest
that's insatiable,
an itch
that's unscratchable,
a disease of the heart
the only cure for which
is to push the fire button
on a regular basis

Perhaps we should
start a foundation
to find an exotic cure
for this deafening passion
While there's still some oceans
that haven't been filled in,
some mountains that
haven't yet succumbed
to the percussion section
of that orchestra of doom

I've got it under control
but there isn't
a Hallowe'en that goes by
where the smell of powder
doesn't catch my nostril –
and like some seagull circling
over a spawned-out salmon
the urge to return
overpowers,
and my thumb
begins to twitch
in anticipation ❖

The Deer???

BY DICK HAMMOND

Author's note: This story may be received with more skepticism than most, for the animal involved is familiar to people who live in the country as well as to many city dwellers and is not usually credited with uncommon intelligence. Therefore I thought it might be well to preface this story with a short account of a trick I saw used by a deer in the wild.

I was walking in the woods one autumn morning. The route led over a ridge of rock separating one small valley from another. The area had been logged not many years before, and most of each valley was visible from the ridge. It is my habit in such a case to crest the ridge as quietly as possible in the hope of seeing something interesting on the other side. In this instance I was able to walk more silently than usual as there were few bushes and the rocks were covered with soft moss damp with dew. A slight breeze was blowing across the ridge, so I knew that my scent wouldn't alert any animals in front of me. As soon as I could see into the valley beyond the ridge, I stopped to look around, and almost immediately saw a deer about fifty yards below and in front of me, nibbling at a clump of huckleberry bushes. It was nothing special, just a two-point buck of average size, but I enjoy watching animals in their natural state when they don't know they are being observed, so I stood very still, breathing as quietly as possible. (This may seem to be an unnecessary precaution, but anyone who has witnessed them in action knows what incredibly acute senses some wild animals have.)

The deer browsed a bit on the huckleberry shoots, took a few steps, nibbled at some other bush, moved on again. Its ears waggled now and then, and once it paused to scratch its shoulder with its hind leg. Its path took it towards and behind a fairly large fir tree – about four feet through – that had been used as a spar tree by the loggers. As the deer measured about five feet from nose to tail, one would expect its head to appear before its tail vanished. Only it didn't. Perhaps it had turned a bit to reach a tasty bush? I waited. No deer. I watched closely but saw no movement. Suddenly suspicious, I shifted a few feet to one side to get a better look. I saw the deer all right , but in

another few seconds I wouldn't have. It was just slipping into the fringe of brush on the other side of the valley, at least a hundred feet away from the fir tree! It had known exactly where I was, and had headed for the nearest cover keeping the tree between itself and me the whole while. Just imagine the skill required to do this while walking over ground littered with the debris of logging, and doing it with your back turned! I know that I couldn't have done it.

It might be objected that deer can quite often be observed acting in a manner that amply justifies the term "dumb animal." To this I can offer no explanation, but might mention that the area I was in had been heavily hunted for many years.

And now, on to the story.

The place, one of the inlets beyond Pender Harbour. I think it may have been Narrows Arm. Why they picked that particular valley, I don't know, but Father had promised to take his friend "Shorty" Roberts on a hunting trip, and this was the place they chose. Probably because neither of them had hunted there before, nor knew of anyone else who had.

They dropped anchor at a creek mouth, in a bay where the water was calm and sheltered. Though it was late in October and the weather stormy, they wouldn't have to worry about the boat.

Father looked around them as Shorty got into the skiff. The mountains were almost covered with clouds which came to within a few hundred feet above the water. There was almost an inch of snow at the beach, and the trees were more white than green. A few small flakes were drifting down. It would be hard, he thought to imagine a more gloomy prospect. Steep hills all around them, grey sky close above, snow.

Shorty was as excited as a hunting dog when its master takes the gun down.

"What a perfect day Hal! Just enough snow, and fresh too. Any tracks will be today's – we should have a great hunt!" He knew that Father was aware of all this, but his excitement had to have an outlet.

"Shorty wasn't much to look at," Father said, "but he was all heart and sinew. He could walk all day with his boots full of snow and his clothes soaking wet and not seem to notice it. He never complained. He loved to hunt. I never saw a man that enjoyed hunting as much as Shorty did. He couldn't get enough hunting."

They rowed ashore, pulled the skiff above high tide level, and headed up the valley. It was quite steep at first, and hadn't been logged except for a few trees near the shore that had been taken out by handloggers. After a hundred yards or so, the slope became more gradual before rising into the foothills of the mountains. The small creek that drained the valley was chattering and gurgling not far away. They kept to the left side where a considerable area had been burned not long before. This would be the most likely place for deer, for they like to browse on the bushes that grow up in a burn and tend to avoid old-growth forest if possible, although they like to bed down on the edge of it.

The two hunters had scarcely entered the burned area when they heard the thump of hooves. The sound was of a heavy deer, and they both spotted it at the same time, a huge buck showing for a second or two between the clumps of young trees.

"Man oh man," breathed Shorty. "Did you see that rack of horns? There's our buck!"

A few moments, and they were looking at the tracks in the snow.

Shorty was awed. "Will you look at those tracks! That deer must go over two hundred pounds. We've just got to get him. Let's go."

They checked their rifles and began to follow the tracks. As they went along, they both scanned the country around them alertly. Sometimes a deer will stand and watch you from some vantage point, curious as to what might be following, especially in a place where they have seldom or never been hunted, such as this valley.

They walked steadily on, not making much effort to be silent, for they could never be silent enough that the deer wouldn't hear them. But suddenly there were no more tracks. They just came to an end halfway across a patch of clear ground. There was – at this height – about two inches of snow.

"He must have made a jump off to the side," said Shorty. "Let's circle."

They separated, each taking one half of a little circle around the point at which the tracks disappeared. But they found no tracks. Aroused now, they coursed the area checking for bare spots where the snow hadn't stayed, or anywhere that a track might be concealed. Nothing.

"Well," said Shorty. "I'm damned if I ever saw anything like this. What do you think of it Hal?"

Now Shorty was a good and enthusiastic hunter, with an average talent for observation, but Father was a superb tracker, by far the best I've ever known.

"I knew I hadn't missed anything," he told me, "and I was pretty sure the deer hadn't suddenly sprouted wings and flown away. There was only one thing left."

So he looked carefully at the tracks in the snow. It wasn't easy, as they had walked over most of them.

"Shorty," he called. "Come here and look at this."

Shorty came over to where Father was standing. "Look there. What do you think of that?"

Shorty looked at the track. Then he got down on his knees and poked at it gently with his finger. He rose to his feet. "That deer has walked backwards in his own tracks. I never even heard of a deer doing a thing like that."

"Neither have I. That must be some smart deer. Probably so old and tough you'd have to chew the gravy."

"Well," said Shorty, "let's backtrack and find where he cut off. Don't see how we missed that."

Back they went, walking slowly, looking carefully at each side of the line of tracks. After they had gone about a hundred feet, Father knelt and examined one of the tracks closely.

"We've missed it. This is a single print," he announced. "OK. You go up, I'll go down. We'll find the spot this time."

Now they walked about fifteen feet away from the line of tracks. They had gone some fifty feet when Shorty called, "Come here Hal."

As Father approached, Shorty pointed. There were the tracks they had been seeking, bunched closely together behind a little clump of brush, where they couldn't be seen from where the other tracks were. Father looked around. Then he walked further uphill to where a small tree had fallen.

Another set of bunched tracks was concealed behind it. They led along beside the tree, then angled off up the hillside.

He shook his head. "A deer that smart, a man could feel like a murderer shooting. But," he continued not fully convincing even himself, "nature is a wonderful thing, and instinct is sometimes just as good – or even better – than thinking. A deer is, after all, just a deer. A wild animal."

Shorty stood there looking serious. Finally he said, "Yeah, I suppose you're right. Let's go after him."

They followed the tracks, paralleling them now, not walking on them. Suddenly Father, who was leading the way, said, "Well I'll be darned. Look at that!"

They had come up to a bushy young fir tree about as tall as a man. The deer had gone behind it, then had turned around and faced back downhill.

"What's so funny about that?" asked Shorty. "He just turned around to see if we were coming after him."

"Look closer. He's been standing there for quite a while. I'd say for all the time we spent trying to find where he went. Just his head sticking out from behind this tree. He knew we couldn't see him, and he was curious. Those tracks are only seconds old. He started off again when he saw we had caught on to him. Not very fast either. He's not much afraid of us."

Shorty made no answer, which was strange for he had always some comment to make about everything.

"Let's go," said Father. "He can't be more than a couple of hundred feet ahead of us. We should be able to spot him in this burn."

But they didn't, and as they went on the reason became clear.

"That deer," he told me, "always managed to keep something between him and us. It was uncanny the way he did it. I know that at any time he was never too far away for us to see him, but we never did."

And now once again the tracks disappeared. Father had been expecting this to happen. He was sure the deer would try something else to throw them off the trail. They stopped where the tracks ceased and looked around them. Father knelt and examined the last few tracks.

"Nope," he announced, "he didn't backtrack this time. I didn't think he'd repeat himself. Let's start looking."

They circled the area, checking everything that could possibly conceal tracks. The ground was wet and soft, spotted with scattered outcrops of rock, most of which had no snow on them, as the ground water kept them just warm enough to melt it. Father passed near one of them, then turned back and looked at it more closely. He beckoned to Shorty and pointed to the rock. There was a small fragment of mud and snow on it.

"He's jumping from rock to rock," Shorty said, "using them as stepping stones." He looked around. "It's going to take us a long time to find which ones he's used."

"No," said Father. "I don't think we'll have to do that."

"Why not?"

"I think that deer is standing out there not far away, watching to see how long it takes us to find his trail again. Probably just over that ridge there. If we spread out a bit and move straight towards it we should jump him and maybe get a shot at him. What do you think?"

"I don't know what to think," replied Shorty slowly. "But I'm game to give it a try."

This didn't sound like the Shorty Roberts that Father knew. He looked sharply at his friend.

"His shoulders were all hunched up," Father said, "and there was no sparkle in his eyes. But I thought, 'He'll perk up when we spot that deer again.'"

So off they went, separating so as to approach the ridge from two different angles. Father whistled at Shorty, and pointed. There were the tracks, leading to just where he thought the deer would be. But they saw no deer. It had been there, and it had been watching them just as it had before, but once again it had slipped away as they approached, taking cover in such a way that they couldn't sight it.

"He's bound to slip up if he keeps on playing tricks like this," Father predicted confidently.

Off they went once more, the tracks leading them on, so easy to follow. The snow was falling faster now, but they could still see far enough ahead to shoot, if their quarry should happen to show himself. The trail led straight up the valley towards the unburned timber, and this time they walked for about fifteen minutes before the tracks came to an end.

Father knelt, looked closely. "Hasn't back-tracked." He walked downhill a bit, looked back. Shorty was standing there, rifle under his arm, shoulders in that uncharacteristic hunch, his hat and jacket powdered with snow, looking up the valley, making no effort to help find the trail. Father watched him for a moment but the puzzle was too intriguing to waste any time wondering about his partner's actions. He cast back and forth like a hunting dog, forward and back, uphill and down. There was no trace. This time the deer did indeed seem to have "sprouted wings and flown away." He went back to where Shorty was still standing.

He said, only half jokingly, "Two pairs of eyes are better than one you know."

"I think we should go home," Shorty replied. "It's too far to drag a big deer like that anyhow."

"Home?" repeated Father, incredulous. "Why, this is just getting interesting. What's the matter with you? How can you even think of going back without finding out what that deer has done this time to throw us off?"

"Hal," said his friend, more serious than Father could remember ever hearing him. "Have you ever heard of 'The-deer-that-is-not-a-deer'?"

"No, can't say as I have. How in heck can a deer be a deer and not a deer at the same time?"

"I just thought you might have. You know a lot of Indians. One of the old ones told me once that in some of the wild places like this valley, if a man is foolish enough to hunt there, he may meet the 'deer-that-is-not-a-deer.' It will lure him farther and farther into the mountains. If he keeps on after it, he's never seen again. You see, it's something more than a deer, though I don't know what. And this thing we're following sure as hell doesn't act like any deer I've ever hunted. It thinks like a man. It knows how we hunt, what we look for. How could a deer know that? And what good would these tricks be up against scent hunters, like wolves or cougars? It's not natural. Let's go back while we can go back."

Father thought for a moment. "Well, if you ask me, your critter is going to a lot of trouble to lose us if he wants us to follow him. A nice plain set of tracks would make more sense."

But Shorty had an answer to that. "If we'd had a nice plain set of tracks, we'd have given up and be heading back to the boat by now." He pointed up to the snow-covered trees dimly visible through the drifting flakes. "Would you follow a straight-line set of tracks up into that? Course you wouldn't. If you hadn't got a shot in by the time we got in there, you'd have turned around and gone home. But as it is now, you're hooked. You can't wait to find out what that thing did this time, and what it's going to do next. That's right isn't it?"

"I looked around," Father told me. "Everything was white or grey or dark green. The only sound was the hissing of the snow. You couldn't see more than a couple of hundred feet. I didn't believe a word of what Shorty said, but I thought suddenly of how the nearest other human was about thirty miles away by boat, how we might be the only people to ever walk into that valley, and in spite of myself, I felt something like a little cold shiver go through me. I had the feeling that we were at the end of the world, and there was no one else."

"Well Shorty," he said, "you know where the boat is. Go back there and wait for me. If I'm not back by dark, don't wait any longer. Something may come looking for you!"

He turned around and scanned the ground intently, trying to think of a way the deer could hide its tracks.

He noticed a little clump of salmonberry bushes about two feet high, and thought that bush should have more snow on it than that. So he went for a look, and sure enough, there were the tracks right in the centre of the clump. "I looked back at Shorty," he said, "and I thought, by Gad, if I was a superstitious man, I could believe there was something in his story at that." That deer had covered about twenty feet in a single jump and landed so as to have hardly disturbed that clump of bushes. It was marvellous!"

Now that he knew the way the deer had gone, he looked around to see where it could have gone next, and spotted a similar clump of browsed-down bushes about the same distance down the slope. When he reached it, there were the tracks in the middle of it. The only cover from there was a brush-covered little creek, but the snow was undisturbed on the bushes lining the bank. He walked slowly up and down examining every possible place where the tracks could be concealed, and finally he found them. They were just over the edge of where the bank sloped sharply down to the stream bed, out of sight unless you walked right along the bank. The deer must have gone into the brush here, even though the snow appeared undisturbed. He saw some odd marks on the ground.

"Shorty," he called. "Come down here and take a look at this."

All this time Shorty had stood unmoving where the tracks had stopped. Now he climbed down to where Father was.

"What do you make of that?" Father asked, pointing to the marks.

Shorty looked closely at the ground and then at the bushes.

"That deer got down on its knees and crawled under those bushes, and it didn't hardly knock off any snow doing it, in spite of carrying a rack of horns about a yard wide. Hal, do you still think that's just a deer you're following?"

"Yes, I do. A smart deer, the smartest deer I've ever hunted, but just a deer, and I'm going after him."

Shorty shook his head slowly. "I'll go along with you for a while, but I know I must be crazy to do it."

They pushed through to the little stream. There the tracks disappeared again. "See there, Shorty. He's not so smart. That's the oldest trick in the book."

"Yah, an old trick for a man," Shorty answered morosely. "Deer don't hide their trail in the water."

Father didn't answer this. He had to decide whether to try upstream or down. He headed up on the theory that the deer would head for the cover of the standing timber. He had guessed correctly. Just when they were beginning to wonder if they had chosen wrongly, there were the tracks showing clearly where the deer had gone up the bank.

"That's strange," Father puzzled. "He could have made it a lot harder for us here if he'd wanted to."

"He wants to keep us interested, not to make us give up and go back," countered Shorty ominously.

Now the trail led straight towards the trees, just as Father had expected. Animals don't care much for snow falling on them and will take shelter if they can. But still the deer took advantage of every little tree, every clump of brush to avoid being seen.

They reached the timber at last, and the land rose more steeply. The trail led directly uphill, and there was less chance of seeing their quarry. Still they pressed on, caught up in that obsessive excitement of the hunting animal that is part of our genetic heritage, and which those who have never felt it can never understand, although they too carry it within them.

But the chase looked hopeless now. If the deer could elude them in the open burn, there was no chance at all of seeing it here unless it chose to let them.

Father knew this, but he also knew that animals – just like humans – grow careless when they feel that they are safe, and he was determined to keep trying for a while yet.

The land levelled out into a bench, an area of flattish ground a couple of hundred yards wide. A fair-sized creek ran through it diagonally before turning abruptly to flow into the valley – fair-sized, that is, in the context of the surroundings. It was about a foot deep and three feet across, the water that deep brown colour of coast forest streamlets. The tracks led to it, but they didn't continue on the other side. The two hunters stopped, looked around.

"The wading trick won't work here," Father said, "the ground is too level. Up or down?"

"You pick," said Shorty, uneasy again.

"Up it is then."

Off they went, one on each side of the stream and about ten feet away from it. They had scarcely gone a hundred feet when they came to a rock face down which the water slid noisily. They looked up it. Almost forty feet of sheer vertical rock, green with moss, a few ferns growing in the cracks. A mountain climber would have a hard time scaling it.

"If he got over that, I'm not going to try following him," joked Father.

They scouted around for signs, found none, and headed back down, this time a bit further from the water in case they had missed something. On they went, past the place where the tracks had led, until their way was blocked by a huge fallen fir tree lying directly across the stream. It was head high, covered with a dense growth of young trees rooted in the rotting bark. These in turn were covered with a layer of unbroken snow. Branches and debris had collected in front of the tree where the swirling, partially blocked water had collected in a deep coffee-coloured pool half covered by several inches of thick yellow foam. There were no tracks anywhere, save those they had followed. Again, Father coursed the ground like a baffled hound. Back to the rock face, down again on the other side to the big log, then back up to where Shorty was standing watching him. As he came near, his friend said in a voice made hoarse with emotion:

"Hal, that's it. I'm finished. If you go on from here, you go alone. For God's sake man, wake up! Surely you don't still think that's a deer standing out there waiting for us?"

Father looked at him but made no answer. He walked over to the fallen tree, then along it to the great upturned root. He went around behind it, back to the stream. He watched the dark water welling up from under the obstruction, then started across, intending to walk right around the tree. He tried once more to imagine what he would have done. Then he saw the answer, for the tracks of the deer showed plainly in the snow a few yards downstream of him, where it had walked out of the water after swimming under the tree through that black and treacherous pool, and surfacing up on the other side. A feat so improbable that it hadn't occurred to Father that it could be done. He looked up, feeling a sudden intuition, and there was the deer, no more than a hundred feet away, standing in full view in an open space between the trees. It was side on, its head turned towards him, looking at him, its body darkly wet, its huge rack of horns shining golden against the snow.

For a long moment their eyes locked. An animal always knows when you see it and runs off as soon as your eyes focus on it. But not this one.

Then Father remembered what he was there for. He swung his gun swiftly to his shoulder, aligning the sights onto that spot by the ear that would bring instant death, as he had done so many times before.

But this time, something stayed his hand. He could feel the deer's eyes riveted on him. He thought about the chase it had led them, the calm intelligence it had shown. And then in a way it never had before, the wildness and beauty of the great animal, so at home here in the snow and trees, hit a soft spot that Father hadn't known he possessed, and he lowered the gun without firing.

"And then," he told me, "the strangest thing happened. I had a sort of vision of an open space under the trees. There wasn't any snow. Against the dark ground was a pile of bones shining white and bare. Human bones. There were skulls lying scattered about. It must have been spring. The leaves were bright green. It was just a flash, a quick glimpse, that passed as quick as an eyeblink. But when I looked up, the deer was gone."

He went back around the root. Shorty was standing near the pool.

"It dove under the log," Father said to him, "and came up on the other side. I almost got a shot at it."

"You mean it turned into a fish. Nothing else could get under that log. Look at it!" He pointed to the pool. "I'm going back now. Are you coming?"

"Shorty was scared," Father told me. "I had never seen Shorty scared before. A wounded grizzly bear wouldn't have scared Shorty. I got that end-of-the-world feeling again, and I thought of that picture of the pile of bleached bones lying under the trees. I thought of that big deer out there, waiting for us to follow him. What would he do next? I thought of what nerve it took to go into that dark pool of water carrying those horns, not knowing if you could make it through or not. I thought, 'Why did he do it?' He didn't have to. He could have made fools of us on that mountain, in those trees. He wasn't scared of us, or why would he stop and watch us? I asked myself these questions, but I had no answers.

"I said, 'Come on Shorty. It's getting late. Let's go home.'" ❖

Kalpalin – an Aboriginal Metropolis

BY HOWARD WHITE

During the 1950s and 1960s when I was growing up in the Sunshine Coast fishing village of Pender Harbour, I was never short of information on the Spanish and English explorers who had first charted local waters in the late 1700s and 1800s. Along the coast there were monuments to Captain George Vancouver, and local place names provided a daily reminder of his personal interests—his heroes (Nelson Island), his moods (Desolation Sound), his family (Sarah Point). Many place names such as Texada Island, Malaspina Strait and Favada Point also commemorated the brief visitations of the Spanish, who churned through the territory alongside their English rivals in such a panic to find the fabled Northwest Passage they failed to notice Sechelt Inlet, Pender Harbour, and a host of other major geographical features. In addition, history buffs were forever rediscovering the explorers' journals and highlighting passages where local landmarks had rated a brief mention. Writers like Roderick Haig-Brown and Hubert Evans wrote juvenile adventure novels based on Vancouver's and David Thompson's brief weeks of disappointment here, and centennial celebrations spotlighted the momentary presence of the long-ago superstars of European colonization.

What I never could find much about was the other pioneers, the ones who had been here for thousands of years before the anxious European visitors and were to remain hundreds of years after—the aboriginal inhabitants. Their presence was hard to ignore in Pender Harbour.

Not that there were many living, breathing Indians still around when I first saw Pender Harbour in 1950—the aged chief Dan Johnson and his wife lived in a tumbledown shack on a reserve in Garden Bay that was said to be laden with graves, ghosts and artifacts; Eugene and Myrtle Paul lived on a landlocked scrap of land in Gerrans Bay and the Julius family lived near the mouth of the Harbour on a barren group of islets locals referred to as the "Indian Islands," ignoring the map name of Skardon Islands. The white people had everything else, but there were abundant signs that it had been very different once upon a time. The much-indented shoreline of the one-and-a-half-mile-long harbour was paved with bones—human bones.

My school chum Ab Haddock and I lived on opposite sides of Gerrans Bay a stone's throw from a small group of islets local legend recorded as an Indian graveyard, and he used to make me jealous with all the nifty artifacts he dug up on them, but the rest of us kids lacked the nerve to disturb them for fear of awakening smoldering embers of the last smallpox epidemic, which to us seemed to lurk still close at hand.

Indian history hovered in the air of the harbour. Clues were everywhere. At Sakinaw Bay you could still trace among the barnacled beach rocks vague outlines of the elaborate stone fish trap which pioneer ethnologist Charles Hill-Tout had described as a masterpiece of stone-age engineering a half-century earlier; shortly thereafter loggers perched an A-frame on the nearby bluff to skid logs out of Sakinaw Lake and promptly obliterated all sign of the ancient wonder. Atop Mount Daniel you could still discern outlines of the stone circles which were placed in worship of the moon by pubescent girls, according to local historian Lester Peterson, but which Hill-Tout described with equal assurance as tombs of the dead. Elders Ann Quinn and Theresa Jeffries say they were simply used by girls "to meditate and prepare themselves for marriage." The stones remain in their circles to this day.

My belief after a lifetime of excavating around Pender Harbour—not as an archaeologist, but as an interested ditch digger—is that there must have been almost continuous settlement around the entire forty miles of harbour shoreline. I once had a job installing a sewer system on the Sallahlus reserve at Canoe Pass and found myself digging down in ancient fire ash and clamshell deposits to a depth of six feet, encountering more than a few human bones along the way. There was another large deposit of bone-laden midden soil at Irvine's Landing at the mouth of the Harbour, and sizable ones at Gerrans Bay and on the fertile mudflats at the head of Oyster Bay, a site known as Smeshalin to the Sechelt (shishalh.) (For old time's sake I have used the more familiar anglicized spellings of Sechelt words but follow with the official phonetic spelling on first usage.) When my father and I were excavating basements around Pender Harbour in the 1960s I became accustomed to rooting up cooking rocks and clamshell anywhere there was a pocket of dirt big enough to sink a muckstick into. Many sites were chock-full of human remains.

I knew from reading about better-documented sites in Huronia that many generations of occupancy upon a single campsite could result in only a few inches of permanent midden soil—and in Pender Harbour there were places the midden soil was eight feet thick. What had gone on here? From my dad's old buddy Clarence Joe, a ranking member of the Tsonai (ts'unay) clan in Jervis Inlet, I learned that Pender Harbour had been a "winter village" where all the far-flung Sechelt communities congregated in the wintertime for dancing and trading. But how many people gathered there? What kind of houses did they have? What did they do when they were all gathered together? Clarence and other contemporary Sechelt were disappointingly vague on these points. When I went to the University of BC, I enrolled in anthropology, hoping I might find some more specific answers.

Alas, my studies only confirmed that information on Sechelt prehistory was extremely sketchy. None of the great ethnologists who had studied the Haida and Kwakiutl in such exhaustive detail had bothered to check in on the Sechelt, for reasons that became clear to me later. However, I did discover the reason for the numerous clamshell middens around Pender Harbour. It had once been the site of one of the largest and most important aboriginal village sites in the Pacific Northwest—an authentic aboriginal metropolis.

Only scattered fragments of this amazing history now remain, and it has taken a good many years of sleuth work to piece together even a general outline of the Sechelt and their magnificent headquarters in Pender Harbour.

Before the arrival of European explorers in the late 1700s, the Sunshine Coast had been shared since the last ice age by three different tribes of native Indians, the Squamish (Howe Sound), the Sechelt (Sechelt Peninsula), and the Sliammon (Powell River). By all accounts they were an exceptional people, each in their own way as unlike the

Early view of Porpoise Bay showing tradional Sechelt dugout.

147

standard run of Northwest Coast Indian as the modern Sunshine Coaster is unlike the pinstriped denizen of Vancouver's Howe Street.

All of the Sunshine Coast tribes belonged to the Coast Salish linguistic family and enjoyed a comparatively prosperous existence owing to their benign climate and an abundance of easily obtained food, principally salmon, herring, venison and berries. The Coast Salish have never enjoyed the renown accorded by white Indian-fanciers to the Haida and Kwakiutl, probably because the Salish didn't erect forests of totem poles, didn't carve sea-going war canoes, and didn't produce world-class art—except on one notable occasion. On the other hand, they didn't use the bodies of freshly killed slaves for boat bumpers. What they did do was create a social order that came closer to that of modern democracies in terms of respect for human life and individual freedom. Among the Northern tribes, only those born to noble families could hope to achieve spiritual power through membership in the cannibal and dog-eating

societies, but every member of a Salish tribe had the opportunity to seek his or her individual "sulia" or "power" through a spirit quest that was open to all comers, and leadership was based on merit as much as on inherited privilege. There was no single, all-powerful chief, but a collective of male and female leaders all honoured with the same respectful term, "si3'm" or in Sechelt, "hiwus."

In their heyday, the Sechelt occupied the bulk of the territory now comprising the Sunshine Coast with some eighty villages. So numerous were the lodge fires of the Sechelt Nation elders used to speak of a time when there was "one big smoke" from Gower Point to Saltery Bay. The main tribal groupings were centred around four principal villages at xenichen (at the head of Jervis Inlet), Tsonai (at Deserted Bay, Jervis Inlet), Tuwanek (in Sechelt Inlet) and Kalpalin (Pender Harbour.) Unlike most other Coast Salish tribes, who stayed put in their ancestral villages year round, the Sechelt congregated for the winter in one composite mega-village at

The Story of Ts'kahl
BY GILBERT JOE

The Sechelt people, in their system, had a purpose for everyone. There was the chiefs, the elders and the warriors. Some of these warriors, by today's standards they would have been called psychopaths. But the aboriginal people along the coast used to be very warlike among themselves, mainly for food.

We had a terrible-tempered man, his name was Ts'kahl (ts`uKal)—a prominent individual respected by all the Sechelt people. He actually killed a couple of Indian people just for standing in his way. But there was a place for men like him in our society, we made them warriors.

During the summer months our forefathers would pack up, dismantle their lodges, and go up the Inlet to collect and preserve their food for winter. The elder men and women stayed home to look after the community.

One summer when the warriors were gone, the Kwakiutl came down from Nimpkish and raided our village, killing all the people except one young woman of high birth, Wipple-Wit, who was taken as a slave.

When the warriors returned they found pieces of their loved ones' bodies hanging from trees and scattered along the beach. They were very angry. The chief and elders decided to retaliate, and when they wanted to retaliate they wanted to do it in good fashion. So they negotiated with the Cowichan for their greatest warrior, Tzouhalem. And they negotiated with the Squamish for their greatest warrior and his name was Luhma.

They gathered all the Sechelt warriors—the strongest and the best—to go up to Nimpkish and retaliate against the Kwakiutls. They got in their big canoes with their provisions and spears and they had Spanish muskets.

Kalpalin (kalpilin) on the shores of Pender Harbour. Although contemporary band publications place their original population at 20,000, scientific estimates range between 5,000 and 8,000. Even if the lowest estimate is correct, it would have made Kalpalin more densely populated in 1800 than Pender Harbour was in 1996 – and that was just counting local residents. During big feasts, potlatches (tl'e?enaks) or trading days, that number would be swelled by other Salish groups visiting from upcoast, downcoast, the Fraser River, the Gulf Islands, Vancouver Island and Puget Sound.

The Sechelt have no tradition of having migrated from anywhere else; their creation myths relate that the creator sent the *spelemulh*, divine but mortal ancestors of the Sechelt people, down to each village from the sky. Other Coast Salish village sites have been dated as far back as 9,000 years but little archaeological work has been done on the Sechelt and most of the midden sites are now gouged up by logging or, like the great Sawquamain site in Garden Bay, paved over with residential subdivisions.

The Salish had an admirable grasp of what really mattered in life. They were tremendous workers and they laboured mightily all summer putting up dried salmon and making salal berry leather as well as thousands of other labour-intensive tasks involved in maintaining well-run stone-age households, like weaving watertight baskets of cedar root and washing used ones with a putrefied fungus known as "thunder shit" (xwat'Klmunach). Everyday dress consisted of aprons made of deer hide or woven from cedar bark. Cedar bark was also woven into blankets and robes, as was wool from special long-haired dogs and mountain goat. Rope and twine for fishing line and nets were woven from nettle fibre. Plentiful stands of red cedar provided easily worked building materials for dugout canoes, feast bowls and plank-walled dwellings, some of which were enormous.

Now Indian people long ago were psychically inclined. Because they had no newspapers or TVs or anything to deter them, they had very powerful minds. They had medicine men that had great psychic powers who could communicate with their minds.

So when the Sechelt warriors headed up to Nimpkish to retaliate, they went by Sliammon at night and they didn't touch their canoes with their paddles. They passed there at night so the Sliammon wouldn't know they were going by. And they did the same at Klahoose. And they did the same at Homalco. Every community between here and Nimpkish they passed without being noticed because if somebody from one of the villages had seen them passing by, they could have sent a message up to the Kwakiutls with their minds. So the warriors didn't want to take that chance.

They made it up to Nimpkish and they waited until dark when the people went to sleep. Then they went onto the beach. Ts'kahl, Tzouhalem and Luhma began their war-whoops in their fierce, enormous voices. They frightened the people of the Nimpkish village so much that they fell into a shambles, giving the warriors enough time to run up the beach and take their revenge.

On the beach, Ts'kahl saw a person rolling toward the water in a cedar blanket as if trying to get away. He went up to the person and was about to spear it when he heard a voice say, "hoy-la tsi-loy wipple-wit." (It's me—Wipple-Wit.") He stopped just in time.

So the warriors brought Wipple-Wit back home. And that was the last time there was a battle between the Kwakiutl and the Sechelt people.

According to Hill-Tout, who studied the Sechelt in the summer of 1902, Sechelt houses had "a platform about two feet high and five or six feet broad erected all around the inside walls. This served as seats or lounges for the occupants during the day, and during the night as beds. Some ten or twelve feet above this platform small isolated cubicles or sleeping rooms were constructed… Each family partitioned off its allotment from the rest by means of hanging mats." Anthropologist Homer Barnett, who visited the Sechelt in 1935, reported seeing only one house which was excavated, and that only to the depth of one step below ground level. In *The Story of the Sechelt Nation* Lester Peterson reports that "Sechelt lodges were filled with dried meats, smoked fish, dried berries and fruits. Chests, *wihk'-ahm*, were filled with regalia – masks, cloaks, drums, rattles, and other paraphernalia needed at ceremonies." Hill-Tout contradicts this, saying "they did not store their winter supplies in the dwellings, but cached them in the woods. Only a few days' supply was ever carried home. This peculiar custom was due to the marauding proclivities of the neighbouring Yacultas, who made periodic forays upon their settlement and carried off all they could lay their hands upon. It was unsafe,

therefore, to keep a large store of food by them." Hill-Tout's informant, Charlie Roberts, was born four decades before Peterson's main informant, Basil Joe, and the inconsistency between generations may reflect fading memories of inter-tribal hostilities during later historic times, but there is no shortage of evidence to indicate that in their heyday the peaceful Sechelt were a favourite target for raiding by leaner and meaner tribes to the north.

The work of the Salish summer was performed with the singular aim of freeing the winter for social activities. Anthropologists are fond of referring to the winter activities of the Salish as "ceremonials" which they manage to depict as some kind of joyless paleolithic ritual. My old Squamish friend Dominic Charlie, who kept performing his sensational leaping deer dance until he was in his eighties, remembered it differently. "In them old times," Dominic told me, "we just dance and dance all winter long. Just dance and dance. Everybody he go to that big house and dance all night long and all day. All winter keep doing that. Oh, we had great times in them old times."

Great times. That's what the Salish winter was really all about. Most people had their own special dance which had come to them in a dream or vision

Sechelt men show off a morning's catch at the white village west of the reserve. Despite closeness, the two villages remain separate worlds. Photo: BCARS D-07509.

accompanied by a song, and often gave them a special power associated with an animal. One renowned hunter imitated killer whales in his dance. He had got this dance when he once approached a beach where people were dancing around a campfire, but turned into killer whales and swam away when he approached. In the dream that followed he got not only the dance and a song, but the killer whale's power to hunt seals, sea-lions and porpoises. Another prominent man had the wolf dance. He got it when he fell and wounded his leg while stripping bark from a tree. When he awoke a wolf was licking his wound. In his dream he received a song featuring the cry of the wolf and a dance in which he ate the flesh of live dogs. Men's dances tended to be associated with major animals like the bear and mountain goat, while women were often left with lesser spirits like the duck, crane, quail, and even the blowfly.

Dances by ordinary Sechelt people didn't go in for the special effects some of the northern tribes used to imitate their animal allies, and generally eschewed masks and costumes in favour of convential gestures (leaping for a deer, flapping arms for a bird). Face paint was used, but costumes tended to be the usual buckskins worn every day.

Winter ceremonials also included events of a more distinctly spiritual nature, initiation rites for youngsters taking possession of their own special dances, and performances by medicine men. Sechelt shamans were particularly noted for their miraculous performances. One involved the handling of red-hot coals and rocks, and the eating of fire. Another featured the dancer making a dramatic bloody slash along the length of his thigh, while another shot blood from his mouth. The ts`unay elder Joe La Dally told anthropologist Homer Barnett of an occasion when an eminent shaman named Kaltopa was called to attend a dying man. He brought with him the skins of seven different animals – otter, mink, raccoon, fox, loon, eagle and marten. After singing his spirit song, he blew on each skin and it came to life, scampering around on the floor uttering its natural cry. He then covered his head with a blanket and began to grope on the floor in search of the patient's missing soul. His own spirit was thought to have departed from his body at this point because at length he uttered a "whoo-ing" noise as if returning from a great distance. Finally the shaman rose, holding the retrieved soul in his hands. When it was returned to its rightful place the patient showed immediate signs of recovery, and his brother asked the shaman if he knew who'd taken the errant soul. The shaman said that he indeed did, whereupon the brother requested the evil-doer be put to death. The shaman again covered his head and began groping on the floor. After about half an hour the sounds of the returning spirit were heard once more, and the shaman lept to his feet to reveal in the palm of his hand a tiny human body. He held the miniature form over the fire and squeezed it till blood ran out between his fingers, then dropped the small shape into the flames. At that moment, according to legend, a well-known Comox shaman keeled over stone dead.

His duties completed, Kaltopa deflated his skins, packed up, and left. The purpose of the skins had been to watch over the patient while the medicine man was out of his body stalking his foe in the spirit realm. Barnett was able to obtain a corroborating version of this story from another Sechelt elder, Charlie Roberts, who added that Kaltopa's return was assisted by other Sechelt shamans who guided him back with choruses of their own "whoo-ing" in answer to his. Roberts said that he'd seen another shaman who could perform the miracle of bringing animal skins to life, and in addition possessed a big quartz crystal he could activate to dance and whirl around on the floor with a whining sound. Shamanic performances of this kind were a regular and popular feature of winter dances, along with feasting and potlatching, the ceremonial giving of property to enhance status. There were also lively trading extravaganzas, especially among the Sechelt, who have always been great wheeler-dealers.

Kalpalin's principal settlement at Sawquamain, on the north shore of Garden Bay, was crowded with seven huge longhouses, four ranked one behind the other while the other three ran crosswise further inland. Some had shed-type single-slope roofs and others the peaked variety. Each had an attached woodshed and a spacious outdoor plat-form suitable for the staging of potlatches, an archi-tectural feature Sechelt elder Gilbert Joe has referred to as "the Sunshine Coast's first sun-decks." Like modern-day leisure homes which announce themselves to passing traffic as "Taki-Teasy" or "Dunworkin" (my favourite is "Sechelter"), each of the Sawquamain lodges had its own nickname. Lodge number one was called "Right On the Beach" and lodge number two, "Back Side House." It had no exterior decoration, but inside, the support posts were carved into seals, sea lions and killer whales. The third house, "Down In the Hole," had a thun-derbird painted on the front. Lodge number four had a single-slope shed roof and was the largest building on the site. Lodge six had a painted welcome figure straddling the doorway and seven had a thunderbird painted across the front. There were no totem poles but "Right On the Beach" had a sea lion head carved onto the end of the ridgepole and lodge five had posts topped with carvings of eagles. The largest house Peterson records as the Kluh-uhn'-ahk-ahwt (tl'epotlatchAenaKawt or "potlatch house"), which he describes as a kind of Sechelt Parthenon, used only when the far-flung affiliate villages were gath-ered together for communal events. Salish houses weren't as finely crafted as those of the northern tribes, but they were bigger. The explorer Simon Fraser observed one near Chilliwack which was 800 feet long and 300 feet wide, and Charlie Roberts told Hill-Tout the greatest of the lodges at Sawquamain towered fifty feet in height.

The Sechelt were highly vulnerable to attack by other Indian tribes, a vulnerability increased by their relative wealth and their nonviolent nature. The word "fort" occurs frequently in Sechelt place names, and according to Peterson a real fort replete with wooden pallisade and moat stood until his-toric times near the head of Jervis Inlet. Another fort existed on Thormanby Island, where the exposed Squawklot (sxwelap) village made frequent use of it to fend off seagoing marauders from Kwakiutl territory. My old school chum Ron Remmem, whose family home in Pender Harbour was close to the Sechelt's long-vanished winter cap-ital of Sawquamain, used to talk about finding what looked like an ancient fort site on the slopes of nearby Mount Daniel. This matches stories Peterson collected of a fort on Mount Daniel which was used to shelter women and children during raids on Sawquamain. Barnett reports the big houses of Sawquamain had "subterranean retreats ready for use in case of surprise attacks...entered by tunnels leading from hidden openings inside." Basil Joe's son Clarence used to tell me his people also kept sentries posted on Mount Daniel – and at many other places including Cape Cockburn to the north and Spyglass Hill to the south – to provide early warning of any suspicious traffic in surround-ing waters. All of which adds up to a fairly pervasive sense of vulnerability.

Most raids were two-bit affairs perpetrated by piratical rovers who picked off small groups of women and elders left unprotected during fishing or hunting forays, but large-scale massacres were not unknown. Peterson mentions a grassy flat east of Cockburn Bay on Nelson Island which got its name, Swalth (skwelh,) "from the fact that much blood was spilt there." He also used to tell me that the rocky knoll next to the property I grew up on at Madeira Park "was forever cursed by a powerful medicine man because of the slaughter suffered there by his people at the hands of early nineteenth century raiders."

The destruction of this once great Native nation began early on. The Roman Catholic mission-ary Father Leon Fouquet of the Oblate Order visit-ed Kalpalin in 1860, urging all to abandon the beliefs of their ancestors and accept the God of the white man. Not surprisingly, Fouquet was sent packing. But only three years later, the Sechelt invit-ed the Oblates back and willingly submitted them-selves to Christian teaching by Father Paul Durieu. By 1871 he had administered the sacrament of con-firmation to the entire Sechelt tribe, a record wor-thy of envy even by his contemporary William Duncan, the Anglican missionary who created a similar "Indian city in the wilderness" among the Tsimshian at Metlakatla. Some writers interpret the Sechelt's remarkable turnabout simply as a case

Sechelt Indian band. After banning traditional winter festivities, priests tried to fill the gap by teaching their converts church-approved pastimes. Photo: BCARS F-02405.

of children of darkness seeing the light, but there is a less glamorous explanation. In 1862 the worst smallpox epidemic in west coast history swept like a tsunami through the coast's Indian population, devastating the Sechelt. It was in an attitude of defeat and despair that they turned back to the missionaries, but they may have had a more pointed reason yet. The Sechelt embraced the belief, universal throughout aboriginal cultures, that the world of the spirit ruled directly and absolutely over the world of matter, and the most persuasive evidence of superior force in the world of spirit was the ability to cause illness in chosen victims. When the white man appeared accompanied by a plague of new illnesses far more devastating than anything conjured up by the most powerful Indian medicine man, wiping out whole Indian nations while leaving whites untouched, Native peoples could not help but view it as evidence of some dread new spiritual super-power on the white man's side. When the

missionaries stepped forward claiming to speak for the Great Spirit of the white man and specifically threatening more illness if the Indians failed to adopt Christianity, native peoples fell on their knees in droves, but not, one would assume, for the love of Jesus. As the plagues continued they must have felt like victims of biological warfare, ready to do or say anything that would spare their families from the wrathful God of the white man.

Duncan made his greatest breakthrough by warning a general assembly of Tsimshian unbelievers they were about to taste God's wrath just as the 1862 smallpox epidemic was sweeping down upon them, and the Oblates apparently seized upon similar tactics. As anthropologist Edwin M. Lemert noted in *The Life and Death of an Indian State*, "sermons delivered by the (Oblate) priests...bore directly on persons and events...Thus epidemics of disease became grim evidence of wrongdoing by the Indians." When the Oblates told the Sechelt in the

Over 2,000 people showed up for dedication of new Our Lady of the Rosary church on June 10, 1890. Threat of flogging assured good attendance at church events.

aftermath of the 1862 holocaust the only way to save themselves was by adopting Christian teaching, it is an understatement to say they probably took it literally.

In 1868 Durieu founded a central mission at an unoccupied site the Sechelt frequented only seasonally because it was so exposed to weather and to attack by marauding Yacultas, it lacked fresh drinking water and generally didn't have much to recommend it from an Indian point of view. This was Chatelech, the site of the modern-day village of Sechelt. Over the next three decades the Oblates forged a Christian community at Sechelt which became the showpiece of "The Durieu System," a theocratic regime featuring police-state discipline, afterward replicated at Oblate missions among the

Sliammon, Klahoose, Homalco, Lillooet and others. Durieu was a strict puritan who didn't allow his own priests to drink wine in private – true privation to a Frenchman – and in one favourite anecdote broke up Sechelt preparations for a soccer tournament with the Nanaimos, confiscated the ball and ordered players and spectators alike to get to work ditching a swamp. Durieu espoused the belief that "Indians are only big children..." and governed accordingly. The whole village was compelled to rise each morning at the first bell and attend church for prayers. An evening bell called them for a second daily round of prayers each evening. Shortly following, a curfew bell was the signal for all lights to be put out. The punishment for missing church was the same as for adultery: forty lashes. On one occasion the flogging got so far out of hand one of Durieu's lieutenants was convicted and jailed by civil court.

Native culture was rigorously suppressed. As Bishop E.M. Bunoz wrote in a warm appreciation of his predecessor's system in 1941, "Our Indians had to give up all of their old fashioned amusements because they contained some traces of paganism and superstition. So they made bonfires with their century-old totem poles. They had to burn rattles, expensive coats and other paraphernalia of the medicine men…'Potlatches' great and small were forbidden. Gambling, dancing and some winter festivities had to be abandoned. Bishop Durieu strictly exacted the abolition of the above practices because they were apposed to pure Christianity, but he knew well that the Indians had to have some amusements and that the pagan feasts had to replaced by Christian ones."

Under Durieu's control the Sechelt made a name for themselves by building a European-style townsite similar to Metlakatla, by touring a brass band and theatre troupe that staged elaborate passion plays around BC, and by diligently applying themselves to such non-traditional economic pursuits as logging, commercial fishing and commercial hunting for the fresh meat trade in Vancouver. Viewing the results of Durieu's cultural makeover of the Sechelt three decades after it began, ethnologist Hill-Tout reported "Of all the native races of this province, they are probably the most modified by white influences. They are now, outwardly at least, a civilized people, and their lives compare favourably with the better class of peasants of Western Europe. Their permanent tribal home, or headquarters, contains about a hundred well-built cottages, many of them two-storied, and some of them having as many as six rooms. Each house has its own garden plot attached to it in which are grown European fruits and vegetables. In the centre of the whole stands an imposing church, which cost the tribe nearly $8,000 a few years ago. Nearby, they have a commodious and well-built meeting room, or public hall, capable of holding 500 persons or more, and a handsome pavilion or band-stand fronts the bay. They possess also a convenient and effective waterworks system of their own…every street has its hydrants at intervals of forty or fifty yards.

"As a body, the Sechelt are, without doubt, the most industrious and prosperous of all the native peoples of this province…they owe their tribal and individual prosperity mainly, if not entirely, to the Fathers of the Oblate Mission."

In fact the Sechelt had not flourished in the charge of the church, but had continued to vanish at an alarming rate until by the time of the first official census in 1881, there were only 167 survivors left from the original population of five thousand or more. The prim little community Hill-Tout viewed so approvingly in 1902 was but a sad remnant of the sprawling aboriginal nation that had united all the inlets and islands of the Sunshine Coast in "one smoke" a hundred years earlier. In the hundred years since, the Sechelt have recovered only slowly. By 1993 official band membership numbered 444 residents, with another 400 living off reserve.

Most of the fabulous repertoire of songs, dances and ceremonial art which had enlivened the great festival season at Kalpalin was lost, but some were transferred to neighboring tribes on Vancouver Island who still perform with them today.

One outstanding artifact remaining from prehistoric times is the "Sechelt Image," a 20-inch tall granite statuette discovered under a tree root by boys playing at Selma Park in 1921. I am informed that Sechelt elders of today view the figure as a mother holding her child *only* – with the emphasis on "only" because other observers, like anthropologist Wilson Duff, describe it as "the very image of masculine strength, stated in the metaphor of sex. His head is powerfully masculine, and he clasps a huge phallus; the whole boulder, seen backwards and upside down, is phallic in form."

I went down to Sechelt just before writing this to check it over once more, and I'm afraid I have to side with Duff. For me, any doubt about the sexual connotation of the work is resolved by taking the rear view, where the whole sculpture appears as a massive phallus replete with bulging veins reminiscent of a work by contemporary Sunshine Coast painter Maurice Spira. But the sculptor of the stone image goes even further, equipping the front of his piece with a prominent vulva as well.

Was some antique wit trying to sum up the entire sexual experience of humankind at one go? Or is it just something in the water Sunshine Coast artists drink? Whatever the answer, Duff pronounced the Sechelt Image "a great work of stone sculpture" and it inspired the Director of the Victoria Art Gallery, Richard Simmins, to make it the centrepiece of "Images: Stone: B.C.", a seminal exhibition of Northwest Coast Indian stone sculpture which toured Canada in 1975. A replica of this enigmatic, powerful masterwork, along with some good examples of Sechelt weaving and carving, can be viewed in the band's Tems Swiya Museum in Sechelt.

Today's Sechelt have maintained their head start in terms of mastering mainstream economic and political life. They have been involved in the operation of an offshore trawler, a local airline, a salmon hatchery, an office and cultural complex, a large gravel-mining project, a McDonalds restaurant franchise and other business enterprises. But it is in the political arena that the Sechelt have most distinguished themselves. From the earliest times when Chief Tom of the ts'unay made land claims representations to Victoria, through the activism of such leaders as Chief Julius, Joe La Dally, Dan Paull, Reg Paull, Stan Dixon and Clarence Joe – a consummate statesman who on different occasions addressed both the Canadian House of Commons and the United Nations – the Sechelt charted their own course through Canadian politics, far in advance of most other First Nations groups. Their first goal was to free themselves from the shackles of the Canadian Indian Act, which deprived them of the full rights of citizenship and greatly encumbered the free exercise of their renowned mercantile abilities, which sometimes outshine their modern-day neighbours on the old Chatelech site. Their long campaign finally culminated in the successful passage of Bill C-93, The Sechelt Indian Band Self-Government Act of 1986, making them the first band in Canada to achieve native self-government.

This in itself proved controversial within the community of First Nations, since the Sechelt had taken a very pragmatic view of self government, one characterized by the Grand Council of Crees as "identical to the model of the municipalities." This is not quite true since the Sechelt are given extra-municipal powers over education, social services, health, and public order, and section 38 of the *Self Government Act* declares that the "constitution of the Band or the law of the Band" can take precedence over the laws of British Columbia. Other bands held out for something closer to full provincial status and denounced the Sechelt solution as a sellout. The Sechelt view the grander claims as impracticable, and hold that freedom to conduct their own affairs as full Canadian citizens free from the strictures of the Indian Act is no small gain. Since 1986 more bands across Canada, whose own campaigns for self-government remain stalled, have been taking a second look at the Sechelt model, and the Nishga settlement of 1996 owes much to it, but for the most part the Sechelt remain defiantly out of step with their brethren on the national stage.

At the same time the Sechelt feel sadly cut off from the traditions of their aboriginal past, and they carry on few ceremonial activities compared to the neighboring Cowichan and Squamish. They pursue a vigorous language preservation project with the help of Dr. Ronald Beaumont of the University of B.C. and several families have revived the practice of giving potlatches (tl'e?enaks) to bestow traditional names, which they research in old church records. Elder Mary Craigan had tears in her eyes as she recounted to me her experience attending a Cowichan ceremony where she witnessed some of the ancient songs and dances which were once performed by her ancestors at Kalpalin. It was the first time she had heard them but they had worked a powerful spell over her she had no words to describe, as if pulling at something deep inside. A traditional medicine man from outside has begun visiting the band, 130 years after shamanistic practices were banned by the Oblates, and Craigan struggles alongside other elders to excavate memories of their people's past to fulfill younger members' reawakening thirst for tribal identity, but it is hard digging. Indian or non-, who can say what their ancestors did and thought over a century ago when there has been no continuing connection and the only written record has been kept by people dedicated to breaking the connection?

Despite that century of cataclysmic upheaval, remorseless cultural domination, near-complete depopulation, and advanced dilution by foreign blood, a very powerful feeling still endures at the village core that the Sechelt are a unique people distinctly apart from the world around them. Despite Professor Hill-Tout's gleeful declaration that Bishop Durieu's master plan had succeeded in acculturating the Sechelt into "a better form of European peasant" at the beginning of this century, to step across the boundary from Municipality of Sechelt onto the Band Lands today is to enter into a special world little suspected by outsiders. How much of this is due to lingering influences of the aboriginal past which managed to seep around the proscriptions of the priests and how much is the stamp of six generations of intense economic and geo-graphical ghettoization, is hard to say. Certainly any closely related family group shaped by the pressures that have crushed down upon the Sechelt over the past 200 years could be expected to emerge with a lot of distinctive characteristics, no matter what their previous cultural history.

Meanwhile, there is no longer one single member of the Sechelt band living on the site of the once mighty Sechelt capital of Kalpalin, and viewing the modest, all-white village of 2,500 reposing on the shores of the landlocked Pender Harbour basin today, it is difficult to picture the same scene rocking under the sway of five or ten thousand buckskinned festival-goers, but if you'd dropped in between October and March a few brief centuries ago, that may well be what you'd have seen. ❖

For their many excellent suggestions in reviewing the foregoing, my special thanks go to Sechelt elders Anne Quinn and Theresa Jeffries and their niece Candy Clark. Excerpted from The Sunshine Coast, *Harbour Publishing, 1996.*

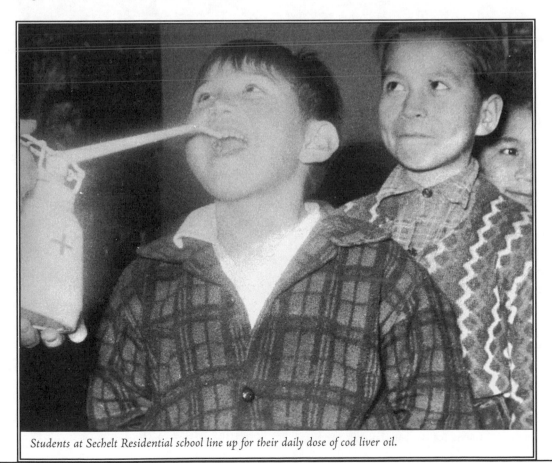

Students at Sechelt Residential school line up for their daily dose of cod liver oil.

Illustrations by Lee Croy

Please Do Not Touch the Gardenias

BY JACK SPRINGS

"*Please do not touch the gardenias. Their flowers will turn brown and fall off.*" The message was written in black marker on an index card affixed to a plastic stake that plunged into the potting soil of a small green gardenia bush. Its flowers are said to be the blooms of unrequited love and a source of symbolic comfort to morose lovers.

I had been thinking, just moments before, about something that happened years ago, when I took a summer job as a tenderman on a fish boat. I was looking forward to it, for I understood tendermen had more time to explore the coast. They were the in-between men who transported the fish from the grounds to the plant, and when not otherwise engaged, they were on their own. I would have more time to smell the flowers.

I would be the engineer! Well, to be accurate, I was engineer in name only, for the skipper, an Australian expatriate, knew the inner workings of all things mechanical. Rolf used me more for discourse than maintenance. An overachiever in the engine room, he was possessed of the industriousness of four men and could probably have run the boat himself if he had figured out how to be in all places at once.

I wanted to make a good impression, so I showed up half an hour ahead of schedule the morning the boat was to leave. Rolf was there ahead of me. Together we fixed something green and cylindrical in the engine room, and later we moved on to the refrigeration system where I learned everything I needed to know about refrigeration systems. (It was my job to keep the fish cool.) When we finally crawled out of the room of pipes and wires I met one of the regular crew members – a "girthy" fellow by the name of Pook.

Pook was of Hawaiian ancestry and did everything he could to be mistaken for a Native Indian. "Pook?" he would say wearily, as if it were the thousandth time he had answered the question. "It's a Coast Salish word that means something like asshole." (Coast Salish was the language his Hawaiian grandmother spoke flawlessly, or so he said.) Pook would wave to every red man aboard a passing boat regardless of whether he knew them or not. The black shirt that never came off his back bore a print of a Haida-style eagle, which only heightened the illusion.

Pook was a hefty fellow, and as lazy as Rolf was industrious, an arrangement that suited him wonderfully. Because Rolf sometimes wanted to tie up the boat as well as docking it, he would often run out on deck and throw the nearest tie-up line. Pook, who also loved to be mistaken for the skipper of our boat, would stay in the wheelhouse and look out the door with his arm braced against the frame, his brow furrowed with authority as he watched the proceedings.

Yet I liked the man. And he liked me, I think, probably because I knew he was more intelligent than his dumbfounded expression would suggest – mouth agape with bottom lip protruding like an overinflated inner tube, which was the natural shape of his face at rest.

Rolf asked Pook if the new cook was here yet, to which Pook replied that he wouldn't know the cook if he saw him. I was working on deck when a woman in her early thirties came down to the boat and asked if she should drive the car down to the dock in order to unload the groceries. Now, a woman doesn't have to be especially pretty to get a lot of attention down by a fish wharf, but this one was pleasant to look at and a lot of eyes followed her back to her car. I thought this must be the delivery girl or the wife of our cook but I never dreamed for a second that she would be spending the summer aboard our boat until she stepped down off the float onto our deck and walked into the galley as if it were her own. Then the realization sank in: there was going to be a woman on board, working with us, cooking for us, eating with us, and sleeping with us. My first experience with a real live female shipmate.

What kind of a woman signs aboard a fish boat with three strange men, I wondered? She must be a woman with unarticulated fantasies about boats and rough men. A fish boat is not the regular domain of women, with the possible exception of those in glossy magazines and calendars. Those of us with vivid imaginations found it easy to suspect women who ventured into our vulgar vessels of subscribing to a non-standard code of sexual morality. Surely our new cook must understand this. We left almost the instant the groceries had been stowed in the fridge and in the ice hole below.

She had a real name but was dubbed "Cookie" almost immediately by our faux Indian deckhand. The name fit and stuck, and I shortly discovered that she was not the tart I had hoped she'd be. For one thing, she had a slight overbite with the two protruding incisors slightly separated by a gap. Not that this gap was ugly to look at. Not by any means. It lent her a girl-next-door-ish form of sweetness that was accompanied by a barely detectable lisp, as if she were perpetually sucking a peppermint candy.

Everything else about her was average in the best possible sense of the word. Her picture could have been the etching sent up in the Voyageur spacecraft, to show aliens what terrestrial females are all about. Her hair was brown and curly and hung down to her shoulders. Average height, medium build, breasts not spectacularly large or small, just right in the middle. I was in my early twenties with my hormones at high tide, so I noticed that she looked healthy, not flabby or muscular, and her bum was perfectly formed.

It didn't take long to get to know Cookie, for she was open and expressive. She liked music and played drums in a band. She was born and raised on the West Coast and she had a love of the ocean. I too had a love of the ocean and although I played no instrument I also loved music. All this I told her, but I soon found out someone else had captured her interest.

Two weeks earlier she had fallen madly in love with a gillnetter who, by happy accident, jammed with her band. She was deliriously happy when she found out our first port of call was Prince Rupert, or 'Rubert as some locals pronounce it. Her beloved would be in 'Rubert (oh joy!) along with the rest of the northern gill-net fleet. And since the first opening was delayed, they would probably be in port the day we arrived. She beamed as I told her. Thousands of plans to delight him flashed in her eyes.

I was blessed with a good grasp of the plausible, so I realized then it was futile to pursue this average-looking woman as my shipboard concubine. Instead, I offered myself as a friend.

But I was left ignorant as to the peace she made with Rolf. In an accent still thick after twenty years in this country, he confided to me his ulterior motive in hiring her. He had heard that occasionally a woman developed a fixation on her boss, doctor, or any other figure of authority. With any luck, it would happen to Cookie. Yet Rolf expressed no intention of actively encouraging her. He was, after all, a married man who would probably be more content with possibilities than realities.

By the time we reached 'Rubert, the entire crew knew about Cookie's beau. Rolf and I had accepted and even teased her about it, but Pook responded by tormenting her. He made fun of the little she knew of navigation and ship stuff. He insulted her cooking and when she got angry he said, "She's PMS-ing." That she didn't bleed to death before the end of the summer must have been a source of wonder to him.

Cookie asked for no special privileges and she slept in the fo'c's'le with the rest of the crew. In her only amendment to the usual sleeping practices of us males, she pinned together the curtains of her bunk while she dressed, undressed and slept. Even when she listened to her walkman the curtains were securely pinned, as much for her own privacy as our comfort. And the only liberty we had to give up was the casual leak over the side of the boat. Yet Pook often complained about the loss of this particular privilege and lashed out in a way that was pure Pook. In fact, I think that was the only time Cookie completely lost control. One morning there was a shriek that blasted through the toilet walls followed by a blood oath to kill the next man to pee on the toilet seat.

And all in all, I think Cookie enjoyed the summer. We travelled north to the community of Port Simpson, or 'Shimshin as it was pronounced locally. There we stayed for a few days and went for walks. Namu was another town we visited, and we hiked along the boardwalk to the lake and then strolled along the white pearly beach. Occasionally we explored the grand old buildings that had been built for a different kind of place than the ghost town Namu had become. These destinations were chosen by Rolf and were suspiciously more appropriate for their beauty than their convenience. Our skipper had revealed himself as a shameless romantic.

Cookie was an eager learner and showed a keen interest in nearly everything. This was her second season on the water, her first being a stint as cook on another fish boat the previous year. In the off-season she had taken a net mending course to better qualify herself as a fisherman. And at night, during the wheel watches we shared, I showed her everything I knew about navigation techniques and equipment. She was a good talker and we filled many lonely hours between daylight with engaging exchanges. There were many more wheel watches I spent alone, remembering how she looked in the green glow of the radar. Very pleasant – the radar emits a carouseling dim light that rivals candles for aesthetic effect. And paired with the hum of the engine, which can gently diffuse the sound of soft speaking voices, a wheelhouse can be an evocative location.

On our way north we passed Butedale. Cookie asked about the lights, and the three men in the wheelhouse that moment poured out the little information we had about Butedale, a small autumnal community that had seen more joyous days. Something about that location touched her in a peculiar way. Nothing out of the ordinary about the place. Lights that looked like the lights of any community, only fewer of them. No interesting features hiding in the landscape. To me the tiny village was completely unremarkable, even under the stars and in the moonlight. However, Cookie asked to be woken every time we were to pass by. This detail has stuck with me for a long time. I found it remarkable that a woman could be so captured by something so completely unremarkable.

She was still impressed by eagles which would swoop to the surface of the water and pluck up cod with expanded swim bladders. When these mega birds would falter and almost head-plant themselves on the surface for overestimating the size of their quarry, she would squeal at the drama. That year was also one of the first of the El Niño currents, which brought exotic finned species up from the tropics. On the fishing grounds one of the nets had disturbed the course of a gigantic sunfish. We men found it swimming alongside our boat propelled by its stubby pectoral fins, a dorky tourist. Our first instinct was to show it, like a jewel, to our cook, as if our own perspectives had become secondary and the true measure of beauty was now more accurately judged by her.

And all the time she professed her growing love for the gillnetter. In 'Rubert they had gone out and had several wonderful times on the town. During one of these dates he officialized things, told her he loved her too. On a slow day we would be outside painting the boat and she would be singing to herself in the galley. She went on and on about what he said and what he did, saying no one has ever said that or done that before. The man could sing, dance, sweet talk and apparently walk on water. I tried my best to foster a grudge against him, but then she brought him by the boat to meet us. The beau was bigger than I had thought, but not nearly as handsome. He turned out to be a very likable guy and, try as I might, I found it difficult not to like him.

So I grew a beard. Not a great beard, for my chromosomes were conspiring against me, producing patches of blond, brown and red hair in a pattern that wouldn't allow the moustache part to join with the rest of the beard. Perhaps I thought it would make me look older, for her, but I had really given up hope. That is the reason for most of my beards – a white flag to the world. It also gave me something else to do besides fantasizing about Cookie. At every opportunity I would look in every reflective surface available – the compass window, the radar screen, the galley window. In some the beard would look fuller than others. But in the mirror I trusted most, in the toilet, it was still the sparse beard of a young man.

When the summer ended I had put on some weight and filled out my shoulders. I had dispatched the beard a week before and was now dealing with a strange facial tan. We had made our last delivery to the fish plant in Vancouver, and although the boat would head out once more, I had to stay ashore and begin my semester at university. It was time to say goodbye to the crew. I shook hands with Rolf and Pook, I would miss them, but when it came to Cookie I stretched out my arms and gave her a hearty embrace.

You know a hug is over when there is that last final squeeze. But in this hug, when I decided to step away at an appropriate interval, I felt a sharp pain in my breastbone. It shot through my entire body and caused the flesh on my back to tingle. At first I thought it must be an amulet or a pin of Cookie's that had pierced my chest, but as I recoiled from the pain a bee flew out from between us.

It wasn't until eight years later that the gardenia metaphor occurred to me. But time has shrunk till it's touched at a few points. The last I heard, Cookie is living a happy life on Lasqueti Island, in a house she shares with her gillnetter. As for me, I try not to think of gardenias, much less touch them. ❖

THE PEOPLE'S HOME MEDICAL BOOK

BOOK I OF THE PEOPLE'S HOME LIBRARY

BY

T. J. RITTER M.D.

GRADUATE OF BOTH THE ALLOPATHIC
AND HOMEOPATHIC SCHOOLS.
FORMERLY ASS'T. TO THE CHAIR OF THE
THEORY AND PRACTICE OF MEDICINE,
MICHIGAN STATE UNIVERSITY,
ANN ARBOR, MICH.

Published by
THE R. C. BARNUM CO.
Cleveland, Ohio—Minneapolis, Minn.
Boston, Mass.

IMPERIAL PUBLISHING CO.
TORONTO, CANADA

1919

The Doctor Book

BY MARGARET McKIRDY

Mama allotted *The People's Home Medical Book* a position in our home alongside the Bible and the Eaton's catalogue. Its influence was greater than either. This book, edited by T.J. Ritter, M.D., formerly Assistant to the Chair of the Theory and Practice of Medicine, Michigan State University, Ann Arbor, Michigan, was published in 1919. We called it the Doctor Book.

Mama was a beautiful woman. When she was ninety, her wrinkles had a softness about them; her pink complexion and silky white curls glowed with health. The very blueness of her eyes lent sincerity to whatever she said, and there was a calmness in her mien as if she had come to terms with life. She had only one imperfection: the nail on her ring finger was slightly misshapen, and all her life there was a hairline scar along the fingertip. Mama explained the scar to anyone who admired her heavy gold ring. "That scar was there when your dad first placed the ring on my finger," she told me, explaining that Dad had chosen her even with her flaw. Actually I was seven years old, and Mama had been married a dozen years, when she got the felon.

A felon, like smallpox, is a disease of the past. I look it up in the Doctor Book.

Felon – Run-Around – Whitlow: It is generally seated immediately around and beneath the finger nail, commencing either at the side, the back, or the end of the finger. The deeper structures are affected and the pain is terrible. The tough covering of the bone is affected and pus appears next to the bone and underneath this tough covering... There is but one thing to do for this kind of felon and that is to open it early and thoroughly.

Trying to remember how Dad and Mama treated it, I read further:

Have a curved knife with both edges sharp and

it should be placed in boiling water for at least 5 minutes before using. Place the patient's hand on the table with the felon side up and this is usually the palm. Put the patient's arm away from the body and stand behind the elbow. Put the knife carefully on the finger a little ways from the felon and on the side nearest the hand. Call the patient's attention to something at the other side of the room and while he is looking away press down hard with the knife and as you press down he will jerk and thus make the cut long enough. As the table is solid he cannot jerk down away from the knife and the cut will go through the covering of the bone as desired and in 10 minutes there will be very little pain.

I can't imagine anyone hoodwinking Mama into accepting this treatment. She would have read the instructions. Neither can I picture Dad being so foolish as to try. Mama did not have a forgiving nature, especially where Dad was concerned.

I look at the scar on the dining room table and remember one night when we waited dinner for Dad, who was out drinking with the boys. On his return, when he carved the chicken his unsteady hand slipped and the knife struck the table. After that, whenever Dad suggested he might be late, Mama rubbed stain into the table's wound.

No! Even when his hand was steady, she wouldn't have let him gouge her finger. So what happened? I read on:

The pus is between this covering and the bone and you must make an opening for it. If you do not, it will, after many days and nights of suffering, burrow through, and destroy much flesh.

Well, her fingernail was destroyed, and the new one was a constant reminder. But what choices did they have?

To prevent a felon apply the white of an egg with 1/2 teaspoonful of salt added. If applied in time no one need have a felon.

Mama had been remiss. With slight precaution, she could have avoided the felon. Did she think of that while she suffered the treatment? Probably, since she never attached blame in the recounting.

Soak the finger or affected part for half an hour in strong lye, or ashes and water, as hot as can be borne. Do this 2 or 3 times a day and apply a poultice of soft soap and turpentine. If the felon comes to head, lance it, poultice with lye and elm bark, and heal with some good salve.

Did Dad lance the thing before it came to a head? I think not. Mama would have attached blame.

No. As I found out eventually, my parents had taken the trip to the doctor. But the felon was slow to heal, and Mama carried the scar, attesting to imperfection, for the rest of her life.

In good Christian homes when Mama was young and well into childhood, the misfortunes we suffered were thought to be our own fault. In God's good grace, the natural state was to be alive and well. If your condition was any other, if you were unfortunate, sick, or dying, you were guilty. There were questions you must answer. How had you been remiss? What rule had you broken? What taboo had you flouted?

Of course there were skeptics even then, and people who felt their systems were too delicate to withstand harsh treatment. For these people, syrups and tonics well laced with alcohol, laudanum or morphine were available, and they were used with sometimes tragic results. But few people in rural communities took the easy way out, and when they did, they were accepting of blame.

Dad was among the skeptics. During a brief period of prohibition in our northern area, Dad could walk twenty miles to find a doctor who would prescribe rum for his cold. He strode out into the biting wind with his collar open, his head

bare. He only covered up when there was no one to witness, and when he entered the doctor's office. Perhaps the bad boy image he maintained lent adrenalin for the walk.

Women were not allowed to enjoy the reputation of being bad. One of our neighbours, whose nerve tonic imparted the whiff of alcohol to her breath, always needed a second and third sip before she informed us that she was "not strong." Her tall body shrunk into her disgrace.

Everyone in the community suffered guilt, Catholics and Calvinistic Protestants alike. The difference was that the Catholic could be absolved by the priest; the Protestant carried guilt to the grave.

When I was six, two of our young friends offered to teach my sister and me about sex. One of the boys was a Catholic, and the next time I went to play with him, he said, "I can't play with you. Father O'Connor says you're bad."

"Well then, you're bad, too."

"No I'm not. I did penance."

I wonder how much of the guilt we suffered was reinforced by the Doctor Book, if not introduced by it. I read through the home remedies. Arsenic, morphine, carbolic acid, strong lye, gunpowder and kerosene – all figure prominently in reliable cures, internal and external. Here's the recipe for Mama's sulphur ointment which cured prairie itch: two parts lard, one part sulphur – brimstone. Give the devil some of his own medicine?

I turn to the index and look for prairie itch, but it's not there, so I scan the skin diseases. Oh! Oh!

Scabies: This is an eruption produced by a parasite and is very "catching." It covers the body in parts but is seen chiefly between the fingers where it often makes a raw surface… Sulphur ointment is a sure cure.

When I came home scratching with the prairie itch, Mama put the washtub in the kitchen and I had to bathe not just Saturday, but every night for the rest of the week. And nobody used the water after me. I had caught it, she said, from those dirty children at school.

Mama scrubbed me with lye soap. She towelled me roughly. She applied sulphur ointment. In the morning she insisted I scrub away all scent of sulphur, and she warned me not to scratch at school. As soon as I got home in the afternoon, she applied the salve again. She hauled water from the well and boiled towels, sheets, and any of my clothing that would stand boiling. But never at any time did she hint that I had scabies.

Some years later Mama discovered a super-effective treatment for almost every sore. Phenol is a form of carbolic acid so corrosive that its production is now banned in every country in the world, but the bottle from Mama's phenol and camphor solution is still in her medicine cabinet. She said she was first introduced to it by her dentist when he applied it to her gums after extracting her abscessed teeth in 1934. Common sense told her that it was safe.

It was more effective for some ailments than the best antibiotic is today. A cold sore? One application. Zap! It was gone. Mama never again felt guilty about her children's sores. Whatever harm it did us, Mama was still alive at ninety, with six of her seven children to come at her call.

My grandmother had a whole different set of cures but they too were based on the evil nature of illness and the need to suffer. Grandma's cure for the croup – also in the Doctor Book – was six drops of kerosene on a teaspoon of sugar. After the first treatment, I avoided going to Grandma's when I felt ill. I can still taste the kerosene. For a head cold, Grandma snuffed salt up her nose and hawked and spat, because she knew how to get rid of evil.

Mama did not hawk or spit; she preferred camphor rubs and bed rest. She was good; she did not need to suffer. I too preferred camphor and bed rest, although I was not sure that I was good.

Being good was very important. Children, too young to hide unacceptable behaviour and too young even to talk, were branded as having depraved minds. Either that or they had depraved

parents. Somebody was guilty. The Doctor Book says:

Sometimes the foreskin or the hood of the clitoris is so tight as to cause irritation and keep the passions excited and perhaps they are a cause of masturbation. When such is the case these operations should be performed. Parents should carefully look after these conditions as they, instead of a depraved mind, are the causes of many immoral practices.

When my brother was about seven, he had to have a small operation. It was not necessary for him to stay in the hospital, so the doctor made a house call. He and Mama went into my brother's bedroom, and through the open door I saw the doctor examining my brother's private parts. Mama would never consider a child of hers depraved (the neighbour's rapscallions, yes – but not us), but my brother was still relieved to find that he still had the thing after the operation.

In the chapter "Diseases of Women," the first disease noted is menstruation. No matter how good a girl was, this was one disease she could not avoid. When a girl is "unwell," says the Doctor Book, she is advised to take bed rest and to avoid any strenuous exercise or dancing. She must not study. She is exhorted repeatedly throughout the text not to study.

However,

A lazy indolent disposition proves likewise very hurtful to a girl at this period. One seldom meets with complaints of menstrual trouble among the properly industrious part of the sex; whereas, the indolent and lazy are seldom free from them. These are in a matter eaten up by greensickness and other diseases of this nature.

I look up greensickness and discover that it is a form of anemia characterized by green pallor, difficult breathing, palpitations and fainting. I doubt that I had anemia, but by the time I reached puberty, I had for so long struggled with the concept of being bad that a sense of unclean guilt smothered me. The shame of menstruation, this mysterious and horrifying body function, tended to make me "unwell." I would have died gladly. I not only felt physically ill, I could not pass the all-important test: I could not look people in the eye.

Some girls and women seem to be able to do almost anything at this time but such is not the case with many and even those who do not suffer at the time are likely to reap the effects in later life.

Not only were we burdened by "the curse," but also our social life was curtailed by caution. In "A Chapter for Young Women," we are advised:

Never have anything to do with a young man who is "sowing his wild oats," or who has sown them. This may mean more than you think.

The first time I read that, I wanted to know what I should think. I read the whole book, but I didn't find out. Mama didn't tell me, but she probably knew almost as little.

Many women, when Mama was young, were irresistibly attracted to young men who were "sowing their wild oats." Upon acquiring some slight knowledge in marriage, women could easily become convinced that their husbands had exposed themselves to unmentionable diseases. A good wife did not admit, even to her doctor, that she suspected her husband. The Doctor Book could tell her that her doctor might find it necessary to remove her internal organs – make her no longer a woman – but he would never tell her about the disease, acquired from her husband, that made the operation necessary.

Since many diseases could not be diagnosed, and everything from a headache or rheumatism to paranoia or insanity was attributed to some unmentionable disease, some women spent much of their lives watching for signs of internal rot.

Internal rot was not as great a danger in rural communities as one might think. Roving husbands had a tendency to seek out neighbours whose reserve had broken. People travelled little, so disease had less chance to spread, and if someone was ill, the neighbours knew it. Nonetheless, the birth of a handicapped child was sure to raise questions among neighbours about the sins of the father. Still, it was usually a woman who was condemned.

Women weren't supposed to discuss sex with their daughters any more than with their friends, husbands, or doctors, yet women were responsible for everyone's moral behaviour. When I went out on a date, although money was extremely scarce, Mama provided me with fare home in case I needed it. I found out from my date why I might need it.

Mama never seemed to doubt that I would refrain from any behaviour that was not nice. Grandma, on the other hand, thought it necessary to give me some warning. The first time a young man started hanging around, Grandma was ready. "I see you've got yourself a boyfriend."

"He's not my boyfriend!"

"Well remember, he won't buy a cow if he gets his milk for nothin'."

It was common advice.

Marriage was the romantic goal of every young girl and a necessary achievement in the eyes of her mother. Then again, the unfit had to be weeded out. A "Chapter for Married Women" in the Doctor Book states:

A woman with poor physical or mental health should not marry, for such a woman as a rule will not bear healthy children. No woman with consumption should marry. Neither should she marry if she has any specific disease… The time will come when the state for its own interest will be compelled to make laws governing marriage. Any mental disease on either or both sides should be sufficient cause for prohibiting marriage, for the offspring of such a marriage are likely to be endowed with a fearful heritage. Women who intend never to bear or rear children have no right to marry for this means the taking of measures to prevent conception or the getting rid of the product of conception and the latter is, in plain English, abortion.

These words were taken to heart in our small town. Mary, a retarded girl, watched as each of her several sisters acquired a boyfriend, courted, married and had children. Mary had a crush on each boyfriend in turn, and each time, she was told that she musn't have a boyfriend. "I can't get married," she said to me. "I wouldn't be able to look after my children." Mary loved her nieces and nephews dearly.

When the family doctor suggested that Mary could be sterilized, her mother was scandalized. She spent the rest of her life protecting Mary from sin. After she died Mary was taken in by relatives. She moved often, because each home in turn tired of Mary and her search for romance.

Abortion and the Prevention of Conception, which the Doctor Book mentions in that order, are lumped together in two very brief paragraphs.

Abortion is frequently caused by women themselves either by the aid of medicines or mechanical means and, to the shame of my profession, it must be said that there are medical men who do it for the sake of financial gain. Whenever abortion is performed, not only the health but the life of the woman is at stake.

As to the prevention of conception, most of the means used are very injurious and especially so to the woman.

But the book offers no hint on these injurious means. Condoms or douches were sometimes used, but to use them was considered immoral; even to talk about avoiding pregnancy was immoral. Many women, after several births, searched frantically for information on the medicines or mechanical means alluded to in the book, guilt and danger be damned, but to no avail. A woman had to accept the fruits of the original sin. If she did not, she suffered accord-

ingly. Contraception was considered injurious to a woman's health. There is little evidence from those days that women were warned of the effect of repeated pregnancies.

At the age of thirty-two, after the birth of her sixth child, Mama was told by her doctor that it was unwise for her to have any more. I do not remember how I acquired this bit of information, and I cannot imagine how Mama could have learned how to prevent pregnancy. Dispensing birth control information was a criminal offence, and in any event, contraception was something nice women did not talk about. Mama had one more child and both mother and baby did survive.

When I was in my early twenties, I nursed my neighbour, Tina, after what she said was a miscarriage. Tina had been laughing and robust in the spring, but gradually she became more withdrawn. Now in the early fall, she lay in her upstairs bedroom, silent and grey. My ignorance was profound, so my nursing amounted to bringing her hot soup and tea and tending the children. Although her three youngsters needed constant attention, and the clatter from below could not have been reassuring, she heeded her doctor's orders and made no attempt to rise. In the afternoon when I primly brought her tea, she confided that her doctor had told her she was lucky to be alive. "I shouldn't have done it," she wept.

I had no idea what she meant. Shouldn't have done what? Copulate? Use some medicines or mechanical means? I was appalled. I did not ask. "Drink your tea," I said, "and have a nice sleep. You'll feel better when you wake." I thought I should put my arm around her. I couldn't. I poured the tea and fled.

The whole book is not devoted to the frailties of women, however. There is "A Chapter For Men," and it is a masterpiece.

It does not pay for a young man to "sow his wild oats"... Do not expose yourself to these loathsome diseases. However, if you have been exposed, at least observe the laws of cleanliness and immediately wash the exposed parts thoroughly with some good antiseptic solution like carbolic acid, corrosive sublimate or permanganate of potash. Do not wait an hour, or even ten minutes.

Carbolic acid and corrosive sublimate are extremely corrosive, yet there is no word of caution. Permanganate of potash may have been the treatment of choice. At least it wouldn't take the hide off. It would, however, leave the exposed part a bright purple – which would, until the colour faded, jog the conscience and be difficult to explain to the wife. But chances were she never looked at his naked body. Modesty was considered becoming to a woman – especially a wife.

Young men are advised that abstinence and cleanliness are the preventives of these diseases. There is no such advice for women. "Boys will be boys," but a sinning woman was so far beyond the pale she wasn't even mentioned in the Doctor Book. Many women were ignorant about disease, but their fear of becoming pregnant protected them somewhat by pressuring them to resist male attentions.

In Mama's day, and when I was young, women were very aware of the stigma attached to an unwed mother. Even an innocent woman deluded by her swain became a social outcast and fair game for every roving male. I learned about that stigma when Amie, a teenage girl in my home town, became a mother. Amie was hired by Johnny McNeil, a widowed farmer to cook for the threshing crew. The pay was meagre, but the farmer was an attractive man and Amie enjoyed a romantic interlude on her first escape from parental supervision. That is, she enjoyed it until she became pregnant, at which time Johnny's ardor cooled. He denied paternity.

Amie was one of a large family of girls, and the disgrace embraced them all. One day in school, I looked up from my book to see my classmate, Amie's sister, blushing from her hair to her fingertips as the teacher, a middle-aged man, walked away. I didn't know what had happened, but Joan's

discomfort was etched in my memory. She and all of Amie's sisters were helpless – guilty by association. Meanwhile, Johnny basked as the butt of male humour. "I hear the baby has flashing brown eyes," Dad joked. "And beautifully curly hair," Dad's friend countered with a laugh.

An old family friend, even Mama considered Johnny innocent and Amie guilty. A few years later when Johnny married Amie, Mama was unable to forgive him for choosing a fallen woman.

Although the Doctor Book reflected the mores of the time, and was widely used, people did not always follow it slavishly. They trusted to Providence or used common sense, and most communities had women with practical health care knowledge who were willing to help. I may have avoided Grandma's remedies, but many of our neighbours bought her their worries. A mustard plaster cured bronchitis before pneumonia could develop. Soda baths, mud packs or crushed berries relieved many an itch. When the sting of iodine didn't prevent infection, a poultice of bread, soft soap and hot milk drew out the poison.

I remember one time when a woman, the mother of six, had pneumonia and stronger medicine was needed. Grandma caught a fat hen, wrung its neck and bound the warm bird to the woman's chest. There it attracted the woman's disease, which it then carried to the nether world. Grandma returned home at dawn and worked till nightfall, buoyed by the knowledge that the woman's children would not be orphaned.

I sit and think – how did my mother survive? All the guilt instilled by church, folklore and literature, and it was only reinforced by her Doctor Book. One day a few years ago, I had this book in my hand when Mama walked into the room.

"What are you reading now?" she asked.

"Oh Mama!" I sniffed and dabbed my eyes. "I was just looking at the Doctor Book."

"That silly thing," Mama said, "I should have burned it years ago. If you are sick, I'll call Dr. MacLeod." ❖

RAINCOAST
CHRONICLES
18

STORIES AND HISTORY OF THE
BRITISH COLUMBIA
COAST

Edited by HOWARD WHITE
with PETER A. ROBSON

Introduction

by Howard White

Apart from the odd rusting anchor on display in Vancouver and the lantern from the old Trial Island lighthouse in Victoria's Bastion Square, British Columbia is oddly devoid of maritime monuments for a province with one of the world's great coastlines. British Columbians can't be accused of wearing their marine heritage on their sleeves, but just the same, it's there interleaving the pages of our lives.

When Claus Botel brought his family from Germany to northern Vancouver Island in 1913, their homesteading tale turned into a story of sea adventure when their small boat shipwrecked them on Cape Cook. Botel's granddaughter Ruth Botel tells the whole story starting on page 210. Even a story of a determined tax collector pursuing an artless dodger turns into a boating story when it takes place on the coast and the scofflaw is a coastal gyppo. The taxman can only track him down by chartering Hal Hammond's gas boat out of Pender Harbour, as Hammond's son Dick recounts in "Svendson and the Taxman" (Page 183).

With so much of our commerce dangling or floating over water, it should not perhaps be so surprising that BC would emerge as a leader in certain technologies like the self-dumping log barge, whose origins David Conn traces in "Booting the Big Ones Home." Nor, given the typical west coast disregard for authority, should it be surprising that in 1963, when three hungry Vancouver scuba divers were told their idea of building the first commercial salvage sub was beyond the capability of all but the world's largest hi-tech manufacturing corporations, they went ahead and tried to do it on a shoestring. What is a little surprising, as Tom Henry describes in "Pisces Ascending" (page 171) is that Al Trice, Don Sorte and Mack Thomson should succeed so brilliantly, establishing BC as a world leader in submersible technology.

One way to get the saltwater boiling in west coasters' blood is to threaten the coast's much beloved lighthouses, as several automation-minded politicians have found to their sorrow. So it shouldn't be surprising that the one event of World War Two still being hotly debated on the west coast is the alleged Japanese shelling of Estevan Point lighthouse. In his book *Keepers of the Light* (Harbour Publishing 1985), lighthouse historian Don Graham contended that the shelling was a hoax perpetrated by the Canadian government to rally support for conscription. In this issue, Lasqueti Island writer Douglas Hamilton returns fire.

Few people carry around with them a stronger sense of the role the sea plays in our lives than commercial fishermen. Hank McBride went to work in the fishing fleet in 1937 when he was fourteen and still does relief duty as skipper on some of the coast's larger draggers and packers. He loves to tell stories, and the stories he tells bear witness to a free and unfettered sea-going lifestyle that has now all but vanished from the coast, as Michael Skog recounts on page 232.

Here on the BC coast, nobody thinks to make a big noise about the sea and its influence on our lives. But when we stop to think, it's all around us.

Pisces Ascending
The Little Sub That Could

by Tom Henry and Ken Dinsley, photos and illustrations courtesy Al Trice

Under the scudding grey clouds of a December morning in 1966, a small workboat towing a wooden scow laboured out of Burrard Inlet, under the great span of Lions Gate Bridge, and set an unsure northwest course into the Strait of Georgia. The little procession was unremarkable in the context of Vancouver's busy port, with its swarming harbour tugs and hulking freighters, though a few experienced seamen did pause to note the incongruity of the obviously underpowered boat struggling with its cumbersome tow. Probably a gyppo logger on a rubber-cheque budget. They blew into Vancouver and scoured the harbour of its marine dreck—the paid-off barges, the fire-sale boats—then bulled them up coast. These seat-of-the-pants mariners, it was said, were either ballsy or brainless. Many thought they were both.

A more colossal incongruity was apparent to the crew of the little workboat. As the *Hudson Explorer* ground past Point Atkinson and leaned into the long, slow pull to Jervis Inlet, they had time to reflect on the magnitude of what they were about to attempt: the first manned deep-water test of their made-in-Vancouver submersible, named *Pisces I*. If successful, they would hurtle past corporate giants like Grumman, Lockheed and Westinghouse, which were all pitching millions of dollars into the race to build the world's first commercially viable non-military submarine.

For twenty-six months, three Vancouver divers, Al Trice, Don Sorte and Mack Thomson, working under the name of International Hydrodynamics Ltd. (HYCo), had struggled to complete *Pisces I*, a teardrop-shaped submarine perched on the lumbering scow. They needed to prove the sub could descend to 600 metres, with a pilot. It was this depth that the US Navy had decreed the vessel must be able to achieve if HYCo wanted in on lucrative work recovering sunken torpedoes from the Maritime Experimental Test Range at Nanoose Bay on the east coast of Vancouver Island. With the *Pisces* project hopelessly over budget, the torpedo recovery contract was a Holy Grail to HYCo. Complete the test and they could pay down their crippling debt, land other Navy contracts, and sell their vessel's technology as the most versatile, affordable salvage sub design in the world. Fail to reach 600 metres and not only would they fulfill the predictions of all the experts who said the sub would never work, but a) one of them would very likely be steak tartare at the bottom of the sea and b) the other two would be commercial diving for the next twenty years to pay off their debts.

In spite of the impressive ring of the name, International Hydrodynamics was anything but a large corporation. It consisted of the three partners: the president, who could not read or write; the designer, whose idea of research consisted of thumbing through back issues of *Popular Mechanics*; and the general manager, who seriously listed as credentials for building a submarine an incomplete apprenticeship building wooden hulls at one of the oldest boatyards on the coast. Filling out the staff of HYCo were a deckhand (who doubled as a bouncer when paycheques were scarce), a secretary and three poodles.

The three poodles belonged to Don Sorte. Sorte (pronounced Sor-tee, or Sor-gee to some) was sometime president of HYCo (in its early days the company did not get tangled in corporate order) and chief spokesperson. For this latter task he was admirably gifted. He was 6'2", exotically handsome, and fond of attention-getting stunts such as hurling off his toupee while dancing at Vancouver's fabled Cave night club. (He kept a table at the Cave, though he did not drink or smoke.) Sorte also loved to flash wads of hundred-dollar bills, which may or may not have had something to do with the non-stop company of impossibly buxom women at his side.

If money and spectacle didn't get attention, then his poodles did. Sorte often dyed the dogs different colours (rose, blue and yellow being favourites) and took them out on business, including visits to the service counters of banks. All three dogs answered to the name Tiger.

"That way," Sorte once explained in his confident, booming way, "I had to yell once and all three came."

For all the bravado, however, Sorte was remarkably secretive. His life was sandwiched between an uncertain birthday in an uncertain part of the USA, and a mysterious death (or at least disappearance) in 1977, while sailing across the Indian Ocean. In dozens of interviews he never gave the same information twice about his age. (If you take the average of the many birthdates he gave to the Vancouver press during construction of *Pisces*, Sorte was probably thirty-eight in 1966.)

Sorte had a lifelong love of money which ultimately, and ironically, led him into the money-gobbling *Pisces* project. This passion may have been the product of a destitute youth. Sorte had a near-phobic dislike of poverty: faced with taking a one-light-bulb room in a cheap hotel or sleeping in his car, he'd choose the car. He was raised in the American Northwest and got a start in business in 1953 by placing what became a controversial ad in a Seattle newspaper—"We will do anything day or night, Don or Mc," followed by a phone number. He was twenty-five, married with two children, and continually short of money.

Sorte was a fan of scuba diving, which in the 1950s was still in its infancy. He was attracted to the frontier aspect of diving: very likely, in the early days, he was looking at a scene no human being had looked at before. Soon, Sorte realized diving was a potential moneymaker. He took a miscellany of underwater jobs, including a regular gig recovering accident victims from submerged automobiles. The police, all too aware of Sorte's immoral imperatives, advised him to stay out of victims' pockets: they needed the wallets for identification.

With no training or experience, Sorte and his partner Mc took on contracts to salvage sunken logs from freshwater booming grounds. Their approach made up in simplicity what it lacked in sophistication. With a heavy set of tongs attached to a crane, they rowed or waded into the water and slammed the tongs into a log. The crane then pulled the log onto land. The water, of course, quickly filled with sludge and goop dragged from the bottom, so they worked by feel, slithering through piles of slime-covered logs on the lake bottom.

If the pile shifted, the men could be trapped or crushed. It was a lucrative business, though, and lasted until Sorte broke up with his wife and moved to Vancouver with a new girlfriend.

Sorte's chance to break into the closed shop of the BC commercial diving scene came in June 1958, when a span of the Second Narrows Bridge collapsed, killing eighteen workers. During attempts to recover bodies trapped in the wreckage, a commercial diver was lost as well when he was carried off by the tidal rip. Whether or not because of the accident—Sorte felt it was—the divers' union opened its doors a crack and Sorte was inducted into the Brotherhood of Local 2404 of the Pile Drivers, Bridge, Dock and Wharf Builders of Vancouver, as a commercial diver.

Sorte became an excellent diver and was paid well. The money was good because the odds of even a small accident turning serious were bad. But diving was dangerous, too. During one job Sorte worked on, a supposedly routine hard-hat chore cleaning up under a Vancouver pier, his air supply was accidentally cut off. The intake hose from the compressor, always placed upwind and well away from the exhaust fumes of the motor, had been left hanging near the surface of the water. Spray was sucked into the hose, shunted down to Sorte by the compressor and detected by the sensor in his helmet. The sensor, designed to cope with a completely severed air hose, immediately clamped shut the air valve in Sorte's helmet. No water was going to get in, but neither was any air. Sorte heard the clunk of the air valve shutting and knew instantly what it was.

"They tell you there is a five-minute air supply inside your helmet but I find you tend to black out after three minutes," Sorte recalled. "I began gathering up all my hoses and such to move out where I would be clear to be drawn up by my tender. I kept calling out to him on my voice line, 'George, are you up there? George! Where are you, George?'"

George was away momentarily, getting coffee.

Sorte regained consciousness flat on his back on the wharf with George slapping his face and crying at him to wake up.

With his diving earnings Sorte bought a home, complete with pool, in the toney British Properties in West Vancouver. He cruised town in flashy cars. He even had an oil painting commissioned: it portrayed a man kneeling in adoration before a huge dollar bill. "One thing about Sorgee," a friend explained, "you didn't take him seriously, you just experienced him."

Sorte met Al Trice through his diving work. Trice, a soft-spoken, pipe-smoking Steve McQueen look-alike, was an early member of the divers' union—and a longstanding regular in Vancouver's waterfront community. After a brief attempt, in his teens, to manufacture wooden sailboats, he drifted through a variety of maritime jobs: fish boat deckhand, towboat skipper and finally, a job as apprentice shipwright at the venerable Mercers Star Shipyard in Queensborough. "Everything

Two of the originators of the *Pisces* submersibles, Don Sorte and Al Trice, in their hard-hat diving gear.

was big—the hammers, the chisels the planes—everything," Trice recalls. "They used to say, 'If it isn't hard work, it isn't Mercers.'"

The yard was not graced by anything that might be called technology. There were no cranes. It took three weeks to put a 2,000-kilo engine in a boat. As Trice explains, "Together with your helper—just one, you always had just one helper—you wedged it up, built a bridge across the deck of the boat, levered it over, then eased it down into the engine room. Scared to death the whole time the thing would get away on you. It was like building the pyramids."

All this was conducted under the eye of Mercers' temperamental foreman. "If you're going to smoke," he once declared to Trice "you're going to smoke tailor-made. You're not rolling on my time."

In May 1953, Trice met Keith Carter, an ex-British Navy frogman. Within a week Carter took Trice diving and Trice was hooked. This, he knew, was his calling. Trice especially enjoyed the three-dimensional freedom of diving—where "up" and "down" lost meaning. He and Carter formed a business, hoping to promote scuba as an alternative to the more prevalent hard-hat diving. But hard-hat divers were intractable. They referred to the aqualung as "mouse gear" and the divers who used it as "frogs." Trice's attempts to sell Vancouver on the merits of the new diving technology failed, and the business folded. But his diving career flourished. By 1964 Trice was one of the most respected commercial divers in the Lower Mainland. That year he was called on to make some of the riskiest dives of his life.

In early spring, *Barge 10*, loaded with heavy bunker "C" oil, turned turtle in heavy seas and sank near Pasley Island in Howe Sound. Trice was asked to do the salvage survey. Compounding the usual dangers of salvage work was the fact that Trice would be diving alone to depths of at least 80 metres. Jacques Cousteau, the French underwater pioneer who essentially made scubas accessible, stated in a book published in 1963 that 61 metres was the maximum depth for, as he called them, "aqualungers." Divers were still using ordinary air, which is 79 percent nitrogen. (Nitrogen gas enters the bloodstream under pressure and is responsible for the crippling, sometimes fatal, bends divers can get when they surface too quickly.) Trice says, "You did lots of dives to 80 metres alone. They wouldn't pay for two divers. That's all there was to it. Some dives you just have to back out of. You just can't do that dive. You'd get too narc'd."

"Narc'd" refers to the other problem dissolved nitrogen causes: nitrogen narcosis, whose effects are often quoted in martini equivalents. For each 20 metres a diver descends, the amount of nitrogen forced into the bloodstream by the increasing atmospheric pressure has an impact roughly equivalent to drinking one martini. At 100 metres, or after pounding five quick martinis, a diver's thought processes become confused. He does foolish things, like offering his aqualung to passing fish or remaining on bottom long after his dwindling air supply should have sent him back to the surface.

Working alone, Trice completed his survey of the wreck. He discovered *Barge 10* was leaking. In his report he noted the barge lay on a slope with its shallow end at a depth of 80 metres and the deep end at 100 metres. Even at 80 metres, each minute a diver spends on bottom requires corresponding minutes of decompression time at various stops while returning to the surface. The difference in depth between the two ends of the barge was only 20 metres, but each of those metres added dramatically to the decompression time. The problem was going to be air supply: a diver needed enough to descend, work, then make the long, slow ascent.

Trice, Sorte and another diver were contracted to do the underwater work. It was to be the deepest diver salvage operation ever undertaken, hard-hat or scuba—anywhere on the west coast. Trice and Sorte had been to such depths only a few times prior to the work on the *Barge 10*. These were sporting test dives off Vancouver's North Shore. The men had done a so-called "bounce" dive, going down to 100 metres and straight back. (Years later a good friend of Trice's drifted to the surface dead after a much shallower bounce dive.)

The underwater work on *Barge 10* proved more difficult than Trice or Sorte had anticipated. After several twenty-five-minute dives at the work site, they had to reduce bottom time to fourteen minutes per dive.

Fourteen minutes was just enough time to secure a shackle or work a pin into place. Then it was time to make for the surface, following a carefully planned schedule. On the support ship they scrambled out of oil-coated suits and into a decompression chamber, where they often slept for hours. They shortened their work schedule to four days on and three off and still they were exhausted.

The *Barge 10* job was successful, but it convinced Sorte and Trice that they needed a submarine. Just as the aqualung freed the hard-hat diver from his awkward gear, so a submarine would free the diver from all the hazards associated with working at extreme depths. A sub would double or even triple the diver's range of operations. The men's ideas were fueled by the fact that Cousteau's submarine *Denise*—or *Diving Saucer*, as she was also known—and her surface support ship *Calypso* were in operation off the coast of California in early 1964, receiving a lot of media and trade journal coverage.

One morning shortly after the salvage of *Barge 10*, Trice appeared in front of Sorte's posh West Vancouver home and announced he was heading south to look at submarines. Sorte didn't even pause. He shot inside, crammed a toothbrush in one pocket and a bulging wallet in another, and the two headed off on an unusual shopping trip.

Now, at lunchtime on that December day in 1966, the *Hudson Explorer* and the scow entered the deep waters near Captain Island, in Jervis Inlet. As Sorte and Trice brought the *Explorer* alongside the barge, HYCo's third partner, Mack Thomson, got ready to go down in the submersible. Unlike hard-hat or scuba diving, work in a submersible requires no special gear. For the occasion, Thomson, 5'8", 135 pounds, had troubled to don his favourite 007 James Bond sweatshirt. Nor did *Pisces* require a lot of preparation: its batteries were charged, its oxygen tanks filled. The only thing that distinguished this dive from many others—besides the extraordinary depth—were the web of stress wires stretching across the submersible's crew chamber. These wires measured microscopic changes in the sphere's dimensions via change in the wires' electrical

resistance. For Thomson, this was an unusual concession to technology. Ever the make-doer, he had tested the hull of the *Pisces* in its first unmanned submersions by lashing pieces of wooden lath together. If the sphere contracted while submerged, the laths slid past one another and Thomson was able to measure the difference when the craft returned to the surface. To date, *Pisces* had exceeded everyone's expectations.

Moving with practised ease, Thomson clambered into the *Pisces* crew chamber and secured the hatch. Outside, the cable from the scow's on-deck crane was hooked to the submersible and it was hoisted over the side. The descent to 600 metres was scheduled to take several hours. Without complicated decompression stages to go through, the craft simply drifted down to the designated depth; then, after blowing water ballast with compressed air, it returned to the surface.

Prior to building *Pisces*, Mack Thomson's closest formal contact with submarines was the Wednesday evening meetings of the Seattle contingent of the US Submarine Naval Reserves. He had joined the reserves not because he was interested in submarines—he was more interested in boats—but because it was an alternative to being drafted into two years of military service. In his four years with the reserves, he never once went down in a submarine. Sea duty consisted of a few cruises in small navy ships on Seattle's Lake Union, during which Thomson was occasionally allowed a turn at the helm. He was told to "steady up on Grandma's Cookies"—a large billboard at the head of the bay. The assignment that carried the greatest burden of responsibility was to teach knot-tying to a more junior class. As soon as his obligatory time was up, he resigned.

Thomson was a nudist and a spiritual brother to Zen mechanic Robert Pirsig, in the sense that he had a near-spiritual affinity for matters technical. "Mack sometimes thinks something, and then, to him, it *is*," said Trice. "He doesn't differentiate."

Like Sorte and Trice, Thomson first got into scuba diving as a sport. Too broke to buy a dry suit, he made his own rudimentary outfit by gluing and stitching together yards of the material used to protect baby mattresses. By

175

wearing a full set of woollen long johns under this plastic suit, he was able to tolerate the frigid waters of Puget Sound. He acquired a secondhand regulator, then made his own K-valve to fit the breathing apparatus to his air tank.

Thomson's inventiveness blossomed in the frontier world of scuba diving. Using salvaged parts, he manufactured an underwater lighting system that, for the first time, enabled photographs to be taken at depths of greater than 10 metres (approximately the limits of full-spectrum light). He showed some of his photos to Don McKuen of KOMO TV, who hosted a popular program called "Exploration Northwest." McKuen was so taken by the photos, and by Thomson's contagious enthusiasm, that they teamed up to produce several programs, one of which garnered the station a prestigious Sylvania Award.

Occasionally inventive beyond recklessness, Thomson once thought he had found a nifty way to ascend from the depths by blowing up his suit like a balloon and rocketing to the surface. A horrendous case of the bends arrested further development of that idea.

Thomson was one of those guys who read technical and trade magazines. In one of these journals he came across an account of how Washington's Grand Coulee Dam was regularly inspected by hard-hat divers. It was risky work. The dam is one of the largest in the world—the waterfall over its spillway is 107 metres wide and falls more than 50 metres—and the terrific currents in and around the areas to be inspected were extremely hard on divers in their cumbersome gear.

Thomson concocted the idea of doing the inspections in modified scuba gear, and immediately focussed all his exuberance in a drive to convince some fellow divers it could be done. Instead of the bulky hard-hat suits, they would use seamless wet suits made—in typical Thomson style—by pouring rubber over manikins. Each diver would wear a small tank of air for emergencies. Connecting them to the surface would be air, hose, telephone and safety lines. With the increased mobility, Thomson reasoned, they could do the inspections much more quickly and much more cheaply than hard-hat divers.

Thomson's bid on the job was successful. The inspection was done in September, when the water level in the dam was as low as possible. The giant turbines were slowed to a minimum and the divers went to work. The water was absolutely clear, so much so that Thomson, working from a platform halfway down the inside of the dam, had an attack of vertigo. He felt he would tumble through the water to the bottom of the dam.

Thomson met Sorte and Trice in Seattle in 1965, at the home of a mutual friend. Trice and Sorte were on the way home from their shopping trip, unimpressed by what they had seen. American Submarine Company of Ohio and Perry Submarine Builders of Florida had both built subs that could dive to 30 metres, but neither was designed for salvage work. In California, Trice and Sorte had visited corporate giants Westinghouse Electric, General Dynamics and General Mills—all working on submersibles—and in every case were welcomed more as colleagues than potential competitors. Executives began calling the Canadians "the T-shirt boys," because of their casual attire. Despite or perhaps because of their unprofessional appearance, Trice and Sorte were ushered into the deepest recesses of the security-conscious research laboratories. (At Lockheed's aerospace research centre they were allowed to watch a prototype moon buggy being put to the test.) Although boggled by the technological excesses of the American submersible programs, Trice and Sorte did note many practical features which they would like to see in a submersible. These ideas would prove invaluable in the future.

Even when they looked beyond North America, the only other sub remotely close to their needs was Cousteau's *Denise*, completed in 1959. A prototype, it was described as "a scrutinizer, a loiterer, a deliberator, a taster of little scenes as well as big," but it was not on the market.

The remaining option was to build a sub, but that too sounded unfeasible. Before leaving Vancouver, Trice had run the idea of building a sub by an engineer at Patterson Boiler Works. "The man was very nice. He sat down with us and carefully explained why building a submersible was impossible." Despondent, Sorte and

Trice asked Thomson if he could build them a sub. Thomson said yes.

Thomson's first step in the design of the sub was to inhale as much of the literature as possible. Among the many texts he consumed was the account of a Swiss man named Jacques Piccard, one of the foremost authorities on submersible design at that time. In 1960, four years before Thomson started on his sub, Piccard, backed by the French Navy, reached a depth of 11 kilometres in a submersible named *Trieste*. The dive, which set a depth record that still stands, was made in the south Pacific Ocean, in a trench named the Challenger Deep. The overall design of *Trieste*, which employed an enormous bag of gasoline to lift the sub to the surface, was totally impractical for a salvage sub, but Piccard's account was invaluable. In particular, Thomson noted Piccard's advice that "the cabin is the vital part of any deep ship; around it all other components must be fashioned."

A submersible's cabin must be capable of withstanding tremendous pressures while keeping its crew not only dry, but at the same atmospheric pressure they left at the surface. The pressure on every square centimetre of the cabin's outside surface increases at a rate of approximately one-tenth of a kilogram per metre of depth. At a depth of 1,000 metres, the pressure is over 100 kilograms per square centimetre. (In Imperial measures: over 1,459 psi.)

The hull design with the smallest surface area—at least the shape which mathematically optimizes the weight-displacement ratio and distributes the pressure most evenly over the surface—is a sphere. Ottis Barton's bathysphere, in which he and William Beebe were lowered on a tether to an ocean depth of 930 metres in 1934, was a metre and a half in diameter, which gave them space enough to see if they could do it, but not enough to provide a working environment for a salvage job. Thomson knew his sub would need room for two crew, plus masses of equipment.

When asked where he had got his information about hull design and materials, Thomson explained: "We just ask our friends. We've got lots of friends who give us information." One of those friends was Warren Joslyn, one of Boeing Aircraft's top stress engineers. Josyln's original contribution to the project was the terse delivery of the comment that the project was impossible. Then, snared by Thomson's limitless enthusiasm (as many, many others would be), he began designing. The engineering specs he prepared for Thomson called for the submersible to be built around two spheres, a larger one for the crew and a smaller one containing various tanks. It would be capable of submersion to 500 metres. Vancouver Iron and Engineering contracted to build the sphere. Thomson took office space in their shop, and the long job of bending metal began in the summer of 1965.

After six months of relentless work, the frame and two spheres were completed. The bill was almost $50,000, thus cleaning out HYCo's entire budget. (The US Navy had paid $50,000 for a submersible named *Intelligent Whale*—in 1872!) HYCo moved *Pisces* from the fabricators to an unused space in the back of a mushroom cannery in east Vancouver. They secured the space in return for helping load crates of tinned mushrooms onto trucks.

Power, steering and breathing systems were completed, but slowly, as Thomson often worked without benefit of engineering drawings. (Incredibly, *Pisces I* was built from a total of forty-four drawings, about the same number, an engineer claimed, needed to build a coat hanger.) Thomson built many parts himself, often at home in the evening. The next day he would show his handiwork to Trice, who would find a way to drop it on the warehouse floor. If the part broke it wasn't any good; if it didn't break, it had passed the *Pisces* quality test.

Originally, HYCo's partners had hoped for the sub to be ready in three months (and $20,000). After fifteen months, Trice and Sorte, in the depths of debt, insisted on seeing the sub tested in the water. Thomson, who had an inventor's disregard for time and budget, said he wasn't quite ready. They would have to wait. By this time *Pisces* had been moved into a little shack at the end of Vancouver Pile Driving's pier in North Vancouver. Desperate to see how their investment was going to perform, Trice and Sorte waited until Thomson was away, ran *Pisces* out on the I-beam and lowered her into the ocean. The submersible did not float straight at all; the

The twin spheres of *Pisces I* were fabricated for HYCo by Vancouver Iron and Engineering.
L to r, Al Trice, Mack Thomson and Don Sorte.

tail end sank. Sorte, who was never big on reining in his emotions, developed a case of the financial bends, declaring the whole venture had been an enormous waste. When Thomson returned, they confronted him with the sub's problem. Thomson was typically philosophical. "Oh well," he said. "We learned a lot." This sent Sorte into even greater paroxysms of anger and frustration. He had been taking every diving job that came along in order to finance the sub, and it wouldn't even float straight. It fell to Trice to defuse the situation. "What are we going to do?" he deadpanned. "I don't know; give up." Disgusted, Sorte and Thomson agreed to carry on.

"There's no magic," says Trice, who has an engineer's patience for mechanical problems. "You can only use what's there. We're always asking for magic. There is no magic."

The problem of *Pisces'* heavy tail proved easy to solve. Thomson bought two hundred Grimsby troll floats at a nearby commercial fishing store and crammed them into every accessible tail section of *Pisces'* fairing. Each float had 3 kilograms' lift and was good to a depth of no less than 525 metres.

Among other problems plaguing the emerging submersible was arc and fire—or, in HYCo lingo, "A & F"—in the electrical system. Electrical problems became so common they were spoken of lightheartedly, but shadowing the jokes was the memory of a fire of catastrophic consequences on board one of Jacques Cousteau's test subs, caused by a short. The sub was quickly lifted onto the deck of the *Calypso*, but when the fire couldn't be put out with carbon dioxide foam it was dropped back into the sea. If there was a serious fire in *Pisces* while Thomson was aboard, even alongside the docks, there was no one to yard the sub out of the water quickly. Testing was a serious business, or at least it was supposed to be.

Thomson often worked on *Pisces'* interior while it was submerged off VPD's dock. With a radio blasting, he painted the hull aquamarine and white, then set to installing an infinity of controls. The chronic shortage of money led to continual compromises. For example, the scrubbers that controlled the critical level of carbon dioxide in the air were driven by a sewing machine motor. Thomson had lifted it from his wife's Singer during a conjugal visit to Seattle. He did splurge on a telephone, which he hooked up inside *Pisces* to save himself the bother of having to clamber in and out whenever he

The final stages of work on *Pisces I* took place in this shed at the end of Vancouver Pile Driving's pier in North Vancouver.

needed to call for parts or advice. People on the other end of the line, listening to Thomson's voice echoing and re-echoing, jokingly asked if he was inside a well. He replied that he was sitting at the bottom of Burrard Inlet.

In the mountainous confines of Jervis Inlet, the crew would need more than a phone line to stay in touch with Thomson, particularly at the depths he intended to reach during the dive. Underwater communication equipment was only marginally effective in those days. Radio waves could not be used, as they spread out rapidly in water and soon became unintelligible. *Pisces'* communication was based on sound. Sound can travel for hundreds of kilometres in water if the conditions are right, but refraction can be a problem; sometimes the sound bends as it travels. As the effect of refraction is minimized on the vertical plane, it was imperative the *Explorer* sit directly above *Pisces*.

Complicating the problems of communication was the proximity of a US Navy vessel also in Jervis Inlet.

After contacting the ship—an innocuous-looking buoy tender—the crew of the *Hudson Explorer* was alarmed to discover it was testing a new generation of anti-submarine torpedo. These torpedoes were being fired out a tube on the stern of the ship, then whizzing away in search of underwater targets.

Thomson irreverently radioed the US ship, explained what HYCo was about to do and asked them to postpone torpedo tests. The Americans, working to schedule, were reluctant to cancel their tests, but stopped just short of refusing. They may have recalled an incident that had occurred before the testing of the American submersible *Deepstar 4000*. Her support boat was mistaken for a target by a Navy ship and had three 5-inch projectiles dropped 200 metres astern of her before she was able to advise the Navy of their error.

The HYCo team and the US Navy ship established what they considered to be a reasonably safe distance between them. It was also agreed the Navy would advise HYCo when they were about to fire a torpedo by raising a

On a cloudy day in December of 1966, Mack Thomson prepared for *Pisces I*'s first test dive to 600 metres in the waters of Jervis Inlet.

red flag. This signal was a near-useless concession as the torpedoes were fired from the deck of the ship: the HYCo crew could watch the launches through binoculars.

During what was supposed to be a long break in the torpedo tests, *Pisces* began its descent. Crouched below the stress wires, Thomson guided the vessel under the surface as easily as he would back his car out of the garage. By this time the fantastic and foreign treats of underwater travel were familiar to Thomson. To the few guests who had been down in *Pisces*, even to relatively shallow depths, it was like a trip to a new world. One American fisheries expert, a guest on a dive in Puget Sound, had taken along a tape recorder and a camera. So dazzled was he by the first-time sight of the rich waters that, as Thomson gleefully noted, he spent much of his time talking into his camera's light meter and pointing his microphone out the view port.

Thomson's first checkpoint was at 170 metres. He reported all was well, although the response from the *Hudson Explorer* was garbled. On the surface, the crew of the *Explorer* were having equal difficulty understanding Thomson's scratchy reports. To Trice, the communication problem hinted at a more serious situation. He realized they were no longer directly above the sub; *Pisces* had drifted out from under them—and toward the torpedo target.

As Thomson continued with his descent someone on board the *Explorer* noticed a red flag raised on the Navy boat. There was no time to call off the dive. Warren Joslyn, along for the ride, tried frantically to advise the Navy to hold the fire, but they suddenly seemed to develop communication problems of their own. Trice advised Thomson to shut everything off aboard *Pisces*. Then, with gut-wrenching horror, the crew of the *Hudson Explorer* watched a torpedo shoot from the deck of the Navy ship, splash into the water and hurtle away.

Far below, Thomson had been recording his thoughts and observations on a tape recorder. He had heard enough of the squawking message from the *Hudson Explorer* to realize his predicament. He shut down all unessential electrical gear. *Pisces* was now still and silent. Thomson even clapped his hand over his wristwatch to muffle its ticking. He left the tape recorder running and on the tape one can distinctly hear the whine of the torpedo's screws as it cuts through the water seeking a target—exactly as Thomson heard it, crouched in the sub, alone, 200 metres underwater, waiting for any change in tone to indicate the torpedo had homed in on *Pisces*. Even though the torpedo was unarmed, he knew it was a toss-up whether it would impale *Pisces* or pass right through.

After an unbearably long time, the sound of the torpedo trailed off and Thomson continued the dive. When he paused at 330 metres to take stress readings there seemed no particular problem other than the discovery that he had lost all communication with the surface. Normally, this would have been cause to call off the dive, but after the business with the torpedo the loss of communication didn't seem that serious to Thomson. Besides, HYCo didn't do things normally.

Shortly after *Pisces* passed the 400-metre mark, an explosion jarred Thomson from the controls and the sub plunged downwards. Thomson's first reaction was to leap up, thus becoming snarled in the strain wires. Fighting to free himself, he struggled with controls to blow the ballast tanks and arrest the descent. There was the familiar hiss of compressed air and gurgle of bubbles as the tanks were cleared, but *Pisces* did not respond. She continued to sink. Thomson could see particles like dust motes, illuminated by the 1,000-watt headlights, snowing upward outside the viewing ports.

Down *Pisces* went, level but uncontrolled, like a feather wafting from a nest. While the depth gauge recorded his plunge toward the bottom, Thomson considered his options. There remained only one possible way *Pisces* was going to return to the surface: releasing an untested 185-kilogram drop weight would have to compensate for whatever buoyancy was lost in the explosion. Had the drop weight mechanism been damaged in the blast?

An emergency drop weight is exactly what it sounds like; a weight that can be dropped from the sub if a large and sudden increase in buoyancy is needed. On *Pisces*, the drop weight was held to the frame by a long, finely threaded crank. Thomson's struggle to release the weight was recorded on tape.

"Fourteen hundred feet and still descending. (Creak, creak, pant, puff, puff.)

"Fifteen hundred feet and still descending. (Puff, puff, puff.)

"Sixteen hundred feet and still descending."

Finally, the weight fell away.

"Thank Christ," said Thomson, to no one. "It's gone."

At this point *Pisces* should have shot up like a bubble. It did not. It merely slowed in its descent. What Thomson had failed to take into account was Archimedes' principle; an engineer had suggested a drop weight of 185 kilos in water. He had made the weight 185 kilos on land.

Still *Pisces* continued to sink, though Thomson, with desperate optimism, thought it might be descending more slowly. Down, down it drifted for another 30

metres, where it came to a standstill, suspended in the black waters. Thomson studied the depth gauge. Six hundred metres. *Pisces* had reached the test depth. But would it rise? *Pisces*' searchlight sent a core into the dark water, but there was nothing to indicate whether the craft was going to hold steady or ascend. Thomson shivered in the chill cabin. The hull ticked under the tremendous pressure.

Again Thomson peered at the depth gauge and considered his immediate future. *Pisces*, designed to take two and even three passengers on day-long expeditions, had enough oxygen to last for forty-eight hours. If Thomson shut down all systems and tried to conserve air, he might last for sixty hours. After that, he knew, would come shortness of breath and blackout. While considering his fate, he kept his eyes on the depth gauge. Slowly, like a minute hand on a watch, the gauge indicated the sub was rising. Thomson could only keep his eye on the controls, and hope there would be no more catastrophes.

Far above on the surface, daylight was dwindling. The US Navy vessel had discreetly concluded its tests and steamed away, leaving the *Hudson Explorer* alone in the inlet. It had been hours since last contact with *Pisces*. With night falling, the crew realized soon there wouldn't be enough light to take bearings. They would be unable to hold *Explorer* over the spot where *Pisces* had descended. Trice ran the boat to the nearby shore, where the scow was secured, and started the power plant to provide light for a reference point. Then all they could do was return to the approximate place where *Pisces* had gone down and wait helplessly for the sub to reappear. Other than to refill a cup of coffee, or search for yet another pack of cigarettes, no one could move. The group huddled on deck, scanning the waters for any sign of *Pisces*. If it did surface, it was important they spot it quickly. *Pisces* rode so low in the water that, between evening winds and tidal currents, it could easily drift away, unnoticed, for miles. The American submersible *Ben Franklin* had drifted six hours on the surface before her support ship located her. Another, named *Alvin*, had been lost for ten hours off Bermuda.

They need not have worried. From the black waters came a light some of the crew later described as an atomic bomb going off, and which others felt was a near religious experience. It was dim for a moment only, then burst into brightness in the black stillness of the waters. It was *Pisces* ascending, led by its powerful headlights. The submersible bobbed to the surface. It was midnight. Thomson had been down for eight hours.

What had caused *Pisces* to sink was an explosion—actually an implosion—of such force it had torn a portion of the fibreglass from the fairing and sucked it into the hole of one of the four smaller 40-centimetre spheres used for ballast and trim control. Thomson had been lucky. If even one more of the spheres had gone, releasing the drop weight might well have been futile. But Thomson was jubilant. The ballast sphere was a simple thing to replace, and *Pisces*, as far as he and the military needed to know, were good to 600 metres.

Although they had no way of knowing it at the time, *Pisces*' inventors had launched a technological renaissance in BC. Success of the little submersible on the torpedo range, and in subsequent salvage operations, led to the building of more *Pisces* crafts—ten in all. International corporations—including some who had entertained the "T-shirt boys," yet failed to complete their own subs—noted the upstarts, and within a few years *Pisces* versions were working on cable-laying projects in the Atlantic and capping oil wells in the North Sea. Experts from all over the world came to visit, including scientists from the USSR, one of whom went on to lead an underwater exploration of the *Titanic*. As HYCo grew, so did the support industries around it—a plethora of Lower Mainland firms specializing in underwater communication, propulsion, navigation and remote control vehicles.

Unfortunately the profit side of HYCo never proved as buoyant as their submersibles. Some of this was the fault of the owners, who insisted on redesigning the sub every time they received an order. Some was the fault of the Trudeau government, which, when HYCo signed a crucial multi-million-dollar deal to sell subs to the USSR, gave in to American pressure and revoked the company's export permit. After fifteen years—from 1964 to 1979—HYCo folded as a business, although its subs, in the hands of other firms, continue to work to this day. So do its former employees, many of whom own and manage firms in Vancouver's elite underwater research firms. Among this crowd, HYCo is referred to as the "kindergarten"—the place where it all began.

But back on the wooden scow that December night in 1966, all that mattered to Trice, Sorte and Thomson was that their idea had worked. As they toasted *Pisces* and each other with glasses of champagne, they swapped jokes about how those aboard the *Hudson Explorer* had debated pouring that same bubbly into the water as a memorial to Thomson. They secured *Pisces* and made ready for the long, slow haul back to Vancouver. For their success they had only themselves to thank. And, perhaps, an American torpedo with lousy ears. ◆

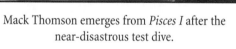

Mack Thomson emerges from *Pisces I* after the near-disastrous test dive.

Tom Henry is the author of The Good Company, *a history of the Union Steamship Co. (Harbour Publishing, 1994).* Pisces Ascending *is from* Westcoasters: the Boats That Built BC, *coming soon from Harbour Publishing.*

Svendson and the Tax Man

by Dick Hammond

ather was working on his boat at the dock in Pender Harbour. This wasn't at all unusual. The owner of an old wooden boat can, if he wishes, spend most of his spare time at this, and Father was fussy about maintenance. The year, probably 1919. Perhaps 1920.

The *Cassiar* had docked and was loading freight and passengers. Immersed in his repair job, Father paid little attention, until there came the hard sound of leather soles on wood. He looked around to see a stranger approach and stop. A cadaverous man, middle-aged, neatly dressed in dark suit and darker tie, a raincoat folded over his left arm. He wore severe-looking rimless glasses and peered through them at the young man rather as if he were examining a bug that was new to him.

"Are you Mr. Hal Hammond?" he asked, in a soft smooth voice.

Father said thoughtfully, "It could be two men you're looking for. One of them's known as Hal; then there's a Mr. Hammond..."

The man regarded him with an icy stare.

"You were pointed out to me as being Mr. Hal Hammond. Now, what kind of foolishness are you up to? Are you, or are you not, he?"

"You look like a government official to me," said Father coolly. "A lawyer friend of mine told me never to admit anything to government officials. But just supposing I was this Hal Hammond, what would you be wanting him for?"

"Lawyers!" sniffed the other contemptuously. "A useful tool but they need watching. As to why I am here, I need transportation and I was told that you could supply it."

"I think," said Father cautiously, "that could be arranged. Just where do you want to go?"

"There is a man called Svendson, who operates, I believe, a logging camp somewhere in the vicinity. I wish to see him on government business. Do you know his whereabouts?"

183

"I know Svendson. He has a camp up in the inlet. I can take you… Take about two hours to get there, though."

Time seemed no worry to the stranger. He agreed readily to the fee, and before long, they were heading up the channel toward Jervis Inlet.

When some time had passed in silence, Father tried a few conversational gambits. They generated only the minimum response. But then the other produced one of his own.

"This Svendson, does he have a profitable business?"

Father considered this, and answered that he really couldn't say.

After a few more tries, the man tried another tack. "A nice boat you have here. Does it bring you much income?"

Some instinct of self-defence stirred in Father's mind, as he hedged, "Oh, I make just enough to pay for fuel and repairs."

The stranger looked dubious. "Then it would not appear to be worthwhile to do it, if that's the case?"

"No," agreed Father blandly, "probably not worthwhile. But it's a living."

There was a long silence as the man turned this over in his mind a few times. His long face assumed the expression of one who has found something in his soup, but hasn't quite decided to call the waiter. He sat there silently, and Father made no more attempts to communicate, so the rest of the trip was made in silence.

At last, Svendson's A-frame came into view, and Father steered in toward it. An A-frame consists of a couple of long trees, usually on a float. They are tied together at the top, but spread wide at the bottom to give stability. Cross braces make it look more or less like an A, and support wires—guy lines—hold it upright. A heavy wire goes from a machine on the float, through a pulley on the peak of the A, and up the sidehill into the woods. Many of the steeper parts of the coast were logged in this way. A-frames can be quite efficient. Svendson's was not one of these.

There was no sign of activity as they eased into the float alongside Svendson's old boat, but as he was tying up, Father saw the man they were looking for appear out of the shed that held the machine. He came across the logs to greet them, wiping his hands on his clothes as he came. Of average build, he was balding, but made up for that with an unusually thick moustache. He wore the usual caulk boots and heavy pants with wide braces, but no shirt, only the grey Stanfield underwear worn by most loggers. This was almost as much hole as cloth, and out of the holes on his chest stuck tufts of hair of the same light brown as that on his lip and scalp. There was black grease smeared on his head and face, and two broad strips of it on his chest where he wiped his hands.

"Hello, Hal." He put out blackened hands. "Guess what I've been doing. Machine's down again." Looking at the man in the expensive suit, he said, "Who's your friend? I'm afraid I'm not hiring at the moment." His eyes twinkled as he almost grinned.

Father, out of his passenger's line of sight, rolled his eyes and shrugged his shoulders eloquently, as the man made his way carefully across the deck of Svendson's boat and onto the big logs of the A-frame float.

Safely there, he said with some dignity, "I assume you are Mr. Svendson? I am not applying for employment, sir. My name is Turner." He held out his hand, but on seeing the state of Svendson's, withdrew it protectively to his pocket. "I represent the government of Canada. To be more specific, the income tax department."

(Income tax had been imposed in 1917 as a wartime measure, with the assurance that it was only temporary. It is said that people actually believed this!)

Svendson withdrew the proffered hand.

"Income tax? What do you mean, income tax?"

"You should know, Mr. Svendson, as a businessman, that you, and all people earning over a certain amount of income, are required to pay a tax on it, as of 1917."

"Ay be not busynessman, ay be logger. Ay make no money, ay pay no tax." Svendson had suddenly acquired an accent. As Father well knew, this was a device that allowed Svendson to misunderstand whenever he chose, and thus give him time to think. He had honed it to a fine point on persistent creditors.

The tax man said patiently, "That may be so, Mr. Svendson, but you must file the papers to prove it. There are no papers filed by you since the tax was imposed. None at all."

Svendson shook his head. "Ay file saws. Ay not file paper. Vat do you mean, file paper?" He squinted his eyes and pursed his lips, which made him look like a caricature Swede.

"Mr. Svendson, I must remind you that this is a serious matter. I am here to audit your books, and to determine how much money you owe the government. Now, show me your office, and we can begin."

"Office?" countered the Swede. "Vot do you tink I am, a doctor? Dere is no office, no books—unless you vant my girlie magazine—and I owe the government notting! Vat has de government done for me, that I should give dem money? Vill you tell me dat, Mr. government man?"

"Why, there is the army to maintain, for one thing. A war is very expensive you know."

"De var is over. For vy do ve need an army? Und dey said de tax vas only till de var vas over."

"Well," said the other firmly, "I'm afraid it's going to last a bit longer. The government needs money to help the country become prosperous. And there's the police, the mail service, the roads..."

"I saw a policeman vunce," mused Svendson, "at a dance. He was drunk. I haf no car, and for de mail, I buy stamps. Und, if de government takes people's money, how can dey be prosperous?"

"But you may want to buy a car, and then there will be roads to drive on."

"Den I vill pay de gas tax, vot is for to build de roads."

By this time, the accountant, having forgotten his original purpose, was now determined to justify his employers. He said earnestly, "Mr. Svendson, you must realize that running a country costs a great deal of money. There are construction works; the parliament buildings, for example. There are a great many government employees who must be paid. People must pay taxes, Mr. Svendson."

But Svendson was having none of it. "By Yeesus, you are right about costing money! Vat do dey need big rock houses for to sit in anyhow. And dere's a lot too many

people vorking for de government should have an honest job, instead of going around bothering oder people vot are trying to earn a living."

This rather low blow had its effect. His opponent flushed, and went on the attack.

"People must pay taxes," he insisted hotly. "You can't just take from the country, Mr. Svendson, you must also give something to it." But Svendson was more than ready for this one.

"I pay stumpage tax on every tree, Mr. Turner, and yust about everyting I buy, the government's got a finger in it somehow. And as for de country, vy vere vould it be witout people like me? De towing boats get vork, de carpenters vot use de vood get vork. Und nailmakers, und hardvare, und everybody. Und vot do I get?" He put a finger in one of the holes in his Stanfields, and out another. "Dese here are my best pair. De other is a bit vorn. And now, ven I make a bit of money to keep, you say dey are going to take some of it away!"

The tax man, taken aback perhaps as much by the decrepit state of Svendson's underwear as by its owner's rebuttal, actually appeared to be sympathetic. "But you should realize, Mr. Svendson, that you are not very likely to have to pay a large amount of tax. In fact, I would estimate that it is not at all likely to exceed ten percent of your net income. You surely must admit that one dollar out of ten is not very much to give for the running of your country."

"It was the wrong thing to say," laughed Father. "Up until now, the talk had been sort of theoretical. Not real, but now it was down to earth; it was real dollars that were coming out of Svendson's pocket. Out of every ten dollars, he was going to lose one, if the tax man was right!"

Svendson blinked with shock. He lost every trace of accent as he said in disbelief, "Ten percent! Ten dollars out of every hundred! Do you mean to stand there and tell me that out of every thousand dollars that I make, they are going to take away one hundred?" As the sums mentioned grew larger, Svendson's voice grew louder, more incredulous.

"Well, not exactly," said the gaunt man in his precise way. "The rate rises with the amount earned—" Then, seeing Svendson's face, he added hastily, "but there is a tax-free minimum, you know."

But Svendson was considering something, and didn't appear to have heard the last bit. "Do you mean to say that some big shot banker that makes a million dollars will have to pay more than a hundred thousand dollars of it to the government?"

The accountant actually smiled at such naiveté, an expression that ill suited his long cadaverous face. "Oh, well, Mr. Svendson. We must be realistic about these things. The wealthy have resources that are not available to people like us."

Svendson nodded thoughtfully. "Yes," he murmured. "I thought so. And what will happen, Mr. tax man, if I don't pay these taxes?"

The other man looked shocked at such a heretical notion. "Why, they will seize your goods, all you own. They will take your machine there, and your logs. You could even go to jail!"

Svendson nodded again, and appeared to come to some decision. "Wait there," he said, with the air of one who has been relieved of a burden. "I'll be right with you. I just have to call my two men."

He turned and went over to the shed, from which a piercing whistle sounded. A shout from up on the hill replied. There was a slight delay, then he reappeared, carrying a battered suitcase. He was now wearing a shirt. "I'll just be a minute. I have to tell the men what's going on, then I'll be ready to go."

"Go, Mr. Svendson? Where are you going?"

"Why, to jail, of course." He waved his hand comprehensively. "She's all yours. Tell the government they can have it, every bit of it. It's not worth a thing. The engine won't run, the lines are shot and the timber's rotten; I've got no money, so I guess it's jail." He seemed quite cheerful about the prospect, rather like someone heading out on a picnic.

"Now, wait a moment, Mr. Svendson. I'm sure you are being too hasty. This isn't at all necessary, you know."

But Svendson had made his mind up.

"I want to go to jail," he insisted. "I need a rest." He held out his hands. "I work my fingers till my hair falls out, and what for? So's someone can take the little bit of money I put by."

"But, ten percent, maybe less, it's not so much to get all excited about."

"Only ten percent, you say. But just look here, Mr. tax man. After a working man has paid for all he needs, about all he has left over is ten percent of what he makes, so what you are asking for is really one hundred percent, and I am not going to pay it!" Svendson's mood had changed. He was now waving his arms and shouting, causing the other to look nervously behind him, making sure of the path back to the boat.

"Take me to jail!" shouted Svendson, red-faced. "I insist you take me to jail. Three meals a day and no worries. A roof that don't leak and no damn engines to break down. I want to go to jail!"

By this time the accountant had made his way across the cluttered deck of Svendson's boat to the comparative safety of Father's. He said, low-voiced but urgently, "Hurry, let's get out of here, the man's gone crazy. You don't know what he might do. Hurry up, he may come after us!"

Svendson was now on the deck of his boat, still shouting that he wanted to go to jail, that the government could have everything.

"Wait for me," he pleaded, as Father shoved off. But he seemed oddly slow in covering the short distance to Father's boat. Then Father shoved the clutch in, and they glided swiftly away as the boat gathered speed. The tax man's back was turned, and he stared resolutely down the inlet to where lay civilization. Father looked back. Svendson was standing on the deck of his boat, waving happily. There was a big grin under the bushy moustache. ◆

Dick Hammond is the author of Tales From Hidden Basin *(Harbour Publishing, 1996).* Svendson and the Tax Man *was excerpted from Dick Hammond's second collection of tales, coming soon from Harbour Publishing.*

Who Shot Estevan Light?
A Traditionalist Returns Fire

by Douglas Hamilton

As summer's dusk settled slowly over the lighthouse at Estevan Point on that memorable night of June 20, 1942, keeper Robert Lally happened to stare out to sea. In the distance, off to the southwest, he made out a "warship zigzagging under heavy smokescreen." The sight was not uncommon during the early days of the war as Canadian naval crews based at Esquimalt frequently trained in these waters. But when the shells began to fly at the big light, Lally realized that this was no training mission. Within minutes of the attack, the keeper had rushed up the 45-metre lighthouse tower and extinguished the powerful beacon. He then stepped out on to the cupola and, from this ringside seat, observed the attack in detail. The shells arrived, at first 500 metres out, then 350, closer and closer. At least six shells landed in front of the light, while others roared over the tower like "freight trains passing over a bridge" and exploded near the Native village of Hesquiat. In all, about seventeen large shells were fired, although some

Looking inland at the Estevan Point light tower. Buildings are painted wartime grey. The fog alarm building is next to the tower and the Lally residence is to the left. *(photo by Robert Lally, circa 1942)*

The evidence suggests that the Japanese submarine *I-26* shelled Estevan Point lighthouse in 1942. The vessel was destroyed near Leyte Gulf in November of 1944 by American Navy planes.

observers later reported as many as twenty-five. Witnesses were unclear as to how many vessels took part in the shelling; many identified the attacker as a large submarine, probably Japanese; some thought they saw other ships as well. There were no injuries and damage was surprisingly slight: only a few windows in the tower were broken by flying debris. The terrified Natives at Hesquiat fled by boat into the protection of Hesquiat harbour. Civilians at the lighthouse were evacuated into the darkening bush in case of a land invasion, while the rest of the staff stolidly remained at their posts.

Fears of a landing party or demolition squad proved groundless: the intruder vanished as silently as he had arrived. Over the next few weeks, authorities examined the evidence, including craters, metal fragments and a dud shell. It was quickly concluded that the fire had come from the 14-cm gun of a Japanese submarine—the first enemy attack on Canadian soil since the War of 1812. Defences at the isolated lighthouse were beefed up and life soon returned to normal there. The matter rested for more than forty years.

Then, in 1985, lightkeeper Donald Graham published *Keepers of the Light*, a book about British Columbia's lighthouses that soon became a classic. In his chapter on the Estevan Point lighthouse, he argued convincingly that the attack had had nothing to do with a Japanese submarine. Some eyewitnesses had claimed that at least two large vessels were conducting the shelling, but Graham ridiculed the notion that the Estevan light was a credible military target for anyone. In fact, he argued that it would actually be an aid to enemy navigators. And how could the "gunners get twenty-five straight misses around that huge 150-foot tower, sticking out like a clay pipe in a shooting gallery?"

Japanese B-1 submarines had a hangar and catapult forward of the conning tower for launching seaplanes. During its 1942 voyage to Vancouver Island, the *I-26* used the hangar to carry supplies instead of a float plane. (*illustration courtesy* Retaliation)

No, it was not the Japanese. Rather, Graham suggested, it was a covert operation undertaken by the federal government (perhaps in collusion with the United States) to unite Canada firmly behind the war effort. Canadian or American warships fired those shells harmlessly to scare the bejesus out of Canadians, and in particular, to wake up those reluctant Québecois and other "lukewarm patriots" to the very real dangers of the deepening war. Shadowy RCMP officers reportedly threatened dismissal or prison terms to any witnesses at Estevan who disputed the official version of the incident. The dud shell bore Japanese ideographs in yellow paint, but according to Graham, the lightkeeper also claimed that English "markings, numerals and whatever" were stamped on the base of the shell. And the entry for June 20, 1942 in Lally's official lightkeeper's logbook has mysteriously disappeared. Even the American intelligence personnel who compiled the official record after the war, using confiscated Japanese documents, felt the sting of Graham's contempt. Commander Yokoda's description of submarine *I-26*'s attack on Estevan was summarily dismissed as a sore loser's evil nonsense: "Yokoda was a questionable confessor at best. There's no more despicable trade in warfare than commanding a submarine. It takes a man with a shrivelled soul to peer through a periscope, put the profile of an unarmed merchant ship on the open sea behind the cross hairs, and order torpedoes away. He can be sure there won't be many survivors."

To cap this argument, Graham pointed out that on June 19, the day before the attack, Parliament was debating a contentious amendment to the 1940 National Mobilization Act which would have permitted conscription. The shelling of Estevan was, he claims, used with great effect by proponents of the amendment, and was instrumental in allowing the bill to pass final reading in July.

This "Great Canadian Conspiracy Theory" soon took on a life of its own. In 1994, CBC-TV aired a segment on "Fifth Estate" that featured Donald Graham. Linden MacIntyre, host of the show, also interviewed two witnesses to the shelling: Myna Peet, then eight years old, and Robert Lally, Jr., about the same age. Then MacIntyre observed: "The Americans even trotted out a submarine commander, Minoru Yokoda, who boasted that he directed the shelling of Estevan Point...For Donald Graham it boils down to a test of credibility. The war stories of a defeated Japanese submarine commander, against the eyewitness account of a lightkeeper with nothing to gain from embellishing what he saw."

It is not surprising that many Canadians believe the attack on Estevan was a grand manipulation, an event staged by agents provocateurs—courtesy of the Canadian government.

Does this hypothesis hold up under careful scrutiny? There is a considerable body of evidence, ignored by both Donald Graham and "Fifth Estate," that a Japanese submarine did attack Estevan lighthouse that night.

A number of daring raids on the west coast of North America were carried out by Japanese submarines in 1942. The effects were minimal, but the attacks represented a serious effort by the Imperial Japanese Navy to cause disruption along the west coast and to sow fear and confusion. Within weeks after the bombing of Pearl Harbor, according to Bert Webber's book *Retaliation: Japanese Attacks and Allied Countermeasures on the Pacific Coast in World War II*, no fewer than nine Japanese submarines had arrived off the west coast to attack shipping vessels moving between the Juan de Fuca Strait and San Diego. Only a handful of cargo ships were sunk before the Allies greatly increased their antisubmarine vigilance. Intense air and ship patrols made life so difficult for the Japanese raiders that military officials in Tokyo decided to take a more drastic step: direct attacks on the coast. On the evening of February 23, 1942, the Imperial Navy submarine *I-17* surfaced off of Santa Barbara, California. Commander Kozo Nishino took the vessel past the resort town and up the Santa Barbara Channel for about 30 kilometres to Ellwood, coming abreast of the Barnsdale Oil Company oil fields at about 7:00 p.m. The sub was only 1.5 km from shore when it lobbed twenty-five 14-cm shells at the oil installations in the space of twenty minutes.

On board *I-17*, the nine-man gun crew under gunnery officer Lieutenant Shimada worked methodically

Built in 1909, the 150-foot Estevan Point lighthouse was not only one of the tallest free-standing concrete structures in the West at the time, but as historian Donald Graham wrote, "the boldest, most beautiful lighthouse in all British Columbia." *(photo by Robert Lally)*

This unexploded 14-cm shell from *I-26* was found in a pile of driftwood after the attack. *(photo courtesy Robert Lally)*

loading, aiming and firing their heavy weapon, while anti-aircraft crews, expecting an air attack at any moment, hovered nervously over two 25-mm machine guns. When the shelling ended, the big sub headed west and slipped silently out to sea. According to Webber's *Retaliation*, US Navy radio operators intercepted a coded report sent to Emperor Hirohito later that night which claimed that Santa Barbara was "a seething mass of flame, with wild panic visible onshore."

Miraculously, damage to the refinery was estimated at only $500. Two dozen oil workers escaped unhurt and no fires were started. A pier, oil derrick and local land values were the only casualties. But fear is quickly contagious, and panic erupted across Los Angeles the next evening as jittery anti-aircraft crews cruised the skies searching for Japanese bombers. On the way home, *I-17* sank two cargo ships within a week. The Allies had their revenge: eighteen months later, on August 19, 1943, *I-17*

met her end off New Caledonia during a running surface battle with a New Zealand minesweeper and two US Navy planes. Out of a crew of ninety-four, six were rescued.

Four months later, according to the *New York Times*, the Imperial Navy shrewdly planned a double hit to achieve maximum psychological effect: Estevan was to be shelled on June 20 by Captain Minoru Yokoda and the crew of *I-26*, and on the next night, Fort Stevens, a US Army fort at the mouth of the Columbia River near Astoria, Oregon, was to be shelled by Meiji Tagami and the crew of *I-25*.

The attack on Estevan was carried out on June 20 as scheduled. The following evening at 11:30 p.m., shells pasted the beach between Fort Stevens and the small vacation community of Seaside, Oregon, leaving seventeen 1.5-m craters. Captain Tagami of *I-25* began firing from an extreme range of 13,000 metres, with a water depth of only 30 m. Because he was using a very old American chart, he mistakenly thought that the fort housed a submarine base. Tagami was also unaware that Battery Russell had the only operational 10-inch (25-cm) guns at Fort Stevens. Fortunately for him they were not pressed into service that night: little damage was done to the base. Nearby residents of Astoria were shaken from their beds by the loud explosions, and hundreds of people watched a spectacular light show far out at sea each time the gun fired. But instead of panicking, most witnesses seemed to revel in the excitement. "The Japs picked a swell place for harmless target practice," one resident commented cheerfully to a reporter. Colonel Doney, spokesman for the US Army, unequivocally blamed a submarine for the attack. He noted that the shell fragments found in the craters had come from high-velocity, low-trajectory shells which appeared to have been fired from several kilometres offshore. The sub drifted or sailed about 5 km during the bombardment. Doney added that an air search for the invader was under way. That search was unsuccessful.

Just hours after the incident in Oregon and barely a day after the shelling at Estevan, Radio Tokyo trumpeted a great naval victory over Canada and America. According to Domei, the official radio news agency of wartime Japan, important military installations in both countries had been destroyed by submarine bombardment, causing dismay and confusion along the entire defence perimeter of the west coast. Citizens from Alaska to Mexico were "panic stricken" by the attacks on Seaside and Estevan, and Canada in particular had been taught a painful lesson. Shelling the lighthouse was but "the first blow at the Canadian mainland…Thus Canada has been shown she is attacked by the Axis navies from the East as well as the West." The story pointed out that Estevan lay very close to Puget Sound and numerous important military bases; more raids should be expected. The attacks were so devastating, said the report, that the Allies would no longer be able to send supplies to Australia, and further air raids on the Japanese mainland were now completely out of the question. Japanese submarines in combination with the

Edward T. Redford found and photographed this unexploded 14-cm shell two weeks after the attack.
(*photo courtesy* Retaliation)

German U-boats in the Atlantic would also cut off supplies to the Russians, thereby preventing the opening of a second front in Europe. These claims were of course inflated into the hyperbole of wartime. But if the attack on Estevan came from Canada's own navy (with the possible help of the Americans), how would the propaganda spin masters at Domei, thousands of miles away, have found out the details so quickly, and used the information with such excellent timing?

The most audacious wartime attacks on North American soil were launched in September 1942. Japanese naval designers had long been fascinated by the idea of a submarine capable of carrying and launching an airplane. The I series, B class submarines used in all of the west coast attacks were very large cruising boats, each with a watertight airplane hangar fore of the conning tower. They were over 105 metres in length, they displaced 3,300 tonnes, and with a range of 25,000 km they could remain at sea for ninety days without servicing. As well, a small float plane provided eyes for the sub (there was no radar on Japan's submarines until much later).

Code-named GLEN by the Allies, the little float plane was a marvel of compactness and ingenuity. The fuselage, wings, floats and fins were detachable and divided into twelve connecting pieces. Flaps and tail folded neatly to fit into the cramped cylindrical hangar fore of the conning tower. Powered by a small 340-hp radial engine, the stubby plane had a top speed of 150 knots and an endurance of about five hours. Its battle load consisted of a small machine gun and two 76-kg bombs—if intercepted, GLEN would have been no match for Allied fighters. Preparation for launching via the compressed air catapult took a tedious hour, as did recovery which was carried out with a special crane located on the foredeck.

Following the attacks on Estevan and Seaside, the two submarines returned to Yokosuka submarine base in Japan for supplies. Then, according to Flight Warrant Officer Nobuo Fujita, *I-25* sailed back to the west coast in early September for what Japan hoped would be the most provocative attacks of all. At dawn on September 9, Fujita loaded two incendiary bombs onto his float plane and catapulted off the deck of *I-25*. Accompanied by petty officer Shoji Okuda, he flew his GLEN low over the well-lighted Oregon coast, dropping his bombs in the large forests 80 km inland near Brookings, Oregon. An alert forest ranger noticed the mysterious dawn raider, with an engine that sounded like a "Model A Ford hitting on three cylinders." He quickly located and doused the flames. When the float plane returned to the waiting sub, it was taken aboard just in time. An American A-29 Hudson bomber with British markings had sighted *I-25*; it dove and straddled the vessel with 135-kg bombs. *I-25* was severely shaken, but only lightly damaged.

Three weeks later Fujita repeated his air attack 18 km east of Port Orford, Oregon at around midnight. There is no confirmation that the bombs even exploded, and no fires spread into the damp underbrush. Fujita, who had experienced the Doolittle bombing raid firsthand in April 1942, later recalled: "That pilot had bombed my homeland for its first time. Now I was bombing his. It gave me great satisfaction." On their return flight, the aviators were led astray by a malfunctioning compass.

> Suddenly I remembered our compass trouble after the Sidney [Australia] reconnaissance. I pulled the Zero [not to be confused with the famous Zero fighter] into a quick turn, and headed directly for the Cape Blanco lighthouse. It could mean interception, but I didn't care. At least I could then die gloriously, crashing into an enemy plane. I might even dive into the lighthouse. Anything, to do the enemy damage through my death, and make it mean something, rather than just waiting for death to find me.

Instead, at the last minute, the two crew members decided to try once more to rendezvous 40 km offshore. Fortunately *I-25* was leaking a streak of oil, which led them to the sub and thus saved their lives.

For some months after the Port Orford incident, the Americans remained puzzled about the little float plane. Almost all civilians of Japanese descent had been interned in resettlement camps in the distant interior;

there was concern that some had been missed. Could the GLEN have been launched from one of the countless lakes in the Pacific Northwest—final proof of a fifth column of Japanese traitors loose on the mainland? Weeks of hard slogging through the bush produced no results. A searcher reported: "We found beautiful mountains, beautiful lakes, good fishing, tall wonderful trees, and mosquitoes and sore, wet feet. We didn't find any Japs." On July 11, 1943, *I-25* was sunk in the Solomon Islands by the American destroyer USS *Taylor*.

Since the first wave of doubt immediately after the Santa Barbara/Fort Stevens shellings and Fujita's bombings, no one has suggested that they were anything other than the work of Japanese submarines. The evidence on both sides of the Pacific is irrefutable. It should not be so

Minoru Yokoda, commander of *I-26*, remembers the night of the attack: "Because of the dark, our gun crew had difficulty in making the shots effective. At first the shells were way too short—not reaching the shore. I remember vividly my yelling at them, 'Raise the gun! Raise the gun!'"
(photo courtesy Retaliation*)*

difficult to believe that the very similar attack on Estevan was also made by the Imperial Navy—especially when veteran Japanese submariners themselves confirm it. In researching *Retaliation*, author Bert Webber made every effort to contact surviving Japanese submariners in the early 1970s and to get them to talk about the war. Most of them had been killed in battle, and some of those who survived were reluctant to talk about their experiences because western writers had misquoted them and treated them with contempt. But Webber did interview several retired Japanese submariners, including Commander Minoru Yokoda of *I-26*, who remained silent until 1973. But his memory of the Estevan shelling was still clear.

> It was evening when I shelled the area with about 17 shots. Because of the dark, our gun crew had difficulty in making the shots effective. At first the shells were way too short—not reaching shore. I remember vividly my yelling at them, Raise the gun! Raise the gun! to shoot at a higher angle. Then the shells went too far over the little community toward the hilly area. Even out at sea we could hear the pigs squealing as shells exploded. [Yokoda may have heard harbour seals, which bark, bray, hoot and bellow when disturbed.] As I watched from the *I-26*, the people were very quick to put out the lights in the buildings but the lighthouse was slow to respond—the last light to turn off.

There is no "boasting" in this fascinating account, as Donald Graham suggests. On the contrary, the mission was a great disappointment to the Japanese commander, as he freely admitted. "There was not a single effective hit that night," he said. Similar stories were told by Nubuo Fujita and Commander Meiji Tagami of *I-25*, among others, and details of their stories have been corroborated by surviving crew members.

The Great Canadian Conspiracy theorists have glossed over or ignored other inconsistencies. First, the Estevan lighthouse was no small mom-and-pop operation in 1942. On the night of the shelling, there were twenty-two people at the isolated outpost—seventeen of them staff. The *New York Times* described Estevan as "one of the largest radio centers on the coast." It housed a telegraph, weather centre, lighthouse and powerful radio station to co-ordinate shipping throughout the north Pacific. The *Victoria Daily Times* observed: "The irony of the shelling of Estevan lies in the fact that for the past 30 peacetime years the Estevan radio station has been giving complete radio services broadcasting weather conditions and handling air traffic generally for Japanese steamships which before the war were regularly operating in the trans-Pacific route."

In fact, Estevan was an excellent military target, and the real question is why Canadian authorities had failed to realize this earlier and provide it with more protection.

Second, if the shelling of Estevan had been an elaborate setup designed to garner support for the war, local governments would have been informed of the ploy and would have made a big fuss over it. But just the opposite was true. After two days of headlines, the matter almost disappeared from view in both Canada and the USA. The mayor of Victoria remarked a day after the attack, "I haven't noticed any change in the people's demeanor…no one is jittery. Why should they be over a nuisance raid such as Estevan or Seaside?" When BC Premier John Hart was asked by reporters if he would issue a message calling for calm, he tartly responded, "No one has the jitters and it would be ridiculous to suggest they needed such a message." Even the *Toronto Globe and Mail* played it down. "This first attack on Canadian soil failed to cause any great excitement on the West Coast made war conscious recently by the sinking of a United States merchant ship off Neah Bay just fifty-nine miles west of Victoria and by the landing of Japanese forces in the outer fringe of the Aleutian Islands far to the northwest." The page two headline declared: Japs' Shelling Held Harmless. Even Prime Minister Mackenzie King seemed more concerned about the fall of the north African fortress of Tobruk than about Estevan. On June 23 he commented: "It is as critical a situation in the Middle East as has arisen since the war commenced. And there have been other evidences in the past forty-eight hours that in this world-encircling conflict Canada is coming more and more into the zone of immediate danger."

Third, the war was going disastrously for the Allies in the early summer of 1942. Tobruk fell to General Irwin Rommel on the same day as the Estevan incident. Twenty-five thousand British soldiers were taken prisoner along with mountains of supplies—enough to keep the Afrika Korps plentifully supplied for almost a year. In Russia, the German steamroller was driving deep into the south. The huge fortress of Sebastopol in the Crimea fell on July 3, after a siege of 250 days—with a loss of more than 100,000 Russian soldiers and thousands of tanks and guns. The Don River was breached the next day, and on July 7, Voronezh surrendered. In the Atlantic, German U-boats were sinking vital convoy ships many times faster then they could be built. In 1942 alone, more than 1,500 ships with a gross tonnage of 6,226,215 were lost to submarines—while U-boat operational strength in the Atlantic surged from 91 to 212. Winston Churchill later wrote, "The U-boat attack of 1942 was our worst evil." In the Pacific, the Japanese occupied Attu, Kiska and Aggatu in the Aleutians by early June, and seemed poised to strike both Alaska and northern British Columbia. With all of this very genuine bad news, there was really no need for any Canadian or American government to stage a phony attack on Estevan.

An interesting question does remain. How does one explain the sightings of several vessels acting in concert off Estevan that night? For days after the shellings, the Allies combed the seas for a "surface raider" or two submarines, which were never found. The observers' stories varied—on the west coast, visibility at dusk in misty June is notoriously poor, and Robert Lally, a key witness, had no binoculars. Contrary to what was reported by both Donald Graham and "Fifth Estate," most of the eyewitnesses reported only a single submarine in the deepening dusk. According to Edward T. Redford, the experienced Officer in Charge, who had lost an arm in World War I:

The submarine surfaced about two miles off shore and was plainly visible. Shelling commenced at approximately 9:40 p.m. and con-

tinued for about 40 minutes. The first shells landed on the beach about 100 yards [90 m] in front of the lighthouse. Mr. Lally, who was the lightkeeper at the time, immediately put out the light. The sub apparently then raised its sights, for from then on the shells went overhead...The submarine pulled out on the surface and everyone could see her and hear the diesel engines quite clearly. While naturally there was some nervousness, everyone, including women and children, took the whole incident in their stride, then spent the following day souvenir hunting.

Captain James L. Detwiler of HMCS *San Tomas* later interviewed a Native woman from Hesquiat. "She was sincere," he reported, "and tried to make me understand that she knew the difference between a whale and a boat. She said that she first thought it was a whale, but when it didn't splash or 'blow' she knew it was a boat." Mrs. Lally, wife of the lightkeeper, had this to say:

Canadian warships passed the lighthouse almost daily. I saw two early in the morning of the shelling, so the sound of gunfire that night didn't bother me. I thought it was target practice. I was just putting the youngest of the children to bed when the first shell exploded on the beach. "That's pretty poor shooting! It came pretty close," I yelled to my husband who had just come down from turning on the lighthouse for the night. "Get the hell out of here! It's a Jap sub and they are shelling the lighthouse!" my husband Mike shouted back. More shells sailed overhead.

All of the eyewitness accounts that night must be taken with a grain of salt. Visibility was just too poor, and the imagination can play strange tricks in times of stress—particularly when events are recalled years later. The spectacular light show produced by the submarine's 14-cm gun, as well as her large and noisy presence, may well have impaired the witnesses' ability to observe events coolly and objectively. Certainly there was a wide variety of conflicting accounts of that exciting evening.

The five submarine attacks on North America demonstrated the weaknesses as well as the strengths of the Imperial Navy's submarine service. Navigating those thousands of kilometres of trackless Pacific expanse for months at a time, launching and recovering float planes at night, and evading endless searches demanded courage, discipline and competence. Yet nothing of importance was accomplished. The attacks were too sporadic and too far apart to make much of an impression—and the marksmanship was abysmal. No doubt the Japanese were hopeful of creating the same kind of sensation that Doolittle's B-25 bombing raid had generated in Japan. But as the war deteriorated for the Japanese, their subs were called back to protect her navy in the home islands; by September 1942, they had left our Pacific coasts forever. Many ended up as supply vessels serving

The night watch. Robert Lally was lightkeeper at Estevan Point the night of the shelling. (*photo by Robert Lally*)

isolated island garrisons in the Pacific. The clear and shallow waters surrounding these islands provided little protection for large submarines. Most were soon lost, and the morale of the Imperial submarine service plummeted.

The Japanese never learned to use their submarines as effectively as other countries during the war. The military also grossly underestimated the danger of Allied submarine fleets and paid a heavy price because of that error in judgement. Half of Japan's maritime tonnage lost was to submarines. American and German submariners sank anything that could carry a cargo, but the Japanese never developed the submarine "wolfpack" hunting technique essential for systematic destruction of the Allies' commerce fleet. After 1942, the huge volume of cargo vessels running between the mainland and the Pacific war zone was left almost untouched.

Instead, the Imperial Navy concentrated its strategic thinking on capital warships.

Japanese submarine commanders were given a strict priority list of what to attack—carriers first, battleships second, cruisers third, and so on. Merchant ships could only be targeted if there was no other warship in the area. There were even stipulations on how many torpedoes could be expended on each type of target. Fire everything if you faced a battleship, three at a cruiser and only one at a cargo vessel.

Bushido, the Samurai code of honour, may well have been a factor in these policies. Bushido taught that it was morally wrong to attack noncombatants randomly. War was fought between warriors who were expected never to surrender and to die for their cause if necessary. Blowing a helpless cargo carrier to kingdom come simply did not fit in with this code of ethics.

Interestingly, Bushido may have also played a role in the selection of west coast targets in 1942. After the war ended, Captain Ryonosuka Imamura, Secretary to the Japanese Naval Ministry, was asked why more populated targets had not been chosen. He replied, "You ask why we didn't shell some coastal United States city rather than Fort Stevens and [the] Santa Barbara oil tanks. At Santa Barbara it was our decision to shell oil tanks because we felt them important war assets. So it was with Fort Stevens. We didn't use these attacks to terrorize your people, but to strike war blows."

There can be little doubt that a Japanese submarine attacked the Estevan complex in June 1942. In his appearance on "Fifth Estate," Donald Graham argued convincingly that in wartime, governments manipulate and even create news for propaganda purposes. Two good examples are the phony Gulf of Tonkin incident in 1964, and stories of Iraqi soldiers removing Kuwaiti babies from maternity wards in 1990. But the theory that the Estevan shelling was nothing more than a setup cannot be supported by the evidence: physical traces, eyewitness accounts, submariners' stories and information on other Japanese military activities in the Pacific all contradict the theory.

And so does Canadian history. Graham's contention that the attack played a major role in the conscription

The lightstation circa 1950. Note that the wartime gray has been replaced with the striking white and bright red paint we see today.

debate is a weak one. The ambiguous results of the conscription plebiscite held on April 27, 1942 led Prime Minister Mackenzie King to waffle and delay any action for as long as possible. "Not necessarily conscription, but conscription if necessary" neatly defined (or obscured) the issue. Every Canadian male over age sixteen had to register for national service, but only volunteers were sent to the front. Not until 1944, when the Allies suffered heavy losses in Italy and France did King send the "Zombies" (the new recruits) to fight overseas.

Canadians today feel resentful and suspicious of our federal government. Who can blame them? Unemployment is alarmingly high in some regions, services are being cut back, national unity seems unachievable, the smell of corruption wafts through many official transactions. West coast lightkeepers themselves have never been treated with proper respect, and now the Canadian government has judged that many of their invaluable services can be replaced by machines and computers. But to extrapolate from state misdeeds that an act of war was staged by the government is to make a serious mistake.

No one can know every detail of what happened at Estevan Point on June 20, 1942. But the evidence shows that there was no political conspiracy: a Japanese submarine attacked Estevan, as well as four other sites on the west coast of North America during the spring and summer of 1942.◆

Sources

Fujita, Nobuo and Joseph D. Harrington. "I bombed the U.S.A.," in US Naval Institute Proceedings, June 1961, pp. 64–69.

Graham, Donald. *Keepers of the Light*. Madeira Park, BC: Harbour Publishing, 1985.

New York Times, June 22, 1942, p. 9.

Toronto Globe and Mail, June 22, 1942, p. 1.

Victoria Daily Colonist, June 22, 1942, p. 5.

Victoria Daily Times, June 22, 1942, p. 1.

Webber, Bert. *Retaliation: Japanese Attacks and Allied Countermeasures on the Pacific Coast in World War II*, Corvallis: Oregon State University Press, 1975.

Webber, Bert. *Silent Siege III: Japanese Attacks on North America in World War II*. Medford, Oregon: Webb Research Group, 1997.

Light at the End of the World
Three Months on Cape St. James, 1941

by Hallvard Dahlie

In August 1786, the French explorer Comte de la Perouse sighted the southernmost tip of what is now the Queen Charlotte Islands and named it Cap Hector. The following year, Captain George Dixon saw it on St. James Day (July 25) and renamed it Cape St. James. He also named the island chain, the Queen Charlotte Islands, after his ship.

A lightstation was established on the cape in 1912–13, and for the next eighty years the island was occupied. It was an isolated outpost, and when the mission ship Thomas Crosby III *visited in 1926, the keeper's wife, Mrs. Lawrence, had not seen another woman for five years! The cape was, and is, one of the windiest spots on the BC coast: in 1985, the anemometer was pegged, recording gusts of over 190 km/hr.*

During the Second World War, just after this story takes place, the site served as one of a chain of early warning radar stations along the BC coast. From the summer of 1942 until the end of the war, up to seventy-five Air Force personnel at a time could be housed in a variety of buildings constructed on every flat bit of rock.

The station was turned over to the Meteorological Branch as a weather station in 1957, and in 1992, the light and weather station were automated and the cape was destaffed. Keeping with government policy, all structures were demolished.

—courtesy Jas. A.C. Derham-Reid, Meteorological Branch, Cape St. James, 1986–1992

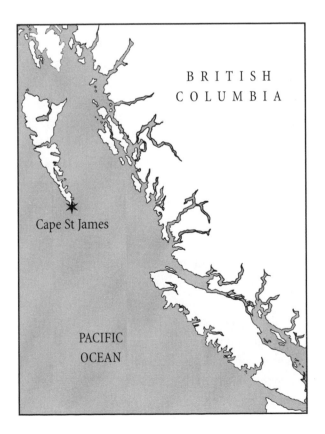

A strange interlude in my brief seafaring life took place in the fall of 1941, when I signed on as assistant lighthouse keeper at Cape St. James, a light perched on top of a three-hundred-foot rock at the very southern tip of the Queen Charlotte Islands. I had quit school earlier that year, at the age of sixteen, and found a job on the CGS *Alberni*, a lighthouse tender operating out of Prince Rupert. But when she had to go into dry-dock at the beginning of September for a new wartime grey paint job and a bit of refurbishing, I chose to take a stint out at the lighthouse rather than scrape barnacles and paint for three months.

From a trip to the Cape earlier that summer, I knew full well how bleak and totally isolated this place was, and as we crossed Hecate Strait to anchor in the deserted

An aerial view of Cape St. James, spring 1941, just before Hallvard Dahlie arrived for his three-month stint as assistant keeper. *(courtesy Jas. A.C. Derham-Reid)*

whaling station of Jedway, I wondered what I had let myself in for. I remembered stories told by one of our deckhands about former keepers. One of them lived there with his companion, a gargantuan woman who hoarded all the food and released small amounts in exchange for sex, until finally starvation overcame his dwindling passion and he chased her out of the house with an axe. Then there was the story about the keeper who had gone mad one day and painted all the rooms in the house a bright marine red—walls and ceilings alike. These stories may have been exaggerated or fanciful, but they always reminded me of the lines from Gibson's "Flannan Isle," one of the few poems I had liked back in grade nine:

> And how the rock had been the death
> Of many a likely lad—
> How six had come to a sudden end
> And three had gone stark mad.

So, as the *Alberni* rounded the last headland of Kunghit Island the next morning, and I saw the tower looming out of the haze, my stomach sank as it came home to me that this is where I was to live, with a complete stranger, for the next three months or so. There was certainly no way to escape from it, for the high rock on which the tower and dwelling were perched was separated from Kunghit Island by a narrow strait. Here the waters of the Pacific and of Hecate Strait met in a steady, roaring maelstrom that must be impossible to cross, and in every other direction there was nothing but open sea.

The captain had assured me that the present keeper, a Newfoundlander by the name of Herb Fitzgerald, was a kind and gentle fellow. But what would I do, I wondered, as we rowed in toward the landing, if he should suddenly go mad? Or if he was a bit fruity, like the chief steward I had worked under for a while on the *Alberni*?

I had seen the keeper briefly on that earlier trip as he checked over the supplies we were unloading from the workboat, but I hadn't talked to him or looked all that closely at him. What I did remember was that he talked all the time, not to anyone in particular, but just talked, as though he had stored up a horde of words for a long time, and now had a chance to release them. As we rowed back to the *Alberni*, my rowing mate had said, "Look at that poor bugger, going back up to that tower all by himself." There he was, climbing slowly up the long tramway, stooped over and limping a bit, steadying himself by holding on to the steel cable, and never once turning to look back at us, as though seeing us depart would confirm something he didn't want to acknowledge.

And now he was busy loading supplies onto the tram car as I stood apart from him at the end of the jetty, watching my mates row back to the *Alberni*. The workboat rose high on the crest of a towering wave that had banked off the rocks, then disappeared into a deep trough, with only the head, shoulders and arms of Second Mate MacKay visible as he stood in the stern controlling the steering oar. "Ye'll be all right," he had comforted me in his soft Scottish burr as they prepared to shove off. "I've known old Herb here for some while now, and he's a right decent fellow. He'll do nothing to harm you, and we'll be back to pick you up in early December." With that, I was struck by the full realization of my abandonment. I waved frantically as the workboat reappeared on the next crest, but no one noticed me, and the boat disappeared around the rock bluff.

All this time I had been vaguely aware of a chattering going on behind me, and now Herb's voice came more clearly. "We'd better get a move on and get these supplies up, for it could be storming soon," he was saying, straightening up from belaying a support rope around the cleats of the loaded tram car. "The glass was falling when I left the house, and storms come up awfully fast around here. We'll come down later for the two fuel drums and the sacks of coal, but I don't want our food to get wet."

He had come down from the dwelling just as we arrived at the jetty, and when MacKay introduced me, he looked surprised, as though he were expecting an older person. He was a tall, thin, grey-haired man with a slight stoop and a mouth that looked as though it was always grinning—which disconcerted me at first, for I thought he was always laughing at me, even when he was talking, which was most of the time.

"I didn't know you were coming today," he had explained, rattling on to MacKay, "and I was sound asleep when your damn whistle woke me up. I was up all bloody night running the foghorn as well as tending the light, and I didn't sleep hardly at all, so when there was no fog at daylight when I put out the light I thought I might as well sleep for a while because it isn't that often I can sleep that long around here, and then that damn whistle woke me up and by the time I started the gas engine and got the tram car down you guys were damn

Sixteen-year-old Hallvard Dahlie at Prince Rupert in 1941. "I chose to take a stint out at the lighthouse rather than scrape barnacles and paint for three months."

near in to the jetty already," and he went on and on, just barely stopping when MacKay told him I was to join him for the next three months.

And though he was puffing heavily as we walked up the long tramway, he kept talking all the way up, even when we stopped to rest so he could catch his breath. In fact, that first day he stopped only when he fell asleep. Even then I thought I heard some sounds coming from his room upstairs, but perhaps it was only the first of many strange noises I was to hear in that house. His sharp blue eyes pierced into mine as he spoke, as though he was afraid I might try to escape; fascinated by him and somewhat afraid, I don't think I said more than a dozen words to him that first day. I remembered parts of Coleridge's poem, for it intrigued me in much the same way that "Flannan Isle" did, and like the Ancient Mariner, old Herb held me "with his glittering eye" and I could not "choose but hear," for there was no escape.

There were, however, a number of specific tasks to learn and to do that first day, and here Herb was efficiency itself, wasting not a word or a motion. He showed me how to start the gas engine in the shed on top of the tramway and how to release and rewind the cable, so we spent a couple of hours hauling up the fuel drums, sacks of coal and remaining supplies. He demonstrated the operation of the foghorn, and most exciting to me, he showed me how to operate the light itself, situated in the concrete tower about a hundred and fifty feet beyond the house, at the very highest point of our rocky island.

"There are two things you must never allow to happen at a lighthouse," he told me as we headed for the tower. "Never let the light burn during daylight hours, and never let the light stop revolving during darkness, for both of these are signals of distress. Any ship that observes these conditions has to come in and check or radio someone for help, for they mean an emergency of sorts at the light." He pulled open the heavy metal door and motioned me in ahead of him. "And if it isn't an emergency, but just a case of our own carelessness, we really catch hell from the Department of Transport. I heard of a keeper down at one of the southern lights who got fired for being careless twice, so we can't afford to make any mistakes."

The ground level area of the tower was dark and

Bleak and remote, Cape St. James light is perched on top of a three-hundred-foot rock. The lightkeeper's house is to the left of the light. Note the tramway and boat landing. *(courtesy Jas. A.C. Derham-Reid)*

cold and damp, and in its hollowness Herb's voice ricocheted off the concrete walls as we climbed the steel steps to the next level. "This is what they call the Fresnel system," he explained as he went up ahead of me, "and up here on the second level is where we keep the fuel tanks and winding mechanism. I'll show you how to operate these in a minute, but let's go up to the top level first, where I'll explain the light itself and the kind of work we have to do during the day."

We climbed the second set of steel stairs, and I was dazzled by the sudden light as I reached the upper level. For here there was nothing but glass—huge curved panels around the circumference of the tower top and massive prisms enclosing the light itself, and the late afternoon sun bathed everything in a brilliant translucence. Herb explained how the prisms gather the light produced by the mantles and concentrate it into a strong ray that passes through the central eye of the prisms, producing the powerful beam that revolves at a certain speed. "Every light on the coast revolves at a different speed," he continued, "so if a captain has to check his position, and can get a glimpse of a light, he can check his directory of lights and figure out where he is. That's why it's so important for us to keep these prisms absolutely clean, and all this surrounding glass, too, on both the inside and outside," and he opened a hinged glass panel so we could step out onto the surrounding catwalk.

"It's not bad out here when it's fairly calm, like today," he said, grabbing the handrail and staring out over the sea, "but sometimes the damn wind almost blows you off as you're washing these panels, so you have to be careful. Believe it or not, in the big storms we get out here, I've seen the spray from the waves blow right up and drench these windows."

I looked down at the ocean, four hundred feet straight below the west side of the tower, and even on this relatively windless day, could see the billowing waves washing high up the side of the cliffs. I scanned the sea in all directions and far off to the west thought I saw a smudge of smoke. But I couldn't be sure; it could have been a cloud or just a mirage. There was nothing else in any direction, and I realized that if we did run into any trouble out here, it could be ages before any help arrived. Off the south shore of our island was a narrow spit of rocks jutting into the sea, on which I saw movement.

"Them's sea lions," Herb explained, following my gaze. "There's thousands of them, it seems, and you should hear the noise they make if something disturbs them. You'd think it was a bunch of babies howling, and in the middle of the night it can really give you a fright.

But let's go back in, and I'll show you how to light the lamp and keep it revolving."

The lamp mechanism was really quite simple, consisting of two rather large mantles, much like the kind we had on our gas lamps back on the homestead, but it was fuelled by kerosene rather than gas, kept in tanks on the second level. Beside the tanks was a drum with a winding mechanism and a thin wire cable wound tightly around it, whose end was attached to a heavy weight. "As soon as you light the lamp," Herb explained carefully, "you have to come straight down here and release this catch so that the weight starts slowly unwinding the cable, which revolves the drum, which in turn through this set of gears rotates the light." All that seemed pretty clear, but Herb went through the whole process again, so I paid close attention, thinking of his earlier warning about carelessness. "And we have to be sure to get up here every two hours to rewind the drum and pump up the pressure in these tanks, otherwise everything will come to a stop. I'll come up with you tonight and watch you light the lamp, and make sure you do everything the right way, but after tonight you're on your own, okay?"

So that's how our routine was set up: I was to take the first shift, from six to midnight, then I would wake Herb and go to bed. Herb would extinguish the light at daybreak, and if there wasn't any fog, he would go to bed for a couple of hours. Then we'd have our breakfast and go about our routines of the day.

It was a ridiculously large house that the two of us occupied, built perhaps in the expectation that lightkeepers would sire many children, but the only large family I saw that summer was over at Triple Island, and that seemed to be the exception. Here there were some thirteen rooms on two floors, a half basement, and a large covered verandah along the south wall where the main entrance was. The front room had two large windows looking out on this porch and a smaller window on the west wall, through which we could see the tower. The kitchen had one large window looking out to the east and north, and as I waited for Herb to come down for breakfast each morning, I would sit at the kitchen table looking out this window and scanning the coast along the east side of Kunghit Island for any sign of a ship, though I knew that the *Alberni* wouldn't be along until early December.

"See anything yet, laddie?" were always the first words Herb said, his mouth turned up into more of a grin than usual, and he repeated these words every day that I was there, though as we got closer to December, I thought his grin seemed less pronounced. He was always partially dressed when he came downstairs, carrying his checkered lumberjack shirt, his heavy black trousers held up over his winter underwear by a pair of bright red suspenders. He would yawn as he peered out the window for a moment, brushing back his thinning grey hair with quick strokes of his hand, then disappear into a small washroom off the back of the kitchen, where we stored our barrel of rainwater for washing and cooking.

The house had no plumbing of any sort, and we took baths in the same galvanized washtub we used for our laundry, rare as either of these activities was. I can't remember Herb ever washing his black trousers—by the end of my stay I'm sure they could stand by themselves—and I wasn't much better. My bed had two sheets and a pillowcase and I would reverse top and bottom sheets, then turn them over and repeat the routine, turn my pillow over when one side got unbearably dirty, then turn it inside out and repeat that routine. All this was done before any washing, and I felt pretty proud of my ingenuity.

And we had a precarious outhouse, the likes of which I had seen only once before, set at the very edge of a cliff beside a prospector's shack up in the mountains above my home town in the interior of BC. But because of the constant winds at Cape St. James, this one seemed even more risky. It was perched on the edge of a ravine a hundred feet or so from our back door and anchored with heavy cables to four concrete-embedded eye bolts. We could look through the hole straight down a couple of hundred feet to where the ravine angled out sharply to a rock outcropping. Sitting there as the roaring winds shook and buffeted this structure was an absolute assurance against constipation.

Off the west wall of the kitchen was a small cubbyhole, sort of like a pantry, with a chair and a small counter that served as a desk. Because we had only a coal oil lamp for light, it was in that room where we passed the long hours of the night, reading whatever we found in some boxes of old books and magazines an earlier keeper had left behind. This room had one long, narrow window whose blind I always pulled down at night, because it was sort of scary to see my reflection looking back at me from outside, the glass distorting my face and head as though my hair was standing straight up.

With the wind almost always howling, the house itself creaked and groaned, with noises seeming to come from all thirteen rooms, or from somewhere outside. I would step out of the cubbyhole into the darkness of the kitchen, hardly breathing, my heart pumping furiously, as I tried to assure myself that there was nothing to be afraid of. But what were those footsteps? Was it old Herb walking about directly over my head? No, his room was at the other end of the house, so I thought about the keeper with the axe, and the madman who painted the rooms red, and I thought of "Flannan Isle" and wondered, was I going mad, too? Then the noises died away and I tiptoed back into my little well-lit room, trying to find comfort in the pile of magazines I had already thumbed through countless times, magazines like *Liberty*, *Mechanics Illustrated* and a 1938 issue of *Life* that showed Chamberlain returning from Munich and what I kept turning back to, an exposé of a Greenwich Village artist's model in various stages of undress.

Then my blood froze, for I heard someone out on the front porch, knocking on the window—or rather, sort of scratching on the windowpanes. I thought stupidly, why don't they knock on the door? I moved silently to my little doorway, the lamp behind me throwing an enormous shadow on the kitchen wall, then I tiptoed cautiously and nervously to the door that led into the front room, from where I could look out the windows to the porch. I yelled in unmitigated panic, for there, up against the window, all dressed in white, was a figure waving its arms and bouncing up and down, as though trying to find a way to get in. I could see him—or it— because the lantern we carried to the tower stood lighted on the porch, but I didn't think I could be seen, for I was in darkness, and that gave me some courage. Then something else took over in my mind and said, there can't be anyone out there, we're on an isolated rock hundreds of miles from any settlement, so where would anybody come from? And old Herb is sound asleep upstairs. And then I said to myself, of course, old Herb, and that white figure out on the porch immediately and with a stomach-filling relief transformed itself into Herb's winter underwear that he had washed that afternoon and hung on the line to dry, now frozen stiff by the icy winds.

It took me some time to work up enough nerve to go out to the porch for the lantern and make my way up to the dark tower and tend the light, a scary enough task without all this extra fear.

That was probably the longest night I spent in that house, and when I woke Herb, he said, "Did I hear someone yell during the night, or was I dreaming again? I have the damnedest dreams about this place." I told him he must have been dreaming, but he looked at me in a funny way, his grin more enigmatic than usual.

In that little cubbyhole, too, we kept our battery-operated radio on which, every morning at nine o'clock

"I yelled in unmitigated panic, for there, up against the window, all dressed in white, was a figure waving its arms and bouncing up and down, as though trying to find a way to get in." *(illustration by Alistair Anderson)*

sharp, we received our daily instructions from the Department of Transport office in Victoria. These instructions were always read by the same person, whom I visualized as a rather frail old man, dressed in tweeds, with a pointed beard and thin lips that barely opened as he read, for the message would come through in a somewhat pinched and shaky tone: "Attention all lightkeepers on the Pacific Coast. Here are your instructions for today. Carry out instructions 'A for Apple.' I repeat, to all lightkeepers on the Pacific Coast, carry out instructions 'A for Apple.' This is the end of today's message."

There would be a bit of crackling static as the gentleman turned off the microphone, and we would immediately shut off the radio, for we knew that the C battery would not last forever and Herb always liked to listen to the six o'clock news before going to bed.

"A for Apple," Herb told me, meant that we were to carry out normal operations for the light and foghorn, and these instructions didn't change the whole time I was there. "If you ever hear instructions 'B for Butter'," he explained, "that means that an enemy is approaching the coast in ships or submarines, and then we can't have the light or any signals operating." That sounded far more exciting to me, but it never happened while I was there. But as things turned out, if I had stayed one day longer, then 'B for Butter' would have been the order of the day, for the *Alberni* came to pick me up the day before Pearl Harbor.

To be more accurate, I should have said that the "A for Apple" message came not for as long as I was there, but as long as the radio's C battery lasted, and I remember precisely the day it died for it was largely my fault. I had always been a baseball fan and it hadn't been that long since my hero, Johnny van der Meer, had pitched two no-hit games in a row for the Cincinnati Reds. Now here it was October, World Series time.

So, in spite of Herb's injunction to keep the radio off except for the news, I would surreptitiously turn it on after he had gone to bed, with the volume on low, to hear as much of the Yankees–Dodgers series as I could. I heard parts of games two and three, but the weakening battery had made each broadcast increasingly faint.

Then, on the fifth day of October, I was listening to game four with my ear pressed hard against the speaker, and it was two out in the ninth for the Yankees, with Brooklyn leading four to three. "It's a swing and a miss for strike three!" I barely heard the announcer say, and then his voice rose in excitement, helping to compensate for the dying battery. "The catcher dropped the ball! Mickey Owen dropped the ball, and Heinrich is running to—" And that is all I heard, for at that moment the battery went absolutely dead, and no amount of coaxing could bring it back to life. I had no idea, until the *Alberni* came two months later, what had happened in the rest of that game or who won the World Series.

The days went by very quickly at first as the novelty of the place kept me intrigued, then more slowly as I waited for the *Alberni* to return. For Herb, all the days must have gone by too quickly. That first evening we had reached a unanimous decision, on the evidence of the meal Herb had prepared, that I would be cook, and his spirits had lifted visibly. "I'm so damn fed up with macaroni and canned tomatoes," he complained, as I looked with some misgivings at the gooey red and white mixture on my plate, "that it won't matter what you prepare, it's bound to be an improvement."

We had countless cans of powdered milk and I was good at making porridge, so that was our breakfast every morning, along with bread and jam and strong coffee. Herb had ordered generous quantities of chops, cutlets, ham steaks and other meat cuts that we stored in the basement, so our dinners didn't stray much from the meat and potatoes variety, which suited both of us. Dessert was no problem, for Herb had ordered two or three cases of his favourite, canned pineapple, but one rainy day I thought I would surprise him with a change—I cooked a rice and raisin pudding. What I hadn't realized was how uncontrollably rice would multiply when cooked, so for a few days we had to forgo the pineapple. I baked bread on two or three occasions, and once I made a batch of oatmeal cookies that not even the dampness of the whole Pacific Ocean could prevent from setting like concrete.

Our other tasks we organized according to the weather, and on the few fine days we had, we spent much of the time gathering firewood, for we had to use our coal sparingly. We picked up pieces of driftwood along the rocky shoreline, hauled them up on the tram car, then cut them into suitable pieces with a Swede saw and axe and stored them in the lean-to off the kitchen. The tide and wind normally brought in a large supply of driftwood every day, but once after a horrendous storm that lasted an entire day and night, we searched in vain. Every stick of wood, and even huge logs that had been wedged behind rocks far up the steep slopes, had been dislodged and carried out to sea.

When we felt we needed a break from this heavy work, we launched Herb's small clinker-built rowboat to try our luck at fishing. Herb would deftly manipulate the boat into suitable spots and I would jig off the stern and usually catch one or two rock cod or red snapper. On one of these fishing trips, a whale surfaced close to our boat, then dived toward us and came up directly underneath us, lifting our small boat almost clear of the water. If Herb had not moved quickly to wallop it with his oar, we would certainly have capsized, and the whale's wide tail flapped dangerously close to us as it shot away like a giant silvery dark arrow toward the swirling current of the narrow strait.

We were always careful in these dangerous waters to stay close to our shore, but one day the sea was unusually calm so we rowed across the strait to Kunghit Island and pulled our boat up on its sandy shore. All around us we found green glass balls, transparent and beautiful, ranging from baseball size to something two or three times the size of a basketball. "These are Japanese fishing floats," Herb explained, "broken free from their nets somewhere out there," and he pointed his thumb toward the west. I wondered if they had floated all the way from Japan, or if they were harbingers of something closer to our shores. But like intruders coming upon some secret cache of treasures, we left them where we found them and headed back to our own island against a stiffening wind.

And one warm, windless Sunday afternoon we were up on the catwalk cleaning the windows of the tower, with Herb talking as much as ever, when over his voice I heard the sound of something else, like an engine, get-

ting louder very quickly—and suddenly we ducked. For coming straight at us from the north, and only fifty feet or so above the tower, was a seaplane, dipping its wings in some kind of crazy salute. It dived down the south side of the island, sending hundreds of squealing, terrified sea lions off the rocks, and then it circled out to sea and came back for a landing in toward our jetty. We had seen the pilot waving at us as he roared past, and we saw the RCAF insignia on the wings and body, so we assumed it was from the air base at Alliford Bay, up at the north end of Moresby Island.

I was quite excited about seeing someone else after all this time, and we hurried down off the tower to go to meet them. My imagination ran wild: Japanese fishing floats, radio going dead—had something happened that we didn't know about? Or were they coming to get me, or perhaps they had a message from my family, for I hadn't seen my mother before I came out here, but had only left a note on the kitchen table: "Have gone out to Cape St. James for three months. Will be back in early December. Don't worry." As we waited at the top of the tramway for them to appear, Herb told me about a German fellow who was a keeper over at Ivory Island during the first war, and who was fired for being a security threat. "Maybe they think you're German instead of Norwegian," he joked, "and they're coming out to check on you!"

But it wasn't nearly that dramatic. The crew was simply out on a routine patrol, had seen us up on the tower and decided on the spur of the moment to drop in on us and present us with a fresh salmon they had caught earlier that day on the west coast of Moresby. They stayed for a half hour or so, had some coffee and a couple of my concrete cookies, then took off up the east coast of Kunghit Island, leaving us to silence and ourselves. It was a welcome visit nevertheless, reminding us that we weren't totally forgotten by the rest of the world after all.

But that Sunday was the last warm day of the fall, and the gloomy days passed slowly after that. The steady rain and wind kept us indoors most of the time, and the decreasing visibility made me feel more trapped and isolated than ever. Herb tried to lift my spirits one afternoon

The light tower at Cape St. James, circa 1957. *(courtesy Jas. A.C. Derham-Reid)*

by giving me a haircut, but he was unpractised and the scissors were dull, so what resulted was a straight line across the back of my head, a series of jagged steps up each side, just missing my ears, then a straight cut across the front that made me look like Ella Cinders. "Will you do mine now?" he asked when he had finished, and I said, "Sure, how do you want it cut?" and he said, "Off." So that's what I did, and for the next little while I don't think either one of us looked in the mirror much.

One morning in early December, Herb slept in longer than usual. I had finished eating my porridge and put the lid back on the pot to keep his warm, and was on my second cup of coffee before he came down. For once he didn't look out the window or say "See anything yet, laddie?" but went straight to the washroom. It was a gloomy morning, with clouds hanging low over Kunghit Island, and I had seen nothing in the hour or so I had been waiting for him. But when he came out of the washroom, cleanly shaven and washed, and dressed in his black trousers and checkered shirt, he said, "Well, today's the day. I feel it in my bones, and besides, I had a dream last night about a ship running aground on those rocks where all the sea lions are, so that must mean something. Maybe they need you back as quartermaster to steer the damn thing!" His grin lit up his face momentarily as he sat down and vigorously stirred his coffee, but his actions all seemed forced that morning. As I cleaned up the kitchen, he sat at the table, slumped over, just staring out the window, seemingly at nothing.

Sure enough, his bones were right. Just before lunch I detected a grey shape coming around the headland of Kunghit Island, barely visible through the haze and rain. It was still too far away to determine whether it was the *Alberni*, and I didn't want to get my hopes up too soon, so I didn't look out again until I had prepared lunch and put it on the table. When I looked again there was no doubt, even though she was now all grey from stem to stern, where before her superstructure had been white and yellow. If nothing else, the huge balloon of black smoke from her funnel gave her away, for only coal-

burners produced such a volume of smoke, and the *Alberni* hadn't yet converted to oil.

I was excited at the prospect of rejoining the crew, but I didn't know what I should say to Herb, who scarcely touched his lunch, saying he wasn't very hungry because he had had a late breakfast. He got up quickly from the table, grabbed his rain slicker and said, without looking at me, "I'd better go out and start the gas engine. You'd better pack your things to send down on the tram car, because they'll be rowing in within the hour."

He knew full well that I didn't have much to pack, only a duffel bag full of dirty clothes, but I knew he wanted to be alone for a while, so I packed slowly, folding each garment carefully, then stripped the bed and swept out my room. I put the two sheets and the pillowcase in a tub of cold rain water in the washroom, where only a miracle soap could ever make them white again. Then I stood in the kitchen and took a last look around, a bit smug, I suppose, over the fact that I had come through these last three months quite unchanged, except for my haircut.

But I couldn't forget how I sat terrified in that little cubbyhole off the kitchen night after night, so afraid at the thought of having to walk up to that dark tower, flickering lantern in hand, not knowing what I might meet behind that heavy door. And then climbing the clanging steps up to the second level to pump up the tank and wind the weight mechanism, lifting the lantern above me to place it on the landing before I stuck my head up, in case there was something there. I remembered how one night, not long after Herb's underwear almost incapacitated me, the long blind on the tall, narrow window suddenly shot up without warning and I leaped out of my chair, paralyzed with fear, seeing my white face in the window staring back at me. No, there were things about Cape St. James lighthouse that I would not miss, and roused out of my memories by a loud, prolonged blast of the *Alberni*'s whistle, I put on my rain gear, grabbed my duffel bag, and went out to join Herb. ◆

Claus Carl Daniel Botel
West Coast Patriarch

by Ruth Botel

Claus Botel was born in 1868 in Schleswig/Holstein, located near the Danish border in northern Germany. He was a farmer like his father before him, and he and his wife raised a large family on a farm with horses, dairy cows and a generous kitchen garden. The income from the farm was not sufficient to support the household and Claus supplemented the farm income by working with his horse and wagon to fill in the approaches of the new railway bridge over the Keil Canal, and by catching poisonous snakes in the fields.

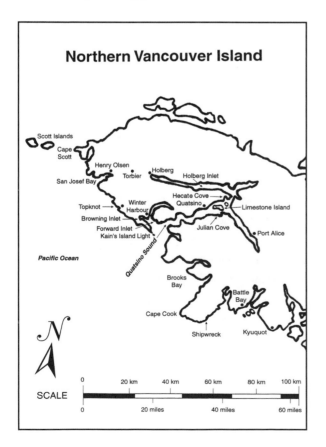

Northern Vancouver Island

He pinned the snakes down with a long forked stick, then kept them in a sack or bottle and sold them to the local pharmacist or chemist, who used the venom for medicinal purposes. The family had a large, comfortable home with a slate roof, brick walls and oak beams. They owned the farm and had no debts.

But times were bleak in Germany in the years preceding World War One, and it became harder and harder to make a living. Claus was very worried about the future. He had seen a number of glowing advertisements about Canada in the newspapers—ads placed by the Canadian government, which was encouraging Europeans to come to this land of milk and honey. The advertisements told of generous grants of free land to those who came and settled. There were opportunities unlimited and jobs galore. In addition, the Canadian Pacific Railway promised free freight and transportation, once they were in Canada, to the nearest point of call to the family's grant. Claus's father and brother had already moved to North America.

Claus Botel studied maps of Canada and decided to look for a homestead in British Columbia, on Canada's west coast. He sold the farm and made the necessary arrangements. On April 9, 1913, the family—consisting of Claus, six children from his first marriage (the three older ones were out on their own), his wife Martha, her two children and their one-year-old son Gustav—departed from the port of Hamburg, Germany on the ship the *President Lincoln*. Martha was eight months pregnant. Besides paying for his own entourage of two adults and nine children, Claus paid another couple's way to Canada. (They repaid the money forty years later.) The journey to Canada took eleven days. They landed in Halifax on April 20, 1913.

After the lengthy procedure of going through customs and medical checks, the family boarded a train which would take them through the United States, then up to Vancouver. The plan was to visit briefly with Claus's father Hans, and his brother and wife, John and Marie, in Omaha, Nebraska.

On April 27, as Claus and Martha rode the train through the Wenatchee Valley in Washington, their baby was born in the passenger car, on one of the hard wooden seats. Claus assisted his wife, whose long voluminous skirts gave her the only privacy to be had during the birth. The family arrived in Vancouver, BC on April 29 and stayed overnight. The next day they headed for Victoria to apply for a homestead.

At the parliament buildings, someone was found to interpret for the Botel family, and a pre-emption of 160 acres was selected for them. They were told that this parcel of land was situated in a nice protected bay on the beautiful west coast of Vancouver Island, not far from Quatsino Sound. Here, they were informed, they could start a farm. A railway would be built nearby in the not too distant future, making it easier to get their supplies in and the produce out. In the meantime they could ship their produce out by boat. The family was enthusiastic about the parcel of land, eager to find it and get settled.

Sixteen-year-old John, the oldest of the children, decided to stay in Victoria and look for employment. They said their goodbyes and the rest of the Botel family boarded the 165-foot CPR boat the SS *Tees*.

The journey up the west coast of the island lasted five days. They put into little settlements along the way, dropping off passengers and freight. Finally they reached Quatsino Sound, then proceeded up the sound to the Botels' dropping-off point, the small wharf at Quiet Cove on Drake Island (then called Limestone Island). As the large family left the boat, having no idea where their homestead was or how to get there, the captain's parting words were: "You're on your own now."

Claus managed to find someone who understood and spoke German, and he arranged for a man named Sorenson to load his family and their belongings onto

Claus Botel with daughter Johanna in 1925.

his boat and take them to Holberg. It was late at night when they arrived at the dock, so the Botels—including Martha and the newborn Wenatchee—bedded down on the rough, cold floor of the freight shed.

The next morning, the family started on their long hike to San Josef Bay and the west coast of the island, where they understood they would find their homestead. The family consisted of Claus, aged forty-five; Martha, thirty; Anna, fourteen; Helene, eleven; Max, nine; Emma, seven; Willy, five; Willi Hecht, seven; Erna Hecht, four; Claus Jr., one; and baby Wenatchee, a week and a half old. The older ones helped the little ones along the trail bordered by alders, high salmonberry bushes and thick salal. They carried all their worldly possessions, including two feather mattresses and a pretty set of china dinnerware.

They reached Torbier's, just below Ronning's, the first day. Mr. Torbier spoke German. The family was exhausted and slept well that night. Up early the next day, they resumed their trek. They reached the mouth of the San Josef River and looked out on a long, wide bay of sparkling water bordered by white sandy beaches stretching out on both sides. Beyond this vista they could see the distant Pacific Ocean. They paused here to drink in the welcome sight, mother and father resting briefly while the children laughed and played and raced about making tracks in the sand.

It was suppertime when the exhausted group reached Henry Ohlsen's homestead, which included the store and post office of the small, remote community of San Josef. Claus and Martha were thankful to have found another family who understood German. The Ohlsen family prepared supper for the Botels and made a corner of their barn comfortable for them to spend the night.

The next morning, Henry Ohlsen and Claus went to seek out the Botel family's homestead, and found the land, fronted by sandy beach, about ten miles south down the rugged coast. Two weeks later the family set out, cutting their own trail through the evergreens of the Pacific rainforest and the extremely dense mossy underbrush and salal.

The pre-emption was at Top Knot—no neighbours for miles. There was some protection from the north and east winds but absolutely none from the south and west. The Botels had the unceasing roar of the ocean surf literally in their front yard, and during storms the noise was deafening.

Immediately the family commenced clearing. At first they had a tent, but it was blown away during a strong southwester a few days after their arrival. Next they built a drafty home from driftwood and weathered planks they found on the beach. Long shakes were made for the walls of the one-room cabin, short shakes for the roof. That first home blew over in a strong wind so they built another. This one had stronger supports, and it was farther up the beach where a sandbank and some tall evergreens gave better protection from the strong winds.

The garden was another priority. Potatoes and turnips were planted as land was cleared and soil was prepared. Come harvest time, these vegetables were excellent. The potato crop was bountiful, the other veg-

etables large and solid. When the turnips were cut open, the syrup literally dripped out.

Clearing the monster spruce and hemlock trees, some of them six to seven feet in diameter, was a mammoth undertaking. To remove some of them, Claus dug down under the main roots, cleared spaces and lit fires there as well as around the base of the tree. The children were kept busy feeding these fires. Sometimes it took up to two weeks of constant burning to bring a tree down. When the tree was finally down, Claus took his little bow saw, brought from Germany, and sawed the limbs into usable lengths. The new bucking saw was used on the massive trunk. With the hammer and the back of the axe, wooden wedges were driven into the sawed-up lengths to split them into manageable pieces, which the children stacked. All this activity gave the Botels a good supply of fuel for cooking, keeping warm and clearing the next trees.

When the family was somewhat settled in, Claus took two of the children, Max and Helene, with him and went to the Ohlsen homestead in hopes of purchasing a cow and calf. Henry Ohlsen was away, but his mother sold the Botels a Holstein cow named Bessy, a yearling steer and a calf. Bessy was young Violet Ohlsen's cow and Violet cried when the Botels took her away. As it turned out, Bessy did not live long. The trail which Claus and the boys had hacked out of the wilderness was crude— too crude for the animals. The cow and the steer each broke a leg and were butchered on the spot. The little heifer was packed back to the homestead on Claus's shoulders. He and his children made trips back and forth to pack home the meat, which was eventually salted down and stored.

Later Claus made another trip and bought a bull and a calf. This time it took a month to get the animals home—as they made their way along the trail, Claus and the children cut out every large root and windfall, making the path safe for the animals.

By the end of that first summer, the family knew they needed to have a boat. Claus took Max and Helene with him and went to buy a boat he had heard was for sale. He took the last of their money from the sale of the property in Germany. The three of them walked the twenty miles through the bush to Holberg, borrowed a skiff and rowed from Holberg to Winter Harbour, a distance of 50 miles. There, Claus bought a twenty-six-foot, round-bottomed cannery skiff. He transferred to it the sack of flour they'd bought at Holberg, a small sail, their meagre remaining supplies and his old gun (a relic from his term of service in the German forces). The winds were strong when they were ready to depart from Winter Harbour. They got as far as the lagoon in Browning Creek, then stopped at a little old shack on the point of the southwest side to wait for better weather. It was almost two weeks before they could make the journey home. While they waited, Claus and the kids trekked through the lagoon's marshes every day, often scaring up ducks and geese. Claus tried to bag a few of the birds without any success.

Finally a favourable day dawned and the eager trio set out for home. They hoped to be able to use the sail some of the time and give their arms a rest from rowing, although none of them had ever sailed before. They travelled down Browning Inlet and out Forward Inlet to Kains Island. Passing Kains Island, they found themselves on the rolling swells of the open Pacific Ocean, with no islands or bays for protection.

As they headed north toward home, a strong north wind came up and quickly built in intensity. The seas heaved higher and higher as the wind rose, and gallons of spray were whipped off the crests and splashed into the boat. As the weather deteriorated, the children bailed constantly while their father did his best to keep them afloat. The wind blew them far out to sea and eventually they lost sight of land. The storm continued

This photo, taken at the Botel's original homestead at Top Knot in the 1940s, shows Claus Botel's stepson, Willi Hecht, at his trapline cabin built with remnants of the original homestead building. Note the pole braces used to support the cabin in big blows.

the rest of the day. They had no idea where they were or in what direction lay the land. The exhausted children bailed all night long.

Finally, toward morning, the wind subsided. Claus still had no idea in which direction to row and the sail had blown away hours ago. All three were soaked, frightened, exhausted and cold. They took turns rowing just to keep warm. Claus waited for daybreak and then, knowing that the sun came up from where the land lay, they headed in that direction. It was evening when they stumbled ashore, happy to feel land under their feet.

They had no idea where they were as they climbed up the rocky shore. The children, in their excitement, forgot their fatigue. Once they got their land legs, they ran here and there scouting the bushline. Just as it was

Raccoons and a cougar skin are part of the bounty from Willi's trapline, circa 1945.

getting dark, they found an old cabin, belonging to Natives from Kyuquot. Inside, on the dirt floor, the exhausted father and children gave silent thanks that they were still alive, curled up together for warmth and fell into a heavy sleep.

While they slept, southeast gales came up, building a mountainous sea. At high tide the powerful storm grabbed the Botel's little skiff and destroyed it completely on the rocks. Luckily they had removed the damp bag of flour and their old axe, but the gun and the ammunition, left in the boat, were gone.

Day dawned and three hearts sank when they saw the scattered wreckage of the boat. Still, refreshed from their much-needed sleep, they began to explore their surroundings. It wasn't long before they spotted a small shake shack at the edge of the bush. It was a Shelter Shed, one of several sheds erected by the federal government in strategic places along the coast, to provide shelter for shipwrecked sailors. Each shed was stocked with

maps, charts and information in several languages. They learned that they were approximately forty miles from Top Knot, and in the lee of Cape Cook. The instructions said that an able-bodied man could walk to Quatsino in twenty-four hours.

The bedraggled, hungry trio packed up a small tent they found in the shed and set off at a fast pace. For two days they trekked the shoreline, stopping to rest by creeks, drinking their fill and then pressing on. As night fell they pitched the tent under the trees and curled up, watching the beam of light from Kains Island lighthouse. In the middle of the second night, a gale came up and tore the tent away, sending it up into the bushes farther along the beach and ripping it badly. Claus assessed their situation the next morning. After two days of walking they had only made it around the cape and could see into Brooks Bay. It seemed hopeless to go on. Disappointed, their enthusiasm gone, they headed back toward the Shelter Shed. On the way, they found their gun washed up on the beach. They picked it up and carried it with them, although it was of little use without ammunition.

What thoughts must have gone through Claus's mind as he trudged over the rocks and sand with his ten- and twelve-year-old children? They'd been away three weeks now. How were his wife Martha and fifteen-year-old Anna managing with the six young children? Was there enough food? Had they begun to fear the worst. Claus's thoughts must certainly have turned to the comfortable home and farm he had left in Germany. Money had been scarce, but there wasn't a shortage of food, the land was cleared and everyone spoke his language.

Back at the Shelter Shed, they read the list of instructions again and learned that if stranded people kept three fires going on the beach, any passing ship would be alerted to send in a boat to investigate and to pick them up. Luckily Claus had a few dry matches in a water-tight brass container which he always carried in his pocket. He, Max and Helene lit the three fires and kept them burning for quite a few days. Keeping the fires stoked must have kept the three of them busy and warm as they ran about hunting for wood and throwing it on the burning piles. Twice during this time they saw the lights of passing ships, but no boat came in.

As the days went by, food became a problem. The Botels basically lived off the land and the shallow water, and when there was nothing else, Claus dipped into his sack of flour and made flour soup. Definitely not tasty, but it put something into three hungry stomachs. One day they spied a hawk flying toward them with a duck in its talons. Grabbing up handfuls of rocks, they chased the hawk all over the beach, pelting it with rocks. The hawk couldn't fly out of reach with its heavy load and one or two rocks hit their mark. At last the bird relinquished its meal and the Botels feasted on bonfire-roasted duck for supper. Another day, several red cod floated up on the beach. Claus figured there was a longliner fishing off the face of the cape, too far away to be seen, and that the crew was shaking off the red cod because they couldn't sell them. Max found some old dried-up fish skins in the shack. He cut them into thin strips with his pocket knife, and tied them together to make two fishing lines. He found some wire which he shaped into hooks, and he and Helene broke some mussels off the rocks and, using the meat for bait, the two of them went fishing off the rocks. They caught little rock cod, shiners and bullheads, which they cleaned and roasted in the fires. Much tastier than flour soup!

Children John, Willy and Max, circa 1919.

They slept in the Kyuquot's shack because it had a dirt floor, and they could keep a fire burning there all night.

Some time into their stay, the Botels started making a canoe, with just a dull old axe and no real idea of how to proceed. Otto Botel, a son born several years later, says it's a damn good thing that they never finished it as it wouldn't have been very seaworthy and there's a good chance the three of them would have drowned.

Finally, after four weeks, help came. The Kyuquot Indians noticed the smoke from the fires and, thinking someone could be burning down their trapping cabin, decided to investigate.

What a frightening sight it was to Max and Helene when they saw the Natives approaching in their large cedar war canoe! They gestured and hollered unintelligible words as they swiftly came ashore, and the children ran as fast as they could into the shelter of the forest and hid. They were sure, after hearing so many stories in Germany, that they would end up in the stew pot if caught. Meanwhile, the Kyuquot realized no one was harming their cabin, and they approached Claus and tried to talk to him. Of course Claus didn't understand their words, but he knew they were friendly and he tried

talking the kids out of the bush. It took a great deal of convincing before they would venture back out on the beach.

The Indians took them to their camp in Battle Bay that night, and treated the shipwrecked Botels exceptionally well. For supper, there was a feast of spring salmon steaks, and later a ceremony in which young Helene was made an honorary Indian princess. The family of three were given their own cabin to sleep in and real blankets on beds. What a change from their rustic beach existence!

The next day, after another ride in the war canoes, which the children enjoyed enormously, they were taken to Kyuquot. The storekeeper there gave the family some work and a shed to sleep in. They got their meals and a little cash as well. By the time the next passenger/freight ship arrived on its trip up the coast from Victoria, the Botels had enough money to pay their fares to Holberg. Imagine their surprise when they saw Claus's son John standing on deck, looking over the rail, as the boat pulled into the dock. After doing a few odd jobs in Victoria, he had decided to rejoin the family. There was no shortage of stories to be exchanged as the boat pulled out of Kyuquot and headed up Quatsino Sound.

The tired, happy group arrived home two months after they had left on their short journey to get the skiff. By then, the rest of the family had given up hope for their safe return. They had managed to feed and care for themselves. One day, after the trio had been gone for a long time and the family had been hungry for several days, Martha took the axe out of the corner of the cabin saying "a person has to eat," and with Anna's help, she butchered the cow.

The family stayed at Top Knot for five years, and through the whole time, getting enough to eat was a big challenge. They

Claus and daughter Beatrice at Julian Cove circa 1946.

lived on what the land and local water could supply—mussels and clams from the beaches, wild game and berries from the woods, a little fish from the ocean and vegetables from their garden. They were always broke. Once in a long while, they were able to sell some of their excellent potatoes and were thankful to get ninety cents for a hundred pounds. With the start of World War One, Claus was classed as an enemy alien and unable to get a job anywhere because of it. The government even sent out a man to pick up Claus's gun. The Botels and some of their neighbours in the San Josef Valley convinced the fellow that the gun was a necessity, that they needed it for protection and for food. Reluctantly, he left the gun with them.

The family checked the beaches regularly while they were at play or at work. Again and again, the ocean cast up usable objects. It was a real bonanza when chunks of paraffin were found. They made candles using string for wicks and tubes of bull kelp for molds. One year, a load of California redwood railway ties washed ashore. The family set to work and built a small cabin for the older kids to sleep in. This made for a little bit more space for Martha, Claus and the younger children in the original cabin, which even then was not roomy.

Sometimes, at night, the family heard wolves howling. It made their skin creep, although they never had problems with wolves. But, cougars were occasionally a bother. One day a cougar took a chicken, and when Claus spotted it heading up a nearby tree, he quickly grabbed his gun and shot the animal. Another time, when the family was rising in the morning, they discovered the bull standing wild-eyed and snorting at the back door. They followed the bull's tracks to his favourite sleeping spot under a tree on the sandy beach. There was a massive area of scuffed-up sand, criss-crossed with bull and

Martha and Claus, circa 1950.

cougar tracks. The cougar tracks led to a tree, from which the cougar must have leaped down onto the bull. About thirty feet away from evidence of the scuffle were a set of cougar prints made by an animal leaping away in a hurry—probably with some help from the bull.

The Botels' daughter Anneliese, born in March 1916 at Top Knot, was the only child born in the five years the family spent at this remote wilderness spot. Martha had had one or two other pregnancies which terminated early, probably due to the very arduous way of life.

The family left Top Knot in 1918. The war was over, and Claus was no longer barred from seeking

Of Carl and Martha's eight surviving children, six got together for a reunion in 1994. Front row (l to r) Claus Botel (born 1912), Anneliese Hole (1916), Helene Sorenson (1902, died 1995). Back row (l to r) Alice Arnet (1918), Johanna Strom (1925), Otto Botel (1920). The two missing survivors are Beatrice Kondrat (1923) and Anna Howich (1898). Anna died at the age of 99 in 1998.
(photo courtesy Marilyn Patterson)

employment because of his enemy alien status. The family needed more money and Claus hoped to find employment in Quatsino Sound. It is likely they were also tired of the isolation and the unending struggle to live in the wilderness.

They transported some of their belongings by rowing them out in a dory. They may also have used Captain Peterson's boat, the *Cape Scott*, with which he did the mail run from Quatsino to San Josef Bay, Sea Otter Cove and Cape Scott. The family went first to Winter Harbour. They stayed for a few months in a cabin by the creek, on the east shore across from the present settlement. Next they moved to Hecate Cove in the Quatsino area and lived in a house belonging to a man named Gill, a pio-

neer of Quatsino who had returned to his homeland. During the three years the Botels lived there, two children were born, Alice in 1918 and Otto in 1920.

Claus and the two older boys, John and Max, found jobs in Port Alice helping to clear the mill site. When the work was done, they were presented with a gift—the cookhouse. It was a very large building and the condition of the gift was that it had to be moved away. The boys and their dad took the building apart. They bought a small boat, which seemed large at the time, and transported the lumber to Julian Cove, south of Drake Island. There they built a house, and the family moved to Julian Cove in the fall of 1921. It was their first nice-sized home since leaving Germany.

The soil was fertile and they grew an abundance of produce. All the family worked the garden and hay fields—including the girls, who managed fine when the fellows were away. Claus made their hay rakes and other tools whenever possible. He also made all their furniture—beds, dressers, a desk, benches and a table. Out of an old oil drum he fashioned a wood stove. When the soles of the family's gumboots were worn through, he made soles out of alder wood and attached the tops of the old gumboots. There weren't enough pairs of boots to go around, so they were shared. When the weather allowed it, the children went barefoot.

Claus and the boys found more work driving piles for the booming grounds at Holberg. Max, John and Claus started beachcombing logs, gathering them into booms of logs and selling them. With their earnings, they bought a Fordson 24-hp donkey—the first gas-powered donkey engine in Quatsino Sound. They built an A-frame and float, and took the donkey out instead of hand-logging. This method was much more productive.

Beatrice was born in 1923 and the Botels' last child, Johanna, was born in 1925. In 1936 Claus decided to move the family to Hecate Cove, where a large piece of land was available. Martha balked. She finally had a nice home and didn't want to leave it. Claus thought it over and decided they could both have what they wanted—they would take the house with them when they moved. He and the boys, with a great deal of labour, put the home on a raft, towed it to Hecate Cove and moved it up onto the land.

Claus then bought another boat and did some commercial fishing, delivering his catches in Winter Harbour. Max, John and Willy joined him. At home they sold beef, eggs and vegetables from the garden. Claus made homemade beer which he sold and traded on the side. The family still kept the hay fields at Julian Cove active and brought the hay home to Hecate Cove for the animals.

In 1946, at the age of seventy-eight, Claus broke his leg. It never healed properly, and he was on crutches until he died at eighty-five, in 1953.

During his lifetime, Claus had supported and helped raise the nine children of his first marriage, the two children of Martha's and the eight children they had together. The family's lives were mostly all work and no play. Claus's children remember some very, very tough times during their growing-up years. But all the children, girls and boys alike, grew up to be wilderness survivors who could always make do with what they had. They were excellent fishermen, hunters, trappers and gardeners, and a couple of them were good boatbuilders. They were all able to repair almost anything and did not have to be dependent on others, yet they have always been willing to help others. Their father was a strong, determined, practical man who believed in hard work and self-reliance. He could be a hard and obstinate driver, yet they also remember him as an honest man with a twinkle in his eye. ◆

Booting the Big Ones Home
Log Barging on the BC Coast, 1922–1998

by David R. Conn

Since the turn of the century, getting logs from upcoast camps to southern mills has been a major task of the forest and towing industries in British Columbia. Log booms got the job done in sheltered waters, and Davis rafts (giant floating bundles of logs) in more exposed waters, but at a cost—logs were damaged and lost. Salt, sinkage, marine borers and storms all took their toll.

As logging operations moved farther upcoast from the southern sawmills, log barges gradually replaced Davis rafts for moving logs out of camps north of Johnstone Strait. Pioneering efforts at log barging began as early as 1922, when marine engineer Bill Ballantyne drew up plans for a towed vessel, resembling a military landing craft, to carry three quarters of a million board feet of timber. The barge was never built.

The 453-foot *Seaspan Forester* (formerly *Island Forester*) is the largest log barge in the world, with a capacity of 4 million board feet. *(photo courtesy Seaspan)*

Laid-up sailing ships and war surplus wooden steamer hulls, called Ferris hulls, could be bought cheaply during the 1920s, and BC logging operators took advantage of that situation. *Drumrock*, a steel barque, was converted by Captain Barney Johnson of Hecate Straits Towing, and the Gibson brothers converted *Black Wolf*, a Ferris hull, to be towed by the *Lorne*.

According to W.G. Crisp, who worked on her conversion in 1924, the 329-foot *Drumrock* was the first

to put his new vessel on a run to the Queen Charlotte Islands and load spruce logs for Vancouver mills.

When the steam tug *Masset* arrived at English Bay, its crew was quick to note the large military number 13 still on *Bingamon*'s bow, and the men convinced Wingate that some work with a can of black paint was needed to improve prospects for the trip. Bill Ballantyne, who was engineer of the *Masset*, settled the discussion by saying, "You want to get there, don't you?"

Laid-up sailing ships and war surplus wooden steamer hulls could be bought cheaply during the 1920s. The 329-foot steel barque *Drumrock* was BC's first self-loading log barge. During the conversion, her four steel masts were shortened, but the lower yards were retained to support cargo booms. Each mast had a winch installed at its base. Logs were loaded through enlarged deck hatches.
(photo courtesy Vancouver Maritime Museum)

self-loading log barge. Captain Johnson had apprenticed on square-riggers like her and he hired tradesmen to alter the venerable barque to his specifications. The four steel masts were shortened, but the lower yards were retained to support cargo booms. Each mast had a winch installed at its base to load logs through enlarged deck hatches.

About the same time, Captain Walter Wingate bought a surplus steamer hull in Seattle and had it towed to Vancouver. Wingate contracted with Burrard Dry Dock to mount a 30-ton capacity derrick on rails along the hatches of the 268-foot *Bingamon*. The captain decided

The *Masset* hooked up the *Bingamon* and headed north. All went well, until two days later when tug and tow were halfway across Queen Charlotte Sound. It was blowing hard, and a series of red flares went up from the barge. As the hull pitched up and down, the travelling crane slid wildly fore and aft along the deck rails. Wingate and his bargees chased it back and forth with the lashing-down gear they had forgotten to install before leaving. The tug crew finally got *Bingamon* into *Masset*'s lee, and the crane was duly secured.

A little later, while bucking a full gale in Hecate Strait, *Masset*'s water tank burst and flooded the engine room. Tug and tow were forced to run before the wind. Then, off Triple Island, the towline parted. *Masset* struggled into Prince Rupert to get repairs, while *Bingamon* drifted into a cove near Barren Island, where the crew dropped anchor.

The vessels were reunited and finally reached Cumshewa Inlet, where *Bingamon* loaded nearly a million board feet of spruce logs. Just as the loading was completed, the crane boom collapsed. Returning south with the loaded hull in tow, *Masset* ran low on coal and barely made Vancouver. It was not an auspicious beginning for log barging, but mariners were still learning how to work with this new type of operation.

Log barges were subject to the same risks as other vessels operating along the west coast, and some were damaged or lost. *Black Wolf* hit a rock in Slingsby Channel and sank in 1926. *Drumrock* broke her back on an uncharted reef in Smith Inlet in 1927. *Bingamon* burned to the waterline near Nootka in 1928, and was towed to Victoria to be scrapped.

In his book *Bull of the Woods*, Gordon Gibson recounted the spontaneous conversion of the five-masted auxiliary schooner *Malahat* for log hauling in 1936. She had already had a colourful career, since World War One had turned the international shipping industry on its head. Built from non-strategic local softwood, the 246-foot *Malahat* and her sisters carried valuable BC lumber to desperate overseas buyers under canvas, saving precious fuel. As soon as the war ended, the big schooners became obsolete. Coal-belching steamships again took over carrying export lumber, and *Malahat* was a white elephant. She made her postwar living as a rumrunner and operated for months at a time in international waters beyond the US territorial limit. She was a mother ship, loaded with thousands of cases of liquor, which other ships and speedboats carried to the coast to be smuggled ashore. The Gibson brothers actually bought the schooner to get spare engine parts for another vessel in their haywire fleet.

While sailing her to the Charlottes in 1936, the Gibsons had some of their loggers cut out the 'tween deck beams, which created sufficient room to load the logs but weakened the ship. On arrival at Cumshewa, the crew discovered the logs awaiting them were too heavy to hoist and too long for the cargo hatches. They decided to chop down one mast and open up a 50-foot hatch, using axes and crosscut saws. The hired captain objected, so the project was completed while he was asleep. The Gibsons also built a heavy-lift cargo boom on the spot, to load 40-ton logs.

Log barges were subject to the same risks as other vessels operating along the west coast, and some were damaged or lost. In 1926, *Black Wolf* hit a rock in Slingsby Channel and sank. *(photo courtesy Vancouver Maritime Museum)*

For a time, *Malahat* was the only self-propelled, self-loading, self-unloading log vessel in the world. Later the Gibsons removed her semi-diesel engines and more masts, reducing her to a barge towed by their converted tugs. *Malahat* finally ended her career off Barkley Sound in 1944, when a deckload of spruce logs broke loose and pounded on her bulwarks, opening the hull seams.

Following a career as an offshore lumber carrier and later as a rumrunner, the 246-foot, five-masted auxiliary schooner *Malahat* was purchased by the Gibson brothers in 1936 and converted to a log carrier. For a time she was the only self-propelled, self-loading, self-unloading log vessel in the world. When this photo was taken, the Gibsons had removed her semi-diesel engines and all but two of her masts, reducing her to a barge that had to be towed by tugs. *(photo courtesy Vancouver Maritime Museum)*

Log barging offered advantages over the cumbersome Davis rafts. Barges could be towed more quickly and in heavier weather, supplying logs to the mills year round. Rafts couldn't be used during storms, when tugs and tows had to run for shelter and wait—sometimes for weeks—until the weather moderated.

On the other hand, old hulls carrying logs could be unseaworthy when lacking hatch covers, complete decks or bulkheads. Their capacity was small, loading logs through deck hatches was inefficient, log cargoes damaged wooden hulls, and crews were needed aboard to load and to steer while under tow. Clearly there was

room to improve the log barge concept.

After World War Two, a new fleet of surplus vessels was available, and this helped BC towing and forest companies move ahead with log barging. Straits Towing bought four steel tank landing craft hulls (LSTs) from Burrard Dry Dock in 1945, and began the practice of carrying logs on deck, lashed between heavy steel bulwarks.

Captain Cliff Eastwood got his start as a bargee with Island Tug and Barge in 1950. His duties included taking the helm of log-carrying hulls while under tow. He crewed the *Riversdale* and *Island Forester*, both converted sailing ships, on runs to Port Alice. The wheels were original sailing ship fittings, seven feet tall. The only heat came from a wood stove in the makeshift wheelhouse. The bargees got groceries from the tugboat and cooked for themselves on board.

Captain Laurie Lusk also began his career as a bargee on the *Island Forester*. He recalls the barge had three cranes powered by a coal-fired steam donkey, and a crew of eleven men. When it was time to load at the logging camps, local fishermen were hired to come in with their boats and corral the logs in the water.

According to Jim Matthew, a marine surveyor with the Salvage Association, MacMillan Bloedel began researching log barge design during the late 1940s. The company was concerned about waste from long tows using Davis rafts, and about the time it took to offload logs from barges. Company researchers were led to the Sause brothers, who ran a small logging operation in Oregon. Iced up and desperate to get a load of logs off a flat deck barge, they had resorted to tipping the vessel, and so had pioneered side-dumping in North America.

The converted sailing ship *Island Forester* had a crew of eleven, and three cranes
powered by a coal-fired steam donkey. While the barge was under tow, the only
heat came from a woodstove in the makeshift wheelhouse. The barge crew got
groceries from the tugboat and cooked for themselves on board.
(photo courtesy Vancouver Maritime Museum)

The technique was used in Europe for small barges
hauling sand or gravel, but the brothers' application of
side-dumping for logs had major consequences for the
BC logging and towing industries.

In 1954, self-dumping log barges came to BC in two
very different ways. Harold Elworthy arranged for Island
Tug and Barge to buy several oil tankers from Venezuela
for conversion to barges which would side-dump their
deckloads. The shallow-draft vessels had been specially
built to work on Lake Maracaibo. They had internal
tanks, and they had the correct hull proportions to be
partially flooded for tipping and then righted. Four were
towed from Balboa to Victoria, a distance of 4,000 miles,
by company tugs *Sudbury* and *Island Sovereign*.

The conversions were designed by local naval architect Robert Allan Ltd. After installation of tipping tanks,
each hull could carry 1.25 million board feet of logs on
deck, and dump the load in an hour. The logs were ori-
ented athwartships, rather than fore and aft.

Cliff Eastwood served his mate's time towing some
of those barges aboard coastal tugs like *Island
Commander* and *Island Navigator*. He recalls, "They
were quite delicate in tide; they could take a sheer and
dump in the middle of a tow." Because the hulls were

narrow, logs might be stacked in a
single tier, which made the load
unstable.

Around the same time,
MacMillan Bloedel hired Robert
Allan Ltd. to design a self-dumping
log barge as a new type of vessel.
Developed with the aid of tank testing at ship model laboratories, the
resulting pair of 342-foot welded
steel barges could be towed at 6.5
knots loaded or 8 knots light. Built
by Burrard Dry Dock, the sisters
Powell No. 1 and *No. 2*, later
renamed *Alberni Carrier* and *Powell
Carrier*, became prototypes for
today's fleet of purpose-built log
barges, increasing efficiency and
raising the technological and financial ante among lumber and towing companies.

The innovative new barges had completely flat
decks with log stops fore and aft, and incorporated tipping tanks in the port sides of their hulls. Their structure was also new, with thick deck and bottom plating,
plus reinforcing webs, girders and pillars within the
hulls. Twin skegs provided stability, at some expense in
drag. The loads were not lashed down; logs were held in
place by being wedged against the log stops.

With self-dumping barges came some tricky new
situations. There were "hang-ups," when the logs refused
to come off, and "jackpots," when they came off in a tangle. Tug crews learned ways to cope. An extreme method
with hang-ups was the "big lift"—or dynamite. Setting
the charge was hazardous, as the listing barge might
depart from under its load of logs at any moment. At
least once, a hole was blown in the deck and the barge
sank. A jackpot meant boom boats and small tugs had
to go into the floating log pile for a giant game of pick-
up sticks, also a hazardous undertaking.

Bill Dolmage, a well-known towboat fleet operator,
claimed to have been the first log barge blaster. He
described the process in Ken Drushka's book about the
BC towboat industry, *Against Wind and Weather*.

In the mid-1950s, self-dumping log barges made their debut. The *Powell No. 1* was one of two 342-foot welded steel barges, built for MacMillan Bloedel, that became prototypes for today's fleet of purpose-built log barges. The innovative new barges had completely flat decks, and tipping tanks were incorporated in the port sides of their hulls. The loads were not lashed down; logs were held in place by being wedged against the log stops. *(photo courtesy Vancouver Maritime Museum)*

Dolmage, who had handled explosives during the war, said he put four or five bags along the high side of a listing barge, with twenty sticks of powder in each. He connected the sticks together with cordex wiring, got well away from the barge, and detonated the charges by remote control.

By 1960, there were a dozen self-dumping log barges in operation, and barging had completely replaced Davis rafts, carrying one-third of the coastal cut. BC Forest Products' *Forest Prince* was launched that year. Equipped with two 35-ton capacity Loraine diesel cranes on buttressed towers, she was the first purpose-built self-loading, self-dumping log barge. The cranes allowed rapid loading independent of shore facilities. Since then, the distinctive silhouettes of log barges with tower cranes have become common throughout BC waters.

The year 1961 saw the last major ship conversion, which came to a premature end. M.R. Cliff Co.'s steel barge, *Log Transporter*, formerly a Great Lakes freighter, sank off Cape Mudge after only a few months' service. The cause was probably structural failure. Despite their

lower cost, ship hulls could no longer compete against the fleet of log barges operated by forestry corporations and major towing companies. The Island Tug tanker hulls were showing their age. *Island Maple* broke in half and sank in spectacular fashion off Cape Flattery in 1963, while being towed by *Sudbury*.

During the 1960s, self-loading, self-dumping log barge design became more standardized, with spoon bow, raked stern and large skegs, fitted with husky Washington pintle cranes on towers. Robert Allan Ltd. designed most of these barges. At least one log barge, the *Straits Traveler*, was equipped with a travelling crane on the afterdeck. The 369-foot *Straits Logger* was the first log barge with a capacity of two million board feet. She was followed by sisters *Rivtow Carrier* and *Island Yarder*. At the end of the decade, a new 453-foot *Island Forester* was launched as the largest log barge in the world, a title she still holds today as the *Seaspan Forester*, with a capacity of 4 million board feet.

Captain Lusk had a lot of experience with the *Straits Logger*, and respects the seaworthiness of the type: "It would take great weather if loaded properly. As long as you could tow it, you were all right." His longtime command, the Mikimiki tug *Johnstone Straits*, was the weak link. She didn't have the power to tow the *Logger* in high winds. Lacking ballast, barges could pound while running light in big seas. Another hazard was fast dumps, which could cause damage. Lusk still remembers a wild dump at Ketchikan, Alaska: "She went up so high I could see the mill underneath the hull." When the *Island Forester* was built, Captain Eastwood towed it with the *Island King*. "You had your hands full in weather and in tide," he says.

Shipyard maintenance crews were also kept busy on the log barges. Fast dumps could cause bent crane booms, and steel decks became dented and cracked from the constant impact of logs and grapples.

Towing companies had to get tugs powerful enough to tow the larger barges safely, and hustle them along at competitive speeds. In 1965, Straits Towing launched the 3,600-hp *Gibraltar Straits*. Island Tug repowered the *Island Sovereign* to handle the *Island Yarder*, and Rivtow bought and repowered a British salvage tug as the *Rivtow Lion*, with 3,200 hp. She was able to tow the *Rivtow Carrier* at 9 knots loaded. Since each tug was different, companies paired the tugs and barges that worked best together. The *Rivtow Carrier* was the first barge to have remote radio control of the diesel power plant, lighting and anchor gear on board.

While the larger, more powerful tugs made a better match with the new log barges, fleet operators also began using water or fuel ballast to stabilize the barges when running light, and running controlled dumps, which reduced damage. It was all part of the learning process in a unique operation. There were no exact precedents to follow.

Some foreign recognition of BC log barging leadership came in 1970. Robert Allan Ltd. designed a pair of 352-foot self-loading, self-dumping barges which were built in Germany and based in Sweden. They were equipped with freighter cargo cranes to handle bundled pulp logs.

Perhaps the ultimate in log barge sophistication was reached in the mid-1970s, with the design of two self-propelled, self-loading, self-dumping log carriers by Talbot Jackson and Associates, for Kingcome Navigation. Once again parent company MacMillan Bloedel took the initiative to advance log transportation development with the 430-foot *Haida Monarch* and 398-foot *Haida Brave*, designed to combine the features of log barge and ship. Both have twin propellers with steerable nozzles, accommodation for a full crew, and the capacity to travel at 12 knots loaded. *Haida Monarch* makes a regular run to the Charlottes, while *Haida Brave* goes to Vancouver Island. These specialized vessels carry through the concept of the converted *Malahat*, though a quantum leap from her capabilities.

Modern log barges have occasionally been grounded, and have proved amenable to salvage efforts. In December 1983, *Seaspan Rigger* escaped from her tug and got stranded on an island in Barkley Sound. The accident broke her back and destroyed much of her bottom plating. The *Rigger* appeared to be on the rocks for good, but salvors hired by Seaspan found a solution. First they cut the big barge in half. Then each half was lifted on a cushion of compressed air and pulled off the rocks. The halves were patched, lashed together again and towed to Esquimalt, still floating on compressed air and without a sound bottom. The continuous deck design of log barges helped make this operation possible, as it was easy to seal the hulls to keep the air inside. Later the repaired barge halves were towed separately to Vancouver and welded back into one unit.

During the 1980s, construction costs became a major obstacle to continued progress in log barge technology. The latest generation of barges is represented by the *Seaspan Rigger* and *Rivtow Hercules*, equipped with heavy-lift hydraulic cranes and other specialized features. The construction of the "package" of *Hercules* and tug *Captain Bob* cost over $20 million.

As log loading practices have gone from loose logs to small bundles to larger bundles, barge operators have been pressured to increase crane capacity. There are now several heavy-lift crane log barges in the coastal fleet, and others are likely to be recraned to handle 50-ton bundles. However, the cost of these custom-built cranes has risen to $1 million each. It has been more affordable to upgrade existing barges by applying

Some consider the ultimate in log barge sophistication to have been reached in the mid-1970s, with the design of the 430-foot *Haida Brave* (above) and the 398-foot *Haida Monarch* (below). These are self-propelled, self-loading, self-dumping log carriers. They were designed to combine the features of log barge and ship. Both have twin propellers with steerable nozzles, full crew accommodation and the capacity to travel at 12 knots loaded. *(photos courtesy Vancouver Maritime Museum)*

The latest generation of log barges is represented by vessels such as the *Seaspan Rigger* (above) and *Rivtow Hercules* (below). Both are equipped with heavy-lift hydraulic cranes and other specialized features. Some companies believe the optimum size of barge to serve logging camps has been reached with this generation of vessels. *(photos courtesy Vancouver Maritime Museum)*

thicker decking made of higher-grade steel, which helps prevent damage from falling logs and grapples.

Operations on one of BC's self-loading, self-dumping log barges begin at a logging camp in some sheltered inlet, where hundreds of logs have been stored in special booms or "bags" ready for loading. Tug crew members anchor an empty log barge in position. The log loaders have flown in by seaplane. As former loggers, they have an intuitive knowledge of how different sizes and species of logs will load.

After stowing their gear on the tug, where they will bunk, the loaders go aboard the barge. Climbing up inside the crane towers, they start up the diesels and swing the cranes around to lift the boom boats off the barge and into the water. Then they work the grapples down among the floating timber, selecting logs or bundles and placing them on the deck. The loaders are in constant radio communication with each other and the tug crew. They pile hundreds of logs on deck in a hill-like mass, which is meant to stay put without being lashed down, yet will dump smoothly at the end of the voyage. The first tier of the load is formed with butted pairs of short logs which overhang both sides. The pile is continued with single short logs, then smaller and shorter logs. As the load is built, the head loader uses a variety of methods to check the changing metacentric height of the barge, to ensure proper stability.

In less than twenty-four hours, there are thousands of tons of timber stacked aboard the barge. The loaders are flown out, and tug and tow head south toward dumping grounds on the Lower Mainland. If the weather is good, the tow itself is uneventful.

At the dumping grounds, the tug crew gets the barge ready to dump. Then comes an awesome sight unique to British Columbia. A radioed command opens valves inside the barge hull and the barge slowly lists as sea water rushes into the tipping tanks. For some minutes, it lists toward capsize, until the load seems to be defying gravity. Very suddenly, with a roar, the barge then slides out from under the logs, restrained by lines

at bow and stern. If the dump is good, the logs float in a row. The barge, freed of its load, rights itself as the tipping tanks empty. The barge is cleaned up and checked for damage. Then it is towed north to another camp, to repeat the whole process.

Over the years, the operation of log barges has done a lot to keep British Columbia forest product prices competitive on volatile world markets. Barging the logs to sawmills or pulp mills, ever more efficiently, has kept transportation costs per unit of wood low, even as tow distances increase. With costs and needs continuing to shift, it is hard to predict the future of log barges. They will evolve along with the lumber and pulp industry, as they have in the past, but they will probably not get larger. Companies believe the optimum size of barge for logging camps has been reached with the *Seaspan Rigger* and *Rivtow Hercules*.

Looking to the future, naval architect Mark Mulligan of Vancouver Shipyards commented, "Camp operators would love to put 70-ton bundles in the water." Each truckload could be bundled as a unit, minimizing log handling costs. Kingcome's marine superintendent, Tom Nixon, sees barges ranging farther north for wood and handling larger bundles. Even further in the future, he suggests, crane loading may be bypassed by the use of submersible barges, like those the oil industry uses.

Naval architect Robert G. Allan speculates that others may follow Swiftsure Towing, which has decraned the *Forest Prince* and now loads with floating derricks. Swiftsure's parent company, Fletcher Challenge, also operates a fleet of flat deck barges, loaded by means of floating cranes. Allan mentions that dryland log sorts could change log barging. Whatever the future holds for the work of getting logs from upcoast camps to southern mills, it is certain that ideas for log-carrying vessels will develop and adapt to coastal economics and conditions. As Robert G. Allan noted, "Log barges are a unique accomplishment—conceived, developed and refined in BC."◆

HIS WORLD TURNED UPSIDE-DOWN
by Duane Noyes

Mike Burke lay stunned where he had been thrown, his body battered and bruised from the impact. Above him on the ceiling, which only seconds ago had been the floor, the huge diesel motor screamed its objection to being upside down and out of lubricating oil, then finally shuddered to a grinding halt. Except for the occasional drip, drip, drip of oil or salt water, the small, dank chamber was deathly quiet.

Despite his pain, Mike struggled to his feet and peered around through the musty gloom. The chilling truth was terrifyingly obvious: he was buried alive in a steel coffin.

The 2,200-ton self-dumping log barge on which he was the first mate had somehow flipped upside down, with him trapped inside. The rusty iron crypt in which he was imprisoned now lay fifty feet deep in the frigid waters of Neroutsos Inlet, and the only way out—if there was a way out—was down.

Mike eased himself to a sitting position on the cold, wet beams of what had been the ceiling. Fortunately the emergency lighting system was still

Mike Burke was trapped inside the *Sealink Rigger* when it flipped over near Port Alice on Vancouver Island in 1995.

functional, the dim glow from its tiny bulbs casting eerie shadows on the steel walls around him. It was fear, not cold, that was making him shiver.

Mike was a skilled and seasoned mariner who had spent most of his life on the water. This particular bargeload of logs had started out no different from the hundreds of others he and the crew of the tug *Arctic Hooper* had successfully towed up and down the coast. Two days earlier, the barge *Sealink Rigger* had been loaded forty feet high from stem to stern with tons of log bundles. The tow from Iceberg Inlet to the pulp mill at Port Alice, on the west coast of Vancouver Island, had been uneventful. And on this drizzly, overcast day in August, Mike had gone aboard the barge as usual to open the tipping tank valves. These valves allow sea water to flood into the port side, tipping the load to about a 45- or 50-degree angle. All the logs slide off the barge into the water, Mike closes the valves, the water is pumped out, and barge, tug and crew are off to some other logging camp to pick up another load. It's as simple as that—at least it's supposed to be.

For some reason this particular load refused to dump. When that happens, the only alternative is to close the valves, pump out the water to level the load, fly in the loaders and unload the bundles with the huge log loading crane that is a part of the barge. That is why Mike had been below decks ten minutes ago, when the load suddenly shifted. It slid partway off and stopped, and those extra tons all on one side, combined with the weight of the water in the flooded tanks, was enough to bring about the unthinkable. The starboard side rose from the blackened sea like a monster and reared over the assist tugs helping with the dump. With a terrible groaning shudder, the barge capsized in a maelstrom of tumbling logs, broken boomsticks, flying cables and shattering machinery.

Now Mike was presumed dead, and on the surface far above, the assist boat crews continued to search frantically through the debris for his body. But Mike was not thinking of that. He was watching as cold salty water rushed into the barge through the only hatchway. Soon the chamber would be completely full. He knew he had only a few minutes to plan an escape and carry it out before his air supply was depleted. He tried to swim through the hatch but the current was too strong. Abandoning his life jacket and shoes, he again dove down through the hatch, only to be forced back. Even if he did get out, he realized, he would have to swim underwater along twenty feet of gangway and through another small engine room before getting out. Once out he would have to navigate through a tangle of ropes, lines, twisted metal and who knew what else before getting clear of the inverted deck. Then, once free of the barge, he would somehow have to get through the heavy logs and other flotsam and jetsam that would be choking the surface after the accident. Mike doubted very much that he could hold his breath for the three or four minutes it would take him to reach safety, but it was his only option.

The water flowing into the barge had slowed enough that on his third attempt Mike was able to swim against the current. But he had only gone as far as the small engine room when his lungs began to feel as if they would explode. With more than a hundred feet to go, he knew he wouldn't make it, but turning back was futile as well. Miraculously, there was a three-foot air pocket in the engine room. It too was slowly disappearing, but it could save his life.

Three times Mike filled his lungs with air before diving out through the doorway and trying to find his way to freedom. Three times he encountered only endless darkness and was forced to return to his rapidly diminishing air pocket. He had no way of knowing which way to turn to get to the surface. His fourth attempt would be his last—the precious air supply had been reduced to only inches. He gulped what might very well be his last breath and dove out the door.

At about the same time Mike was preparing for his last dive, the tide changed, and it cleared the surface just as another twist of fate occurred. The sun, which hadn't shone for days, broke through the heavy cloud cover and cut down through the murky gloom like a lighthouse beacon. Mike had the guidance he needed. With lungs aching and sore muscles straining, he plunged forward through the maze of tangled junk toward the light and followed it to the surface. The astonished tug crew dragged a sputtering, gasping Mike on board as the sun slipped back behind the clouds.

Some people would like to be lucky enough to win a big lottery, others want the good fortune to be famous, still others crave the good luck that brings health, happiness, power and status or some combination of these. Mike is not much different from his fellow human beings, except that he seems satisfied with nothing more than tide changes, small air pockets and sunlight overhead—lots and lots and lots of sunlight overhead. ◆

They Don't Make 'Em Any More Department
Fisherman Hank McBride

by Michael Skog

Hank McBride has been involved in the fisheries since the late thirties when he began his career on the decks of his uncle's boat. He is perhaps best known as the skipper of his last boat, the ninety-eight-foot steel dragger *Gail Bernice* (now the *Viking Storm*), but during his life he has harvested a lot more than bottom fish. He started out fishing for salmon, then skippering salmon tenders (packers) for BC Packers, and began trawling in his later days.

Hank well remembers his first trip up the coast in 1937. His folks sent him up to Rivers Inlet on one of the Union Steamships when he was fourteen years old, so that he could work with his uncle on a fishing boat.

No sooner was he aboard than a troop of rowdy loggers adopted him. As he sat with them awaiting his first meal, he was awed by their reckless debauchery. They bellowed loudly, gestured grandly and drank heavily, including Hank in the conversation and making him feel like he belonged in their world. "I'm feeling pretty good because I'm one of them," he says

Although he says he's retired, Hank still manages to get a bit of fishing in each year as a relief skipper.

232

An early postcard showing Namu. The fishermen's floats are to the left and one of the many bunkhouses to the right. The bunkhouses provided modest accommodation for the hundreds of BC Packers seasonal employees. The highest dwellings built onto the hill above the bunkhouse were cabins for married office workers. The boardwalks were essential to carry pedestrian traffic over the rocky shores and inland bogs.

years later. Finally the food came and Hank and his companions flew at the feast. Unfortunately, one of Hank's dinner companions had gone a little heavily on the apéritifs and, in Hank's words, "the silly son of a bitch pukes all over the table. All over his plate, my plate. I was hungrier than a bear and thought, Oh shit. After that I was still hungry. And then the skipper walked in."

The captain observed the spectacle unfolding over at the loggers' table and shouted "Get that kid out of there. Put him at my table." Hank couldn't believe his luck. "Well now I get to sit at the skipper's table, with the chief engineer, the skipper, the radio operator and all the officers, see…then, o'course, the engineer, he says, 'Laddie, you'll come down to the engine room to see the engine.' That's just what I wanted to hear, so I sez 'You bet!'" The captain, not to be outdone by one of his subordinates, extended an invitation to visit the bridge of

the large, classy vessel any time Hank wanted. Finally, the radio operator followed suit. "I had the run of the ship," Hank grins.

As it happened, there was another boy on board, about Hank's age. "He was rich—he had a tutor. So me being a kind of friendly type—I walk up to him and goes 'Hi.' He frowned at me, sneered, and walked off. Me and my rubber boots, my dungarees, and one shirt—didn't impress him one bit. I remember thinking, 'son of a bitch!' Then I went into the wheelhouse and he followed. The old skipper, he kicked him out." The memory of the little snob getting his comeuppance still brings on a deep belly laugh.

Payback time makes Hank think of another time when his boat was unloading bottom fish. When time came to deliver, the boat made its way to the Glenrose Cannery, which lay at the south end of Annacis Island in the Fraser River. It was owned in part by a fellow named

Dougal Bartlett, "Old Dougal—quite religious old Dougal Bartlett—just a tiny little guy," Hank remembers. Hank figured Bartlett didn't have the best rapport with his men, clinging to a puritanical work ethic and always dressing in a white pressed shirt with collar and tie. His shore crew thought him an insufferable, self-righteous pain in the butt who milked every misdeed for its moral lessons. On that day a group of fishermen had gathered for some recreation. Among them was an old-timer Hank knew as Old Nelson, who in addition to being a fisherman was also part owner of the Glenrose. "This old Nelson, he was a real old bugger. They were all down at the boat, you know, drinking. And of course Bartlett comes down and he sees them out there, and sees that everybody down at the cannery, they're all drunk. The whole goddamn cannery was drunk, it didn't matter who you were. Dougal comes down and he starts to squawk at everybody sitting there drinking, not doing anything."

It was a weekend, and the fishermen had nothing to do while they waited for their fish to be unloaded, but Bartlett went on and on. At the zenith of his sermon, Old Nelson decided to remind him of the days before his religious conversion. "Jesus Christ, Dougal," he bellowed, "remember years ago when you and I was young at Ewen's Cannery, when you used to make silver dollars out of seine leads, and shine 'em up and give 'em to the klootches for a piece of tail?" Whether or not it was true didn't matter—the crowd surrounding the men were convinced by Bartlett's ghostly complexion, and they enjoyed a good guffaw at his expense.

"Old Dougal, he was all embarrassed," says Hank as he jiggles with laughter. Then he becomes solemn, remembering that Bartlett was also "a fine old gentleman. He worked hard all his life." Bartlett eventually sold his share of the enterprise to Canadian Fishing Company and bought two tickets for an around-the-world cruise. As he stepped up the gangplank with his wife, he dropped dead. Bartlett's wife never recovered from the shock and spent the rest of her life in an institution. The Glenrose, Bartlett's sole legacy, is still there and still owned by Canadian Fish. Only now the building serves as a storage locker.

Hank worked hard and became a well-respected skipper for BC Packers. One night he was travelling to Vancouver with a full load, accompanied by another boat, the *Mermaid*, skippered by a man named Jack. It was late at night, and the only aids to navigation were lighthouses, the lights on their boats and the glow from shoreside communities. As they chugged along, Hank and Jack talked to each other on the radio, keeping each other awake. They were heading into Johnstone Strait and approaching Alert Bay on their left-hand side when Hank noticed another boat. It seemed to be heading across the channel toward Port McNeill, and Hank realized with alarm that it was on a collision course with the *Mermaid*. Hank held his breath and prepared for the worst as the two sets of lights slowly converged, "getting closer and closer and closer and closer and closer till the two boats merged into one, and then they parted and each went its own way."

It must have been a week later when a group of tendermen were tied up in Namu waiting for fish and Jack, who had recovered from the shock enough to talk about it, treated them to a rant about the near miss. "S-s-s-stupid son of a bitch come out of Alert Bay—pretty near hit me!"

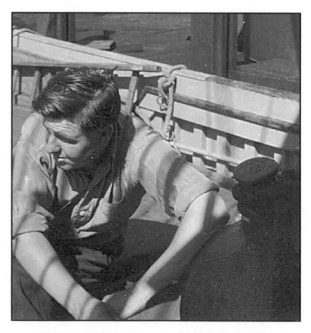

Hank McBride, at leisure on the back deck of his salmon tender, the *Sharon M*, c. 1950.

This prompted another skipper to describe a similar event that had happened to him. "Stupid son of a bitch comin' down the channel pretty near hit me the other morning!" Hank couldn't help noticing how much the two tales had in common. "The two guys finally get to talking," he says, "and they figure out, Jesus Christ, it's each other!" The two skippers got so mad they nearly came to blows. Hank still laughs about it.

Another of Hank's favourite stories starts on a fine summer night when he and a highliner friend of his named John were partying on the boats in port. John went to the rail, retched violently and "puked out his teeth." The poor man could only watch them sink to the bottom. Soon afterwards the two friends got together once again, this time in the more civil environment of John's living room, with their respective spouses. While they sipped coffee and sampled cookies, John's son, a cute ten-year-old, asked the guests if they wanted to hear how his dad had lost his false teeth. The boy recounted the heroic life-and-death tale that had unfolded the week before. High seas and gale force winds had mercilessly pummelled his father's boat, and

suddenly one of the savage waves had heaved the boat so far to the side that a skiff broke free of its lashings and rammed the back of his brave daddy's head, knocking out his teeth, which were quickly swallowed by the sea.

Hank and John exchanged glances. For a man who appreciates a joke, it was a long moment and an enormous temptation. Yet Hank resisted. "Oh ya, I remember now," he said. The memory of it still gives him a good laugh.

In the late forties, Hank and his wife Ruth met in Namu, where she worked at the only cafe in town. It was just the beginning of Namu's golden age. The Namu operation saw a great deal of activity, and required a huge number of seasonal workers who came from all over. Most of them were young, eager people of all races who worked together all day but socialized only within their own groups. There were separate bunkhouses for men, women, married, single, European, Native, Chinese and Japanese workers. Married couples occupied a section of town called Tunerville, consisting of small cottages, but the single workers slept two to a room in enormous bunkhouses. For consenting adults, the social calendar

Inside the Namu Cafe, where Ruth McBride worked. She is behind the counter, at the fountain, with a scarf tying back her hair. The cafe was a popular meeting place and nearly always busy during the fishing season.

Ruth McBride sitting with Hank's father Bert, aboard the *Sharon M*. This photograph was taken at Wadhams Cannery in Rivers Inlet, during the Rivers Inlet salmon run. Typical packer paraphernalia, including scales to weigh fish, can be seen in the stern, opposite the dory.

featured weekly dances at the far side of town and the local bowling alley provided further distraction. Namu was the ideal place for hormonal expression. Most romances were of the respectable variety. Competition was fierce—men overwhelmingly outnumbered women. "You had to be pretty on the ball to keep a woman in Namu at that time."

Hank remembers fondly one early morning when he stole away to visit a woman during the dark hours before work. As he tiptoed back to his boat in the first light of dawn, he encountered another man, also carrying his shoes and trying to be silent as he moved along the wooden promenade. This man was an office lackey, universally unpopular among fishermen, as Hank puts it, "a hoity-toity son of a bitch." The two men exchanged a nod of recognition and continued along their way. But just a few yards later, they were both startled by the cheerful voice of "Mac" Maclean, the camp manager, wishing them both a loud "Morning, boys!"

Hank was delighted, but the other gentleman was horrified. Not only had he been caught with a smoking gun, he had been lumped into the same category as a lowly boat person.

Namu was accessible only by fish boat, packer or coastal steamship. The isolation often contributed to reckless behaviour, as if the camp's physical distance from civilization was also a moral one. "You didn't have to go far to get in a goddamn fight." Fuelled by booze and boredom, fighting became an integral part of life in Namu. It was a tough neighbourhood when everyone got boozed up. The non-Natives threatened to kill all the Natives and the Natives vowed to kill all the non-Natives. There was continual talk of racial wars. In practice, however, the lines of combat were not so neatly drawn. Both Natives and non-Natives got just as much pleasure fighting amongst themselves as with each other.

As the province had Judge Begbie to keep order in its untamed years, Namu had Mac Maclean. Hank remembers this fellow as a respected manager, a good friend and a legendary disciplinarian. The delicate peace in Namu was maintained entirely by Mac, who was the "head honcho" and knew everyone personally. Perhaps more important, they knew him—and his legendary mean side. "Boy, was old Mac tough," says Hank.

Inevitably, people sometimes exercised bad judgment by challenging Mac Maclean to a scrap. Usually the fellow was drunk, otherwise he might have thought better of it. Hank recalls being in a machine shop one day when the camp testosterone was at high tide, and an ornery machinist named Bill picked up a hammer and began smacking it into the palm of his hand, hollering "Where's that goddamn Maclean? Where the hell is he? I'll fix him up."

With the perfect timing that was characteristic of Mac, he chose that moment to rear around the corner of the machine shed. Fortunately for Bill, his position was considered valuable: Mac only put him in the hospital for a few days. This was quite charitable as Mac was rumoured to have torn men's ears off for less.

Namu did have provincial police officers, but they were ineffectual. The only real law and order there was

The famous Mac Maclean, (right) manager of the BC Packers Namu plant. His fists were legendary among the young fellows, including Hank. In their minds, Mac was a tough guy and a hero—which could not be readily observed in his kind smile. Hank remembers the man next to Mac as another fine fellow, but he doesn't remember his name.

Maclean. According to Hank, who wouldn't say no to a good party, there were times when the whole town was drunk and fighting and the police never left their boat. "They were scared to," says Hank. One morning after a town-wide brawl, Mac woke him up and asked him to go with him down to the police vessel. Mac was livid—his whole town had nearly been torn apart the night before by revelers. "He kicked the side of the boat," Hank says. "Boom, Bong, Boom! The cop poked out his head and Mac said, 'Get back inside and get out of here. Don't want you around here—you useless bunch of bastards.'"

Hank remembers another evening in Namu, a notorious Saturday night. It was about 9:00 p.m. when he nosed his packer into the dock. "My gang was sober," he says, "we were the only sober ones in town." Namu was already blind with celebration—all the fish had been delivered and there was no opening until late the next evening. But all was not good fun. There had been an altercation in which, as Hank puts it, "Somebody ran a fish pugh through somebody's guts. Run right up to the hilt." The pugh, a pole with a spike on the end for spearing fish, was none too sanitary and the man needed medical attention. Mac Maclean had an old rumrunner with an enormous aircraft engine. It was called the *Black Hawk* and could do 40 knots. Mac, who was also partying that evening, entrusted its operation to the only skipper in town with a clear head. Hank was instructed to take the pugh to the hospital in Bella Bella and get it removed, for its owner needed it back. "I opened up the throttle," Hank says. "Forty-some knots up that goddamn Fitz Hugh Sound." Wind-induced tears slid across Hank's cheeks as he roared up the channel listening to the soft moans of his passenger, who lay beside him bleeding from the belly. The pugh was safely returned to its owner.

Hank is now officially retired, but finds fishing about as easy to give up as he does telling stories. He misses life at sea and is easily induced to go back on board whenever somebody needs a relief skipper. The old skipper doesn't find the modern industry compares very well to the one he knew. In his view, the proliferation of new government rules and regulations relating to the fishery have spoiled this last frontier, where a person could once be entirely in charge of his own destiny. ◆

Under Fire and Under Pressure
West Coast Shipbuilders in World War II

by Vickie Jensen with Arthur McLaren

The steel shipbuilding industry in British Columbia has undergone plenty of ups and downs, but the most powerful impact on the industry was World War II. Small naval vessels were ordered and built early on, but the war was primarily a battle to control ocean transport, and it gave rise to an increased need for merchant cargo ships.

In the early years of the war, enemy submarines and aircraft took a toll of forty to eighty merchant ships every month. Despite new construction from British yards, the transfer of ships and crews from Norwegian, Danish, Dutch and Greek merchant fleets, and the release of World War I vessels from the American reserves, it was obvious that an enormous amount of merchant tonnage must be replaced if Britain was to survive. The British government had already purchased a number of older US merchant vessels from the 1920s, and for new construction, the Ministry of War Transport sent a team of shipbuilders and engine builders to the USA and Canada. They came armed with drawings for a 9,300-ton coal-burning cargo steamer made of steel.

The drawings were prepared by the North Sands yard of Joseph L. Thompson & Sons Ltd.; hence the wartime cargo vessel became known as the North Sands ship. The design was similar to that of hundreds of British tramp steamers and presented a simple, efficient ship capable of carrying bulk, baled and deck cargo. The design, which became the basis of all the emergency "Liberty" and "Ocean" ships produced in the USA and the "Fort" and "Park" ships built in Canada, called for a riveted shelter deck vessel with machinery amidships.

The lines incorporated "V" rather than "U" sections forward and a "canoe" stern. The hull was an easy form to build, requiring no furnace plates. The Americans kept the identical hull form, but adopted welded construction. Canadian practice was to rivet the longitudinal seams and weld the transverse butts.

By late 1940, the British government had ordered eighty North Sands ships—sixty to be built in the USA and twenty in Canada. The Canadian order saw twelve assigned to the St. Lawrence yards and eight to Burrard Dry Dock in North Vancouver. Shortly afterward, the US government placed orders for an additional 100 North Sands ships, to be owned by the US Maritime Commission but built in Canada and delivered to the British Ministry of War Transport under the terms of the US Lease Lend Act. Later, ships were built for the Canadian government account. Some were loaned to the British Ministry of War Transport, while others were delivered to the Park Steamship Company, a Canadian Crown corporation.

The ships built for Britain in American yards had the prefix "Ocean" in their names; those built in Canada had the prefix "Fort." Canadian-built and -operated ships were assigned the suffix "Park." All of the Canadian vessels were paid for by the British government and transferred to the Ministry of War Transport. The Ministry assigned each ship to a British shipping company which would operate it. Between 1942 and 1945, 320 cargo ships were constructed in Canada—some 255 of them in BC.

By the summer of 1941, some twenty-two shipbuilding berths had been prepared in seven steel shipyards in

West Coast Shipbuilders yard was located on the south shore of False Creek in Vancouver, just east of what is now the Cambie Street Bridge. This photo was taken looking north from 1st Avenue. Hamilton Bridge was adjacent to the shipyard. West Coast was one of seven BC shipyards producing 10,000 ton steel merchant ships during World War II.

the province: Burrard Dry Dock (North Vancouver), North Vancouver Ship Repairs Ltd. (North Vancouver), Burrard South Yard (Vancouver Harbour, south shore), West Coast Shipbuilders (Vancouver, False Creek), Victoria Machinery Depot (Victoria, outer harbour), Yarrows Limited (Esquimalt) and Prince Rupert Dry Dock Ltd. (Prince Rupert). During 1940–41, the early naval shipbuilding program employed about 1,800 men, who learned basic shipbuilding skills while constructing 190-foot patrol vessels (later designated Corvettes), 180-foot steam, twin-screw minesweepers (Bangors) and 118-foot wooden motor launches (Fairmiles). But the expanding merchant shipbuilding program required twelve times that many production employees, and altogether the seven yards employed some 25,000 men and women.

Shipyard production was only part of the wartime story. An additional 5,000 workers were employed in manufacturing components. All boilers, steering gear, winches, windlasses, masts, shafting, etc. were manufactured in BC. Steel came from three mills in eastern Canada, engines were built by three eastern Canadian firms and pumps were produced by the machine shops of the gold mines in northern Ontario. Before the start of the war, Canada had been a producer of raw materials; now the country was being transformed into an industrialized society.

Delivery of ships started in March 1942, and by July, the combined output of the Vancouver yards was an astounding two new ships per week. This level of production was maintained through 1942 and 1943. When the Battle of the Atlantic turned in favour of the Allies, shipbuilding was cut back and deliveries extended to one vessel per month in each of the Vancouver yards. In the latter part of 1943, when there was a critical demand for tankers, twelve ships of the standard design were built with tanks instead of holds. By 1944 the demand for cargo ships had lessened, and the western Canadian shipbuilding effort was directed to the war in the Far East. The final wartime program was the construction of fifteen Type "B" China Coasters. None of these 214-foot 'tween deck steamers was complete at war's end, so all were taken over by private owners.

W.D. McLaren and his son T.A. (Arthur) McLaren share a common work history at West Coast Shipbuilders, one of the seven BC yards that built North Sands ships during the war. The J. Couglan & Sons shipyard on the south shore of False Creek in Vancouver had been destroyed by fire in 1923, and adjacent to it was Hamilton Bridge, a structural steel building plant owned by the Walkem family. Peacetime construction pursuits such as bridges and office buildings were put on hold as soon as war broke out; the Walkems set up a modern 4-berth shipyard on the Couglan site at First Avenue and Columbia Street and named it West Coast Shipbuilders.

The owners of the new yard then opened negotiations with Wartime Merchant Shipping for a share of the North Sands ships, but they were told to stand by while the "established" yards received orders. Some of the

existing builders opined that there was not enough labour to man another yard. West Coast's directors argued that the Hamilton Bridge company next door was much better equipped to fabricate steel than any of the existing shipyards, and that with commercial bridge building at a wartime halt, the plant was operating at less than 10 percent capacity. Their logic won out. Arthur McLaren recalls:

Although it was never written down, the federal government at that time was also concerned about labour stability. The steel shipyards were heavily unionized with agreements for every trade. Burrard Dry Dock had twenty-two separate agreements with steelworkers, shipwrights, machinists, pipefitters, coppersmiths, crane operators, etc., with new employees being recruited daily. So the federal government, through Wartime Merchant Shipping, offered West Coast Shipbuilders orders for North Sands ships, provided they kept an open shop agreement. This challenge was accepted.

Of course, we paid the wages and honoured the same terms of the union agreement as the other yards, but ours was the open shop. This matter of the open/closed shop was seen as a holy war by some. As a result, my father was portrayed as a rabid anti-unionist. He was not. He was merely carrying out his orders.

A week after completing his engineering studies at UBC in 1941, Arthur McLaren went to work as a shipbuilder—but not before trying to enlist in the armed services.

During the war, all the young guys eighteen to thirty years old either enlisted or were conscripted into the services. So it

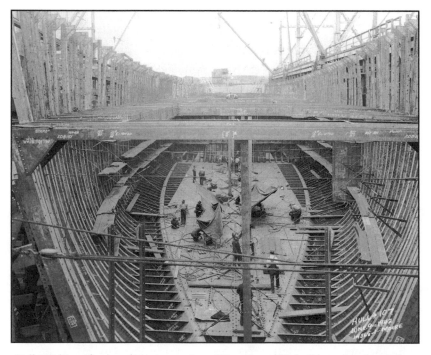

Hull 107 (*Fort Slave*) under construction at West Coast Shipbuilders, showing girders and deck beams. During 1942 and 1943, the four Vancouver shipyards collectively delivered two 10,000 ton freighters every week.

was the men over thirty, basically, who made up the crews working in the shipyards. I got drafted myself and spent a whole day down in Little Mountain barracks, but they kicked me out and sent me home because I can only see with one eye. I reminded the officer that Nelson only had one eye, but he said Nelson started out with two good eyes. So that was it for volunteering with the Navy. And it turned out the Army wasn't interested either, so I went to work for West Coast Shipbuilders. They were just starting up, and my first job was to help lay out the yard so that four of the 10,000-ton wartime freighters could be built at the same time.

In about 1943, the Walkems sold out to Frank Ross and Victor Spencer. They bought the shipyard as well as the assets of Hamilton Bridge and brought the two False Creek firms under common ownership. W.D. McLaren, who had been general manager of West Coast Shipbuilders, was asked to continue with that company and handle Hamilton Bridge as well. His son Arthur also stayed on.

Prior to 1939, shipyards, shops and foundries all worked a forty-four-hour week, which meant five weekdays and Saturday morning. Wages in heavy industry in the Vancouver/Victoria area for tradesmen (machinists, boilermakers, moulders) employed fairly steadily under shop conditions was 75 cents per hour prior to World War II. Helpers received 50 cents per hour. Those carpenters, riveters, and shipwrights employed in outside work subjected to inclement weather earned 90 cents per hour, with specialists getting 67 cents. At the beginning of the naval shipbuilding program in 1940, wages of 90 cents per hour were established for all tradesmen, with a rate of 67 1/2 cents for unskilled workers. In 1942, rising living costs were recognized by the government, and a cost-of-living bonus of 10 cents per hour was added to all wages.

Arthur recalls that after the attack on Pearl Harbor in December 1941, Ottawa instructed Canadian shipyards to carry out continuous production, twenty-four hours per day, seven days a week. Each employee was to work eight hours per day, six days a week, with one day off per week, but not necessarily Sunday. Maintaining the seven-day production week was extremely difficult at a time when the Lord's Day Act was enforced. No shopping or commercial activities were permitted on Sundays. For many employees, Sundays were for church attendance and family activities. For some, Sunday was a day of rest following a bacchanal Saturday night.

At that time, union agreements were based on a forty-four-hour week. Men were now told to work forty-eight hours, so the additional four hours were paid at time and a half. Thus, the weekly wage was based on fifty hours' pay. This gave a tradesman $45 per week (later on $50 per week). For most, this was a bonanza compared to pre-war wages.

In the early days of World War II, tradesmen were pursued with offers of employment. But every morning there were also some two dozen men standing at the gates, waiting to be employed. These men usually were not tradesmen. They came from farms, logging camps and mines. Many had not found employment during the Depression. Others had left mundane, low-paying jobs, hoping for advancement. This was the raw material we had to work with in order to produce, if not tradesmen, then at least specialists who could build ships. The task was not so much to find workers as to fit them into a productive role.

West Coast Shipbuilders' first ship was definitely the toughest to build and launch—and the one that caused the hardest feelings. The keel of No. 101 was laid in August 1941; six months later—on March 8, 1942—it was launched, with delivery in May. The nine-month building period was governed by the six months it took to build and equip the yard, the lack of steel, holdups in the supply of templates, and the learning time necessary for all employees and supervisors.

By February 1942, the yard was under heavy stress to get the first hull launched. Hulls Nos. 102, 103 and 104 were all under construction and rapidly catching up. Hamilton Bridge had already fabricated half the steel for Hull No. 105, which was to follow No. 101 on the berth. A launching at the earliest possible date was imperative, but there were still no deckhouses erected on the first hull except the boundary bulkheads of the engine casing. Since it was apparent that deckhouse construction would have to be undertaken after the hull was afloat, all the plating stiffeners and beams for this construction were dropped helter-skelter on the upper deck.

The drawing of the deckhouse, issued by the builders of the original ship, had been done on a scale of a quarter inch to the foot. This was rather small to reveal clearly all the steel work detail and to include the markings for plates, frames, beams, etc. Furthermore, this particular drawing was difficult to decipher since it had been blueprinted from a sepia print of the original tracing. With the clarity of the drawing compromised, deciphering the data was indeed a challenge.

After launching, attention was given to shipping the three boilers and main engine. The piles of deckhouse steel were picked over, but the whole problem remained a Chinese puzzle. A week went by with no action on the deckhouses. The erection crew stood around as though waiting for guidance from some mystic spirit.

In those days, the yard ran continuously on a three-shift basis. The day shift was fully manned by senior and older men. Younger men with less experience but more get-up-and-go ran the afternoon shift, and the graveyard shift was for catching up.

One particular afternoon, we assembled gangs to blitz the deckhouses on Hull No. 101. The plan of attack was to retrieve the coaming bars for the deckhouses from the tangled piles of steel dumped on the deck. These would be bolted to the upper deck, flange up, thus establishing a datum for further erection. Next we'd tackle the look-out plates that formed the deckhouse sides. These were relatively small plates about eight by eight feet, with seams on every third stiffener. A lot of the house sides, subdivision bulkheads, etc. could be manhandled into place. A crane was used for handling deck beams and deck plating.

Using a gang of some forty fitters and ten welders, we started at 4:00 p.m. and worked through to 4:00 a.m. During that time we managed to erect 60 percent of the six deckhouses—indeed an overnight wonder.

In the course of erecting the steelwork, the pile of plates and angles was diminished and the task of locating a given plate or steel section became much less arduous. The day shift erectors who had been baffled were now in a position to continue and complete the deckhouse structures. Within two more days, deckhouse steelwork was completely erected, ready for welding and rivetting. This exercise was a challenge to teams of younger men working on their first ship. They tackled the job with great enthusiasm, knowing it was vital that deckhouses be complete for joiner and electrical work to proceed. Nonetheless, the overnight wonder caused bad feelings amongst the senior men on the day shift to whom the work was originally entrusted. They felt humiliated that a crew of young men had done on one twelve-hour shift what they had failed to get started in one week. As Arthur sums it up:

Should we have consulted with the seniors first, I doubt such parley would have made any difference. We were a bunch of smart alecks who had gone out of our way to embarrass older, experienced men. We didn't apologize. There was a war on and ships were being sunk at twice the rate of replacement. We had cleared a stoppage on the building of Hull No. 101!

Each subsequent West Coast ship, starting with Hull No. 105, was turned out from keel to launching in eight

Hull 141 (*Atwater Park*), being launched at West Coast Shipbuilders. She was one of 225 10,000 ton cargo ships built in BC for the war effort.

on one ship during its passage out of False Creek.

We always made the run from the east end of False Creek to open sea at English Bay on Sundays, so as to cause the least inconvenience to traffic held up by opening the various swing span bridges. On this particular Sunday, we had cleared False Creek and were sailing toward First Narrows. The army had installed a coastal defence gun at Ferguson Point in Stanley Park, midway between False Creek and the First Narrows. As we proceeded, a signalling lamp at the gun emplacement rattled out a speedy Morse code message. Those of us on the ship's bridge asked, "What's up?" There was another unintelligible dash of code, then another. Finally there was a puff of smoke, a scream through the air and a splash in the water about a quarter of a mile ahead of us—all quickly followed by the explosion of a gun firing!

We had an Aldis Lamp on board, so somebody who at least understood Morse code tapped out, very slowly, "What's the matter?" The reply came back flashing at a mile a minute. So our Aldis man tapped back, requesting the sender to signal slowly. That did the job. Back came the request, painfully slow: "What ship is that?" We showed our name board and that was that. End of story

One of Burrard Dry Dock's ships was not so lucky. Returning from sea trials, the vessel was similarly challenged from a gun emplacement at the north side of First Narrows, under the Lion's Gate Bridge. A warning

weeks. From keel to delivery took only twelve and a half weeks. With the second series of hulls, West Coast workers delivered a new ship through the False Creek bridges every second Sunday until the program eased off. Crews in the other three Vancouver yards met the same schedule, and from mid-1942 to late 1943, two new ships per week were dispatched from the Port of Vancouver.

Under wartime regulations, no name or any other form of identification could be exhibited on a ship. Atop the wheelhouse on each side of the rails was a heavy board bearing the ship's name. This board was hinged so that when it was folded, the top half covered the lower portion and the name was obliterated. Arthur McLaren recalls one very alarming event involving these boards that occurred

Hull 127 (*Fort Boise*) during sea trials. At the top of the photo is the old lighthouse at the mouth of the Capilano River, adjacent to First Narrows and Vancouver Harbour.

10,000 TON CARGO SHIP OUTPUT FROM BC SHIPYARDS DURING WORLD WAR II	
Burrard Dry Dock North Vancouver & Vancouver Yards	111
West Coast Shipbuilders False Creek	55
North Van Ship Repairs North Vancouver	54
Victoria Machinery Depot Victoria	20
Prince Rupert Dry Dock Prince Rupert	13
Yarrows Ltd. Esquimalt	2
Total	255

shot ricocheted off the surface of the water and actually punctured the hull of the brand new cargo ship. The vessel was beached on the sand bank on the north side of First Narrows. Fortunately, it was refloated with only minor damage.

"So," Arthur concludes, "if you ask if I've ever been under fire, I'd have to say yes, but presumably only from friendly forces!"◆

Vickie Jensen and Arthur McLaren are collaborating on a book that chronicles four generations of McLaren shipbuilders and the history of British Columbia's steel shipbuilding industry.

RAINCOAST
CHRONICLES
–19–

Stories and History of the
British Columbia
Coast

Edited by
HOWARD WHITE

WITHOUT DEED OR PERMIT

Squatters in the Lower Mainland

SHERYL SALLOUM

On September 14, 2002, a group of homeless people and housing activists occupied the old Woodward's building on Hastings Street in Vancouver, empty and unused since the department store went bankrupt in 1993. They were angered by the failure of repeated attempts to broker a deal that would convert some or all of the block-sized structure to social housing.

A week later police evicted about 25 occupants, but soon afterward a throng of squatters erected a community of sorts on the sidewalk surrounding the building. For three months the "Woodward's Squat," as it came to be known, focussed the entire city's attention on issues of social housing, homelessness and the general neglect of Vancouver's Downtown Eastside.

At its peak the squat was home to an estimated 280 people, but their numbers had dwindled to about 100 by December 14, when a new, left-leaning city council, with federal help, arranged temporary quarters for 54 of the squatters and promised to find a more permanent solution to the inner city's housing crisis.

As squatters' settlements go, the Woodward's Squat was more of a political statement than a

Tim Cummings, the last sanctioned squatter in Stanley Park, chops firewood outside his Brockton Point shack. Born in the area in 1881 to one of the original squatter families, Cummings snubbed negotiations to relocate squatters, noting that no one consulted his family before it became a park. He stayed put until his death in 1958. *Photo courtesy Vancouver Public Library*

The squatters' community on Deadman's Island in Stanley Park, seen around 1898-1900, when it was more than a decade old. Most of the homes were built on logs, floating at high tide, resting on the beach at low tide. Their occupants fished in the harbour for a living; some grew vegetables and even raised livestock. *Photo courtesy City of Vancouver Archives*

serious attempt at homesteading, but it takes its place in the rich, varied and almost unbroken tradition of squatting in the Lower Mainland over the last 140 years. In the words of Malcolm Lowry, perhaps the region's most famous squatter, the homes of squatters "with their weathered sidings [are] as much a part of the natural surrounding as a Shinto temple is of the Japanese landscape."

Squatters' communities have evolved in Greater Vancouver for various reasons, including poverty, rebellion against social conventions and the yearning for a way of life that harmonizes with natural surroundings. A temperate climate and the ready availability of unused property, water, food and fuel have made settlement feasible for even the poorest residents. Local waterways provided fish for eating and selling; driftwood could be gathered for home heating and cooking; boats provided transportation. While many of the settlements were established in isolated areas, they were close enough to Vancouver and its satellite municipalities that service industries were always nearby.

The history of squatters in Vancouver goes back at least as far as 1860, when Portuguese and Scottish sailors jumped ship in Vancouver's harbour and settled in what is now Stanley Park. The land was an ancestral burial and fishing ground for the Coast Salish Indians, heavily forested and inhabited by bears and cougars. The sailors married aboriginal women and built one-storey homes of axe-hewn lumber near the sandy beach at Brockton Point. At that time, the harbour was teeming with herring and the sailors made a living fishing the abundant waters. The squatters supplemented their food supply by planting gardens and raising chickens and other livestock. Their community was known locally as Fishermen's Cove, Fishermen's Village, Squatters' Village or Indian Portage.

In 1888, the year that Stanley Park officially opened, a smallpox epidemic swept through Vancouver. The health inspector had the squatters' houses razed; compensation was $150. The families rebuilt, but their tenancy became more difficult. A roadway was built around the park and more people used the lands more often. Inevitably, those who saw the houses as eyesores and those who were interested in developing the area commercially applied pressure to have the squatters evicted. Their lobby was not successful until 1921, when the city

began legal eviction proceedings against the park's inhabitants: nine descendants of the original Stanley Park squatters.

To establish squatters' rights, the residents had to prove 60 years of continuous occupancy, a difficult task without deeds or other written documentation. Tom Abraham, a Native thought to be 110 years old at the time, testified that he "had made no record like the white man, but remembered by events, such as the Cariboo gold rush." Abraham recalled that at that time (1859–1865) there were "four buildings on land now occupied by the squatters." But an 1863 map prepared by Corporal George Turner of the Royal Engineers did not show the homes of the defendants, and Mr. Justice Murphy declared the

On the north shore of False Creek in 1934, a squatter saws driftwood for his stove aboard one of the boats and float homes moored near the CPR roundhouse. Railway workers, First World War veterans, families and hoboes coexisted peacefully in squatter communities on both sides of False Creek during the Depression. Although civic authorities grumbled about the 'eyesores,' they seldom enforced eviction notices, preferring not to add to the relief rolls. *Photo courtesy City of Vancouver Archives*

evidence of all but one squatter inconclusive and "unsatisfactory." Mariah Kulkalem was the only one who managed to prove 60 years of uninterrupted residency. The others appealed their cases, but lost in 1925. They were allowed to remain in their homes for one dollar a month until they were evicted in 1931, their homes and outbuildings burned by the Vancouver Fire Department.

Tim Cummings, who was born in 1881 and whose family had been among the first squatters, did not participate in the court battle. He felt that since his family had not been consulted when the land they inhabited was turned into a park, he did not have to comply with eviction orders. Instead, Cummings came to an "understanding" with the parks board, and he and his sister Agnes were granted continued tenancy for the sum of $5 a month. Both lived in Stanley Park until their deaths, Agnes in 1953 at the age of 69 and Tim in 1958 at the age of 77.

Some time after the squatter community at Brockton Point was built, another illegal village took shape on the small finger of land south of the park—Deadman's Island. Most of the homes there were built atop logs on the foreshore; at high tide they would float and at low tide they would rest on the shoreline. In 1909, all of the squatters, numbering close to 150, were evicted. They soon returned and on April 30, 1912, their shacks were raided. "Men from the sheriff's office carried the firebrand...and burned to the ground" about 40 dwellings. In 1924, squatters again began settling on the island. Most were fishermen, some of whom had been evicted from Stanley Park. Many moored houseboats on the small island. They were evicted in 1930 but some people stayed on in their houseboats until the early 1940s.

Meanwhile, a number of other squatter communities were developing. In the November 7, 1936 issue of the *Daily Province*, Ogden H. Hershaw wrote that a community established in about 1900 was burgeoning beneath the Burrard Bridge, on the foreshore of the Kitsilano Reserve and should

be "preserved." The tumbledown dwellings of "Bumtown" or "Bennettville" (a derisive reference to Depression-era Prime Minister R.B. Bennett) were home to some 300 proud but poor people, a city within a city. One man, a Swedish immigrant of 10 years, made his living by fishing, screening sand and salvaging logs. He proudly stressed,

I have never been on relief, but should the government evacuate us...the majority of us will become a public liability...If they really wanted to help us, let them give us sewers and sidewalks, house numbers and the odd coat of paint. If, then, the Parks Board would give us some flower seed, we could work wonders around here.

Eviction notices were regularly given to the "Bumtown" residents, but neither the city of Vancouver, nor the province, nor the federal government seemed interested in enforcing the notices. In the *Daily Province*, Norman Hacking wrote that most residents attended to "their own business, sawing up wood for the winter, building additions to their homes, patching up tar paper, mending boats." They had been receiving eviction notices for at least nine years, and as one man explained, "They don't mean nothin'. Government's gotta get rid o' them notices, so they paste 'em up here." The squatters were right. No one was going to be dispossessed during the Dirty Thirties—Vancouver did not want to add to its relief rolls. New ramshackle dwellings appeared. Shantytowns developed on the banks of the Fraser River east of Nanaimo Street and stretched as far as New Westminster. Others were built on False Creek, along the northern and southern shores of Burrard Inlet, and in Richmond. Most of the communities lasted for decades.

The one exception was a "jungle" of unemployed and desperate men who congregated on property belonging to the Canadian Pacific Railway, east of Dunlevy Avenue, on the edge of Burrard Inlet.

Founded by Finnish immigrants in 1892, Finn Slough is the oldest squat in BC. Its modest floating homes have always been comfortable and well maintained, albeit Spartan—washing machines and refrigerators did not appear in the community until 1959. *Photo courtesy John Skapski*

During the 1930s, hundreds of destitute men rode freight trains into Vancouver in search of employment. Upon arriving, they found little work and took to squatting near the rail line. Col. R.D. Williams, the harbour commissioner, witnessed the formation of the squatters' "jungle." On a day of torrential spring rain in 1931, he saw "the legs of a man disappear under a pile of rails which lay on the CPR right of way... The rails were stacked four or five high... [and] the men had added some paper in sheets to add to the protection from the elements afforded by the rails." When he investigated, Col. Williams found 14 men huddled under the makeshift shelter "and two of them were without boots." He found out that some were veterans of the Great War, and he immediately tried to help by securing donations of food, clothing and cigarettes. However, their numbers continued to increase, and at the

jungle's peak there were approximately 240 men living there. By the autumn of 1931, Col. Williams said, an outbreak of typhoid closed the encampment, and its "improvised...nondescript...[and] wonderfully unique architecture; old boards, sheet iron, packing cases, and whatnot went up in flames."

At their height, squatter communities in Vancouver were home to about 1,800. Taxpayers complained that the illegal residents had city benefits without having to pay taxes. In fact, most cabin dwellers had no running water or electricity, no sewage or garbage disposal. For the down-and-out there was simply no other place to go than the city's slum areas—not an appealing alternative for those with children.

The Biiroinens were one such family. Mr. Biiroinen, who had been a logger, fell ill and then suffered years of unemployment. By 1941, he and his family had lived in their shack for five years. Mrs. Biiroinen said that living in their waterfront shanty had been a "godsend," which allowed them to remain independent and off relief. A reporter from the *Daily Province* noted:

> [The Biiroinen] "cabin" is a far cry from a squalid room in a tenement… It's only three rooms—but they're three airy, sunny rooms, clean and scrubbed, attractive as ingenuity can make them on a small income. There are flower boxes by the window and a large well-fenced veranda where Roy [the baby] can play in the sunlight and breathe the fresh salt air, away from the smells of the city.

Members of the harbour squatters' community did enjoy running water for a time: it was piped in from a home on nearby Wall Street until a new owner moved in and refused to continue what he consid-ered an illegal activity. When one of the squatters, Mrs. Eva Pick, asked the city to provide water, the city engineer answered with eviction notices. Mrs. Biiroinen commented that her family would likely have to move to an east end rooming house: "We can't pay a high rent… We'd like to stay here, even if we do have to carry our water." Another squatter, an elderly veteran of the Great War who existed on a small pension, lamented that if he moved into a rooming house he could not keep his only compan-ion, a terrier.

The waterfront residents won a small reprieve when port manager K.J. Burns told an investigating committee that the squatters were "completely law-abiding." He was "amazed at the cleanliness" of their homes. Nevertheless, 40 of the shacks were removed. The Harbours Board and the Canadian Pacific Railway then agreed to consider leasing property to the cabin dwellers or giving them a temporary easement.

Laundry hangs on clotheslines among squatters' homes viewed from the Burrard Bridge in the late 1930s, the twilight of squatting in False Creek. Industry and a wartime expansion of RCAF activity on the Kitsilano side of the inlet would soon put teeth into the perennial eviction notices. *Photo courtesy City of Vancouver Archives*

In 1937, Vancouver City Council again wanted to eradicate the communities, which council members and others considered unsightly, but the Second World War and a severe housing shortage stopped them from taking action. By 1947, *Maclean's* magazine reported the councillors were again complaining, calling the squatters "water rats" and describing their villages with terms such as "eyesore...potential fire hazard...potential health hazard," pointing to improper sewage facilities (even though the city was dumping its sewage into the inlet). Inexplicably, to city authorities, the squatters and their children enjoyed extremely good health; some shacks did burn down, but other property was not destroyed.

Some Vancouverites prospered because of the squatters. In the colony at the foot of Cardero Street, known as "Shaughnessy Heights" (named after a prestigious Vancouver residential district), landowners put out wharves and collected moorage fees of 20 cents per foot per month for boats, and $10 a month for houseboats. Water and electricity usually cost more. Accommodation here was as swank as the name of the community implied. Mil Smith, a 61-year-old who worked part-time in a cannery, had an electric refrigerator, radio, and oil-burning stove. Some floating houses contained hot showers. A grey-haired grandmother named Elizabeth Sharp owned a 50-year-old missionary boat, the *Sal Lal*. She found her accommodation much less expensive and more cheerful than the rooms she had rented uptown for $55 a month. Another boat, the *Kia Ora*, was built as a ferry in 1913 and provided her owner with a beautiful home. The only drawback to "Shaughnessy Heights" was its smelly black mud, in which garbage such as mattresses, tin cans and broken glass was embedded.

Vastly different from "Shaughnessy Heights" was the cluster of cabins in the False Creek settlement. There, according to *Maclean's* in November 1947, "weather-beaten boards, broken shingles and rusted tin signs covered the shapeless houses, the whole conglomerate assembly vaguely joined together by

a tangled line of floating walk and shaky handrail." Not all False Creek squatters were happy about their situation. One couple, Mr. and Mrs. Penny, lived there only because they were "not old enough for the old-age pension, and not rich enough to buy retirement on solid ground." They had the comparative luxury of electrical service from BC Electric, but had to haul water: there was "the paradox of people carrying fresh water 100 yards in pails to fill up their slick new washing machines."

Those on the Kitsilano Reserve side of False Creek had to contend with "a mixture of smells, all unpleasant." Life there was "primitive—no rent, no wharfage, no electricity, no running water." Similar settlements existed farther up Burrard Inlet: one on the south side stretched from the foot of Boundary Road to the Belcarra area of Burnaby; one on the north side had been built near Deep Cove, North Vancouver.

In September 1946, two young veterans of World War II and their families became squatters in another area of town. After 17 months of searching for a proper home for his wife and three-year-old son, John Robert Cox decided to move his family into the unused army huts at the Little Mountain Military camp near Heather and 41st Avenue in Vancouver. They were joined by another veteran, Bill Mooy, his wife and their 16-month-old son. Both men were from the Prairies and were given no priority for accommodation at a time of severe housing shortages.

The corporal guarding the gate was not prepared to deal with the arrival of two young women, their babies and their bedding. The *Daily Province* reported that the squatters entered and "tried the doors of empty huts till one opened...They took the first four rooms, two to each family, in an H-shaped hut already partitioned into 30 small bedrooms, two communal bathrooms...and one laundry room." The young men managed to turn on the water, but the barren rooms were without electricity and heat, and their mattresses had to be placed on the floor. Even so, their new quarters were preferable to their last ones in Gastown. Nellie Cox said, "It was terrible at Water Street...There were a lot of old men, and they would shout at us to shut up whenever the children made a noise." Cox was pleased that they could "turn around without wondering if the kids...[had been] killed by a car or truck." They made their first pot of coffee "with hot water borrowed from the Sergeants' Mess." Shortly after the squatters moved in, some of the army huts were turned over to the University of BC, where they were used as housing. Nine buildings were retained by the reserve army; six were allotted to the Department of Veterans Affairs. The *Province* noted that "trained social workers" were brought in to help squatters relocate, but the records do not indicate the fate of the Cox and Mooy families.

In 1950, a False Creek squatter, Frederick Roger Ducharme, was convicted of murdering a woman, and Vancouver ratepayers clamoured to have the shantytowns removed. In the *Vancouver Sun* of March 22, 1950, the squatters' homes were described as "disease-breeding, vermin-producing hovels;" the residents were said to be "unbelievably filthy" and a "nest of perverts." The *Daily Province* of October 3, 1951, however, described the majority of the squatters as "ordinary citizens."

Despite protests that the communities were health hazards and eyesores, most squatters managed to stay put. But in 1955, the False Creek squatters were issued their final eviction notice, as the site was required for a new government wharf. By June of that year only a few squatters remained. As Norman Hacking reported in the *Province*, they were the "last ditch survivors" and "the happy-go-lucky type." Some moved "just around the corner...to the other side of the bridge." For many, their homes were not worth moving; their choices were limited. One man lamented, "Try to find a house where me and the old woman can live on $40 a month." Another expressed concern that he might have to go back to his wife, who liked "beer parlours...If I move out tomorrow maybe she'll take me back. Maybe she won't. I hope she won't."

A community near Deep Cove, North Vancouver,

was first inhabited by fishermen and employees of the Dollar Mill and McKenzie Derrick. Later, some of the jerry-built structures at Dollarton served as summer cabins for Vancouver families. For Malcolm Lowry and his wife, Margerie, life in a shack became an affordable refuge that removed Lowry from the temptation of beer parlours and liquor stores. Their 14 years as squatters provided Lowry with enough serenity to complete his most famous novel, *Under the Volcano*. He worked on other writings in the shack, including a book of short stories that received the Governor General's Award in 1961, four years after his death. The Lowrys' tenancy drew other writers such as Earle Birney, Dorothy Livesay and Al Purdy to the ramshackle beach homes. But the community was evicted in 1960, the shacks bulldozed and burned, and the foreshore became part of Cates Park. In 1958, eviction notices were given to the Burnaby squatters on the other side of the inlet; in 1960, the last members of that community moved and their shacks were destroyed.

Another Burrard Inlet squatter community sprouted on the Maplewood mud flats in 1971. Earlier squatters on the muddy estuary were forced out in 1961 when L&K Lumber purchased the property. Ten years later, hippies discovered the picturesque foreshore, moved in and set up tents, shacks and lean-tos. Some lived in vehicles. The BC sculptor Tom Burrows lived on the tidal flats for two years, taking inspiration from "the environmental setting, source of material, observation point (mainly the window of my cabin), the machinations of my squatter community, [and] the lunar rhythms of the tide."

The owners of the mudflats property, Lyttle Brothers Ltd., evicted the illegal tenants but reached an agreement with five people who were refusing to vacate. The firm agreed to pay them $500 "if they remove[d] a quantity of garbage" and moved. One occupant, 73-year-old Mike Bozzer, was allowed to stay because of his age. Bozzer had lived on the flats for 36 years. His four-room home was built from scrap lumber that had drifted onto the beach; so were

Malcolm and Margerie Lowry's third and final shack at Dollarton, North Vancouver, where they lived for 14 years. They moved here after their second home burned to the ground, taking with it the manuscript for Lowry's greatest work, *Under the Volcano*. *Photo courtesy UBC Library Rare Books & Special Collections, Fisherman Publishing Society*

his small veranda and his woodshed. Ironically, in 1980, the aged squatter himself had to evict his own squatter, a transient male who took up residence in his upstairs bedroom. Bozzer enjoyed his solitary existence until 1986 when, at the age of 88, he was forced by ill health to move to a care facility. The bulldozers were brought in and his shack was destroyed.

For 10 months in 1990, a group of people began occupying six empty houses on Frances Street in East Vancouver. Most of the squatters were homeless, young and single; a few said they were trying to escape "the rent rut." Others were "trying to make a point about housing, that this was good housing... and that it shouldn't be empty," according to John Shayler of the Tenants Rights Coalition. As many as 50 people at a time sought shelter in the buildings. In November, a violent confrontation took place between the police and the illegal tenants, "ordinary citizens on one side and... police and helicopters on

A fisherman tends his nets in Finn Slough, where a few of the 30-odd residents still work on gillnetters. Some say the settlement on Richmond's Gilmour Island is the oldest continuously working fishing community on the Fraser River. *Photo courtesy John Skapski*

the other," in the words of Ald. Libby Davies. The squatters were arrested and city council ordered the homes demolished within 61 days. The owner said he planned to build 36 condominiums on the site.

Finn Slough, on Gilmour Island at the end of No. 4 Road in Richmond, has hosted squatters since 1892. Finnish immigrants were initially attracted by the beauty of the river flats, but the price of raw land was $40 an acre, a princely sum. The newcomers decided to build on Crown land and to fish the abundant waters of the Fraser River. Mikko Jacobson was one of the first, and built a scow-house to house his boat with a room at the back serving as makeshift living quarters. As more Finns heard about the community, the population grew, and in 1927, the municipality of Richmond ordered the occupants to pay property taxes or be evicted. Matti Lampi spoke for the squatters when he emphatically replied that as he was living on Crown land, he would not pay taxes.

A year later, the community moved 400 metres west. The new settlement became known as Finn Slough and, as Eric Sorila wrote, the scow-houses began "popping up like mushrooms in the rain." They were built with wood washed in by the river, or brought in by barge and horse-drawn cart from a sawmill in New Westminster. Residents added rooms to the scow-houses to make living in them more comfortable, "although a separate bedroom was . . . considered a luxury." Wood for heating and cooking was picked up along the riverbanks. Rainwater was collected for drinking and the river provided washing water. Saunas were an early and distinctive feature of the settlement. Washing machines and refrigerators were not acquired until 1959. Sewage went back into the river.

In the 1940s, the municipality again gave the residents notice to evict. According to Toivo Boren, the last of the Finns to leave the community, "the fishing company which bought the fish from the community fishermen became infuriated...because the fishermen were very productive and their evictions would mean less profit for the company." Thanks to the company's lobbying, the residents of Finn Slough were allowed to stay.

From 1950 to 1960, the population swelled to about 70 residents. But after 1960, the population began to decline, and from then until 1980, "funerals were the main social event" in the community. In 1984, municipal planners declared the community was unlikely to continue, in light of drainage problems and the fact that the area was zoned for agricultural, not residential, use. Nineteen years later, a community of about 30 individuals still exists. They are an eclectic mix including artists, pensioners and Vancouver business people. Like those before them, however, these residents are again threatened with eviction. A Toronto development company, Smith Prestige Properties Ltd., has proposed a multi-million-dollar development for the area.

Meanwhile, residents and concerned individuals have created the Finn Slough Heritage and Wetland Society. They want to protect the natural environment, to implement alternative methods of waste disposal for the community and to maintain an area for cyclists, walkers, equestrians, sports fishermen and naturalists. According to one resident, David Dorrington, those currently living at Finn Slough wish to preserve "the memory of how things were" in squatter communities. They see Finn Slough "as an important three dimensional, living part of that memory." To them "the village is not only a historical artifact...[but] an example of a possible way forward to find more creative solutions to...non-stop urbanization."

Should the Finn Slough homes and their inhabitants disappear in favour of suburban ranchers and townhouses, an integral part of the cultural and geographic history of the Vancouver area will be lost. Squatter communities will, however, always be a part of our heritage. In Malcolm Lowry's words, they will be remembered as symbols of "an indefinable goodness, even a kind of greatness." ◆

Sources and Further Reading

Burrows, Tom. Biography file, UBC Fine Arts Gallery (February 15, 1974).
Dorrington, David. "A Small History of Finn Slough." www.finnslough.com
Lowry, Malcolm. *Hear Us O Lord from Heaven Thy Dwelling Place*. New York: Lippincott, 1961.
Masson, Hal. "Sea-borne Shantytown," *Maclean's* (November 15, 1947).
Matthews, J.S. *Early Vancouver*, vol. 1. City of Vancouver Archives.
Sorila, Eric. "From Finland to Finn Slough." Unpublished paper, Richmond City Archives (1984).
Daily Province (Vancouver), Apr. 30, 1912; Nov. 17, 1923; Nov. 26, 1923; Oct. 29, 1936; Aug. 21, 1941; Aug. 26, 1941; Sept. 20, 1946; Sept. 25, 1946; June 14, 1955.
Province (Vancouver), Feb. 27, 1973; Nov. 28, 1990.
Vancouver Sun, July 25, 1953, Apr. 22, 1994.

NEVER SAY PIG

West Coast Fishing Superstitions

MICHAEL SKOG

"What the hell are ya bringin' that aboard for?"

That less than welcoming query came from a deckhand as I attempted to board a seiner, my arms loaded down with the bulging garbage bags and canvas duffels of the journeyman crewman. I was hoping to spend the summer salmon season replenishing my sorely undernourished bank account.

I was taken aback. I thought I had made a good impression the day before, my first with the boat's crew. I had shown up half an hour early and, over the course of the afternoon, sweated away two cans of Pepsi helping the seine net aboard and making other semi-voluntary preparations.

I silently reviewed every detail of the previous twenty-four hours, trying to figure out what I might

Illustration by Nick Murphy

have done to arouse this hostility. I followed the eyes of my accuser down my arm to the canvas gym bag containing my clean clothes.

"Ya can't bring a black bag on a boat. It's bad luck."

"This thing?" I asked, waggling the little bag dangling from my left hand. Being well past my rookie season on the boats, I knew about the black bag taboo, but I had always pictured a bad-luck bag as one that was black all over, like a black cat. This one had a colourful beer logo on it, and racing stripes. Only the background was black.

I was tempted to try arguing that this particular bag was not of the ill-omened variety, but what then? At the first sign that the trip was not measuring up, the blame would fall on my shoulders for packing aboard the Jonah bag. I would become the target of black looks and hostile silences, and nothing I could say about logos or racing stripes would do me the slightest good. I unpacked all my clothing and took the scorned object back to the car.

I have often had occasion to ponder just how it is that case-hardened skeptics who wouldn't entertain a supernatural thought if the archangel Gabriel visited them in person will nevertheless enforce the most bizarre shipboard taboos with the unshakeable conviction of a banker enforcing the terms of a mortgage. What is it that comes over normally rational people when they set foot on a boat, especially a fish boat? In the face of logic and science, they fall back on a primitive, warped logic: We observe these taboos and we're still alive, so the taboos must work. It's pure cause and effect.

Like every greenhorn eager to avoid the scorn of older hands, I once devoted a lot of brain volume to discovering and observing the superstitions of the trade. I concluded that the part of the cranium used to store this (dis)information must be the same area usually allotted to common sense, because the more superstitions one catalogues, the more difficult it becomes to resist even the most ridiculous ones.

The list is lengthy. Whistling is a widely forbidden activity. Years ago a shipmate told me to pipe down when he heard me unwittingly "whistling up the wind." Some forward-thinking people maintain that this prohibition applies only in the wheelhouse, but the prudent will stick to humming even these days, to be on the safe side.

Everyone has heard the saying, "Red sky at night, sailor's delight; red sky at morning, sailors take warning." But did you know that if you see a seagull taking a bath it means that the wind is about to howl? And if the gulls start moving inland it is really time to batten down the hatches.

Most will have heard of the proscription against leaving a hat on the galley table. The ban on opening the wrong end of a milk tin has also gained widespread notoriety. Less known is that the taboo applies to all food containers: All cans and boxes must be opened right side up or they have to be thrown over the side—no exceptions. Price is no consideration, so a tin of artichoke hearts gets tossed as fast as a can of consommé. Some interpretations of the dogma are stricter than others. One cook I sailed with threw out two jumbo cartons of milk in one week because he had inadvertently parted the waxed seal on the wrong side.

Today's fisherman stores most garbage in plastic bags atop the cabin instead of chucking it all overboard as in unenlightened times. But when this civilized practice comes head-to-head with the ancient juju about upside-downness, there is no contest. The defiled container is purged from the ship by the most direct route possible, as if it had suddenly become radioactive.

Many a hungry fishermen has come into the galley only to recoil in horror because some ignorant cook has roasted a turkey, otherwise known as "Blow Bird," or has laid before his crew a steaming bowl of pea soup, known as "Storm Soup." Whether it blows or not, few cooks make that mistake more than once.

Still on the subject of food, never, never mention the name of that low-slung, mud-loving animal that provides us with bacon. (Hint: it is a three-letter word which, enunciated backwards, sounds like "gip.") Refer to it only as "curly tail."

Some crews enforce a ban against mentioning all barnyard animals by name. The extent of this farm-critter taboo differs from boat to boat. Some fishermen just bring up the superstition if such a word is used and laugh at it, as if it were a curious piece of trivia that might interest others, but the cautious greenhorn might be well advised to take a hint and avoid repeating the profane terms in any case. Sometimes it seems these taboos are falling into obscurity, but there is always an old-timer ready to infect the younger crew members and perpetuate the anxiety for another generation.

There is also a long tradition about not being entirely prepared for the best, as if that would be presumptuous in the eyes of fate. Large catches are what we are talking about, more fish than a crew knows what to do with. Everyone hopes for that big haul, and there are special bits of extra heavy tackle required if it comes. In salmon seining a brailer is needed for the biggest sets when there are too many fish to pull over the stern ramp.

But to prepare it beforehand is to ensure it won't be needed. Big hauls are more likely if the dipper is left down in the hole or "all confused in the rigging." The same goes for the other fisheries where the Boy Scout motto applies in reverse: Be not prepared, and maybe you'll be lucky enough to wish you were.

Then there is the dreaded hoodoo—a trade term describing any object or person believed to cause ill fortune. I have experienced the uncanny vibrations felt from these. One was another boat that caused us to pull in repeat water hauls (the seining equivalent of a "skunk") whenever it fished within sight. After we discovered the source of our bad luck we did everything possible to avoid this vessel, yet it continued to shadow us as if it knew its presence hexed us.

Superstition is probably linked in most people's minds with fear, and the most frequent explanation of ritualistic behaviour is that it is undertaken to ward off disaster. What this theory conveniently overlooks is that rituals intended to summon good luck are just as common as those intended to avoid bad. Maybe commoner. I have never actually seen a ritual being cooked up to ward off bad luck, but I've seen plenty of the other variety.

One of my skippers had a green baseball hat he insisted on wearing whenever he set the seine net. He'd been wearing it when he made his first big haul, and after that he wouldn't make a set without it, even though it was rancid with fish slime. He was convinced that the absence of that hat would be fatal to our hopes of a good season, and the entire crew shared that belief. We wouldn't let him take it off the boat, lest he forget it at home, or lest his wife—horror of horrors—launder it and remove its fishy mojo.

This kind of thing is common on the boats. I once wore a sour-smelling, sweat-marinated bandana to bed because I thought untying the knot would break a recent streak of good luck. Near asphyxiation from the stench eventually put an end to that, but most fishermen I know have fallen prey to similar quirks. Some compulsions run throughout the fleet like a collective neurosis. Most men don't shave or shower until the fishing trip is finished. Then there is the grand old belief that nothing bodes better for a prosperous trip than to have a dark-skinned woman come down and piss on the net. It's commoner than you might think, even today.

In fishing, where an entire season can be made in a single set, or lives may be lost in a single swell, there is much that remains beyond mortals' control. It is to avoid seeming totally helpless before these superhuman forces that fishermen cling to talismans and fetishistic rituals. A popular saying holds that there are no atheists in a foxhole. Neither are there unbelievers on the fishing grounds. ◆

ANGELS IN CAULK BOOTS

Tug Skippers in the Days Before Search and Rescue

DOREEN ARMITAGE

In addition to their regular chores of berthing ships and hauling booms and barges, BC's tugboats are often called upon to assist in emergencies, often working with the Coast Guard and fireboats to save lives and retrieve damaged vessels. In fact, until Coast Guard and Search and Rescue units were invented, tugs were the first—and sometimes only—help on the scene when mariners were in danger.

Two boys get a closer look at the *Unimak* as it is beached at Davis Bay August 7, 1960, more than a week after it sank off Gower Point. All four aboard were killed, the last trapped in an air pocket and banging on the hull as would-be rescuers looked on helplessly. Repaired and relaunched, the *Unimak* later collided with a tanker off Prince Rupert and went down for good. *Photo courtesy UBC Library Rare Books and Special Collections, Fisherman Publishing Society*

On March 6, 1945, the *Green Hill Park*, a 10,700-ton freighter, was loading at Pier B in Vancouver harbour. Longshoremen were stowing a variety of cargo such as newsprint, chemicals, distress signals, food and aircraft spare parts. Skipper Cyril Andrews and crewman Cec Phillips were awaiting orders on the Gulf of Georgia tug *Cuprite*, tied up at the BA Oil dock. Just before noon they received a phone call from their office directing them to go to the *Green Hill Park* and turn the lumber scow around. The men were finished loading from one side, and needed to have the scow turned so that they could reach the rest of the lumber.

The next few minutes would change the rest of Cyril Andrews' life.

"We went in there, and I had the deckhand letting go the lines off the scow. We were touching it and up against the *Green Hill Park*—and she blew. It sounded like a shot out of hell. When I saw the first explosion go straight up, it blew the hatch-tender with it. He went as high as the Marine Building and landed back on the deck. There were three blasts altogether and they blew me out of the wheelhouse every time. I had to be in close because there were men in the water and I had to get them out. The lumber barge was on fire, roaring away. We backed out away from it, and started pulling people out of the water. It was strange because we didn't know who they were. Men were climbing down ropes dangling from the ship's side, but were dropping like grapes from a vine at each explosion. I backed up to the dock and let the men off that we'd pulled from the water. A newspaper photographer jumped on board and went out with us as we looked for more survivors."

For most of the war Vancouverites braced for a Japanese attack that never came. Then on March 6, 1945, the freighter *Green Hill Park* blew up with enough force to shatter windows downtown. *Photo courtesy Doreen Armitage*

Debris was raining on buildings and streets. Pickles from the cargo fell like green hail. Hundreds of windows shattered in buildings from the waterfront to Georgia Street. Capt. Andrews continued: "We finally got the *Green Hill Park* away from the dock. Some people on the wharf had let the lines go. In the midst of the smoke and flames we pushed and pulled, then a bunch of boats came in to help. George Grey on the *Sumas* took the burning scow out into the middle of the harbour so we could get at the flaming ship. We got her pushed out a little bit, and turned her around. The *RFM*, a big tug, went in and put a line on her and started towing her out. We headed out of the harbour. She was turning this way and that and I was right alongside of her, pushing on her port side trying to keep her straight. We tried to put her on the beach where Vancouver Wharves are now, in North Vancouver, but the tide washed her off. She was burning furiously, and we didn't know if she was going to explode again or not. I said to my deckhand, 'I don't know if she's going to blow again.' We were only about 15 feet from her. 'Well,' he said, 'maybe we won't know this time if she blows.' They tried to stop us from pushing her under Lions Gate Bridge in case she blew and destroyed the bridge, never mind about us. The bridge controller was attempting to divert water traffic by shouting through his megaphone but no one could hear him. We finally got her up on the beach at Siwash Rock, and three fireboats pumped 35 feet of water in her over the next three days and nights to get the fire out.

"Afterwards Gulf of Georgia Towing provided the official boat for investigations. We were around there for about a week, with a representative from the underwriter firm Lloyd's of London. Every time a body was found he and I had to go up on board to verify its location. It wasn't a very nice job. In one place a guy had tried to climb up a ladder inside and he got caught. His arms were burnt off at his elbows, his legs were burnt off at his knees and his head was burnt off. He was hung on the ladder under his armpits."

The federal government investigated the disaster, and, based on available evidence, found that the explosion was caused by "improper stowage of combustible, dangerous and explosive material in No. 3 'tween decks and ignition thereof by a lighted match." The commission's assumption, confirmed years later by a deathbed confession, was that some longshoremen had broached barrels of overproof whiskey and dropped a match while attempting to illuminate the area. Flares stowed on top of the barrels ignited.

The explosion killed six longshoremen and two crewmen. Another 19 men were injured, and flying glass sliced into dozens of office workers. One serious injury not counted at the time incapacitated Andrews. Not realizing that he had a concussion, he couldn't understand what was happening to him later that month.

"I began having severe dizzy spells and collapsing. I hadn't known I had a concussion from being blown out of the wheelhouse. So the company took me off the tugs and I worked for the Towboat Owners' Association that had a hiring hall of their own called the Towboat Employment Agency at 220 Alexander Street in Vancouver. I couldn't work on a boat, but I needed employment. I was in and out of the hospital so many times and they were really trying to do something for me. I felt like I saw every doctor in the country. I was fed up with it. My head hurt so much. Everything would go black in front of me. One doctor told me it was all in my mind. An Air Force doctor took me on and worked with me for years and eventually got me halfway straightened out. They finally found out that my pituitary gland had been squashed by the explosion. I had to have an injection every day of my life for several years. I finally felt better."

In December, 1953, another disaster changed the course of search and rescue on the BC coast. Again, Capt. Andrews was involved. A tug called the *C.P. Yorke*, with eight crew, was running light up the coast one night. "The crew members were all good friends of ours," Cyril Andrews recalled. "We'd see them in the office regularly. Every time a crew would leave they'd come into the office and say, 'Hi you guys. Just saying hello.'" Only a few hundred yards from Secret Cove, going up through Welcome Pass, the *Yorke* hit Tattenham Shoal. Skipper Roy Johnson apparently wasn't too worried when the boat first grounded, expecting it to float off with the tide. But when a wild southeaster came up, the waves and rocks ground a hole in the hull. The *Yorke* rolled over and sank. There were several boats nearby, but in those days tugs' radios were usually tuned to music, probably *Bill Ray and his Roundup*. So they didn't know *C.P. Yorke* was in trouble as her mayday couldn't get through to them.

"The company sent me by car, and also a diver on a salvage boat, up there to search for bodies. I had a phone in the car, one of the first ones. I told George Unwin, who was the diver, that we'd meet him in Pender Harbour. Next day we went out on the boat looking for bodies. And we found six of them, unfortunately. The captain and engineer had made it to shore but it was the middle of winter. The engineer, who couldn't swim, had climbed onto the overturned lifeboat. Water kept washing over him. Freezing! Freezing! He had only pieces of the canvas cover for protection. Finally the boat washed up on shore, and he had to pull himself onto the beach with his elbows because his legs were paralyzed with the cold. Local residents found him and took him into the hospital in Pender Harbour. The captain was also found on the beach. He had a flashlight clutched in his hand, turned on. That's how they happened to find him. He was alive but unconscious. The nurse told me at the hospital that they had a terrible time

Views from a tug's deck as explosions rip through the *Green Hill Park*. Capt. Cyril Andrews recalls three explosions, 'and they blew me out of the wheelhouse every time.' *Photos courtesy Doreen Armitage*

prying the flashlight out of his hand. Both men came through all right. The rest died. We got the bodies and the boat. It was raised from about 80 feet of water by Straits Towing and was running again after a complete overhaul. This catastrophe, in my mind, is what started Search and Rescue. In those days the government wasn't willing to establish Coast Guard on the coast.

"I thought, it's so ridiculous, all the boats have radios on them, but most of the crews are tuned to a music band and can't hear a mayday call. So I went to see my board of directors who were elected every year from the towboat companies, and I told them that I'd like to take all those radio bands with music on them out of the wheelhouses so the crews couldn't listen to music there, and put a radio in the galley for amusement. In the wheelhouse the radios would be tuned to 2182 kilocycles, the distress frequency. The directors thought that was a good idea, so the board sent out messages to all the companies about what they were going to do. And they did it in April 1954. Then we had framed notices made up for all the tugs with what to do in case of emergency and the steps to go through. Printed across the bottom was this: 'The life you save may be your own.'"

This marine rescue arm worked closely with the RCAF base at Jericho beach in Vancouver. Combined air and sea rescue services could be called on when necessary. Capt. Andrews was still working out of the towboat office but could not receive direct calls from the boats. Their mayday calls would go out to any government radio station that could pick them up, who then relayed them to Andrews on the radio telephone in the office, his car or his home.

In December 1953, the tug *C.P. Yorke* sank in a storm in Welcome Pass. Six of its eight crew members died. There were other tugs in the area, but none of them heard the *Yorke*'s mayday—probably because they had their radios tuned to music programs. Cyril Andrews was determined to make sure that wouldn't happen again. *Photo courtesy Vancouver Maritime Museum*

He then contacted any vessels in the vicinity of the accident and the captain of one of them was appointed search master. Andrews was on call 24 hours a day, and was not comfortable with the fact that the boats could not contact him directly. Finally he came up with a solution: "I used to go down to Second Narrows Bridge on my day off, and would sit and chew the fat with the boys while they were working. I thought: 'Their radio is only five watts, but why can't we use that?' So they got permission from their office for me to use it. But the government representative refused: 'You cannot use that radio, period!' But I said, 'I'm damn well going to use it.' He said, 'I'm ordering you.' But I told him I was going to use it anyway. After all, men's lives were at stake. He said it wouldn't reach up the coast but I asked him how come I could speak to the Coast Guard in Alaska on it. There was a write-up in the paper about the feud. Finally I asked Bob Cole what if someone jumped off the bridge or fell off a boat. Would I have to use a special lifebuoy to throw to that man in the water because we couldn't use your lifebuoys? There was a regular war going on, but I kept using the radio. Of course the towboat owners were behind me. The Second Narrows Bridge radio was a monitoring station and listening all the time. If something went wrong they phoned my office right away and I would jump into my car and boil on down to the bridge and use their station. Finally the rescue service got going so well that they formed a committee of companies involved. There was one representative each from the towboat owners, the pilotage, the CPR, Union Steamships, the Fishing Vessels Association, the CNR, Northland Navigation and me. They all agreed that if we needed any of their boats I had the authority to take them and use them; it didn't matter for how long, and for no cost. Nobody paid anything.

"We later went to the insurance companies and asked them what they were going to do to help us with our rescue efforts. They said, 'If you go to a rescue, first save the lives. But, if one of your tugs salvages the boat and tows it into Vancouver, we'll give you double the daily rate of the boat that's towing it.' The rate depended on the horsepower of the tug. For instance, if it had 1,500 horsepower they charged $1,500 an hour. But the insurance company cut down their insurance fees for those hours the guys were working on a salvage. But paying half of it was a good deal.

"The American Coast Guard liked it so much they came up here to see how we worked and we met with them once a month. We worked all over the province, even the lakes. If you were in distress you would switch to 2182 kilocycles and call 'mayday, mayday, mayday.' We had all the lighthouses on the same frequency. That's how it started, and it got so big that they decided that I shouldn't be in the towboat office; I should be in an office of my own. In the spring of 1956, the Department of Transport granted $10,000 toward my salary and some other expenses, and I was moved to an office at the Air Force base at Jericho. It was a highly secure building because it was the end of the radar line and was guarded. My past and my relatives had to be checked. I still hold the pass for it. It was a little awkward in a way because the Air Force didn't like a beastly civilian ordering them around. But I never really ordered them around; I was marine adviser to the Air Force. Then we went to the government to ask for marine telephones so I could talk to the boats

to direct what was going on. They had a five-watt government station at Point Grey, so they hooked a line from that into my office, and when something happened I could talk to all the boats and the Air Force. It was so nice, because as soon as we had an emergency, I'd switch over to the 2366 frequency that all of the tugs talked to each other on, and say 'Hello the ships. Hello the ships. Hello the ships. This is Search and Rescue calling. This is a mayday call.' They'd all answer back. They were always rude to me, of course. On the waterfront you're always rude to each other. If you're not, there's something wrong. Jack Fish was a mate on the *Kenora*. I'd be on the air calling the ships and Jack Fish would call back 'We're out here, Curly [Andrews is bald]. What do you want us to do?' They'd give me their positions, and I'd check them on my huge chart.

"The Air Force boys were interested in plane rescues, but with me there they were also involved in marine rescues. No helicopters were used, just sea planes or wheeled aircraft. They would throw over lifesaving equipment, or lower a line and winch the people up. They did a very good job. The only trouble with the Air Force was that they had an hour's standby. You had to give them an hour's notice. I told the Air Force that it was wrong. You can't expect a guy to hold his breath for an hour. We found out from the doctors how long a guy could live in the water: they gave him at the best 30 minutes. So they brought the Air Force at Comox into it and they had a standby plane there at all times. The Air Force was always the one that spoke to the planes.

"When we got our boats lined up we always appointed a Search Master. He took the orders from me, although I never ordered, I always asked, 'Can you help?' I arranged for a moving line of boats ahead, and the Air Force would drop flares. L&K Lumber in North Vancouver gave us their airplane to use if we needed it. Larry and George Lyttle said I could have that plane anytime I wanted, with a pilot."

One highlight of Capt. Andrews' rescue efforts involved the disappearance of five men on the

Capt. Cyril Andrews

Hilunga, an 82-foot federal works department vessel. Capt. Herbert Dale-Johnson had radioed at 2:30 a.m. in a raging blizzard in February 1956: "I'm going to have to abandon ship. She's breaking up." He gave their location as Cape St. James, the southern point of the Queen Charlotte Islands. After one mayday call their radio was swamped. The Air Force sent planes out looking for any sign of the boat or the men, but after two days found nothing.

After the Air Force contacted him for assistance, Capt. Andrews took action. "I put out a call to any ship that had seen the *Hilunga*," he said. "The closest I could come was the report that one boat phoned in saying that he had seen it just about at the top end of Vancouver Island, and gave the day and the time. We worked out where that was, and I could calculate the speed of the *Hilunga* from the time it

was seen to the time the captain got the distress out, the state of the tide and the weather, and there was no possible way she could be near Cape St. James. I drew an arc on the chart. If he had been on the port side of the arc he would have been in wide open seas. So he had to have been on the starboard side. I drew a mark across there and said, 'There it is, on Aristazabal Island, south of the Queen Charlottes.' When the Air Force went up the next day, there they were, on Aristazabal Island, waving from the rocks on the beach. The tug *Sea Monarch* picked them up that afternoon and they were transferred to a Canso rescue aircraft on the lee side of the island. It was very nice to get thank-you letters from the crew's wives. The *Hilunga* is still sailing. They brought her down to Vancouver and put a new bottom in her."

Despite his co-ordinated efforts, not all rescue attempts were successful. When, on November 10, 1954, the *Salmon Queen* sent out a distress call that it was sinking, Andrews had dozens of boats searching the Strait of Georgia near the mouth of the Fraser River for the missing fish boat with two crewmen aboard. "One boat, the *Master*, got it on his radar, but before the rescue boat could get there the signal disappeared. You know, they would load these wooden fish boats up with so much fish that the vessels would sink to below the regular water line, and, of course, the seams were open where the wood had dried out."

Capt. Andrews and the search and rescue team did enjoy some light moments during their serious searches. One day he requested assistance from some naval vessels in a search area. They radioed their position to the rescue team, who had difficulty interpreting it. "I finally sent a message to Victoria requesting confirmation of the latitude and longitude sent to us," Andrews smiled. "They agreed that it was correct.

"So I sent them a return message: 'Please confirm that the *Restigouche* is in Abbotsford.' That's what they had given us," he chuckled.

In 1960, the Dominion government began to make plans for a Canadian Coast Guard service, and

Capt. Howie Keast

the Department of Transport took over control of the West Coast marine search and rescue co-ordination after seven years of this successful service.

Capt. Howie Keast and Capt. Cyril Andrews were both present at the July 1960 sinking of the *Unimak*. Keast was also involved in the boat's salvage:

"We came across the gulf one night from Gabriola Island on the *Jean L.*, and we crossed over to [Cape] Roger Curtis. During our crossing we came across a fishing vessel heading for Vancouver, towing a reefer barge that carried canned fish and things like that, loaded up-coast. Just east of Gower Point, the vessel towing the barge had gotten into an accident with a fishing vessel called the *Unimak* that had crossed the stern of the tow vessel in front of the barge. Consequently the towline flipped the fishing vessel over, and it then caught up on the bridle gear. You can imagine the position that the skipper of the towing vessel was in. What do you do? Do you slow down? If you slow down it might sink. If you keep going you might hold it up. It was a difficult situation and a hard decision to make.

"As we were getting in past Roger Curtis with our log tow, a westerly wind had started coming up with a swell. There were several vessels including the CPR vessel *Princess of Vancouver* to give some assistance. Several tugs were in the vicinity and came to give a hand, but to no avail. These people in the boat were trapped upside down and had no way of knowing which way the boat was because of blackness. If the rescuers tried to cut a hole in the boat with a chain saw there was some chance that the vessel might sink because the air inside would escape. So with the swell, and increasing westerly wind, the vessel was getting lower in the water. You couldn't beach it properly because of all the problems with the masts, stay wires and so forth. Consequently the vessel sank, but had drifted far west of Gower Point towards White Islets. A diver named Frank Wright went down and tried to see if there was anything he could do. He found a girl but she was already drowned. The vessel took two men down, and there was little they could do in that situation."

Cyril Andrews: "God it was rough! The *Unimak*, a big fish boat, had hit a scow at night near Sechelt, and rolled over. Someone was banging from inside the hull. I brought in the CPR ship *Princess of Vancouver*, on its way from Nanaimo to Vancouver loaded with passengers, to make a breakwater beside the fish boat so that we would be able to get the guy out. We had quite a dilemma. We couldn't cut a hole in the bottom of the boat or it would go down as soon as the air came out. The only thing we could do was hope to hold it up and get a diver to go inside, a pretty risky move. The guy inside kept hammering away. It was a horrible feeling. The water was getting rougher all the time. The guys tried to string towlines between two tugboats and under the fish packer to hold it up, then we could run it ashore and cut a hole in the bottom. Of course we would still be taking the chance of hitting the fuel tanks, or steel plates. One of the rescue boats, the *Brentwood*, had a mast and derrick, and we hooked that up to the *Unimak*. It was so heavy that the weight tore the *Brentwood's* mast out. All of a sudden the fish boat righted itself, then went down. We found out later that two men inside, and another man and a girl also drowned. That would have been a horrible death, in the dark— terrible. But what else could we have done? The CPR ship left then and proceeded to Vancouver. We had held up the transcontinental train for about six hours because they were waiting for the passengers. That was all okay."

Howie Keast: "A few weeks later we took on the job of salvaging the *Unimak*. We used a barge with a logging donkey from L&K Lumber, a Caterpillar and an arch that they used for hauling logs out of the woods. The grappling gear involved the barge, assisted by the *Kathy L.* and our tug, the *Jean L.* We had a big sweeping line going from the barge to our tug, and we dragged along the bottom in a large loop. When we thought that we had hold of something, we'd use what we called a haulback line attached to a logging block or shiv, which would tighten up the loop and go around the vessel, or whatever we had hold of on the bottom. Then we would haul up what was attached. Eventually we found the *Unimak*, but we didn't know what we had ahold of. So we brought it up and the RCMP patrol vessel gave us a hand with their depth-sounder to show us the best way to get in to the beach. While we were holding this vessel just below the surface of the water, we used an inch-and-an-eighth cable, which was rubbing on the angle iron on the barge's bumper. The steel stranded the cable and it broke. Back down goes the vessel. It was so heavy. The wood was just saturated, impregnated with water, and it was down 450 feet, very deep to find without using electronics. We checked the amount of water pressure later with someone at UBC who said it was 198 pounds per square inch, so you can imagine the pressure that was on it. When we did get ahold of it the first time a lot of the penboards floated to the surface. They're eight feet long, six or eight inches wide, two inches

thick and used for making various pens for fish in the hole of the fish boat, and they were just barely floating. A propane tank came flying up from the bottom and blew off all the propane, and gallon cans came up that were squished, crushed together. There was a lot of pressure there.

"So after losing the boat, and trying for the second time, we rearranged our grappling gear, and shortened up the line to the logging donkey to give us a better purchase on the winch. We caught the boat again, and this time we brought it up and held it. The sweeping line must have come up over its stern and the loop tightened on the drag boards cabled to the deck. They are used on fishing boats to drag along the bottom, attached to the fishing nets that are above and behind them. We were worried that the boards would come loose. If our line had come up over the bow, it would have slipped off over the stay lines. We took it in to Davis Bay at Sechelt, beached it, and waited for higher water to float it further in. In the meantime we got some barrels from the Chevron at Sechelt and put them in the fishing hole of the vessel. They helped to give it more buoyancy at the next high water. When the tide came in we moved it in a little further and when the tide went down the RCMP were there to get the bodies out. This was a Sunday morning, and the priest came down and told me that we had a bigger congregation than he did at the church. We patched the boat up and towed it into the shipyard at Coal Harbour. It was repaired and went back to sea again. However, the last I heard of that vessel was that it was hit by an Imperial Oil tanker up off of Prince Rupert and went down with no loss of life. But the boat went down and never came up again.

"I still have a shotgun and a lifebuoy as mementos from the *Unimak*. The shotgun today is rusty, I would never use it, but it is a treasure. We found out later that the *Unimak* was one of the deepest wrecks on the coast brought up to the surface without electronics to aid in locating." ◆

OAR, PADDLE AND SAIL

Nineteenth-Century Transit Along the BC Coast

Lynn Ove Mortensen

Intricately decorated ceremonial canoes are rafted together to form a floating stage for potlatch dancers at the home of Chief Wakas of Alert Bay. This totem pole stood for years at Stanley Park in Vancouver before it was restored and installed in the Canadian Museum of Civilization. *Painting by Gordon Miller, courtesy Canadian Museum of Civilization*

Well into the 20th century, movement around the British Columbia coastline relied on oar, paddle and sail. Even after the advent of scheduled steamer routes and outboard engines, most people depended mainly on human power and the whim of the wind for everyday travel.

Small boats were the workhorses of the coast and one of the cheapest and most available forms was the Native canoe, hand-hewn from local cedar. Pioneers often bought dugouts or, for money or trade goods, hired them, complete with Native guides who acted as navigators, translators and/or fellow paddlers.

Coastal lore brims with tales of robust rowers and lengthy journeys. Skookum Tom Leask of Quadra Island rowed to the Queen Charlottes and returned with a bride. Hans "the Boatman" Hansen lost a hand in a hunting accident while working at Hastings Mills in Vancouver. Undaunted, he had a hook fitted to his arm, which connected into his oars. Finally settling at Port Neville on Johnstone Strait, Hansen thought nothing of rowing and sailing to Vancouver and back again for supplies or medical care when necessary. Once he offered a friend a ride home. The friend thought he'd reach Port Neville faster on the Union boat but Hansen arrived first and was there to greet him when he stepped ashore.

Ernest Halliday explored the coast by rowboat in search of a farm for his wife and two children and finally settled on expansive meadows near the mouth of Kingcome Inlet. Nearing the arrival of her third child, Lilly Halliday helped Ernest row from Kingcome to Comox for the baby's delivery. The trip lasted 14 days and the small family was forced to negotiate Seymour Narrows in a blinding snowstorm.

Contemporary accounts of these remarkable feats speak of time elapsed, weather and blisters, but rarely describe the sights, sounds and smells travellers encountered. We hear little about their supplies and gear, their impressions of the countryside through which they passed or the

Snuneymuxw (Nanaimo) band paddlers pose behind the *Patricia*, an 11-man racing dugout.
Photo courtesy Snuneymuxw First Nation

problems caused by cultural and language barriers. Most were too busy eking out a living to leave chatty written records. Fortunately, several unusually detailed accounts of early travels along the coast remain to lend glimpses of what these early trips were really like.

In the spring of 1862, Reginald Pidcock, barely 21, arrived from England with several other upper-middle class young men to try his luck in the Cariboo goldfields. Six years later, Pidcock wrote the story of his first year in the new colony. Its immediate tone and attention to detail—if not to spelling—seem to indicate that he'd kept a journal.

While Pidcock's upbringing and status certainly influenced the quantity and quality of his initial supplies, his packing lists suggest an idea of goods available in Victoria and contemporary advice for such an undertaking. Pidcock's later revisions reflect practical adjustments learned from experience.

At that time, well-off travellers surrounded themselves with a sea of trunks, bags and luggage of every kind. Even before he left Victoria for the Cariboo, "Pid" had some misgivings about his travelling gear:

In starting for a Colony…I should advise every one to take nothing but a very portable portmanteau as boxes and other baggage are a source of great expense and trouble & hinder & delay in a most terrible manner…& then half the contents is useless & the other half seems too good for the Country.

Pid advised "several pairs of strong lace up boots with good knitted stockings, two or three suits of good tweed of a grey or light brown colour…but a good gun or rifle is indesspensible [sic]."

After a brief, unsuccessful foray toward the Cariboo, Pidcock and friend Harry Blaksley backtracked to Victoria, concocting plans for a canoe trip up-island. They hoped to reach Comox, the new island settlement fast becoming an important northern outpost. By then Pid had rethought his supplies.

"We invested in a blanket shirt apiece…the very best thing to travel & hunt in…& we took a half dozen flannel shirts & two pair of fustian trousers, as these last stand the ware & tear of the bush better than

272

Cloth." The strong cotton-linen twill, usually with a pile face, may have bettered Pidcock's original tweed, but still would have been very weighty, especially when wet. The young men wore "rather heavy lace-up boots" when venturing ashore, but soon learned to make Native-style rawhide moccasins for hunting and paddling, "as a Canoe will not bear to be roughly used."

They bought a dugout and made a sail, which would double as a handy addition to "Indian mats to lie on & also to form a…tent…We bought two pair of heavy blankets, two light axes, a frying pan, & some tin pots or 'billies'…to boil & stew in…."

Provisions included four or five bags of flour, bacon, salt, pepper, yeast powder, and whisky. Hot grog proved "a great treat…if we had got very wet during the day." They carried a rifle, "double barrel gun" and a good stock of powder and lead to insure fresh meat. Pidcock's rifle stood four feet, 10 inches in length. It weighed 12 pounds and had a hair trigger. He also carried a thin, easily sharpened sheath knife to use for every purpose, "either skinning a dear, or eating ones meal or cutting a stick."

The adventurers set out on a "fine morning in September…We had to start early…to catch the tide which runs very strong just outside Victoria & for many miles beyond…" Pidcock records passing Natives trolling for salmon, digging and drying clams, which he and Blaksley relished.

It is a Curious sight to see a party of Indians moving about. If only going to a short distance for a short time they do not move their houses but take their boxes and all their goods and chattels including, cats, dogs & children all stowed away in a wonderful manner, with their brass kettles of which they are very fond. Large mats of different descriptions some made of Cedar bark others of very large Rushes…form very comfortable mattresses…and also make capital dry & warm huts to live in. They travel very slowly in Summer time…and sing a Sort of monotonous Chant which is heard at a great distance in Calm weather.

A party of Natives heading for Nanaimo warned the pair that Dodd Narrows were "hyas skookum" or very strong. Pidcock's account shifts into the present tense as he recalls the excitement of the crossing:

Moving between seasonal fishing grounds or visiting relatives, coastal Natives routinely take the entire family, household goods and all, aboard the dugout. *Photo courtesy Snuneymuxw First Nation*

Dugout canoes, whether the ocean-going whalers and war canoes pioneered by the Haida 1,000 years ago or smaller versions for everyday use, required weeks or months of highly skilled craftsmanship to construct. Recognizing their superiority as 'commuter' vessels for coastal travel, 19th-century Europeans commonly hired or bought Native dugouts.
Photo courtesy Maritime Museum of BC

The tide had just begun to run against us... it was a question whether to try it or not but as our Indian friends wanted to get through and we should have to wait till next morning if we wanted daylight...we determined to try it. The Indians gathered themselves together and paddled all the time. [We] put our best hand forward and prepared for the struggle. Now we are in the middle of it paddling for our lives, the Indians strain every nerve and give a shout to every stroke. We make hardly any headway and all at once the canoe is caught by a strong eddy &

back we both go like lightning & have some trouble in keeping clear of the rocks. Now we try it again always keeping in the wake of the Indians & with a tremendous shout and great straining we hold our own and stand quite still so strong is the current, until another whirl comes and we make a desperate effort and are through...

While they were camped at Nanoose Harbour "two canoes, attracted by the smoke of our fire came over to see who we were...They asked for a little tobacco and seem very much pleased when we gave them each a small piece & offered us some oysters...not anything at all equal to our English oysters either in size or flavour."

With some difficulty Pidcock shot a deer. Stumbling under the load, the novice hunter managed to get it back to camp. "The beast was very fat & weighed...80 or 90 lbs." Blaksley meanwhile had cut firewood, shot a goose and several ducks, and cooked supper. "We had a most comfortable camp and sat rather late over our fire."

In Victoria the men had learned to make thick beds of evergreen boughs to achieve "a nights rest as it is not the lot of many persons to enjoy." Amid other nighttime sounds like "porpoises blowing & seals crying..." Blaksley awakened Pidcock to a "chorus of the most doleful yells...which made us both put our hands to our guns & sit up. The howling proceeded from a pack of wolves who had no doubt followed on my trail...I never heard such a melancholly noise in all my life..."

In the morning they feasted on "venison steaks and kidneys...then cooked some bread with yeast powder stowed all again in the Canoe and started off."

In 1884, the Norwegian B. Fillip Jacobsen arrived on the BC coast to collect "artifacts & curiosities" for European display. Barely 20, he had much experience under his belt. Under the command of his 14-year-old brother Adrian, six-year-old Fillip had helped pursue shark livers off Norway's northern coast. As a teen, he again followed Adrian's lead, becoming a curio collector for a German zoological firm.

Starting along Pidcock's route, Fillip "...took a canoe and one Indian...on my collecting trip..." When the wind was right, they hoisted a sail made from flour sacks still bearing colourful advertising labels. This amused Jacobsen and "...the Indian was...very much pleased with it as it was a regular picture gallery all through."

The Natives' stores seemed even leaner than Pidcock's. They carried bacon, beans and rice; but breakfast and dinner often consisted of salmon cooked the Native way, splayed between sticks angled over a fire, which Fillip "got to leike...very much..."

Jacobsen spoke no English and met few white men along the way "...but the Indian was talking chinok [Chinook] to me all the time and by the time we richet Allert Bay I was fair in chinok...and there for when I meet a whiteman...I tolket chinok."

Alert Bay was as far as his Native companion had agreed to go, so Jacobsen found a Native family to accompany him through the intricate maze of waterways leading from Broughton Strait. Here lay villages steeped in the rich traditions of the Kwakwaka'wakw culture. Because it was forbidden to part with dance masks, rattles and other ceremonial regalia,

During their coastal travels, Pidcock and Jacobsen would often stay overnight at Native settlements such as this one at Cape Mudge on Quadra Island. Relations between Natives and whites could be unpredictable, however; Jacobsen claimed his life was threatened by his paddlers.

he traded secretly at night at Mamalilaculla and nearby villages. Here also he learned that sharply-pointed Kwakwa-ka'wakw paddles, made of stout yew, doubled as spears.

Adrian had suggested great caution in this region. Paddling up Knight Inlet with an old woman, her son and teenage grandson, Filllip grew apprehensive. The woman muttered a steady stream in Kwakwala, and near evening the others began sharpening their paddles.

Finally, Fillip recognized a signal; "like lightening" they attacked...Fillip drew his "6 shotter and...they got so scaret that they droppet right down in the canno. I could not swer in Chinok as there is not such a word, but I certainly told them whot I would do to them if they did not behave..."

Jacobsen maintained command. Leaving the others ashore he anchored and attempted to sleep in the canoe. In the morning he demonstrated his skill at target practice before the four continued on to a village at the head of Knight Inlet.

Appearing hostile, the Natives there sported faces "paintet black and [red]" but Jacobsen managed to make trades and attend a potlatch. While he feasted "...Indians had cut all the buttons out of my coot and over coot and another tried to open my trunk." Jacobsen secured two reliable guides back to Alert Bay. As they started downstream in a downpour, a mudslide rolled into the canoe, splitting the bottom. The men managed a quick repair and continued through relentless, heavy rain. Coming up the inlet, Fillip had noticed a small house. Drenched, they beached nearby as dark fell, and gobbled "dry salmon and water sooket hard tack."

Anticipating a dry night's rest, Jacobsen headed for the tiny house, but he couldn't convince his companions to join him. Not finding a door, he clambered through a loose board and

> laid myself down to sleep...but mighty litle did I have on account of the wet blanket. When daylight com...to my astonishment I noted the leg bone of a skeleton stiking trough the end of one of the boxses...I had sleept in an Indian grave house.

While Pidcock paddled the coast for pleasure and Jacobsen for profit, a third early traveller made a canoe trip for very different reasons:

In April of 1880, 26-year-old Helen Kate Woods set out with her younger brother Edward to visit their older sister, Alice, wife of Robert Tomlinson, the Anglican missionary in Ankihtlast, near Kispiox. Irish born, Helen Kate was raised in comfortable circumstances in Victoria, unaccustomed to the kinds of challenges she was to face—especially the intense cold.

Dugouts were remarkably seaworthy in the hands of expert paddlers. Here two Egmont men brave Skookumchuck rapids. *Harbour Publishing photo*

Kate and Edward left Victoria aboard the *Otter* bound for Kincolith, where they rested and prepared for a trip up the Nass River and overland to the mission. After provisioning and despite some misgivings about bad weather, the small party left against a strong wind at 2 p.m., "when the tide would serve." The Natives of the village, gathered to bid them farewell, wondered "much at my strong heart."

"[T]hrough rough water we forced our way for about three hours...had it not been for the extreme cold, the journey so far would not have been disagreeable," she wrote. Around 7:30 they encountered ice. Arthur, the head Native guide, explained they must lift the canoe and contents on to sleighs. Following Arthur's instructions, they walked "by the side of the canoe, holding on to it...Most places [the ice] was soft, plashy thaw stuff—we sank sometimes five or six inches..."

After about an hour a smell "steals slowly, gently—not sweetly—over our tired senses." It was "...the refuse of the Indian 'river harvest' of fish, fish oil and grease. I never did so heartily enjoy a bad smell!...We can see...bright fire lights shining through door-ways and walls of [Native] houses..."

Stopping at a fish station "established by our countrymen...our first care is to make tea. TEA—hot from a billycook and sipped from tin mugs—it is life, strength, rest, refreshment—all in one..." After the Woods' first night of roughing it, the cannery workers served up a breakfast of "porridge carried round in a huge milk pail...small fish and fried potatoes, hot rolls, bread and coffee and last but not least, a large china washing basin full of dried apples and peaches stewed together."

Morning presented even worse travel conditions. With a cry of alarm, Arthur and the sleigh broke through. Helen Kate had been quite close to

Nearly a month after leaving Victoria, the intrepid Helen Kate Woods and her brother arrived at remote Ankihtlast, where their older sister and her husband ran a mission—depicted here in a sketch by Kate.
Illustration courtesy BC Museum and Archives

Arthur and was splashed with the freezing water. She "thought it safer to abandon the canoe and keep as close along shore as possible, and so hand in hand with a [Native] woman named Catherine I make for the shore, jumping...from hummock to hummock of the rough ice."

The difficulty now is to get the bow-sleigh out of the hole ... [which is] only accomplished by hauling the canoe back far enough to free the sleigh. In doing this the stern sleigh breaks through, Edward going...with it... not an encouraging omen for the beginning of our journey.

This day's trip presented strange sights. "We met a sleigh piled with packages and boxes, on top of which an Indian woman sits holding a pole in her hand as a mast, on which was stretched an old black petticoat as a sail...while her husband (ran) behind" with a rope to guide it, "the wind and the petticoat carrying it forward."

Reaching solid ice, the men packed Kate "in the middle of the canoe with tents and blankets rolled round me while the snow-shoes were arranged fan-wise to shelter me from the wind." The men "rush along full speed, jumping, running and shouting..."

Helen Kate recorded the dress of some Native women in a village they passed:

Their feet were encased in moccasins, the blanket leggings fitting nearly tight, then blanket skirts reaching to the knees, and a blanket jacket of many colours; it being not unusual to see the front of a jacket made from a scarlet blanket while the back will be green and the sleeves of an ordinary white blanket—then outside of all a blanket worn as a shawl or a marmot robe 'skinny side out, woolly side in'—with blanket hoods closely covering the head and greater part of the face.

At the end of the ice, tea was prepared "in the shelter of an Indian house as it was blowing too hard to prepare anything outdoors." They canoed on in open water until 7:30 p.m. when they reached their camping ground. "Having first cleared away the snow to the depth of about two feet we pitched our tent, spread dry branches" in front and "lay with our feet towards the fire while supper was being prepared."

In the morning, they "took to our canoe again, the river here being narrow and very swift it took all our strength to paddle and pull up … toward evening it grew intensely cold and threatened snow." Helen Kate and Edward hoped to camp out rather than sleep in the nearby Indian village, but Arthur advised them to seek the "shelter of a roof."

Settled in the house selected for us, we set about preparing supper as quickly as we could, being somewhat afraid of having a meal prepared for us, which Indian etiquette would not have permitted us to decline … The house was about forty by fifty feet all in one room, and each occupant sat or stood or lay down just where he or she liked—Edward and I lay apart towards the top of the room, wrapped in our blankets. [The Native guides] lay on the floor but carefully within the four posts of a bed-stead from which all the laths have been removed. The "use" of the bedstead had been offered to me but I had declined....

I found in this my first night in an Indian house plenty of warmth, pure air, and no bad smells. To prevent ashes from the open

Reginald Pidcock became the prosperous and respected patriarch of a prominent family in the Campbell River area, and his offspring inherited his passion for paddling. Here Herbert Pidcock takes the King of Siam fishing.
Photo courtesy Museum at Campbell River

fire falling on my head I made a cap of one of Edward's red handkerchiefs... and I more than once asked myself "What would folks at home have thought had they seen me that night?"

The next day navigation proved still more difficult and Arthur, who "having hurt his feet... felt he would not be up to the work on the trail which we now must take to. We were fortunate in finding a Skeena Indian to take his place."

Soon after, the party reached ice again. Edward and one of the guides fell through, getting so wet they determined to stop even though it was still afternoon. The camp was an old Chinese stopping place on the trail to the Omineca. There was firewood cut and dry branches for bedding. The guides found a Chinese shoe and spent the evening imitating "the chatter of Chinamen" as well as performing "tricks of strength and skill." The next morning they left the canoes, dividing the stores and gear, and started up the river.

Their hike over the rugged grease trail to Tomlinsons' mission at Ankihtlast lasted from April 17 to April 29 and provides a story of dogged hardiness all its own.

Helen Kate planned to stay only for the summer but weather prevented her return to Victoria until the following year. She married in 1882 and remained in that city until her five children were grown. Reginald Pidcock originally settled in Comox and became a respected leader among the upcoast villages. And Fillip Jacobsen, who continued his collection of artifacts as far north as Tongass, Alaska, returned to homestead in the Bella Coola Valley. ◆

Reginald Pidcock eventually settled in the Comox area, becoming an Indian agent and, as this photo of his estate shows, a prosperous landowner.

Source Notes

Faa, Eric. *Norwegians in the Northwest*. Funestad, 1995.
Pidcock, Reginald Heber. "Adventures in Vancouver Island. Being an Account of 6 years residence and of hunting & fishing excursions with some Account of the Indians inhabiting the Island." 1868. BC Archives. Add Mss 0728, Vol 4.
Woods, Helen Kate. Diary, Spring 1880. BC Archives Add Mss 773.

The Lightkeeper and the Crow

Pete Fletcher

Being a lightkeeper should have been a contemplative job, and so it was but for a few irritants: a shortage of fresh reading material, an always-empty larder, severe water restrictions...and that bloody crow.

East Point lighthouse perched on a cliff's edge at the end of a long finger of land protruding from Saturna Island's eastern shore. An American lightstation, Patos Island, faced us across five kilometres of boiling ocean, Boundary Pass. It was a cauldron of churning tidal upwellings streaming back and forth with sudden rushes. Talkative persons, not valuing the moment and wishing to compete with nature, would often have to shout above the roar.

The sea here is deep. A drop-off of 37 fathoms was half a stone's throw from the kitchen window. As a consequence, waving at the crew of deep-sea freighters was commonplace, our own goodwill effort. We exchanged fractured languages, big smiles, and friendly gestures. I recall one Russian freighter passing close by, its crew lined up on deck doing calisthenics; in a quick rush their ranks broke. Twenty good-natured seamen were calling out cheers and flailing their arms in greeting. Lining up in front

Fervently I waited for departure day—a day that never came . . . Plainly, he had settled in for a lengthy visit.
Illustration by Carolyn Houg

The ghost of East Point's original wooden tower, demolished in 1967, is superimposed over the open-frame metal tower that replaced it. The light was automated in 1996. *Illustration by Graham Scholes*

of the tower in fine military fashion, my wife, my son, my daughter and I waved our jackets in response. It was a grand spot—the centre of the universe, at least to me.

Our house was a tired veteran built in 1888. Once its peak had sported a lantern, but that had been relocated to a steel tower and the roof closed over. It was cold and drafty and flying a flag indoors during a breeze was no great trick. But it was home.

Nature was the backdrop to each day, and my bonds with the old girl had always been deep. My acquaintance with crows, for example, had always been cordial. Their comings and goings could be noisy, but on the whole, we got along. Privately, I considered them the motorcycle gang of the bird world. But that was just a thought.

On a day of ill fortune I found a bald sausage stuck with pin feathers under a fir tree. Fallen from the family nest, it was a squawking baby crow.

A picture of nursing and nourishing clouded my reason. A scene appeared, in soft water-coloured, fairy-dusted splendour, depicting an adult bird, released, flying free with a thankful heart beating praise for my kindness. I picked the bird up and carried it to the house.

Immediately, I was faced with a feeding problem. Food stocks were sparse at the best of times. Supply tenders sent to revictual the station were, at that period, infrequent and unreliable. Canned food was the family staple, augmented by meat, fowl and seafood taken from nature's larder at the back door. So a balance was struck. I fed the ugly fledgling on bread soaked in tinned milk, dog food, which became his favourite, and strips of venison and rock cod. He flourished.

Anyone who has stood beneath a tree listening to the incessant begging for sustenance which makes up a young crow's life will appreciate the demands now placed upon my time. Any movement in the house—a door being opened or closed, a pot rattled, or perhaps a sneeze—brought a clamour from the cardboard box by the kitchen woodstove. Turning on the foghorn or closing the gate outside would produce the same result. I became a creature of stealth, padding about in bare feet, even tiptoeing quietly from room to room. Objects were picked up in slow motion, carefully, with firm grasp, so as to allow no sound to trigger the raucous demands that would surely follow.

When at last he became fully fledged I removed him to the outdoors. Thankfully I watched him learn to fly. Fervently I waited for departure day—a day that never came. Having grasped the rudiments of flight, he now possessed the ability, and most certainly the inclination, to follow me. Everywhere. Appearing suddenly from an empty sky he would alight upon my shoulder and issue his catalogue of requirements. I had my own feathered Walkman. Plainly, he had settled in for a lengthy visit.

Seconds after the smiling pose was recorded on film, the crow would suddenly clamp his beak on the soft earlobe of his host.
Photo by Pete Fletcher

Trolling for salmon one pleasant summer's day, I was interrupted by an ominous silhouette. Moments later I had a crow on the cabin top. He cast covetous eyes on the herring strip lying on the stern seat. He made a half-hearted grab for it and I waved him off. Just then the bell on one of the cedar poles jingled. A fish! And while I was engaged hauling in the hand line and securing the all-important supper, he quickly saw his opportunity and made off with the bait package and all its contents.

It was the opening salvo in what would be a long and troublesome war. And what a one-sided contest it was.

He had a peculiar habit that became more noticeable with time. When deeply satisfied with himself, as he often was, he would hunch over in low profile, white lids blanking out his eyes. Thus sightless, he would bob up and down chortling with a "nyuk, nyuk, nyuk" identical to the snicker of Curly of Three Stooges fame—except that it was steeped in malice, as I was to learn.

Underneath the open-framed steel light tower lay a large pile of fine sand intended for a future project. My four-year-old son had constructed a miniature world of mountains, ravines, lakes, tunnels, bridges and roads, all nestled in the bosom of this inviting mound. Along these roads travelled his much loved collection of metal cars and trucks. Matchbox toys, as they were called, were highly prized collectibles and the very centre of this young lad's life.

Swooping down from the rooftop, the crow selected a splendidly-painted, red double-decker bus. He poked his beak through the passenger windows and fled with the prize. His next move was hard to witness. As straight as the storied crow flies he flew out to sea and dropped his plunder. A tiny splash below marked the spot. Returning, he landed on the clothesline where he bobbed about in a self-congratulatory rhythm. His young victim burst into tears. Despite a careful watch, the four-wheeled fleet was soon decimated. A few survivors were moved indoors, and the once bustling metropolis on the sandy hill fell silent. The crow cast about for further adventure.

Saturna Island's dry climate made potable water a carefully rationed commodity. Rainwater was funnelled from the roof into a meagre 5,500-litre concrete cistern. For a family of four, especially one with young children, this was a pitiful amount. The taps were turned on with care. Bathwater was shared. Seawater was hauled up the cliff in buckets for the toilet. Washdays were critical exercises in cleaning the maximum piles of clothing with the minimum amount of water.

Sitting inside eating lunch one washday, we were interrupted by the dreaded sounds of sinister chuckling. They were coming from the clothesline outside the screen door. On examination of this sure-to-be-crime, we found all the wet, freshly cleaned laundry lying in heaps upon the dusty ground. One by one, working with devoted dedication, the crow had pillaged his way along the line, releasing clothes pegs as he travelled.

It came to be that with all future washings, one family member was assigned as a broom-waving sentry. And what a rigorous occupation it was too; calling for speed and precision as well as cunning and dexterity. The foe's interest in the gleaming wash never diminished. Frequently, flagging guards had to be relieved due to exhaustion.

Painting season at the lighthouse meant that all the nine buildings that made up the station were to be painted white, and the roofs red. It was a big job, made harder by the constant intrusion of a feathered nuisance. He developed a knack for judging when a paint can was empty enough, and consequently unstable enough, that he could perch on its edge and tip it over. As summer progressed, he took on a colourful red and white coat. He also liked to roost on freshly painted spots where he could mince back and forth to ensure a continuity of blemishes. For awhile he looked like a skunk, sporting a broad white stripe on his back where I had flung a paint brush at him.

One day while I was mowing the pathetic patches of grass we called a lawn, a rock flew out and shattered a large pane of glass in an engine room window. Scouring the supply shed, I discovered I did not have another pane, or a piece large enough to cut. So I boarded up the window and set out on the long trek to buy a replacement.

East Point was 18 kilometres by road from a ferry terminal, small grocery store, post office, and that most vital of all links, a telephone. Calling the narrow clearing through the trees a road was really stretching it. No rock fill or ballast had ever been used in its construction. As a result the dirt had been worn into deep ruts, a railway as it were, where one could take the hands off the steering wheel and motor slowly along enjoying the scenery. Usually the trip took an hour and a half each way.

I phoned the hardware store on Saltspring Island and ordered the glass. Making further arrangements, I asked the mate on the ferry to look after my fragile cargo, and met the vessel the following day to pick it up.

With the new pane at the ready, I proceeded with repairs. Cleaning out the old putty, I carefully scraped a flat surface for the new. The pane was then held in place by freshly moulded sealant around the frame.

Inside the workshop, I was hammering the lid back on to the can when I was startled by the noise of breaking glass.

Running out to the engine room I was just in time to see the crow fly off with a long strip of putty in his bill. He had managed, by dint of evil industry and an ability to hover like a hummingbird, to remove it all. My new glass lay in ruins at my feet.

I kept a boat moored on the Tumbo Channel side of the light, where its exposure to westerly breezes caused many an anxious night. Even more worrisome was the temperamental engine, a sullen lump of metal that required constant upkeep. I despised it, catered to it, and kept it alive.

Removing the cylinder head one day and tinkering with the petulant innards, I realized I needed a few more tools. Rowing the skiff back to the beach I saw the black shape of my arch-enemy entering the boat. My first thoughts were for the welfare of the shiny new, chrome-clad, open-end wrenches. I have broad shoulders, having grown up in a watery world where I learned to row at about the same time I learned to walk. I cranked the skiff around in its own length and flailed those oars. The skiff was planing by the time I arrived back alongside. But it was too late.

Ignoring all the enticing plunder lying about the deck, the crow had selected instead the cylinder head bolts. Eight of them. They were all neatly deposited over the side. Three months passed before I was able to secure replacement parts. Fish swam unmolested in the sea, ducks bobbed about with impunity, and large fir logs eminently suited for the kitchen stove drifted majestically past.

Visitors to the station were fascinated with the crow, delighted to see him perch close at hand and show no fear. Invariably they would ask to have a photograph taken with this feathered ham. Obligingly he would hop onto the offered shoulder. Seconds after the smiling pose was recorded on film, the crow would suddenly clamp his beak on the soft earlobe of his host. He would quickly retreat to a nearby treetop and chuckle heartily.

One year my brother visited the station, and upon his departure was delaying the final goodbyes. Knowing the ferry's sailing time and the condition of the road, I urged him not to be late. He was leaning on the car, twirling the keys around his finger. The crow alit on the car's roof and sidled slowly to the edge, pecking at fir needles and other minor debris as if nothing at all was on his mind. Reading the signals correctly, I warned my brother of the impending raid. Too late! At that very instant the crow seized the keys and flew to the top of the house. But instead of indulging his customary burial-at-sea ritual, he decided to twist the knife and enjoy some quality gloating time on the roof.

Taking a can of dog food, I fetched the extension ladder, climbed to the eavestrough and peered over the edge at my adversary. With his eyeballs blanked

out, he was deep into some real belly laughs. It was tough to mouth all those sweet nothings I cajoled him with, all the while tilting the can invitingly to show off its yummy interior.

Just as in the fable of the fox and the crow, greed and vanity prevailed. He dropped the keys, which slid down the roof into my waiting hand, and flapped to my side for an expected reward. I told him what I really thought of him, which felt good, closed the lid and returned the can to the pantry. Finally a last laugh had been reserved for me. Dashing off for the ferry my brother left in a cloud of dust, counselling me as he left to "shoot that damn bird."

We sometimes felt our kids were deprived of many pleasures considered commonplace by the average child. So we ordered from the mail-order catalogue a red vinyl, inflatable, wading pool. Determined not to limit its use due to water shortages I lugged salt water up the cliff, two buckets at a time. It took, as I recall, sixteen pails to fill it. Then I collapsed in the shade to recover. Within minutes the crow arrived for an exploratory bounce on the rim. He circumnavigated the pool two or three times, had a half-hearted bath by fluttering his wings in it, then he retired to think the matter over. I went into the house to find something cool to drink, returning in minutes to find flattened vinyl and a wet lawn. Strategic holes were revealed around the pool's outside perimeter, at ground level. It was a good replication of machine gun fire.

For a number of years I had applied for a highly sought-after lightstation up north. My application was finally accepted. As there were no roads within 40 kilometres of this particular site, I was forced to sell my beloved truck. Driving as hard a bargain as was possible, I managed to sell it to a fellow who boated in to the beach one afternoon. He came back a week later with the agreed-upon $700. Seven crisp, new, hundred-dollar bills. I put them on the kitchen table for safekeeping while we conducted business. We were drawing up the transfer papers on the hood of the truck, when a glimpse of familiar trouble was framed fleetingly in the corner of my eye. The dreaded dark invader had swooped down to the open kitchen window and hopped inside.

Running as fast as I could, I bounded up the stairs three at a time and threw open the door. There in his black bill was the money, all $700 of it. I threw the only thing I had in my hand, a pen, which hit the table with enough clatter to startle him into dropping the load. He beat a hasty retreat through the window and one of the $100 notes fluttered out in his wake. I raced outside and we arrived at the floating currency in a dead heat. A brief tug-of-war ensued in mid-air and the money, minus a beak-shaped bite, was mine.

The new purchaser of the truck was standing nervously by the vehicle. I explained my mad dash; he in turn was fascinated by the bird and insisted on having his picture taken with it. Months later,

by mail, he sent me a copy of the photo. There this fellow stood, transfer papers in hand, face contorted in pain, the crow tugging viciously on his ear.

Crowless in my new abode, 480 wonderful kilometres from my tormentor, I received a letter from the replacement keeper. He related some of the villainy he had been forced to endure, and was relieved to report the crow had taken up with a female of his own abominable race. As a result the bird was busy now foraging for food for their young. Stepping out on the porch I filled my pipe and gazed upon the endless expanse of Pacific Ocean and heard the rolling southwest swells breaking ashore. In the moonlight I grew reflective and a picture of a nest high up in a tree appeared, filled with demoniacal spawn, being instructed in the fundamentals of iniquitous behaviour. I was overwhelmed with an urgent desire to send this poor unguarded man a shotgun for Christmas.◆

East Point lightstation, established in 1888, sits at the southeast corner of Saturna Island, close to the US border. *Photo courtesy Russ Heinl*

AFLAME ON THE WATER

The Final Cruise of the Grappler

DOUGLAS HAMILTON

HMS *Grappler* was Britain's muscle on the BC coast during the 1860s, quelling a miners' strike, suppressing Native 'threats' and countering American influence. *Painting by Bill Maximick*

On the night of April 29, 1883, the steamer *Grappler* burned and sank in Seymour Narrows with a loss of over 100 passengers. It was the worst fire aboard ship in British Columbia's maritime history, yet it remains little known.

The tragedy entailed a shameful combination of poor planning, panic and cowardice, but from it arose the beginnings of safety regulations on the West Coast.

The *Grappler* was originally built in 1857 as a Royal Navy gunboat designed to patrol the shallow rivers of the Black Sea during the Crimean War—which was over by the time she was launched. HMS *Grappler* was a handy little steamship—32.3 metres (106 feet) long, 6.1 metres (20 feet) wide, with a draught of only 198 centimetres (6.5 feet). On the cutting edge of the technology of the day, she was powered by a 60 nominal horsepower reciprocating engine (about 240 of today's horsepower), driving

Stripped of munitions and military livery, the *Grappler* was sold for $2,400 in 1868 and began its career as a coastal freight and passenger carrier. *Photo courtesy BC Museum and Archives*

a screw propeller, which pushed her along at a steady 6.5 knots. When the winds were fair, a fore and aft square rig turned her into an adequate sailor. *Grappler* was also well armed, with two of the Royal Navy's most modern breech-loading guns on revolving carriages. Her very name suggested determination and aggression, and several examples of the type were built with similar names including the HMS *Forward*.

With the end of the conflict in the Crimea, Britain looked for a place where the mobility and power of these gunboats could be put to good use. Accordingly, in 1859, *Grappler* and *Forward* were

both dispatched to the uncharted coastal waters of British Columbia to counter Indian "threats" and growing American influence in the area. Both gunboats were busy over the next nine years, enforcing law and order, rigorously suppressing any sign of Native rebellion and holding the line against American ambitions in the northwest.

Their most noteworthy moment came during the Lamalcha incident in April 1863. The *Forward* was attempting to apprehend the murderers of three white settlers when it was repulsed with a hail of bullets from the fortified Native village of Lamalcha on Kuper Island. A "boy second class" seaman was killed, and the Royal Navy suffered a major loss of face. Two weeks later both *Grappler* and *Forward* returned to the village and, finding it deserted, burned it to the ground along with several canoes. A large naval force, including the two gunboats, was then quickly assembled to track down the murder suspects hiding on the neighbouring islands. The *Grappler* also served the fledgling coal industry by delivering militia to suppress a bitter, four-month strike against Dunsmuir, Diggle and Company in Nanaimo.

These small warships, crowded and uncomfortable, were not popular with their crews. With the machinery and boilers taking up over half the space between decks, the crew of 36 were squeezed into what remained at the extremities, officers aft, the men forward. Even in an age when seamen had nothing in the way of luxuries afloat, life on these little craft was well below the already low standard.

By 1868, the boilers of both ships were deemed too worn out for repair and they were auctioned off. The *Forward* was sold for $7,000 to agents acting for a Mexican firm. During a period of revolution in that country in the 1870s, she was captured by rebels and burned.

The *Grappler*, being in worse shape, fetched only $2,400. The new owners thought she would be perfect for the rapidly expanding coastal trade. For the next seven years the *Grappler* led a varied career as a freighter jack-of-all-trades, passing through several owners. In late 1875, the steamer was purchased by the famous American, Capt. William Moore, later to be one of the first sourdoughs in the Klondike. Moore proved a better gold digger then shipping tycoon, as the vessel soon became involved in a number of dangerous and unlucky incidents—a portent of the future.

In March of 1876 she went aground on Beacon Rock in Nanaimo Harbour and was beached on the mudflats of the Millstone River for repairs. She was soon aground again, on Sidney Spit near Victoria, causing one shipbuilder to dismiss her as "rotten." However, a steamship inspector disagreed, pronouncing her "sound, staunch, and seaworthy in every respect." Then, in July, while towing the barque *Henry Bruce*, she ran up on D'Arcy Island. The heavy towing rope pulled the *Grappler* over onto her starboard beam, filling her with water, and the old gunboat remained on the rocks for another three weeks.

In November 1880, the ship was hauling a load of heavy machinery from Victoria to Nanaimo when she encountered a fierce southeast gale. The battered hull sprang a leak and she barely made it to Northwest Bay before sinking to her guardrails. Miraculously, the crew was able to patch the hole, and the tug *Pilot* pulled her to safety during a lull in the storm. These repeated groundings undoubtedly played a role in the final tragedy. Although the hull and boiler remained certified, the boiler and firebox were set in brickwork that may have been fatally weakened by this series of mishaps.

In late April 1883, the *Grappler* departed Victoria for points north with a crew of about eight whites and several Native coal carriers. Her captain, John F. Jagers, was experienced, having served as mate and then master of the Hudson's Bay Company *Beaver*. The old gunboat was packed to bursting with lumber, cannery supplies, 50 kegs of blasting powder, 30 white passengers, and more than 100 Chinese cannery workers. On April 29, she docked in Departure Bay to take on 40 tons of coal and unload the blasting powder—a good thing, as it turned out. Anxious to maintain schedule, the ship took on a new pilot and was back on her way by 4 p.m.

At about 10 p.m. during slack tide with a calm sea, the steamer was plodding towards Seymour Narrows and approaching the infamous Ripple Rock, when the mate reported "the smell of fire." Most of the white passengers were sleeping in the few staterooms and temporary berths between decks, while the Chinese had stretched out on the freight wherever they could. Jagers went forward and opened the hatch for inspection.

Steam and sail moor side by side in Nanaimo in the late 1800s. Despite the burgeoning maritime activity on the West Coast, there were no safety standards or inspections—until the catastrophe of the *Grappler*. *Harbour Publishing photo*

"I went below and found a strong smell of fire, but no flame; I went from the after part of the ship along the boiler to the forward part of the ship to the back connection of the boiler. I smelt smoke; I naturally went to look for fire where there was most heat... I went to call the mate, and did not go below after that; I could not get down."

Unfortunately, the brick firebox was inaccessible due to the heavy bulkheads and freight stored below. A large iron plate used for cooking was fitted over the firebox, and it was later surmised that something carelessly stowed had fallen on the plate. But, spontaneous combustion in the coal bunkers or a coal oil lamp may also have been responsible.

Whatever the cause, the fire moved with horrifying speed. Crew members tried ineffectually to haul coal away from the spreading inferno, but were quickly driven topside by the heat and smoke. Capt. Jagers ordered the hatches sealed, sounded five short blasts of the whistle, and set course for nearby Duncan Bay on Vancouver Island. "For God's sake, say nothing about it to the passengers—keep it quiet!" his first mate, John Smith, urged the captain. It was a strange and futile admonition, as the smoke, yelling, and clatter of running feet made it clear to all that something was going very wrong.

Attempts to fight the growing conflagration were seriously hindered by the darkness and lack of available equipment. Only a small lantern in the stern lit the scene; and buckets, hoses and axes were either missing or impossible to locate. James Jones, a passenger, reported:

> The crew were not sufficient; two hands, a mate, and an Indian were all that I saw. There was only one light in the after part of the boat; I did not hear anyone ask for lights until the time of the fire…There was no effort to stop the fire; there was hose, but I saw no water raised. I should judge there were 120 persons between decks; there was a hatchway aft, where it would be easy to escape; I can't say whether any went that way; by the other ways the passengers went over each other's heads. After the fire was discovered, it was about eight minutes until the ship was in flames.

It quickly became apparent that there was a severe shortage of lifejackets and lifeboat space aboard. *Grappler* had originally been equipped with three lifeboats, but the largest had been left in Victoria. Three flat-bottomed fishing skiffs stowed on deck were considered a sufficient replacement. Unfortunately, these ungainly boats were missing oars and oarlocks, and their draining plugs had been removed for the trip north. The remaining two lifeboats had places for only 22. Sixty life preservers were supposedly on board, but few of the survivors reported finding any.

Meanwhile the old gunboat was steaming on full ahead, completely out of control. Her wheel ropes had burned through and the throttle controls were firmly jammed. Chaos reigned as everyone rushed the boats in a panic. Passenger Robert K. Hall described the scene.

> Men, some of them half-dressed running frantically to and fro, half bereft of reason, calling on others to save them, the cries of the horrified Chinamen adding to the fearful confusion…As fast as a boat was lowered men jumped into it—whites, Chinese, Indians—the coolies actually attempting to save their property, throwing clothing and bags of rice into the boats which capsized almost as soon as they were lowered. I could see there was no chance of saving my life by these means and took a set of steps, made it fast to a line, and threw it overboard, allowing it to tow alongside. When I saw the vessel had become completely unmanageable and there was no possibility of running her ashore I dropped overboard, cast off the line and supported by the steps was rapidly borne away with the current.

The crew made little effort to organize an evacuation. David Jones and several panicked passengers attempted to launch boats from the speeding ship with predictable results.

Opposite: Chinese labourers were in great demand in the late 19th century as dockworkers, miners, railway workers and canners, but they were often ill-treated. Racial attitudes and the language barrier added to the chaos when fire swept the *Grappler*. *Photo courtesy Vancouver Maritime Museum*

We swung the boat out, and started to lower her. They let go very quick at the forward tackle, and we could not clear the rope. The after fall fouled, and the boat hung at an angle, she was...8 or 10 [feet above the water]. I said to somebody "cut that fall." After they cut it, the boat turned somersault; I came up and grasped a rope from the ship, and asked to be hauled up; they hauled me a short distance, and let me fall into the water again. I then struck out to swim to shore...

Henry McCluskey was awakened by his nephew and immediately ran on deck searching for a bucket and hoses. He found no hose and only one bucket, which was half full of fish soaking for the cook. McCluskey lashed two barrels together and was about to go over the side when "...I saw Mr. Steel [the engineer] with one lifebuoy and one life-preserver. I said 'You are pretty well fixed for life-preservers.' I did not ask for one; he said nothing. I saw one life-preserver on the captain; this was after I saw Mr. Steel with two life-preservers; I saw a deck-hand named Conlan with a life-preserver; that makes four, all the life-preservers I saw."

Indeed, Capt. Jagers seemed more concerned with salvaging the ship's strongbox than with passengers.

I then told the captain it was getting warm and was time to be getting ashore. I saw the safe, at the end of the windlass, close to the captain. I saw something like a stocking with money in the captain's hand. When I said it was time to go, the captain said "I won't go yet."

McCluskey then went looking for an axe to chop down the foremast, which would have floated 15 to 20 persons, but he was forced to retreat before the flames and entered the water with no flotation. He swam partway to shore and came upon several men clinging to a spar.

Mr. Steel, with his life-preserver on, came up and got on the spar; then a Chinamen came and got on the spar; that made four altogether. I told the men who had life-preservers to get off and let the spar float lighter; they did not get off.

Fortunately, they were soon rescued by Capt. John McAlister, one of the few heroes of this debacle. This experienced sea captain was on his way north to the fishing grounds as a passenger, and it was he who owned the three skiffs stowed on deck. He accompanied Capt. Jagers below, and sizing up the situation, ran back on deck to organize a bucket brigade. When this proved impossible, McAlister raced forward and tipped one of his skiffs into the rushing sea. He jumped in after it, clambered aboard, and was soon followed by a white man and a Chinese. They salvaged a bamboo cane and broom from floating debris and painfully began to paddle their way towards Quadra Island (then called Valdes Island), picking up "five or six men...and two or three Chinamen," as the Victoria *Daily Colonist* later related.

Suddenly, without warning, the *Grappler* turned and bore directly down on their fragile craft, passing within a few yards and singeing all with her fiery breath. The steamer kept going backwards and forwards in an erratic manner, the passengers shrieking and yelling for assistance and the flames spreading rapidly over the vessel.

The courageous McAlister ferried his passengers to shore, and immediately set out once again using broken bits of lumber for oars. He pulled aboard "a Chinaman, a Siwash, Steel, the engineer, and several other white men" and returned to shore to build a fire for the survivors. Further rescue attempts soon became impossible as the already desperate situation took a severe turn for the worse. At about 11 p.m., the tide began to ebb.

HMS *Grappler* (foreground) rests at anchor in Vancouver's harbour in the early 1860s, along with two more British warships, *Shearwater* and *Malacca*. *Photo courtesy Vancouver Maritime Museum*

Even today, the tidal rips in Seymour Narrows run at over 15 knots, making it one of the most dangerous stretches of water on the coast. In 1883, Ripple Rock lay in the centre of the channel, creating a boiling maelstrom for the unwary or unlucky. (Ripple Rock was destroyed in 1958 with 1,237 tonnes of explosives.) As the tidal flow strengthened, the struggling survivors were relentlessly sucked into a frigid hell of roaring white rapids that had consumed many a full-sized ship over the years.

David Brown clung to one of McAlister's upturned skiffs and drifted "among some Chinamen who were supporting themselves with various articles. Two or three grabbed my legs and I felt my hold slackening. I exerted all my strength and managed to free myself." However, on sighting an exhausted white man clinging to a plank, Brown helpfully pulled him aboard.

I had long before this lost sight of the ill-fated *Grappler*, but my companion and I kept our spirits till we heard the roar of rapids and felt the increased strength of the current. We were spun round and round in the whirlpools, sometimes under water and sometimes above, but held on like grim death. At last, about an hour after sunrise we drifted ashore on an island and were found in the afternoon by a couple of Indians in a canoe, who took us to a camp of loggers.

Passenger John Cardano broke his arm trying to launch one of the boats. He described using his remaining fist to punch his way on board one of McAlister's skiffs, occupied by two terrified Chinese. Around midnight the steamer's engine finally stopped and she grounded near Duncan Bay "wrapped in flames from stem to stern." A number of small explosions were heard as the *Grappler* burned through most of the night.

This was clearly one of those terrible disasters in which just about everything that could go wrong did so with a vengeance. So many contributing factors—an irresponsible crew, the darkness of a cold April night, the dearth of lifejackets, buckets, axes, hoses and lifeboat space, the ship barrelling along out of control, the vicious tidal rapids—all combined at the worst possible place and time. The clash of language and culture between the scores of Chinese workers and the 30-odd white passengers and crew then turned a very bad situation into a catastrophe. Most of the Chinese were very recent arrivals with little understanding of the language and customs of the new country. The resulting lack of communication between the two groups made it impossible to stem panic and issue coherent directions for firefighting and a safe evacuation.

British Columbia was wracked by racial tension in the early 1880s. Burgeoning mines, roads and railways required more manpower than the province could furnish, so contractors were forced to import large numbers of workers from China and other Asian countries. It was said that two Chinese miners could do the work of three whites—and do it for less money per worker. The influx reached a peak in 1882 when 8,083 of these Chinese workers arrived in the province, compared to 6,679 white immigrants. An ugly racist backlash developed as whites moved to secure their position in the workplace. The railway work camps in particular seethed with discontent, and less than two weeks after the disaster one Chinese was killed and several critically injured in a violent confrontation at Camp 37 near Lytton.

On the doomed *Grappler*, each race viewed the other as if from another planet—jabbering nonsense, worshipping false gods and looking to steal each other's livelihoods. With all these barriers, co-operation between the two groups was clearly impossible.

At dawn the next day, McAlister made his way to the Kwakwaka'wakw Native village near Cape Mudge for help. Canoes were immediately sent out to scour the beaches, and the survivors were brought back to the village, where they were very well treated before being transferred by steamer to Nanaimo. Twenty-one Caucasians, two Indians and only 13 Chinese survived the sinking. Ten to 12 whites and about 100 Asian passengers perished, but the true number is unknown because there was no official passenger list and many bodies were never recovered. One crew member was lost. At the inquest, even Capt. Jagers seemed to have had little idea as to how many were onboard at the time. "I think I had 100 passengers as near as I can tell, besides those belonging to the ship; I suppose there were about 30 white men and 70 Chinamen..." As we have seen, a passenger estimated 120 were between the decks before the fire. More would have been topside.

The hulk of the *Grappler* was found drifting with the tide, her hull burned to the waterline, and "thin as a wafer." She remained afloat for another half hour while Salmon River Natives clambered aboard to salvage what they could. Of particular concern was the ship's safe, which was said to contain at least $1,000. The Natives found and hauled out the strongbox, and $170.50 was salvaged in "half-melted silver coinage." The remainder, no doubt safe in Capt. Jagers' sock, was never recovered. *Grappler* then suddenly flooded and sank, almost taking two Natives along with her. She went down in 30 fathoms, about 1.5 kilometres southeast of Ripple Rock. The next day the receiver of wrecks arrived and thanked the Natives for their kindness and gallant service.

Almost immediately, questions were raised about the safety of the vessel and the competence of its crew. Although most of the victims were Chinese, it was the death of passenger Donald McPhail that prompted a coroner's inquest. After several days of testimony from survivors (no Chinese or Natives were called), the jurors concluded that McPhail had died by drowning caused by the "accidental burning" of the ship. Arthur Vipond, BC's inspector of steamships, noted that the *Grappler* and her boiler had been examined just a few months before and found sound. "I should think the *Grappler*, as to her hull and machinery, at the time I inspected her, was fit to carry passengers, but not as to her equipment."

Capt. Jagers lost credibility when he revealed that his mate's certificate had been confiscated. "I have lost it: not in this country." Under no legal obligation, he declined to tell the jurors when, where or how. Jagers noted that there were few requirements for operating a passenger vessel in British Columbia waters, and that, as captain, he needed neither a mate's licence nor a certificate from the Board of Trade. In fact, ship passenger travel was almost completely unregulated in the province.

The coroner's report, while critical of the captain and crew, was not damning in its findings. No serious laws had been broken, and the steamship line was neither fined nor required to pay compensation. The coroner ruled that the ship was not licensed to carry passengers, and that it had not made sufficient provision for their safety. The owners and officers were found to be "guilty of culpable negligence in allowing said steamer to leave this port in the condition she was, and [we] respectfully call the attention of the Government to the absolute necessity of having a duly authorized Inspector appointed for that purpose."

That was the one positive outcome of this tragedy: The lackadaisical approach to safety at sea, and the absence of regulations and inspections for passenger vessels was no longer acceptable. Marine transportation in rapidly growing British Columbia had become too important to be left to chance. No more catastrophes on this scale would be tolerated. ◆

Source Notes

Arnett, Chris. *The Terror of the Coast*, Talonbooks, Burnaby BC, 1999.

Daily Colonist, Victoria BC, May 4–20, 1883

Gough, Barry M. *Gunboat Frontier, British Maritime Authority and Northwest Coast Indians 1846–1890*, UBC Press, Vancouver: 1984.

Morton, James. *In the Sea of Sterile Mountains, The Chinese in British Columbia*, J.S. Douglas Ltd. Vancouver: 1974.

Paterson, T.W. "*Grappler's* Fateful Voyage," Canadian West Magazine, Number 10, pp. 152–155, Winter 1987.

Pemberton, A.F. *The* Grappler *Disaster, Proceedings Before the Coroner*, May 15, 1883, Pamphlet at Provincial Archives of British Columbia.

MEMORIES OF CEEPEECEE

Life at a West Coast Cannery

ALDER A. BLOOM

It was late August in 1937 when I first sighted Ceepeecee, or should I say when I first smelled it. I was on the *Princess Maquinna*, bound for Zeballos, the gold-mining boom town on the west coast of Vancouver Island, in search of a job. When the boat tied up at the little dock on the north side of Hecate Channel, behind Nootka Island, a few girls and women rushed on board to buy goodies and I went ashore to see the cannery and reduction plant.

The plants were in full operation, the cannery on salmon and the reduction plant on salmon offal and pilchards (sardines). It was very smelly, but so are most industrial towns, each in its own way. To someone looking for work, the smell meant money. Zeballos was 10 miles or so away, so I just took a cursory look, filed it away for future use, and returned to the boat. Little did I know that I would spend four years at this plant and meet the girl I would marry.

When the boat pulled out I was at the rail waving goodbye with the rest of the tourists. We travelled maybe two miles up-coast to McBride Bay and tied up again. At this site a big sawmill was being built and the boat had a lot of freight to unload so I went

ashore to have a look around. I found the boss, asked for a job and was hired. They were expecting carpenters on the boat and none had shown up, so I was the lucky one. I spent 10 months at McBride Bay, then worked for the Gibson brothers at their logging camps and for Nootka Packing Company at Nootka, and then at Port Albion before returning to Ceepeecee in the fall of 1941 to work for Delbert Lutes.

Ceepeecee, or CPC, was short for California Packing Corporation, the American company that built the plant in 1926 to process pilchards. In 1934 they sold it to Nelson Brothers Fisheries, who added the salmon cannery. Richard and Norman Nelson had been trolling and packing fish on the West Coast for some years; in 1933, they bought the St. Mungo cannery on the southern shore of the Fraser River near Annieville. After their purchase of Ceepeecee they went on to become one of the major fishing companies in the province.

At Ceepeecee, in addition to the cannery and reduction plant, there was a manager's bungalow with a couple of VIP visiting rooms, a two-storey staff house, a couple dozen houses and apartments

Pages 56–57: Wartime view of Ceepeecee leaves no doubt of the hamlet's purpose. The long, white-sided building with dark roof jutting into the inlet is the cannery and fish house. Beyond are two warehouses and the reduction plant. A freighter is tied up at the end of the dock, while a flotilla of fish boats stretches out beside it. Along the shore are the workers' houses and bunkhouses; the China House, and Native village are to the lower right. Midway up the right side of the photo is a long, dark building with white trim—the company store and office. Above and perpendicular to it, the long, white building is the recreation hall. And the taller white building at the right, half obscured by trees, is the church.

Opposite: For most of its life Ceepeecee was accessible only by water, and this was the first scene to greet all arrivals: A cluster of wood-frame buildings huddled between the forest and the shore at the north end of Tahsis Inlet.

Below: Ceepeecee was founded at the head of Tahsis Inlet, a long and dangerous voyage from Victoria. In the days before factory ships and refrigeration, however, canning had to take place close to the fishery.

for married people, and the bunkhouses and cookhouse. Everything was very Spartan but they did have running water, a sewer running out to the saltchuck and electric lights. Mr. Lee, the Chinese cook, and his helper served tasty and abundant meals for the crew; outsiders could get a meal by buying a voucher at the office.

Del Lutes was the manager and Mac McLean was the plant foreman. Lutes grew up around the canneries in Steveston and, like McLean, was a real coastal character. He had a voice and vocabulary suitable for a muleskinner and I guess he came by it naturally, because he did drive freight wagons from Steveston to Vancouver over a road, cut through the forest, now known as Granville Street. Lutes was everything at Ceepeecee: plant manager, office manager, postmaster, storekeeper, cannery and reduction boss (he had a foreman in each of these plants but they didn't dare make a move without first consulting him), oil agent, shipping agent, and harbourmaster.

He was virtually king over Ceepeecee and the boats that operated out of his plant. The only contacts he had with head office were the *Maquinna*'s bimonthly trips and a radio wireless that transmitted only in Morse code. Lutes and the boat skippers were left to make all the day-to-day decisions on their own.

Small wonder, then, that Lutes became a bit autocratic. He was Mr. Ceepeecee, loved and respected by some, hated by others. His word was law. He got into many scrapes around the town and mines of Zeballos. But he had good fish sense and

I think he made money for the company that far outstripped his indiscretions. I ended up working for him for 20 years.

I was the local carpenter and with one or two helpers we took care of all the buildings and plant repairs. Apart from the actual machinery, everything

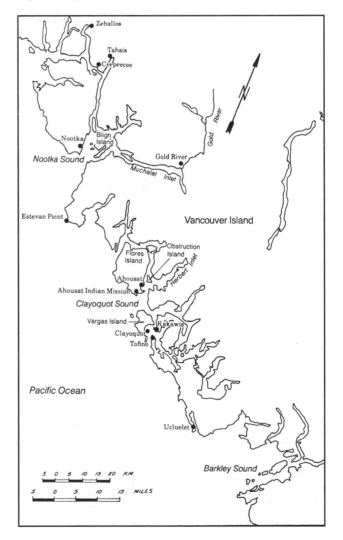

301

in the cannery was built of wood, so we were kept busy. We built and repaired houses, added onto the store and office, drove piles and repaired docks, built fish bins and flumes, erected a big recreation hall, put in a marine ways—and did boat repairs in our spare time. When the plants were running I often worked alone; when they were slack I often had several helpers as Lutes tried to keep the crews busy.

Neil McLeod, the storekeeper, had at least one of everything one might need. Somehow he could always find the required article in the store or warehouse. And while he was looking, he often found a half-empty bottle of Scotch that he had stashed away and forgotten about, so he was always happy to go on a scrounging spree away from prying eyes.

His assistant was a guy named Joe Hicks. Among other things, he was the butcher. The meat came in bulk—quarters, halves or in boxes—every 10 days and Joe kept it in the store freezer, the only cold storage in the camp. Joe had the job of doling out the meat to the cookhouse, boats, families and others. He had standing orders to take care of the cookhouse and the boats first and the rest of us were to share the remainder, but somehow he managed to keep everybody happy—and all for 25 cents a pound in the early 1940s. With his meat supply and his hearty laugh, Joe was a popular guy. He also had an affinity for the bottled goods and could put away more than his share at a sitting with very little effect.

When I moved to Ceepeecee, Joe was living alone in a company house and I moved in with him. There was a bedroom that Joe used and I had a cot in the living room. My job was strictly from eight to five, except for an emergency, but I soon found out that a storekeeper had no such hours. There were bangs on the door at all hours and Joe would get up to give a boat its grub and supplies.

Women make the most of a sunny spell and a break from cannery work to get a little exercise on Ceepeecee's main street. That's Florence Bloom skipping double dutch.

During the pilchard run the plant never stopped. Pilchards are a very oily fish and wouldn't keep for long in a boat. As a packer loaded with pilchards came within sight of the plant, the skipper would blow his whistle to alert the unloaders and they would be waiting to drop the marine leg (a bucket-type conveyer system) into the hold as soon as the boat tied up. The packers often came in with deck loads, barely floating and with the bilge pumps going full blast. The four-man unloading crew started work right away, shovelling the deck load into the hold so the marine leg's buckets could pick up the fish. The marine leg would clamour and groan, powered by a little steam engine, as it dug its way down through the fish. When the fish quit sliding into the buckets the unloaders pulled their hip boots up to their belts, clambered into the hold and plied their big scoop shovels with all their strength, never stopping until the hold was empty. Then they raised the marine leg out of the hold and back on the dock as the fishermen washed down the boat. By then the boat would have its supplies on board, along with any mail or messages, and it would head back to the fishing ground.

Fishermen delivered their catch on a per-ton basis and that's how the unloaders worked, too. They made good money, compared to the plant workers, but few people envied them the job. They were on call night and day and as long as there was room in the plant they were expected to keep working, because the packers had to get back to the grounds as soon as possible.

The head unloader in my day was Oscar Olsen, a medium-sized man but tough as nails. When a packer arrived it was his job to lower the marine leg into the hold and start it operating. When the elevator rested on the bottom of the hold Oscar would climb down and join the other three men shovelling. He also had stomach ulcers and when he started to shovel he invariably became sick and had to empty his stomach over the rail before he could get down to business with the old shovel. But he never complained or failed to do his share. Because

of their odd hours the unloaders had their own bunkhouse but Oscar had his wife and his 14-year-old, Ronnie, in camp so he had a company house. They were exceptional neighbours.

The reduction plant crews worked a 12-hour shift, then returned after supper for another two hours piling meal in the warehouse—100-pound (45-kilogram) bags piled 14 high. It was hard work and all for 35 cents an hour, all straight time. An average of 13 people worked each shift. There were five or six skilled positions and these men were paid by the month regardless of the hours worked. They almost always were white men. Natives were assigned some of the more menial jobs, not because they weren't capable of doing better, but they weren't considered dependable enough. The key men all had to be on the job or the plant couldn't operate, as the meal and oil moved from one process to the next continuously until the meal was in the big sacks and the oil was refined and in the tanks ready for shipping.

To refine the fish oil, the press liquid was pumped to tanks and heated by steam coils in the tank. The lighter oils went to the top and the sediment stayed at the bottom. As more liquid was added to the settling tank it filled to the top and the oil spilled down a trough to another tank, and then another, and finally it was refined. Later they developed mechanical separators that were used in the last stages. The sediment in the bottom of the tanks was washed out onto the beach and this had a lot to do with the rotten smell around reduction plants. Later the fish companies were forced to put in expensive evaporator plants to process this sediment and turn it into fish meal. The operator on the oil deck also became permeated with this smell. It steamed right into his pores, and when an oil deckman sweated, he smelled like a codfish. At the end of the season it took many steam baths to remove the smell and even then one never knew for sure.

The fish oil was stored in a number of steel tanks around the plant, most of them on solid ground, but there were a few smaller ones on pilings over

Left to right: The men's bunkhouse, manager's bungalow, staff house and, at the far right, part of the Native village. Not visible behind the staff house is the China House. The pipe on trestles banking from the centre to the bottom left carries water from a creek behind the town.

the beach. One night, the foundations under two of the tanks collapsed and thousands of gallons of refined oil, ready to be shipped, was spilled out on the beach.

For many years the 100-pound burlap fish meal bags were toted to the warehouse on steamer trucks and stood on end, close to but not touching the neighbouring sacks. This allowed the meal to oxidize and cool off. This method took up a lot of space as the bags often had to stand for more than one shift before they were cool enough to move to the warehouse, where they were piled in a solid mass 14 high. But it worked.

During the war years they started using special paper bags; supposedly these could be piled immediately without standing around to cool. It made for big savings in both labour and space, so Lutes adopted the new system. At first it was okay, but then they must have had a batch of oily meal and the bags began burning in the pile. The

warehouse was more than half full and it was a terrible thing. Lutes got crews of men to dig down into the pile until they came to the hot spots—always near the bottom—removed the bags that were hot and hoped for the best. In short order there would be smoke from another area and they would dig again. Finally, in desperation, Lutes called in a freighter and shipped out the meal. They were heading for Vancouver but the meal started to burn again and the freighter pulled into Victoria and unloaded the works. Nelson Bros. opened up all the sacks, reground the meal—by this time it was like concrete—and resacked it. The company took a big loss on that deal and Lutes wasn't anybody's fair-haired boy for some time.

The cannery took many more people to operate than the reduction plant. In the early days the reduction plant workers were mostly single white men, but the addition of the cannery required a lot of female help. Counting the machine men, the Chinese men, Native men and women, Japanese women, and the white girls, I suppose there were 75 or more people in the cannery crew. The machine men, like their counterparts in the reduction plant, were paid by the month regardless of hours worked. The other white men got 35 cents an hour, while Chinese men and women got 25 cents an hour.

During the fall fishing season there were always fish waiting to be canned, usually on scows tied up to the floats with swarms of screaming gulls overhead and on the scows. It was not an appetizing sight. The cannery ran from eight in the morning till 10 at night and then the cleaning crew and maintenance men took over to steam clean and prepare the cannery for another day. As long as there were fish, there were no weekends; every day was the same. People got tired but they didn't mind the long hours. They were just thinking of the paycheque and winter coming on.

All out-of-town canneries, like Ceepeecee, had a bunkhouse for Japanese girls and Ceepeecee was no exception. Japanese men fished for the canneries and Japanese women worked in them, usually washing fish and filling cans. The Japanese women had unfailing good humour and their smiling faces brightened the cannery shed. Their bunkhouse crowded in 15 to 20 girls and a very strict house mother, and every once in awhile a Japanese fisherman would drop in to see how things were going and to read the riot act if required. They kept strictly to themselves when not in the cannery and there it was all work. The only thing that the white folks thought a little strange— and secretly envied—was their hot tubs. These were wooden tubs about six feet in diameter, with walls about four feet high, set up outside, filled with water and heated with wood fires under the tanks. The Japanese stood in these tanks and soaked away their aches and pains. And the elite of today with their spas and their wine glasses think they invented the hot tub!

When war was declared on Japan, the Canadian Japanese were herded to camps in the Interior of BC and in southern Alberta. Their boats and property were confiscated and a bunch of hardworking, capable and frugal Canadians were treated like prisoners of war. They soon became valued residents in their new home territories. The fruit growers had the most knowledgeable workers and pickers they could ever hope for. The canneries suffered the most, other than the Japanese themselves, of course. The white fishermen licked their chops in glee. There had long been enmity between the two factions; now the whites had things their own way as well as the chance to pick up good boats for a song. Also, once more the Indian fisherman had a chance to get back on an equal footing with the white man. They got better boats, but it was still hard for the individual Indian fisherman to get his boat and gear ready to go fishing when the season opened. He was always a few days late whereas the Japanese were ready and waiting days ahead. When the war ended the canners made a concerted effort to get the Japanese back on the coast and into the fish boats where they belonged.

Usually when there was a shortage of cannery women, the Native women took up the slack, but there was an accommodation problem. They lived in the Native village: two long buildings facing each other with a plank walkway between them. They were built on piles over the water to make sanitation easy. The houses were divided into two-room suites. One room had a small wood-burning cook stove, a table and some chairs or benches and a work counter. The garbage went out the door or sometimes through a hole in the floor. The toilets were separate, built over the water. The Indian women never travelled alone but brought their entire family with them, men as well as kids. Often each suite had 10 or more people living in it but only one or two cannery workers. The Native women had to take care of them all, even if they worked long hours in the cannery.

The other main labour force at all canneries were the Chinese men, who were the mainstay of BC canneries from the start. They had finished their labours on the railroad in 1885 and the canneries were a lifesaver for many of them. Very few could speak English so a bilingual foreman was required and this led to the contractor system, whereby a Chinese businessman would contract to supply most of the cannery labour for so much a case. Each company had its own contractor and the amount paid was usually kept secret.

The company supplied the China House, a two-storey building with a kitchen lean-to. The kitchen always had a big, brick wood-burning stove, built on site, with two or more woks built into the top. All the cooking was done in these woks; rice and tea were their main dishes. The main floor had the office and a room for the foreman and the dining room with its little four-man tables for dining and playing domino gambling games.

The upstairs was a big open ram pasture [men's dormitory], filled with single bunks made from wooden boards and hung with gunny sacks to give a little privacy. The first Chinese worked for $30 or $40 a month, for three or four months, but later it changed to 25 cents an hour. They were willing and able to do most any job that came up, and with a good foreman they could accomplish almost any task.

When Lutes put in a new 12-inch wooden pipeline from the dam to the plant—a distance of about two miles—the job of transporting the wood stave pipe and laying it out along the proposed line fell to the Chinese men. They had to carry it over the rocky creek bed, a horrendous job. They managed it with ropes under the pipe and four men on each side of a 20-foot length of pipe, with the ropes tied to sticks across their shoulders. They would rest in a squatting position and at a signal they would all straighten up, lifting the pipe clear of the rocks, stagger up the creek a few yards and then drop it again for a rest. Eventually they reached their goal and could return downhill for another pipe. It was quite an accomplishment. The wooden supports were cut on the site and the pipes were hammered into place by a couple of out-of-work fishermen. Once more Ceepeecee had a water supply with enough pressure to operate a water wheel for night lights so the diesel generator could be shut down.

During the war years when young male help was hard to get, the companies went after white girls and the more stable married men. To attract them, they offered almost year-round work. To accommodate these couples and the white girls, the company built and moved in more bunkhouses and small houses and somehow managed to house everybody. The single women took care of their own quarters but took their meals in the cookhouse with the men, though at separate tables. Most of the time with married couples, the wife worked in the cannery also. In spite of the low wages, the long hours resulted in a good yearly family income.

Lutes ran a very strict camp but he had to relent a little during the war years. Esperanza Hotel, just 15 minutes away by boat, was a modern building with a good-sized beer parlour, built in 1938 to tap the sawmill trade from McBride Bay. When the sawmill shut down, they found that the loggers, cannery workers and fishermen gave them an adequate business. The town of Zeballos had more to offer with hotels, cafes, shows, bootleggers—and the frontier necessity, a bawdy house. The cannery crews patronized Zeballos very little. It was hard to get to and the cannery hours were prohibitive. We built a big recreation hall to help occupy their time but Lutes' dry laws still sent many of them to the hotel for weekend bashes.

There was a little Scotsman working in the reduction plant and he could squeeze out some very swingy music on his little accordion. He went to the hotel on weekends and the girls spent the night doing their fast jazzy steps with any of the boys who could move that fast. I couldn't so I sat, talked and drank beer whenever I was present, which wasn't very often. They were happy nights and there was no trouble.

One Sunday morning, Scotty didn't check in for his reduction plant shift so a search was started. Scotty travelled in his own little skiff and tied it up at the unloading dock. He had to climb a ladder to get to the dock and somehow he fell. We found him at low tide resting on the bottom below the ladder. Scotty was everybody's friend and he gave more

The young Bloom family—Alder, Florence and son Bob—in Ceepeecee, 1946

pleasure to the crew than anyone in camp. In a place where radio reception was very poor, his little accordion was a godsend. It was sad that he had to go so tragically and alone after having spent hours entertaining an appreciative audience.

Back in the fall of 1940, before I started working at Ceepeecee, I was at the cannery picking up supplies. It was in the fall, when there was a lull before the winter herring started. Most of the crew had gone for holidays but there were maintenance men working and a few of the girls had stayed on to paint machinery. One of them was Florence French, from Vancouver. Florence noticed me going by and gave me a big smile, which I returned. A few minutes later when I was in the Ceepeecee store, she glided in, smiled again, bought her cigarettes and went back to work. I bought my supplies and went back to camp. Once I started working at Ceepeecee, we spent much time together. On October 31, 1942 we were married. We were the first of several Ceepeecee couples to get married; like ours, most of those marriages turned out well. Our son Bob was born in Port Alberni on August 27, 1943.

During the war years I was kept busy with building and repairs. Fishing was seasonal. First we had the salmon from the trollers in the spring, then pilchards for both the cannery and the reduction plant all summer, and herring after Christmas for both plants. It was a year-round deal. Ceepeecee was considered essential to the war effort as the government wanted the canned fish, especially the herring put up in oval cans with tomato sauce.

The only indications of a war at Ceepeecee were the blackout curtains, the absence of the neat and smiling Japanese girls to brighten up the drab cannery and camp, and, a little later, the food rationing. However, the store had such good quotas that we hardly noticed the rationing. Radio reception was very poor so we weren't bombarded with war news and we only received mail once every 10 days. The Air Force had a listening post at the mouth of Esperanza Inlet—at Ferrer Point, I think it was—so we had an occasional Canadian airman as a visitor.

The fishermen's navy was our only real protector. The government took 40 of the biggest and best packers and seine boats from the fishing companies to make up this force and the ex-fishermen and skippers had the time of their lives patrolling the coast. I'll bet that, had the coast been invaded, they would have put up a good fight and gone down with their ships.

With our big recreation hall and the arrival of the white girls Ceepeecee became a regular call for the Navy. They enjoyed our dances and I have to admit that they were a credit to the Navy and behaved in an orderly fashion.

One day, an Army man arrived to alert us about the Japanese incendiary balloons that were being sent over on the prevailing winds to try to set BC forests on fire. It sounded very farfetched to us, but apparently they took the threat very seriously, as they did the shelling of Estevan Point, a mere 20 or 30 miles south of us. At any rate this fellow organized a Ranger unit and each man joining up was given a 30-30 rifle and shells.

There were always accidents that kept Mrs. Davies, the Ceepeecee nurse, busy: hands jammed in gibbing [fish-head-removing] machines, cuts, bruises and burns, hands pierced by fish bones and infected. One time the cannery lineman's leg was burned by steam and he went around on crutches for a long time. Another poor fellow stepped in a screw conveyor and lost a foot. A Chinese man sat down to rest and didn't get up again. The Chinese were very superstitious and they refused to touch the fellow. The cannery maintenance people had to seal him in an airtight container for shipment south on the *Maquinna*.

There was a doctor at Zeballos, but that was two hours from Ceepeecee by boat. Dr. McLean, the mission doctor, was only half an hour away and he did some exceptional things in emergencies but he always maintained that he would rather save souls than bodies, so most people were reluctant to visit him if they had an alternative. Jack McKay was one fellow who had no alternative. He developed terrible stomach pains and lay in his bunk for a number of days with no relief. We had a couple of guys in camp with ulcers who lived on baking soda; Lutes insisted that Jack was in the same category and left him in Mrs. Davies' care. Ritchie Nelson paid us a visit, took one look and ordered Jack taken to the Mission Hospital. Dr. McLean operated that night under the most primitive of conditions, with people holding lamps and flashlights, and removed a badly infected duodenal ulcer and undoubtedly saved his life. That was one of the fantastic things that McLean did, but he often messed up smaller things.

McLean travelled around the camps in his far-from-safe little boat, often overloaded with his people, giving sing-songs and preaching in good old evangelical style. He eventually built a church at Ceepeecee and held regular services.

In the early '40s the pilchards became scarce and then disappeared completely. Everyone—the plants, the fishermen and the crews—were geared up for a big year and then there was nothing. The fishermen staggered about the ocean like chickens with their heads cut off, not willing to believe that millions of tons of fish could just disappear. Some of them rigged up poles and tried to catch some tuna that showed up in coastal waters. That wasn't enough to keep the ambitious fishermen happy so they turned to the salmon. Before long their efficient fishing machines took a toll on the salmon also.

With the pilchards gone the fishermen were in a quandary, but the shore worker was left destitute.

They expected a four-month session of 12-hour days so their 35 cents an hour would grow into a winter's stake. Instead they were given a few hours of work now and then to pay for their board and tobacco. The salmon cannery still operated but the plants depending on the pilchards, including Ceepeecee, were very dismal places. The crews had no money to pay their way out. Some managed to work their way out on the *Maquinna*, but the rest just had to sit back and wait.

Ceepeecee struggled on for a bit, but was shut down for good in 1951. Fish boats using refrigeration or freezers could stay out longer and deliver their fish right to the cities. New regulations were imposed and government inspectors took a dim view of the old, wooden canneries. Up and down the coast, companies found it too expensive to renovate the out-of-town canneries so they abandoned them. Some were torn down, some were sold, but the others were just left to rot. Nelson Bros. built a reduction plant at Steveston and got big, fast packers and barges to haul the fish. Other companies also built modern canneries in the major cities. Over the years, the canning industry was consolidated and now a few companies control the whole industry.

Most of the buildings at Ceepeecee were destroyed by fire in 1954. Only the little boat ways remains. ◆

We are sad to report that while we were compiling this issue of Raincoast Chronicles, *author Alder A. Bloom passed away at his home in Vancouver. Mr. Bloom spent 40 years in the fishing industry, starting in 1938. He worked at Ceepeecee from 1940 to 1946, then went on to work at all the Nelson Bros. plants and camps in BC. Mr. Bloom was very familiar with the BC coast, its history and many of its most notable characters. He spent the years after his retirement from BC Packers documenting the colourful history he lived through. He has left the people of BC a rich legacy in his writing.*

THE CANNING LINE

A Working Salmon Cannery in Photos

In addition to his lucid writing about Ceepeecee, Alder Bloom left behind this remarkable photographic record of Ceepeecee's cannery, documenting the processing of salmon from fish floor to warehouse.

1. With only a few boxes and planks holding back a sea of salmon on the cannery floor (later the fish would be stored in bins) three men work a Smith Butchering Machine, dubbed the iron chink, in the early 20th century because it replaced 30 Chinese men on the butchering table. The man on the right wields a long-handled, one-tined fork called a pew (or pugh), skewering fish and heaving them up to the table beside the machine. The fellow on the far left sorts the fish and places them head-first on a conveyor, which takes them past a knife that removes the heads. The man in the middle then feeds the butchering machine, which has a large spiked wheel that grips the back of the fish and holds it while knives remove the fins and open the belly. Brushes and water gut and clean the fish. The head, tail, fins and offal drop through a hole in the floor to a flume that floats them to the reduction plant, while the roughly cleaned fish is deposited on a belt that leads to the washers. There are electric lights, but everything else is powered by a steam engine, so that shafts, countershafts, belts and pulleys clank and shimmy from one end of the cannery to the other. It looks messy, but the whole place is cleaned with live steam and hot water at the end of each shift.

2. From the iron chink, a belt takes the fish to the washing line, 10 or more young women assigned to individual work stations. A door opens as required to deliver more fish to the worker's trough, filled with running water. She thoroughly cleans, scrapes and washes the fish, then puts it in the bin behind her, which is monitored for both quality control and worker productivity. These girls are on their feet for 12 hours or more a day, for 25 cents an hour, all straight time. Even so, they fare better than their predecessors, Japanese girls who were paid on a piecework basis—so much per bin—before they were rounded up and sent to internment camps. According to author Alder Bloom, it was always a sore spot with the canners that it took so many girls to wash the fish, but they were never able to devise a different way to do it, even in the modern-day canneries.

3. This machine, one of the first modern cannery machines, cuts the salmon into pieces sized to fit either a one-pound or half-pound can. The circular knives on top are very sharp and can be spaced as required; the worker here is operating the left-hand side, set up for half-pound cans. The blades on the right side are spaced farther apart, for one-pound cans. Rectangular buckets, with slats aligned with the knives, are bolted to a continuous chain that loops around sprockets at the top and bottom of the machine. As the bucket comes up from the bottom a worker throws a fish into it, and as it goes over the top the rotating blades pass through the slats, slicing the salmon. The resulting pieces of fish are collected in a hopper, loaded onto a push cart and taken to the canning line.

4. (page 70) On the canning line, cut-up fish are loaded into galvanized buckets perched at an angle in front of the fillers. Each worker takes half-pound cans from a basket behind her, fills them with fish and puts them in the trays on the middle shelf in front of her. This is piecework: When the tray is full a tally man patrolling the filler stations will remove it and punch her card. Only the half-pound tins are filled by hand; most fish are loaded by machine into one-pound cans.

5. (page 71) Workers empty trays of full cans onto the conveyor chain that takes them to the steam box. Salt is added before the lid is loosely fastened. Other women across from these workers are the patchers, who remove from the line any can that looks light, weigh it, add fish if required and return it to the line. Patching is a specialized job that goes to more senior workers. They get the same pay, but a bit more respect from both the women on the line and from management.

6. Filled cans with loose lids are loaded into the matt steam box, about 6 ft. wide, 16 in. deep and 50 ft. long. Steam boxes are made of planks, caulked to make them waterproof and steam-proof, with steam heating pipes below and heavy hinged doors on top that can be raised for cleaning and inspection. The cans pass slowly through the steam box and emerge after 20 minutes. This doesn't cook the fish, but simply heats the can and forces out excess air prior to sealing.

7. Cans slowly emerge from the discharge end of the steam box and slide down a metal guideway to a conveyor that will take them to the crimping machine, where the lids are sealed tight.

8. Half-pound tins are sealed as they come off the filling line. From here they are loaded onto buggies and shunted into the retorts for cooking. If this machine and others on the half-pound line look small for such a large operation, it's because 60 years ago only the choicest fish were sold in half-pound cans. These were mainly coho; West Coast troller operators of this era did

not fish for sockeye, believing they could not be caught with hooks in the open sea. Other fish were sold in one-pound cans, and the cannery has two long packing lines dedicated to the larger size.

9. A woman operates a machine filling one-pound cans. She feeds a cleaned, whole fish into the machine, which uses a series of plungers to push the fish into open cans descending from the can loft, (right). These are used in the fall for the big dog salmon (chum) run. Note the wooden shield protecting the operator's head from oil from the shaft bearing.

10. A mechanic and his helper adjust a filling machine as it runs, while filled cans are conveyed to the patchers (next photo). The women in the background are operating a second filling machine.

11. Native women work on the patching line from the filling machine. During the fall 10,000 or more cases of chum are canned at Ceepeecee, and every tin in every case must pass these women. They remove light cans from the line, add the correct amount of fish and return the tins to the line. From here the cans move through a salter and then to the closing machine.

12. The closing machine loosely crimps the lids on the cans before they enter the vacuum machine.

13. The vacuum machine at the end of a tall-can line sucks the air out of the cans and seals them airtight. This method replaced the steam box.

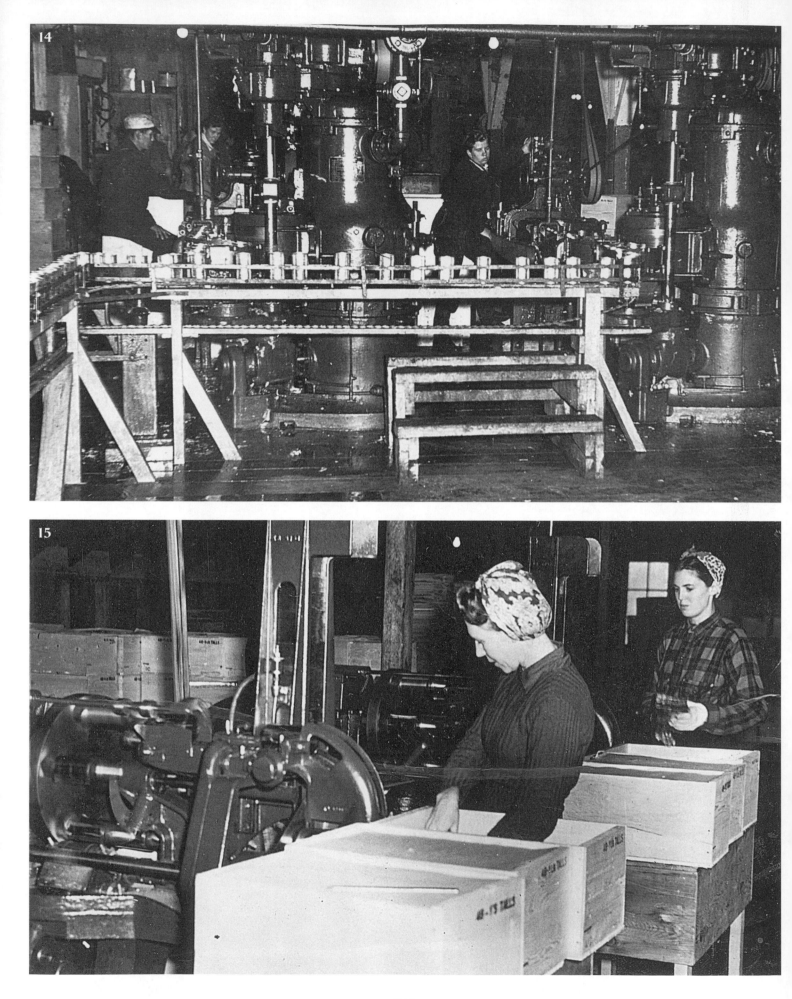

14. Both vacuum machines working full-tilt at the end of either one-pound line.

15. Cans are shipped to Ceepeecee in pieces—one box containing the sides, packed as flattened cylinders, another box containing the round ends. These women are loading the flattened sides into a machine that restores their cylindrical shape.

16. In the can loft, the machines in the foreground receive the re-formed cylinders from the machines to the left and rear of the picture, attach one end to each can, then pass it to the canning line below. These machines are leased from the can supplier.

17. The man to the right is either raising or lowering the door to one of Ceepeecee's five or six cannery retorts, or steam cookers. Visible in the retort is a dolly loaded with seven trays of sealed tall cans; behind it are four more loaded dollies. The door is locked in place before the steam is turned on, and the canned fish is cooked for 70 minutes or so.

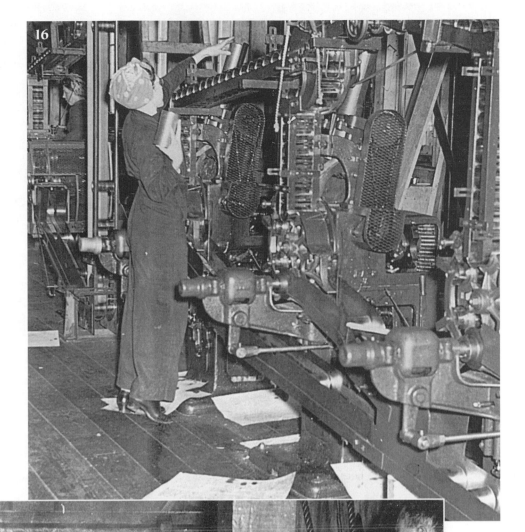

18. Using a long hook that grips the axle, men pull a hot dolly out of the retort, then push it to the box-up warehouse where the cans are left to cool. As their temperature drops, the vacuum in the cans pulls in the ends with a sharp ping. Protruding lids signal a faulty seal; packers will set such cans aside for recanning or disposal.

19. Filling crates is murder on the back, but the box-up warehouse is clean, dry and warm, so the job usually goes to older women with seniority.

20. Chinese box makers nail the tops on full boxes of canned salmon. They are paid an hourly rate for this, but the assembly of the crates in the box loft is piecework, and the men work long hours to make a good wage. In the 1950s cardboard cartons will replace the wooden boxes.

21. Before the advent of forklifts, boxes are shunted to the warehouse by steamer truck and piled by hand. It's no easy job, as each box weighs about 50 lb.

SALT, SALMON AND PSALMS

Wes Huson and the Growth of Alert Bay

PAT WASTELL NORRIS

Sometimes, before I was old enough to go to school, I spent days with my grandparents in Alert Bay. In the afternoons, after my grandmother had scrubbed clothes, cooked a lot of wonderful food on a wood stove, washed and trimmed the oil lamps and done her bookkeeping (for she was the family's financial officer) she changed into a

Left: Oblivious to the charms of scenery or tribal art, boys hang out on the waterfront sometime during the 1920s, throwing stones and generally looking for mischief. *Photo courtesy Pat Wastell Norris*

Opposite: A towering totem, emblem of Alert Bay's Kwakwaka'wakw culture, alongside one of the clapboard structures that began to replace traditional bighouses. *Photo courtesy Pat Wastell Norris*

fresh pair of lisle stockings, put on a navy "afternoon dress," did up her hair and we went out. I took her hand and together we walked along the wide gravel path that followed the shoreline. Our route led us right through a Kwakwaka'wakw Indian village. On one side of the path was a row of longhouses fronted by towering totem poles so that we walked beneath the cruel, proud gaze of thunderbirds and passed bears exhibiting ferocious teeth. We developed a nodding acquaintance with huge naked figures with pursed lips, extended arms and sightless eyes that stared out to sea. On the opposite side of the path were dugout canoes pulled up on the pebbly beach and, in season, big beach fires ringed with intricate racks of drying salmon. On these excursions we met barefoot children clutching tiny kittens with crusted eyes and dodged half-starved dogs scratching and nipping at their limitless supplies of fleas. Neither my grandmother nor I found anything noteworthy in these surroundings. She had lived in Alert Bay since 1909 and I had never known anything else.

Alert Bay offered other, more unsettling, experiences for a small girl from a virtually teetotal household. If our boat was tied to one of the docks in "downtown" Alert Bay on a Friday or Saturday afternoon, and if I accompanied my father up the street on an errand, I had to edge around the drunks who lay sprawled on the side of the road mumbling and shouting (fortunately unintelligible) curses.

Inevitably their faces were covered with blood—the result of a difference of opinion with their fellows.

"The Bay is a terrible place," said my mother.

What it was, of course, was a rip-roaring fishing village. Before Charlie Pepper built the Rainbow Theatre, he showed movies every Saturday night in Alert Bay's Anglican Church Hall. More often than not they were shoot-'em-up "cowboys and Indians" films which were, in the days before political correctness set in, extremely popular with the audience. The real Indians yelled encouragement to the phony Indians on the screen. And small boys, sitting on wooden benches in the front row, totally caught up in the action on the screen, stared up in wonderment. When the story line got particularly exciting, they shrieked and pummelled each other until the bench fell over, throwing them all on the floor.

The audience gave little thought to the fact that they were watching Hollywood's version of the Wild West while right outside the door of the hall the real Wild West was going full tilt. Outside was a rickety little village that included, not the Last Chance Saloon, but the Nimpkish Hotel. The steeds weren't tied to hitching posts outside the bank but were moored five deep at the string of docks lining the shore. And since it was Saturday night in fishing season and everyone had just been paid, the good guys and the bad guys were locked in combat—rolling around on the gravel road that formed the main drag. Fueled by alcohol and testosterone, they flailed away, barely noticed by the passersby.

It started out quite differently. It started, you could say, in 1792.

At 10 p.m. on July 19 of that year, Captain George Vancouver's ship *Discovery* arrived at the mouth of what is now the Nimpkish River and anchored just outside a stretch of sand and sedge grass that formed a small island. At that latitude, at that time of year and at that hour there was just enough light left for the crew to distinguish the mouth of the river and, across the strait, the long mound of an island. And there was just enough light for the native inhabitants

323

of the village at the river's mouth to witness the arrival of the *Discovery*.

As impressive as the ship's appearance must have been to people who travelled by canoe, it probably wasn't the first time they had seen a sailing ship, for in the last quarter of the 18th century Spanish, British and French explorers had all found their way to the coast of what was to become British Columbia. In unwieldy sailing ships the explorers fumbled their way through the coast's narrow channels, ferocious tides and rock-choked passages, its reefs and its fog. They navigated without the aid of GPS, the sweeping line of radar or the flashing numbers of a depth sounder. They didn't even have a chart for, in time, the unwieldy ships' purpose was to survey this coast and *produce* charts.

These foreign explorers substituted seamanship and local knowledge for technology. For this wasn't a totally empty wilderness, however much it might have appeared to be. Scattered bands of Natives lived in villages lost in the vast jigsaw puzzle of land and sea, kept at the water's edge by immense trees and a jungle of undergrowth. Their sustenance came from the sea, so they were skilled seamen, wise in the ways of this treacherous coast and its complicated tides. Consulted by officers of various majesties' ships, the Natives gave advice, warned of hazards and shared knowledge hard won by a people who had paddled their canoes here for thousands of years.

It was another 50 years before the ships of the Royal Navy began to map the area. For 13 years HMS *Alert* and HMS *Cormorant* and later the steam-powered HMS *Plumper* undertook a detailed survey of British Columbia's coastal waters. By 1860 Johnstone and Broughton Straits, Queen Charlotte Sound, Knight Inlet "and adjacent channels" had been surveyed and mapped in the London offices of the British Hydrographic Service. For three shillings the Royal Navy produced a chart that could be used with confidence today. The village at the mouth of the Nimpkish River was identified as Cheslakee, after its chief, and the sandy islet became Flagstaff Island.

The island across the strait was named after HMS *Cormorant* and the curve of bay after HMS *Alert*.

And then, some 10 years after the island and its bay were identified on charts, Westly Alden Huson stepped ashore in Alert Bay. An early resident of Alert Bay, now long gone, remembers hearing that years before, "Wes" Huson had arrived on a sailing sloop, possibly one of many owned by traders plying the coast with goods to sell to the Native people. Huson, an American from New York state, had come to the West Coast convinced he would find a fortune in gold and other minerals.

Huson, the only white man in this village of 400 Native Indian people, promptly set out to explore the surrounding country. Almost immediately he had a brush with success. At Fort Rupert he was told of a coal deposit at Suquash, just north of the Nimpkish River. He obtained a lease for the property from the Crown and worked hard to develop "The North Pacific Coal Company." And he nearly succeeded; he came within a hair's breadth of becoming a coal baron. If it hadn't been for Robert Dunsmuir, who found better quality coal much nearer the markets, Wes Huson might have been the one to build himself a castle in Victoria. Instead he went back to his search for another mineral bonanza. Periodically he boarded the SS *Beaver* and travelled to Victoria with samples of copper and iron ore, marble and granite.

In 1874, the first cannery was established on the lower Fraser River and canned, salted and pickled salmon was produced and exported for the first time. Perhaps, Huson thought, there was an opportunity offered by this new industry. He and his friend and partner Stephen Spencer pooled their slender resources and built a primitive little saltery on the waterfront at Alert Bay where there was deepwater mooring for steamships and easy access to the huge salmon runs in the nearby Nimpkish River.

As a location, Alert Bay had an incomparable advantage. Not only were the Nimpkish River salmon plentiful, they were superior to the salmon caught elsewhere. The Japanese, discriminating consumers

Salmon from Wes Huson's cannery made its way to market under a variety of brand names.

from the very beginning, had discovered that salmon from the Nimpkish River and from Simoom Sound had a firm texture ideal for salting. So, by 1878 a Mr. Fujiyama and a Mr. Sukiyama, knowledgeable in the customer's preferences, were in charge of Spencer and Huson's saltery. Before long steamships were calling to take the five-foot wooden boxes of fish to Vancouver and then to Japan.

Early on the enterprise ran into an unexpected problem, however. There was a modest market and a bountiful supply of fish but not enough people to process them. In this sparsely populated wilderness the only available labourers were the peripatetic Natives who moved back and forth to the Cheslakee village—much farther afield if there was a wedding or potlatch to attend. The paper *Kwakwaka'wakw Settlements 1775–1920* states: "There is conflicting evidence about when the inhabitants of Whulk (the native name for the Cheslakee village, meaning bluff) crossed to Alert Bay. Part of the problem is that Whulk continued to be a fishing site after it was abandoned as a winter village." Whether they lived at Whulk or at Alert Bay, which was also a seasonal village, persuading these inhabitants to come to work in the saltery on a regular basis was more difficult than Huson and company had expected. They found

themselves introducing a radical idea—"working for a living"—to a people for whom the concept was entirely foreign. The First Nations people worked only enough to exist on a subsistence level; their days, then, weren't workdays as such but days in which work, play, art, music and celebration all blended seamlessly into a whole. Untouched by the Puritan work ethic, the men found nothing shameful about spending whole days talking or gambling or simply sitting in the sun and doing nothing at all. So these people paddled across to Alert Bay and turned up at the saltery out of curiosity or when the spirit moved them, but the concept of a regular workday had no appeal at all.

It took a combination of religion and materialism to solve the problem. First Wes Huson persuaded the Reverend Alfred Hall, who had established a mission at Fort Rupert, to move to Alert Bay, noting that Alert Bay was more central in relation to the surrounding villages than Fort Rupert. Huson also promised to supply the mission with land and to build a mission house. Thus persuaded, the Reverend and Mrs. Hall moved to Alert Bay the same year that the saltery was established.

The second lure came in the form of material goods. There was a store in Alert Bay; periodically a steamer called with supplies and goods of all kinds which could be bought with wages. This proved an irresistible attraction. Alert Bay might owe its name to the survey ship HMS *Alert* but it owes its existence to people like Wes Huson and his partner Stephen Spencer. Capitalism had arrived and the Native way of life was changed forever.

By the late 1800s, a footpath followed the pebble beach that curved along Cormorant Island's wide bay, stretching a mile or two from the mission house and the little sawmill at one end to John Robilliard's log house at the other. In between lay the Kwakwaka'wakw village marked by a row of massive longhouses that stood shoulder to shoulder, their great flat facades facing the sea. Their distinctive shallow-pitched roof line proclaimed their heritage as did the totem poles that towered in front of them, the fierce faces of wolves, bears and thunderbirds glaring down at passersby. Their only break with tradition was the milled siding that covered their log frames in place of long split cedar shakes. Here and there a Native inhabitant of the village had opted for the more "modern" style of a conventional frame building and here and there the gigantic log frame of a longhouse under

construction raised its bulk. For this was a community still taking shape.

Lying in front of the longhouses or pulled up on the beach below were high-prowed dugout canoes. And all along the waterfront was a raised wooden platform built out over the beach. This was the Native equivalent of the Englishman's club and its philosophy was "carpe diem." This was where the men indulged their passion for gambling games and carried on interminable conversations.

The beach itself was the domain of the grandmothers. As they did on the beach at the mouth off the Nimpkish River, the women built big fires that burned continuously in the months when the salmon were running. The fires were encircled by an intricate network of saplings and filleted fish and, as at Cheslakee, a gaggle of barefoot boys kept them supplied with driftwood.

Establishing this village within a village caused some difficulty. The Crown, blithely assuming ownership of the whole coast, had given Wes Huson a lease for the whole of Cormorant Island. Now some of this land had to be extracted from the lease agreement and designated as a reserve for the people who had lived there first.

A spacious mission house was sited on a portion of this reserve land and when it was completed the Halls left the wilds of Fort Rupert for the dubious charms of Alert Bay. They arrived in a bleak little settlement that could dispirit the cheeriest of souls. The incessant rain bleached the sea, the beach, the piles of driftwood, the handful of frame buildings and the row of longhouses to a weathered grey. Even the dark trees were greyed with mist. And then the impenetrable darkness of a wilderness night obliterated it all, except for windows glowing from kerosene lamps or a bobbing lantern carried by someone walking along the waterfront.

Kwakwaka'wakw fishermen soon became a vital part of the new industry. Paddling across the strait to the mouth of the Nimpkish, they trolled the tides from their dugout canoes and delivered their catch to the saltery where Native women cleaned, salted and packed it. By 1881, only three years after its establishment, the saltery's owners became convinced that canned salmon was the product of the future. So they bought some early canning equipment and converted the saltery to a cannery. The little mission sawmill, originally intended to teach skills and supply the community with lumber, became a bona fide box factory and the man-and-wife trollers were soon catching the first Nimpkish River salmon to be put in tins. In Victoria, Stephen Spencer did his best to sell this new product. He was not particularly successful.

In 1901, the Right Reverend W.W. Perrin, bishop of the diocese of BC, visited Alert Bay as part of his clerical duties. This man was one of an astounding group of clergy that fanned out across the world promoting the religion of Victorian England, an era that was prim, narrow-minded and utterly convinced

of its superiority. Eager to minister to "the heathen," the Right Reverend disembarked from one of the Union steamships and plunged into a busy round of activities.

He was distressed, he noted later, by Kwakwaka'wakw marital arrangements. "The whole question of their marriage customs is full of difficulties. A girl is sold at a very young age to her husband but as soon as she has paid back the purchase money, she is free to leave her husband without disgrace and to be married to another who may be willing to give a larger price for her. In this way a young woman of twenty-one may have lived with four different men and the result is disastrous." (From today's vantage point this arrangement may seem an enlightened response to the problems of monogamy but to a Victorian Englishman it certainly did not.)

Left: Bighouses crowd the waterfront at Alert Bay. The European concept of 'work' as a daily routine with fixed hours was alien to the Kwakwaka'wakw whose everyday life combined fishing, cultural and leisure activities in whatever mixture seemed appropriate. Seeing that money did not motivate his workforce, Huson set up a mission in town to spread Christianity—and with it, the Puritan work ethic.

Above: A dog naps during a quiet afternoon on the waterfront—a contrast to the rip-roaring celebrations when the fishing fleet comes in.

Spectacular totems are juxtaposed with laundry lines along Alert Bay's boardwalk, circa 1912.
Photo courtesy Pat Wastell Norris

On the other hand, the Right Reverend Perrin was considerably buoyed by his visit to the school: "The school children are quite equal to any white children in secular knowledge," he said. "And I only wish that other school children in Canada and England had an equal knowledge of their Bibles."

He was concerned, as many after him were, about the liquor problem. But all in all, he thought, it had been an encouraging visit. He commended Reverend and Mrs. Hall for their devoted service and reboarded the steamship on its return trip to Vancouver.

Wes Huson was still struggling to keep his fledgling business afloat. The government official who had approved his lease for the Suquash coal property noted that Huson and his partners "possessed little means." Lack of capital was certainly one of Huson's problems; another was lack of business contacts. But perhaps his biggest obstacle was his predilection for prospecting. Stephen Spencer was having great difficulty interesting people in Victoria in canned salmon and it seemed to a discouraged Huson that

canning fish was nothing more than a sideline that distracted him from the possibilities that prospecting offered. So in 1884, three years after the saltery became a cannery, Wes Huson sold his lease on the 600 acres of property on Cormorant Island that he had obtained in 1870 and left the business for good. Stephen Spencer and his new partner, Thomas Earl, bought out the lease for $1,000. In Earle, Stephen Spencer had found what was needed: a partner who had capital, business experience and invaluable contacts in London.

In 1873 Wes Huson had married Mary Ekegat, a Tlingit woman originally from Alaska. He and his wife were to have 10 children, but in the 19th century a child's chance of reaching adulthood was far from assured. In infancy and early childhood, five of the Huson children succumbed to illness. In 1892 Mary died, too. She was only 44. After her death, the older Huson sons scattered, picking up work where they could find it—in the Yukon and on the Skeena River; crewing on ocean-going steamships and logging on Swanson Island. They always kept in touch with their father, always kept their eyes open for prospecting opportunities and occasionally helped him with his ventures. A younger brother, Spencer, named for his father's friend and former partner, made his contribution by becoming a first-rate hunter. He kept the family supplied with deer, ducks and geese and sold the excess.

As with most householders of the time, theirs was a hand-to-mouth existence. But Wes Huson remained the eternal optimist. Until blindness made it impossible, he continued to file mineral claims and collect ore samples, convinced that one of them would prove to be the motherlode.

In the census of 1881 Wes Huson's profession was listed as "trader" but when he died on December 19, 1912, the Record of Burials listed his profession as "canner" which was perhaps more appropriate. For although Wes Huson never did grasp the fortune that seemed so attainable in his youth, the little saltery that he established with his partner Stephen Spencer changed the lives of the inhabitants of Alert Bay forever. ◆

Although his first love was prospecting, Wes Huson's entrepreneurial skills created a stable economy for Alert Bay. *Photo courtesy BCARS*

Source Notes

Akrigg, G.P.V. and Helen. *BC Place Names*. University of BC, 1997.

Chart (copy) Johnstone & Broughton Straits and Queen Charlotte Sound with Knight Inlet and Adjacent Channels. Admiralty, 1867 (Courtesy B. McClung).

Galois, Robert Michael. *Kwakwaka'wakw Settlements 1775–1920*. Joint publication of University of BC Press and University of Washington Press, 1994.

Gregson, Harry. *A History of Victoria 1842–1970*. The Victoria Observer Publishing co., 1970.

Huson, David. Family correspondence and documents in A.M. Wastell, ms, Provincial Archives, Victoria.

Marshall, James Stirrat. *Adventures in Two Hemispheres: Captain Vancouver's Voyage*. Telex Printing Service, Vancouver, 1955.

Newell, Dianne and Roberts, Arthur. "B.C. Canning Industry," article from *Western Fisheries* Vol. 110 No. 3. University Projects document, March 1984.

Perrin, R.R. Article in *The Church Missionary Intelligencer*. Anglican Church Publication, London 1901.

Vancouver, George. *The Voyage of George Vancouver 1791–1795*. The Hakluyt Society, London, 1984.

A Story in the Snow

Bus Griffiths

You know, when you are in the woods in the wintertime, there are lots of stories to be seen in the snow, if you are observant.

I remember one winter we'd been shut down for snow. On this particular day, I'd just gone out to the woodshed for an armload of wood when the boss's pickup swung into the yard. He climbed out of the truck and I wondered what he had on his mind.

He said, "Buster, you know that series of rock bluffs just past the S-curve in the logging road? Did you ever hunt over them bluffs?"

I said, "Yeah! I've got the odd buck in there. Quite a few does seem to hang around in that area."

The boss laughed. "I'm not interested in the deer," he said. "What's the ground like, and how's the timber?"

I said, "Well, actually it's pretty flat. The rock shows in lots of places, but it's not bad. There's quite a few trees in there. Along the front there's mostly them peewee firs, but when you get in a ways there's some nice stuff."

The boss seemed excited. "Look, I'll pick you up in the morning and run you down to camp. You can take the GMC truck and go up them bluffs. I want you to cruise that timber to see if it would make a worthwhile Cat show. I'll see you in the morning."

With that, he took off.

I was up early the next morning, because I knew the Old Man would expect me to be up in the bush by the regular starting time. Margaret and I had finished breakfast when I saw the lights of the pickup as it swung into the yard, so I grabbed my rigging and headed out.

When I was warming up the GMC truck in camp, the Old Man came to me and said, "I want you to really look over that area and see just how much timber we can get with the Cat. You know the elevation isn't too high and there shouldn't be too much snow. It might make a bit of a winter show for some of you boys. I may be up later."

There was a little snow on the road as I neared the rock bluff area. I pulled into a turnout and parked the truck. I grabbed my axe, and I figured I'd take my lunch bucket. That way I wouldn't have to come back to the truck at lunchtime.

There was about three inches of snow on the ground. I worked my way through, studying and estimating the timber and also the ground. I noticed some old deer tracks and, later in the morning, old tracks of a big cougar. There were lots of signs of squirrels and also marten tracks.

I began to feel the pangs of hunger, so I thought I'd better check the time. I shoved my hand down the waistband of my Bannockburn pants and pulled out my old turnip. Sure enough, chow time. I slipped the strap of my lunch kit off my shoulder, then cut some bark off the dry side of a fir snag, including a large piece for a dry seat. I soon had a nice little fire going, so I cut a forked stick from a blueberry bush for toasting my sandwiches.

I'd barely got seated and had just started to open my lunch bucket when two whisky-jacks came sailing in and plunked in the snow, one on each side of me: A couple of volunteers to help me eat my lunch.

It has always amazed me that these birds are so tame. Even the young birds, that have never seen

I'd barely got seated and had just started to open my lunch bucket when two whisky-jacks came sailing in and plunked in the snow, one on each side of me: A couple of volunteers to help me eat my lunch.

people before, seem devoid of fear and will come down and take food from your hand.

I broke a piece off a sandwich and held it out for one of the birds. It took the piece of bread and flew away. I turned just in time to see the other bird taking off with one of my sandwiches clutched in its feet. When it was about to land in a tree it transferred the sandwich to its bill.

When the whisky-jacks collected their booty they would fly up and tuck it in any handy crotch, where a limb came out from the trunk of the tree.

Close by, and being very secretive, was a Steller's jay. It was watching this performance with great interest. Finally, while the whisky-jacks were down collecting more loot, this wily bird was up pilfering their caches. One of the whisky-jacks,

returning to the treetops with more booty, caught the blue thief taking off with its ill-gotten prize. A great squawking match started between the two birds, and they were joined by the other whisky-jack. Shortly, two more whisky-jacks appeared on the scene and the blue jay was lucky to escape with just a few ruffled feathers.

But it was time to get back to work, so I put out my lunch fire and went back to scaling timber and studying the country.

Around mid-afternoon the Old Man showed up. By that time I had a pretty good idea of the lay of the land and the amount of timber available. When I told him what I'd come up with he said, "That's great! There's more than enough wood to keep several of you boys busy until the snow goes and we're ready to start loggin' up on the mountain. I think in the morning you better start blazing out the Cat roads.

I said, "Okay, and I'll mark them out so the fallers can herringbone the timber to the roads, as much as possible."

The next morning there was a little fresh snow, and there's nothing that makes the woods look prettier than a fresh fall of snow.

As I worked back through the timber, marking out the first Cat road, I saw a few fresh deer tracks. These were joined farther along by the tracks of a cougar. Later I saw where the cat had sprang at a deer, but hadn't made a kill.

I was amazed, later in the day, to see the tracks of a fair-sized bear. I thought all bears should be asleep by now. Generally, when a bear doesn't hibernate, it's because it's hungry.

I thought I'd better study the tracks; maybe this fella was hurt. After following the bear's tracks for about a hundred yards, I discovered two things. The bear was injured in the hind quarters—you could see by the tracks that it was dragging the right hind foot. Also, the bear was definitely following the cougar, probably hoping the cat would make a kill, and he'd invite himself to a meal. Sort of an uninvited guest.

The thought struck me that maybe I'd better leave the area and blaze a road in another part of the bluff.

The next morning there was a skiff of fresh snow, and I was blazing a Cat road through a stand of big, scattered fir. I could feel a cold breeze blowing on the back of my neck as I worked through the timber.

Suddenly I came into an open area in time to see the back end of a big bear disappearing into the trees on the far side of the opening. In the snow were the sad remains of a two-point buck deer, and there in front of me was the "story in the snow."

You could see the marks where the cougar had made the kill. The bear must have been quite close and downwind. The cat had started to feed when the bear charged, but there was no sign that the cougar had put up any fight—almost as if it thought, "I'm outta here!"

When a cougar makes a kill, it's what you might call a "tidy diner." It eats what it wants, and if there's snow on the ground, it covers the remains with snow. If there's no snow, the cat will cover the remains with leaves and brush.

On the other hand, a bear is anything but a "tidy diner." This bear had already dragged the carcass of the deer away from the spot where the cougar had made the kill, and before it was through the remains would be spread over quite an area.

I thought I'd better leave and blaze a Cat road into another spot, and let nature take its course.

In the next few days I finished laying out the Cat roads. When I got into the spot where the cougar had made the kill, I could see that the bear had cleaned things up, but had scattered the remains over quite an area.

Nowhere could I see any fresh sign of either animal.

A short time later the fallers moved in and started dropping the timber. I questioned several of them about the animals, but none of them had seen any fresh sign of either the bear or the cougar.

Over the years I've often thought about my "story in the snow," and what a great painting it would make. I could have the cougar lying on the deer, snarling and with a paw up in defensive position, and show the bear rushing in. If I gave the painting a title, it could be along the lines of "Whose Meat?", "Disputed Possession" or "The Uninvited Guest."

However, so far all I've done is think about the painting. Oh well, maybe one of these days...? ◆

The cat had started to feed when the bear charged, but there was no sign that the cougar had put up any fight—almost as if it thought, 'I'm outta here!'

THE TUGBOAT ANNIE METHOD

HOWARD WHITE

I never came across a truer saying than the one about a boat being a hole in the water into which you throw money. I often wondered what kind of person thought it up. It seemed like it should have been someone I knew.

It isn't the idea of the money going in that strikes me quite so much, since most of my boats have been on the do-it-yourself side, as much as the idea of the hole, a temporary disarrangement of the natural order, an offence to oceanic pride

Illustration by Nick Murphy

334

on which it concentrates its vast resources day and night, trying to set it right. There is only one final aim secretly harboured by any boat, and that is to relinquish its unnatural void by going to the bottom with as much inconvenience as possible to its owner. Some boats will wait whole lifetimes for the chance. I was reminded of this on a New Year's day a few years back.

Our family had this old jointly owned diesel cabin cruiser, the *Pywackett*. It was old enough that its previous history was pretty much lost in the mists of time, but there was a theory it had been built some time in the 1930s in the "foredeck cruiser" style that was popular back then. These boats had great high flush-deck hulls extending back three-quarter way to the stern, where they were punctuated by a skimpy wheelhouse and a small open cockpit. Some do-it-yourselfer had gone at it in the meantime and hacked off most of the foredeck, replacing it with a squarish wheelhouse and after cabin that owed more to carpentry than boatbuilding. (Carpenters think in straight lines; boatbuilders don't.)

Like most pleasure boats, the *Pywackett* lay idle at the dock month in and month out. I knew just by its look it was getting in the mood to sink, but I redoubled my determination to head it off by checking it every day as I drove by. I watched it like an eagle, egged on by my all-too-vivid vision of carpet soaked with crankcase oil and electrical equipment oozing turquoise mush. I began to flatter myself with the notion that perhaps I had reached the stage of grizzled experience where it was no longer possible for a boat to get the best of me. I had to leave it at New Year's for two days, but my sister and her family were holidaying in the cabin beside the dock and Alan and Sharie Farrell, who had lived on boats all their lives, were anchored beside it. They were all watching it especially closely because of the bad weather. I explained to them how you could tell how full the bilge was by watching the waterline at the bow. The bow always settled first.

It made it through the night, apparently floating as normally as it had for fifty years. Both parties of

watchers particularly noticed this as late as 10 a.m. But at 10:30 my sister looked out and there it was, its life mission fulfilled, the two-inch high combing around the cockpit the only part of the hull still above water.

I don't get seasick from sailing on boats, but the way sufferers describe it gives a good indication of the sensation I had standing on firm ground taking in that sad sight. I have a job that doesn't give me much time off and I treasure the brief respite of the Christmas–New Year's break. I make the most of it and spin it out as long as I can. Now it was going to be cut short. Worse, my precious downtime was going to be supplanted by a particularly ugly and frantic species of labour.

The usual drill when a boat goes under involves a lot of panicky around-the-clock work as you inch the hulk up the beach over a series of tides. You get logs or empty oil drums alongside and run lines under the hull so the floats are taking as much weight as possible. At the top of the tide you drag the arrangement as close to shore as you can before it hangs up. As the tide falls and the boat grounds, you take up slack on the ropes. When the tide comes in again, the logs lift the hulk higher, and you bump further up the beach. By the second or third tide, if you're lucky, you have the boat sitting up on dry ground. But there's a lot that can go wrong.

When you get the boat up far enough that it starts to come out of the water on a falling tide, if it has a deep-keeled hull like the *Pywackett*'s, it will naturally try to fall over on its side. Not only will this risk smashing the brim-full vessel on the rocks like a water balloon, it means that the rising tide will just flood in over the low side and you won't get it refloated. Like as not it will become one of those disgraced old hulks that adorn the beaches of so many coastal harbours, to the chagrin of the beautification advocates and the delight of Sunday painters.

To avoid this fate you have to get around the side and just at the crucial moment when it begins to heel over, jam a bunch of sturdy timbers in with one end against the rub rail and the other in the mud. Usually the balance point comes when the water around the stern is still over a tall man's head, and I have never discovered a way of navigating through this phase without spending a lot of time underwater. Being made of nice buoyant cedar, the timbers don't really want to keep their heads in the mud. They'd rather tease you by popping up just when you think you've finally arranged the physics of the situation so there's enough lean on the boat to hold them down. The first couple always go in fairly well, but when you get to the last one, you have to rock the boat back up a little to set it in place, but when you do this you take the pressure off the others, and up they pop. It never gets done without at least half a dozen trials, and hysterical cursing only helps so much.

In hypothermic January temperatures and having long since out-matured the wetsuit bought in svelter times, I wasn't looking forward to this part. Nor was I looking forward to the part that comes immediately after, when the tide exposes the hull and fifty tons of trapped water comes to bear on a structure that is designed to hold it out, not in. The stress can break a boat's back, or at least spring the fastenings. You have to go crazy bailing and pumping trying to lower the level of the water inside at the same speed the tide is going down outside, and it's amazing how fast that tide can vacate the premises once it makes up its mind. At this stage the boat is still teetering back and forth, threatening to eject its props, and oily floorboards are floating around inside denying good foothold to frantic bailers. Wet and cold is one thing, but wet and cold and greasy has it beat by a nautical mile.

All of this familiar activity was streaming through my mind as I stared in disgust at the old *Pywackett* that New Year's morning. The gorge rose in my throat, pushed partly by anger and partly by the remains of some stuff I'd put down it the night before. Way too much stuff, as Premier Campbell might say. It was one of those moments, far too frequent in my life, when you get thinking a nice clean lightning strike between the eyeballs might not be such a bad thing.

It was an ugly prospect, but there was no use sulking about it. Your only chance of surviving stuff like that in your right mind is to get up a big head of steam and bull through it, and that is what I resolved to do. Almost.

In my desperation, I began to entertain a goofy idea aimed at avoiding most of the foregoing scenario. It was based on my observation that at this point the old girl had not quite gone under. It was trying desperately, but in those days the family dock was still floating pretty high, and the tie-up ropes on the boat were pretty skookum. They had come tight in just the right way, and were holding the ship just high enough that there was about a half an inch of deck combing still staying dry around the stern.

There's an old story I read years ago in the *Saturday Evening Post* when I was a kid, and it always comes back to me at times like this. It was based on my favourite fictional character, Tugboat Annie, who was the only person in the whole world of mainstream culture who had the faintest shred of plausibility in the eyes of a kid growing up in a logging camp like I was. Most stories you read featured people riding around on underground trains or going up 200-foot-high buildings in things called elevators, and it made for good fun but you couldn't take it seriously. But Tugboat Annie—here was somebody who did something real.

On this occasion she was, as usual, trying to outsmart her arch rival, old Capt. Bullwinkle. Something big had sunk, a barge or a steamship or some such, and the first one who could figure out a way to get it refloated was going to have a big pay day. More important, they were going to have the pleasure of seeing their rival be really, really pissed. Bullwinkle, being better capitalized, had the jump on all the conventional remedies as usual, and Annie's only chance was to employ her superior wits. As usual.

She got on the blower to Seattle's biggest sporting goods supply and ordered three truckloads of ping pong balls. Of course everybody figured the strain had finally got to her, and she had to unleash a

Howard White, his son Silas and friend John Skapski (left) prepare for a voyage aboard the Pywackett in happier, pre-submersion days. *White family photo*

couple of her patented body slams to quell a mutiny. But the ping pong balls showed up just in time, she hooked a big air hose to the sunken barge and with the aid of her on-board air compressor blew those ping-pong balls down into that sunken barge until their collective buoyancy made it pop to the surface. Boy, was that Bullwinkle cheesed...

I didn't have a million ping pong balls handy, but I took inspiration from Annie's example and started toying with the idea that maybe there was some tricky newfangled way of taking advantage of that half-inch of freeboard to make that boat come back up on its own, without going through the three-day hell of dragging it up the rock-bound beach.

I knew it didn't have a big hole in the bottom or anything. The reason it sank could only have been that it took on enough rain to lower that heavy bow down well below the normal water line. The old fir planking on this particular hull had long ago been treated to the "final solution"—a jacket of watertight fibreglass, which stopped sea water from even thinking about leaking in through the bottom. The only trouble was that the fibreglass ended just a few inches above the normal waterline. Above that you were back to the original fir planking chinked between the seams with cotton caulking, which had been allowed to dry out and become about as watertight as the average fishnet. Once the water level came up to that area, swoosh, down she went.

Realizing this, I also realized I only had to think of some cagey Tugboat Annie way of raising her back up to where the dry planking was out of

337

the water, and I could walk away happy. The diesel motor would be fine after this brief a dunking, if you rinsed it with fresh water and changed the oil, and got it running. The rest of the cleanup could wait till the holidays were well past and I was back to being miserable full-time anyway.

I knew where I could rent a couple of high-volume barge pumps capable of sucking the boat dry in short order, if only I could stop new water from washing in through the un-glassed part of the hull, which was so porous the dock's resident herring school was probably swimming through it. I tried to imagine Annie slowing down the incoming water by stiffening it with five tons of Jell-O. Naw, you'd need something stiffer than that to clog these holes . . .

Then it came to me. Poly. Get a nice new 100-foot roll of three-mil poly from the lumberyard and make an envelope of it around the boat. But how to hold it against the sides tightly enough to form a seal against the inrushing water? Maybe, just maybe, when you got the barge pumps going full blast, the tiny current of the water being sucked in through the seams would be enough to draw the poly in against the hull and plug it up.

Well, I know for sure it's not from living right, but that day the Gods were in an uncharacteristic forgiving mood and they smiled on me. The barge pump-and-poly ploy worked so slick I spent about a nanosecond wondering how you could go about filing for a patent on something like that. I just pushed the plastic down around the hull with an oar—being careful not to cause a half-inch ripple that might finally swamp the old girl and send her the rest of the way to the bottom—pulled it tight and fastened it with roofing nails. Then I cranked up the big pumps.

You could almost hear that poly snap as it clamped up against the sides. It wasn't five minutes before the gunwales started to rise, and inside of an hour I had the *Pywackett* sitting up on top of the water like a seagull. I still spent most of my New Year's ripping out oily carpet and roasting salt-soaked electrical gear alongside the turkey, but it sure wasn't as bad as it could have been.

I did manage to save the starter, a nice bonus since those diesel starters cost a bundle, and the little Nissan motor was so tight the water hadn't even got inside it. But the house wiring, which had been cranky enough to start with, never worked again without sparking and smoking. When we got it all scrubbed down, the boat wasn't much funkier than it had always been, but we never really used it again. Once a boat has been underwater you can't relax on it. Eventually we sold it to an oyster farmer on Nelson Island for $1,000, and he rebuilt it into a beautiful yacht, but it sank on him too, and he gave it up for good. You can see her barnacled old hulk today adorning the beach of Blind Bay.

Still, I always keep a boat. Living on the coast without a boat is like living in the Swiss Alps without a pair of skis, in Los Angeles without a car, or in Merritt without a 4X4. You can't quite feel you belong. People come to visit, and what do they think? You're not in tune with your surroundings, not receiving what your place has to offer. If I went to visit someone living in a Wyoming cowtown, I would expect to find a horse. I would expect people there to say that riding through the pine scrub on horseback was in their blood, and that was why they would never live anywhere else. I would expect to feel the pull of this way of life coming through them, pulling at me. Living here in a coastal fishing town, I feel the same way about having a boat, even if the only time I go on it is to bail it and charge the batteries. ◆

RAINCOAST CHRONICLES 20

LILIES & FIREWEED

FRONTIER WOMEN OF BRITISH COLUMBIA

STEPHEN HUME

PHOTO RESEARCH BY KATE BIRD

1 Pioneering through the Ages

Caril Chasens dwells in the same weather-beaten log cabin she built at McCully Creek with her own calloused hands about 30 winters ago at a place so far off the urban map that most of her fellow British Columbians couldn't find it if they tried. Living in a tent for shelter and later moving into a small lean-to that now sees duty as a recycling shed, she felled trees, bucked the logs with a chainsaw, then dragged them back to the building site with a long-departed Land Rover. Petite and still wiry as she approaches her sixties, her black hair now shot with silver, she winched the logs into place by hand using a come-along and then chinked the gaps between them with moss—although she later found that spun glass insulation tamped into the cracks does a far better job of keeping out the December wind.

Caril Chasens' pioneering spirit reaches back to B.C.'s origins. Leslie Barnwell

This tough frontier homesteader is a contemporary example of those courageous pioneer women whose often overlooked contributions shaped the cultural landscape, reformed our politics, defined who we are and made BC into a fully realized province. Like the lilies that settlers planted in their gardens, these women brought a domesticating, even exotic, aesthetic that spoke to the assumptions of a male-dominated society on a rough frontier. Yet the experiences of newcomers quickly meshed with the experiences of those who were

Chasens' 30-year-old log cabin, with more recent additions rising behind, is far from urban comforts.
Leslie Barnwell

A gun, a dog and a pack horse—pioneer Mattie Gunterman leads her son and husband into the bush.
Mattie Gunterman Photo Vancouver Public Library VPL 2213

indigenous and their collective influence eventually proved as pervasive and as hardy as the native fireweed that flourishes everywhere—and most especially in the aftermath of trial and hardship.

Today, Caril's original hexagonal structure is graced with interesting add-ons, one of them the studio where she creates lustrous three-dimensional metaphors from native woods. A naked human form emerges from a carved birch burl. A wood slab is transformed into a bird perched on a log. A round burl is sculpted into the flat realism of a crab putting its claws up as it skitters sideways through the ripples on a sandy bottom. To reach this artist's modest

homestead in BC's remote outback, a visitor by road must be prepared to travel close to 1,200 kilometres north from Vancouver, passing out of the electrified, highly domesticated landscape of the

Caril Chasens' tools transform slabs of wood into luminous metaphors of the wilderness life around her.
Leslie Barnwell

Lower Mainland, through Prince George, westward to Hazelton and north, into a rugged world still illuminated mostly by starlight and sunshine.

This is a country where householders encounter grizzlies in the garden, a place where myths still have a tangible presence and the landscape itself thrums with artistic intensity. Even the glittering mountains have names and legends. They thunder skyward out of the dark shawl of the boreal forest with its lower elevation embroideries of white birch and crimson ground maple. Below them, in villages like Kispiox, Kitseguecla, Kitwanga and Kitwancool, is found the richest concentration of totem pole art in Canada. The jagged peaks of Hagwilget and the more distant Seven Sisters are high enough to make their own weather. Their crags and icefields trail semi-permanent plumes of cloud and the icy meltwater from their glaciers primes the vast hydraulics of a dark green Skeena River and its cold, swift, salmon-bearing tributaries. But for now, the focus comes down to this logging road, our muddy four-by-four still bouncing and juddering northward over ruts and potholes as the gravel surrenders to dirt and the bridges dwindle to a narrow single-lane span. Telephone poles and cables vanished some time back. Now the bush closes in. Another 50 kilometres of this, up over the ridge and we'd be into the upper Nass watershed.

I'm here looking for the woman I hope will provide one of those elusive, living connections between ourselves and the frontier experienced by pioneer women 150 years ago. "Frontier" is a loaded word, of course. It comes charged with the energy of countless justifying icons from North America's paternalistic and colonial past. Traditionally, the frontier is the edge along which "wilderness" defines "civilization." It is also the place where the colonizing culture that presumes itself predestined for dominance most often encounters the unwelcome reality of that dispersed rural "other" that continues to pose vigorous alternatives to urban comfort and refinement. When I set out to try and shape some kind of narrative from the diverse experiences of women whose lives on the geographical frontier had helped bring into being the modern province we call British Columbia, I soon discovered that these women also dwelt on a metaphysical frontier.

Their lives were lived at the boundaries of what would come to shape our notions of a just, pluralistic and egalitarian society, of economic culture and political philosophy as well. And all had one clear thing in common: except for a few exotic celebrities, they were virtually absent from the historic records assembled, for the most part, by their male contemporaries.

The records of missionaries, fur traders, literary men, and the keepers of church and government documents, the writings of brothers, sons, fathers, and husbands are the main sources of women's history, point out Beth Light and Alison Prentice in their 1980 collection, *The Pioneer Women of British North America, 1713–1867*. "Unfortunately, where the women themselves have been totally silent, such records are sometimes our only sources and we must read between the lines for the reality of women's historical lives," they note.

I soon discovered that the story of BC's frontier women was fragmented, scattered and sometimes difficult to find, even "between the lines." Some

Mattie Gunterman ventured into BC mining camps, working as a cook, trapper and subsistence farmer, while documenting life in a collection of glass-plate negatives. The pre-World War I images recorded by Gunterman—seen here near Beaton about 1900—came into wider circulation thanks to Henri Robideau's *Flapjacks and Photographs: A History of Mattie Gunterman, Camp Cook and Photographer.* Mattie Gunterman Photo Vancouver Public Library VPL 2215

Poet Pauline Johnson dressed as a Mohawk Princess, a nickname many people used for her.
BC Archives A-09684

of it I found in dusty, long unopened record boxes in city and provincial archives, some in museum exhibits, some in microfilmed obituaries and wedding notices, some by dogging used bookstores for long-out-of-print local histories. Until recently, women's own voices often emerged from the history of the day only as footnotes, brief asides, amused anecdotes, secondary references or quotations from forgotten journals, letters, memoirs, household accounts and family stories. Yet, as I stitched my quilt together from these brightly coloured bits and pieces, the narrative began to take on a fascinating and astonishing texture of its own.

"The History of a Country is written from the lives of Men, but from the lives of the Women we learn best of a Nation's soul," observes one rare, detailed, early account of women's stories dating back to 1843 that was found for me, perhaps appropriately, in a quaint glass cabinet at the back of his store by Adrian Batterbury, proprietor of the quirky antiquarian establishment in Sidney named The Haunted Book Shop. Published in 1928 by the Women's Canadian Club of Victoria and out of print ever since (a planned second volume apparently foundered with the stock market crash of 1929 and the onset of the Great Depression), The Pioneer Women of Vancouver Island, 1843–1866 was written "In order that we, and those who follow us, may remember the courage, strength of purpose and nobility of character which governed the lives of the pioneer women of Vancouver Island." Women of British Columbia, the next comprehensive look at their collective history, was undertaken almost half a century later by Jan Gould, the popular Vancouver Island historian. Indeed, before the 1970s—just about the time Caril Chasens was building her cabin—there was little serious study of women's history as a formal discipline. Between the publication of that first

volume and Gould's book, the history of frontier women in our province had largely moved out of living memory and into the archival record.

In recent years, however, the rise of an assertive feminist scholarship has brought new perspectives and a new appreciation of women's history to the fore. Today few universities have no women's history component in the curriculum and, in the tradition of BC's own Margaret Ormsby, some of our best historians are now women—Jean Barman, Patricia Roy, Lynne Bowen and the generation that will succeed them. And yet in the bigger sweep of things, the study of women's history remains a relatively fresh phenomenon. On my writing table, the books from which I've gleaned much of the background about BC's remarkable frontier women now number well over 100. Many mention no women in their indexes, even when the books contain references in their narratives—the assumption being, I guess, that nobody would want to look them up. But some offer dramatic first-person accounts of great adventures, of incredible hardships, of courage, of bravery, of tenderness and indomitable will in the face of tragedies and tribulations that would have broken many.

A Nakoaktok chief's daughter.
BC Archives D-08311

Front, from left: Agnes McKay, Lilias Spalding. Rear: Charles Lowe, Gerry Payne, Arthur Spalding, Arthur Lowe on Pender Island, 1889
BC Archives B-07186

to battle their way around Cape Horn, or beating eastward against the tireless North Pacific trade winds, the frontier ranged from the elegant boudoirs of a new colonial capital to the brothel cribs of brutal mining camps.

The frontier was multicultural long before we invented the word, an amazing mosaic of more than 35 aboriginal nations and languages, of Iroquois, Cree and Ojibway women who came with the fur trade, Scots who travelled the lonely back country like fur-clad ghosts, Métis paddlers, Hawaiians, Chinese miners and Japanese mill hands, Portuguese and Italians, English officers, American merchants, Finnish fishermen and Swedish loggers, German dance hall girls, Blacks turning their backs on a slave state, Sikhs and Hindus, Muslims and Jews, Roman Catholics, Anglicans and Methodists. The frontier for women was found equally in classrooms and medical wards, on the factory floor and at the pithead, in painting, poetry, politics and sports. While

The frontier for women left a complicated legacy of many changeable faces. For First Nations women, it wasn't a frontier at all. It was a contemporary modernity that was about to change forever. To find Native pioneers, you'd have to look back to 6,000, or perhaps even 10,000 or 20,000, years ago. For women from Europe and Asia who came so long afterward, initially crossing the oceans in vermin-infested sailing vessels that had

Graduating class of nurses at Vancouver General Hospital in 1909.
City of Vancouver Archives CVA 677-**507**

An antique by uptown standards, the wood-fired cookstove is a reliable essential in the backcountry.
Leslie Barnwell

much is made today of women's hockey, who remembers that the game in BC was pioneered by a feisty women's team that travelled from Victoria to Dawson City to play in 1904?

Then there were the questions of where the frontier era ends and whom among the hundreds of candidates to include in the narrative. I decided, somewhat arbitrarily, that World War I marked the great transformation of BC from its rural, agrarian roots to the industrialized urban giant it is today. So I made 1914 the cutoff point. As for whom to mention, that too was necessarily arbitrary because of the volume of material. Generally, I opted for those less well known, except for women whose ground-breaking work insisted upon their inclusion. And to further complicate things, it turns out that the frontier isn't an artifact that's been fossilized in an unchanging past. It's with us yet, in both geographical and metaphysical terms.

Caril Chasens is an example of this. I found her deep in the forest, far from the

entertainments and diversions most of us take for granted, where she lives cheerfully under conditions that most of her big-city sisters couldn't abide. She hauls water for washing and cooking from the tumbling creek beyond her back door, tramping the summer trail with a pair of plastic buckets until freeze-up. Then she switches to the winter trail, which leads to a more distant point where the current in McCully Creek is swift enough to preclude ice formation. Even the most rugged individuals generally balk at chopping their water at 30 below zero. What Caril and her partner Geoff Watling do have to chop are the many cords of firewood and bales of kindling necessary for cooking and heating their cabin during the long, dark, often bitter months they must spend waiting out winter deep in the northern Interior. At the time I met with Caril, winter had been holding off. "In the old days, you had snow by the first of November," she says. "Winters were fiercer then. But this winter's just not happening. It makes it gloomy around here when all the leaves are gone and there's no snow on the ground. Maybe it's global warming. Maybe not. It's amazing how different the climate is from spot to spot."

Caril lives well beyond the ubiquitous electricity grid that most of us assume is essential for normal life. To communicate with the outside she uses a radio telephone. The only street lights are the shimmering green and yellow curtains of the aurora borealis. The only electrical energy comes from a small gasoline generator supplemented by some solar panels and it's husbanded for power tools and the computer. There's no dishwasher, no electric range, no baseboard heaters, no PlayStation 2 to while away a dreary evening. "One plus is that you don't give a damn when the power goes out or the phone service quits," says Caril, dark eyes flashing, shrugging a little deeper into her red plaid shirt. "The worst thing is trying to fix your truck and breaking a part and having to drive an hour of gravel to get another one." Behind her, the kitchen counter is fragrant with new loaves. She bakes her own bread every week, one more way of avoiding the fuel costs of that long drive to the nearest convenience store. That's in Kispiox, a Gitksan village of

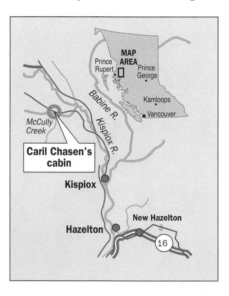

651 or 553, depending upon whom you ask. "These roads just beat vehicles to death," she says. Indeed, the hulks of several that have already died are out at the fringes of the yard. Willows sucker up through the windows.

And yet, despite similarities that her pioneer sisters from two centuries ago would recognize instantly, any woman who chooses the frontier life in BC in the 21st century has a far different experience from one who lived in the early years of this province. "I'm as much in the 21st century as any woman in Manhattan—a little less worried about bombers, perhaps. I'm marketing my art on the Internet. It connects me directly into the mainstream," Caril says. Her partner, on the other hand, a 20-year veteran of the forest industry who says he reinvented himself as a computer nerd when the bottom fell out of logging, uses the household computer to operate a digital recording studio for musicians scattered up the Kispiox Valley.

"We're not separate from the world here. There was a time when I believed you could get back to nature, get back to that hippy-dippy paradise we thought was over the horizon," she says. "Now, I know, problems are global. I used to think I could get away from them, but you can't. You are part of it wherever you go." In fact, she points out, this very afternoon there's an air quality warning out from Environment Canada for the whole zone between Terrace and Smithers, an area the size of some small European countries. People are warned to avoid strenuous activity outdoors because of the particulate matter in the air from mills and slash burning. "Yes, it's a different way of living out here on McCully Creek but it's definitely not the 1800s," she observes, waving a hand dismissively. "Actually, I'm thankful for that. I wouldn't want to go back there, anyway. It was real crappy for women back then." Born in Dayton, Ohio, in 1945, she came to Canada in 1966 and drifted north until she wound up here, in a curve of this little singing tributary of the Kispiox, surrounded by the forests, mountains and sky that inspire and infuse her art.

Like Caril, many of those earlier pioneer women came to BC in search of greater freedom, with dreams of a new life beyond the reach of stifling conventions, a chance for greater prosperity, for the opportunity to fulfill themselves creatively and make a better future for their own children than they had faced in Europe, Asia and America. Like her, they encountered unimaginably hard work and difficult conditions, which they accepted, then mastered, then turned to their own advantage. Yet a woman on the frontier today is still within a helicopter flight of first-class medical treatment, even if it means slamming over frozen ruts in a four-by-four to get to a landing site. A century ago, many rural inhabitants might have had to travel a week to find a doctor. For women of childbearing years, this added risks to their lives that most young women today would consider unacceptable. For every 1,000 births, five women and 120 babies would die. In 1871, the average woman could expect to have 6.8 children and the majority of those women lived on rural farmsteads, in logging shows, fishing outports and mining camps—far beyond the reach of medical care and technology that we today assume as a birthright. What they endured is a reminder of the significance of their contributions to the creation of this province.

As for Caril? How far is she from town?

"How far? I don't know," she says, bemused by the question. "I've never measured."

And that, perhaps, is the true measure of a frontier woman—one who's gone so far beyond the comforts and predictabilities of urban life that she can't remember the distance back.

Camp life meant hard work and difficult conditions for women.
Mattie Gunterman Photo Vancouver Public Library VPL 2214

2 Mothers of the Old World

I n its official form, the documentary history of women in British Columbia can be said to begin at Tatoosh Island, where a honey-shouldered wedge of cretaceous sediment tilts out of the storm-tossed entrance to the Strait of Juan de Fuca. Bearing the name of an aboriginal chief, this island is the most westerly location in Washington State and therefore a point of pilgrimage for Americans who northwest up the Olympic Peninsula to the territory of the Makah—famous in the past as great whalers, infamous to some in the present for their impertinent renewal of that whaling tradition.

The tourists stop to pick up their $11 recreation permits in the Makah community at Neah Bay, where the pavement finally gives way to potholes and gravel, continue past the fish nets drying in the wind outside an old military base recycled for tribal administration purposes, then park their cars and hike the rest of the way to Cape Flattery along a trail maintained by the band. The footpath winds through waist-deep salal, nodding ferns and a sighing rain forest

Nootka women on the beach with clam baskets on their backs, awaiting the tide to fall and uncover the clam beds.
BC Archives D-08313

A Clayoquot girl smiles from under a blanket (left), while another (right) gazes from beneath cedar branches. It was the custom for girls to wear a mask of boughs for one year upon reaching womanhood.
Glenbow Archives NA-1700-79 and NA-181-69

that was already old when the images of the wives of Chief Tatoosh were graven by a Spanish explorer over 210 years ago. Today, chainsawed tree rounds make stepping stones through soft spots and boardwalks, constructed from planks as thick as Danielle Steel paperbacks, lift walkers over fragile ground and past cedars still bearing marks where bark was stripped to make clothing and baskets for rituals and ceremonies.

Eventually, hikers emerge at a spectacular clifftop lookout. To the north, the ragged graveyard coast of Vancouver Island continues westward, the shore fringed with white lace, the mountains scabbed with vast clear-cuts and draped in cloud. Below, translucent green swells off the Swiftsure Bank boom into sea caves and cause the whole promontory to shudder underfoot.

Most visitors come to take in the scenery and look for the bright orange bills of the exotic tufted puffins that nest on the cliffs, maybe even spot a big shark or sea mammal drawn by the abundant marine life that congregates to feed on nutrients welling up from the underwater canyons just offshore. Few of the visitors that I asked knew that it was from this precise lookout that the Makah first saw the ships carrying European mariners who would give us our earliest documentary glimpse of the society of women who occupied the unknown landscape west of the Rockies.

Traders and explorers from the French and American colonies had penetrated deep into the interior of the continent by the mid-18th century, but BC was unknown, unmapped and as remote from Europe as the dark side of the moon. Yet before the first adventurers arrived, this area of the continent was a quilt of nations, their territories defined by geography, by linguistic affiliation, by trading hegemonies, by

Women of Ahousat on Flores Island in Clayoquot Sound gather on a bench with the next generation.
BC Archives H-07195

transportation routes, by political alliances and by war. Women, as they still were for European royalty and had been for Bronze Age warlords, Chinese and Roman emperors, Egyptian Pharaohs, Persian satraps, African rulers and Aztec god-kings, were a crucial factor in forging dynastic alliances by marriage. In short, women of rank were a political commodity as well as a vital and sustaining part of the community. They were also prized booty, frequently taken and held as slaves in war. In fairness, there are some early Russian references from the North Coast, a fleeting description of Haida women and their dress in the journals of Juan Josef Perez Hernandez who sailed from California to the Queen Charlotte Islands in 1774 and a brief account of Nuu-chah-nulth culture by James Cook four years later at Friendly Cove. For the most part, despite their importance aboriginal women are even less of a presence in the documentary record than their European sisters. Even

today, after a full generation of feminism and raging gender politics in the academy, entries for women are to be found in few indexes of current anthropological and sociological studies of aboriginal cultures.

In the sketches of Manuel José Antonio Cardero, however, an artist attached to a Spanish expedition that stopped at Neah Bay in 1792, some of that missing history springs to vivid life in the faces of the wives of Tatoosh. He had three that we know about—evidence of his wealth and stature—and we know that his relationship with them was infused with affection. When he was invited aboard a Spanish ship and offered a cup of cocoa, Tatoosh drank some and then insisted on taking the rest to one of his wives waiting in the canoe alongside—the crew called her Maria—so that she could share in the novel taste.

Back then, of course, there was no BC, no Washington State, no Canada,

even the United States of America was a precarious experiment involving 13 tiny colonies on the far side of the continent. But there were the Makah, the southern cousins of the powerful Nuu-chah-nulth nation whose political, linguistic and cultural hegemony extended down the entire western shore of Vancouver Island. So it seems appropriate that any narrative about pioneer women, their lives and their accomplishments should begin at Tatoosh Island because, like the astonishing array of nations and cultures that existed here before the influx of Europeans, Asians, Africans and South Sea Islanders, the society of women sprawls across the artificially imposed boundaries of politics, ethnicity, geography and history.

The notion of "pioneer" women in BC is an oxymoron that begins with an assumption that history here is short and commences with the arrival of those whose cultures subsequently came to dominate the social and political

Maria and her husband Chief Tatoosh as sketched by Manuel José Antonio Cardero in 1792.
University of Washington Special Collections U23484Z and NA23483Z

A Cowichan woman tying a bundle of reeds, 1912.
Glenbow Archives NA-1700-49

landscape. But history here is ancient. Radiocarbon datings from the earliest excavated sites of human habitation in BC average more than 10,500 years before present. Some from a large animal kill in Washington push the date back another 2,000 years. To put that into historical perspective, women had already been looking after their families and maintaining their households in BC for at least 7,000 years by the time Moses led his people out of Egypt.

For me, the idea of the earliest pioneer women in BC evokes two images. The first is from a remarkable series of films about the Netsilikmiut of the Central Arctic made half a century ago by the brilliant National Film Board producer and cinematographer Doug Wilkinson. In a segment entitled "Going to the Weir," the camera focusses on a vast panorama of brown tundra beneath a cold sky. Only after many minutes does the observer become aware that there is indeed something happening. Those specks on the horizon looming larger and then dwindling again in the distance are a family walking toward the camera on their way to a favoured fishing spot. This is how it must have been for the first pioneer women trekking across the land bridge of Beringia, burdened

with equipment and supplies, keeping track of children, entertaining them, setting up and breaking down camp while the male hunters ranged ahead in the immense, hostile landscape in search of the next meal, sometimes not returning for days and expecting to be fed and serviced when they did. Work may differ in a wage economy, but divisions of labour respecting the family today are not so different from then, if the sociological surveys can be believed. Women still run most households, particularly with respect to food acquisition and preparation, and manage the nurturing and education of children.

On the other hand, a growing number of scholarly adherents supports the theory that the first pioneers to the West Coast came not by land but by sea. Some North Coast stories among aboriginal

peoples make references to a specific number of people crossing from Siberia to Alaska in a skin boat in flight from some dimly remembered tribal conflict—which brings to mind the second image, shared by an RCMP officer on the Arctic Coast. He told of watching a skin kayak with a lone paddler making its way to shore. At the beach, he said, the paddler disembarked, followed by his children, then five dogs and finally his wife—a reminder that the first woman to pioneer here may well have arrived the same way.

But how did these women live? Indications can be gleaned from the artifacts on display at the Makah Cultural and Research Center in Neah Bay. This stunning assemblage of 30,000 pieces was excavated at the Ozette River, where six houses from a village of 800 Makah

Preparing meals was a daily task for both women and children.
Glenbow Archives NA-1141-19

A Nakoaktok woman gathers abalones in the Seymour Inlet area. Glenbow Archives NA-1700-63

were buried in a mudslide 500 years before Christopher Columbus and then exposed again in 1970. The clay tomb sealed out oxygen and preserved perishables that would otherwise have long ago rotted away. It also created an intimate archeological snapshot of life in each house at the moment of burial—a record made of tools and implements, clothing, furniture, housewares, foodstuffs, ornaments and weapons. They suggest a strenuous life dictated by the coming and going of fish, birds and sea mammals. If the men were whalers and warriors, the women were custodians of family life. In stratified coastal societies that ranked people as nobility, commoners and slaves—a hierarchy not so different from those of the European newcomers—it's probably safe to conclude that aboriginal women had influence, but not power. And that influence would be graduated according to the rank and power of one's family and husband.

One North Coast woman, the daughter of a chief, took the name "Chief of All Women" when she was married by arrangement to another powerful chief to cement a dynastic alliance. Another, whose name is lost to history, was herself chief of the Nahannis when she intervened to save Fort Liard factor Robert Campbell from starvation in 1837. "She was a fine looking woman above the middle height and about 35 years old," Campbell reported to the Hudson's Bay Company. "She had a pleasing face lit up with intelligent eyes, which when she was excited flashed with fire. She was tidy and tasteful in her dress. At our first meeting she was accompanied by some of her tribe and her husband, who was a non-entity." The Nahanni chief must have been a powerful and respected leader because she openly defied Chief Shakes, who controlled the flow of furs from the Stikine watershed and was forcing trade to the Russians, for whom he served as the regional middleman. It's interesting to note that Campbell's observations focus on her beauty rather than her political power. Perez, too, commented on the beauty of Haida women he observed but also noted that "they gave signs of meekness and good

Upper Kootenay woman and baby in a cradle board in Windermere. Glenbow Archives NA-1135-18

Nakoaktok woman paints a hat of a form borrowed from the Haida. The Nakoaktok were a Kwakiutl tribe residing at Seymour Inlet. Glenbow Archives NA-1700-64

At Birth

I used to help at times of birth, yes,
I used to help all the women around here.
I learned it from my book, my blue doctor's book.
I used to read it all the time.

I made up my mind that if she needs help,
I will help her. I'm not scared.
You've got to be awfully quick. There's two lives there.
The baby and the mother.

Yes, two lives, and what you got to do it with
Those days? You've got to be quick
To cut the cord, keep the bed clean, take out
The afterbirth, discard it, burn it.

Yes, you've got to be quick, fix the baby,
Tie its navel so it will not bleed

Photograph taken in 1973 of Mary Augusta Tappage, author of *The Days of Augusta*.
Robert Keziere

To death—cut it about that long.
When it heals there's nothing left, you know.

Then you bandage the mother, pin her up,
Keep her clean, keep her in bed ten days.
The doctor told us this—but if I leave
I guess she got up.

I never had to spank a baby
To make him cry—they always cried.
They were always alive and healthy.
Yes, mother and baby, alive and healthy.

by Mary Augusta Tappage 1888–1978

Baskets woven by West Coast Native women were beautifully designed but also practical for daily use.
Glenbow Archives NA-1807-8

disposition," qualities doubtless desirable to the male-dominated cultures of Europe. A Spanish botanist and naturalist named José Mariano Mozino kept notes when he was dispatched to do scientific work for Juan Francisco de la Bodega y Quadra, who had been sent to explore the "limits to the north of California" in 1792. He described in detail the dress and ornamentation of Nuu-chah-nulth women.

But it's the Makah museum—with its assemblage of baskets, each designed for a special purpose, its specialized utensils for food preparation and presentation, its examples of cedar bark clothing, a dog-hair blanket adorned with woodpecker feathers and woven in a plaid pattern reminiscent of old Highland tartans, and even the loom on which such fabric was woven—that tells the most exact and engaging story of women's lives. It's clear that women had a central role in the collection of raw materials for the manufacture of these utensils and in gathering, preparing and putting up foodstuffs for the winter. There were clams to be

smoked, berries to be picked, seagull eggs to be gathered, fish to be cleaned, dried and smoked, the mysterious little "Ozette potatoe" to be dug, cedar bark to be stripped and processed, blankets to be woven.

According to Makah custom, much of the food preparation and the protocols of hospitality were supervised by the senior female member of the family. This was complicated, since each dish was governed by rules regarding preparation, presentation, service and appropriate ceremony. She and her subordinates were responsible for ensuring that visitors were served according to the strict privileges of their rank, that small children were fed next and finally that none of the remaining guests left hungry. This responsibility was a daunting one, considering that Nuu-chah-nulth chief Maquinna, for example, expected 36 different dishes to be served to guests at his formal banquets. One of those events sat Captains Quadra and George Vancouver at the same table and helped defuse the tensions that had brought the empires

of Spain and Britain to the brink of war over their colonial claims to the West Coast. The name of the Nuu-chah-nulth woman who managed that banquet of international diplomacy that helped lay the foundations for what's now BC is lost to formal history, but like the wives of Tatoosh who greeted the Spanish in what's now Washington, she can certainly be said to have helped pioneer the birth of a new world.

3 The Accidental Tourist

Scattered across Barkley Sound like jade and silver beads from a shattered necklace, the Broken Group archipelago provides a stunningly beautiful maze of sheltered passages and white shell beaches in waters that teem with marine life. And it was near here, at Bamfield, just before mid-summer almost 220 years ago, with the light of the northern latitudes lying long on the swells rolling in from China, that the sailing ship Imperial Eagle dropped anchor and the first non-aboriginal woman of whom we're certain—Frances Hornby Barkley—arrived in what would become British Columbia.

First Nations households like the one sketched by John Webber at Nootka Sound were large and demanded complex management skills of the women who ran them.
BC Archives PDP 00235

There is a legendary tale from Clooose that in the mid-1700s a Spanish ship visited the west coast of Vancouver Island. It might possibly have been an early voyage of exploration—some believe both Sir Francis Drake and a Spanish expedition piloted by Juan de Fuca visited these shores more than 400 years ago. More likely, however, any such vessel would have been a galleon sailing between South America and the Philippines that had been blown off course by a storm and found itself with BC's graveyard coast as a fatal lee shore. In any event, the legend goes that the crew was killed and a group of Spanish women were made captives by the Nitinat people, became integrated into tribal life and later bore children. But many decades afterward when another Spanish vessel passed, the captives stole a canoe and fled. There's no mention of this in any known Spanish maritime records, so the story is likely apocryphal or the anachronistic appropriation of some other incident. On the other hand, it's reported that some Ditidaht and Nitinat people have found glass, bits of jewellery, fragments of gold chain and even a Spanish lady's comb in the San Juan River.

the glare of a tropical Sun on the Sea in which Element, they pass so much of their time the Women have no pretentions to beauty but they are very active and lively, and also healthy, I did not see any vestages amongst them of Leprosy, which we remarked amongst the Men of Awhyhee. we were surprised to find so few articles of curiosity amongst them but the Feathered Cloaks & Helmets are only worn by the Chiefs and the King. who appears to Rule the whole of the Groups of Islands called by Cap.ᵗᵗ Cook Sandwich Islands the Kings name when we visited Owhyhee — was Tomahomahaa a perfect savage —

The last page of Frances Barkley's "Reminiscences." [from *The Remarkable World of Frances Barkley: 1769–1845***]**
BC Archives

Captain Charles Barkley took a teenaged bride on his trading voyage into the unknown.
Vancouver Public Library VPL 39031

For the more formal purposes of history, however, the first female European for whom documentary proof exists arrived on the west coast of Vancouver Island in late June, 1787. Frances Barkley was 17 and newly wed to Charles W. Barkley, the master of a 20-gun square-rigger of 400 tonnes sailing under Austrian colours to evade British trading licences. In the previous 18 months, Barkley had sailed halfway around the world to barter for the sea otter pelts he planned to sell in China before backhauling exotic Oriental cargoes to Europe. On the voyage, Barkley accidentally discovered the "lost" Strait of Juan de Fuca—Nuu-chah-nulth, Nitinat, Ditidaht and Makah mariners laugh at the notion it was ever either lost or discovered in the first place—and left his own name on the enormous sound that lies between Ucluelet and Bamfield.

Fanny, as she was called by her husband, must have been a feisty teenaged bride.

While there was a robust history

Opposite: Frances Barkley cast off a life of luxury when she moved into the cramped quarters of the *Imperial Eagle* and set off on a journey around the world.
Illustration by Captain Steve Mayo

of British women going to sea—from the notorious pirates Anne Bonny and Mary Read to women serving as cooks on whaling ships and trading vessels, at least a dozen female sailors are known from the 18th and early 19th centuries—a mariner's life was brutal, dangerous and frequently abbreviated by the privations of wretched food, bad water, storms and attacks by Natives. The Imperial Eagle, for instance, lost six men to a Makah ambush at the mouth of the Hoh River in 1787 and the following year John Meares was approached by a strange canoe in Friendly Cove and offered the mummified hand of what he thought must be the remains of one of the victims since one of the paddlers was wearing an item that had belonged to Barkley's second mate.

It was, however, far from common for a proper young English lady to accompany her husband to sea in the face of such possibilities. Indeed, British admiralty regulations issued in 1731 and again in 1756 expressly forbade women from going to sea aboard Royal Navy ships without specific orders from the most senior officers. Fanny was only 16 and a clergyman's daughter fresh out of convent school when she met Charles William Barkley, then aged 25. Five weeks later, on October 27, 1786, she

married him in the chapel at Ostend and, defying tradition, insisted on joining him on his voyage, since naval regulations had no bearing on a merchant ship under a foreign flag. And so, about 1 p.m. on November 24, she waved farewell to her father as the Imperial Eagle slipped its moorings and caught the ebb tide.

It would not be a pleasure cruise. Even the best ships of the day were foul, leaky, rat-infested tubs, the bilges reeking of filth, the sleeping quarters often soaked and the rations dreadful. Although scurvy was in retreat by the time Fanny Barkley followed her husband to sea, sailors were routinely afflicted by various fevers, respiratory infections, dysentery and smallpox. A Royal Navy casualty report of the day shows that between 1776 and 1798, less than 2,000 men died in the 10 battles fought by its fleets during the Revolutionary and Napoleonic wars while 85,000 died of disease, shipboard accidents and shipwrecks.

Living in a tiny cabin with all her domestic possessions in a single locker beneath her hard, narrow bunk, sharing the cramped saloon with the first mate as well as the captain, she circumnavigated the world twice with her husband, bore and buried children at sea and kept

"Our dear little Patty died on board. . ."

My beloved Husband was attacked with a dreadful disease, which is common to these Climats, a violent Colic but with the most extraordinary symptoms, and excruciating pain, attended with fever and distortions of every kind. Two Men could hardly restrain him, so as to prevent his hurting himself. He turned all colours, sometimes appearing as if Actually dead. After a time the symptoms abated, and he got over it, but it left him in a dreadfully debilitated state. But a similar disease deprived us of our dear little Patty, then a twelve Month old, saving one day. She died on board the Halcyon on the 15th day of April, 1791 or 92. A Leaden Box was prepared for her remains in order that they might be kept until we could Inter her remains in consicrated ground, in some Dutch settlement, and accordingly we made for the Island of Celebes. When after much negociation with the unfeeling Dutch Resident, and extortions of every kind, She was laid in a burying Ground situated opposite the place where we were at Anchor, from whence we watched the Ceremony, not being allowed to go on shore to pay the last duties to our dear Child. The spot where she is deposited is one of the most beautiful in the World—as are all the Spice Islands. There she lies under the Shade of a Grove of Cocoa Nut Trees.

—from Frances Hornby Barkley's *Reminiscences* (as quoted in the Beth Hill text), written at the age of 66 and based on the diary of her circumnavigations of the globe

Vancouver Island's remote west coast soon became the hub of a vigorous trans-Pacific trading network.
BC Archives A-02688

a vivid and lively diary of her experiences. The surviving correspondence between Fanny and Charles reveals a deep and abiding affection over 46 years of marriage. Although Frances Island, Mount Hornby and Trevor Channel, the main entrance to Port Alberni, were all named in her honour by her husband, Fanny Barkley fell into obscurity. Like the enigmatic legend of the Spanish women at Clo-oose, however, Fanny Barkley's story has its own mystery.

When the late Beth Hill, a Victoria writer known for her studies of Indian petroglyphs, was researching a rock carving of a sailing ship found at Clo-oose, she noted that Captain Walbran said he had consulted Frances Barkley's diary in the preparation of his great scholarly work from 1909, British Columbia Coast Names, 1592–1906. He'd borrowed the diary from her grandson, Captain Edward Barkley, who had settled at Westholme, near Crofton on the east side of Vancouver Island. Then Hill found a story in the Victoria Daily Colonist newspaper reporting that shortly after Walbran returned the diary in 1909, Barkley's house had caught fire. Barkley was killed when he rushed back into the burning building in an attempt to retrieve some papers of great importance. The Barkley diary vanished and was presumed destroyed in the blaze.

But when Hill travelled to England to interview descendants while researching her book The Remarkable World of Frances Barkley: 1769–1845, she found correspondence that makes a compelling case that this diary survived until at least 1952. Today it's possibly sitting on the bookshelf of someone who doesn't know its importance. The literary trail petered out when Hill died in 1997, leaving unsolved the conundrum of Fanny Barkley's lost diary, a mystery as fascinating as the story of the castaway Spanish women of Clo-oose.

"They came singing their War Song. . ."

Once, in particular, Captn B. saw several War Canoes with his Night Glass, stealing along under the shadow of the land on a fine moonlight Night, and as we were very indifferently Man'd, he was suspicious of their intention, and therefore he had a whole Broad side fired off over their heads, which made a great noise amongst the trees. We heard them scuttle off, but kept perfect silence on board that they might not think we were alarmed. Early the next morning they came alongside dreassed in their War dresses, and singing their War Song & keeping time with their paddles. When they had paddled three times round the vessel they set up a great Shout, then pulled off their masks and resumed their usual habits, and exhibited their sea otter skins, and gave us to understand they had been on a war expedition and had taken them from their Enemies. They never alluded to the firing, but went on trading as if nothing had passed, firing off their own Muskets in the Air, and then giving a great Shout.

—from Frances Hornby Barkley's *Reminiscences*, on an incident at Nootka Sound in 1792

4 The First, First Lady

Over 175 years ago, just beyond the palisades of the fur trading outpost Fort St. James, established by Simon Fraser in 1806, the courage of a shy young woman who kept a cool head during a terrifying crisis was to change the course of history. Situated on the southeast end of Stuart Lake, about 950 kilometres by road north of Vancouver, this small community of 2,046 people is an important Carrier First Nations settlement. But Fort St. James also ranks as the second-oldest continuously inhabited European settlement in the province. For nearly 40 years before Victoria was founded far to the south, Fort St. James would serve as the capital of New Caledonia, the British colony that comprised much of the Interior. Indeed, the British Columbia we know today might not have come to pass without the intervention of that young woman.

Amelia was the daughter of William Connolly, the Hudson's Bay Company's chief factor at Fort St. James, and Miyo Nipiy, a Cree woman. In 1828 she married a junior fur trader serving at the fort named James Douglas. Douglas had destiny printed in his soul. He would later found Fort Victoria, help blunt the American expansionism that would wrest much of the Oregon Territory from the Crown, secure British interests on the Pacific Slope, manage the turbulent gold rush of 1858, sign treaties with First Nations in a far-sighted policy later abandoned by greedy politicians, serve as midwife for the union of New

Fort St. James village, shown in the 1890s, had been a fur trading post since 1806 and was the capital of New Caledonia for almost 40 years.
BC Archives A-04241

Caledonia with Vancouver Island and end his career as the governor who presided over the birth of responsible, democratic government. But in 1828, Douglas was merely a brash and ambitious young clerk whose intelligence and skill had already come to the attention of his superiors but whose worth had yet to be proven.

The story of James and Amelia Douglas points to a fascinating moment that winked into existence about 200 years ago on the west side of the Rocky Mountains and then flickered out in the ruins of a human catastrophe of epic proportions. For a moment, it seemed that the collision of European and aboriginal cultures was about to bring forth some-

Portrait of Lady Amelia Douglas, circa 1865.
BC Archives A-02834

Indian women packers at Moricetown, near Smithers, in the early 1900s.
BC Archives A-06062

thing entirely new. A common language was being born—Chinook, the language of commerce forged from French and Mowachaht, Spanish and Halkomelem, English and Tsimshian, Hawaiian and Haida—and a generation like Amelia's was emerging from marriages between First Nations and fur traders.

Life was hard on the fur frontier. Providing and preserving food for the long, bitter winters and manufacturing clothing for the harsh climate often dominated family life and much of this responsibility fell to the women. Childbirth and child-rearing often took place in isolation and under primitive conditions of sanitation and hygiene. Faced with long absences by their menfolk on trading missions and voyages of exploration, fur traders' wives had to be tough, resilient and

resourceful in an often hostile environment.

Aboriginal women who had been born into just such conditions understood the complexities of local politics. They had extended kinship groups upon which they could call for help in emergencies and they brought invaluable skills to marriage with a European man, many of which were marriages of convenience. For European men in the fur trade, the frontier was devoid of opportunities for a domestic life unless they turned to aboriginal women. Single men lived in military-style barracks, their Spartan lives punctuated by periods of excessive drinking and dangerous voyages. A number of these marriages were essentially political. In a landscape where the dominant society was aboriginal, powerful chiefs and astute fur traders sought in an age-old fashion to cement alliances, formalize access and expand trading relationships through marriage. As a result, much of BC's non-Native and Native populations share common ancestries to an extent that many have either forgotten or prefer to repress.

For example, after British trader Robert Hunt's European wife died around

1850, he promptly married Ansnaq or Mary Ebbetts, granddaughter of Shakes, a chief who monopolized fur trade routes to the Interior on the Stikine River. Mary's mother, Chief of All Women, had been married to Abbitts, a Tlingit chief who controlled territory at the mouth of the Nass River. These women were typical in that they brought to their marriages the political weight of their rank and the prestige of family ties in a society that was deeply stratified with respect to class. Among Mary Ebbetts's possessions when she married, for example, was a Haida slave. It has been pointed out by historians that many European traders set aside their "country wives" once they were no longer useful in economic or political terms and then travelled east to formally marry European women. William Connolly, Amelia's father, was one who did.

Adele Perry, who delves into this complex social history in a brilliant piece of scholarship entitled On the Edge of Empire: Gender, Race and the Making of British Columbia, 1849–1871, provides evidence that attitudes toward First Nations, and particularly aboriginal women, became an expression of racist prejudice largely following the influx of British and American settlers. The Americans brought the prejudices of their Indian wars and many of the British newcomers aspired to status denied them at home and seized the opportunity to bestow rank upon themselves. Stereotypes were born when they encountered the ruins of once rich and powerful societies demoralized by successive epidemics that had depopulated the landscape, shredded cultural legacies and shattered their economic underpinnings.

Yet many of these personal relationships were also based in genuine love and proved remarkably resilient and durable, as did the affectionate marriages of James and Amelia Douglas and Robert and Mary Ebbetts Hunt. Mary and Robert had 11 children. One daughter, Sarah Hunt, married Alexander Lyon and helped him found the city of Port Hardy on Vancouver Island in 1904. Another daughter, Annie Hunt, married Stephen Spencer, an American cannery operator at Alert Bay. They had seven children and moved to Victoria in 1900, becoming part of the social establishment. And a brother, George Hunt, became the chief assistant of famed anthropologist Franz Boas.

Few of these cross-cultural relationships, however, had the impact on BC's history that Amelia's marriage to James Douglas was to have. In 1828, young

Beaver woman and child in Fort St. John, 1904.
Glenbow Archives NA-494-25

James was temporarily in charge of Fort St. James when he apprehended a man wanted for the murder of two Hudson's Bay Company traders five years earlier at

The first citizen of Port Hardy

If rugged self-reliance was the watchword for frontier marriages, there are few better examples than that of Alexander Lyon and Sarah Hunt. They left the Hudson's Bay Company trading post at Fort Rupert by rowboat in 1904. The couple was bound for Hardy Bay in windswept Goletas Channel, about 30 kilometres north of present-day Port McNeill, along a wild and sparsely settled coast.

Alexander had taken a liking to the sheltered anchorage fed by the Quatse and Tsulquate rivers at the north end of Vancouver Island. The bay had been named by an equally admiring George Richards, captain of HMS *Plumper*, to commemorate Vice Admiral Thomas Masterman Hardy, who was captain of Lord Nelson's flagship HMS *Victory* at the Battle of Trafalgar in 1803.

Sarah was one of the tough, resilient daughters of Robert Hunt, who had been a fur trader at Fort Rupert for 20 years before buying the post outright in 1883, and Mary Ebbetts, a Tongass Tlingit woman from the North Coast. And

although Sarah was pregnant and approaching term, she didn't hesitate to accompany her husband on the long row to their new home. On landing, however, she slipped on the wet stones and went into premature labour. Alexander got her up into the one-room cabin he had built, then set out to get the nearest doctor from the Anglican mission in the village of Alert Bay, about 35 kilometres to the south.

Rowing like a demon, he made it as far as Fort Rupert when a storm blew up and drove him ashore with many kilometres of heavy seas still separating him from the doctor on Cormorant Island. His mother-in-law, however, called on her relatives in the emergency and a sea-going canoe sped him the rest of the way through heavy weather to get the doctor and then bring him back up the coast to Hardy Bay.

When Alexander and the doctor returned, they found Sarah lying on the floor of the cabin. She was exhausted but otherwise all right. Cradled in her arms was newborn Douglas Lyon, the first citizen of what would become Port Hardy, the commercial and industrial hub of northernmost Vancouver Island.

Fort George. Unfortunately, the suspect was killed when he tried to stab Douglas with an arrow. Even worse, the rash young clerk had gone into the house of the Carrier Chief Kwah to make the arrest. By violating the chief's prerogative to offer sanctuary he had caused the chief to lose face. Kwah seized the fort, overpowered Douglas and was preparing to kill him with a knife when Amelia intervened. She began throwing bales of recently arrived trade goods at the feet of the Carrier chief and his warriors. Kwah accepted them and, his honour satisfied, released his captive. Amelia's marriage to the hotheaded Douglas was to last 49 years and produce 13 children. She would have a private audience with Queen Victoria. And if her life ended in the tranquil obscurity she sought, it might also be argued that her legacy is the province itself, for without her understanding of Kwah and her calm diplomatic solution, British Columbia might never have come to pass.

Lady Amelia Douglas and her family at their Victoria home. Aboriginal women understood local politics and brought invaluable skills to marriage with European men.
BC Archives G-03584

Opposite: Lady Douglas donned widow's weeds and withdrew from society after her husband's death.
BC Archives H-04909

5 Miners' Angels and Dance Hall Queens

A cold wind sighs through the evergreens. They cast deep, gloomy shadows across the old burying ground on the outskirts of Barkerville where weathered wooden headboards, time-darkened stone and rusty wrought iron straggle along the steep hillside. Almost 750 kilometres north of Greater Vancouver by road, this lonely little cemetery is where the luckless of Cameronton and Richfield staked their final claims—although by the 1880s those mining camps were gone, absorbed by Barkerville, the now-restored Cariboo boom town just up the road that is one of British Columbia's famous tourist destinations.

This old graveyard is one of BC's most important pioneer historic sites, for here lies the flotsam and jetsam of the gold rush in whose crucible of greed, brutality, courage and vision the province and its destiny were forged. And there are few more poignant reminders of the roles that women played in that grand adventure than the simple memorials raised to those who came in search of fortune and found only six feet of cold ground.

There is Jessie Heatherington, the "Scotch Lassie," debauched by a drunkard husband, abandoned and then murdered by an unknown assailant. And Marie Hageman, who probably came to work in the saloons, bestowing her favours for $1 a dance and a commission on every drink she could coax from a besotted miner. There's Margaret Blair, a much-loved wife who died giving birth to her fourth child at the desperately young age of 21. There's Isabella Hodgkinson, the camp washerwoman whose epitaph, "Sleep, Bella, Sleep," is her husband's bittersweet farewell to the wife who rose every day before dawn. And there is Janet Allen, "Big Jennie," the saloonkeeper who "dressed like a man, drank like a man and died like a man" in a carriage

Alturas Gold Mining Co. in Stout's Gulch, near Barkerville, circa 1868, by photographer Frederick Dally.
BC Archives A-04919

Dance hall girls, circa 1900. They bestowed their favours for $1 a dance and a commission on every drink they could coax besotted miners to buy.
Glenbow Archives NA-3439-3, NA-3439-2 and NA-3439-1

crash but for whom every flag flew at half-mast and who was eulogized in the *Cariboo Sentinel* as "nurse and friend to the miner" for her kindness toward the sick, injured or distressed.

These women were among the remarkable few carried by the gold-crazed tide of humanity that flooded up the Fraser River in 1858, spilled along its tributaries and seeped across the mountain passes, opening the remote and barely known regions of the Chilcotin, the Cariboo, the Kootenays and the Cassiar to European settlement. They came by steamboat and pack train from California, like Nellie Cashman. Born in Ireland the year before the great famine, she later immigrated to Boston, followed the California gold rush to San Francisco and then went on to BC, where she ran boarding houses and restaurants. The "Angel of the Cassiar" was legendary for her good works with the poor, the sick and the indigent. Although

Nellie never married—"Why child, I haven't had time for marriage. Men are a nuisance anyhow, now aren't they? They're just boys grown up," she told an American reporter—when her sister Fannie died, she raised five nieces and nephews. Yet the Angel was as tough as any sourdough. In 1874, she and six men packed more than a tonne of fresh supplies through deep snow to Dease Lake to avert an outbreak of scurvy and at the age of 78 she mushed a dog team 750 kilometres in Alaska. She died of pneumonia in Victoria in 1925 and is buried in Ross Bay Cemetery with the Sisters of St. Ann where her gravestone reads: "Friend of the sick and the hungry and to all men. Heroic apostolate of service among the western and northern frontier miners. Miner's Angel."

Others, no less tough than Nellie Cashman, came overland from the Prairies, struggling from valley to valley. The most famous of these was Catherine Schubert, born in Ireland in 1835. Four months pregnant, with three children

Nellie Cashman, circa 1874: The "Angel of the Cassiar" ran boarding houses and cared for the sick.
BC Archives D-01775

aged one, three and five in tow, she and her husband Augustus set out for the Cariboo from Fort Garry in 1862 with a

party of gold seekers later known as the "Overlanders." It was a perilous journey beset by hardships. Two drowned and the rest almost starved. But Catherine survived and while travelling down the Thompson River by raft she went into labour. She was cared for by the women of a First Nations settlement and her baby girl, Rose, was the first non-aboriginal citizen to be born in BC.

The catalyst for all these adventures—and more—can be traced to February 1858, when James Douglas delivered 800 ounces of gold dust from the Thompson River to the Hudson's Bay Company. When that gold was refined at a San Francisco mint, prospectors who had played out their diggings or had bad luck in California drifted north. On April 25, 1858, the American ship Commodore arrived at Fort Victoria,

"That was almost heaven. . ."

I used to waken in the morning to the sound of rushing Williams Creek and the song of the anvil from the O'Neil blacksmith's shop across the street and the sound of Billy Hodgkinson's pack horse with a bell carrying milk up town from the milk ranch down the road.

Another cheery sound was the water dripping into the water barrel in the wood shed. This had to be brought from the springs on the hillside in overhead wooden troughs and to the backs of the various homes by smaller troughs. Can't you hear the arguments and tempers rising on wash day when the first house took more than its share of the precious water?

On the cold, cold days the sound of the frost and snow crackled beneath our feet and the sidewalks as we ran home from school for our lunches. On those bitter days mother usually had a big pot of hot pea soup on the stove in the front room. Most of the house had to be closed off to keep us warm.

I recall the anxiety lest the snow should not have gone by May 24th so that we girls might wear our summer dresses for the usual picnic at Joe Mason's meadows up at Jack O'Clubs Lake.

Lottie Mabel Bowron and company enjoying a sleigh ride. Lottie was born in Barkerville in 1879 and became inspector of social welfare for about 800 female teachers, most of whom worked in rural one-room schools.
BC Archives C-09760

And then the lovely walks with Mother up to Richfield, through Chinatown, past Stout's Gulch and the canyon, where Billy Barker sank his shaft. The walk was to bring my father home. His office was in the old courthouse. . .

The exciting arrival of the stage on Thursday evening and its departure Saturday morning—everyone was excited when the stage came in—the children watched for it behind the church—then the cry being carried from one child to another—"Here, here's the stage, here's the stage."

If you've never travelled by the "BX" Barnard's Express then you've never travelled. Four days from here to Ashcroft—the lovely, spirited horses, the heavy red coaches. And to get to sit next to the driver on the box—that was almost heaven.

—Lottie Bowron, a native of Barkerville whose father, John Bowron, was an Overlander, quoted in *Barkerville: A Gold Rush Experience*, by Richard Thomas Wright

Ann and Rose Williams wash dishes at the Nettie L. mine in Ferguson in the Kootenays. Opportunities for women to work for wages were limited.
Mattie Gunterman Photo Vancouver Public Library VPL 2266

population less than 300, carrying 450 passengers bound for the goldfields. By the end of August, 1858, 20,000 people had arrived in Victoria and another 13,000 were moving into the Lower Mainland from the American side of the 49th parallel. In 1858, those miners took 106,000 ounces of gold from the Fraser River system, an amount worth more than $50 million at today's prices and a discovery of mind-boggling richness for its time.

It was essentially a male invasion—by 1861, there were still only 192 non-Native women living on the mainland,

The Flynn brothers and their wives at the Williams gold claim at Mosquito Creek in the Cariboo, 1903.
BC Archives A-03838

an area the size of Western Europe—and this distorted demographic resulted in what historian Adele Perry describes as an intensely homosocial culture. It was a society, she says, that continued to circumscribe women's lives in traditional ways. In an economy dominated by resource extraction and back-breaking labour, women's opportunities to work for wages were severely limited. A few entrepreneurs found themselves in business running laundries, boarding houses, saloons, bakeries and eating establishments or making clothes. Others took positions as governesses or teaching in public schools for pitifully small salaries that encouraged them to marry as quickly as the opportunity arose. Some were recruited as "hurdy-gurdies" who nominally provided dances and socializing for a fee but were often forced to provide sexual services on the side, although more than a few wound up married to former clients.

For all but the establishment elite in Victoria, life was hard, dangerous and unforgiving, as the grave markers at Barkerville attest. And yet, by the time these women were laid to rest, the social and demographic landscape of BC had been utterly transformed and a new province had been born, phoenix-like, amid the ashes of their endeavours.

The Hotel de France in Barkerville, circa 1863. Life was hard, dangerous and unforgiving, as the grave markers in the town attest.
BC Archives A-02051

"Brought to America by some speculating, conscienceless scoundrel . . ."

Hurdy-Gurdy damsels are unsophisticated maidens of Dutch extraction, from "poor but honest parents" and morally speaking, they really are not what they are generally put down for. They are generally brought to America by some speculating, conscienceless scoundrel of a being commonly called a "Boss Hurdy." This man binds them in his service until he has received about a thousand per cent for his outlay. The girls receive a few lessons in the terpsichorean art, are put into a kind of uniform, generally consisting of a red waist, cotton print skirt and a half mourning headdress resembling somewhat in shape the topknot of a male turkey, this uniform gives them quite a grotesque appearance. Few of them speak English, but they soon pick up a few popular vulgarisms; if you bid one of them

German dancing girls, known as hurdy-gurdies, Barkerville, 1865. They provided dances for a fee, but often were forced into sex.
BC Archives G-00817

good morning your answer will likely be "itsh sphlaid out" or "you bet your life.

The Hurdy style of dancing differs from all other schools. If you ever saw a ring of bells in motion, you have seen the exact positions these young ladies are put through during their dance, the more muscular the partner, the nearer the approximation of the ladies' pedal extremities to the ceiling, and the gent who can hoist his "gal" the highest is considered the best dancer; the poor girls as a general thing earn their money very hardly.

—letter to the *Cariboo Sentinel*, September 6, 1866 (quoted in *British Columbia: A Centennial Anthology* edited by Reginald Eyre Watters)

6 Homesteads and Hard Women

Some languid evenings, when the late autumn light slants into the grasslands where the Nicola River tumbles toward the great, green glint of the Thompson at Spence's Bridge, everything seems burnished with gold, just as it must have appeared almost 120 years ago to homesteader Jessie Ann Smith. She'd come from her Scottish village as a bride in 1884, one of the multitude pulled into the unmapped interior of a remote and little-known colony on the far side of the world by a gold rush that began in 1858 and continued into the 20th century.

If raw gold is what prospectors sought in the Fraser Canyon, flooding up the two forks of the Thompson, up the Bonaparte and over the dry ridges into the Tulameen and the Similkameen valleys, some travellers looked on the land and saw wealth of another kind in the bunch grass and the dark loam of the creek bottoms. Boom towns like Barkerville, Fairview and Camp McKinney had to be fed and their hunger meant instant markets. Markets meant opportunities for producers. The gold rush launched a demand-driven expansion in frontier ranching and farming that lasted until World War I. Unlike the chic, sophisticated, urbanized province of today, 100 years ago 80 percent of BC's population lived rural lives under conditions that most city dwellers have difficulty imagining. There was no electricity, no telephones, no television or radio, no libraries. Schools, where they existed, were one-room affairs and children travelled far to attend. Few homesteads had running water and the only source of heat

Left: Children watch a pot suspended over a fire in the Windermere Valley in the East Kootenay. Glenbow Archives NA-1135-55

Right: Jessie Ann Smith in her wedding dress. Her legendary apples, winners of gold and silver medals in the US and Canada, were fit for a king. Photo courtesy Nicola Valley Museum Archives Association PF 913

was the wood stove. Transportation was on foot, on horseback or by rowboat and save for a few non-perishable staples, households were expected to produce their own food. And, without doctors or hospitals, women were expected to give birth at home.

Pioneer rancher, world-renowned fruit farmer, wife, widow and tenacious single mother, Jessie Ann Smith rode that astonishing wave for more than 60 years, a small yet symbolic player in the great game of empire—although her charming autobiography, *Widow Smith of Spence's Bridge*, deftly edited and published by Murphy Shewchuk of Merritt in 1989, reveals it is doubtful she held that perception of herself.

While the mining camps were characterized by their transience, farming required families to put down roots—for generations in the case of orchardists. And in contrast to the almost exclusively male society of the gold creeks, farms desperately needed women and children if they were to function effectively as economic units. Farms also secured territorial rights. The mining camps were full of bellicose American adventurers and the British authorities understood that to secure their colonial hold, the land had to be occupied and made productive. To persuade men to settle required the society of women; achieving imperial ambitions required white women. But in 1861, there were fewer than 100 European women in BC for every 1,000 men. The first effort to

Clearing land in Beaton, near Revelstoke, circa 1900.
Mattie Gunterman Photo Vancouver Public Library VPL 2319

Drawing by Emily Carr entitled *The Women Tell Her of Such Woes As How The Wind Won't Dry The Clothes.* BC Archives PDP05894

"Drudgery so awful. . ."

For women in the rural and frontier regions maintaining a home offered few challenges as horrific as the weekly laundry.

Monday was considered "Wash Day."

Beginning early in the morning water had to be brought from its source, often a creek or well. As many as 200 litres might be necessary for the family wash—water that had to be boiled over whatever heat source was available.

Homemade lye soap, so hard on the hands, rubbed skin raw as women separated the items by color and fragility, scrubbed and scoured, sometimes over several changes of boiling water. Rinsing several times was often necessary. Then the laundry had to dry, usually outside no matter what the weather.

The process lasted well into the evening. Husbands were accustomed to cold dinners on Mondays.

Tuesday meant ironing. This was another challenge since irons also had to be heated. The "sad iron" was a succession of hot irons which were heated to replace those that had cooled. Each iron weighed between seven and eight pounds but some weighed up to 14.

This drudgery was so awful that even women of lower income would scrounge together funds to hire washerwomen. A woman of higher income would use a commercial laundry. Destitute women who took in laundry could do it at their own home and at their own pace.

Washing machines and electricity ended the pioneer's curse.

—exhibit notes, Clallam County Museum, Port Angeles, Washington

redress this imbalance involved the free transportation of wives with the Royal Engineers to New Westminster and the promise of 150 acres of free land for each soldier or his widow who stayed in the new colony. The offer of a quarter section of land to homesteaders prepared to clear and "improve" the property was a compelling incentive.

Yet the demand for women who would transform a fur trade and gold rush culture into a settler society soon took a more exotic form. In 1862, the first of what became known as the "Bride Ships" began arriving at Fort Victoria loaded with young single women recruited in Britain. One sailing ship, The Seaman's

First ranchers in the Elk Valley, 1905. Back row, from left: Joe Fristal (pointed hat, gunbelt, long gun); Elizabeth Musel; Anna Kiasner (striped blouse); Harry Kiasner Sr. (white shirt, pipe, soft cap); Emil Fristal. Front row: Phil Musel Sr. (little girl's head on his knee); Phil Musel's daughter Emily Musel; Anna Fristal (white pompom necklace); John Fristal (bowler hat, large gun); Jerry Kiasner; Millie Fristal (with mandolin); Harry Kiasner Jr. (little boy in front with gun in his lap). Glenbow Archives NA-1320-4

Bride, put in at San Francisco after a Pacific crossing from Australia only to have the women "stolen" by American gallants and married before the vessel could leave again for BC, much to the fury of British Colonist editor and future premier Amor de Cosmos. When the Tynemouth arrived at Fort Victoria that September with 59 women aboard, the town went into a near frenzy. Royal

An early farmhouse in Richmond, circa 1908.
City of Richmond Archives photo
no. 1984 17 71

Marines and Royal Navy bluejackets had to be mustered to permit the passengers to walk from the docks to their accommodation.

The youngest—some were orphans as young as 12—were found positions as domestic servants until they were of an age to marry. The eldest found positions as teachers and governesses. Those who could marry frequently did so quickly, some the same day they arrived. Few of these women and those who fol-

lowed had the faintest idea of the hardship, loneliness and privation they faced beyond the bustling little fort. Land had to be cleared, preserves put up for the long winter, living conditions were primitive, husbands were often away for long periods, babies were often born with little more than the assistance of neighbours. In addition, pioneer women faced the challenging task of keeping clean not only the bed and table linens but a bewildering array of crinolines, camisoles, petticoats, pantaloons, corsets, gloves, stockings and the white lace dresses required for fashionable summer wear. Some, even those who came long after the Bride Ships had ceased, found only heartbreak and

despair, turning to suicide or abandoning families. Yet many more women found satisfying futures in the new colony. Vancouver teacher Peter Johnson's book Voyages of Hope: The Saga of the Bride-Ships traces the bountiful, richly fulfilled lives of a number of them.

Mr. and Mrs. W.H. Grassie stand next to a felled tree on Georgia Street in Vancouver around 1886, the year the city was incorporated.
Charles S. Bailey photo, City of Vancouver Archives CVA SGN 152

The Bride Ships were one extreme of a trend that would see the number of non-Native women in BC increase by 1,500 percent over the next decade. The majority however, came by more conventional means, often accompanied by husbands and children. One of them was Jessie Ann Smith. In 1858, just as authority was passing from the Hudson's Bay Company to the newly minted colony of British Columbia in a muddy yard at Fort Langley, she was six and sitting in her first class in Scotland, where her father was a comfortable member of the upper middle class. Twenty-eight years later, with a toddler and a baby, she was moving into a four-room log cabin on a half section homestead 30 kilometres beyond the end of the road. The ranch was four days' ride from the nearest store. She'd already seen grizzlies, cougars, wolves and black bears in the valley and lay awake her first nights trembling with fear.

"The wild grass was abundant and grew shoulder high. John bought a few cows, two horses and some pigs and I raised chickens," she wrote later. "We made butter for sale and traded butter, eggs and pork at Mr. Carrington's store at Nicola Lake and the store at Coutlee." Ten years later, the family was raising fruit at Spence's Bridge. When her husband died, she kept the fruit farm going. Her apples were legendary and

Mrs. Chancy Smith milks a cow on her Elk Valley farm in the East Kootenay. W. Bovin and Chancy Smith are in the background.
Glenbow Archives NA-1320-5

won many gold and silver medals for the British Empire and in the United States and Canada. Her moment of fame came in 1909 when King Edward VII insisted on seeing her gold medal entry of Grimes Golden Apples at the Royal Horticultural Society Exhibition in London. The exhibit had been misplaced and the king was not amused. "The apples which I have come to see are those of the Widow Smith of Spence's Bridge," her autobiography recounts. She died at the age of 93 in 1946 and was buried beside the husband she had outlived by more than 40 years.

If the gold rush had unleashed political, economic and ideological forces that transformed the landscape, women like Widow Smith and the girls of the Bride Ships came to domesticate transient males who were more interested in striking it rich and moving on. Pioneer women who fashioned a permanent home in the wilderness and encouraged those men to settle down were ultimately to prove more significant in the making of what was to become British Columbia than the men that history usually credits.

7 The Search for Eden

A sudden, cold slant of rain spatters across the glossy leaves of salal with a brisk, plastic rustle. The wind picks up, hissing and roaring through the high canopy. One more weather front is moving in across San Josef Bay toward the bleak northern tip of Vancouver Island. Blows like this were lethal in the days of sail. The brig *Consort* was wrecked in San Josef Bay in 1860. The *Henry Denis* and the *Hermit* were both lost here within days of one another in 1892, the schooner *Wanderer* sank in 1896, the *Hilmeny* in 1906 and the *Suzie M. Plummer* foundered with all hands in 1910.

Yet at Cape Scott, just northwest of here, hardy Danish settlers sought to establish a farming and fishing colony in 1897. They were inspired by similar settlements of Norwegian immigrants at Quatsino Sound and Bella Coola and served in their own right as an inspiration for Finns settling at Sointula on Malcolm Island in 1901.

Explore the dripping, moss-muffled woods up here, a good hike beyond the end of the Island Highway, and you'll find the assorted bric-a-brac of long-vanished human habitation. There are faint signs of the ancient Lalasiquala village of Nomch, abandoned before Europeans arrived. And more obvious evidence of those long-departed new-comers: a rusting bed frame, stray buttons lost between the floorboards of a post office rotting back into the forest floor, log rounds corduroyed into boggy ground, the trails leading off to unseen destinations in the gloom.

Ever since James Douglas looked on the flower-laced meadows and Garry oaks of south Vancouver Island and declared he was building the new Hudson's Bay Company fort in "a perfect Eden," it's been said of British Columbia that two kinds of people sought to lose

Men carved clearings from the forest but women built communities, like these early Norwegian settlers on BC's coast.
BC Central Coast Archives

themselves in its wilderness: those wanting to play God and those wanting to hide from God. A third group might be added: those wanting to re-create that same Eden that momentarily blossomed in the mind of the future governor when he looked on the blue brocade of camas blooms spread across rippling fields of grass under spring sunshine.

Few statements of that intent are quite as explicit as "The Cape Scott Song," a homegrown saga of the time about the paradise in which the settlers proclaim that "slowly we will here an Eden make."

So this place, still at the far fringe

of human habitation in Canada's third-largest province, seems a good spot to contemplate the often nameless and frequently overlooked women who put up with privation, loneliness and isolation in helping efforts to create Heaven on Earth, or at least to assist earthly sinners to find a way of climbing more easily to the metaphysical realm.

Since the early days of the colony, BC has been a blast furnace of missionary zeal, of fervent searches for Utopia and of a series of experiments in social engineering in the name of God, whose consequences—both uplifting and destructive—the province is

still trying to sort out here on Earth. Christians from the Roman Catholic, Anglican and other Protestant faiths perceived the landscape west of the Rockies as a country filled with pagans, heathens, wicked men and fallen women requiring the ministrations of salvation. Others—from Finnish freethinkers on the West Coast to Doukhobors fleeing Russian persecution into the mountain valleys of the Kootenays—saw, in a wilderness they perceived as uninhabited,

"How to knit a sock. . ."

She would be alone for months at a time, with nothing but the Indian women up there. They were Nishga Indians, so Robert, my husband, as a boy learned the Nishga language and could rattle it off before he could talk English, because they had girls in the house working for them so Grandma could teach the girls how to do things. She had never done much sewing herself because they were pretty well protected. They came from Ireland and they belonged to the gentry in Ireland and moved over here. So she'd never done much housework and she'd never knitted in her life. But now she had to teach the Indians how to knit a

sock. The only way she could learn how to knit a sock was to unravel a sock that was made by a machine. The heels are turned entirely differently than a homemade sock. So she and my father-in-law figured out how these socks were made, and so they taught the Indians how to knit. So the Indians up the Skeena and on the Nass knit their socks with the heels the same way as the boughten socks, which comes in from the side. The homemade comes square up. And, of course, they had to make their own candles; they had to do a lot of things that she had never done in her life.

—Mrs. Robert Tomlinson, daughter-in-law of Alice Tomlinson, a missionary in the Nass Valley in the 1870s

the possibility of their own redemption in founding and perfecting communities of the like-minded at a remove from the corrupting temptations of the secular world. Women have played significant roles in all of these organizations as willing participants, unwitting victims or well-meaning perpetrators. Their sometimes central participation has tended to be overlooked because the deep-rooted social values and assumptions of

their time pushed them from the rugged foreground reserved for men into the comforting background of romantic stereotypes and expectations.

For example, the first woman to arrive at Sointula, the Finnish Utopian settlement launched about 300 kilometres northwest of Vancouver, was the newly married Anna Wilander. This young woman from New York proved crucial to the establishment of the colony, cooking and washing for 14 men and bringing them hot food in the winter bush while they furiously cleared land and built shelter for the families and 15 children who would follow. Sointula was founded on principles of women's equality. Founder Matti Kurikka was a student of Minna Canth, a leading Finnish suffragette. At a time when they were denied the vote and even status as persons in mainstream society, women at Sointula held their own meetings to determine their role in the community. (They cre-

Missionaries brought more than new religious beliefs, they brought new fashions for these young Muchalat women. BC Archives I-31553

"We crawled. . ."

We landed at Clayton's store [in 1894]. There was about 40 of us, mostly women and children and two or three men. I can picture them leaving Clayton's. They all had packs on. My father had my blanket, I had my suitcase, and the little children were riding on top of the packs on the men, and there was a long string of us went up. The trail was narrow, crooked. We crawled on trees across the creeks; especially we had to cross a big river, that they call Nusatsum; it [the bridge] was just poles and my father led me across. We all got as far as what we call Hagensborg now. My uncle, Ole Gaarden, lived this side of Snootli Creek and we stayed at his place.

—Annie Engebretson, among the first at the Norwegian settlement in Bella Coola
BC Archives tape 4032:1 Sound Heritage Series

ated a day care facility so that women were free to work, although it proved less successful than planned when those committed to the ideal decided to stay home when it came to their own babies and toddlers.) Even in Utopia the growing self-determination of the women created fault lines. Some men resented their autonomy as derailing the male vision of a perfect community. Perhaps as a result, Anna is reduced to the merest footnote in the official narratives. Of two recent histories, one doesn't mention her and the other identifies her only as Mrs. Wilander, effectively defining her as an extension of her husband's persona.

Indeed, across the contemporary historic record, female missionaries are often seen largely as helpmates, submerged in their husbands' valiant strife in a war for souls. The humdrum work of nuns as nursing and teaching sisters is eclipsed by the illustrious work of conversion by priests and bishops. And yet, agree with their objectives or not, the social impact of these women was significant. The provincial archives are rife with photos of aboriginal women

Sister Mary Providence was 22 years old when she arrived in Victoria in 1859 to join the first four Sisters of St. Ann as their Superior.
BC Archives A-02419

abandoning their traditional dress for Victorian corsets and taking up the new feminine labours of weaving, spinning and sewing that were introduced by missionary wives.

The group of missionary women that was to have the most profound influence came from Montreal. Salome Valois,

Angele Gauthier, Virginie Brassard and Mary Lane answered a plea from Bishop Modeste Demers for teachers at a school for girls in Fort Victoria. These four members of the Sisters of St. Ann—a religious order founded in Montreal in 1850—had taken the veil as Sister Marie du Sacré-Coeur, Sister Marie Angèle, Sister Marie-Luména and Sister Marie-de-la-Concepcion. They arrived in Fort Victoria on June 5, 1858, took residence in a vermin-infested hut with dirt floors in the midst of a gold rush and had St. Ann's School for Young Ladies up and running in less than three weeks.

Enrolled were Hélène Lavoie, Emma and Henriette Yates, Emélie Morel, Emélia Desmarais, Elizabeth Dodd, Elizabeth Anderson, recently arrived from India, Virginia Gurta and Lucy Angèle. And six years later, at a time when advanced education was not thought particularly necessary for future wives and mothers, the British Colonist newspaper was not-

Schoolgirls, nuns and school officials gather for a Passion Play at St. Mary's Church in Mission, circa 1894.
City of Vancouver Archives CVA LGN 579

ing that the results of examinations in natural philosophy, English grammar, modern and ancient history, geography and mythology were a testament to the girls' teachers from Quebec. By 1870, the sisters had established a convent and later St. Ann's Academy, which was expanded to provide commercial studies for young women in 1913. Although the academy closed in 1973, the nuns continued at Queenswood House of Studies, where they offered retreats for prayer, study and contemplation. They also provided a chapel for University of Victoria students and remained active in ministries concerned with social justice, rehabilitation, prison work and care for the sick and the elderly.

The nuns serve to remind us that while buildings may tumble and the forest reclaim scores of failed Utopian dreams from Cape Scott to Creston, much important spiritual work was done in the service of those dreams by unrecognized and under-appreciated women. Their vital legacy endures and continues to shape the social and cultural fabric of the province they helped bring into the world.

Four girls at the Coqualeetza residential school in Sardis, which was established by the Methodist Church in 1888. BC Archives I-51769

"A right to speak at meetings. . ."

We arrived here late at night. It was pitch-black and all the bay was covered with these big kelps—these great big snakes in the water with these great big heads on them. The boat tied up to some sort of a slip and we had to walk along these logs to the shore where this little shack was.

In this log cabin were five double bunks for all these families. Hay was piled high on these bunks for a mattress and my husband and I and two children got one of these bunks for our own.

They were going to share everything. Everyone would be working for the common good. No one owned anything separately and individually. They planned to farm and log and all the proceeds would be divided equally.

I think the main idea was to have a free society. Especially, they emphasized that women should have equal rights with men. At that time, women had no property rights, they had no rights whatsoever in wages, so this was one thing that applied here. The women had a-dollar-a-day wages, as the men did, and they had a right to speak at meetings and they had a right to vote. And they had to work. Everyone had to work.

Another thing they wanted was a society where there would be no government church. There would be no liquor vending and no women would have to sell themselves. . . . They could have religion, but no one would be forcing any particular religion and anyone could believe as they wished. The company was to look after the children—all the expenses, clothing, food and schooling. No one would be charged extra for children. The idea was that later on the children would be the workers and they would look after the elders. All the women went to work in the kitchen or laundry or wherever they were needed and they had a nursery where their children were sent.

—Kaisa Raisman, arrived at Sointula, aged 22, on June 3, 1902

BC Archives tape 4032:1 Sound Heritage Series

8 Women at Work

Except for the ruin of a stone chimney under blackberry brambles and fading memories in the surrounding community, little remains of the Hudson's Bay Company outpost at Fort Rupert where British Columbia's formal labour history began. It was here, in 1850, that the wives of eight Scottish coal miners brought in to work a seam for the company prodded their husbands to stand up for their rights, prompting the first job action in BC.

The miners and their families had been enticed to make the dangerous journey around Cape Horn with promises of steady work and daily rations of beef, mutton, beer, grog and new wine. Once they arrived, however, they

Women and children behind a marching band leading a United Mine Workers of America parade in 1913 during the Big Strike, which paralyzed Vancouver Island coalfields between 1912 and World War I.
BC Archives E-02631

Anne Muir and her coal miner husband, John, came to Fort Rupert where in 1850 harsh conditions triggered BC's first serious labour dispute.
BC Archives E-02392

discovered that things weren't quite as the company had promised. Housing was wretched, they were expected to live off the land because the company could make more money exporting the beef and mutton from its farms at Fort Victoria. (The workers were assured they'd soon come to prefer "wild food.")

Their tools weren't suitable, the coal seam proved to be only a hand's span in thickness and the miners, who prided themselves as professionals, were expected to work as common labourers. To make things worse, no sooner had the wives and children landed than a 16-canoe Kwagiut war party hauled up on the beach, erected 16 poles and placed a human head—trophies from their raid on the south coast—on each one. Annie Muir, wife of the mining contingent's leader John Muir, was offered her choice of any two heads. She was not amused.

When the miners decided they'd rather move their families to California and take their chances in the goldfields, the company had the men thrown in irons. The captain of the trading ship England, which was standing off the fort, was instructed to refuse passage for their families. The women were having none of that. They gathered their children, defied the company's authority and boldly swept aboard the ship, refusing to be dislodged. Annie later settled at Sooke where the Muirs proved one of the most industrious pioneer families in BC history.

Women like those who came to Fort Rupert more than 150 years ago were

Along with the gospels, missionaries brought new technologies to the North Coast, like these spinning wheels.
BC Archives B-03573

no strangers to work, of course. Nor were the women who already occupied the landscape. Helen Meilleur, whose poignant memoir of Fort Simpson, *A Pour of Rain*, opens a window on the lives lived in and around the coastal fur trade forts, recounts the burden of being a wife in that male-dominated society. "She loaded and unloaded his canoe, cleaned the fish he caught, skinned the animals he trapped, made gear and clothing and mats and baskets she carried," Meilleur wrote of one aboriginal woman she observed as a girl. "She carried home firewood from distances of two miles; she carried baskets and cedar mat rolls full of possessions and cedar boxes full of food," she noted of her childhood observations at the dawn of

Our First Teacher.

Miss Georgia Sweney, a "voice in the wilderness" who, in a land of virgin forest, instituted teaching at our first public school at Hastings Sawmill on primeval Burrard Inlet, 1872, now Vancouver. An accomplish⁴ musician, a skilled artist, she could also milk a cow. Portrait presented, 1941, by her daughter Esther Cummings, Santa Paula. City Archives J S⁵ᵐ

Miss Georgia Sweney, the first teacher at Vancouver's first public school at Hastings Sawmill, 1872. City of Vancouver Archives CVA PORT P556N235

First Nations women were a crucial part of the work force, whether using the old technologies of cedar bark baskets and digging sticks or the new ones brought from Europe and Asia. Glenbow Archives NA-1700-80

the last century.

And yet, perhaps the perception that things were harder for aboriginal women than they were for the wives of Europeans of the period reflects a cultural bias. Scholar James Axtell, in his study *Natives and Newcomers: The Cultural Origins of North America*, notes that one of the repressed social problems of the colonial period was that many "white" women captured or rescued by Natives

"She rules through the affections. . ."

Female teachers, as a rule, possess greater aptitude for communicating knowledge, and are usually better disciplinarians, especially among young children, than males. Woman's mission is pre-eminently that of an educator. Her softening, refining, and elevating influence contributes largely to the success in the classroom. Patient and painstaking, she rules through the affections, her authority being thus based upon love, this trait of character is reciprocated by those with whom she comes in contact.

—John Jessop, *Second Annual Report on Public Schools*, (quoted in *Their Own History: Women's Contribution to the Labour Movement of British Columbia* by Betty Griffin and Susan Lockhart, United Fishermen and Allied Workers' Union/CAW Seniors Club, 2002)

Native cannery workers on Cormorant Island, about three kilometres off the northeast coast of Vancouver Island, early 1900s.
BC Archives E-07419

came to prefer their new life and resisted returning to so-called civilization. "The great majority of white Indians left no explanation for their choice," he writes. "Forgetting their original language and their past, they simply disappeared into their adopted society. But those captives who returned to write narratives of their experiences left several clues to the motives of those who chose to stay behind.

"They stayed because they found Indian life to possess a strong sense of community, abundant love, and uncommon integrity—values the English colonists also honored, if less successfully. But Indian life was attractive for other values—for social equality, mobility, adventure and, as two adult converts acknowledged, 'the most perfect freedom, the ease of living and the absence of those cares and corroding solicitudes which so often prevail with us'."

It can also be argued that the crucial moment in 1850 when some strong Scottish women at Fort Rupert defied the powerful Hudson's Bay Company marked a sea change in the role of women at work for both Natives and non-Natives. Pioneer women of all ethnic backgrounds ran ranches, carried the mail, bore children in the bush, hauled

freight and shot game for the table as a matter of course, but by 1911 more than 6,000 women in BC—about one in five—had made the transition from subsistence economics to the wage economy

Telephone switchboard and operators at British Columbia Telephones Ltd. in 1898. Dominion Photo Company, Vancouver Public Library VPL 23795

Teacher Dorothy Alison and her class at the Model School in Vancouver, 1907. C. Bradbury photo, City of Vancouver Archives CVA SGN 1586

and formally entered the workforce. This shift in labour and economics proved to be the early harbinger of a series of changes, later accelerated by two world wars, that would utterly change the structure of British Columbian society and women's roles in it.

For Native women, the transition began when their labour became the assembly-line engine of the fish-processing business in canneries that sought to exploit huge salmon runs returning to remote rivers on the wild coast. At the time, these women were at the cutting edge of technology and mechanization. "Native women cleaned fish and filled cans amid clanking tinning machines, alongside steam vats and tray boilers, near conveyor and transmission belts, amid steam, and pipes, and foremen," observes Rolf Knight in Indians at Work: An Informal History of Native Labour in British Columbia, 1858–1930. "Those canneries may seem primitive by today's standards, but they were the industrialism of the resource frontier." Non-Native

women were not far behind. Japanese, Chinese and European women soon moved into the canneries, too, part of a multicultural mosaic that those ignorant of history have come to believe a recent phenomenon.

And the expansion of urban life around seats of government, seaports and resource industries created demand

"A storm-tossed ship with a group of drunken miners. . ."

Mabel Blake came to Vancouver in 1913 armed with an English teaching certificate but had to wait until the following January before she found work at Minto on Vancouver Island. She had taught only a few days when a government replacement teacher arrived who had seniority over her. It was back to Vancouver on a storm-tossed ship with a group of drunken miners as fellow travellers. Another offer soon arrived, however, and she went off to Sand Creek School near Grand Forks, in the Kootenays. That fall she found herself in yet another school, this time in a Swedish logging community of five families at Hilltop, situated some 2,000 feet up from Fife, a whistle stop on the Kettle Valley Railway.

The schoolhouse was a square building with a large classroom in front, while the teacher's bedroom and kitchen were at the back. Mabel taught all grades, including one or two beginners who had to learn English first.

At her next posting in Bridesville, she had to ride a horse to get to the school, going down a steep bank to the creek below, riding through the creek, then up another bank to the road. It was while teaching there that she met young Juliet Bell, a deaf student who changed her career. In order to help Juliet, Mabel decided to investigate what government programs were available for deaf children. She discovered that classes for the deaf were being held in Vancouver; by the following fall she had joined the staff at what was to become Jericho Hill School.

—from *Women of British Columbia* by Jan Gould, Hancock House, 1975 for domestic servants, nurses, teachers and the light manufacturing of garments among women of European, Asian and aboriginal descent. Later, women occupied positions as telephone operators and retail clerks. Some scholars suggest these women received shabby treatment from a sexist union movement that perceived them as a threat to male prerogatives. Some unionists even lobbied for government restriction of female access to the labour market. However, in December 1911, the labour newspaper The Federationist was arguing vigorously against such short-sighted folly and in favour of giving women the franchise. "Women are going to get the ballot," the paper warned. "They will have power to wield and whether they use it wisely or not depends upon how we educate them."

Indeed, women persevered and continued to fight for the very unions that sought to shunt them into unskilled, low-paying job ghettos. One such ghetto was the teaching profession. But it was here that what proved to be among the most transformative developments for women took shape. In 1872, a new Public Schools Act replaced the moribund system begun by the Hudson's Bay Company. Two years later, almost half the teachers in BC were women and they took their ideas of equality to the most remote reaches of the province.

One of them was a spirited campaigner for equal rights for women who had been born in Victoria in 1863 and at the age of 27 became the first female high school teacher in BC. Four years later Agnes Deans Cameron was appointed the first female principal but was fired in 1906 for insisting that women deserved the same pay scales as men in the teaching profession. No quitter, she responded by working as a journalist

Agnes Deans Cameron, at age 27 in 1890, was the first female high school teacher in BC, and soon the first female principal.
BC Archives F-08820

and by trekking down the Mackenzie River with her niece in 1908, becoming the first woman to reach the Arctic by an overland route. Her book about this trip (The New North, 1910) became a literary sensation. When Cameron died suddenly of complications following surgery for appendicitis in 1912, the Victoria Daily Colonist (May 14, 1912) described her as "the most remarkable woman citizen of the province." She was 48.

By 1909 the tough, resourceful and resilient pioneer women of Cameron's generation had organized themselves into the Women's Educational Club. Betty Griffin and Susan Lockhart point out in Their Own History: Women's Contribution to the Labour Movement of British Columbia that from an early initiative of that organization arose the powerful BC Teachers' Federation, a social and political institution that still has a profound influence on public policy almost a century later. And it all began in Fort Rupert, where the angry pioneer wives of a handful of ill-treated coal miners said "Enough," faced down the bullying of a powerful colonial employer and ignited a women's movement that is still active today.

9 Elite Excess & Riff-Raff Reality

If many pioneers came to early British Columbia in flight from the stifling conventions and social stratification of Europe, others came intent on establishing the same society in the colonies—but with themselves on top. So, less than a decade after the union of Vancouver Island with the mainland, the colony had developed its own Upstairs-Downstairs class structure. At one end of the spectrum was a genteel life of high teas, debutantes, calling cards and fancy balls for gowned ladies and gentlemen in glittering military attire. At the other were the brothels and dance halls where another class of woman tried to survive in a world without safety nets, in a world in which women were not considered legal persons and had few property rights.

The Victoria police chief's report for 1886 says that in addition to a cruel traffic in female slaves by Natives and 100 women working in Chinatown, there were four brothels in the downtown run by European madams employing 38 women. These brothels were licensed by the city as "dance halls." One long-standing rumour, wrote the late historian Terry Reksten, who cited the police report, held that a passage connected some of these establishments to the exclusive Union Club. Nevertheless, a local newspaper drew an editorial bead on the dance halls as "sinks of iniquity and pollution" where "prostitution and kindred vices, in all their hideous deformity and disease in every form, lurk."

That was Downstairs. Upstairs, "society" women like Julia Trutch, polished wife of Lieutenant-Governor Joseph Trutch, her brilliant sister Caroline O'Reilly, wife of the province's commissioner of both gold and Indian reserves, and the elegant Sarah Crease, wife of Judge Henry Pering Pellew Crease who drafted most of the new province's first laws, were creating their own hothouse culture in Victoria. The snobs of this arriviste establishment now felt comfortable snubbing the likes of

Tea in the garden at Pentrelew, 1201 Fort St., Victoria, 1897. The four children of Frederick George Walker and Mary Maberley Crease with their aunt, Josephine Crease.
BC Archives F-06877

Left: Mae Field was a dance hall girl at Dawson. Women of the gold rush demimonde, the world of prostitutes, dance hall girls and entertainers who lived on the outskirts of respectable society, were a fiercely independent lot, defying post-Victorian society to travel north and endure incredible hardship, and sometimes heartbreak, as they, too, sought their fortunes.
© Canadian Museum of Civilization, negative no. J6215

Above left: The artist Josephine Crease (1890), daughter of Sarah and Henry Crease, the attorney general.
BC Archives F-06875
Above: Caroline Trutch married Peter O'Reilly and emerged as a bright, vivacious spirit of Victoria's high society, renowned for her singing abilities.
BC Archives G-09394

Amelia Douglas. The former governor's Cree wife seemed to prefer her social eclipse and a life of relative seclusion from the new social whirl. Reading the racist attitudes toward Natives and the social bigotry revealed in the Trutch correspondence, one can understand why she might have enjoyed her own company rather more than that of the new establishment. Small wonder that Robert Melrose, a working-class fellow

at Craigflower Farm, should note wryly in his diary (held in the collection of the Provincial Archives of BC): "Great Ball held at Victoria, riff-raff excluded."

Yet many of these newly arrived pioneer women came from Irish and Scottish families that were themselves excluded from England's upper crust by similar ethnic prejudice. In BC, they suddenly found themselves enriched by cheap land, the torrent of wealth flowing from the gold camps, coal mines, sawmills and ranches and the new markets this wealth created.

The evidence of a hunger for social status among the upwardly mobile middle class and the aspiring lesser gentry in exile is found both on the skyline of the capital's still exclusive Rocklands

Diamond Lill Davenport, a dance hall girl of the gold-rush era.
Yukon Archives, Canadian Museum of Civilization Collection 3829

neighbourhood—and in the pretentious names settlers gave the new homes they carved from rain forest and rangeland. Joan Dunsmuir's husband, Robert, a coal baron who became BC's first millionaire and one of the wealthiest men in North America, built her a grandiose castle in Rocklands and named it "Craigdarroch." Captain Walter Colquhoun Grant built a great, curved carriage road to his log cabin at Sooke and named what visitors described as a shanty "Mullachard," after his ancestral home. Mary Ann Raby was living on a farm in Saanich when sailor

Downstairs

The Prostitutes: On the creek—nine in number—put on great airs. They dress in male attire and swagger through the saloons and mining camps with cigars or huge qwids of tobacco in their mouths, cursing and swearing and look like anything but the angels in petticoats heaven intended they should be.

Each has a revolver or bowie knife attached to her waist, and it is quite a common occurrence to see one or more women dressed in male attire playing poker in the saloons, or drinking whiskey at the bars. They are a degraded set, and all good men in the vicinity wish them hundreds of miles away.

—*Victoria Daily Colonist*, September 10, 1862, cited in *Barkerville* by Richard Thomas Wright, Winter Quarters Press, 1998

Left top: Lady Aberdeen, centre, settled on the Coldstream Ranch near Vernon in the Okanagan.
BC Archives A-01071

Left bottom: Victoria garden parties like this one on Rockland Avenue just weeks before the First World War began were often lavish and elegant affairs.
BC Archives A-02885

William Thompson found her so irresistible he jumped ship, proposed marriage and, when she accepted, cleared 400 hectares, bought 19 pigs and named his new estate "Bannockburn." There was a Fairfield and a Fintry, a Trebatha and a Roslyn, a Regent's Park and an Armadale, an Erin Hall and a Pentrelew, a Cary Castle and a Hatley Castle—the last also built by the Dunsmuir family with clear instructions to architect Samuel Maclure: "Money doesn't matter, just build what I want." G.P.V. and Helen Akrigg argue convincingly in their British Columbia Chronicle that it was deliberate British colonial policy to "recreate on Vancouver Island the social structure of England, a stalwart squirearchy with the working class properly relegated to an inferior station."

In addition to minor bureau-crats hoping to clamber up the colonial administration to acceptance in England, high society in Victoria was fuelled by an influx of second sons of landowners seeking their fortunes in the

Above: Craigdarroch Castle, built by Robert Dunsmuir, BC's first millionaire.
Harbour Archives 3246

Below: Beautiful Kathleen O'Reilly, seen here with a friend.
BC Archives I-51791

colonies, well-connected junior officers of the Royal Navy and adventurous spirits from the aristocracy who saw the new province as a place to experiment with scientific agriculture. For example, Isabel Gordon, the Countess of Aberdeen, settled with her husband on the Coldstream Ranch near Vernon in the Okanagan. Winifred Ashburnam set out for a 200-hectare homestead on Cowichan Lake that her husband had purchased sight unseen. And a member of the Bowes-Lyons—that's the late Queen Mother's family—is said to have wound up teaching music at Cowichan

Station following an ill-starred love affair that earned disapproval at home. An urban gentry flourished around the seats of political power and commercial wealth in Victoria and later Vancouver, while a rural gentry took root in the pleasant landscapes of the Gulf Islands and the Okanagan, Cowichan, Comox and Kootenay valleys.

But the heartland of the establishment remained the capital and south Vancouver Island. "San Francisco on the Solent," Emily Carr called it. Terry Reksten describes it as a peculiar hybrid of English social values and American

brashness with a population that included English, Blacks, Chinese, Scots, Irish, Germans, Indians and Americans. The social scene was vigorous. For the ladies of the establishment, whether rural or urban, there were polo matches and regattas to attend, there were lawn tennis and croquet—and, of course, the round of balls, garden parties, soirees and levees where their daughters might meet the Royal Navy man with the right family connections in the Old Country. The Cowichan Valley Amateur Athletic Club, for example, boasted the best dance floor in BC. Three hundred or more could

"Everybody came to the ball. . ."

We gave a ball to the fair ladies here; two of the men-of-war the *Satellite* and *Plumper* with ourselves, determined to join together and give a grand ball to the ladies of Vancouver Island. . . the only house we could find was the market place, a most dismal-looking place, enough to drive all thoughts of dancing out of ones head, however we got all the flags we could from the ships & turned in 30 or 40 sailors & in a short time a fairy palace of flags was erected, so that not a particle of the building was visible; we then rigged up some large chandeliers & sconces of bayonets and ramrods wreathed with evergreens which when lighted up produced a regular blaze of light & made it quite a fairy scene. We also got up a large supper room in the same style & managed to provide a first-rate supper. Everybody came to the ball from the governor downwards nearly 200 in all & we kept the danc-

Fancy dress ball at Government House in Victoria, circa 1914. Of such gatherings, Robert Melrose, a working-class man, noted wryly in his diary: "Great Ball held at Victoria, riff-raff excluded."
BC Archives G-00947

ing up with great spirit until half past three in the morning. Everybody was quite delighted with it & it goes by the name of "the Party" par excellence; nobody says ball in this part of the world, it is always party. The ladies were very nicely dressed & some of them danced very well, they would look much better if they would only learn to wear their crinoline properly, it is most lamentable to see the objects they make of themselves, some of the hoops being quite oval, whilst others had only one hoop rather high up, the remainder of the dress hanging down perpendicularly. . .

—quoted from Lieutenant Charles Wilson's journals of service. BC Archives MS-0368

Kathleen O'Reilly in flower garden at Point Ellice House, circa 1900.
BC Archives C-03922

dance there and young women would row in from the Gulf Islands, waltz all night with officers from visiting warships and then row home as dawn broke.

For all the socializing, life was intensely focussed on the family. The O'Reillys perhaps best represent both their class and their time. Peter O'Reilly was Irish. He met Caroline at a dinner at the Trutches. She was described as extremely bright, vivacious and a seasoned world traveller. They were married on a snowy day in 1863 and soon had four children. But rank and privilege were no guarantee of protection from the perils that stalked everyone in an age before antibiotics and advanced medical care. Among the touching artifacts from the era held by the provincial archives is Caroline's frantic letter to Peter about the illness of their seven-year-old daughter, Mary Augusta. "My dearly beloved husband," she wrote on October 26,

1876. "I have left writing to the last hoping that I might be able to tell you that our darling is better. I grieve to say I am not able to say so with any certainty. I am in so much anxiety that I feel difficulty to write with calmness." Mary died November 6, 1976, and is buried in Victoria.

Like most upper-class families, the O'Reillys sent the kids, Frank, Kathleen and Jack, to good schools in England to be educated. When they returned, their home at Point Ellice House was already a hive of social activity for Victoria's elite and was where Prime Minister John A. Macdonald dined during his visit to BC in 1886. The O'Reilly household was also a hotbed of Victorian romance. Daughter Kathleen had blossomed into a stunning beauty. Among her suitors was Royal Navy Captain Robert Falcon Scott, who later led the doomed British dash to the South Pole in 1912. Another

suitor was Lieutenant Commander Henry Scudamore Stanhope, heir to the Earldom of Chesterfield. But Kathleen spurned them both and never married. She died in 1945 at the age of 78.

Point Ellice House is a rambling structure on Victoria's Inner Harbour. It is now preserved as a museum where visitors may still take a strawberry cream tea in summer, play croquet on the lawns or walk the lovely gardens with the ghosts of Kathleen, the bold young Scott of the Antarctic, Sir John A. Macdonald, Julia Trutch, Caroline O'Reilly and the other forgotten women of the establishment.

There is, of course, no historic monument to the women consigned to the "dance halls."

10 A Rainbow Society

Most of them never met. Most of them knew little of each others' homeland. Yet women from around the world stitched their diverse cultures together across the broken landscape of this province like the panels of a many-coloured quilt. From Africa by way of the United States, from the South Sea Islands, from China and Japan, from the ghettos of Eastern Europe and from the dusty Punjab, the women who came to settle British Columbia's frontier came from everywhere. Some came in search of freedom, some came to a fate of bondage, some came as dutiful wives, some as concubines bound for a grim life in the sex trade. Some were welcomed and some were denied.

But those who came, persevered and prevailed, and embroidered upon the fabric of a new society the rich brocade of their own distinctive traditions and the experiences all women shared as wives and mothers in a patriarchal society and an unforgiving environment.

They brought their own religions and their own recipes. They modified practice in both temple and kitchen to accommodate the new realities of a different world in which they would have to nurture families and raise children. They watched those children marry across ethnic and religious boundaries, helping to bring into being the new culture that is still being forged here on the western slope of the Rockies. Descendants of those women have served as mayors and lieutenant-governors, as judges and cabinet ministers, as university chancellors and labour leaders, as intellectuals and as all-star athletes.

One of the first intersections of these varied cultures occurred on the rumpled landscape of Saltspring Island with its sheep paddocks, sunny upland meadows, pastoral lifestyle and still-liberal sensibilities. Evidence of this early multiculturalism exists in more than the

In the late 1800s the congregation of St. Paul's Church on Saltspring Island was fully integrated.
Salt Spring Archives

Above left: Hannah Estes was one of a contingent of free American Blacks who brought their families to Victoria at the invitation of James Douglas. Middle: Kini Kajiyama performing with the traditional instrument known as the koto in Cumberland, where the Japanese community built a tea garden. Right: Gracie Benjamin was one of the early Hawaiian settlers arriving in Canada in the late 1800s.
Salt Spring Archives, Estes/Stark Collection; Cumberland Museum; Salt Spring Archives, Cathy Roland Collection

genealogies of old island families. Swing left on the Ganges Road as you disembark the ferry from Vancouver Island and you'll pass one enduring symbol of that brief moment in BC's early history, when it still seemed possible to avoid the Old World prejudices and bigotry that would visit its curse on later decades: it is St. Paul's, a little stone church nestled in the shadow of Mt. Tuam at the head of Fulford Harbour. If you should take the time to look carefully at the photograph from its consecration in 1885 you will see a congregation in which, among the women at least, the white faces are far from the majority.

Among the first women from visible minorities to arrive in BC were those called Kanakas, a Polynesian word that means human beings, but which was used in a disparaging sense by white Europeans of the time. Today, however, the word has redeemed its original dignity and is used by Hawaiians themselves to refer to indigenous islanders. Disparaged or not, these Natives of what were then called the Sandwich Islands were much

Cecile Naukana, whose father William Naukana was born in the Sandwich Islands in 1813, married Ganges farmer George Napoleon Parker. This 1890s picture shows them with five of their children.
Salt Spring Archives, Cathy Roland Collection

in demand as sailors. Tough, hardy, able to navigate by the stars, consummate readers of the North Pacific weather, Kanakas were prized crewmen for the sailing captains of the late 18th and early 19th centuries. Herman Melville mentions Kanakas in his novels. When the first Kanaka women arrived on the West Coast isn't entirely clear, but we do know that one left Hawaii to accompany Frances Barkley on one leg of the 1787 voyage of discovery to Vancouver Island. Unfortunately, the young woman known as Winee became homesick and sailed for Hawaii from Macao with John

Maria Mahoi Douglas (later Fisher), born on the Saanich Peninsula about 1856 of a Native mother and Hawaiian father. Hawaiian families displaced from San Juan Island in 1859 settled on Saltspring Island.
Salt Spring Archives

Meares. She fell ill and died during the crossing of the China Sea.

During the early years of the fur trade, the number of Hawaiians working on the West Coast for the Hudson's Bay Company and arriving aboard trading vessels numbered in the many hundreds. Whether Hawaiian sailors jumped ship in BC or were marooned by captains cheating them of their wages is a matter of argument, but by the time Fort Victoria was established, they had their own street. Kanaka Row was found where the stately Empress Hotel now stands. A Kanaka Ranch was established in what's now Stanley Park and others farmed up the Fraser Valley.

But it was on Saltspring Island, where Hawaiian families displaced from San Juan

Mrs. Sylvia Estes Stark was born a slave and came to BC in 1857. She died in 1944 at the age of 106.
Salt Spring Archives, Estes/Stark Collection

Island following a boundary dispute in 1859 had resettled, that the Kanakas formed a community. One of the matriarchs was Maria Mahoi, or Mahoy, or Mahoya, depending upon the source. She'd been born about 1856 in what was then the remote, rural outback of the Saanich Peninsula. Her father was a Hawaiian, an employee of the Hudson's Bay Company, and her mother a Native woman. She was beautiful and spirited and at 15 became the "country wife" of a New England whaling captain named Abel Douglas. Maria bore seven of his children before Douglas departed. She subsequently married another Saltspring Islander, George Fisher, with whom she had six more children. Like most women of her generation, she was resourceful, self-reliant and capable of packing up the kids in a small open boat and sailing it single-handed to Sidney for a day of shopping, much like the way modern moms take the mini-van to the mall. Maria died in 1936.

Hawaiians were not the first visible minority to arrive on Saltspring Island, however. Even before the gold rush that was to transform BC, freed Black slaves from Kentucky and Mississippi had begun to settle here with the blessings of Governor James Douglas. The first arrived at Vesuvius Bay in August, 1857. By 1859 the Black community numbered more than 100. Among them was Sylvia Estes, who was born into slavery. Her father, Howard Estes, had first bought his own freedom and then his family's, paying $900 to free his daughter, before moving them to California, where the racism was cruel. Douglas sent the Black community in San Francisco an invitation to immigrate. At 20, Sylvia was already the mother of two children and pregnant with her third when she accompanied her husband, Louis Stark, to carve one of the first farms in the Gulf Islands from the bush on Saltspring near Vesuvius Bay. She died in 1944 at the age of 106.

Hard on the heels of Black and Hawaiian settlers came the first Chinese woman to BC. Mrs. Chong Lee came to Victoria with her young child in 1860 when her husband, an enterprising merchant, arrived from California to open a store. By 1868, he had a chain of shops in Barkerville, Yale, Lillooet, Quesnelle Forks and Quesnel, that advertised "groceries, provisions, rice, tea, sugar, cigars, tobacco, opium, clothing, boots and shoes, hardware and mining tools which are offered for sale at reasonable rates." His wife's arrival marked the beginning of Chinese family life on the frontier, but she was a rare sight. Although one-half of Victoria's exploding population was Chinese, in 1860 that segment was 99 percent male. By 1902, when Victoria's Chinese population was 3,283, only 96

Mrs. Lee in Victoria wearing Ching dynasty clothing circa 1910.
Glenbow Archives PA-344-2

of that number were women.

Not all of the women who came from China were respectable wives. A less scrupulous class of merchant recognized that in a society of lonely men, there was money to be made selling sex. Women from Hong Kong were brought over ostensibly to work as waitresses but soon found themselves in a world of opium addicts and prostitution. By 1883 the problem was sufficient that BC had one of its first transition houses. The Methodist Home for Chinese Girls opened in Victoria specifically to provide sanctuary for those escaping the sex trade, slavery and cruel marriage contracts.

The first Japanese woman to arrive in BC was Mrs. Washiji Oya, who followed her husband in 1887 after he came to work at Hastings Mill. She was the harbinger of a tsunami. Between her arrival and World War I, almost 20,000 immigrants would come from Japan. Men who took lonely jobs in the fishery and logging communities frequently wrote home to have parents arrange marriages with suitable women. After courtships by mail and an exchange of photographs, the "picture brides" would join them, bringing old customs to help civilize the rough male community of a new frontier. The coal mining camp of Cumberland on Vancouver Island,

Yip Sang family members, 1906. An immigrant from China, Yip Sang worked for the CPR and later became a successful Vancouver businessman. He had 23 children—19 sons and four daughters.
Photo courtesy Henry Yip

明治式拾壹年八月渡加　元治元年八月五日生
縣川奈神
ウヨ屋大

Mrs. Yo Oya, the first Japanese woman to settle in Canada. She came to join her husband in 1887.
Japanese Canadian National Museum

for example, had both a Chinese opera house and a formal Japanese tea garden. Soon after the Japanese, Sikhs began to arrive from the Punjab, eventually founding the settlement of Paldi in the Cowichan Valley on Vancouver Island.

Not all the minorities were so easily visible, of course. A group of about 100

Jews arrived in Fort Victoria in 1858 to open businesses and, in 1863, established Canada's longest-serving synagogue. Highly educated, they soon became an essential part of the new colony's merchant and administrative establishment and their wives and daughters helped refine and civilize society in the rough frontier fort. Cecelia Davies, who had come from Australia with her prosperous parents, married Francis Sylvester in 1869 and quickly established herself as one of the capital's leading hostesses, renowned for her piano recitals. Over on the mainland, in the other would-be capital, New Westminster, Mrs. Simon Reinhardt was a social whirlwind before she moved to Victoria.

Although there was an overt anti-Semitism in some quarters, the frontier proved remarkably tolerant in some ways. In 1860, Selim Franklin was elected to BC's legislative assembly, the first Jew to hold political office in Canada. His brother Lumley was elected mayor of Victoria in 1865, the first Jew to hold such office in a North American city. He later led the Confederation move-

ment in the new province of BC. And in 1871, Victoria elected Henry Nathan to Ottawa—the first Jew elected to the House of Commons.

Unlike Cecelia Davies and others, not all Jewish women found an easy niche in Victoria's upper crust and palatial homes in high-end neighbourhoods. Hannah Director wound up homesteading at South Fort George, where she raised three small children in a log cabin with a dirt floor. She persevered, too, becoming the first woman elected to the school board, which she eventually chaired, in Prince George. The quilt she and all these women made of their collective lives and laid upon the dramatic frontier landscape of BC still offers a profound lesson in the principles of faith, hope and charity as our province of many cultures learns to live in a climate of tolerance and mutual respect.

Hannah Director homesteaded about 35 km south of Prince George in 1914.
Jewish Historical Society of BC **Archives**

Old recipes and new seasonings

The frontier was nominally a man's world, but women ruled the kitchen and learned quickly to make do with what was at hand. Appetites were large, children were many and supplies were often spare, which meant relying on non-perishable staples and whatever game the shotgun and fishing rod produced to supplement the larder. As women from different backgrounds met, old recipes were spiced up with new seasonings. Here are some standard recipes that would have been a part of every pioneer-era woman's culinary repertoire. Readers who want to try a pioneer dinner can substitute chicken or turkey thighs for game birds or rabbit.

Small Bannock

3 cups flour
dash of salt
1 tsp. baking powder
2 tbsp. lard
enough water

Combine dry ingredients in bowl. Make a little well and pour in water, not too much to start. Mix into a dough and knead it. Flatten it out and put it in the greased frying pan. Cook on hot ashes over open fire or bake in a 400 degree oven. Eat it hot with bacon drippings or lard.

Smoked Salmon Soup

1 lb. smoked salmon
1 quart water
1/4 tsp. fresh ground pepper
1 cup baby spinach leaves

Break salmon into bite-sized chunks and place in large saucepan. Add water and pepper. Simmer on low heat for 15 minutes until hot. Add the spinach and cook five more minutes at simmer.

Curried Spruce Hen

2 spruce hens (you can substitute skinless, boneless chicken thighs or chunks of turkey thigh)

1/2 cup flour
4 tbsp. butter
2 medium onions, minced
1 tsp. curry powder
3 tbsp. flour
3 cups chicken broth or bouillon
1 apple, diced
salt

Skin and draw the spruce hens, cut into serving pieces, wash and drain. Melt butter in a heavy cast iron skillet. Dredge meat with flour then cook in hot fat until browned all over. Remove each piece as it browns. Cook onions in the same fat until soft and golden. Add the curry powder and stir to coat. Add the flour and stir. Add the broth and stir. Bring to a boil. Add the meat pieces and the diced apple. Cover and simmer for 90 minutes. Serve with wild rice.

Fricaseed Rabbit

1 rabbit (you can substitute 4-6 skinless, boneless chicken breasts)
1 package bacon strips
1/4 cup flour
1/4 cup butter or lard
dash salt
dash pepper
1 cup milk
1 tbsp. finely minced onion

Wrap bacon strips around each piece of meat and skewer with toothpicks. Roll in flour. Melt butter in heavy cast iron skillet or Dutch oven and brown meat. Sprinkle on salt and pepper. Add milk, pouring very slowly to keep meat from sticking to pan. Cover and simmer until tender. Remove meat and make gravy with remaining liquids. Add onion. Cook. Pour over meat.

Camp Cabbage

1 package bacon, chopped into squares
1 medium onion, chopped
1 bunch green onions, chopped
1 medium head cabbage cut into 8 pieces

3/4 cup water
1 tsp. salt
1/4 tsp. pepper

Brown the bacon in a large cast iron skillet or Dutch oven. Add onion and green onions. Cook until soft and golden. Add cabbage and sauté briefly. Add water, salt, pepper. Cover and simmer 35 minutes. Stir and serve.

Salmonberry Sweet

4 cups salmonberries
4 cups sugar

Add equal amounts of berries and sugar and slowly cook together for about 15 minutes, stirring constantly. Remove berries with slotted spoon and reserve. Boil remaining juice 15 minutes, stirring constantly. Return berries and bring back to boil, stirring constantly. Serve right away over hot biscuits.

Strong Coffee

Put 1 quart water in a clean billycan. Add 12-16 tbsp. ground coffee. Bring to full boil then remove from heat and let stand five minutes. Add two tbsp. cold water to settle grounds. Pour and drink right away. Add sugar and canned evaporated milk to taste.

Molasses Candy

2 cups molasses
1 cup sugar
1 tbsp. vinegar
chopped walnuts
baking soda

Cook sugar and molasses together in a saucepan until it goes brittle when dropped in cold water. Stir in a pinch of baking soda and three cups of chopped walnuts. Pour onto a greased cookie sheet. Break it into pieces when cold.

11 Painters, Poets and Politicians

In 1791, just as courageous young Frances Barkley sailed for the second time toward the uncharted coast of British Columbia, women in New Brunswick were being formally deprived of the right to vote. This exclusion of women from the political process would not end in Canada until women in Quebec finally obtained an unrestricted franchise in 1940, almost 150 years later.

But the first victory in women's long battle for political equality was won through the determination of Maria Pollard Grant, in the capital of a newly minted province that Frances Barkley could barely have imagined. Today, in a province where women have held the offices of prime minister, lieutenant-governor, premier, cabinet minister and mayor, where they sit on the bench and lead great universities, it's difficult to imagine they were once thought unfit to participate in the suffrage or political life.

Frontier women were tough enough to drive dog teams 500 kilometres at 40 below zero or to give birth alone at remote homesteads. They could skin and butcher a moose or climb the Chilkoot Pass. Yet, in the eyes of most male contemporaries they symbolized frailty and fragility—both physically and psychologically. During the pioneer era most doctors, educators and legislators defined women by their biology, creating a self-fulfilling stereotype. Before effective birth control, when women were denied full property rights and therefore had to be identified through their legal relationships with

Women's Building at a fair in New Westminster, circa 1900. Note the banner for the Local Council of Women, an organization set up to push for political equality.
Philip Timms Collection Vancouver Public Library VPL 6692

Victoria College women's basketball team, 1912. Where women's physical recreation had previously been limited, they began to take up more robust sports.
BC Archives E-02868

Mohawk poet once travelled the entire Cariboo Wagon Road to Barkerville, declaiming her romantic verse in roadhouses. She would switch from buckskins to a brocaded silk evening gown depending upon the audience. At Soda Creek she performed in a barn and her dressing room was the oat bin. The next night she performed at Lac La Hache, her silk dress still bristling with oats. But smitten miners showered her with gold nuggets. There were sentimental melodramas, blackface minstrel shows and the erotically charged burlesques of "Klondike" Kate Rockwell, who was with the Savoy Theatrical Company in Victoria before taking her act to Dawson City in 1900.

As women reshaped the performing arts on the frontier, they were doing the same in the studio. As early as 1862, Victoria's Hannah Maynard was radically expanding the artistic envelope of a new technology known as photography. She had one of BC's first portrait studios and experimented with multiple exposures, perspective, mirror images, infinity and surrealism. She travelled the province—as did her husband Richard, also a photographer—for four decades, recording landscapes, portraits of people and leaving an important photographic legacy when she died in 1918. Not far from Hannah Maynard's photo studio, a young Emily Carr was formulating the ideas that would cause her to abandon the expectations of where and

Unidentified woman actress photographed by Richard Maynard in the 1880s in Victoria.
BC Archives F-06219

Left: Miss Russell as Maid Marian, 1899.
BC Archives G-00170

how a woman should paint. Travelling to remote places on the coast alone, her bold brushwork, vibrant hues and sweeping curves would capture the fecund energy of the BC landscape as no painter before or since.

Where women's physical recreation had previously been limited to walking, a bit of riding and occasional forays by canoe or rowboat, they began to take up more robust sports. At first these involved relatively sedate versions of lawn tennis and croquet—sports that could be played in the garments of the day. The venturesome soon took up golf and then more competitive pursuits. Women's walking competitions became popular. Women joined alpine expeditions, climbing beyond the treeline to paint and take photographs. Zoe Gayton, the actress who had warmed audiences at Victoria's New Royal Theatre, left on a cross-country hike in 1890. She crossed the United States in 213 days, averaging more than 28 kilometres per day. By the late 19th century, more than a million women in North America owned bicycles—racing them as well as riding them for errands or for touring. They raced horses, too. Isobel Stanley, whose husband was Governor General of Canada and had donated the Stanley Cup, challenged the ladies of Rideau to a hockey game against the ladies of Government House in Ottawa. Rugged team sports now had an imprimatur and there was an explosion in the number of

Production of *The Bridal Trap* **in Victoria, 1908. From left: Miss Stoddart as Marion, Miss H. Kent as The Marquise and Miss Carter as Rosette.** BC Archives G-00198

women playing ice hockey, field hockey, baseball and lacrosse. Within a decade of the first airplane flight, Alys Bryant had qualified as a pilot and on July 31, 1913, became the first woman to fly over Vancouver.

Growing social acceptance of these new and expanded roles for women in everyday life was accompanied by a rising demand for political equality as well. Maria Pollard Grant used a new provincial act (passed in 1872) that extended property rights to married women to argue successfully that women who met property qualifications had the right to a vote in municipal elections. She cast her ground-breaking ballot in 1875. In 1885, she drafted a petition demanding the vote for women in BC and led a delegation to present it to the all-male legislature, a symbolic journey she would make every year until women were finally granted the franchise 32 years later. Her successful candidacy for school board was advanced by the Victoria Council of Women, organized in 1894 at a meeting presided over by Lady Ishbel Gordon, wife of Lord Aberdeen. In January of 1895, she became the first woman elected to public office in BC. Three years later, school trustee candidate Mrs. Duncan Roderick Reid became the first woman elected in Vancouver. In 1908, the Victoria Council of Women became the first in Canada to endorse the campaign for women's universal suffrage. Ten years later, BC voters would elect Mary Ellen Smith to the provincial legislature and she would become the first woman to hold cabinet rank in Canada.

If the ascent to genuine power launched the 20th century with a new beginning for women, it marked the symbolic closing of the pioneer era in BC. And yet, as the 21st century begins, it's also fair to argue that the pioneering spirit was never laid to rest and that bold women still live rugged lives in remote places, challenge conventions and continue to drive for social reforms across this vast and diverse province.

"Here was nothing but loveliness. . ."

Life Class, Westminster School of Art, 1899

The curtains of a little recess parted, out stepped the model and took her place on the throne.

I had dreaded this moment and busied myself preparing my material, then I looked up. Her live beauty swallowed every bit of my shyness. I had never been taught to think of our naked bodies as something beautiful, only as something indecent, something to be hidden.

Here was nothing but loveliness...only loveliness—a glad, life-lit body, a woman proud of her profession, proud of her shapely self, regal, illuminated, vital, high-poised above our clothed insignificance...

Every eye was upon her as she mounted the throne, fell into pose. Every student was tallying her with perfection, summing up balance, poise, spacing, movement, weight, mood.

Charcoal began to scrape upon paper and canvas... swishing lines, jagged lines, subtle curve, soft smudge.

Tremblingly my own hand lifted the charcoal—I was away, lost in the subtlety, the play of line merging into line, curve balancing curve.

—Emily Carr, in her autobiography, *Growing Pains,* Oxford University Press, 1946

Above: Playing tennis in Vernon, 1895.
BC Archives I-55785
Left: Photographer Hannah Maynard bicycles with friends in Beacon Hill Park in Victoria in the 1890s.
BC Archives F-05070

men—either husbands or fathers—they were made hostage to their reproductive systems. Without legal status as persons, their choices were often the economic security of marriage and its stifling social restrictions, the "freedom" of spinster-hood and economic dependence on patronizing relatives or being marginal-ized as women of questionable morals. And yet, for all these constraints, from the mid-19th century many women in BC were fashioning a stunning revolu-tion in which they would transform the cultural landscape by taking up sports once reserved for men, excelling in the arts and forcing profound political reform.

Oddly enough, the year of the gold rush and the making of British Columbia was a signal year for this revolution. In 1858, an American woman created an overnight stir by climbing four kilome-tres to a mountain summit in Colorado. She was wearing bloomers. This dar-ing British alternative to crinolines and starched petticoats worn by a female American mountaineer would mark the beginning of the end for the hoop skirt that women still felt compelled to wear, even on the gold diggings. Bloomers, sensible and designed by a woman, would free women to partici-pate in active sports and eventually kill the whalebone corset, that stiff conserva-tive symbol of control.

By 1858, women had only just begun to challenge convention and appear on the stage. A few years before, theatre in Fort Victoria was an all-male affair, usu-ally performed by visiting Royal Navy crews. But two decades later, the Fanny

Morgan Phelps Dramatic Troupe was headlining shows from Oregon to BC and performers like Lizzie Morgan, Zoe Gayton, Annie Pixley and Minnie Pixley were on their way to celebrity status. In an age before radio, television or mov-ies, almost every town from Barkerville to Vancouver had its own theatre, often several, including an opera house. For

Mrs. Duncan Roderick Reid (nee Christina Campbell) was elected as Vancouver's first woman school trustee in 1898.
City of Vancouver Archives CVA Port P757 N338

highbrows there were Shakespeare and readings by E. Pauline Johnson. After arriving in BC in 1894, this statuesque

12 The Last of the First

Is it true that the first non-aboriginal child born in Vancouver was a baby girl named McNeil, I was asked by Angus MacNeil of Vancouver as I plugged away at my research into the often unattributed contributions women have made to British Columbia. The archives showed that there was a Margaret Florence McNeil born in Vancouver on April 27, 1886, the year the city was both incorporated and burned down—but whether she was actually the first-born I couldn't attest. The more I asked around, the more frequently I heard in anecdotal terms that her parents had moved after the fire and she wasn't located again until 50 years later, thanks to the diligence of a city archivist who doggedly traced her to Portland, Oregon. That yarn was too good to ignore.

Then I got some unexpected help from Erin Sweeney of Richmond, who wrote to me—"at the urging of my uncle, Jake Sweeney, and my father Ed Sweeney"—to help clarify what turns out is not a mystery at all, although it began as one. And my 12-year-old daughter broke off from designing her website to track down for me a posting to a genealogical site in Cape Breton that provided some further interesting background. It was written by a Vince MacNeil, who himself thanks the research of Carol MacLean and quotes

Burned to the ground in 1886, by the late 19th century Vancouver had surpassed Victoria as the social hub of the province.
BC Archives C-05627

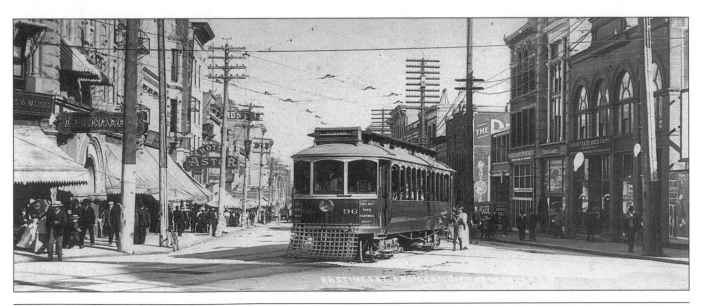

Margaret Florence McNeil, the first non-aboriginal child born in Vancouver, was tracked down by the city's archivist 54 years later and brought home for a birthday party in her honour.
City of Vancouver Archives CVA LP 129

from sources as far afield as the long-defunct Vancouver News Herald, the Oban Times in Scotland (a place I've actually visited, but only in search of the perfect Scotch) and the Vancouver Province.

As I say, the Vital Events Registry at the provincial archives corroborates that on April 27, 1886, exactly three weeks after the town of Granville was incorporated as the City of Vancouver and two weeks before the first meeting of the first city council—at which the first order of business was to ask Ottawa to turn over the land that would create Stanley Park—a Margaret Florence McNeil entered the world and was baptized by Father Patrick Fay at Holy Rosary, the humble predecessor of the present cathedral. The date was certainly right and the name was similar to that offered by Angus MacNeil, who wasn't sure exactly how she spelled her surname and thought she lived in Portland, Oregon, but was descended from stock on the Isle of Barra in the Outer Hebrides.

Which brought me back to Erin Sweeney. She told me that her grandfather, M. Leo Sweeney, had served as the General Chairman of Vancouver's Diamond Jubilee. The committee apparently produced a splendid souvenir booklet of Vancouver facts from which the following excerpt is taken:

By way of contrast to the dim beginning of cities in "old" countries, there sat down to a dinner in the Stanley Park Pavilion on April 30, 1946, nine of the 16 men and women born in Vancouver in 1886.

These "Jubilarian" guests included Miss Margaret Florence McNeil, first white baby born in the year of incorporation, whose birthday was April 27, 1886. Other "1886 babies" present on this unique occasion were: A.C. Reid; C.F.H. Steele; E.G. Sumner; Mrs. Edward Brown, formerly Edna Ludlow; Mrs. W.W. Hatfield, formerly Irma Chase; Mrs. J.B. Abrams, formerly Beatrice Jagger; J.D. McPhalen; Mrs. George Sims, formerly Flora Johnston.

But there's more to this story than the birthday party that took place the year before I was born. It turns out we owe the presence of Vancouver's first-born at the celebration to the tenacity and skill of Vancouver's first city archivist, Major J.S. Matthews, a hero of Ypres who came home and had a brief stint in business before retiring in 1924. His hobby—perhaps we should say obsession—was collecting and recording early Vancouver history and, according to Donna Jean MacKinnon's short essay about him in Chuck Davis's The Greater Vancouver Book, his Kits Point house was soon jammed to the rafters with memorabilia. He was made the city's first archivist in 1932 and his personal collection is still at the heart of our early documentary record of the city's genesis—another triumph, I always like to point out, for the publicly spirited amateur in this age that seems overly impressed by formal credentials and the notion that you need a PhD before you can think.

Major Matthews, it seems, was blessed with an uncanny ability to remember names long-forgotten by others and a reporter's skills in ferreting out information about them, which probably explains why he was so chummy with the reporters of his day. As I poked about looking for information, I came across letters in the papers of my late father-in-law, Bill Mayse, who was a reporter for both the Vancouver Province and the Vancouver Sun more than 75 years ago, with news tips from the archivist scrawled in the margins.

According to Vince MacNeil's posting on the Cape Breton site, the major wrote more than 900 letters in a relentless 20-year search to track down Vancouver's vanished first-born. Then a reporter drew his attention to a 1909 newspaper story that seemed to indicate that her parents, Alexander McNeil and Anna Springer McNeil, had moved to Portland after losing their home in the ferocious fire that wiped out most of Vancouver just six weeks after the baby was born. That fire was so hot it melted the church bell at St. James to cinder slag. Our intrepid archivist next wrote to the city comptroller in Portland. He obtained a municipal government list of every McNeil in the American seaport and then worked his way through the addresses. He found Margaret working as a glove buyer for a big department store.

In 1940, 54 years after her departure, the city brought her home. She was greeted at city hall by Mayor Lyle Telford, presented with a gold necklace and pendant bearing the city's coat of arms and treated to a spectacular birthday cake decorated with roses to represent Portland and a maple leaf to represent Canada. Major Matthews, who died in 1970 at the age of 92, undertook to ensure that Vancouver's long-lost birthday girl was never again forgotten. Every year until her own death in 1972, she received a cake, a present and a phone call from the City of Vancouver.

Postscript:
A Woman of Fortitude

When Linda Allison swings into the saddle of her trusted palomino, Molly, and ambles out across the rolling hills of her ranch in the Similkameen Valley to bring in calves for branding, you might be forgiven for thinking you were in the presence of an apparition. Her great-grandmother, Susan Allison, came into this valley as a girl. And now she sleeps for eternity in the family cemetery of the old Allison Ranch near Princeton, snuggled in beside her beloved husband beneath the rustling of the amber bunch grass. More than 130 years ago, Susan rode this same burnished country on Cream Kate, a horse of the same colour as Molly, for the very same purpose as the great-granddaughter who would not even be born until 12 years after the remarkable old lady was laid to rest at the age of 92.

A picture of a young Susan Allison shows her beauty, but not her adventurous spirit. From *A Pioneer Gentlewoman in British Columbias: The Recollections of Susan Allison*

"She must have been a woman of great fortitude and strong character," Linda says, relaxing after another long day tending the 200 cattle that range across almost 65 square kilometres of her deeded land and grazing leases. "I really enjoy these mountains. I always enjoy being out there. I often think if I'd been here 100 years ago [in Susan's time] how amazing it must have been to

Linda Allison, owner/operator of the Allison Creek ranch, feels a strong connection to the adventurous young woman who rode this land before her.
Glenn Baglo *Vancouver Sun*

come through this country with almost nobody here."

Susan Louisa Moir was a beautiful, vivacious teenager celebrating her fifteenth birthday when the paddlewheeler Reliance nosed in at a muddy landing on the Fraser River on August 18, 1860. She and her sister Jane, 17, broke away from their mother Susan and ne'er-do-well stepfather Thomas Glennie and scrambled—"joyously" was the term she later used to describe the moment—up the embankment toward the wooden palisades at Hope. The young woman, clad in the constricting corsets and puffy white petticoats that were the proper attire for proper ladies even in the wilderness, understood that she had arrived at a real frontier and that beyond it lay a vast unknown and the grand adventure that would consume the rest of her astonishing and fruitful life. This was as far as the riverboats could yet travel on the great waterway, which boiled through towering canyons. It flowed from an uncharted interior which, in many ways, was as mysterious to the newcomers as the Darkest Africa of the pulp novels that entertained city dwellers in London, Paris and Berlin.

Barely 18 months before, what became known as the Fraser Canyon War had ripped like a wildfire through the inaccessible country beyond the little settlement. When American adventurers panning for gold refused to countenance First Nations doing the same and sought to drive them off with violence, they got more than they planned. For weeks, the bodies of miners picked off from ambush had floated down the river, pitched gun battles had been fought and British arms had finally been dispatched from the Royal Navy base at Esquimalt to restore order and bring the troublemaking Americans to heel. But in 1860, more trouble was brewing at Rock Creek, where American miners refused to abide by the colonial administration's licensing rules. Governor James Douglas had ridden to the mining camp dressed in full uniform, faced down 300 surly miners in a saloon, told them flatly that

"He rode a superb chestnut horse. . ."

I shall never forget my first sight of a Hudson's Bay Company Brigade train coming in from Colville. I had gone for a stroll on the Hope–Similkameen trail. There were still a few berries and I was getting a "feed" when I heard bells tinkling and looking up saw a light cloud of dust from which emerged a solitary horseman, the most picturesque figure I had ever seen.

He rode a superb chestnut horse, satiny and well-groomed, untired and full of life in spite of the dust, heat and long journey. He himself wore a beautifully embroidered buckskin shirt with tags and fringes, buckskin pants, embroidered leggings and soft cowboy hat.

He was as surprised to see me as I was to see him, for he abruptly reined in his horse and stared down at me, while I equally astonished stared at him. Then, as the Bell Boy and other horses rode up, he lifted his hat and passed on. I never met him again, but was told he was a Hudson's Bay Company Officer in charge of the Colville train and that he said he was never more surprised in his life than to see a white girl on the trail—he had lived so long without seeing anyone except Indians.

—from *A Pioneer Gentlewoman in British Columbia: The Recollections of Susan Allison*, edited by Margaret Ormsby, University of BC Press, 1976

he was building them a road from Hope but that they had damn well better abide by the law or he'd be back with 500 Royal Marines to give them a taste of British justice.

Doubtless, the air was still electric with tension when Susan took her first walk through the Native village adjacent to the little settlement, marvelling over the bales of salmon dried for winter, the beautifully patterned dog-hair blankets and the intricate baskets, so tightly woven she could carry water in them. Inadvertently, this friendly, curious, irrepressible girl found herself mingling with the who's who of high society in the new colony of British Columbia, itself not yet two years old. At Fort Victoria, she'd already been introduced to Douglas, to the governor's charming son-in-law Dr. John Helmcken and his wife Cecilia and to the tolerant, reform-minded Reverend Edward Cridge of Christ Church Cathedral. Travelling with her on the riverboat were Judge Matthew Bailey Begbie, Lieutenant Colonel Richard Moody and Edgar Dewdney, the future lieutenant-governor who was then a young surveyor about to embark upon the building of the promised wagon road from Hope through the Similkameen that would make his name. Dewdney would soon be so smitten with Susan's older sister that his mooning over her became

a source of ribald amusement among the fur traders, merchants and Royal Engineers in the little community. But he was determined, love prevailed and he successfully courted and, in 1864, married Jane. Waiting on the riverbank as the two excited girls scrambled up in 1860 were Peter O'Reilly, the witty Irish surveyor whose home would become the centre of social life in the capital, and William Yates, the canny entrepreneur whose name now graces one of Victoria's main streets.

The unpretentious teenager, rather than being intimidated by her physical and social surroundings, absorbed her encounters with them with such intensity that decades later her memoirs still crackle with the vividness of her impressions, with the sense of awe, wonder and privilege at what she was witnessing and of which she had become part. Her dreams of adventure were soon tempered by the reality of the endeavour upon which she had embarked and for which neither she nor her gentrified parents were very well equipped. Her stepfather had squandered the family fortune yet still had delusions of setting himself up as a country squire in the colonies. "None of us knew how to wash clothes," she wrote. "We had a tin tub that we brought out with us that we used for a wash tub and as we were

Susan Allison's older sister Jane met and married a young British engineer who was building a wagon road at Hope. Edgar Dewdney was later appointed Lieutenant-Governor of BC and Jane became Chatelaine.
BC Archives A-01179

one essential skill of frontier life, proved a daunting mystery until a trailwise man named Kilburn taught Susan how to make sourdough and bake it in a skillet. She learned how to sew and found there was a market for petticoats in the muddy settlement. She taught school.

And she met a young miner named John Allison who had learned Chinook, was on friendly terms with the Natives and had been venturing inland on the fur brigade trail where he had taken a 65-hectare homestead near Vermilion Forks at the confluence of the Tulameen and Similkameen rivers. The "red earth" from which the place took its name was in great demand for ceremonial paint by the Okanagan, the Shuswap and even the fierce and much-feared Blackfeet, who were then engaged in a bitter war with the Americans across what is now Montana. The Natives visited the ochre deposits often, but they considered Allison a friend. He'd quickly

ignorant as to the use of wash boards, we bent over the bath and rubbed with our hands until they bled and our backs felt broken. As we always wore white embroidered petticoats, we had rather a bad time on washing day." Baking bread,

The Allison children pose with dogs and horses in the Similkameen Valley. Susan Allison gave birth to 14 children, the last at age 47. All of the children lived to maturity.
BC Archives D-08228

Her husband and the ranch hands were often away on cattle drives or tending the livestock. With only the local Native women for companionship she soon decided she must learn Chinook, did so, and became an important authority on the aboriginal customs, folklore, legends and history in the Similkameen Valley. She found that the role of a rancher's wife on the frontier was variable. At times she served as hostess to travellers—General William Tecumseh Sherman, the US Civil War hero, passed by and presented her seven-year-old son with his sword after a demonstration of horsemanship—as well as postmistress, fur trader and bookkeeper. In addition were the usual cooking, housekeeping and child rearing duties, of which there were many. Without the benefit of medical assistance and with only her husband and a Native midwife in attendance, Susan Allison gave birth to 14 children, the last at the age of 47, all of whom lived to maturity.

When the Allisons held a big family reunion several years ago, more than 300 of her descendants turned up. Today, the bloodlines established by this remarkable frontier woman reach across both BC's landscape and our pioneer history. Perhaps the most poignant is the one that now resides in the clear, steady gaze of Linda, the great-granddaughter she never knew, a woman astride a pale horse just like her own, riding across the beautiful, still-empty landscape where Susan Allison's spirited dreams have fused with the eternal earth of British Columbia.

discovered there was more satisfaction in raising cattle and driving them to the coast than there was in chasing gold dust. He spent most of his time in the saddle, so perhaps it was not unexpected that the handsome young man had soon given the pretty teenager the horse she named Cream Kate and was teaching her to ride.

One evening, riding with him at dusk, she realized she must get home to mother before dark or there'd be hell to pay, so she set out at a brisk canter while he continued to his destination at Powder Camp. She was knocked from her horse by a branch, her skirt snagged on the saddle horn and she was dragged for two kilometres with the horse kicking her all the way. Finally, the skirt tore off and she stumbled to a neighbour's house. Fortunately, her mother was away and the neighbour was discreet and didn't report her bruises and state of dress the next day.

In any event, the experience didn't dampen the romance and when John proposed to her during one of his cattle drives in 1868, she accepted and set out with her new husband to his remote ranch beyond the mountains. "Then began my camping days and the wild, free life I ever loved till age and infirmity put an end to it," she would write fondly when she was near 80. "On the journey out we rode the two Kates, Cream and Grey. My husband sent the three packboys on ahead to fix camp...

"I went to the creek and washed and did up my hair in the darkness and when I regained the camp, Tuc-tac had spread a canvas in front of the fire with fried trout, grouse, bacon and bannock. That was washed down with tin cups of delicious-tasting tea. We sat and talked until late, the Indian boys sitting with us and telling us stories of the place."

Afterword

In the sun-burnished August of 1914, as trains laden with excited recruits bound for the First World War wound their way through the Interior, young women in big hats and white summer dresses would make their way down to the station stops with baskets of cherries for the laughing, khaki-clad soldiers. Did those women imagine, then, that half those handsome young men would become casualties; that none would return unmarked in mind or spirit? The image lingers as a poignant metaphor. For, as the remarkable era covered in this book drew to a close and British Columbia slid toward the bloody engagements that would irrevocably transform the province, most women still stood at the margins of public life as they had once stood on the fringes of a wild frontier.

True, a few had been elected to school boards and a few had voted in municipal elections—if they met the stringent rules that defined them as land owners. Some had carved out a niche as activists and intellectuals. Increasingly women moved into the work force and would soon do so in unprecedented numbers as the war claimed more and more of the male population. Yet for all their profound contributions to the shaping of BC, women were still denied the vote in general elections at both federal and provincial levels. Few outside the upper classes had the benefit of a higher education. For those who did, education was largely viewed as an accessory to life in cultured society. Even to women of means, the university-trained professions remained essentially closed.

Women were not expected to pursue careers—or even to wish to—but rather to dedicate themselves to making homes for families.

And yet in the years that lay ahead, those women, their daughters and their granddaughters would turn their efforts to reshaping the social, political and economic landscapes yet again. By 1917, the suffrage movement had finally obtained the vote—although only for some. Women of Chinese, Japanese, Hindu, First Nations and Doukhobor descent were still denied the franchise and would continue to be denied it for another 30 years or more.

Still, in a by-election held on January 24, 1918, Mary Ellen Smith of Vancouver became the first woman to run for a seat in the provincial legislature. She won. In the general election of 1920, one of three female candidates among 155 province-wide, she went on to top the Vancouver polls and was rewarded with a cabinet post, the first ever held by a woman in the British Empire.

Today, BC women have achieved acclaim in politics, science, the arts, sports, industry and commerce. A BC woman has served as prime minister of Canada. Another as premier of the province. Yet another as lieutenant-governor. Women serve in senior cabinet posts and as First Nations chiefs, as supreme court justices and as mayors of cities big and small. They lead powerful labour unions and run major corporations. They work as plumbers and software designers, systems analysts and university presidents. They are award-winning novelists and newspaper editors, poets and historians, medical researchers and deep ocean scientists, pilots and police detectives, visual artists and mathematicians, mountaineers and movie stars, musicians and Olympic champions.

Where higher education was once the nearly exclusive preserve of men, women have made it their highway to success. In 2003, girls outnumbered boys among graduates of BC's public education system and 83 per cent who entered kindergarten graduated from grade 12. Over half the graduates of universities are now women. One in three graduates in higher mathematics is now a woman.

Few young women contemplating a career today regard any field as being closed to them. This confident sense of entitlement—which may be the most significant gift that any generation can bestow upon its successors—they owe to those grandmothers and great-grandmothers who encountered an often unforgiving frontier, confronted its turbulence and change and from it shaped the world of marvels their great-granddaughters now inherit.

Source Notes

Page 74. Reprinted with permission of the publisher from *A Pioneer Gentlewoman in British Columbia: The Recollections of Susan Allison* by Margaret A. Ormsby © University of British Columbia Press 1976. All rights reserved by the publisher.

Page 37. Exhibit notes are reprinted with permission of the Clallam County Historical Society, Port Angeles, Washington.

Pages 41, 42, 44. Selections from Tape 4032 are reprinted with permission of the BC Archives.

Page 56. Selections from Archives MS-0368 are reprinted with permission of the BC Archives.

Pages 30, 53. Reprinted with permission of the author from *Barkerville: A Gold Rush Experience* by Richard Thomas Wright (Winter Quarters Press, 1998).

Pages 21, 22. Reprinted with permission of the publisher from *The Remarkable World of Frances Barkley 1769–1845* by Beth Hill with Cathy Converse (Touch Wood Editions 2003).

Page 47. Reprinted with permission of the author from *Their Own History: Women's Contribution to the Labour Movement of British Columbia* by Betty Griffin and Susan Lockhart (United Fishermen and Allied Workers' Union and CAW Seniors Club, 2002).

Page 49. Reprinted with permission of the publisher from *Women of British Columbia* by Jan Gould (Hancock House, 1975).

Page 68. Reprinted from *Growing Pains* by Emily Carr (Oxford University Press, 1946).

Page 17. Excerpt from "At Birth" by Mary Augusta Tappage from *The Days of Augusta* © 1973, 1992 by Augusta Evans and Jean E. Speare. Published by Douglas & McIntyre Ltd. Reprinted with permission of the publisher.

Bibliography

Akrigg, G.P.V. and Helen B. *British Columbia Chronicle, 1778–1846; 1847–1871*, 2 vols. Vancouver: Discovery Press, 1977.

Axtell, James. *Natives and Newcomers: The Cultural Origins of North America.* London: Oxford University Press, 2001.

Barman, Jean. *The West Beyond the West: A History of British Columbia.* Toronto: University of Toronto Press, 1996.

Bowen, Lynne. *Boss Whistle: The Coal Miners of Vancouver Island Remember.* Nanaimo: Nanaimo and District Museum and Rocky Point Books, rev. ed., 2002.

Bowes, Gordon E., ed. *Peace River Chronicles: Eighty-One Eye-Witness Accounts from the First Exploration in 1793 of the Peace River Region of British Columbia, Including the Finlay and the Parsnip River Basins.* Vancouver: Prescott Publishing Company, 1963.

Carr, Emily. *Growing Pains: The Autobiography of Emily Carr.* Toronto: Oxford University Press, 1946.

Davis, Chuck. *The Greater Vancouver Book: An Urban Encyclopaedia.* Vancouver: Linkman Press, 1997.

de Bertrand Lugrin, N. *The Pioneer Women of Vancouver Island, 1843–1866.* John Hosie, ed. Victoria: Women's Canadian Club of Victoria, 1928.

Fish, Gordon, ed. "Dreams of Freedom: Bella Coola, Cape Scott, Sointula." *Sound Heritage Series*, Vol 36. Victoria: Public Archives of BC, 1982.

Francis, Daniel, ed. *Encyclopedia of British Columbia* Madeira Park: Harbour Publishing, 2000.

Glavin, Terry and Former Students of St. Mary's. *Amongst God's Own: The Enduring Legacy of St. Mary's Mission.* Mission, BC: Longhouse Publishing, 2002.

Gould, Jan. *Women of British Columbia.* Saanichton: Hancock House Publishers, 1975.

Griffin, Betty and Susan Lockhart. *Their Own History: Women's Contribution to the Labour Movement of British Columbia.* Vancouver: United Fishermen and Allied Workers' Union and CAW Seniors Club, 2002.

Gunther, Erna. *Indian Life on the Northwest Coast of North America as Seen by the Early Explorers and Fur Traders during the Last Decades of the Eighteenth Century.* Chicago: Univ of Chicago Press, 1972.

Hamilton, Bea. *Salt Spring Island.* Vancouver: Mitchell Press Ltd., 1969.

Hill, Beth and Cathy Converse. *The Remarkable World of Frances Barkley, 1769 – 1845.* Victoria: Touch Wood Editions, 2003.

Ito, Roy. *The Japanese Canadians.* Van Nostrand Reinhold Ltd., 1978.

Johnson, Peter. *Voyages of Hope: The Saga of the Bride-Ships.* Victoria: Touch Wood Editions, 2002.

Knight, Rolf. *Indians at Work: An Informal History of Native Labour in British Columbia 1858–1930.* Vancouver: New Star Books, 1996.

Koppel, Tom. *Kanaka: The Untold Story of Hawaiian Pioneers in British Columbia and the Pacific Northwest.* North Vancouver: Whitecap Books, 1995.

Leonoff, Cyril Edel. *Pioneers, Pedlars and Prayer Shawls: The Jewish Communities in British Columbia and the Yukon.* Victoria: Sono Nis Press, 1978.

Light, Beth and Alison Prentice. *Pioneer and Gentlewomen of British North America, 1713–1867.* New Hogtown Press: 1980.

Meilleur, Helen. *A Pour of Rain: Stories from a West Coast Fort.* Victoria: Sono Nis, 1980.

Mitchell, David and Dennis Duffy, eds. "Bright Sunshine and a Brand New Country: Recollections of the Okanagan Valley, 1890–1914." *Sound Heritage Series,* Vol 8, No 3. Victoria: Public Archives of BC, 1979.

Perry, Adele. *On the Edge of Empire: Gender, Race and the Making of British Columbia, 1849–1871.* Toronto: Univ of Toronto Press, 2001.

Reksten, Terry. *More English than the English: A Very Social History of Victoria.* Victoria: Orca Book Publishers, 1986.

Smith, Jessie Ann. *Widow Smith of Spence's Bridge.* As told to J. Meryl Campbell and Audrey Ward. Murphy Shewchuk, ed. Merritt, BC: Sonotek Publishing, 1989.

Tappage, Mary Augusta. *Days of Augusta.* Jean E. Speare, ed. Vancouver: J.J. Douglas, 1973.

Toynbee, Richard Mouat. *Snapshots of Early Salt Spring and Other Favoured Islands.* Ganges, BC: Mouat's Trading Company Ltd., 1978.

Walbran, J.T. *British Columbia Coast Names, 1592–1906.* Vancouver: J.J. Douglas, 1971.

White, Howard, ed. *Raincoast Chronicles First Five.* Madeira Park: Harbour Publishing, 1977.

White, Howard, ed. *Raincoast Chronicles Six/Ten.* Madeira Park: Harbour Publishing, 1983.

Wright, Allan A. *Prelude to Bonanza: The Discovery and Exploration of the Yukon.* Sidney, BC: Gray's Publishing, 1976.

Wright, Richard Thomas. *Barkerville, Williams Creek, Cariboo: A Gold Rush Experience.* Winter Quarters Press, 1998.

Index